Nuclear Politics

When do states acquire nuclear weapons? Overturning a decade of scholarship focusing on other factors, Debs and Monteiro show in *Nuclear Politics* that proliferation is driven by security concerns. Proliferation occurs only when a state has both the willingness and opportunity to build the bomb. A state has the willingness to nuclearize when it faces a serious security threat without the support of a reliable ally. It has the opportunity when its conventional forces or allied protection are sufficient to deter preventive attacks. This explains why so few countries have developed nuclear weapons. Unthreatened or protected states do not want them; weak and unprotected ones cannot get them. This powerful theory combined with extensive historical research on the nuclear trajectory of sixteen countries will make *Nuclear Politics* a standard reference in international security studies, informing scholarly and policy debates on nuclear proliferation – and U.S. nonproliferation efforts – for decades to come.

ALEXANDRE DEBS (PhD MIT, 2007) is Associate Professor of Political Science at Yale University, where he is also Co-Director of the Leitner Program in International and Comparative Political Economy. His work centers on international security and applied game theory. Specifically, it investigates the causes of war, nuclear proliferation, and democratization, and has appeared in such journals as the *American Political Science Review*, *International Organization*, *International Security*, and the *Journal of Conflict Resolution*. Alexandre received a Rhodes scholarship in 2000 and was a Stanton Nuclear Security Junior Faculty Fellow at the Center for International Security and Cooperation (CISAC), Stanford in 2011–2012.

NUNO P. MONTEIRO (PhD University of Chicago, 2009) is Associate Professor of Political Science at Yale University, where he is also Director of Research of the Brady-Johnson Program in Grand Strategy. His work centers on International Relations theory and security studies, specifically great-power politics, power transitions, nuclear studies, the causes of war, deterrence theory, military occupations, and the philosophy of science. He is the author of *Theory of Unipolar Politics* (Cambridge University Press, 2014) as well as articles published in *International Organization*, *International Security*, *International Theory*, and *Perspectives on Politics*, among other venues.

Cambridge Studies in International Relations: 142

Nuclear Politics

EDITORS

Evelyn Goh

Christian Reus-Smit

Nicholas J. Wheeler

EDITORIAL BOARD

James Der Derian, Theo Farrell, Martha Finnemore, Lene Hansen, Robert Keohane, Rachel Kerr, Jan Aart Scholte, Peter Vale, Kees van der Pijl, Jutta Weldes, Jennifer Welsh, William Wohlforth

Cambridge Studies in International Relations is a joint initiative of Cambridge University Press and the British International Studies Association (BISA). The series aims to publish the best new scholarship in international studies, irrespective of subject matter, methodological approach or theoretical perspective. The series seeks to bring the latest theoretical work in International Relations to bear on the most important problems and issues in global politics.

Cambridge Studies in International Relations

Series list continues after index

Nuclear Politics

The Strategic Causes of Proliferation

ALEXANDRE DEBS
Department of Political Science
Yale University

NUNO P. MONTEIRO
Department of Political Science
Yale University

CAMBRIDGE
UNIVERSITY PRESS

CAMBRIDGE
UNIVERSITY PRESS

One Liberty Plaza, 20th Floor, New York, NY 10006, USA

Cambridge University Press is part of the University of Cambridge.

It furthers the University's mission by disseminating knowledge in the pursuit of education, learning, and research at the highest international levels of excellence.

www.cambridge.org
Information on this title: www.cambridge.org/9781107108097

First published 2017

Printed in the United States of America by Sheridan Books, Inc.

A catalog record for this publication is available from the British Library.

Library of Congress Cataloging-in-Publication Data
Names: Debs, Alexandre, author. | Monteiro, Nuno P., author.
Title: Nuclear politics: the strategic causes of proliferation / Alexandre Debs, Associate Professor, Department of Political Science, Yale University, Nuno P. Monteiro, Associate Professor, Department of Political Science, Yale University.
Description: New York: Cambridge University Press, [2017] | Includes bibliographical references and index.
Identifiers: LCCN 2016027169| ISBN 9781107108097 (hard back) | ISBN 9781107518575 (paper back)
Subjects: LCSH: Nuclear nonproliferation. | Nuclear weapons – Government policy. | Strategic culture.
Classification: LCC U264.D444 2016 | DDC 355.02/17–dc23
LC record available at https://lccn.loc.gov/2016027169

ISBN 978-1-107-10809-7 (hard back)
ISBN 978-1-107-51857-5 (paper back)

À mon père, Chaouki (1945–2016).

–AD

Para a minha mãe, Odete da Piedade.

–NPM

Building an atomic bomb here would be stupid. We have no threats.

–Admiral Maximiano da Fonseca
Minister of the Navy of Brazil, 1979–1984

If we are satisfied with our security requirements in conventional armaments, ... we would not hazard our economic future and promote an economic and social upheaval by diverting vast resources for a nuclear program.

–Zulfikar Ali Bhutto
Prime Minister of Pakistan, 1974

Contents

Figures and Tables

Figures

Tables

Cover illustration: atomic explosion photographed by Harold Edgerton of EG&G, on commission for the Atomic Energy Commission, likely at the Nevada Proving Grounds circa 1952. Taken using a Teletronic camera shooting at ultra-high speed (1/100,000,000-of-a-second exposure) with a 10-foot long lens from seven miles away, this photograph reveals the anatomy of the first microseconds of an atomic explosion. © 2010 MIT. Courtesy of MIT Museum.

Preface

This book is the product of a wonderful intellectual journey that started when we both arrived at Yale as assistant professors in 2009. Coming from backgrounds that could hardly be more different – Alexandre had been trained as an economist at MIT; Nuno, as an IR theorist at Chicago – we quickly found overlapping interests. Substantively, we were both keen to understand the dynamics of the nuclear age – the long shadow cast by nuclear weapons on world politics since 1945. Conceptually, we both wanted to refine existing theories of international politics by placing states' security interests in their strategic context and analyzing their interaction. Methodologically, we both sought to further the use of historical research to test theoretical propositions, especially causal mechanisms. Professionally, we both aimed to encourage further dialogue between formal and informal approaches to theorizing world politics, as well as between theory and history. More than a half dozen years later, we are both happy to realize that our objectives have remained largely the same. (And we take that as evidence that we are on to something important, rather than as proof that we have so far failed to achieve our goals!)

What started as a series of brief discussions over lunch quickly turned to informal chats in front of a white board, then to research memos bouncing back and forth, until by early 2010 we thought it was time to work on something together. Neither of us was happy with the literature on power transitions. So we set out to write a paper on the question of when power shifts lead to preventive wars.[1] After work-shopping it around, we realized that we had focused on only half of the broader problematique that interested us. While focusing on preventive wars, our theoretical framework also offered predictions on when power shifts actually happen, despite these preventive dynamics. We therefore decided that after wrapping up our original paper, we

[1] This ultimately became Debs and Monteiro (2014).

should write another, looking at this second question in greater depth. At the same time, it gradually became clear to us that the magnitude of the power shift introduced by a state acquiring nuclear weapons – in the jargon, horizontal proliferation – is qualitatively different from most (perhaps all) other shifts in military power. This, in turn, made us realize that our real interest was in the causes of nuclear proliferation, a topic on which neither of us had done any serious thinking.

By 2011, then, our work together was expanding to cover the question that animates this book: under which conditions do states acquire nuclear weapons? We started modestly – or was it hubristically? – thinking that one more paper would allow us to "say our piece" and move on.[2] Alas, as often happens, the more we dug, the more we realized we had more to learn and more to convey. To begin with, the literature on the topic was, well, sizeable. There was a multitude of theoretical arguments to grapple with. This was less of a problem, as we had clear views on what we wanted to do: to place the security interests of all states affected by one state's possible nuclear acquisition within a strategic interaction context and analyze the conditions under which proliferation was more likely to occur. The bigger problem was the gradual realization that the field of nuclear studies occupies this middle ground between the study of rare events (such as, for instance, hegemonic wars), of which the number of cases is small enough that there is little doubt the researcher can (and is expected to) master all of them, and the study of frequent events (such as, for instance, interstate crises), of which the number is large enough that no researcher could (or would be expected to) master the historical details of them all. In between these two positions, the field of nuclear studies covers enough historical ground that a researcher can spend a lifetime struggling to master its historical domain; while not including a sufficiently large number of cases that mastery of the historical record is unthinkable – or, some might say, unnecessary – and instead most research consists of uncovering regularities in large-n data using statistical tools. In short, nuclear studies, when properly done, require the researcher to master the history of the nuclear age. Perhaps this explains why most experts on the topic devote their entire careers to it. It certainly explains why this book was four years in the making.

---

[2] This paper became Monteiro and Debs (2014).

This issue manifested itself in practice as a scholarly version of the infamous "Nth country" problem in nuclear politics. Just like policy-makers have long worried about "the possibility that more and more countries might acquire nuclear weapons," we found ourselves worry-ing about the possibility that more and more countries might acquire a place in our book.[3] Whenever we presented our already burgeoning drafts or sent them out to someone who had kindly volunteered to read them, we almost invariably received a comment of the form: "What about country N, on which you have no case study? How does N fit into your theory?" So we started trying to preempt these criticisms by attempting to guess which would be the Nth country that people would ask about next. If we wanted to bring together theory and rich empirical accounts, we needed to wrestle with a seemingly unending number of cases of (attempted as well as actual) nuclear prolifera-tion. In the end, this dynamic accounts for the considerable length of the book.

Looking back, and much as we may have despaired along the way every time someone brought up another case and, with it, another large set of materials to master, this was the right thing to do. Our theory matured as a result of being exposed to this expanding set of cases. Our understanding of the nuclear age also changed appreciably. But it took us a while. In the end, this need to cover a relatively large universe of historical cases – the more than two dozen states that, at one point or another, had an active nuclear program with a military component – dictated the need to write a book. And so we started writing the pages that follow. Four years later, we are thrilled to finally abandon them. (As Paul Valéry said of poems, so with books: they are never finished, only abandoned.)

A book always involves fighting many battles, some larger, others smaller. (We hope to have won the one we fought against the par-ticularly stubborn auto-correct function in our word processor, which insisted in giving France a *force de frappé*.) Nevertheless, we are happy to report that our overall experience was a joy for both of us. Perhaps this is owed to our own approach to coauthorship. Seen from the outside, one might be led to guess that one of us does "the math" and the other brings in the historical knowledge; or that "the math" drives the theory and the other does "the chatty bits;" or that one puts

---

[3] Iklé (1960, 391). See also: Wohlstetter (1961).

"numbers" on the other's arguments or ideas; or that each of us covers half the ground; or whatever. Instead, we decided to do it in what is perhaps an inefficient method: each of us read and summarized existing work; dug up archival materials; helped manage our platoon of intrepid research assistants; then together we debated and refined our theory, while discussing its fit with the cases; finally we each drafted different sections of the manuscript, then swapped our rough drafts back and forth and edited each other's writing, until – we hope – the whole thing has a coherent style, such as it is. This process was not the result of a particularly conscious decision. Rather, it emerged organically from our shared interests in writing the book: each of us was determined to learn more about the politics of the nuclear age – and about the workings of the dialogue between formal theory, natural-language theory, and history. In our view, this approach to coauthorship may take longer to get things done, but it also, at least in our case, makes for a better final product. And it was certainly more fun.

We hope this will be the first of many books we write together – and we already have ideas for at least a couple more, on nuclear matters and beyond. The obvious sequel would be another book covering nuclear politics after proliferation. How do states react to another state's acquisition of nuclear weapons? How do nuclear weapons – and the omnipresent danger of escalation – shape state behavior in and beyond crises? We have started exploring these matters in a working paper and feel that we will soon have enough to present on this to make for a second volume on nuclear politics.[4] So, stay tuned.

This book would not have seen the light of day without the support of many – indeed, so many that the first order of business here is to apologize in advance to any whose names we may have unwittingly omitted in these pages.

For having graciously agreed to read different sections of the manuscript, and for sending us helpful comments and suggestions, we thank Dimitris Bourantonis, Jonathan Caverley, Andrew Coe, Martha Crenshaw, James Fearon, John Lewis Gaddis, Richard Gillespie, Eliza Gheorghe, Feliciano Sá Guimarães, Jolyon Howorth, Robert Jervis, Thomas Jonter, David Kang, Jonathan Kirshner, Jiyoung Ko, Matthew Kocher, Andrew Kydd, Adria Lawrence, Christine Leah, Philip Lutgendorf, Sean Lynn-Jones, John Mearsheimer, Costanza

---

[4] See: Anderson, Debs, and Monteiro (2015).

Musu, Vipin Narang, Behlul Ozkan, David Palkki, Carlo Patti, Benoit Pelopidas, Barry Posen, Robert Powell, Or Rabinowitz, Samuel Rajiv, Frances Rosenbluth, Andrew Ross, Joshua Rovner, Bruce Russett, Scott Sagan, Nicholas Sambanis, Jayita Sarkar, Anne Sartori, Kenneth Schultz, Duncan Snidal, Matias Spektor, Aaron Stein, Oliver Stuenkel, Milan Svolik, Michael Tomz, Panagiotis Tsakonas, Jessica Varnum, Hikaru Yamagishi, and Anne-Mart Van Wyk.

We also received excellent comments and suggestions from the discussants, participants, and audiences at workshops held at Cornell University, George Washington University, Harvard University, MIT, Stanford University, the University of Chicago, the University of São Paulo, the University of Wisconsin-Madison, Yale University, the October 2013 conference of the Nuclear Studies Research Initiative, the annual joint conference of the International Security Studies Section of ISA and the International Security and Arms Control Section of APSA, the International Studies Association annual convention, the American Political Science Association's annual meeting, and the Peace Science Society annual meeting.

For providing us with a great working environment here at Yale, and with valuable feedback on many bits and bobs in the book, we thank our colleagues David Cameron, Allan Dafoe, Samuel DeCanio, Thomas Donahue, John Lewis Gaddis, Susan Hyde, Sigrun Kahl, Stathis Kalyvas, Paul Kennedy, Paulina Ochoa, John Roemer, Ian Shapiro, and Steven Wilkinson. Our life was also made much easier by the excellent staff we were lucky to have supporting us, including, in the Department of Political Science, Lani Colianna, Mary Sue FitzSimons, Blaine Hudson, and Karen Primavera, and at the Jackson Institute for Global Affairs, Elizabeth Gill, Alice Kustenbauder, Larisa Satara, and Cristin Siebert.

The pages that follow were made much better by feedback we received over two days in New Haven back in May 2014, during which an earlier draft was subjected to unrelenting (though gentlemanly delivered) criticism by Frank Gavin, Charlie Glaser, Colin Kahl, Robert Powell, Daryl Press, Scott Sagan, and our editor, Robert Dreesen. We are tremendously grateful to all of them – as well as to David Holloway, Leopoldo Nuti, and Marc Trachtenberg, who could not be present but sent us detailed comments on the whole manuscript. This workshop would not have been possible without significant financial support from the Leitner Program in International and Comparative Political Economy and the Edward J. and Dorothy Clarke Kempf Memorial Fund at the Whitney and Betty MacMillan Center for International and Area Studies, Yale University. We thank both for their generous funding.

For superb research assistance, without which we would not have been able to write this book even in the long time we feel that it took us, we thank our principal research assistant, Nicholas Anderson, as well as all the other members of our research team: Jonathon Baron, John Bentley, Gabriel Botelho, Will Bruno, Jackson Busch, Julia Butts, Omegar Chavolla-Zacarias, Elisabeth Cheek, Richard Chung, Cole Citrenbaum, Stefan "Reed" Dibich, Kelsey Ditto, Edmund "Ned" Downie, Alexander Ely, Emmet Hedin, Stephen Herzog, Donna Horning, Connor Dezzani Huff, Alexander Jacobson, Umm-e-Amen "Amen" Jalal, Mason Ji, Matthew Kim, Jiyoung Ko, Jéssica Leão, Bonny Lin, Jacob Lundqvist, William Nomikos, Chad Peltier, Mark Pham, Mehmet Saka, Matthew Sant-Miller, Noah Siegel, Teodoro Soares, Hayden Stein, David Tidmarsh, Vivian Wang, Yoonji Woo, and Mujtaba Wani. All errors remain, of course, our own.

For providing hospitable environments during part of the drafting of this book, Alexandre thanks the Center for International Security and Arms Control at Stanford University; and the Berkeley Center for Economics and Politics at the University of California, Berkeley. Nuno, for his part, is grateful for the warm welcome he received as a visiting scholar at the Center for Advanced Study in the Social Sciences at the Juan March Institute, in Madrid, Spain; the Center for Research and Documentation on the Contemporary History of Brazil of the Getúlio Vargas Foundation, in São Paulo and Rio de Janeiro, Brazil; and the Institute for International Relations at University of São Paulo, also in Brazil.

Finally, we would like to thank all those who helped put this book between covers at Cambridge University Press, starting with Robert Dreesen, a model of efficiency and a true supporter, and including also Brianda Reyes and Cassi Roberts, plus our copy editor Ramesh Karunakaran at Newgen, and Mary Harper, who compiled the index.

An earlier, compressed version of the arguments laid out in Chapter 2, as well as shorter versions of our case studies on the Soviet Union, Iraq, Pakistan, South Korea, and West Germany, and some of our conclusions in Chapter 7 appeared in Nuno P. Monteiro and Alexandre Debs, "The Strategic Logic of Nuclear Proliferation," *International Security*,

Vol. 39, No. 2 (2014), pp. 7–51. Furthermore, an earlier version of the model discussed in Chapter 2 and the appendix, as well as a shorter version of our case study of Iraq, appeared in Alexandre Debs and Nuno P. Monteiro, "Known Unknowns: Power Shifts, Uncertainty, and War," *International Organization*, Vol. 68, No. 1 (2014), pp. 1–31. We gratefully acknowledge permission from MIT Press Journals and the IO Foundation to elaborate on those ideas here.

Personally, Alexandre would like to thank Daron Acemoglu, his PhD thesis supervisor, for generous feedback throughout his graduate studies, and for helping him discover his passion for political questions. Alexandre would also like to thank his wife Mira, and children Francesca and Gabriel, for filling his life with love and laughter. He observes that when reviewing the major events of the day at the dinner table and dividing them up into happy, hopeful, and challenging moments – the "rose," the "bud," and the "thorn" – he always has an abundance of choices for the "rose" from his time spent with them. Finally, Alexandre would like to thank his mother Diane and sister Marie-Estelle for their unconditional love and support.

Alexandre dedicates this book to his father, Chaouki (1945–2016), who is most responsible for Alexandre's love of history and ideas. While he did not have a chance to see the book in its final form, he was very much present at its creation.

While finishing this book, Nuno became even more deeply indebted to John Mearsheimer, mentor and friend, who generously provided unfaltering support through trying times. Nuno hopes he will one day be able to pay this forward; he is sure he will not be able to pay it back. Nuno also wishes to thank his wife, Audrey Latura, for always finding a way to prevent the lid on the pressure cooker from sealing him inside. He can only hope to reciprocate when her turn to write a book arrives, he trusts soon. Finally, Nuno wants to express his gratitude to his son, Sebastian Miguel, who, having arrived as we were putting the finishing touches on this manuscript, was far more cooperative than his early age warranted us to expect.

Nuno dedicates this book to his mother, Odete da Piedade, who taught him the central role that dreams play in life, and provided him with unflinching support in pursuing his own.

Abbreviations and Acronyms

ABACC	Brazilian-Argentine Agency for Accounting and Control of Nuclear Materials
ACDA	Arms Control and Disarmament Agency, of the United States
ADD	Agency for Defense Development, of South Korea
AEA	Atomic Energy Authority, of Egypt
AEB	Atomic Energy Board, of South Africa
AEC	Atomic Energy Commission, of both the United States and South Africa
AEOI	Atomic Energy Organization of Iran
AERC	Atomic Energy Research Committee, of India
ANC	African National Congress, of South Africa
ATOP	Alliance Treaty Obligations and Provisions data set
BJP	Bharatiya Janata Party, of India
CANDU	Canadian Deuterium nuclear reactor
CASP	Country Analysis and Strategy Paper, of the U.S. Department of State
CCP	Chinese Communist Party
CDA	Common Development Agency, between the United States and the United Kingdom
CDU/CSU	Christian Democratic Union of Germany/ Christian Social Union of Bavaria
CEA	Atomic Energy Commission (*Commissariat à l'Énergie Atomique*), of France
CENTO	Central Treaty Organization
CIA	Central Intelligence Agency, of the United States
CINC	Composite Index of National Capabilities data
CIRUS	Canadian-Indian Reactor, United States, of India
CNEA	National Atomic Energy Commission (*Comisión Nacional de Energía Atómica*), of Argentina

CNEN	National Commission for Nuclear Energy (*Comissão Nacional de Energia Nuclear*), of Brazil
CNPq	National Council of Scientific and Technological Development (*Conselho Nacional de Desenvolvimento Científico e Tecnológico*), of Brazil
COW	Correlates of War data set
CSEM	National Center for Military Experiments (*Centre Saharien d'Expérimentations Militaires*), of France
CSN	National Security Council, of Brazil
CSSI	Chung-Shan Science Institute, of Taiwan
CTBT	Comprehensive Nuclear-Test-Ban Treaty
DMZ	Demilitarized Zone, separating North and South Korea
DOM-TOM	Overseas Departments and Territories (*départements et territoires d'outre-mer*), of France
DPRK	Democratic People's Republic of Korea, commonly known as North Korea
DTD	Directorate of Technical Development, of Pakistan
EDC	European Defence Community
EEAE	Greek Atomic Energy Commission
EMIS	Electromagnetic Isotope uranium enrichment
EURATOM	European Atomic Energy Community
F-I-G	France-Italy-Germany treaty
FNLA	National Liberation Front of Angola (*Frente Nacional de Libertação de Angola*)
FOA	National Defense Research Agency (*Försvarets forskningsanstalt*), of Sweden
Frelimo	Front for the Liberation of Mozambique (*Frente de Libertação de Moçambique*)
FRG	Federal Republic of Germany, commonly known as West Germany
FRUS	Foreign Relations of the United States series
GDP	Gross Domestic Product
GOP	Government of Pakistan
GRC	Government of the Republic of China (alt. GROC)
HEU	Highly-Enriched Uranium
IAEA	International Atomic Energy Agency
IAEC	Indian/Iraqi/Israeli Atomic Energy Commissions

ICB	International Crisis Behavior data set
ICBM	Intercontinental Ballistic Missile
IMF	International Monetary Fund
INER	Institute of Nuclear Energy Research, of Taiwan
INR	Bureau of Intelligence and Research, of the U.S. Department of State
INUS	Insufficient but Necessary part of a condition that is itself Unnecessary but Sufficient to produce an outcome
IRBM	Intermediate-Range Ballistic Missile
ISIL	Islamic State of Iraq and the Levant
JAEC	Japan Atomic Energy Commission
JCPOA	Joint Comprehensive Plan of Action, on Iran's nuclear program
JCS	Joint Chiefs of Staff, of the United States
JDA	Japan Defense Agency
JPOA	Joint Plan of Action, on Iran's nuclear program
KAERI	Korea Atomic Energy Research Institute, of South Korea
KANUPP	Karachi Nuclear Power Plant
KEDO	Korean Peninsula Energy Development Organization
LDP	Liberal Democratic Party, of Japan
LEU	Low-Enriched Uranium
LWR	Light-Water Reactor
MAD	Mutually Assured Destruction
MLF	Multilateral Force, of NATO
MPE	Markov Perfect Equilibrium
MPLA	People's Movement for the Liberation of Angola (*Movimento Popular de Libertação de Angola*)
MW	Megawatt
MWe	Megawatt Electric
NAM	Non-Aligned Movement
NATO	North Atlantic Treaty Organization
NDPO	National Defense Program Outline, of Japan
NIE	National Intelligence Estimate, of the United States
NMC	National Military Capabilities data set
NNPA	Nuclear Nonproliferation Act, of the United States
NPG	Nuclear Planning Group, of NATO

NPT	Treaty on the Non-Proliferation of Nuclear Weapons, commonly known as the Non-Proliferation Treaty
NSC	National Security Council, of the United States
NSC-#	National Security Council report #, of the United States
NSG	Nuclear Suppliers Groups
OB-#	Supreme Commander's (*Överbefälhavaren*) recommendation #, of Sweden
OPEC	Organization of Petroleum Exporting Countries
P5+1	The Five Permanent Members of the UN Security Council, plus Germany
PAEC	Pakistani Atomic Energy Committee
PARR-1	Pakistani Atomic Research Reactor
PATN	Autonomous Program of Nuclear Technology, of Brazil
PBE	Perfect Bayesian Equilibrium
PINSTECH	Pakistani Institute of Nuclear Science and Technology
PKK	Kurdistan Worker's Party
PLO	Palestine Liberation Organization
PNE	Peaceful Nuclear Explosion
PPE	Perfect Public Equilibrium
PRC	People's Republic of China, commonly known as China
PTBT	Partial Nuclear Test Ban Treaty
RAFAEL	Authority for the Development of Armaments, of Israel
ROC	Republic of China, commonly known as Taiwan
ROK	Republic of Korea, commonly known as South Korea
ROKG	Republic of Korea Government
SADF	South African Defense Force
SAFARI	South African Fundamental Atomic Research Installation
SAP	Swedish Social Democratic Party (*Sveriges Socialdemokratiska Arbetareparti*)
SEATO	South East Asian Treaty Organization
SETAF	Southern European Task Force, of the United States

SNEPP	Study of Nuclear Explosions with Peaceful Purposes, of India
SNIE	Special National Intelligence Estimate, of the United States
SWAPO	South-West African People's Organization, of Namibia
TAEK	Turkish Atomic Energy Authority
TRR	Taiwan Research Reactor
UF6	Uranium Hexafluoride
UN	United Nations
UNGA	United Nations General Assembly
UNITA	National Union for the Total Independence of Angola (*União Nacional para a Independência Total de Angola*)
UNMOVIC	United Nations Monitoring, Verification, and Inspection Commission
UNSC	United Nations Security Council
UNSCOM	United Nations Special Commission
USG	United States Government
USSR	Union of Soviet Socialist Republics, commonly known as the Soviet Union
WMD	Weapons of Mass Destruction

1 | *Introduction*

The history of international politics since 1945 is to a great extent the history of nuclear politics. A robust nuclear arsenal can obliterate an enemy's state and society in a matter of weeks, days, perhaps even hours. This staggering devastation potential is part of the background against which international politics are conducted. Considerations about nuclear weapons permeate diplomatic exchanges on a wide range of topics, from military deployments and alliance management, to technological cooperation, trade and economic integration, and even international finance. Above all, nuclear weapons have reconfigured the relationship between military power and international influence – in one word, they have reshaped statecraft. So profound is the transformation of world politics since the first nuclear device was detonated in the Trinity test of July 16, 1945, that we often refer to the historical period that started that day as the "nuclear" or "atomic" age. In the seven decades since their introduction, nuclear weapons have become the military equivalent of Adam Smith's "invisible hand": they regulate behavior, impose constraints, and shape preferences while remaining largely out of sight.[1]

The signal importance of nuclear weapons for international relations has gradually pushed one problem to the top of the U.S. foreign-policy agenda: nuclear proliferation.[2] From the inception of the nuclear age, the United States has been at the forefront of efforts to stymie the spread of nuclear weapons. In the domestic plan, the U.S. government has passed a wide array of legislation aimed at preventing the transfer

---

[1] For a contrasting view, see: Mueller (1989).

[2] By nuclear proliferation we mean "horizontal" proliferation, i.e., an increase in the number of political units (so far exclusively states) that possess nuclear weapons, not "vertical" proliferation, i.e., an increase in the capabilities of the political units that possess a nuclear arsenal, typically by building more or more sophisticated nuclear weapons. Throughout the book, we use "nuclear proliferation" interchangeably with "nuclear acquisition" and "nuclearization."

of sensitive nuclear technology to other states, going back to 1946 with the (McMahon) Atomic Energy Act. Internationally, the United States spearheaded numerous multilateral efforts aimed at limiting proliferation, also going all the way back to the Baruch Plan of 1946 and reaching its zenith in the 1968 Treaty on the Non-Proliferation of Nuclear Weapons (NPT). Furthermore, all through the nuclear age, Washington spent considerable effort engaging bilaterally with potential proliferators, friend and foe alike, attempting to lead them to abandon their nuclear aspirations in the military realm. Against unfriendly states, Washington has often contemplated preventive counterproliferation strikes.[3] High-ranking U.S. officials defended the need to attack the Soviet Union before it would acquire nuclear weapons – which it did in 1949.[4] Less than two decades later, U.S. officials considered a strike on the Chinese nuclear program.[5] After the Cold War ended, proliferation concerns led President Bill Clinton (1993–2001) to the brink of war with North Korea in 1994, were central to President George W. Bush's (2001–2009) case for invading Iraq, and pressed grave dilemmas on President Barack Obama (2009–2017) concerning Iran.[6] When dealing with U.S. allies, Washington has also vigorously tried to persuade and, when necessary, coerce most of its protégés not to nuclearize, either by making additional commitments to their security or by bluntly threatening to abandon them.

Today, it is difficult to identify a tenet of U.S. foreign policy more solid than the belief that nuclear acquisition by any state is intrinsically bad for U.S. interests and should be avoided at all costs, if necessary by threatening allies with abandonment and adversaries with

---

[3] For the purposes of this book, we label "counterproliferation" any attempt to prevent a country from acquiring nuclear weapons by threatening it (implicitly or explicitly) with military action. In contrast, we label "nonproliferation" any measure designed to deter proliferation without the threat of military action. Whereas counterproliferation tends to be used vis-à-vis adversaries, nonproliferation is the usual approach toward nuclearization attempts by allied and friendly states.

[4] See: Buhite and Hamel (1990).

[5] See: Burr and Richelson (2000–2001).

[6] See: "President Delivers State of the Union Address," January 29, 2002, White House Archives. Available at: http://georgewbush-whitehouse.archives.gov/news/releases/2002/01/20020129-11.html. Last accessed: April 29, 2016; Lee and Moon (2003).

military force. All in all, nuclear proliferation remains one of the deepest concerns and thorniest problems facing the United States.

Questions and Puzzles

The historical spread of nuclear weapons is riddled with puzzles. To begin with, why does the United States worry so much about the spread of nuclear weapons when the pace of proliferation is so slow – indeed much slower than most predicted?[7] More than seven decades after nuclear weapons were invented, only eight other states possess them, of which at least three (Britain, France, and Israel) are U.S. allies – five, if one includes friendly states such as India and Pakistan. Among U.S. adversaries, only China, North Korea, and Russia possess the bomb. Why does Washington devote so much attention to a foreign-policy problem that materializes so seldom?

Relatedly, this small number of nuclear powers is the result of many states having eventually given up their nuclear development efforts. But if most countries ultimately stopped their nuclear program, why did they at one point or another engage in nuclear development? Besides the ten states that ultimately built nuclear weapons – the nine current nuclear powers plus South Africa, the only state that so far dismantled its nuclear arsenal – more than a dozen other countries have possessed nuclear programs with a military dimension at some point in time. Why did they start if they eventually decided to stop?

Furthermore, it is puzzling that although security is intuitively the foremost reason why a state would seek nuclear weapons, there are many states facing serious threats to their survival that have, nonetheless, remained nonnuclear. West Germany, for instance, despite having been until 1989 on the front line of the Cold War, never acquired nuclear weapons. Saddam Hussein's (1979–2003) Iraq, notwithstanding consistent security threats, also failed to acquire the bomb. South Korea has eschewed nuclearization even after the North went nuclear during the last decade. Taiwan has forfeited nuclear weapons despite dwindling U.S. security guarantees in the face of a mightier China. What accounts for these puzzling cases of nuclear forbearance? Why is it that although nuclear weapons are weapons of the weak, few weak states possess them?

---

[7] See: Yusuf (2009, 4).

Existing scholarship is unable to make sense of these puzzling patterns in the spread of nuclear weapons. In fact, these paradoxical patterns of proliferation have led the scholarly literature to practically discard security as the primary motivation behind a state's quest to develop nuclear weapons, and turn instead to non-security motivations for proliferation in an attempt to make sense of these puzzles. This in itself is perplexing, for nuclear weapons are, after all, weapons. Shouldn't we expect security considerations to be the foremost driver in states' decisions to build or eschew them?

To solve these puzzles of nuclear proliferation, we must go back to basics and once again ask the fundamental questions: Why do states acquire nuclear weapons? How does the security environment shape a state's decision to go nuclear? Are there particular strategic conditions that make states more likely to go nuclear? Conversely, are there strategic circumstances that make nuclear forbearance more likely? When is a nuclear power, such as the United States, more likely to be successful at preventing another state – friend or foe – from acquiring the bomb? Our book answers these questions in a manner that solves the puzzles highlighted in the preceding text.

The Argument in Brief

This book is based on one simple insight: nuclear proliferation affects the security of the state acquiring nuclear weapons, as well as the security of its adversaries and allies, which may attempt to prevent it. This observation entails two elements. First, nuclear proliferation is shaped by a process of strategic interaction involving the state that is considering the development of nuclear weapons, its adversaries, and, when present, its allies. Second, this process is shaped mostly by the security interests of the states involved. These are the two key wagers we make in this book.

A Strategic Theory of Proliferation

Our first theoretical wager, then, is that in order to understand nuclear proliferation we need a strategic theory, one that focuses on the interaction between all the states involved in, and affected by, the spread of nuclear weapons. To grasp the proliferation process, we must consider not only the interests of the state that is deciding whether to build a nuclear deterrent, but also those of the states whose security goals would be affected by such nuclear acquisition. We must then combine the interests of all these parties during the period in which one of them is considering nuclear acquisition, and analyze how their strategic interaction conditions a state's decision to build the bomb.

In looking at the interaction between all these actors, we follow in the footsteps of David Lake and Robert Powell, who invite scholars of international relations to take "the *interaction* of two or more states as the object to be analyzed," seeking "to explain how this interaction unfolds," thereby recognizing "the strategic interdependence of actors."[8] Focusing on only one of these strategic actors cannot but yield a partial view of the proliferation process – a problem common to much existing scholarship on the topic, which focuses either on the incentives of the state contemplating nuclearization or on those of the states that try to oppose its nuclear acquisition. Nuclear proliferation is a process through which a military technology spreads as the result of a strategic interaction between the state that wants it and those that have a say in whether it will get it: its adversaries, which would face a loss in relative power; and its allies, which might lose some of their influence and face higher odds of entrapment. Our strategic theory focuses on the interaction of these three sets of actors.[9]

---

[8] Lake and Powell (1999, 4), Lake and Powell's emphasis.
[9] Previous works on proliferation have claimed the label "strategic." See: Gartzke and Kroenig (2009); Kroenig (2010). What these authors mean by strategic, however, is that their work focuses on the consequences of nuclear proliferation for a particular state's "strategic" concerns. For example, key to some existing accounts of proliferation is the intuition that a state capable of projecting power over another state will face "strategic" losses if the latter acquires nuclear weapons, whereas a state that is unable to project power will have little to lose. See: Kroenig (2009a, 2009b, 2010, 2014). According to this line of reasoning, and we concur, states with great power-projection capabilities are more likely to oppose proliferation for "strategic" reasons. But in order to understand the conditions under which the opposition of power-projecting states will actually deter the spread of nuclear weapons, we need to allow their interests to interact with those of the would-be proliferator and determine which set of interests, so to speak, trumps the other. In other words, we need to take into account not the interests of one or another state taken separately, but their interaction within their strategic context.

A Security Theory of Proliferation

Our second key theoretical wager is, when analyzing this strategic interaction, to focus on security interests. Because proliferation is the process through which states acquire a particular *military* technology – nuclear weapons – it should come as no surprise that the most important factors conditioning it are the security interests of the states affected by it. Echoing Scott Sagan's words, we too believe that most proliferation cases "are best explained by the security model."[10] What we need – and what this book provides – is a more refined security-based theory of nuclear proliferation.

The Willingness and Opportunity Constraints on Proliferation

Proliferation only happens when a state has both the willingness and the opportunity to acquire nuclear weapons. A state will be willing to nuclearize only when it believes that a nuclear deterrent will yield a security benefit, leading to an improvement of its security outlook vis-à-vis its adversaries. In order to determine whether a state is willing to proliferate, we must compare this security benefit of proliferation to the cost of a nuclear program. A state will be willing to proliferate only when the security benefit of proliferation is greater than this cost.

Although willingness is a necessary condition for nuclear acquisition, it is not sufficient. An attempt to acquire the bomb could be thwarted by an adversary's counterproliferation effort – a credible threat of preventive attack or an actual military strike against the state's nuclear program. By striking preventively, an adversary can avoid the unfavorable shift in the distribution of capabilities that would result from the state's nuclearization. Whether a state will be able to nuclearize despite these preventive dynamics depends on the credibility of its adversaries' threats of attack against its nuclear-weapons program.

Preventive counterproliferation military action is always costly, however. Therefore, it will only be rational for an adversary to launch a counterproliferation preventive war if this action is less costly than the consequences of allowing the state to build nuclear weapons.

[10] Sagan (1996–1997, 85).

Moreover, when this is the case, the threat of preventive war will be credible, even if implicit. The potential proliferator may nevertheless attempt to develop nuclear weapons undetected, and may end up being targeted by an actual preventive strike.[11] Or it may drop its nuclear efforts for fear of being targeted. Either way, the state will lack the opportunity to acquire nuclear weapons. (These dynamics help account for the puzzling observation that many states start their nuclear efforts only to abandon them without having acquired nuclear weapons.) As the cost of prevention rises relative to the consequences of nuclear acquisition, threats of preventive action will become less credible. If these threats are not credible, the state will gain the opportunity to build the bomb and, having the willingness to do so, will nuclearize.

Whether a state satisfies the willingness and opportunity constraints, in turn, depends on three underlying strategic variables: the level of security threat it faces, its relative power vis-à-vis its adversaries, and the level and reliability of allied commitments to its security.

The Role of Security Threats

A state will attach a security benefit to nuclear weapons only when it faces a high level of threat to its security. A relatively benign security environment may lower the benefit of proliferation to the point at which it becomes smaller than the cost of a nuclear program, extinguishing the state's willingness to proliferate, and accounting for why most states have never attempted to develop nuclear weapons. Among states that have started down the nuclear development path, an improvement in their security environment may undermine their willingness to nuclearize, leading them to forfeit their nuclear ambitions and abandon their program.

---

[11] For an analysis of the conditions under which preventive strikes become more likely, see: Debs and Monteiro (2014). Theoretically, the only way a state could acquire the bomb under these conditions would be for its nuclear program to remain undetected such that it could present nuclear acquisition to its adversaries as a fait accompli. This scenario has never materialized historically and, given existing surveillance and inspection technology, is highly improbable in the future.

The Role of Conventional Power

The balance of conventional power between the potential proliferator and its adversaries prior to nuclear acquisition conditions both the state's willingness and its opportunity to build the bomb.

High relative power during the nuclear development phase dampens the security benefit of proliferation. Conversely, the weaker a potential proliferator is, the more nuclear acquisition would improve its security outlook. By lowering the security benefit of proliferation vis-à-vis the cost of a nuclear program, conventional power undermines a state's willingness to build the bomb. Among states that are strong vis-à-vis their adversaries, only those facing the direst security threats will attempt to acquire a nuclear deterrent.

At the same time, the balance of conventional power between the potential proliferator and its adversaries prior to nuclear acquisition also conditions the cost of preventive military action and, through it, the state's opportunity to build the bomb. If the state considering nuclear weapons is stronger relative to its adversaries, the cost of preventive war is greater. All other things being equal, it is less likely that a preventive attack will be the adversaries' rational option. Powerful states therefore rarely face credible threats of preventive counterproliferation military action launched by their adversaries. Consequently, whenever they face security threats dire enough to make them willing to build the bomb, powerful states will be more likely to have the opportunity to cross the nuclear threshold.

If the state contemplating nuclearization is weaker than its adversaries, in contrast, the cost of preventive counterproliferation military action is relatively lower. At the same time, the state's conventional weakness increases the security benefit that it would extract from nuclearization. This makes it more rational for an adversary to launch a preventive attack. Threats of counterproliferation military action are therefore more likely to be credible, removing the state's opportunity to nuclearize.

Proliferation among states without allies thus requires an empirically rare combination of strategic factors: high relative power plus a serious threat to the state's security. This logic accounts for one of the puzzling patterns of the spread of nuclear weapons – the absence of nuclear proliferation among weak unprotected states facing dire security threats. Nuclear weapons may well be the weapons of the weak, but the weak (and unprotected) cannot get them.

The Role of Allies

Having characterized the strategic interaction through which a state's adversaries condition its ability to nuclearize, we then focus on the role a state's allies play in the proliferation process. Allies may affect a state's odds of proliferation in two ways.

First, an ally can help alleviate a security threat faced by its protégé. This would decrease the protégé's willingness to acquire nuclear weapons. In fact, if the ally reliably guarantees all of the protégé's security interests, the protégé should not be willing to nuclearize. Under these conditions, nuclear weapons would not present a security benefit that would justify their cost. A state protected by a security sponsor has the willingness to build the bomb only when this sponsor does not reliably cover all of the protégé's security interests.

Second, the presence of a security sponsor increases the costs that an adversary would face if it were to launch a preventive counter-proliferation strike. Therefore, a security sponsor lowers the credibility of threats of military action against its protégé. Even when the protection of the sponsor is not sufficient to undermine the protégé's willingness to nuclearize, it may nevertheless be enough to give it the opportunity to build the bomb. When this combination occurs, proliferation will ensue.

Factoring in both of these effects, the presence of an ally suppresses proliferation when it reliably covers the protégé's security interests, undermining its willingness to build the bomb. At the same time, the presence of an ally enables proliferation when, absent the added deterrent power of the sponsor, the protégé would be vulnerable to preventive military action, and would therefore lack the opportunity to acquire nuclear weapons.

Sticks, Carrots, and Proliferation

Our theory of nuclear proliferation is also a theory of nonproliferation. In fact, our analysis of the role of allies in the proliferation process helps ascertain the relative effectiveness of different nonproliferation policy tools. We group all such tools into two broad categories: sticks and carrots. A sticks-based approach to non-proliferation includes all coercive measures such as inspections of nuclear facilities, limits to the supply of nuclear materials and technology, sanctions, and so forth. Underpinning these coercive efforts is the threat of withdrawal of the sponsor's support. Such an approach aims at removing the protégé's opportunity to build the bomb. The effectiveness of a sticks-based nonproliferation policy therefore depends on the consequences of carrying out this threat. What would happen if the protégé would be left on its own? A protégé that is relatively strong vis-à-vis its adversaries would nevertheless retain the opportunity to proliferate even if abandoned by its sponsor. It would therefore be immune to sticks-based nonproliferation efforts by its sponsor. Only protégés that are relatively weak vis-à-vis their adversaries can be coerced into maintaining their nonnuclear status through a sticks-based nonproliferation policy.

Now consider a carrots-based approach. This includes the set of policies through which an ally boosts its security commitment to the protégé through public pledges of protection, troop and nuclear weapons deployments, military aid, and sales of conventional weapons. Such an approach aims at removing the protégé's willingness to build the bomb. Therefore, it will be easier to implement with a protégé that is already relatively strong vis-à-vis its adversaries, requiring less support to reach the point at which it no longer views an investment in nuclear weapons as worthwhile. Protégés that are weaker vis-à-vis their adversaries, in contrast, will require a greater level of support before they lose their willingness to build the bomb. As with power, so it is with the breadth of the protégé's security interests. If these are broader, the protégé will require a greater level of support before a carrots-based approach to nonproliferation leads it to abandon its nuclear ambitions. A protégé with narrower security interests will be easier to satisfy with this approach, making nonproliferation efforts more likely to succeed.

Taking stock, a sticks-based nonproliferation policy, entailing no additional security commitments on the part of the sponsor, is the most adequate to guarantee the continuation of the nonnuclear status of weak protégés. Costly carrots-based approaches to nonproliferation, which result in greater security commitments on the part of the sponsor, will be reserved for relatively strong allies, which cannot otherwise be deterred from acquiring nuclear weapons.

Empirically, proliferation occurs in a limited range of strategic environments. Specifically, we find two sets of strategic circumstances – or pathways – to nuclear acquisition. First, a high level of security threat combined with high relative conventional power on the part of the proliferating state. Second, a high level of security threat combined with the presence of an ally that is deemed unreliable. All other strategic settings result in the maintenance of a state's nonnuclear status.

Empirical Patterns

Our theory highlights the deep continuity in the strategic logic of proliferation that has governed the spread of nuclear weapons since the dawn of the atomic age in 1945. Despite frequent claims about the changing dynamics governing proliferation in different historical periods – say, before and after the NPT, or before and after the end of the Cold War – a focus on the strategic environment reveals the enduring role of power, threats, and allied commitments in conditioning the odds of nuclear acquisition.

In doing so, the strategic logic of nuclear proliferation sheds light on several hitherto underappreciated historical patterns. First, states that do not face a high-level security threat have not acquired the bomb. The presence of a significant security threat is a necessary condition for nuclearization. Historically, no state has acquired nuclear weapons without perceiving its security environment as highly threatening, regardless of how strong other pressures to acquire the bomb – including considerations of domestic or international prestige, the psychology of leaders, or the economic preferences of ruling elites – may be.

Second, among states that are not protected by a great-power sponsor, only those that are strong vis-à-vis their adversaries have acquired the bomb. There is no historical case of a relatively weak state ever succeeding in nuclearizing without having a powerful ally committed to retaliating against a preventive counter-proliferation strike. We should therefore be cautious about claims that nuclear weapons are the "weapon of the weak," the "great equalizer" in international relations.[12] No doubt, the atomic bomb would enable a weak state to stand up to more powerful adversaries. So far, however, no weak unprotected state has ever managed to obtain it.

---

[12] Paul (1999, 2012).

Third, among states that possess a powerful ally, only those whose security goals are not entirely covered by this sponsor have acquired nuclear weapons. Put differently, states whose security goals are subsumed by their powerful allies' own aims do not possess the willingness to acquire the bomb. This means that, among weak states, proliferation only occurs under two narrow sets of strategic circumstances: either the state's security sponsor is unwilling to ensure reliably the future protection of the protégé's territory; or the protégé has secondary security goals that the sponsor does not share.

Fourth, threats of abandonment issued by a security sponsor – what we call a "sticks-based" nonproliferation policy – are effective in curtailing proliferation only by protégés that are relatively weak vis-à-vis their adversaries. If a protégé is strong vis-à-vis its adversaries, it has the opportunity to proliferate on its own, even if its security sponsor were to abandon it. In this case, the sponsor can only effectively deter proliferation by taking away the protégé's willingness to acquire nuclear weapons, which it can do by extending additional security assurances – what we call a "carrots-based" nonproliferation policy. In other words, whereas sticks can deter proliferation by weak protégés, only carrots will prevent stronger protégés from building nuclear weapons. This, in turn, means that when Washington is faced with a strong protégé that is willing to acquire the bomb (because some of its security interests are not reliably guaranteed by the United States), U.S. decisionmakers must choose between extending additional security commitments to that state or allowing for the spread of nuclear weapons.

Fifth and finally, the spread of nuclear weapons slowed down after the end of the Cold War in 1989. Despite much concern about "nuclear cascades" and proliferation "tipping points,"[13] only two states – Pakistan and North Korea – have acquired nuclear weapons in the era of U.S. military power preponderance.[14] U.S. allies face few if any

[13] See: Campbell, Einhorn, and Reiss (2004); Potter and Mukhatzhanova (2008); Bracken (2012); Miller (2014b).

[14] By all accounts, Pakistan already possessed nuclear weapons before the Cold War ended. For example, the list of nuclear programs we use in the empirical sections of this book places Pakistani nuclear acquisition in 1990, while the Soviet Union still existed. See: Way (2012). Still, since Pakistan only tested a nuclear device in 1998, we prudently list it here as a "post–Cold War" proliferator. If we were to categorize it as having proliferated during the Cold War, this empirical pattern would be even more pronounced.

significant security threats that nuclear weapons could placate and on which they do not trust Washington's continued protection. U.S. adversaries, lacking a nuclear patron, risk a preventive strike against their nuclear program.[15] As long as U.S. conventional power preponderance endures, therefore, we should expect the rate of proliferation to remain exceedingly low.

Existing Scholarship

Concerns about nuclear proliferation are not only one of the foremost topics in the U.S. foreign-policy agenda. They have also percolated through the scholarly world. Although during the early Cold War most thinking in nuclear studies was devoted to avoiding escalation between nuclear powers, an increasing effort has been devoted to understanding the motivations and constraints driving the spread of nuclear weapons. Particularly since the end of the Cold War, which lowered the likelihood of nuclear conflict involving the United States, the causes of nuclear proliferation have been the object of much theorizing and empirical study. The resulting scholarly literature evolved in three waves, which we discuss in turn.

Security Sources of Demand

The first wave of proliferation scholarship focused on security explanations, arguing that a state's nuclearization results from its need to mitigate threats to its survival.[16] As Bradley Thayer put it in an early work on the topic, "security is the only necessary and sufficient cause of nuclear proliferation."[17] The higher the threat level a country faces, the more it is likely to acquire nuclear weapons. Furthermore, and given the threat posed by an adversary's nuclear acquisition, proliferation might itself beget more proliferation, leading to predictions of

---

[15] For a survey of such attacks, see: Fuhrmann and Kreps (2010). This option became more attractive and effective since the end of the Cold War and has been used to account for the Iraq War. See: Debs and Monteiro (2014).

[16] See: Epstein (1977); Mearsheimer (1990); Betts (1993); Frankel (1993); Thayer (1995). For a literature review of early security explanations of nuclear proliferation, see: Sagan (1996–1997).

[17] Thayer (1995, 486).

nuclear "dominos" or a "strategic chain reaction."[18] Reviewing this literature in the mid-1990s, Sagan noted:

Although nuclear weapons could also be developed to serve either as deterrents against overwhelming conventional military threats or as coercive tools to compel changes in the status quo, the simple focus on states' responses to emerging nuclear threats is the most common and most parsimonious explanation for nuclear weapons proliferation.[19]

This line of reasoning stemmed from neorealist approaches to the study of international politics, which emphasize the role of the security environment in conditioning state actions.[20] Prominent neorealist scholars such as Kenneth Waltz argued that, because nuclear weapons offer great security benefits in the self-help international environment, efforts to deter proliferation are doomed to fail. In Waltz's own assessment, "in the past half-century, no country has been able to prevent other countries from going nuclear if they were determined to do so."[21]

The pessimistic predictions made by these early security-based theories of proliferation did not come to pass, however. The number of nuclear states remained relatively steady over time and "the pace of proliferation has been consistently *slower* than has been anticipated by most experts."[22] Today, only nine states possess nuclear weapons.

The realization that these early security arguments overpredicted the pace of proliferation led to a shift in focus toward explaining nuclear "forbearance" – i.e., why states forego nuclearization. Mitchell Reiss argued that when the security threats that prompt a nuclear program wane, so will the program itself, resulting in nuclear abandonment.[23] But some countries – such as Iraq, South Korea, or Taiwan – faced continued threats and have nonetheless maintained their nonnuclear status. In another account of nuclear forbearance, T. V. Paul argued that it happens when a state anticipates that nuclearization will generate negative externalities for its own security.

[18] See: Epstein (1977, 19).
[19] Sagan (1996–1997, 57).
[20] See: Waltz (1979).
[21] Waltz (2003, 38).
[22] See: Yusuf (2009, 4), Yusuf's emphasis.
[23] See: Reiss (1995).

Specifically, a state will eschew its nuclear ambitions when it fears that proliferation will worsen its security outlook by causing abandonment by an ally or triggering an arms race with an adversary.[24] This line of reasoning is an important step in the direction of incorporating into our analysis of nuclear proliferation the interests of all the states it affects. Yet, some countries – e.g., the Soviet Union and Pakistan – chose to proliferate even though their nuclear acquisition was likely to trigger an arms race. Furthermore, whereas in some cases great powers have been able to persuade their protégés to remain nonnuclear by threatening them with abandonment (e.g., the United States vis-à-vis Taiwan), in other cases such threats were ineffective and the protégé ended up acquiring nuclear weapons (e.g., the United States vis-à-vis Israel). Finally, whereas Paul predicts that states located in high-conflict regions and which do not possess robust allied security guarantees will tend to proliferate, in some cases (e.g., Iraq and Sweden) they have not.

Overall, the arguments put forth by Reiss and Paul represent important advances toward understanding how a state's security incentives may push both toward *and against* nuclearization.[25] Nonetheless, existing security-based arguments are unable to account for why some states build the bomb while others choose to remain nonnuclear.

Non-Security Sources of Demand

Reacting to these limitations of security arguments in accounting for the patterns of nuclear proliferation, scholars in the 1980s started to search for other, non-security "sources of the political *demand* for nuclear weapons," resulting in a second wave of literature.[26] Just like the first wave of explanations for nuclear proliferation stemmed from a broader research program, this second wave itself derives from alternative approaches to the study of international relations. Specifically, this second wave of proliferation research stems from neoliberal theories of world politics, which focus on the role of domestic and international institutions in driving, or constraining, state behavior; and from

---

[24] See: Paul (2000, 15–27).
[25] See: Reiss (1995); Paul (2000).
[26] Sagan (1996–1997, 56), Sagan's emphasis.

constructivist theories of international relations, which focus on the role of identities, culture, and norms in shaping state action.[27]

In what is perhaps the most directly neoliberal view of proliferation, Etel Solingen's work offers an account of the spread of nuclear weapons based on the political and economic preferences of ruling elites.[28] Contending that existing security-based arguments are unable to account for variation either in states' nuclear behavior or in their responses to U.S. efforts to stem the spread of nuclear weapons, Solingen explains these behaviors based on how ruling coalitions believe state security and prosperity can best be produced, namely, through inward-looking military means or outward-looking economic integration. Inward-looking elites who favor import-substitution or purely autarchic developmental models will favor militarization and, often, nuclearization. In contrast, outward-looking, internationalizing elites who favor economic integration and growth through interdependence will frown upon nuclear acquisition, which is likely to bring with it regional isolation and geostrategic instability. The odds of proliferation – as well as decisions about starting and stopping nuclear development – depend on the relative power of these two types of elites within a country's political system.[29] In Solingen's own words, open "internationalizing models" are "likely to be sufficient for denuclearization except under two circumstances: (a) when neighboring inward-looking regimes seek nuclear weapons (or other weapons of mass destruction [WMD]); and (b) when nuclear weapons were acquired prior to the inception of internationalizing models."[30]

Solingen makes a valuable contribution to our picture of the nuclear proliferation process. Certainly, economic integration may bring with it better security relations with one's neighbors and alleviate security concerns.[31] Nonetheless, Solingen's theory, as noted, includes caveats that introduce serious questions about its broader applicability. First, per caveat (a), the presence of an inward-looking neighboring state developing nuclear weapons is sufficient to dissolve the predicted

---

[27] On neoliberalism, see: Keohane (1984); Moravcsik (1997). On constructivism, see: Wendt (1999).
[28] See: Solingen (2007).
[29] Ibid., 40–47.
[30] Ibid., 46.
[31] See: Polachek (1980); Crescenzi (2003); Martin et al. (2008); Polachek and Xiang (2010).

power of her model, by making even an outward-looking ruling coalition likely to attempt to develop nuclear weapons. But clearly not
all states that are faced by inward-looking neighbors that are trying
to nuclearize have themselves attempted to develop nuclear weapons. In fact, one of Solingen's case studies focuses on a country, South
Korea, that did not attempt to develop nuclear weapons even though
its inward-looking neighbor, North Korea, nuclearized in the 2000s.
Second, per caveat (b), Solingen exempts her theory from explaining cases of proliferation that occurred while an inward looking elite
ruled a country. As we just saw, the general prediction of Solingen's
theory for these cases is that they will be likely to develop nuclear
weapons. Still, what explains the decision to acquire the bomb made
by some inward-looking regimes (the Soviet Union in 1949, China
in 1964, South Africa in 1979, Pakistan in the late 1980s, and North
Korea in the mid-2000s), whereas many other such regimes (such as
Egypt, Iraq, or Libya) never built a nuclear weapon? In our view, to
understand the conditions under which states that are threatened by
a nuclearizing neighbor will themselves develop a nuclear arsenal, we
need to look at their strategic interaction. In effect, Solingen's theory
itself points to this need, by allowing for a state's nuclear decisionmaking to be affected by the nuclear behavior of a state's neighbors.
Our theory generalizes this insight.

Inspired by constructivist theories of international relations, Maria
Rublee puts forth an alternative account of why states acquire or eschew nuclear weapons that focuses on emerging international nonproliferation norms.[32] For Rublee, the nonproliferation regime that
emerged in the 1960s, and the international norms it has helped
spread, have influenced the nuclear behavior of states, bringing the
pace of proliferation close to a halt.

Certainly, nonproliferation norms have frequently been invoked
by states that decide to eschew nuclear weapons. Furthermore, these
norms are often part and parcel of nonproliferation efforts led by the
United States and others. But it is hard to see how one could build
a general theory of the spread of nuclear weapons by focusing on
nonproliferation norms. To begin with, much of the history of how

---

[32] See: Rublee (2009). For other treatments of norms in the context of nuclear
studies focusing on the question of nuclear use, see: Paul (1995); Tannenwald
(1999).

the current nuclear states acquired their nuclear arsenals took place before those norms emerged. Of the nine current nuclear states, six (the United States, Soviet Union, United Kingdom, France, China, and Israel) nuclearized before the NPT went into force in 1970. A theory of proliferation based on the spread of nonproliferation norm has little to say about why these six states acquired nuclear weapons between 1945 and 1970 whereas many others did not. Furthermore, to state the obvious, the remaining four states to have acquired nuclear weapons (South Africa, India, Pakistan, and North Korea) have done so after the NPT regime was already in place. What explains their failure to internalize nonproliferation norms? Finally, could it be that the norm of nonproliferation itself and the regime that was set up to enforce it result from strategic considerations made by the nuclear powers?[33] There is considerable evidence that the emergence of the NPT was to a great extent driven by the determination of both superpowers to guarantee the nonnuclear status of the Federal Republic of Germany (FRG).[34] In fact, much of what Rublee describes as persuasion and norm-internalization could be redescribed as coercion or manipulation by nuclear states of their nonnuclear peers. To understand a state's decision to acquire or eschew nuclear weapons, we need to place the emerging norm against proliferation in the strategic environment that proliferators face.

In another view on the non-security sources of nuclear proliferation, Jacques Hymans' work draws on the tradition of political psychology to account for the spread of nuclear weapons based on the psychological makeup of leaders and their conception of their nation's identity. Specifically, Hymans argues, leaders that have an oppositional nationalistic identity conception will be more prone to drive their countries toward nuclear acquisition.[35] This oppositional view makes leaders feel both fear and pride, his argument goes, resulting in "a higher threat assessment, which motivates a serious commitment to enhance the nation's

---

[33] See: Craig and Ruzicka (2013).
[34] See: Swango (2009); Coe and Vaynman (2015).
[35] See: Hymans (2006). For a different – institutional rather than psychological – take on how autocratic leaders may be more inclined to pursue the bomb, see: Way and Weeks (2014). This study differs from ours in that it focuses on leaders' propensity to pursue nuclear weapons, whereas we are interested in nuclear acquisition, not just pursuit. On how leaders' conceptions of national "roles" condition the odds of proliferation, see: Chafetz et al. (1996); Grillot and Long (2000).

defenses," along with "a greater urgency to act, to do something to improve the security situation," all the while wanting to impress themselves, "a goal that can hardly be better achieved than through the terrible beauty of a homemade mushroom cloud."[36]

We have little doubt that a leader's psychological makeup and national-identity conception may encourage certain behaviors and discourage others. But whence do these conceptions come? Could it be that they are insulated from the strategic environment the state faces? To be sure, a leader's threat assessment, though perhaps liable to be shaped by their psychological makeup (to say nothing of multiple other factors), must be at least somehow related to the strategic circumstances their state faces, including the presence of adversaries and allies, and their relative military capabilities. We wager that more explanatory leverage can be obtained by focusing on the features of the security environment a state faces than on the psychological makeup of its leaders.[37]

Finally, building on organizational theory, Hymans lays out a second argument accounting for the patterns of proliferation centered on "nuclear weapons project efficiency." Hymans focuses on varying levels of managerial acumen and types of macro-institutional environment in order to explain why some states have been able to acquire nuclear weapons whereas others pursue them for decades to no avail.[38] Using this theory, Hymans shows that, since 1970, states that attempted to develop nuclear weapons have taken a great deal longer to achieve their nuclear ambitions.

In our view, these managerial and institutional constraints on nuclear development may affect proliferation in three ways. First, they increase the cost of nuclear acquisition, making it less likely that a state deems a nuclear investment to be productive in terms of yielding a security benefit. Second, by delaying nuclear acquisition, these constraints may facilitate nuclear forbearance if the security environment improves during this longer nuclear development period. Third, they augment the period during which the state is vulnerable to preventive action by its adversaries. In short, managerial and institutional constraints explain why states may take longer to proliferate, but they

---

[36] Hymans (2006, 35).
[37] Solingen (2007, 104).
[38] See: Hymans (2012, 27).

cannot account for a state's decision to abandon the pursuit of nuclear weapons, which requires a transformation in its security environment during the period of nuclear development; nor for an adversary's decision to act preventively, which requires a strategic evaluation that a counterproliferation strike is preferable to proliferation.

Taking stock, this second wave of proliferation studies has put forth such a wide variety of non-security explanations for states' nuclear decisions that today "the overwhelming majority of scholarly work on nuclear proliferation argues that states do not directly respond to the international environment in making their nuclear weapons choices."[39] This burgeoning wave of scholarship on the causes of nuclear proliferation has no doubt added much to our knowledge of how these non-security variables may contribute to a state's willingness to nuclearize. Yet, this wave of literature finds itself in an ironic situation. Having emerged from a sense that security-based theories could not explain proliferation because they led to contradictory predictions, non-security-based explanations are now themselves the source of myriad different predictions about what causes different nuclear behaviors.[40] We wager that this predicament is a consequence of the premature turn away from what is intuitively the most important determinant of nuclear acquisition: a state's security environment.[41] Surely, the economic, political, psychological, institutional, or normative preferences of leaders and ruling elites are conditioned by the security environment they face. To understand their role in the proliferation process, then, we must determine how the security context in which they operate shapes the incentives to pursue or forfeit nuclear weapons. The theory we lay out in the following text gives this strategic context its due importance, placing it at the center of the proliferation problem.

Supply Constraints and Strategies of Inhibition

More recently, a third wave of scholarship on proliferation has focused on "strategies of inhibition."[42] These are the strategies great

[39] Hymans (2011, 154).
[40] For an extensive criticism of security-based arguments on the causes of nuclear proliferation based on the observation that they make different predictions, see: Solingen (2007, 24–28).
[41] See: Hymans (2006); Solingen (2007); Rublee (2009); Way and Weeks (2014).
[42] For an overview of the literature on these strategies, see: Gavin (2015).

powers employ to inhibit the spread of nuclear weapons.[43] This wave of research shifted the analytic focus from a state's willingness to its opportunity to proliferate, being largely responsible for a renaissance in nuclear studies.[44]

This line of scholarship started out by applying quantitative research methods[45] and focusing on supply-side constraints on nuclear proliferation.[46] The resulting "supply-side" literature emphasizes the role of powerful states in limiting access to nuclear technology and materials as key in determining the odds of proliferation. The higher a state's power projection capability, the more likely it is to oppose attempts to assist others' nuclearization efforts, thus undermining them.[47] Supply-side explanations correctly emphasize how nuclear acquisition is also a supply problem. In order to obtain nuclear weapons, a state must want them, but it must also be able to get them. In highlighting this second half of the proliferation problem, supply-side theorists make an important contribution.

Yet, existing supply-side explanations of proliferation suffer from several notable shortcomings. To begin with, an exclusive focus on restrictions to the supply of nuclear materials and technology ignores other tools states use to limit proliferation, including threats to withdraw support from an ally or to use military force against an adversary. In fact, restrictions to the supply of nuclear materials will rarely be applied on their own. To the contrary, they usually are accompanied by sanctions or threats of military force in the case of attempted proliferation by an adversary, or by inspections and threats of abandonment in the case of attempted nuclearization by an ally. Given that the success of supply restrictions may depend on them being underpinned by these other efforts, the efficacy of the toolkit deployed to deter proliferation must be evaluated in toto.

Moreover, supply-side theories cannot account for the slower pace of proliferation of the past two-and-a-half decades when compared

---

[43] For a provocative argument on U.S. nonproliferation efforts, see: Maddock (2010). For a review of different states' attitudes toward the NPT treaty, written soon after its implementation, see: Quester (1973).

[44] See: Sagan (2014).

[45] See: Singh and Way (2004); Jo and Gartzke (2007).

[46] See: Fuhrmann (2009a, 2009b, 2012); Kroenig (2009a, 2009b, 2010, 2014).

[47] See: Kroenig (2010).

with the Cold War. By these theories' own logic, as the Soviet Union lost much of its power-projection capability, it "became more willing to provide sensitive nuclear assistance."[48] Additionally, states such as Pakistan were, for part of the post–Cold War period, suspected of supplying would-be nuclear powers with technology and materials.[49] Therefore, it is unclear whether the supply of nuclear materials and technology is more restricted today than in the past. And even if we were to grant that this supply is more restricted today than in the past, it is not clear why this would slow down the rate of proliferation. If one takes the demand-and-supply framework seriously, a reduction in supply would only alter the rate of proliferation if demand for nuclear weapons were elastic. A small number of nuclear weapons, however, has a large effect on a state's ability to guarantee its own survival. Therefore, few security-related goods should have a *less* elastic demand. Attempts to restrict nuclear supplies may thus lead only to an increase in the cost that states have to pay for nuclearization. Indeed, looking at the empirical record, we see that several of the states that have acquired nuclear weapons were the target of consistent supply-side efforts to restrict their ability to make progress toward the bomb. They nonetheless managed to build a nuclear deterrent, showing how an exclusive focus on the supply of nuclear technology and materials is insufficient to predict the patterns of proliferation.

Finally, supply-side restrictions – and, conversely, offers of nuclear assistance – are often endogenous to demand-side considerations. In other words, a power-projecting state is likely to put greater effort to curtail the availability of nuclear technology and materials to a state that exhibits a high demand for nuclear weapons and is making a great effort toward acquiring the bomb. Conversely, a non-power-projecting state is more likely to offer assistance to a state developing the bomb if this state asks for assistance because of its high level of interest in acquiring nuclear weapons. Demand and supply are, in nuclear weapons as in the production of any other security or non-security good, inextricably linked. Which of the two forces "trumps" the other in a particular case – resulting in nuclear proliferation or forbearance – can only be established by analyzing both.

---

[48] Kroenig (2009a, 128). Kroenig notes that China's rise may counter the effect of Russian decline, but this is theoretically indeterminate.

[49] See: Corera (2006).

Overall, although supply-side theories of nuclear proliferation are useful to explain which states are more or less likely to offer or withdraw nuclear assistance to aspiring nuclear states, they are unable to account for why some states go nuclear whereas others do not. After all, many nuclear states developed their program while circumventing others' efforts to limit their access to nuclear technology and materials – by finding alternative suppliers or doing most development effort themselves. At the same time, many other states received a great deal of nuclear assistance and yet never acquired the bomb.

Beyond restrictions to the supply of nuclear materials and technologies, this latest wave of scholarship on proliferation has also looked at other policies through which powerful states attempt to deter proliferation. Specifically, the latest scholarship has tried to tackle the role of alliances on proliferation, analyzing the effectiveness of different nonproliferation tools available to a security sponsor such as the United States when one of its protégés displays an interest in acquiring the bomb.[50] This work looks both at the policy instruments with which security sponsors attempt to undermine their protégés' demand for nuclear weapons (e.g., public pledges of protection, troop deployments, nuclear-weapons deployments, and sales of conventional weapons) and at the tools with which security sponsors attempt to curtail their protégés' opportunity to develop nuclear weapons (e.g., inspections of nuclear facilities, efforts to limit their access to nuclear materials and technology, threats of ending support, and sanctions). Overall, the resulting scholarship has yielded a multiplicity of predictions about what are the most effective ways to deter proliferation among allies, reinforcing the criticism that earlier opponents of security explanations had advanced: security factors, such as the presence or absence of an ally, have no simple predictive effect on nuclear proliferation.

For example, whereas according to one study U.S. troop deployments to a protégé's territory have no effect on the protégé's nuclear status,[51] a close examination of important historical cases (e.g., South Korea and Taiwan in the 1970s) highlights the role of concerns about U.S. troop withdrawals as a crucial motivation behind the willingness

---

[50] See: Kogan (2013b); Lanoszka (2013); Fuhrmann and Sechser (2014); Miller (2014a); Reiter (2014); Gerzhoy (2015).

[51] See: Reiter (2014).

of a U.S. ally to pursue nuclear weapons.[52] Similarly, whereas some recent work finds little support for nonproliferation as a rationale driving the foreign-deployment of U.S. nuclear weapons,[53] other scholarship finds that the deployment of U.S. nuclear weapons to allied territory has an overall dampening effect on the odds of proliferation.[54] Finally, although one recent study claims that intrusive U.S. inspections of nuclear facilities have led some U.S. allies (such as Taiwan in the 1970s and 1980s) to abandon their nuclear program, other U.S. allies (e.g., France in the 1950s, Israel in the 1960s, or Pakistan in the 1980s) have proliferated without being exposed to such intrusive inspections regimes.[55] In sum, the debate on the effect of alliances on proliferation remains wide open.

Although this most recent wave of empirical work advances our knowledge of the effects of alliances on nuclear proliferation, in our view a better understanding of this question requires a combination of rigorous historical analysis with additional theoretical development. Specifically, only by developing a strategic theory of nuclear proliferation – one that takes into consideration the security interests of a protégé considering nuclear acquisition, its security sponsor, and their common adversary – will we be able to understand the conditions under which the protection offered by a security sponsor will deter or, to the contrary, encourage nuclear acquisition by the protégé. Put differently, we need a theory that allows us to understand when alliances will lower the protégé's willingness to proliferate more than they increase its opportunity to do so, and vice versa.

Summing up, we possess a multiplicity of scholarly views on what accounts for the patterns of nuclear proliferation. To be sure, this scholarly debate has spilled over to the policy world, where different communities echo different arguments. Perhaps unsurprisingly, the U.S. defense community tends to endorse security explanations for why states want nuclear weapons. Members of the U.S. defense establishment, moreover, spend a great deal of effort deliberating about the most appropriate policies to deter further nuclear proliferation, if necessary by military means. But without a proper understanding of

---

[52] See: Lanoszka (2013).
[53] See: Fuhrmann and Sechser (2014).
[54] See: Reiter (2014).
[55] See: Kogan (2013b).

the role played by the strategic environment in the process of nuclear proliferation, U.S. policymakers lack a basic framework within which to compare the relative effectiveness of different policy tools. At the same time, the arms control community is largely motivated by neo-liberal and constructivist arguments about the role of institutions and norms in shaping the proliferation process. Well intentioned as its efforts often are, their success will be more likely if they incorporate a strategic-interaction perspective into their analysis of the motivations each state has to acquire or forfeit nuclear weapons.[56]

Today's scholarly debate on the causes of proliferation, for its part, is largely organized between demand- and supply-side explanations.[57] Each of these perspectives contributes to our understanding of the proliferation process. Yet, they each suffer from the same limitation: they focus either on a state's willingness to acquire nuclear weapons (demand-side explanations) or the motivations of other states to prevent it from having the opportunity to do so (supply-side explanations). That each existing theory accounts for only one aspect of the proliferation process – demand or supply – explains why despite having developed a multiplicity of arguments on economic, political, sociological, organizational, technological, and psychological variables, we are still not capable of accounting for the overall pattern in the spread of nuclear weapons. At the same time, although most scholars agree that security matters greatly as a driver of proliferation, we possess no systematic treatment of how security concerns and, more broadly, the strategic environment shape the spread of nuclear weapons. In our view, these two problems are connected: to understand the role played by security concerns on the odds of proliferation, we need to look at how both demand *and* supply interact in a state's strategic environment, analyzing their net effect.[58] Only when we do so will we be able to develop a theory of nuclear proliferation that (i) accounts for why some states acquire nuclear weapons whereas others eschew nuclear ambitions and (ii) compares the relative effectiveness

---

[56] For a skeptical view of the arms control community, see: Craig and Ruzicka (2013).

[57] See: Gartzke and Kroenig (2009); Montgomery and Sagan (2009); Müller and Schmidt (2010); Sagan (2011).

[58] See: Sagan (2011, 240).

of different tools with which the United States can try to deter other states from acquiring nuclear weapons. This book sets out to present and test one such theory.

Implications of Our Argument

It should be clear by now that our theory of proliferation is also a theory of nonproliferation. As such, our argument has implications for policymakers. To begin with, one might be tempted to think that given the low rate of nuclear acquisition, the United States should not rank proliferation among its most pressing international problems. We show how this view has it backward. Consistent U.S. efforts to stymie the spread of nuclear weapons underpin the low rate of proliferation, accounting to a great extent for the surprisingly small number of nuclear-weapons states seven decades after the beginning of the nuclear age.

Furthermore, we show how despite rare *explicit* U.S. threats of military action or allied abandonment, the military dimension plays a key role in preventing the spread of nuclear weapons. Threats rarely need to be implemented or even issued explicitly, because their targets internalize them and give up nuclear development efforts. As the historical record shows, in many of the cases in which U.S. policy played a role in successfully stopping the spread of nuclear weapons, credible threats of military force (against, e.g., Iraq and Libya) or allied abandonment (vis-à-vis, e.g., Taiwan or West Germany) were key in producing this outcome. As in many other domains of international politics, credible threats tend to be internalized by their targets and therefore do not need to be carried out, producing successful coercion.[59] Specifically, the effectiveness of counterproliferation threats largely accounts for why there is no historical case of proliferation by a relatively weak state that does not have the protection of a great-power sponsor. In this sense, our theory lends support to the claim that leaving "all options on the table" when dealing with potential proliferators decreases their

---

[59] For the seminal treatment of this issue in relations among nuclear states, see: Schelling (1960, 1966).

odds of nuclear acquisition even when no explicit threat of military attack is ever issued.

While emphasizing the importance of military threats in shaping proliferation, our theory also underlines the risks inherent in a forceful counterproliferation approach. Particularly in an era of U.S. military power preponderance, the costs of a preventive counterproliferation strike on an adversary of the United States may be seen as sufficiently low to justify an attack even when it is doubtful that the target is indeed pursuing nuclear weapons. As we saw in the case of the Iraq invasion of 2003, this strategic setting is likely to result in mistaken preventive wars against presumed proliferators that are not, in fact, developing nuclear weapons.

Moreover, our theory sheds light on how, in order to understand the effect of alliances on proliferation, we need to determine the baseline ability that a state would have to acquire nuclear weapons in the absence of protection from an ally. U.S. threats of abandonment are unlikely to prevent nuclear acquisition by a protégé that would, because of its high relative power vis-à-vis its adversaries, have the opportunity to nuclearize anyway even if Washington terminated its support. With such a relatively strong protégé, a successful U.S. nonproliferation effort would likely require taking away its willingness to go nuclear by providing it with more robust security guarantees, up to and including troop and nuclear-weapon deployments. In contrast, proliferation by a protégé that is relatively weak vis-à-vis its adversaries – and would therefore not have the opportunity to acquire nuclear weapons if U.S. security guarantees were withdrawn – can be deterred by threats of U.S. abandonment. In short, our theory provides insight into the circumstances in which efforts to stymie proliferation by U.S. allies are more likely to be successful using carrots or sticks. While dispelling arguments in favor of this or that particular policy – say, inspections or sanctions – as a silver bullet in all cases, we provide a nuanced picture of the strategic conditions under which different U.S. nonproliferation tools are more or less likely to be successful.

Road Map of the Book

The remainder of this book proceeds as follows. In Chapter 2, we lay out our strategic theory of nuclear proliferation. The chapter describes how the key features of a state's security environment – its relative power and security goals, plus the level and reliability of the support it may enjoy from a great-power security sponsor – condition its willingness and opportunity to acquire nuclear weapons and, ultimately, its odds of nuclear acquisition. After laying out the causal logic of our argument, we examine the different nonproliferation tools that allies can use, and characterize the conditions under which each of them is more likely to succeed in preventing nuclear acquisition – a topic of particular interest for U.S. policymakers. We then lay out different paths to nuclear acquisition, explaining how in each case the decision to acquire nuclear weapons or abandon the state's nuclear ambitions is shaped by the strategic environment surrounding it. After highlighting the strategic conditions more likely to lead to nuclear proliferation or forbearance, the chapter concludes by laying out the observable implications of our argument.

In Chapter 3, we bring these observable implications to bear on the overall historical record on the spread of nuclear weapons. We begin by laying out our empirical research design and justify our decision to test our theory using case studies. Then, we highlight five hitherto underappreciated patterns of proliferation. First, we show how facing a dire security threat is a necessary condition for nuclear proliferation. Second, we demonstrate how no weak state without a great-power ally has ever acquired nuclear weapons. Third, we emphasize how, among states that possess a powerful ally, the only ones to build nuclear weapons are those that have security goals not entirely covered by their security sponsor. Fourth, we underline how threats of abandonment are an effective nonproliferation tool only when they target protégés that are relatively weak vis-à-vis their adversaries. Protégés that are relatively strong, in contrast, require additional security assurances in order to remain nonnuclear. Finally, we shed light on the slowdown in the pace of nuclear acquisition since the end of the Cold War.

Then, in Chapter 4, we present an initial set of case studies, exploring the first pathway to proliferation delineated by our theory, which focuses on states that do not enjoy the protection of a security sponsor and for which, therefore, the odds of proliferation are conditioned by their interactions with their adversaries. The cases in this chapter demonstrate two claims. First, we look at the Brazilian nuclear program to illustrate how a serious security threat is a necessary condition for nuclear proliferation. Possessing abundant natural uranium reserves and sizeable industrial and technical capabilities, Brazil worked relentlessly until it mastered the technology necessary to produce weapons-grade fissile material by the 1980s. Still, absent a serious security threat – and despite having great motivation to accrue international prestige – Brazil never built a nuclear weapon. Instead, under benevolent strategic circumstances, Brazil opted for maintaining its nonnuclear status, as our theory predicts. Second, we use three case studies – of the Soviet Union, Iraq, and Iran – to demonstrate how, among states that face a serious security threat and do not benefit from the protection of a security sponsor, only those strong enough to deter an attack on their program ultimately acquired nuclear weapons. The Soviet Union was sufficiently strong to raise the costs its adversary would incur in case it decided to launch a preventive counterproliferation attack on its program. The combination of a clear national security threat – emanating from the United States, which enjoyed a nuclear monopoly since 1945 – and sufficient relative power to deter a preventive U.S.-launched counterproliferation attack was enough to lead to nuclearization in 1949. In contrast, neither Iraq nor Iran possessed sufficient relative power to be able to cross the nuclear threshold without being targeted by a counterproliferation strike. Both countries were relatively weak and isolated. Iraq, despite facing significant security threats coming from Iran, Israel, and, later, the United States, was ultimately coerced into maintaining its nonnuclear status by a series of measures – including preventive strikes, sanctions, and ultimately a ground invasion – taken by its adversaries. Iran, for its part, faced a serious nonproliferation effort spearheaded by Israel and the United States, which included the threat of military action, and ultimately agreed to a negotiated settlement by which it suspended the components of its nuclear program that might enable it to build an atomic bomb.

Chapters 5 and 6 analyze another set of case studies, this time focusing on the second pathway to proliferation described by our theory. Chapter 5 introduces eight cases of "loose" allies, states that enjoyed some degree of protection from a great-power sponsor. We start with Sweden, which illustrates that a serious security threat and concerns about the reliability of support from a security sponsor are necessary conditions for proliferation among allies. While Sweden abided by an official policy of neutrality, in practice it worried mostly about a Soviet threat, the only contingency for which nuclear weapons might prove useful. Despite having been at the forefront of nuclear technology in the 1950s, Sweden forfeited nuclearization when tensions receded in Europe and when it realized that U.S. protection would be forthcoming in case of a Soviet attack. We then turn to the case of China, which nuclearized in 1964 as a consequence of the vital threat to its regime posed by the United States, particularly after the loss of Soviet support following the Sino-Soviet split of the late 1950s. Our third case, Israel, faced a hostile security environment and in the 1950s and 1960s was unable to obtain robust U.S. security guarantees. Given the limited level of U.S. protection it enjoyed, Israel proceeded with its nuclear development, acquiring nuclear weapons in the late 1960s. We then analyze the case of India, which developed nuclear weapons in the run-up to its 1974 test, fearing Chinese aggression and lacking reliable protection from either superpower. Next, we turn to the case of South Africa, which faced a growing regional threat after the rise of pro-Soviet regimes in Angola and Mozambique in 1975. Unable to rely on U.S. support, particularly after the Carter administration took office in early 1977, Pretoria proceeded to develop a nuclear weapon by 1979. North Korea, for its part, nuclearized in the 2000s, in the face of a serious security threat coming from South Korea and the United States, along with a deteriorating – but nonetheless robust – ability to inflict damage in South Korean territory by conventional means (and independently of its unreliable ally, China), thereby deterring a counterproliferation strike launched by either Washington or Seoul. Taiwan is our seventh case. Given its weakness vis-à-vis China and the dwindling support it enjoyed from the United States after the 1970s U.S.–China rapprochement, Taiwan was keen to acquire nuclear weapons. Still, its weakness made it dependent on U.S. support, however small, allowing Washington to coerce Taipei into remaining nonnuclear. Finally, we examine the case of Pakistan, another relatively weak state that was willing to build the bomb to deter the security threats emanating from its powerful neighbor, India. During the 1980s, while enjoying a moderate degree of protection from the United States and doubting that it would last, Pakistan pushed toward nuclear acquisition, building the bomb in the later part of that decade.

Our last empirical chapter – Chapter 6 – looks at four states possessing "close" allied support. We start out with Japan, a country that, like Sweden, illustrates how a serious security threat and concerns about the reliability of support from a security sponsor are necessary conditions for proliferation. Japan had limited foreign policy objectives and remained firmly in the nonnuclear camp as a result of robust U.S. security guarantees, which effectively addressed security threats from the Soviet Union and, later, from China. We then turn to the case of South Korea, which seriously considered the nuclear option against North Korea, in part because of a reduction of U.S. commitments to East Asia announced by the Nixon Doctrine, but remained nonnuclear due to reinvigorated U.S. security guarantees. Next, we deal with West Germany, which remained nonnuclear as a result of U.S. coercive pressure. German nuclearization raised serious concerns among European North Atlantic Treaty Organization (NATO) allies and, especially, in Moscow. This hostile reaction led Washington to fear that German nuclear pursuit would unravel its alliance and lead to entrapment in a war with the Soviet Union, prompting a serious U.S. nonproliferation effort targeting Bonn's nuclear aspirations. In contrast, France, our concluding case in this chapter, acquired nuclear weapons in 1960 determined to achieve greater foreign-policy autonomy from the United States in pursuit of its broader strategic goals. French nuclearization happened despite its NATO membership because it did not prompt a Soviet reaction strong enough to lead Washington to fear entrapment as a result of Paris's nuclear pursuit. In fact, both the Soviet Union and the United States acquiesced to France's nuclear acquisition.

The main body of the book concludes with Chapter 7, in which we lay out the theoretical and policy implications of our argument. Additionally, we include four appendices. Appendix I lays out our rules for coding each case of nuclear development in terms of relative power and the presence of a security sponsor. Appendix II contains brief vignettes of all cases of nuclear development that do not feature in the main text: Algeria, Australia, Egypt, Italy, Libya, Romania, Switzerland, Syria, the United Kingdom, the United States, and Yugoslavia. Appendix III presents abbreviated cases of four states that, according to existing theories of proliferation, should have attempted to develop – or even acquire – nuclear weapons and yet did not: Greece, Saudi Arabia, Spain, and Turkey. Finally, Appendix IV formalizes our argument with a game-theoretic model and presents proofs of the formal results.

2 | *A Strategic Theory of Nuclear Proliferation*

This chapter introduces a strategic theory of nuclear proliferation. We account for the spread of nuclear weapons by determining the overall effect of the security environment on the likelihood of nuclearization. While our theory is anchored in the "security model" of proliferation, we depart from existing security explanations for the spread of nuclear weapons by shifting and broadening the focus of analysis. Instead of looking at the consequences of nuclear acquisition for the subsequent security of the state, we focus on the security environment a state faces while developing nuclear weapons.[1] Furthermore, instead of looking only at the security incentives of the proliferator, we include those of all the key strategic actors – the potential proliferator, its adversaries, and, when present, its allies.

The chapter starts by broadly characterizing the strategic setting in which nuclear proliferation takes place. We then delineate the two constraints a state faces when considering nuclear acquisition – willingness and opportunity – each of which captures one strand of the existing literature, demand and supply. Next, the core of the chapter lays out the strategic logic of nuclear proliferation. We identify the key actors and explanatory variables shaping the odds of nuclearization and lay out the causal mechanisms through which the strategic interaction among these actors shapes the odds of nuclear acquisition. We then evaluate the different tools that a state's adversaries and allies may use to deter its nuclear acquisition and specify the two different causal pathways that a state may follow toward nuclearization. The chapter concludes with the empirical implications of our argument.

---

[1] Supply-side theorists also focus on the period of nuclear development. See: Kroenig (2010); Fuhrmann (2012). We differ by broadening the analysis from nuclear assistance to the overall set of strategic interactions among the relevant states during this period.

The Strategic Setting of Nuclear Development

Our theory focuses on the strategic interactions that take place during
the nuclear development period between a potential proliferator and
the states that would be affected by its nuclear acquisition. This shift
in analytic focus toward the period prior to nuclearization is justified
by the fact that nuclear acquisition requires a prolonged investment
in nuclear technology. Historically, no state has ever acquired nuclear
weapons without first developing them for a period of time during
which it invested in its nuclear program.[2] In fact, states spend a period
of time – years, often decades – exploring and pursuing the nuclear
option before acquiring the bomb. Since nuclear acquisition requires a
costly investment in science, technology, and industry that only yields
a return after a significant span of time, proliferation can be deterred
by the efforts of other states. Therefore, the security environment the
potential proliferator has to face prior to the moment of nuclear acquisition must be factored into its decision to nuclearize, conditioning
the state's odds of nuclear acquisition.

During this nuclear development period, our theory centers on the
strategic interactions among three key actors: the potential proliferator, its adversaries, and, when present, its allies. A state may gain
much from nuclear acquisition in terms of its ability to pursue its security goals vis-à-vis any adversaries. At the same time, its adversaries
may stand to lose much as a result of its nuclearization. Therefore, if
a state wants to nuclearize, its adversaries will likely want to thwart

---

[2] Three former Soviet republics – Belarus, Kazakhstan, and the Ukraine –
"inherited" nuclear weapons from the USSR upon its dissolution in 1991.
Until they concluded returning these weapons to Russia by 1996, however,
they had no operational control over them, disqualifying them as cases
of nuclear acquisition. As Robert Norris wrote in the context of the 2014
Ukraine crisis: "Ukraine was never a nuclear power. Ukraine did have several
thousand Soviet/Russian warheads deployed within its borders, but the button
was always in Moscow. The weapon systems were guarded and manned
by Russians. Ukraine had no operational control over them or any way to
launch or fire them. Had the Ukrainians tried to seize the missiles, bombers
or warheads, there would have been a bloody confrontation with the Russian
military." See: Robert S. Norris, "It's Not Just Ukraine, It's What Russia May
Try Next," *The Wall Street Journal*, March 21, 2014. Available at: http://search.
proquest.com/docview/1509131010?accountid=15172. Last accessed: May 2,
2016. See also: Sagan (2011, 227).

this effort. To do so, they will resort to different counterproliferation measures, up to and including preventive war.

Similarly, the acquisition of nuclear weapons may improve a state's ability to make decisions autonomously from its allies. Yet, this will often lead its allies to try to stymie its nuclearization for fear of entrapment and regional instability.[3] To do so, an ally will resort to different nonproliferation tools, including boosting its commitments to the security of its protégé or, alternatively, threatening it with abandonment. To understand the overall effect of the security environment on nuclear acquisition – and the relative effectiveness of different policies aimed at deterring proliferation by both adversaries and allies – we synthesize the interaction of these competing forces.

The key to understanding nuclear proliferation is to characterize the attractiveness of nuclear weapons for the potential proliferator, the credibility of an adversary's threats of preventive war, and the effectiveness of an ally's guarantees of protection and threats of abandonment. To do so, we need to take two analytic steps. First, we need to focus our analysis on the strategic interactions among all relevant actors. Second, within these interactions, we need to focus on the role played by security interests. In fact, the first of these steps begets the second: when we analyze a potential proliferator's strategic interactions, the central role played by security interests becomes readily apparent. The following sections unpack this logic, uncovering different strategic circumstances that may push a potential proliferator to nuclear acquisition or forbearance.

---

[3] By "entrapment," we mean, as Glenn H. Snyder puts it, "being dragged into a conflict over an ally's interests that one does not share, or shares only partially." See: Snyder (1984, 467). By "regional instability," we mean an increase in the likelihood of a major conflict involving the new nuclear country. Recent work has questioned whether entrapment and entanglement are valid concerns, given the postwar historical record, which shows that the United States is rarely if ever entrapped in conflicts by its allies. See: Kim (2011); Beckley (2015). Our point is precisely that security sponsors will work hard to avoid getting entrapped, including going to great lengths to deter nuclear proliferation by their protégés, especially when it would increase the risks of conflict with their adversaries. These efforts may help account for the low incidence of entrapment.

Willingness and Opportunity Constraints on Proliferation

Our analysis of the strategic dynamics at play during the period of nuclear development shows that proliferation only happens when a state satisfies both willingness and opportunity constraints. Here we account for the role that each of these two constraints plays in shaping the spread of nuclear weapons. The next section focuses on the variables that condition whether a potential proliferator will be able to overcome the willingness and opportunity constraints and acquire nuclear weapons.

To acquire nuclear weapons, a state must first satisfy what we label the "willingness constraint" on proliferation. When a threat is sufficiently serious, the beneficial effect of nuclear acquisition on the potential proliferator's security is likely to exceed the cost of a nuclear program. In this case, the willingness constraint is satisfied, unless the need for nuclear weapons is made redundant by credible security assurances from an ally. Such assurances would eliminate the beneficial effect of nuclear acquisition, leading a potential proliferator to abandon its nuclear ambitions despite facing a serious security threat.

While other factors, such as a quest for domestic or international prestige, may contribute to a state's desire to build the bomb, they are not, in the absence of a serious security threat, sufficient to lead a state to overcome the willingness constraint. In short, a state will only possess the willingness to nuclearize when it faces a serious security threat that is not met by reliable security assurances extended by an ally.

At the same time, whereas the willingness constraint is a necessary condition for nuclear acquisition, it is not sufficient. A state might be willing to build the bomb and yet not have the opportunity to do so. When the negative impact of nuclear acquisition on the security of the potential proliferator's adversaries is greater than the cost of a preventive war, acquisition will be thwarted by the incentives these adversaries have to prevent it. When this is the case, the state will not have the opportunity to build nuclear weapons. In other words, the "opportunity constraint" is not satisfied. The proliferator may internalize this logic, forbearing its nuclear ambitions, or, in case it does not, become the target of preventive military action. Either way, proliferation will not occur.

In order to satisfy the opportunity constraint, a state must either possess high relative power or benefit from the protection of an ally, each of which would raise the cost of a preventive counterproliferation war. At the same time, when an allied security guarantee grants the state the opportunity to proliferate, it may also undermine the state's willingness to acquire nuclear weapons. When an allied security guarantee meets the state's security needs, an investment in nuclear weapons is no longer productive. This means that a potential proliferator who enjoys the protection of an ally will only be willing to use the opportunity to nuclearize if that guarantee is not entirely reliable. A guarantee will not be deemed reliable if it is insufficient to protect the state's homeland, unlikely to last in the long term, or too narrow to cover all of the potential proliferator's security needs.

In sum, states that do not face a serious security threat or that are protected by a reliable ally do not have the willingness to proliferate. Weak unprotected states do not possess the opportunity to go nuclear. The existence of a "prevention" window during the nuclear development phase means that a state's willingness to nuclearize may be thwarted by other states' efforts to deny it the opportunity to acquire the bomb. It is only when a state faces a dire security threat that is not met by allied security assurances and enjoys the power or protection sufficient to deter preventive military action that nuclear acquisition takes place.

The Strategic Logic of Nuclear Proliferation

This section unpacks the causal logic in our theory.[4] To understand the overall effect of the security environment on nuclear acquisition we must synthesize the interaction of competing forces for and against proliferation. Our theory sets out to do so, determining the strategic conditions more likely to result in nuclear acquisition. In what follows, we unpack the causal logic that determines whether a state will be able to satisfy the willingness and opportunity constraints on nuclear acquisition. We start by laying out the key actors and variables that shape these constraints. Then we focus on how the strategic interaction between a potential proliferator and its adversaries shapes its ability to overcome the willingness and opportunity constraints. Once we have laid out that baseline logic, we turn to the role of allies in shaping their protégé's willingness and opportunity to build nuclear weapons.

---

[4] A formal presentation of the argument can be found in Appendix IV.

Key Actors and Variables

As we noted, our analysis focuses on the strategic interaction between the state that is developing nuclear weapons, its adversaries, and any allies it may possess.

For the purposes of our theory, an "adversary" is a country that constitutes an independent and direct threat to a state's security. Two countries are considered independent adversaries of a state if they pose different direct security threats to the state, such that they each could engage in war against the potential proliferator without the other's support. These are the countries against which a nuclear deterrent would provide additional security. These are also the countries most likely to consider a preventive attack against the potential proliferator during the nuclear development phase.

Similarly, an "ally" is a country that, given its past behavior, is expected to support the potential proliferator in a crisis against its adversaries, regardless of whether the two possess a formal alliance. For simplicity, we operationalize our notion of a "powerful" ally by restricting our attention to nuclear allies, which are the most effective deterrers of a preventive counterproliferation attack.[5] We say that an ally is "close" if its commitment to the state's defense, as expressed through formal pledges of support and deployments of troops or nuclear weapons, is high. Otherwise, we say it is a "loose" ally.[6]

Nuclear acquisition improves the security of a state vis-à-vis its adversaries and its autonomy vis-à-vis its allies. To prevent it, both adversaries and allies may use a variety of tools. We focus on the most powerful tools at their disposal: credible threats of preventive war launched by an adversary; and credible commitments of protection or threats of abandonment made by an ally.[7]

In our view, the efficacy of softer counter- and nonproliferation measures depends on the underlying credibility of threats to use

---

[5] See Appendix I for explicit coding rules for allies.

[6] This means that we take the robustness of the alliance between the state considering nuclear weapons and its security sponsor to be exogenous to the nuclear proliferation dynamics on which our theory focuses. In reality, both alliance partners may, and often do, attempt to manipulate the robustness of their partnership. On how states may attempt to draw an ally closer after acquiring nuclear weapons, see: Narang (2014).

[7] On how credible commitments and coercive threats of abandonment are connected, see: Wirtz (2012).

military force against or in support of the potential proliferator. For example, a potential proliferator's adversaries may attempt to halt its nuclear development by imposing sanctions on it. If these sanctions fail to persuade the potential proliferator to abandon its nuclear aspirations, however, military force would be the last chance to avoid its nuclear acquisition. This logic underpins recurrent pronouncements by U.S. leaders about how "all options are on the table" when dealing with recalcitrant regimes that may be pursuing a nuclear weapon. All else equal, the greater a state's capacity to hurt, the greater its ability to coerce its adversaries to remain nonnuclear. Similarly, a potential proliferator's ally may demand inspections or threaten with the withdrawal of military aid in order to stop its protégé from getting the bomb. Yet, these attempts at coercion are only likely to succeed when the protégé would face significant adverse consequences for its security if it were to lose the ally's support. All else equal, the greater an ally's capacity to protect its protégé from being hurt, the greater its ability to coerce it into abandoning its nuclear aspirations.

Our theory focuses on the period of nuclear "development." This period includes two phases: nuclear "exploration" and nuclear "pursuit." We follow Singh and Way's definitions for these two types of nuclear activity. Nuclear "exploration" involves the "political authorization to explore the [nuclear] option" or "linking research to defense agencies that would oversee any potential weapons development." Nuclear "pursuit," in turn, involves "[a] political decision by cabinet-level officials, movement toward weaponization, or development of single-use, dedicated technology."[8] Whereas some states have first explored the nuclear option for some time and only then turned to nuclear pursuit, others have pursued nuclear weapons vigorously since the inception of their nuclear program. Either way, nuclear acquisition has always been preceded by a period of nuclear development.

We are interested in whether nuclear development leads to nuclear acquisition or forbearance. Our dependent variable is a country's "nuclear status," which can either be "nuclear" or "nonnuclear." A country's status can go from nonnuclear to nuclear in one of two ways: the conduct of a nuclear test, which is the most common way states announce their mastery of nuclear-weapons technology; or,

---

[8] Singh and Way (2004, 866–867).

alternatively, by the construction of a first nuclear bomb.[9] If development ends without nuclear acquisition, and the country status remains nonnuclear, we say that development resulted in nuclear forbearance. Forbearance, therefore, is compatible with a range of different levels of nuclear development: a state may dismantle its entire nuclear program but it may also opt to maintain an advanced latent capability that would enable it to break out and build a nuclear weapon in a relatively short period of time. In either case, we would label this outcome nuclear forbearance. In short, our outcome variable changes only with nuclear acquisition: whether countries that start developing nuclear weapons make it to the finish line.

When accounting for whether nuclear development leads to nuclear acquisition or forbearance, our main focus is on the "security benefit of proliferation." This concept refers to the magnitude of the shift in the distribution of capabilities that nuclear acquisition would produce vis-à-vis the state's adversaries. The security benefit of nuclear possession is the object of heated scholarly and policy debates.[10] Minimalist conceptions of the benefits of nuclear possession emphasize the value of nuclear weapons for deterring attacks on the state's core interests – its territory, population, and economic base.[11] More maximalist understandings of the utility of nuclear weapons also include coercive advantages vis-à-vis adversaries.[12] Our theory is agnostic about, and compatible with, different views on whether nuclear weapons yield offensive advantages. We rely solely on the consensual insight that nuclear possession boosts the ability of the state to deter aggression on its territory and on the uncontroversial view that a nuclear arsenal is also of some use in deterring escalatory threats issued against the state in response to actions it undertakes in pursuit of its other goals. Our theory assumes, therefore, that a nuclear deterrent

---

[9] Israel and South Africa were acknowledged as nuclear powers by the international community without them publicly testing a bomb. On U.S. efforts to avoid nuclear tests by these and other countries, see: Rabinowitz (2014).

[10] See: Snyder (1961); Waltz (1981); Betts (1987); Huth (1988); Mueller (1988); Jervis (1989); Kapur (2007); Ganguly (2008); Kapur and Ganguly (2008); Gartzke and Jo (2009); Ganguly and Kapur (2010); Sobek et al. (2011); Sagan and Waltz (2012); Anderson, Debs, and Monteiro (2015); Bell (2015); Bell and Miller (2015).

[11] See: Sechser and Fuhrmann (2013).

[12] See: Kroenig (2013).

virtually ensures the state's survival and territorial integrity, may better enable it to pursue any secondary security goals it may have by providing it with the ability to meet any threats of nuclear retaliation against it, and might even provide it with added coercive capabilities vis-à-vis its adversaries.

We let the security benefit of proliferation depend on three underlying strategic variables. The first is the proliferator's "relative power." This reflects the balance of military power between the country that is considering nuclear acquisition and its adversaries. A crude measure of this balance would rely primarily on the size of the state's military forces and the magnitude of its defense expenditures. In Chapter 3 we test our theory using these basic indicators. Still, factors such as training and technology deeply affect a state's ability to succeed in the military missions it needs to perform in order to achieve its security goals. Therefore, in Chapters 4–6, we test our theory using case studies that enable us to capture these more nuanced assessments.

Our second underlying strategic variable is the "level of security threat." This captures the likelihood of future conflict between a country and its adversaries, as evaluated by a country's decision-makers.[13] By security, we do not mean only the survival of the state and the integrity of its territorial mainland. Whereas some states may have such narrow security goals, other states may include in their security needs the protection of overseas possessions and the pursuit of broader security interests. Therefore, our definition of security is not restricted to the maintenance of the international status quo. Rather, it encompasses any goal or interest in pursuit of which the state might benefit from having higher relative military power.[14]

The third underlying strategic variable is the "level and reliability of allied commitment to the state's defense." This variable captures first whether a powerful state is allied with the potential proliferator

---

[13] In order to increase the replicability of our results, Chapter 3 analyzes the historical patterns of proliferation using some "hard" measures of material power, threat, and commitment. In the case studies we present in Chapters 4–6, however, we take policymakers' perceptions of these variables at face value. In this sense, our theory incorporates possible leadership psychological biases. See: Jervis (1976); Hymans (2006).

[14] As such, our use of the term "security" should not be seen as reference to the dichotomy between security-seeking and revisionist states used, e.g., in Glaser (2010). Security goals can, in our usage, include revisionist aims, as long as they require the threat or use of force.

(either formally or informally) and, if so, the reliability of its commitment to the defense of its protégé. A simple analysis of the reliability of an ally's commitment might look at whether the two possess a defense pact as well as the number of troops and nuclear weapons the ally deploys on its protégé's territory. The higher these numbers, the greater the reliability of the ally's commitments to the security of the protégé. We use these straightforward indicators of allied commitment to test our theory in Chapter 3. A more sophisticated analysis involves softer issues of reliability based on political assessments of credibility, reputation, and so forth.[15] Thus, in Chapters 4–6 we incorporate these more nuanced factors in our historical analysis of multiple cases.

We compare the security benefit of proliferation to two costs associated with nuclear proliferation: the "cost of a nuclear program" and the "cost of preventive war." The cost of a nuclear program corresponds to the value of the material resources necessary to develop nuclear weapons. Although one might prefer a more encompassing notion of cost that would include, say, the opportunity costs of a nuclear program and the costs incurred as a result of other state's opposition to nuclear development, broadening our notion of cost in such a manner would weaken the analytic power of our theory, making it harder to falsify. For example, we do not include in this variable the costs deriving from nonproliferation sanctions imposed on a state by its adversaries or allies, which might indirectly be considered part of the cost of a nuclear program. This allows us to have a cleaner analytic distinction between the willingness and opportunity constraints on proliferation.

The cost of preventive war corresponds to the total value of the resources destroyed in a preventive counterproliferation war launched by an adversary against a state that is developing a nuclear capability. We label "preventive war" any military action that aims at preventing proliferation, including a whole range of options, from surgical strikes against a limited target set to full-scale invasion of the target country.[16]

---

[15] See: Schelling (1966); Press (2005).

[16] For a literature review on preventive war, see: Levy (2008). On preventive war debates in the context of proliferation, see: Fuhrmann and Kreps (2010); Gavin and Rapp-Hooper (2011). Notice that, following the standard rationalist bargaining framework, the cost of preventive military action includes the total value of the resources destroyed by both sides in a war, given the possibility of side payments. See: Fearon (1995).

We now lay out the causal mechanisms connecting all these variables, thereby highlighting the strategic causes of proliferation.

Adversaries, Threats, Power, and Proliferation

We start by characterizing the odds of proliferation among states that do not possess a powerful ally. The key strategic dynamic in these cases takes place between the proliferator and its adversaries.

To acquire nuclear weapons, a state must first satisfy the willingness constraint. A potential proliferator has the willingness to build nuclear weapons only when the security benefit of proliferation is greater than the cost of a nuclear program.

For states that do not possess a security sponsor, the security benefit of proliferation hinges on our first two underlying strategic variables: the state's relative power vis-à-vis its adversaries prior to nuclear acquisition and the level of security threat it faces. The lower a state's relative power prior to proliferation and the higher the level of threat it faces, the more nuclear acquisition will improve the state's strategic outlook by shifting the distribution of capabilities in favor of the proliferator. If a state is already relatively strong vis-à-vis its adversaries, nuclearization will add relatively less to its ability to pursue its security goals. In short, the weaker and more threatened a state is, the greater is the security benefit it will extract from proliferation.

To determine whether a state is willing to proliferate, we must then determine whether the security benefit of proliferation is higher than the cost of a nuclear program. A relatively benign security environment, by lowering the benefit of proliferation, may make it smaller than the cost of a nuclear program, reducing a state's willingness to proliferate and helping to account for why most states have not acquired or even tried to develop nuclear weapons. Likewise, an improvement in the security environment during the nuclear development phase may also undermine the potential proliferator's willingness to nuclearize, leading it to abandon its nuclear ambitions. Finally, an increase in the relative power of the potential proliferator would also undermine the state's willingness to build the bomb. In sum, a state's willingness to proliferate increases with the level of security threat it faces and decreases with its relative power and with the cost of a nuclear program.

Willingness is a necessary condition for nuclear acquisition. It is not sufficient, however. To nuclearize, a state must also satisfy the opportunity constraint on proliferation. Whether it will be able to do so depends on the relationship between the security benefit of proliferation and the cost of preventive war. A state will have the opportunity to proliferate when the security benefit of proliferation is smaller than the cost of preventive war.

If nuclear weapons present a security benefit for the state that acquires them, they also undermine its adversaries' ability to achieve their own security goals. When this impact is smaller than the cost of preventive war, the potential proliferator's nuclearization is, from the perspective of its adversaries, less disadvantageous than fighting a war to prevent it. In this case, the threat of preventive war is not credible and the potential proliferator has the opportunity to nuclearize unimpeded. As the security benefit of proliferation increases relative to the cost of preventive war, however, the threat of preventive military action gains credibility, reducing the likelihood of proliferation. Some states internalize this threat, refraining from pursuing nuclear weapons. Others may launch a covert nuclear program, hoping to remain undetected, and may suffer a preventive strike.[17] Either way, when the security benefit of proliferation is higher than the cost of preventive war, a state that is willing to nuclearize is likely to lack the opportunity to get the bomb. In theory, a weak and unprotected country could only proliferate if its nuclear development efforts were not detected by others prior to its nuclear acquisition. The dual nature of nuclear technology makes it impossible to rule out this sort of proliferation by stealth. If a state were able to hide its nuclear development efforts – or

---

[17] See: Debs and Monteiro (2014). The acquisition of nuclear weapons would produce a large and rapid shift in the balance of power that would justify a preventive war. For previous arguments on preventive war dynamics, see: Fearon (1995); Powell (1999); Copeland (2000). Our theory does not account for which states internalize the threat of preventive strike, abandoning their nuclear efforts, and which do not, and end up being targeted by counterproliferation military action. The better is the available surveillance and detection technology, the higher the odds that a state would be caught attempting nuclear development and, consequently, the lower the odds that a vulnerable state would nuclearize when its adversaries have incentives to launch a preventive strike. Our conclusions on the relationship between relative power and proliferation, presented in the following text in the context of perfect information about a state's decision to develop a nuclear weapon, generalize to the case of imperfect information. See Appendix IV.

procure a ready-made nuclear weapon from another country – the strategic dynamics on which we focus would not apply, and so the state would have the opportunity to acquire the bomb regardless of any incentives for others to deter its nuclearization. Nevertheless, given existing technologies of surveillance and detection, plus the capacious inspections regime to which NPT members adhere, nuclearization by stealth has never happened and remains exceedingly unlikely.

As we have seen, among states without a protecting ally, their relative power vis-à-vis their adversaries conditions the security benefit they would extract from proliferation. The more powerful a state is, the smaller the benefit it will get from acquiring nuclear weapons. At the same time, relative power also determines the cost of preventive war. The higher a state's relative power, the greater is the cost of a preventive war against it. Combining these two effects, we can establish that when the balance of power favors the potential proliferator, the overall cost of preventive war will be higher relative to the security benefit of nuclear acquisition. This lowers the credibility of threats of preventive war, making stronger states more likely to have the opportunity to proliferate whenever they are willing to do so. For a potential proliferator not protected by a nuclear ally, then, the greater its relative power prior to nuclear acquisition, the greater the odds of proliferation.

In contrast, when the balance of conventional power favors the adversaries of the potential proliferator, the security benefit of proliferation will be high. Nuclear weapons would vastly improve the security outlook of the potential proliferator and worsen that of its adversaries. At the same time, the potential proliferator's relative weakness makes preventive war relatively less costly. Consequently, preventive war is more likely to be a rational option against a relatively weak potential proliferator.[18] This, in turn, boosts the credibility of preventive threats, making relatively weak and unprotected states unlikely to have the opportunity to nuclearize.[19]

---

[18] See: Debs and Monteiro (2014).

[19] This dynamic accounts for why strong states have no need to dissimulate their effort to develop a nuclear-weapons capability. Given the high cost of a preventive war relative to the consequences of allowing the state to acquire the bomb, it is not rational for an adversary to initiate counterproliferation military action. Weak and unprotected states, however, can only acquire the bomb if their adversaries do not suspect their nuclear development efforts. For a comparison between the behavior of strong and weak states when

Therefore, the relationship between relative power and the odds of proliferation is not as intuitive as one might first think. To be sure, low relative power increases the security benefit of proliferation relative to the cost of a nuclear program, contributing to the state's willingness to build nuclear weapons. At the same time, low relative power increases the security benefit of proliferation relative to the cost of a preventive war, undermining the state's opportunity to nuclearize. Likewise with the relationship between the level of security threat faced by the potential proliferator and its odds of proliferation. On the one hand, a high level of security threat, by increasing the security benefit of proliferation relative to the cost of a nuclear program, contributes to a state's willingness to proliferate. On the other hand, a high level of security threat, by increasing the security benefit of proliferation relative to the cost of a preventive war, may also hinder the state's opportunity to build the bomb.

Herein lies an important difference between our theory and existing security-based accounts of nuclear proliferation. Beyond a certain point, as the security benefit of proliferation increases, the likelihood of proliferation decreases. Certainly, the more nuclear weapons would boost a state's ability to achieve its security goals, the greater that state's willingness to nuclearize. Traditional security-based explanations of proliferation, which focus on states' willingness to acquire nuclear weapons, center on this effect and end up overpredicting proliferation. Nuclear weapons are often described as "weapons of the weak" or the "great equalizers."[20] Yet, the weak are unlikely to get them.

Likewise, extant security explanations predict that a worsened security environment will make a state more likely to proliferate – for example, in response to proliferation by an adversary.[21] Crucially, however, the more nuclear weapons would boost a state's ability to achieve its security goals, the greater the incentive of the state's adversaries to strike preventively. Because the acquisition of nuclear weapons results from a costly investment with delayed returns, any potential proliferator must go through a vulnerable period of nuclear development.

---

attempting to acquire nuclear weapons, see our case studies of the Soviet Union and Iraq in Chapter 4.

[20] See: Paul (1999); Paul (2012).

[21] See: Epstein (1977).

The adversary has the advantage: it can launch an attack before the moment of nuclearization. Therefore, when preventive action is rational, the adversary's interest trumps that of the potential proliferator, and nuclearization is averted.

Proliferation occurs when the willingness and opportunity constraints are both satisfied. These constraints can be expressed in terms of the main cost and benefit variables of our analysis. Figure 2.1 below depicts the security benefit of proliferation, growing from left to right, and compares it to the cost of a nuclear program and the cost of preventive war. For simplicity, we describe the canonical case of perfect information, i.e., when a state's decision to build nuclear weapons can be observed by its adversaries and allies without fail. When the security benefit of proliferation is greater than the cost of a nuclear program, a state will be willing to launch a nuclear-weapons program. Put differently, the willingness constraint is satisfied. Therefore, the cost of a nuclear program represents the "willingness threshold" of proliferation. Likewise, when the security benefit of proliferation is smaller than the cost of preventive war, a state could complete a nuclear-weapons program. Put differently, the opportunity constraint is satisfied. Thus, the cost of preventive war represents the "opportunity threshold" of proliferation. When the security benefit of proliferation is smaller than both these costs – Zone 1 – a state will have the opportunity to proliferate but lack the willingness to do so. Conversely, when the security benefit of proliferation is greater than both these costs – Zone 3 – a state will have the willingness to proliferate but not the opportunity

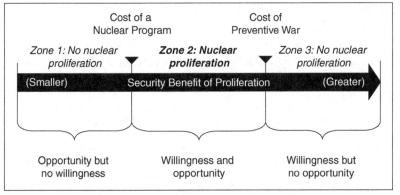

Figure 2.1. Willingness and Opportunity Thresholds of Proliferation

to do so. It is only when the security benefit of proliferation is greater than the cost of a nuclear program but smaller than the cost of preventive war – Zone 2 – that a state has both the willingness and opportunity to acquire nuclear weapons, leading to proliferation.[22]

Since the security benefit of nuclear proliferation decreases with a state's relative power, our theory predicts a positive relationship between the relative power of a potential proliferator and its odds of proliferation, *once the willingness threshold is met.* As relative power increases relative to the cost of preventive war, the security benefit of proliferation decreases, and a state desiring nuclear weapons can move from Zone 3 to Zone 2. In other words, among states intent on obtaining nuclear weapons, stronger states are better able to shield themselves against counterproliferation threats, and therefore more likely to nuclearize. This conclusion generalizes to the more realistic situation in which a decision to nuclearize is imperfectly observed by other states.[23]

Allies, Assurances, and Proliferation

We now turn to the role played in the proliferation process by our final independent variable: the level and reliability of an ally's commitment to the state's defense. Alliances affect a state's odds of proliferation in two ways, each of which relates to one of the relevant constraints on nuclearization: willingness and opportunity.

The first effect of an alliance with a powerful state is to mitigate the protégé's security threats. The more reliably a powerful ally commits to defend its protégé's security interests from their common adversaries, the lower the security benefit of proliferation will be for the protégé. When the powerful ally shares all of the protégé's security threats and reliably offers a level of protection that is sufficient to mitigate them, the protégé is unlikely to see a benefit in nuclear acquisition

---

[22] We depict the cost of a nuclear program as being smaller than the cost of preventive war, the most likely empirical situation. When the opposite is true, proliferation never occurs.

[23] See Appendix IV. In addition, when the enemy bases its decisions about war and peace on imperfect information, the theory can accommodate "mistaken" preventive wars, i.e., wars launched against states that are suspected of having, but in fact do not possess, an active nuclear-weapons program. See: Debs and Monteiro (2014).

that is greater than the cost of a nuclear program, and will thus lack the willingness to nuclearize. Taken alone, this effect makes states that possess a powerful ally less likely to go nuclear, for lack of willingness.

At the same time, the presence of a powerful ally raises the costs of a preventive war launched against its protégé, thereby increasing the protégé's opportunity to nuclearize. Therefore, whenever an alliance fails to take away the protégé's willingness to go nuclear, it will boost its opportunity to get the bomb. Overall, then, the effect of alliances on proliferation may be indeterminate: lower willingness but greater opportunity.

In order to ascertain the effect of alliances on proliferation, we need to determine the conditions under which each of these two effects will trump the other. We start by examining what determines the magnitude of the effect of alliances on the ability of the potential proliferator to satisfy the willingness constraint. We then turn to examining what determines the magnitude of the effect of alliances on the potential proliferator's ability to satisfy the opportunity constraint. Finally, we compare the two.

If the powerful ally's commitment to the potential proliferator's security credibly covers all of the protégé's interests, the protégé will have no willingness to nuclearize. Therefore, proliferation will not occur. A protégé will possess the willingness to go nuclear only when its powerful ally fails to mitigate all of its security threats reliably. In other words, proliferation by a protégé requires insufficiently reliable security guarantees on the part of its security sponsor.

In practice, a protégé may be dissatisfied with its security sponsor's guarantees of protection for one of two reasons. First, the potential proliferator may find that its ally is insufficiently committed to the security of its homeland territory, either because it provides only a limited amount of protection or because the long-term reliability of this protection is questionable.[24]

The reliability of a sponsor's commitment to its protégé's survival can vary widely. At a minimum, a sponsor can offer private security guarantees while declining to make any public pledges of support, eschewing any deployment of troops or nuclear weapons to the

---

[24] Our theory is agnostic regarding the existence of a "multiple audiences" problem in extended deterrence, according to which it may be easier for an ally to deter an enemy than reassure a protégé. See: Crawford (2012).

protégé's territory, and withholding any military aid. Furthermore, it is possible that the sponsor's level of support for the protégé be contingent on broader strategic factors that may vary over time, giving the protégé good reason to doubt the long-term reliability of the sponsor's protection. In this situation, the sponsor's commitment will likely not undermine the protégé's baseline willingness to proliferate.

At the other end of the spectrum, a sponsor may be willing to extend public formal guarantees about the security of its protégé, deploy a sizeable troop contingent and numerous nuclear weapons to its territory, and provide it with lavish military aid. In this case, the high level of commitment demonstrated by the sponsor to the security of its protégé is more likely to undermine the protégé's willingness to acquire nuclear weapons. Ultimately, when the protégé's security goals are limited to the survival of its state, a high level of commitment to the defense of its homeland on the part of the sponsor is likely to remove the protégé's willingness to nuclearize. This would be sufficient to deter proliferation. In sum, the first way in which the protégé of a powerful state may nevertheless possess the willingness to nuclearize is when the support it receives from its sponsor is insufficient to guarantee the long-term security of its homeland territory. Among protégés that possess security goals limited to the protection of their homeland, proliferation is likely to take place only among those that do not trust the reliability of their security sponsor.

The second situation in which the protégé of a powerful state may have the willingness to build the bomb is when it possesses broader security interests that its ally is unwilling to guarantee. For example, the protégé may have revisionist foreign-policy goals not shared by its sponsor; or it may have an interest in protecting colonial possessions that is not shared by its sponsor. When this is the case, even a high level of commitment by the sponsor to the protégé's survival and the protection of its homeland is unlikely to eliminate the protégé's willingness to build the bomb. According to this logic, the wider the range of security goals of the potential proliferator that an ally does not protect, the higher the likelihood of nuclearization. States with broader security goals may possess the willingness to go nuclear even when their powerful allies reliably protect their homeland.

Taking stock, an alliance with a powerful security sponsor will take away the protégé's willingness to acquire nuclear weapons unless it is unreliable – either because it is unlikely to cover the protégé's homeland in the long term, or because it is unlikely to protect the protégé's broader security interests. In either of these situations, we expect a protégé to possess the willingness to build a nuclear deterrent.

We now turn to an analysis of what determines the magnitude of the effect that an alliance has on a protégé's opportunity to proliferate. As we saw in our examination of the strategic interaction between the potential proliferator and its adversaries, a state will have the opportunity to build nuclear weapons when the cost of a preventive counter proliferation war is greater than the security benefit of proliferation. When, on the contrary, a preventive war is less costly than the consequences of proliferation, we expect an adversary to launch a counterproliferation military strike – or the potential proliferator to internalize the risk of a preventive strike and abandon its nuclear ambitions.

Through security guarantees, troop and nuclear-weapon deployments, conventional arms sales, intelligence sharing about possible preventive attacks, and so forth, a security sponsor may increase the cost of a preventive war, thereby augmenting its protégé's opportunity to proliferate. The magnitude of the effect of the sponsor's protection on the protégé's opportunity to acquire the bomb is a function of the protégé's relative power vis-à-vis its adversaries during the nuclear development phase. When the protégé is relatively strong, it already has the opportunity to nuclearize even in the absence of a security sponsor. In this situation, the sponsor's presence has little or no effect on the protégé's opportunity to build a nuclear deterrent. When the protégé is relatively weak vis-à-vis its adversaries, however, it will lack the opportunity to proliferate in the absence of a security sponsor's protection. Therefore, a weak protégé benefits more from the presence of a security sponsor, which may raise the costs of preventive war enough to give it the opportunity to nuclearize.

Summing up, the presence of a powerful ally will have a relevant impact on the odds of a state acquiring the bomb in two situations. First, if when left on its own the protégé would have had the willingness to proliferate but, because of its ally's protection, is no longer willing to build the bomb, the alliance can be said to discourage proliferation. Second, if in the absence of a powerful ally the protégé would have had no opportunity to nuclearize but, as a

Table 2.1. *Willingness, Opportunity, and the Effect of Alliances on Proliferation*

| | | If abandoned, would protégé have opportunity to nuclearize? | |
		Yes	No
If abandoned, would protégé have willingness to nuclearize?	Yes	Alliance deters proliferation *iff* sponsor removes protégé's willingness	Alliance enables proliferation *iff* sponsor does not remove protégé's willingness
	No	Alliance has no effect on proliferation	Alliance has no effect on proliferation

consequence of the ally's protection, can now safely proliferate, the alliance can be said to enable proliferation.[25] Combining these two effects of alliances on proliferation, we conclude that states protected by an ally are likely to acquire the bomb only when this ally fails to guarantee all of its protégé's security goals, thereby failing to remove its willingness to nuclearize, while nevertheless shielding the protégé during the period of nuclear development, thereby giving it the opportunity to go nuclear. Table 2.1 above summarizes the effects of alliance protection on a protégé's odds of acquiring nuclear weapons.

Combining the strategic interactions between a potential proliferator and its adversaries that we laid out in the previous section with the strategic interactions between a potential proliferator and its allies that we discussed in this section, we can now understand the strategic logic of nuclear proliferation, which we summarize in Figure 2.2 below. From left to right, this figure represents the connections between the strategic variables on which our theory focuses and a state's nuclear status. Positive connections are represented by solid lines; negative

[25] When the protégé would have been unwilling to nuclearize on its own anyway, we cannot say that the alliance prevented proliferation. Likewise, when the protégé would have maintained the opportunity to go nuclear without the protection of a powerful ally, the alliance cannot be said to cause proliferation.

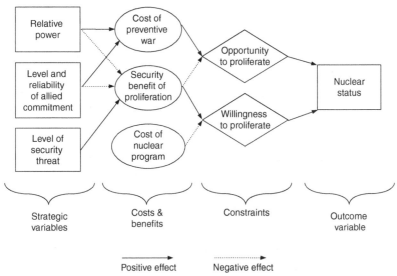

Figure 2.2. The Strategic Logic of Nuclear Proliferation
When the state considering nuclearization possesses no security allies, the
"level and reliability of allied commitment" is null and its effect is void.

ones by dotted lines. Our strategic variables condition a state's nuclear
status through a three-step process. In the first step, our strategic variables condition the security benefit of proliferation and the cost of
preventive war. Then, in the second step, this cost and benefit, together
with the cost of a nuclear program, condition the odds that a state
will satisfy the willingness and opportunity thresholds. Finally, these
two thresholds condition the country's nuclear status, determining the
odds of nuclear proliferation.

For the strategic causes of proliferation – and nuclear forbearance –
to be complete, we need to take one last analytic step. When laying
out the strategic interaction between a potential proliferator and its
adversaries, we allowed these adversaries to attempt to deter proliferation by using their most effective policy tool: threats of preventive
counterproliferation military action. But so far, our argument has not
taken into consideration the nonproliferation policy tools with which
allies can try to maintain their protégés nonnuclear status. The following section examines this last component of the strategic dimension of
nuclear proliferation.

Nonproliferation Policy Tools

Our strategic theory of proliferation places front-and-center the role that a state's adversaries and allies play in curtailing its nuclear ambitions. In doing so, we highlight how the strategic environment shapes the odds of successful counterproliferation attempts by adversaries, and the odds of successful nonproliferation efforts by allies. As we have seen, under certain conditions – when the security benefit of proliferation is greater than the cost of preventive war – counterproliferation efforts led by a state's adversaries can take away its opportunity to build the bomb. In this section, we focus on establishing the conditions that shape the relative effectiveness of the different nonproliferation policy tools with which the allies of a potential proliferator can undermine their protégé's willingness or opportunity to build a nuclear arsenal.

Allies have two basic sets of tools with which they can attempt to ensure their protégé's nonnuclear status: sticks and carrots. We say that a nonproliferation policy is "sticks-based" when it aims at taking away the protégé's opportunity to proliferate by issuing threats of abandonment. These threats are usually accompanied by demands for intrusive inspections of the protégé's nuclear facilities, so that the ally can verify the end of its development activities. The effectiveness of this nonproliferation approach depends on the consequences that carrying out such threats of abandonment would have for the protégé's opportunity to nuclearize. To be effective, a sticks-based nonproliferation policy requires that, if the threats of abandonment were to be carried out, the protégé would lose the opportunity to build the bomb.

In contrast, we say that a nonproliferation policy is "carrots-based" when it revolves around undermining the protégé's willingness to proliferate by boosting the ally's commitments to its security. Such carrots-based policies may include public pledges of protection, troop deployment, nuclear-weapons deployment, military aid, and sale of conventional weapons. To be effective, a carrots-based nonproliferation policy requires that the sponsor reliably mitigate all threats to the protégé's security goals.

The relative effectiveness of sticks- and carrots-based nonproliferation policies depends on two factors that we already began to examine in the previous section: the relative power of the protégé vis-à-vis its adversaries and the magnitude of the protégé's security interests.

The stronger a protégé is, the harder it will be for its security sponsor to remove its opportunity to proliferate using a sticks-based policy.

If the protégé is sufficiently strong to possess the opportunity to nuclearize even if abandoned by its powerful ally, a sticks-based approach to nonproliferation is unlikely to succeed. Because the protégé is sufficiently strong to nuclearize on its own, it can choose to pursue nuclear weapons despite its sponsor's threats of abandonment. Consequently, a relatively strong state will proliferate whenever it is willing to build the bomb, regardless of whether it possesses a security sponsor.

Under these circumstances, a carrots-based nonproliferation policy offers greater promise of success. Certainly, a carrots-based approach will only succeed if it removes the protégé's willingness to proliferate. But doing so will be easier with a stronger protégé than removing the willingness to nuclearize from a protégé that is relatively weak vis-à-vis its adversaries. Since greater relative power lowers the security benefit of proliferation, all else equal, the willingness of a strong state to proliferate is likely to be relatively lower compared with that of a weaker state. In sum, a protégé that is relatively strong vis-à-vis its adversaries makes it harder for a security sponsor to undermine its opportunity to proliferate by using a sticks-based approach. At the same time, high relative power makes it easier for a sponsor to undermine its willingness to nuclearize by using a carrots-based nonproliferation policy.

The contrary is true of a relatively weak protégé that is considering nuclear weapons. In this case, relative weakness boosts the security benefits of proliferation. Therefore, to remove the protégé's willingness to build the bomb, the sponsor would have to make greater commitments to its security. A high level of commitment to the protégé's defense may not be in the sponsor's interest, however, making a carrots-based approach to nonproliferation often unworkable toward weak protégés. At the same time, threats of abandonment are more effective when issued to a protégé that is relatively weak vis-à-vis its adversaries. A weak protégé would not, if abandoned, have the opportunity to build the bomb. The protégé's weakness thus makes it easier for the sponsor to remove its opportunity to proliferate by employing a sticks-based approach to nonproliferation.[26] In sum, a protégé that is relatively weak vis-à-vis its adversaries makes it easier for a security

---

[26] To be rigorous, a relatively weak protégé only possesses the opportunity to proliferate when protected by a security sponsor, so the conditionality of the sponsor's guarantee does not strictly "remove" the protégé's opportunity; it removes the opportunity that it would have were it to possess an unconditional guarantee of support from the sponsor.

sponsor to undermine its opportunity to proliferate by using a sticks-based approach. At the same time, it makes it harder for a sponsor to remove its willingness to acquire nuclear weapons by using a carrots-based approach.

The breadth of the protégé's security interests also conditions the relative effectiveness of sticks- and carrots-based nonproliferation policies. A protégé with broader security interests requires wider commitments from a powerful ally before losing its willingness to build the bomb. Narrower security interests, in contrast, facilitate the effectiveness of a carrots-based approach by lowering the overall level of commitment necessary from a security sponsor. We therefore expect carrots-based nonproliferation approaches to be relatively easier to implement, and thus more likely to succeed, with protégés whose security interests are narrow, preferably limited to the defense of their territorial homeland. Protégés with broader security interests are less likely to drop their nuclear ambitions as a result of carrots-based efforts; whether they will forfeit nuclear development as a result of sticks-based efforts, as we saw, depends on their relative power vis-à-vis their adversaries. In sum, relatively strong protégés with broad security interests present a particularly thorny nonproliferation problem for their sponsors. Their strength undermines the effectiveness of sticks-based policies; their broad interests require capacious carrots-based security commitments from their allies.

Taking stock, the effectiveness of sticks-based nonproliferation efforts increases as the relative power of the protégé vis-à-vis its adversaries decreases. Conversely, the effectiveness of carrots-based nonproliferation policies increases as the relative power of the protégé vis-à-vis its adversaries increases, and its security interests narrow down. Broader security interests increase the scope of the security commitments that an ally has to extend to remove the protégé's willingness to nuclearize. Higher relative power decreases the magnitude of these security commitments, while also decreasing the ability of the ally to resort to threats of abandonment in an attempt to remove the protégé's opportunity to go nuclear.

Before wrapping up, there is one last aspect of the effect of allies' nonproliferation efforts that we still need to address: the conditions under which an ally is more likely to oppose proliferation by its protégé. Nonproliferation policies, either carrots- or sticks-based, are costly for a security sponsor to implement toward a protégé.

A carrots-based policy entails further commitments to another state's security, bringing with them additional costs (of deployments, military aid, etc.) and higher risks of conflict. A sticks-based policy, for its part, may damage a strategic relation that is valuable for the security sponsor. Therefore, an ally may opt for turning a blind eye to its protégé's nuclear efforts, allowing its nuclear development to proceed unimpeded, even if it eventually leads up to proliferation. When is an ally more likely to look the other way? When is it more likely to be willing to incur costs to stymie proliferation by a protégé?

The answer to these questions depends on the odds that the protégé's attempt to acquire the bomb will make conflict more likely, heightening the chances of entrapment for the sponsor. When the existence of the protégé's nuclear program is unlikely to lead to conflict with their adversaries, the sponsor will have a lesser motivation to engage in a nonproliferation effort toward its protégé in order to avoid entrapment in a conflict. When, however, the protégé's nuclear ambitions would be likely to lead to conflict, the sponsor will be highly motivated to ensure the continuation of the protégé's nonnuclear status by implementing the most effective nonproliferation policy, in order to avoid entrapment. In sum, the key factor determining whether a security sponsor will go to great lengths to prevent its protégé from developing nuclear weapons is the likelihood that proliferation will beget conflict. The more likely conflict becomes, the harder the sponsor will work toward ensuring the maintenance of its protégé's nonnuclear status.

Causal Pathways to Proliferation

The strategic logic of proliferation laid out in the previous sections specifies two causal pathways to nuclear acquisition. These are the only configurations of the strategic environment that are likely to result in nuclear proliferation.

First Pathway: Threat and Power

The first pathway to nuclear acquisition applies to states that possess no security sponsor, and whose odds of proliferation are therefore entirely shaped by their strategic interaction with their adversaries. This first pathway conjoins the following elements:

- Sufficiently high threat to the state's interests to yield a security benefit of proliferation that is greater than the cost of a nuclear program, thereby giving the state the willingness to proliferate and
- Sufficiently high relative power to make the cost of a preventive war higher than the security benefit of proliferation, thereby giving the state the opportunity to build the bomb.

When a state that has no security sponsor faces a serious security threat, it has the willingness to nuclearize. When it also has sufficient relative power to make a preventive counterproliferation war so costly that it is not a rational option for its adversaries, it also has the opportunity to go nuclear. Together, these two conditions result in nuclear proliferation.

Second Pathway: Threat and Unreliable Allies

The second pathway to nuclear acquisition applies to states that possess a security sponsor and whose odds of proliferation are shaped by the state's strategic interaction with both its adversaries and allies. This second pathway conjoins the following elements:

- Sufficiently high threat to the state's interests, and an insufficiently high level and reliability of allied commitments, thereby giving the state the willingness to proliferate and
- Sufficiently high relative power or a sufficiently high level of allied commitment, thereby giving the state the opportunity to build the bomb.

When a state faces a serious security threat and does not possess a sponsor whose security guarantees are sufficiently great and reliable, it has the willingness to nuclearize. This may happen because the protégé worries that the sponsor's commitment could wane over time; or because the sponsor does not cover all of the protégé's security interests. When, furthermore, the sponsor's present commitment to the protégé's security is nevertheless sufficient to make a preventive counterproliferation war so costly that it is not a rational option for its adversaries, the protégé also has the opportunity to go nuclear. Together, these two conditions result in nuclear proliferation.

When the protégé's attempt at nuclear development meets little opposition from its adversary, its ally is also unlikely to devote much effort to attempt to thwart its protégé's nuclear ambitions. When, on the contrary, the protégé's nuclear development risks generating conflict with its adversaries, its sponsor will go to great lengths to press it in the direction of nuclear forbearance.

When the protégé is relatively weak vis-à-vis its adversaries, the sponsor may be able to deter its nuclearization by employing a sticks-based nonproliferation policy and making its security guarantees conditional on the maintenance of the protégé's nonnuclear status. When the protégé is stronger vis-à-vis its adversaries, however, it possesses a greater independent opportunity to nuclearize even in the absence of the sponsor, making it more difficult for the sponsor to deter proliferation using a sticks-based approach. In this case, the most effective way for the sponsor to deter proliferation is to employ a carrots-based policy, boosting the security guarantees it extends to its protégé. When such deeper security commitments are not in the sponsor's own interest, a carrots-based policy will prove unworkable and proliferation is likely to ensue.

Observable Implications

Our theory yields several observable implications, or predictions. First, a serious threat to the security of the state is a necessary condition for nuclear proliferation to occur. States that do not face serious security threats will not possess the willingness to acquire nuclear weapons, and will therefore not proliferate.

Second, among the states that face a serious threat and possess no ally, there will be a strong positive relationship between their relative power vis-à-vis their adversaries and their odds of proliferation. Among threatened states, powerful states are more likely to nuclearize. Since high relative power is a sufficient condition to provide a state with the opportunity to nuclearize, a state that faces a highly threatening environment while possessing the power to make a preventive counterproliferation war sufficiently costly will have both the willingness and the opportunity to nuclearize, and will therefore acquire nuclear weapons. Weak unprotected states may have the willingness, but will not have the opportunity to acquire the bomb.

Third, amid those states that face a serious security threat and possess an ally, the relationship between power and proliferation will be less straightforward. Among these states, the protégé will only have the willingness to build the bomb when it considers the security guarantees offered by its ally to be unreliable. This can manifest itself in two ways. The protégé may consider the level of protection that the sponsor extends over its homeland to be insufficient or unlikely to last. Or the protégé may possess other security goals beyond the protection of its homeland that the ally fails to ensure. Either of these cases will be sufficient for the protégé to have the willingness to build the bomb.

Fourth, the relative effectiveness of carrots- and sticks-based nonproliferation policies employed by allies to keep their protégés nonnuclear will vary with the protégés' relative power vis-à-vis their adversaries. Carrots-based approaches, consisting of greater allied commitments to the security of the protégé, will be more likely to succeed in averting proliferation when employed with protégés that are relatively strong vis-à-vis their adversaries. Sticks-based approaches to nonproliferation, consisting of threats of abandonment, will, in contrast, be more likely to succeed in averting proliferation when employed with protégés that are relatively weak vis-à-vis their adversaries. Put differently, whereas strong states facing a serious security threat can only be kept nonnuclear if the ally implements a carrots-based nonproliferation policy and reliably covers all of their security interests, weak states whose ally is determined to keep them nonnuclear can be effectively targeted by a sticks-based nonproliferation policy, which will deprive them of the opportunity to build the bomb.

The following four chapters test these predictions; first, in Chapter 3, against the broader empirical record; and then through a series of sixteen case studies of nuclear proliferation or forbearance in Chapters 4 through 6.

3 | *The Historical Patterns of Nuclear Proliferation*

This chapter performs three functions. First, we lay out our empirical research design, elaborating on the reasons behind our choice to test the observable implications of our theory by looking at a series of historical case studies of nuclear development. Then, we turn to the broader empirical patterns of nuclear proliferation and show how the observable implications of our theory are supported by the historical record on the spread of nuclear weapons. Finally, we explain the organization of our chapters covering historical cases of nuclear development and stipulate our case selection criteria.

Empirical Research Design

Our empirical research design consists of a two-pronged approach. We begin, in this chapter, by analyzing the broad historical record on nuclear development. We use this analysis to highlight how the patterns of nuclear proliferation largely conform to the observable implications of our theory. Then, in Chapters 4 through 6, we conduct sixteen historical case studies of nuclear development. (Additionally, Appendices II and III contain vignettes of all other cases of nuclear development as well as short historical cases of four countries whose decision not to attempt nuclear development might be considered puzzling.) Within each case, we conduct a process-tracing analysis to show the causal mechanisms postulated by our theory at work. Furthermore, we conduct structured between-case comparisons – both within and across chapters – to demonstrate the role that changes in our explanatory variables (threat, power, and allied commitments) have on our outcome of interest (a country's nuclear status).

Focus on Nuclear Development

The empirical analysis that takes up most of the remainder of this book centers on cases of nuclear development: states that at some

point in their history explored or pursued a nuclear program with
military goals, leading either to nuclear acquisition or forbearance.
Our decision to restrict our empirical analysis to this list of cases of
nuclear development could prompt concerns about strategic selection,
which might invalidate our findings.

Certainly, strategic selection presents a problem for the study of nuclear politics. Only countries that are sufficiently motivated – in our
terminology, that possess the willingness to proliferate – will start a
nuclear program. Therefore, one cannot study the reasons that lead
states to *start* a nuclear program by looking only at countries that
have an active program. That would indeed configure a case of "selecting on the dependent variable."[1]

This problem does not impact our analysis, however. First of all,
our dependent (or outcome) variable is nuclear status, so our theory
explains nuclear *acquisition*, not development. We therefore examine
all nuclear-weapons programs and evaluate the conditions under
which they are completed successfully or abandoned. Many, indeed
half, of the states we examine in the following chapters did not acquire
nuclear weapons. Instead, they abandoned their nuclear ambitions –
some willingly, others coerced. This reflects in part the inclusiveness
of our standards. Nuclear exploration is a low threshold for inclusion
in an analysis of nuclear proliferation, which does not presuppose a
significant investment toward nuclear acquisition. All the countries
that "seriously considered building nuclear weapons, even if they
never took major steps toward that end," are included in our analysis.[2] Empirically, no state has ever acquired nuclear weapons without
going through a phase of nuclear development,[3] so no historical case
of nuclear acquisition falls outside the scope of our analysis.[4] In sum,
our focus on cases of nuclear development presents the advantage of
looking at all the relevant cases of states that considered building a

[1] On the problems raised by selecting on the dependent variable, see: Achen and
Snidal (1989, 160–161); Geddes (1990); King, Keohane, and Verba (1994,
151); Geddes (2003).
[2] Singh and Way (2004, 867).
[3] See Chapter 2, footnote 2 on the former Soviet republics of Belarus,
Kazakhstan, and Ukraine.
[4] Furthermore, our theory would still apply to hypothetical cases in which
technological or other developments shorten the period that a state would
take to obtain the bomb. As long as the potential proliferator's adversaries and

nuclear weapon without including states that were not even remotely close to the point at which they could consider doing so.[5]

Second, in addition to covering all cases of nuclear development, we examine the history of five "near misses" – states that were at different moments and for different reasons perceived to represent a high risk of proliferation but nevertheless did not even start a military nuclear program. These include one of our full-length case studies (Japan) as well as the four abbreviated cases we discuss in Appendix III (Greece, Saudi Arabia, Spain, and Turkey). Our analysis reveals that our logic is consistent with the historical evidence and that, at least in these cases, our theory also offers a good account of their decision not to start nuclear development.[6]

What benefit might we have extracted from extending our analysis to other countries? Should we have covered all states in the international system since the inception of the nuclear age in 1945 or, somewhat less ambitiously, a random sample of those states that never engaged in nuclear development? If we were to analyze all these other cases and find only instances of states that lack either the willingness or the opportunity to proliferate, this would pose no

---

allies both understand that nuclearization is possible, the strategic dynamics we discussed in the previous chapter continue to shape the odds of proliferation. An extreme case would be a state acquiring the bomb by purchasing it from an established nuclear power. This possibility has been discussed in the context of Saudi Arabia possibly acquiring a nuclear weapon from Pakistan in response to hypothetical Iranian nuclearization. See: Mark Urban, "Saudi Nuclear Weapons 'on Order' from Pakistan." BBC.com, November 6, 2013. Available at: www.bbc.com/news/world-middle-east-24823846. Last accessed: December 1, 2015. But even in this case, the fact that we are aware of this possibility means that the relevant actors know that Saudi Arabia might nuclearize in this way, and so both its adversaries and allies possess a window of opportunity to attempt to deter it from doing so using threats and assurances.

[5] On the problems generated by the inclusion of such cases in quantitative analyses of proliferation, see: Montgomery and Sagan (2009, 311–313). For example, according to Montgomery and Sagan, if Singh and Way (2004) had used the most empirically adequate regression model specification, their number of observations would have been cut down by over 95 percent and the causal effect of *all* of their variables would have become statistically insignificant. Jo and Gartzke's (2007) article presents similar problems. According to Montgomery and Sagan, simple, plausible tweaks to their variables not only undermine confidence in their results but actually produce *opposite* results.

[6] This is not to say that the mechanisms at the core of our theory *cause* states to opt out of exploring the nuclear option. We do not make any general claims about the determinants of nuclear development.

problem for our theory, as our prediction is that these states would not acquire nuclear weapons anyway even if they would engage in a period of nuclear development. Such cases would therefore pose no challenge to our claims about how the strategic environment affects a state's odds of nuclear acquisition. Extending our analysis to other cases would only generate problems for the causal inferences we make if we were to find a state that, according to our theory, possessed both the willingness and opportunity to acquire nuclear weapons, and yet never engaged in nuclear exploration. But if a state were to possess the willingness to build a nuclear arsenal, it would likely discuss the option of exploring nuclear weapons – the threshold for inclusion in the list of states that engaged in nuclear "exploration" – and would therefore be included in our analysis. In fact, our analysis shows many states that possess the willingness to acquire nuclear weapons rapidly moving to nuclear exploration. Positing that out-of-sample cases would possess both the willingness and opportunity to nuclearize and yet eschew any consideration of nuclear development presents a cotenability problem, given the evidence we present in the following text. Furthermore, even if it were to happen that a state had the willingness to nuclearize and yet never explored the nuclear option, how would one find evidence of this? If a state is not included in our case list, it is because no historical evidence has been uncovered of a "political authorization to explore the [nuclear] option" or of the state ever "linking research to defense agencies that would oversee any potential weapons development."[7] How then would we know that the state possessed the willingness to acquire nuclear weapons? We conclude that states outside our sample are highly unlikely to have overcome the willingness threshold necessary for nuclear acquisition.

Focus on Historical Process Tracing

The most adequate method to study the causes of nuclear proliferation and test a strategic theory such as ours is the careful analysis of historical cases. The several existing case lists of nuclear development – which include all countries that at one point or another explored or pursued the nuclear option – encompass between twenty-six and

---

[7] See: Singh and Way (2004, 866–867).

thirty cases.[8] This number of historical cases is both sufficiently low that scholars can acquire in-depth knowledge of a wide sample and sufficiently high that researchers have enough degrees of freedom to test even relatively complex theories.[9] Taken together, these two factors mean that nuclear proliferation is a rare phenomenon in which the number of relevant historical cases fits the sweet spot between too few to make reliable causal inferences and too many to allow for qualitative in-depth knowledge about them.

The method of structured, focused comparisons across multiple case studies consists of asking a set of general questions of interest for the theory at hand from each of the multiple cases and focusing our analytic narrative on these questions, abstracting from other aspects of the historical record.[10] Formally, the case-comparison method aims at approximating statistical "matching" techniques, in which cases are similar in all aspects except their exposure to the "treatment" – i.e., to different values of the explanatory variables, such as, in the case of our theory, the level of threat faced by the potential proliferator, its relative power vis-à-vis its adversaries, and the credibility of the security assurances made by a security sponsor.[11] These conditions are hard to obtain in historical cases, however. Any given pair of cases to which we can turn in order to, say, test the proposition that higher relative power in the presence of a security threat and in the absence of a security sponsor will increase the odds of nuclear proliferation, will exhibit differences not only in these variables of interest but in myriad other factors. The robustness of the inferential claims we can make about the causes of nuclear proliferation using the case-comparison method on its own is therefore limited.

In order to circumvent this problem and boost our standard of causal identification, we complement this cross-case comparison with deep historical within-case process tracing. Process tracing consists of reconstructing each case study while focusing on the causal connections between our explanatory variables (threat, power, and alliances) and our outcome of interest (nuclear status). Since our theory posits

[8] See: Bleek (2010b); Sagan (2011); Way (2012).
[9] On degrees of freedom, see: Brady and Collier (2004, 284).
[10] On the "structured focused case-comparison" method, see: George and McKeown (1985, 43); George and Bennett (2005, 67–72). On analytic narratives, see: Bates et al. (1998).
[11] On statistical matching, see: Diamond and Sekhon (2013).

the existence of two different pathways to proliferation, process tracing is particularly well suited to test its observable implications.[12]

Specifically, by tracing the process through which the level of security threat, relative power, and the presence of a security sponsor condition nuclear decisionmaking in each of our sixteen full-length cases, we are able to establish the different causal roles played by each of our variables. As we conclude, a high level of security threat is a necessary cause of proliferation. When a high-level security threat is absent, proliferation will not occur. Other than the level of threat, the explanatory variables in our theory play the role of INUS causes.[13] An INUS cause refers to a factor that is "an insufficient but necessary part of a condition which is itself unnecessary but sufficient for the result."[14] For example, our theory postulates that high relative power is, together with a high level of threat, sufficient to cause proliferation. But high relative power is not necessary for proliferation because a state that possesses an unreliable security sponsor may also acquire nuclear weapons even if it is relatively weak vis-à-vis its adversaries. This means that high relative power is an INUS cause of proliferation. By itself, it is neither a necessary nor a sufficient cause; together with a high level of threat, it forms a sufficient but unnecessary causal pathway to nuclear acquisition. Likewise with the presence of an unreliable security ally. These nuanced causal roles are particularly well suited to being tested using the process-tracing method.

Moreover, the historical cases we analyze in subsequent chapters allow us to make use of counterfactual analysis, further boosting our confidence in the causal relations captured by our theory.[15] Within each case, counterfactuals are useful because they enable us to think about how changing the value of one explanatory variable might have produced a different outcome – say, how a strong Iraq would have been likely to acquire nuclear weapons and a weak Soviet Union would have likely been deterred from doing so. Across cases, counterfactuals can help us understand how changing the value of explanatory variables might have led historically dissimilar cases – say, the Soviet Union

---

[12] On process tracing, see: George and Bennett (2005, 205–232).

[13] On different types of causation and, specifically, INUS causation, see: Mahoney (2008, 418–419); Mahoney, Kimball, and Koivu (2009, 124–126).

[14] Mackie (1965, 246).

[15] On counterfactuals, see: Fearon (1991); George and Bennett (2005); Brady (2008).

and Iraq, which were, respectively, strong and weak vis-à-vis their adversaries – to become similar in terms of outcome. Although we leave across-case counterfactual analysis largely implicit, we delineate the most relevant within-case counterfactuals at the end of each chapter.

Process tracing in qualitative historical cases is an especially useful method for testing strategic-interaction theories more generally.[16] Put simply, theories that posit outcomes shaped by the strategic dynamics that take place between two or more actors cannot be adequately tested using statistical correlations between explanatory variables and outcomes. At the core of any such theory is a set of complex causal mechanisms that often include second-order strategic effects and multiple causal pathways connecting explanatory variables to the outcome of interest. These causal mechanisms are difficult to corroborate – or invalidate – using statistical tests. Only by tracing them in relevant historical processes can researchers elucidate how a given constellation of explanatory factors produces the outcome of interest.

Furthermore, the sort of deep historical within-case process tracing we conduct in the following chapters is particularly important when testing theories that, like ours, incorporate leaders' perceptions of the key explanatory variables. In our historical analysis, we therefore take into account how the leadership in the relevant countries perceived the values assumed by our explanatory variables – the level of threat faced by the state considering the nuclear option, its relative power vis-à-vis its adversaries, and the reliability of the security guarantees extended by a security sponsor, when present.

A qualitative empirical research design is thus preferable to a test of the theory's observable implications based on quantifiable "objective" measurements of our variables of interest. Existing quantitative data sets that measure our explanatory variables present serious limitations for testing our theory. Data sets that attempt to measure the level of security threat objectively tend to focus on the states' involvement in militarized disputes or enduring rivalries. But these are imperfect proxies for assessing the level of threat a state faces. Often, the leadership in one state will perceive a high level of threat emanating from another state despite the absence of militarized disputes in their recent past. Furthermore, given the fluidity of the international security

---

[16] See: Lorentzen et al. (2014).

environment, a state may face a serious threat to its survival without being part of an enduring rivalry.[17] The use of enduring rivalries as a proxy for a high level of threat is problematic because rivalries require a relatively long period of animosity before they are identified as such. Yet, a state may seek nuclear weapons to placate a threat emanating from an adversary with which it does not share a long history of conflict. For example, while in 1945 the Soviet Union started its quest to build nuclear weapons in order to deter possible U.S. aggression, the two superpowers are not considered to have an enduring rivalry until 1966, twenty years after their earliest post–Second World War confrontations. By then, the hottest part of the Cold War was arguably over.

Likewise, quantitative measures of relative power, such as the National Military Capabilities (NMC) data set that is part of the Correlates of War (COW) project, present important limitations for analyzing the strategic causes of nuclear proliferation.[18] Although we use these measures in the following text when discussing the broad patterns of nuclear proliferation, we find that in some important cases, leaders' perceptions of a country's relative power – and of its ability to impose costs on its adversaries in case of military conflict – differ markedly from these "objective" values. For example, if one focuses on the Composite Index of National Capability (CINC) coefficient of power, which aggregates factors such as territory, population, and military power, Israel will appear particularly weak vis-à-vis its adversaries. Yet, as we show in Chapter 5, U.S. decisionmakers during the run-up to Israeli nuclearization thought that the country would likely prevail in a conflict against its Arab neighbors. Moreover, if we measure power using the military expenditures variable included in the NMC data set, then Israel looks relatively stronger. At the same time, using this more restrictive indicator of power, China appears to be too weak to impose heavy costs on the United States in case of a preventive attack during the run-up to its nuclear test of 1964, again in marked divergence from the assessments made by U.S. policymakers at the time.

Existing data sets of military alliances, such as the one collected by the Alliance Treaty Obligations and Provisions Project (ATOP), face

---

[17] On enduring rivalries, see: Bennett (1998); Klein et al. (2006). For applications to the study of nuclear proliferation, see: Singh and Way (2004, 873); Jo and Gartzke (2007, 176); Bleek (2010b, 178–179).
[18] See: Singer (1987).

similar limitations.[19] On the one hand, several of the formal defense agreements that are most relevant for our purposes were highly questionable during the run-up to an alliance partner's nuclear acquisition. For example, the formal Sino-Soviet alliance had all but collapsed by the time Beijing tested its first bomb in 1964, and its impact on Beijing's nuclear decisionmaking reflected this strategic reality. On the other hand, several of the states that have explored nuclear weapons – e.g., Sweden and Israel – received implicit or private security guarantees from nuclear powers during their period of nuclear development, and yet these guarantees do not show up in existing data sets of formal defense treaties. A focus on formal treaties would therefore be inadequate to test the role of allied support in conditioning the odds of nuclear proliferation.

Given these measurement issues, the most accurate way of testing our theory is by looking at the assessments of threat, power, and the reliability of alliances made by the key decisionmakers involved in the relevant strategic interactions. Although this approach is not without problems – sometimes different decisionmakers have diverging assessments of a country's level of threat, power, or protection – we believe that it nonetheless yields results that are superior to the available, more "objective" measurement alternatives.

One final issue limits our ability to test our theory using existing quantitative data on proliferation. There is often considerable uncertainty about the precise moment a state stopped exploring or pursuing nuclear weapons. In the cases of India, Israel, Pakistan, and North Korea, there is uncertainty about the exact timing of their nuclear acquisition. In these cases, we cover the span of possible dates by which the country may have acquired its first nuclear weapon. For cases of nuclear forbearance, we continue to cover the country's nuclear decisionmaking even after, according to existing case lists, it has ceased its military nuclear program. This approach allows us to evaluate whether leaders maintained the willingness to build a nuclear arsenal, as was the case for some time after West Germany and South Korea shut down their nuclear programs.

Overall, our qualitative historical approach allows us to paint a more complete picture of the incentives and constraints that each

---

[19] See: Leeds et al. (2002).

country faced in its nuclear decisionmaking over time. We agree with Vipin Narang when he argues:

the causal inference revolution in quantitative methods may lead to a resurrection in the discipline's valuation of qualitative methods in nuclear security, since qualitative methods in this particular area are much better suited to identifying and teasing out causal mechanisms and processes than the big-data enterprise.[20]

This is not to say that the quantitative study of nuclear proliferation is entirely without virtue. Much to the contrary, quantitative analysis allows us to provide a broad first-cut overview of the patterns of proliferation. Furthermore, it presents the important advantage of being more easily replicable. Therefore, in the following section, we look at all cases of nuclear exploration listed in existing quantitative data sets to show how our theory provides a plausible account of the overall patterns of nuclear proliferation – i.e., of what leads states that have at some point considered the nuclear option eventually to acquire nuclear weapons or forfeit their nuclear ambitions.

Historical Patterns of Nuclear Proliferation

This section tests our theory against the overall empirical record on nuclear proliferation. We evaluate whether the historical patterns of nuclear proliferation match the observable implications of our theory regarding the role played by the three underlying strategic variables in our analysis: the level of security threat faced by a potential proliferator, its relative power vis-à-vis its adversaries, and the level and reliability of any commitments an ally may make to its security.

We base our analysis on Sagan's canonical list of states that have at some point in time been involved in nuclear development.[21] This list includes both countries that demonstrated their willingness to acquire the bomb by pursuing a nuclear-weapons capability as well as those that were merely exploring the nuclear option without having made up their mind on whether a nuclear weapon would be beneficial.[22] Table 3.1 below lists, in its first two columns, all countries

---

[20] Narang (2013, 5).
[21] See: Sagan (2011).
[22] For start dates of nuclear powers' development phase, unavailable in Sagan's case list, see: Way (2012). Way's case list incorporates two countries not

Table 3.1. *Nuclear Development, Adversaries, and Allies*

Country	Period of Nuclear Development	Adversaries	Relative Power Latent	Relative Power Military	Allies	Formal Defensive Pact	Allied Troops Deployed	Allied Nuclear Weapons Deployed
Algeria	1983–93	Libya, Morocco	0.82	0.37	–	–	–	–
Australia	1956–61	Indonesia, China	0.06	0.06	United States	Yes	<1,000	No
Australia	1967–72	China	0.07	0.05	United States	Yes	<1,000	No
Brazil	1953–90	–	–	–	–	–	–	–
China	1955–64	Taiwan, United States	0.50	0.21	Soviet Union	Yes	<1,000	No
Egypt	1955–67	Israel	4.45	1.25	Soviet Union	No	<1,000	No
France	1946–60	Soviet Union	0.19	0.11	United Kingdom, United States	Yes	40,000	No
India	1954–74	China, Pakistan	0.44	0.09	Soviet Union	No	<1,000	No
Iran	1974–78	Iran	2.51	4.32	United States	Yes	<1,000	No

(continued)

Table 3.1 (Continued)

Country	Period of Nuclear Development	Adversaries	Relative Power Latent	Relative Power Military	Allies	Formal Defensive Pact	Allied Troops Deployed	Allied Nuclear Weapons Deployed
Iran	1984-	Israel, United States	0.09	0.01	–	–	–	–
Iraq	1972–91	Iran, Israel, United States	0.07	0.04	–	–	–	–
Israel	1949–67	Egypt, Iraq, Jordan, Syria	0.13	0.43	France, United Kingdom, United States	No	<1,000	No
Italy	1957–58	Soviet Union	0.11	0.03	United States	Yes	18,000	Yes
Libya	1970–2003	United States	0.01	0.01	–	–	–	–
North Korea	1965–2006	South Korea	0.45	0.31	China	Yes	<1,000	No
Pakistan	1972–90	India	0.18	0.27	United States	Yes	<1,000	No
Romania	1985–93	–	–	–	–	–	–	–
South Africa	1969–79	Angola	7.17	5.36	United States	No	<1,000	No
South Korea	1959–76	North Korea	1.65	0.73	United States	Yes	40,000	Yes

Soviet Union	1945–49	0.55	1.01	United States	—	—	—	—
Sweden	1954–69	0.02	0.02	Soviet Union	United States	No	<1,000	No
Switzerland	1946–69	0.01	0.01	Soviet Union	—	—	—	—
Syria	2001–	0.03	0.01	Israel, United States	—	—	—	—
Taiwan	1967–77	0.05	0.04	China	United States	Yes	2,000	No
Taiwan	1987–88	0.07	0.99	China	United States	No	<1,000	No
United Kingdom	1945–52	0.34	0.17	Soviet Union	United States	Yes	26,000	Yes
United States	1942–45	2.08	2.94	Germany, Japan	—	—	—	—
West Germany	1957–58	0.22	0.07	Soviet Union	United Kingdom, United States	Yes	229,000	Yes
Yugoslavia	1954–61	0.04	0.02	Soviet Union	—	—	—	—
Yugoslavia	1974–87	0.03	0.01	Soviet Union	—	—	—	—

Data for Iran and Syria are based on 2005–2007, the latest available years. Data for North Korea is based on 2001–2003, the latest available years. Data for Angola 1977–1978 and Libya 1993 are not available, hence replaced by the average of the closest preceding and succeeding years for which data is available.

included in our analysis ordered alphabetically, along with the start and end dates for their nuclear programs.[23] Countries presented in bold have acquired nuclear weapons; all others have forfeited their nuclear ambitions.

Within this set of states, we investigate the conditions under which they successfully acquire nuclear weapons. We make four empirical claims supporting the observable implications of our theory. First, the presence of a significant security threat is a necessary condition for successful nuclearization. Historically, no state has acquired nuclear weapons without perceiving its security environment as highly threatening. Second, among states without a nuclear ally, there is a strong relationship between power and successful nuclearization – that is, no weak unprotected state has so far acquired nuclear weapons. This relationship between power and proliferation is weakened by the presence of an ally, such that some protected states that are weak vis-à-vis their adversaries have acquired nuclear weapons. Third, among states that enjoy the protection of an ally that ensures all of their security interests, none acquired nuclear weapons. States protected by a powerful ally only build the bomb when this protection does not reliably cover all of their security interests. Fourth, a powerful ally can only ensure the nonnuclear status of a protégé that is relatively strong vis-à-vis its adversaries by employing a carrots-based nonproliferation approach that provides the protégé with additional security assurances. Sticks-based nonproliferation policies are effective only when applied to protégés that are relatively weak vis-à-vis their adversaries.

To test our predictions, we start by focusing on the level of security threat a state faces. For each case of nuclear development, we

included by Sagan: Argentina and Indonesia. We include neither in our analysis. Argentina lacked a clear security threat; its program was not aimed at producing an atomic weapon. See: Hymans (2001). Indonesia, although it announced publicly its intention to acquire nuclear weapons between late 1964 and mid-1965, does not appear to have considered any investments in nuclear technology.

[23] Several countries are listed twice in Table 3.1, as they had two periods of nuclear development. Japan is not included in the table, as it does not figure in the list of countries that have engaged in nuclear development on which we base our study. See: Sagan (2011). As a "near miss" case, we include a case study of its nuclear policy in Chapter 6.

identify the set of significant security threats against which that state might have perceived the acquisition of nuclear weapons to bring benefits. To identify these threats, we research each of these historical cases, canvassing the secondary and, often, primary literature in order to determine which countries, if any, were perceived by the leadership of the would-be proliferator as the source of a serious independent security threat. The case studies included in Chapters 4–6 lay out this analysis for sixteen of the historical cases of nuclear development. The remaining cases are treated in abbreviated form in Appendix II.

We focus on two features of threats to a state's security. First, we determine the existence of independent security threats – i.e., countries that possess security interests that make them independently willing to engage in a conflict against the potential proliferator. Second, we evaluate the significance of the threat – i.e., whether a threat is serious enough that the potential proliferator perceives nuclear weapons as yielding a security benefit in mitigating it. Given that our underlying strategic variable is the perceived level of threat, we rely on the perception of policymakers in the state engaged in nuclear development. In sum, we say that a state faces a significant security threat against which nuclear weapons might produce a positive effect only if we can identify at least one independent and significant security threat against it.

Temporally, the analysis in this chapter focuses on the three years leading up to nuclear acquisition or forbearance. This is the period during which decisions about weaponization of a nuclear program – or the abandonment of the state's nuclear ambitions – are most likely to have been made and, therefore, the period in which the strategic dynamics on which our theory focuses are most likely to have played a role in nuclear politics. (This means that we do not consider states that were adversaries only earlier in a country's process of nuclear development. Such was the case, for example, of West Germany, which was an adversary of France prior to 1955; and of Iraq, which was an adversary of Iran prior to 2003.) In its third column, Table 3.1 lists, for each country that engaged in nuclear development, the states that constituted significant independent threats to its security during the last three years of its nuclear program.

Having identified significant security threats, we can test the first observable implication of our theory: that the presence of a significant threat to a state's security interests is a necessary condition for it to acquire nuclear weapons. We find that this is indeed the case.[24] Each of the ten states that have acquired nuclear weapons perceived its security environment as highly threatening in the lead-up to nuclear acquisition. More broadly, twenty-four of the twenty-six recorded cases of nuclear development we study also involved a significant security threat.[25] The two exceptions are Brazil and Romania. We know of no security motivation behind Romania's nuclear exploration. Although Argentina and Brazil are often portrayed as the security threat behind each other's nuclear program, the two cooperated extensively in their quest to master nuclear technology, and neither faced a significant security threat.[26] The fact that these countries did not possess a significant threat helps explain why their nuclear programs did not ultimately lead them to build the bomb. Furthermore, several states have started a nuclear program but eventually dropped their nuclear ambitions because of improvements in their strategic environment – caused by international or domestic transformations – that undermined their willingness to build the bomb. These include Algeria, Egypt, Iran (until 1978), Libya, Sweden, Switzerland, and Yugoslavia. We examine the case of Iran in Chapter 4 and the case of Sweden in Chapter 5. In sum, the first observable implication of our theory is borne out by the historical data: no state has ever acquired nuclear weapons without facing a dire security threat.

We now turn to the effect of the two other underlying strategic variables: relative power and security alliances. We start by organizing all cases of nuclear development according to the relative power of the potential proliferator vis-à-vis its adversaries and the level of allied protection the potential proliferator enjoyed.

To measure relative power, we follow quantitative studies in using the COW data set. We use both measures of latent and military power. For a country's latent power, we use COW's CINC scores, an aggregate

---

[24] For evidence that security concerns correlate positively with nuclear proliferation, see: Montgomery and Sagan (2009, 306); Bleek (2010b, 178–179).

[25] Based on the case list in Way (2012).

[26] On Argentina, see: Hymans (2001); on Brazil, see Chapter 4; on Romania, see Appendix II.

indicator of a country's demographic, economic, and military capabilities. For military power, we use COW's military expenditures index.[27] Since we are interested in a country's relative power, we divide the power coefficients of each potential proliferator by the sum of its adversaries' coefficients. We then average this ratio for the three years leading up to nuclear acquisition or abandonment of the country's nuclear program. We display these ratios in columns four and five of Table 3.1.

To measure the role of alliances, we construct our own coding of the level of allied protection each potential proliferator enjoys. We focus on the security commitments of nuclear powers, which would be the most likely to possess the ability to mitigate security threats that the potential proliferator deems worthy of nuclear acquisition. As with adversaries, we focus on the last three years of a country's nuclear program.

The quantitative literature typically favors formal treaties.[28] Such a restrictive definition may miss important dynamics that occur in the context of informal security pledges, however. For example, as we show in Chapter 5, in 1957 Israel received private assurances from the United States, which refused to formalize them.[29] Implicit U.S. support, along with Israel's doubts about its reliability, were important dimensions of the strategic environment in the run-up to Israel's nuclearization. More broadly, an alliance can facilitate nuclear acquisition when it provides a modicum of protection against preventive attack but is considered unreliable by the protégé either because the sponsor cannot be trusted to maintain its protection in the long term or because it does not support the protégé's broader security goals. To capture these dynamics, we go beyond formal defensive commitments and look also at each nuclear power's behavior in past crises involving the potential proliferator and its adversaries. To do so, we canvass crises included in the International Crisis Behavior (ICB) data set.[30] This allows us to better grasp the expectations of, and preparations for, assistance between potential proliferators and each nuclear power.[31]

---

[27] See: Singer (1987); Jo and Gartzke (2007).
[28] See: Singh and Way (2004); Jo and Gartzke (2007).
[29] See: Little (1993, 565).
[30] See: Brecher and Wilkenfeld (2000).
[31] We code formal defensive alliances based on the Alliance Treaty Obligations and Provisions (ATOP) v3.0 alliance data set. See: Leeds et al. (2002). The

We also record whether the alliance is based on a formal pact according to the ATOP data set.[32] We present our complete protocol for coding allies in Appendix I. The sixth column in Table 3.1 identifies each potential proliferator's allies, when present.

This allows us to separate those potential proliferators that had at least some allied support in mitigating the security threats posed by their adversaries, and those that did not. We conclude that among the countries that at some point engaged in nuclear development, the following did *not* benefit from any allied protection: Algeria, Iran (post-1984), Iraq, Libya, the Soviet Union, Switzerland, Syria, the United States, Yugoslavia; plus Brazil and Romania, which faced no serious security threats. The remaining countries listed in Table 3.1 above enjoyed some level of allied protection vis-à-vis their adversaries.

Our analysis supports our second theoretical prediction: among those states that face a security threat serious enough to give them the willingness to proliferate, and which do not enjoy the protection of a nuclear ally, high relative power is necessary to provide them with the opportunity to build the bomb. In accordance with the second observable implication of our theory, there is a strong positive correlation between power and proliferation among states that do not possess a nuclear ally.

Historically, among states without security sponsors, only two states have proliferated. These are the United States and the Soviet Union, each of which possessed relatively high latent and military power vis-à-vis their adversaries during the run-up to their nuclear acquisition – Nazi Germany and Japan in the U.S. case; the United States in the case of the Soviet Union. Both followed the first pathway laid out in our theory: a threat to the state's security interests serious enough to give it the willingness to nuclearize; plus sufficient relative power to give it the opportunity to build the bomb. None of the seven states that engaged in nuclear development without the protection of an ally while being weaker than their adversaries acquired nuclear weapons. Two – Iraq and Syria – launched a program hoping it would go undetected and suffered a preventive strike. The remaining five – Algeria, Iran (post 1984), Libya, Switzerland, and Yugoslavia

International Crisis Behavior (ICB) data set is introduced in: Brecher and Wilkenfeld (2000).

[32] See: Leeds et al. (2002).

– abandoned their nuclear programs due to one of two reasons. Either changes in their strategic environment made an investment in nuclear weapons no longer productive (Algeria, Libya, Switzerland, and Yugoslavia), or they were coerced into remaining nonnuclear (Iran). In Chapter 4, we examine several of these cases to demonstrate the role of threat and relative power in shaping the odds of proliferation among states that do not enjoy allied protection.

Taking stock, strong states that possessed the willingness to build the bomb had the opportunity to proliferate unimpeded. Furthermore, all of the preventive counterproliferation strikes in history have been carried out against weak states without a nuclear ally: Iran during the Iran-Iraq War; Iraq (in 1981 and 2003); and Syria.[33] No weak unprotected state has ever acquired nuclear weapons. Figure 3.1 displays all cases of nuclear development arranged according to their relative latent power and whether or not they enjoyed allied protection.

Figure 3.1 also allows us to make a preliminary evaluation of the effect of security alliances on nuclear acquisition. When we compare the left and right columns in the figure, we notice that the relationship between relative power and proliferation is weakened by the presence of an ally, which can give a weaker state the opportunity to nuclearize. China, France, India, Israel, Pakistan, and the United Kingdom were all relatively weak vis-à-vis their adversaries and yet managed to acquire nuclear weapons. (South Africa acquired the bomb to mitigate unrest in its region, while enjoying great relative power vis-à-vis its adversary, Angola.) Clearly, alliances can give weaker states the opportunity to build the bomb.

In order to test the two remaining observable implications of our theory, however, we need to investigate the relations between potential proliferators and their allies in greater depth. To begin with, we must distinguish between different levels of allied support. To do so, for each potential proliferator that has a nuclear ally, we measure the degree of commitment this sponsor had made to its protégé's security by the last three years of the latter's nuclear program. We look at three variables. First, we consider whether the ally offered a formal, public security guarantee.[34] Second, we determine the number of troops

---

[33] See: Fuhrmann and Kreps (2010, 831–859).
[34] See: Leeds et al. (2002).

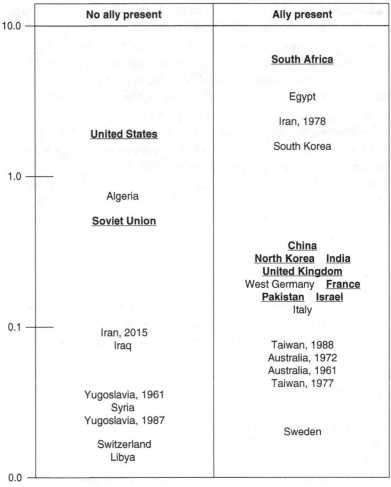

Figure 3.1. Power, Alliances, and Nuclear Proliferation
Bold underlined cases note nuclear acquisition; others are cases of nuclear
forbearance. Case list and program dates from Sagan (2011). We omit Brazil
and Romania for lack of clear security threats during their nuclear programs.

the ally has deployed in its protégé's territory.[35] Finally, we investigate
whether the ally had nuclear weapons deployed on the protégé's territory.[36] (We also include information on these indicators in the last
three columns of Table 3.1.)

[35] For data on deployments of U.S. troops between 1950 and 2005, see: Kane (2006).
[36] For data on deployments of U.S. nuclear weapons, see: Reiter (2014).

We consider the level of protection offered by an ally to be high when the ally deploys nuclear weapons or more than 5,000 troops to the protégé's territory; and to be low otherwise. Whereas deployment of nuclear weapons to a protégé's territory, even in small numbers, is a strong signal of an ally's security commitment, our criterion is somewhat arbitrary in setting the necessary number of troops at 5,000. Fortunately, in practical terms, no potential proliferator had between 2,000 and 18,000 allied troops deployed in its territory during the last three years of its nuclear program. Therefore, our coding of individual countries would remain the same regardless of where our threshold level of troops was set within that range. Fewer than 2,000 allied troops is clearly insufficient to make a protégé comfortable relying on its sponsor; more than 18,000 allied troops no doubt represents a great level of present commitment from a sponsor.

Using this criterion, we identify eleven potential proliferators – Australia, China, Egypt, India, Iran (until 1978), Israel, North Korea, Pakistan, South Africa, Sweden, and Taiwan – that enjoyed limited allied protection. We label them "loose allies." We also identify five potential proliferators that enjoyed a high level of allied protection of their homeland during the last three years of their nuclear development: France, Italy, South Korea, the United Kingdom, and West Germany. We label these countries "close allies."

This distinction between loose allies and close allies helps us understand how potential proliferators may doubt the reliability of their security sponsor. Since they receive weak support, loose allies can seriously question whether their sponsor is committed to the defense of their primary security interests. Close allies should be more confident in the reliability of their security sponsor. Nevertheless, they may worry that their sponsor's support could wane over time or that it does not cover all of their security interests.

This distinction between loose and close allies helps us test the third observable implication of our theory: that among states that enjoy the protection of an ally that ensures all of their security interests, none acquired nuclear weapons. Indeed, we find that among protégés that have a reliable security sponsor covering all of their security goals, proliferation has not occurred. Of the eleven potential proliferators that enjoyed the protection of loose allies, all six that acquired nuclear weapons – China, India, Israel, North Korea, Pakistan, and South Africa – doubted the reliability of their allies' commitment to the protection of their territory. Likewise, we find that among the five potential proliferators that possessed a close ally during their nuclear development phase, the only two that acquired the bomb – France and the United Kingdom – deemed the United States an unreliable guarantor of their overall "vital interests," which they defined broadly.[37] In Chapters 5 and 6, we examine several of these cases to demonstrate the role of allied security guarantees in shaping the odds of proliferation. Overall, we conclude that, per our third prediction, only protégés that doubt the reliability of their allies' security commitments will proliferate.

We now turn to the fourth and final observable implication of our theory: that sticks-based nonproliferation policies through which a security sponsor threatens its protégé with abandonment are only effective when the protégé is weak relative to its adversaries; a protégé that is relatively strong will only be effectively stopped along its pathway to nuclearization by a carrots-based nonproliferation policy that enhances its security assurances.

Looking at the historical cases of proliferation, we find that of the eight states that enjoyed the protection of an ally during their nuclear development phase and ultimately abandoned their nuclear ambitions – Australia, Egypt, Iran (until 1978), Italy, South Korea, Sweden, Taiwan, and West Germany – two were successfully coerced by the United States into remaining nonnuclear (Taiwan and West Germany) and one (South Korea) was ultimately induced to remain nonnuclear through greater U.S. security assurances. Taiwan and West Germany were considerably weaker vis-à-vis their adversaries (China and the Soviet Union, respectively), and so Washington was able to coerce them into remaining nonnuclear by deploying a sticks-based nonproliferation approach and issuing threats of abandonment. South Korea, in contrast, was stronger relative to its adversary (North Korea), and Washington was therefore unable to guarantee the end of its nuclear efforts by threatening to abandon it. In order to ensure the continuation of South Korea's nonnuclear status, the United States ultimately had to implement a carrots-based approach, reinforcing the security guarantees it offered Seoul.

To summarize, the empirical patterns of nuclear proliferation are consistent with all four observable implications of our theory. The

---

[37] See: Goldstein (2000).

strategic dynamics on which our theory centers condition the spread of nuclear weapons by shaping each state's willingness and opportunity to build the bomb.

Our theory can also shed light on another hitherto underappreciated historical pattern of proliferation: the decline in the rate of proliferation since the end of the Cold War. Whereas, during the Cold War, one new state entered the nuclear ranks every five years on average, since its end more than two-and-a-half decades ago, only two states have gone nuclear: Pakistan in 1990 and North Korea in 2006. Moreover, the number of active nuclear programs has decreased significantly in the post–Cold War period, such that today no state is suspected of actively pursuing nuclear weapons.[38]

Seen through our strategic interaction prism, the end of the Cold War had two effects on proliferation. First, it ameliorated the security environment for U.S. friends and allies, thereby lowering the expected security benefit they would extract from nuclearization and undermining their willingness to go nuclear. In fact, South Africa, which had developed nuclear weapons to counter regional communist threats, terminated its program shortly after the end of the Cold War, producing the only case of nuclear reversal to date.[39] Second, the demise of the Soviet Union limited the potential costs of U.S.-launched preventive attacks, boosting the credibility of U.S. threats of military action, thereby decreasing the opportunity to nuclearize among non-U.S. allies. As we shown in the following text, the United States was able to impose crippling sanctions against Iraq that – along with the ever-present threat of force – effectively terminated its nuclear-weapons program. There is some evidence that Libyan leader Muammar Qaddafi (1969–2011) ended his nuclear

---

[38] It is unlikely that Syria has continued its nuclear development since the onset of its civil war in 2011. On Iran, see Chapter 4.

[39] South African president F. W. de Klerk (1989–1994) noted that the fall of the Soviet Union and the subsequent resolution of the conflicts in Angola and Namibia meant that "a nuclear deterrent had become, not only superfluous, but in fact an obstacle to the development of South Africa's international relations." See: Pabian (1995, 10). There is some controversy about the importance of domestic politics in South Africa's nuclear reversal. See, for example, Albright and Hibbs (1993); Liberman (2001); and Van Wyk (2010b). Recently, Van Wyk concluded: "there is no evidence to back the suggestion that the de Klerk government did not wish to risk seeing a potentially radical Black Nationalist government in South Africa armed with nuclear weapons." See: Van Wyk (2010b, 69).

program in part as a reaction to the U.S.-led invasion of Iraq in 2003, reportedly confiding: "I will do whatever the Americans want, because I saw what happened in Iraq, and I was afraid."[40] Syria had its nuclear reactor reportedly struck preventively by a U.S. ally, Israel, in 2007.[41] Combined, these two effects account for why, despite claims to the contrary,[42] proliferation has slowed down with the emergence of U.S. power preponderance.

Having laid out our empirical research design and highlighted how the broader historical patterns of proliferation are compatible with our theory, we now turn to the criteria we used to select and organize the sixteen case studies we present in the following three chapters.

Case Selection and Organization of Historical Chapters

The chapters that follow are organized to reflect the two causal pathways to proliferation identified by our theory. Chapter 4 focuses on cases in which the potential proliferator was not relying on an allied guarantee of protection during the nuclear development period, and in which therefore the key strategic dynamics took place between the state developing nuclear weapons and its adversaries. To proliferate, these states would have had to follow the first pathway to nuclear acquisition. They would have to face a dire security threat and possess high relative power, as was the case with the Soviet Union, the only case of successful nuclear acquisition we cover in this group. The remaining potential proliferators either lacked a dire security threat and did not have the willingness to build the bomb, as was the case with Brazil, or were relatively weak vis-à-vis their adversaries and did not have the opportunity to nuclearize, as was the case with Iran and Iraq.

In Chapters 5 and 6, we study states that relied at least in part on an allied guarantee of protection during the nuclear development period, so that the key strategic dynamics took place between the potential proliferator, its adversaries, and its allies. To proliferate, these states would have had to follow the second pathway to proliferation. They would have had to face a dire security threat and be able to deter a

---

[40] Palkki and Smith (2012, 272–273).
[41] See: Makowsky (2012).
[42] See: Jo and Gartzke (2007, 187).

preventive counterproliferation attack through a combination of their own power with whatever support they received from their sponsor. At the same time, they would have had to deem their sponsor's support to be unreliable.

In Chapter 5, we analyze cases of "loose allies," states that enjoyed a modicum of protection from an ally during the final phase of their nuclear development. Such states could clearly doubt the reliability of their sponsor's commitment, and would acquire nuclear weapons if they could thwart preventive attacks. Such was the case with China, Israel, India, South Africa, North Korea, and Pakistan. The other states we analyze in this group either lost the willingness to nuclearize because their allies offered de facto guarantees of protection against serious security threats, as was the case with Sweden; or lacked the opportunity to build the bomb, because their allies threatened them with abandonment if they continued to pursue their nuclear ambitions, as was the case of Taiwan.

We conclude our historical analysis in Chapter 6, where we analyze cases of "close allies," states that possessed robust security guarantees from their sponsors during their period of nuclear development. Despite the robustness of their sponsors' security guarantees, these states might nevertheless doubt that such support would continue over time, or that it would cover all of the state's security interests. Among these states, the only one that proliferated was France, which wanted to pursue broader security goals than its ally, the United States, was willing to protect. The remaining states we cover in this group lost their willingness to nuclearize in return for firm guarantees of allied protection, as was the case with Japan and South Korea; or lost their opportunity to build the bomb when their allies threatened them with abandonment, as was the case with West Germany.

For each of these three chapters, we select cases based on two criteria. First, we have at least one case that illustrates each of the possible combinations of values for two of our explanatory variables: high and low levels of threat; high and low relative power. (Variation in the level of support a state receives from an ally – our third underlying strategic variable – is reflected in the organization of cases into different chapters.) Second, within each of these sets of states, we select for in-depth case studies those that are most relevant from both historical and policy perspectives. We look at the remaining cases of nuclear development in brief vignettes laid out in Appendix II. In Appendix III we cover the cases of four states that are considered by existing statistical examinations of proliferation to have been "puzzling misses" among the list of states that attempted to develop nuclear weapons.[43]

---

[43] See: Singh and Way (2004, 879–880).

4 | *Adversaries and Proliferation*

In this chapter, we introduce a first set of four historical case studies: Brazil, the Soviet Union, Iraq, and Iran. We use these cases to explore the first pathway to proliferation delineated by our theory.

We demonstrate two claims. First, using the history of the Brazilian nuclear program, we show how a serious security threat is a necessary condition for nuclear proliferation. The Brazilian case highlights the role of security threats in conditioning a state's willingness to build the bomb. Despite having abundant reserves of natural uranium, a sizeable industrial and technological complex, and a manifest desire to accrue prestige on the world stage, Brazil never acquired nuclear weapons. As our theory predicts, facing a benevolent strategic environment, Brazil opted for maintaining its nonnuclear status. Once the country had mastered nuclear technology by the 1980s, it integrated the global nuclear order as a nonnuclear-weapons state.

Second, turning to the nuclear histories of the Soviet, Iraqi, and Iranian nuclear programs, we demonstrate how, among states facing a serious security threat but lacking a security sponsor, nuclearization is only within reach of those that are strong enough to deter a counterproliferation strike.

In the run-up to its nuclear acquisition, the Soviet Union possessed the capability to inflict significant cost on its adversary, the United States, were Washington to launch a preventive counterproliferation strike. Therefore, U.S. leaders considered the effect of Soviet nuclear acquisition to be smaller than the cost of a counterproliferation war. Having the willingness to proliferate, Moscow was unimpeded in its opportunity to obtain the bomb.

In contrast, Iraq and Iran were relatively weak vis-à-vis their adversaries – beyond the rivalry between the two, their nuclearization was also opposed by Israel and the United States – and, therefore, notwithstanding their willingness to go nuclear, both were denied the opportunity to acquire the bomb. In the case of Iraq, and despite its great effort to maintain the secrecy of its nuclear program, the country was targeted by preventive counterproliferation strikes, was constrained by a robust regime of nonproliferation sanctions, and was ultimately invaded by the United States in 2003. In the case of Iran, the country was also targeted with robust international sanctions and repeatedly threatened with counterproliferation military action by Israel and, less explicitly, the United States. In the end, by 2015 Tehran agreed to limit its ambitions in the nuclear realm, signing the Joint Comprehensive Plan of Action (JCPOA) with several international partners, and pledging to maintain its nonnuclear status for at least a decade more.

Taken together, these three cases display the role of relative power in shaping a state's opportunity to acquire the bomb. The Soviet case illustrates the first causal pathway to proliferation laid out by our theory: powerful states that face a high-level security threat and lack a security sponsor are likely to acquire nuclear weapons.

Brazil

Despite having mastered the nuclear fuel cycle by the 1980s, Brazil has elected not to develop nuclear weapons. To the contrary, the country's rulers consistently opposed conducting a nuclear test.

Brazilian nuclear forbearance can be explained by the country's benign strategic environment, which undermined Brasília's willingness to nuclearize. Despite Washington's perception that Brazil and Argentina were serious security rivals engaged in a nuclear race, relations between the two countries were mostly cordial during the atomic age. In fact, Brazil and Argentina cooperated in the nuclear domain in a joint attempt to overcome U.S. attempts to deny them nuclear technology and materials.[1] But this cooperation aimed at mastering nuclear technology for peaceful purposes. Faced with no serious regional threats to its security and protected by the United States from any extra-regional threats, Brazil's strategic environment has throughout the nuclear age been one of abundant security. Therefore, Brasília has had no willingness to build a nuclear deterrent.

Brazil's nuclear ambitions were largely driven by considerations of economic and technological development as well as national

---

[1] For an overview of Brazil-Argentina relations up to the 1980s, see: Hilton (1985).

independence and autonomy, particularly vis-à-vis the United States. Given the country's wealth in natural uranium, Brazilian leaders thought the nuclear sector could play a key role in the country's growth, bringing other sectors in tow. Security considerations played only a secondary role in driving the Brazilian nuclear program. They did so in two ways. First, until the late 1970s, Brazilian elites thought that Argentina might see in nuclear acquisition a means of compensating for its relative conventional weakness vis-à-vis Brazil. Therefore, Brazilian decisionmakers in this early phase decided to acquire the technology necessary to build a nuclear weapon, so that if at any point in the future Argentina decided to go nuclear Brazil could quickly follow suit. As would become clear to Brazilian elites, however, Buenos Aires had no intention to develop a nuclear weapon either. Second, security played a supporting role in Brazil's nuclear endeavors because the country was – and remains – determined to develop a nuclear propulsion system for submarine vessels in order to improve its ability to project power in the South Atlantic.

Were Argentina to have represented a serious threat to Brazilian security, Brazil would have had the opportunity to proliferate. Argentina is conventionally weaker than its neighbor and, particularly given Brazil's vast territory, would have found it difficult to prevent Brazilian nuclearization by force. In the three years running up to Brazilian nuclear forbearance in 1990 – the period in which Brazil was highly likely to have weaponized its nuclear effort if it so wished – Brazilian military expenditures were more than triple those of Argentina.[2]

This relative strength vis-à-vis its regional rivals, combined with the low level of threat that the Soviet Union presented to the security of South American countries during the Cold War, also made Brazil relatively immune to a sticks-based U.S. nonproliferation policy. U.S. efforts – denying Brazil nuclear technology transfers; pressuring those countries, such as France and West Germany, that offered to supply Brazil with these technologies; and repeatedly attempting to coerce Brazil into joining the NPT – were therefore limited in their effectiveness.

---

[2] See: Singer (1987).

Brazilian Interest in Nuclear Weapons

The Brazilian nuclear program was started under the civilian governments of the postwar era and intensified under the military dictatorship that ruled the country between 1964 and 1985. After Brazil transitioned to democracy, it mastered the nuclear fuel cycle in the late 1980s. Since then, Brazil eschewed building nuclear weapons and instead joined the global nonproliferation regime.

**Brazil's Civilian Nuclear Program under the
Republican Regime, 1951–1964**

President Getúlio Vargas (1951–1954) started Brazil's nuclear program in 1951.[3] The newly created national research council (CNPq) outlawed exports of atomic minerals except those resulting from bilateral government agreements.[4] During the initial years of the program, Brazil sought an arrangement with the United States that would allow it to obtain nuclear technology.[5] When Washington declined its request for a processing plant, Brasília turned instead to scientists in West Germany.[6] In 1953, Brazil contracted with research centers in the FRG to obtain uranium enrichment centrifuges and provide training for Brazilian personnel.[7] At the same time, Brazil tried to make a nuclear deal with France on the joint development of uranium mining and extraction technologies. Finally, Brazil attempted to purchase heavy water reactors from Norway.[8]

President Dwight D. Eisenhower's (1953–1961) announcement of the "Atoms for Peace" initiative in December 1953, along with Vargas's death and replacement by João Café Filho (1954–1955) – a more pro-American leader – repositioned the United States as Brazil's potential technological supplier in the nuclear realm.[9] Facing U.S. pressure, Café Filho canceled the nuclear deal with West Germany[10] and, in August 1955, signed an agreement with Washington for the joint development

---

[3] See: Patti (2014, 4).
[4] See: Patti (2012a, 36).
[5] See: Patti (2013a, 4–6); Patti (2012a, 37–39).
[6] For an overview of Brazilian-West German atomic collaboration during the 1950s, see: Patti (2013a).
[7] See: Ibid., 8.
[8] See: Ibid., 5.
[9] See: Ibid., 10.
[10] See: Ibid., 11.

of peaceful nuclear technology and uranium exploration.[11] The United States would supply Brazil with a research reactor and the necessary nuclear fuel in exchange for minerals with atomic use.[12] A step forward in Brazil's nuclear path, this deal also generated a nationalist backlash, with a Brazilian congressional inquiry concluding that the country was fully dependent on the United States in nuclear matters.[13]

Riding this nationalist sentiment, the newly elected president Juscelino Kubitschek (1956–1961) decided in 1956 to push for Brazilian autonomy in the nuclear realm.[14] Apart from developing nuclear energy, Kubitschek's "Plano de Metas" (Goals Plan) aimed at producing nuclear fuel (enriched uranium), training nuclear personnel, and producing radioisotopes for medical purposes.[15] With those ends in mind, Kubitschek created the National Commission for Nuclear Energy (CNEN) and froze exports of uranium and all other "strategic" minerals.[16] He also reoriented Brazilian nuclear policy back toward collaboration with West Germany, from which Brazil would again unsuccessfully attempt to purchase centrifuges in 1957.[17]

Brazil's nuclear effort would continue under President João Goulart (1961–1964), with the government establishing a state monopoly over radioactive materials[18] and pursuing negotiations with France to procure a heavy water reactor that would use natural uranium and thus free Brazil from dependence on American enriched uranium.[19] In 1963, the first experimental reactor partially built by Brazil with U.S. help under the Atoms for Peace program began to operate.[20]

This early interest in nuclear technology was restricted to civilian purposes. In 1962, Brazil presented a proposal at the United Nations General Assembly (UNGA) for the creation of a nuclear-weapons-free zone in Latin America. This proposal would gain momentum with the Cuban Missile Crisis of October that year, but would ultimately be

[11] See: Malheiros (1993, 11–12).
[12] See: Patti (2013a, 14).
[13] See: Malheiros (1993, 20).
[14] See: Motta (2010, 118).
[15] Ibid.
[16] See: Malheiros (1993, 20); Motta (2010, 118).
[17] See: Patti (2013a, 15).
[18] See: Patti (2012a, 51).
[19] See: Myers (1984, 884); Patti (2013b, 213). Negotiations with France would be frozen by the military coup of 1964 in Brasília.
[20] See: Myers (1984, 884).

defeated by Cuban and Soviet opposition.[21] Brazil would pick up the issue again the following year by joining the Five Nations Declaration for a denuclearized Latin America.[22]

Brazil's Civilian Nuclear Program under the Military Regime, 1964–1975

In 1964, a coup turned Brazil into a military dictatorship. Under Marshal Humberto Castelo Branco (1964–1967), Brazil would accelerate its nuclear development, investing in "efforts to master two highly sophisticated and essential technologies for the nuclear fuel cycle: uranium enrichment and plutonium reprocessing."[23] Among other nuclear deals, in 1965 Brazil signed an agreement with the United States, securing access to uranium supplies for three research reactors.[24]

At the same time, Brazil opposed the 1967 Treaty of Tlatelolco, which established a nuclear-weapons-free zone in Latin America and the Caribbean. In fact, Brazil and Argentina coordinated their nuclear policies during negotiations for this agreement.[25] From then on until the early 1990s, the two countries would work together to oppose the nascent nonproliferation regime. Brazil's opposition to Tlatelolco did not reflect the country's determination to acquire nuclear weapons. Rather, as army general Danilo Venturini, who would later become the Brazilian National Security Council (CSN) chief (1979–1982), put it, the problem with Tlatelolco was its "recognition of castes among countries," making the United States the only legal nuclear power in the Western Hemisphere.[26]

Nuclear coordination between Brasília and Buenos Aires continued during the administration of Marshal Artur da Costa e Silva (1967–1969), with the two countries presenting a joint position in NPT negotiations. Here too, they opposed the agreement on the grounds that it established a discriminatory regime, which impinged on state sovereignty and hindered the technological development of nonnuclear states, aiming at what Brazilian and Argentinian diplomats called the "disarmament of the disarmed."[27] When the NPT opened for signature

---

[21] See: Patti (2012a, 55–56).
[22] See: Ibid., 56–57.
[23] Kutchesfahani (2014, 27).
[24] See: Malheiros (1993, 22).
[25] See: Redick et al. (1994, 110–111); Mallea (2013a); Coutto (2014, 5).
[26] Quoted in Barletta (1997, 25). See also: Hurrell (1986, 91).
[27] Kutchesfahani (2014, 43). See also: Hurrell (1986, 112–113); Goldemberg and Feiveson (1994, 12); Camargo (2006, 281–284); Patti (2012a, 66–74).

in 1968, Brazil refused to join based on the need to maintain the right to conduct peaceful nuclear explosions (PNEs) for civil engineering works.[28]

Also in the late 1960s, the view that nuclear energy would be necessary for satisfying growing demand resulting from economic development gained traction in Brasília. Brazil started plans to build its first nuclear power plant, eliciting bids from Canada, France, the United Kingdom, the United States, and West Germany.[29] Costa e Silva saw nuclear energy as "the most powerful resource that can be made available to developing countries so as to reduce the distance that separates them from industrialized nations" and therefore considered all issues related to the nuclear sector as a matter of national security.[30] His successor Emílio Médici (1969–1974) followed in his footsteps and started building a nuclear power plant in Angra dos Reis, fifty miles south of Rio de Janeiro.[31] Despite lobbying by Brazilian nuclear scientists, who favored the development of indigenous technology, the government chose to purchase the reactor from foreign vendors.[32] In 1972, U.S.-based Westinghouse won the public bid for Angra I, a pressurized water reactor, to operate under International Atomic Energy Agency (IAEA) safeguards.[33] Fuel for the plant would require England to turn South African yellow cake into uranium hexafluoride, which would then be enriched through gaseous diffusion in the United States.[34]

By 1974, however, partly in response to the Indian Smiling Buddha nuclear test, Washington halted exports of enriched uranium to Brazil.[35] Brazilian officials had good reason to suspect that "the United States might not provide the necessary enrichment services in the long run."[36] As General Hugo Abreu, secretary-general of the CSN (1974–1978),

[28] See: "Minutes of the Fortieth Session of the Brazilian National Security Council," October 4, 1967, Wilson Center Digital Archive, Brazilian Nuclear History.
[29] See: Patti (2012a, 87).
[30] Costa e Silva, speech at the Itamaraty Palace, April 5, 1967, quoted in Andrade (2006, 130), our translation. For the guidelines of Brazilian nuclear policy during Costa e Silva's government, see: "Minutes of the Fortieth Session of the Brazilian National Security Council," October 4, 1967.
[31] See: Malheiros (1993, 27).
[32] See: Goldemberg and Feiveson (1994, 13).
[33] See: Solingen (1996, 26); Squassoni and Fite (2005, 16); Coutto (2014, 7).
[34] See: Malheiros (1993, 29).
[35] See: Reiss (1995, 49–50); Nedal and Coutto (2013).
[36] Patti (2012a, 108).

would reflect later, the "solution adopted in Angra I would leave us entirely dependent on the North Americans and we did not want to remain dependent in the energy field."[37]

At the same time, the Indian test prompted Brazilian decisionmakers to reiterate the importance of taking all the steps necessary to build a bomb if a security threat were to emerge in the future. In one of the most explicit discussions on nuclear weapons at the highest level of the Brazilian government, the president, General Ernesto Geisel (1974–1979), told the top brass of the military on June 10, 1974 – a mere three weeks after the Indian test – that Brazil should "develop the technology necessary for a peaceful nuclear explosion, which will even allow us, if necessary, to possess our own weapon." At the same time, Geisel cautioned against a "passionate approach" to the issue, which would be "capable of leading to hasty decisions, influenced by the supposed possibilities and intentions of Argentina."[38] In other words, there was no need for a bomb at present; but Brazil should keep its freedom of maneuver in the nuclear realm. That a putative security threat from Argentina did not exist is further confirmed by the fact that, when faced with the United States' tighter post-1974 nuclear controls, Buenos Aires suggested deepening nuclear cooperation between the two countries. President Geisel docked this proposal until the dispute between the two countries over hydric resources in the River Plate basin was settled.[39]

Brazil's Cooperation with West Germany and Secret Military Nuclear Program, 1975–1987

Washington's growing efforts to limit Brazil's access to nuclear technology and materials came at a critical juncture for the Brazilian nuclear effort. The oil embargo ensuing the Yom Kippur War of 1973 had resulted in higher energy prices. To meet the expected growth in demand, the Brazilian national electricity company Eletrobrás released *Plan 90*, calling for twelve nuclear power plants to be operating by

---

[37] Abreu (1979, 43), our translation.
[38] Marcelo de Moraes, "Geisel admitiu a possibilidade de construir a bomba atômica brasileira." *Estado de São Paulo*, August 11, 2013. Available at: http://internacional.estadao.com.br/noticias/geral,geisel-admitiu-possibilidade-de-construir-a-bomba-atomica-brasileira,1063015. Last accessed: May 2, 2016, our translation.
[39] See: Mallea (2013b).

1990.[40] Against this background, Geisel's administration was keen on acquiring autonomous control over nuclear fuel production technology through cooperation with the FRG.[41] To that effect, on June 27, 1975, the newly created Brazilian public nuclear corporation Nuclebrás reached an agreement with West German Kraftwerk Union for "the first sale of a complete nuclear fuel cycle and one of the largest transfers of nuclear technology to a developing nation."[42] Specifically, the agreement included a joint uranium mining venture, experimental "jet nozzle" enrichment technology, facilities for nuclear fuel production and spent nuclear fuel reprocessing, and the construction of four pressurized water reactors.[43] Notably, the agreement excluded participation of the Brazilian military in any of its components, and included safeguards considered stricter than those called for by the NPT.[44]

In 1977, the United States ratified the Additional Protocol I to the Treaty of Tlatelolco, pledging not to threaten or use nuclear weapons against other treaty members. This was the United States' "first self-limiting agreement of this nature" and strengthened Washington's hand in negotiations over regional nuclear matters.[45] That same year Geisel secretly agreed with Washington to "abandon the sensitive part of the nuclear deal with Bonn [in exchange] for receiving a package of substantial economic aid from Washington."[46] Moreover, in an attempt to address Washington's concerns about rivalry in the Southern Cone – or, failing that, circumvent the barriers Washington was erecting – Brazil and Argentina issued a joint communiqué calling

---

[40] See: Patti (2012b).
[41] For an outline of Geisel's nuclear policy, see: "Memorandum, Information for the President of Brazil, No. 055/74 from the National Security Council," August 13, 1974, Wilson Center Digital Archive, Brazilian Nuclear History. See also: Hurrell (1986, 218, 224); Barletta (1997, 14); Motta (2010,125).
[42] Kutchesfahani (2014, 35). See also: Myers (1984, 883); Barletta (1997, 2); Patti (2012a, 110).
[43] See: Kutchesfahani (2014, 35).
[44] See: Barletta (1997, 4); Pinheiro da Silva (2010, 25); Patti (2012a, 117–118).
[45] Redick (1978,181).
[46] See: Patti (2012a, 154). This primacy of development over military goals was part of the broader, though perhaps counterintuitive, policy of the military government. Brazilian leaders saw their strategic environment as one of abundant security, so the regime did little to modernize Brazilian armed forces. See, e.g., Geisel's speech to the representatives of the Inter-American Defense Council, November 19, 1976, Presidential Library of Brazil. Available at: www.biblioteca.presidencia.gov.br/presidencia/ex-presidentes/ernesto-geisel/discursos/1976/75.pdf/view. Last accessed: April 29, 2016.

for nuclear collaboration and the "initiation of systematic technological exchanges."[47] Three years later, this communiqué would be translated into an "Agreement on Cooperation for the Development and Application of the Peaceful Uses of Nuclear Energy," which called for "systematic coordination of nuclear policy in all international forums."[48] In his speech on the occasion of the agreement's signature, Argentinian president General Jorge Videla (1976–1981) attempted to lower U.S. concerns – and the pressures they generated – by stating his hope that the agreement would "silence forever the legend that there is an arms race between Argentina and Brazil in the nuclear field."[49]

In the meantime, doubtful that Bonn (facing strong U.S. pressures) would transfer reliable centrifuge-based enrichment technology, in 1979 the Brazilian government gave the military permission to establish a parallel nuclear program with the support of the CNEN. Anticipating Washington's continued opposition, this program – dubbed the Autonomous Program of Nuclear Technology (PATN) – was shrouded in secrecy.[50] Its goals were to "develop the national capability for the broad use of nuclear energy, also including naval propulsion and the production of peaceful nuclear devices."[51] By the end of the 1970s, then, Brazil in effect had two programs – a civilian nuclear program based on the agreement with Germany and the secret military PATN – competing over the direction of Brazilian nuclear policy.[52]

Within the PATN, and resorting to "undemonstrated purchases in the black market" from other non-NPT members such as China, Iraq, and, to a lesser extent, South Africa, each of the three branches of the military pursued a different method of obtaining fissile material.[53] Among the three, the navy, focusing on ultracentrifuges, would

[47] Kutchesfahani (2014, 46).
[48] Redick et al. (1994, 111). See also: Carasales (1995, 39–40).
[49] Quoted in Kutchesfahani (2014, 57).
[50] See: Barletta (1997, 5). For the proposed goals of the PATN, see "Notice No. 135/79 from the General Secretariat of the Brazilian National Security Council," June 18, 1979, Wilson Center Digital Archive, Brazilian Nuclear History.
[51] Quoted in Patti (2012a, 203). See also: Barletta (1997, 5–6, 14); Pinheiro da Silva (2010).
[52] See: Coutto (2014, 12).
[53] Patti (2012a, 204).

achieve the greatest progress.[54] According to some in the navy's top brass, its nuclear effort was squarely grounded on a desire to enhance Brazil's international stature – and that of the military within Brazil – by displaying its mastery of nuclear technology.[55] Vice admiral Othon Pinheiro, in charge of the navy's program during the early 1980s, would later present a broader view, describing it as part of the country's "war against underdevelopment,"[56] aiming at energy independence, economic development, scientific and medical research, and security – this last one through the development of a nuclear naval propulsion system for a submarine.[57] For physicist Rex Nazaré Alves, head of the CNEN between 1982 and 1990, this last aspect was the most important: for the navy, "the goal was the construction of a nuclear propulsion submarine."[58] The 1982 Falklands War – in which the Royal Navy's nuclear-powered task force, operating thousands of miles from its home bases, imposed heavy losses on the Argentine Navy – had demonstrated the unequivocal advantage of having nuclear-propulsion naval forces.[59] The other two branches of the Brazilian armed forces were less successful in their nuclear endeavors. The air force program, using laser enrichment technology, went nowhere; and the army program, aimed at building a graphite reactor capable of producing plutonium, was never a priority and received limited resources.[60]

Evidencing Brazil's nuclear progress, in late 1984, while the regime prepared a transition to democracy, air force officials suggested testing a nuclear device in March 1985, as a way of displaying the achievements of the military dictatorship. However, President General João Figueiredo (1979–1985) declined on the grounds that "Brazil's

[54] See: Barletta (1997, 6).
[55] Ibid., 16–17.
[56] Pinheiro da Silva (2010, 91), our translation.
[57] See: Ibid., 44, 70, 110, 126. Interestingly, Pinheiro considered the energy component of the program as also having a security dimension: "nuclear energy will help settle our energy accounts without needing other countries, that is, without needing additional military power to back up contracts or invade other countries. ... [E]veryone thinks of nuclear energy through the prism of destruction. In our case, it will guarantee we won't need any." Ibid., 129, our translation.
[58] Quoted in Motta (2010, 129), our translation.
[59] See: Reiss (1995, 50); Barletta (1997, 7–8); Motta (2010, 129–130); Pinheiro da Silva (2010, 55); Patti (2013b, 127).
[60] See: Barletta (1997, 7–8).

interests were to master the enrichment cycle and to avoid any activity that would be perceived as a bomb."[61]

In April 1985, Brazil again became a democracy, led by President José Sarney (1985–1989). The new administration was made aware of the PATN and initially approved all existing nuclear projects.[62] By then, Brazil had mastered two key nuclear technologies: "yellow cake conversion into pure uranium hexafluoride (UF6) gas suitable for use in enrichment operations ... and uranium enrichment."[63]

Since a transition to civilian rule had also taken place in Buenos Aires, with President Raúl Alfonsín's (1983–1989) rise to power, there was room for reinvigorated cooperation between the two countries.[64] Brazil and Argentina therefore entered a new phase in the nuclear rapprochement they had started in the late 1970s, with their new civilian presidents working together to boost their mutual level of control over their own nuclear programs in order to diminish the power of the military and strengthen civilian oversight of the armed forces.[65] In November 1985, Sarney and Alfonsín met at Iguaçu and signed a Joint Declaration on Nuclear Policy, establishing a "standing joint committee on nuclear policy chaired by their foreign ministers."[66] From this moment onward, the nuclear dimension "became a fundamental vehicle for bilateral integration."[67] The following year, the two countries would commit to creating an integrated free-trade area (Mercosur), anchoring their nuclear cooperation on a broader context of economic partnership.[68] Then, in July 1987, Sarney and Alfonsín issued the Viedma Declaration promoting mutual confidence in the nuclear realm "within the framework of the immovable commitment made by both nations to use nuclear energy exclusively for

[61] Ibid., 19.
[62] See: Ibid., 10. For an updated description of the PATN in 1985, see "Notice, Information for the President of Brazil, No. 011/85 from the National Security Council, Structure of the Parallel Nuclear Program," February 21, 1985, Wilson Center Digital Archive, Brazilian Nuclear History.
[63] Patti (2012b).
[64] See: Carasales (1999, 56).
[65] For an excellent oral history of nuclear cooperation between Brazil and Argentina, see: Mallea et al. (2015).
[66] Redick et al. (1994, 112). See also: Carasales (1999, 57).
[67] Gamba-Stonehouse (1991, 233). See also: Carasales (1999, 57).
[68] See: Redick et al. (1994, 112); Vargas (1997); Alcañiz (2000).

peaceful purposes."[69] Clearly, this was not the behavior of two security rivals engaged in a race to acquire nuclear arms.

On September 4, 1987, after Brazilian nuclear scientists were certain their enrichment methods worked on an industrial scale, President Sarney announced on television the country's mastery of the nuclear cycle saying that "Brazil already dominates uranium enrichment technology using ultracentrifuges."[70] His speech emphasized the peaceful objectives of the country's nuclear effort and its significance as a step toward the country's "scientific and technological autonomy."[71] Military officials confirmed that they did not see a military benefit in acquiring nuclear weapons. For example, navy minister Maximiano da Fonseca (1979–1984) had earlier that year told *Veja* magazine that "[w]e don't need the bomb now, since there is no foreign enemy in sight. What we need is to retain the technology to have the capability to fabricate it should circumstances require."[72] Before his public announcement, Sarney privately informed Buenos Aires.[73] That same year, the two presidents embarked on a series of state visits to previously restricted nuclear facilities in each other's country.[74] Then, in March 1988, Brazil and Argentina signed another nuclear cooperation accord, the Iperó Joint Statement on Nuclear Policy.[75]

Given Brazil's advancements in nuclear technology, it is not surprising that the 1980s also witnessed increased speculation about a Brazilian bomb. Already by 1983, officials in the military regime were stating to the press that Brazil would soon be able to build a nuclear weapon.[76] On December 10 that year, the *Estado de São Paulo* newspaper quoted Brigadier Waldir Vasconcellos claiming

[69] Quoted in Kutchesfahani (2014, 59).
[70] Quoted in Malheiros (1996, 82), our translation.
[71] José Sarney, "Ao Anunciar a Vitória do Programa Autônomo de Tecnologia Nuclear," Speech to the nation on September 4, 1987. Available at: www.biblioteca.presidencia.gov.br/ex-presidentes/jose-sarney/discursos/1987/76.pdf/view. Last accessed: October 29, 2014, our translation.
[72] Quoted in Barletta (1997, 16), quoting *Veja*, April 22, 1987, p. 94. See also army minister Pires Gonçalves' comments in ibid., quoting *Jornal da Tarde*, June 1, 1987.
[73] See: "Cable on Ambassador Rubens Ricupero's Meetings with President Alfonsín and Ambassador Jorge Sabato about Nuclear Cooperation," September 4, 1987, Wilson Center Digital Archive, Brazilian Nuclear History.
[74] See: Redick et al. (1994, 112).
[75] See: Malheiros (1993, 134–137).
[76] See: Malheiros (1996, 77).

that Brazil "may build armaments, including the atomic bomb."[77] That same day, the *Jornal do Brasil* published an interview with Brigadier Hugo de Oliveira Piva, a top official in the air force's nuclear program (1984–1989), in which he stated: "The prediction that after 1990 Brazil may decide to build the atomic bomb is valid."[78]

Then, in 1986, the *Folha de São Paulo* newspaper made the world aware of the existence of a purported underground nuclear test site prepared by the air force in its remote Serra do Cachimbo air base.[79] This revelation gave new weight to the earlier pronouncements. All of these claims are speculative, however. Indeed, Brazil, as a threshold nuclear state, "might" develop nuclear weapons. At the same time, there were no signals that a decision to weaponize the Brazilian nuclear effort had been made.[80]

Overall, we find no evidence of a plan or decision to build a Brazilian nuclear weapon as the country approached the technological

[77] Quoted in Malheiros (1993, 67), our translation. In 2005, the Associated Press reported that former president Sarney had admitted that Brazil had pursued nuclear weapons during the military dictatorship. The report, however, only contains Sarney's statements about having been informed of the supposed testing shaft at the Cachimbo airbase, on which more details are given in the following text. See: Michael Astor, "Brazil Nearly Built Atom Bomb in 1990s, Scientist Says," *Free Republic*, August 30, 2005. Available at: www.freerepublic.com/focus/f-news/1473263/posts. Last accessed: May 2, 2016; Harold Olmos, "Brazilian Military Dictatorship Was Working to Develop Nuclear Arms, Ex-President Confirms." Associated Press, August 8, 2005. Available at: www.highbeam.com/doc/1P1-111937635.html. Last accessed: May 2, 2016.

[78] Quoted in Malheiros (1993, 67), our translation.

[79] "Newspaper Article 'Serra do Cachimbo May Be Nuclear Test Site,' " August 8, 1986, Wilson Center Digital Archive, Brazilian Nuclear History. Local press in the state of Pará had reported on the facility since 1981. See: Hibbs (2014). See also: Barletta (1997, 2); Motta (2010, 132). Rex Nazaré Alves, head of the CNEN at the time, later insisted that "the shaft at Cachimbo was not suitable for a bomb test." See: Motta (2010, 133), our translation.

[80] To the best of our knowledge, the only official connected to the Brazilian nuclear program who ever advocated publicly for a nuclear detonation is Admiral Maximiano da Fonseca, minister of the navy between 1979 and 1984. *After leaving office*, he declared that if he had the power he would "build an atomic bomb and explode it in front of an international audience as a way of demonstrating our national technological capability." Even such a nuclear hawk added: "It is absurd to spend money stocking atomic bombs, but to explode one and then accept international inspections could contribute to demonstrating that Brazil is a sovereign state." Quoted in Malheiros (1993, 70), our translation. See also: Spector (1987, 206); Kutchesfahani (2014, 28).

capability to do so.[81] As Brazilian diplomats Georges Lamazière and Roberto Jaguaribe argue, "[a]t no stage was there a government directive to build nuclear weapons in Brazil."[82] To the contrary, Brazilian and Argentinian officials with roles in the two states' nuclear programs "consistently denied that their countries had been working towards a nuclear weapons program."[83]

Brazil's Nuclear Forbearance and Accession to the NPT Regime, 1988–1997

By the late 1980s, Brazil was a nuclear threshold state, possessing virtually all the capabilities necessary to build a nuclear weapon. A 1990 report by the Brazilian Physicists Society concluded that the navy's "Aramar enrichment plant could enrich uranium to 90%, that such material might be used to construct an explosive within one month of a decision to do so, and that a limited-yield device could be tested in the shaft at the Cachimbo Air Force base."[84] Clearly, Brazil had the opportunity to nuclearize, and whether it would build the bomb would depend on the willingness of Brazilian decisionmakers to go nuclear.

Such was the situation when President Fernando Collor de Mello (1990–1992) took office. Collor felt that the military's covert nuclear program undermined his political authority and risked reinforcing suspicions of nuclear competition with Argentina, harming relations with the United States.[85] Since the country had achieved its objective of mastering the nuclear fuel cycle, the PATN could be shut down. After one week in office, Collor effectively ended it.[86] Then, in September 1990, Collor announced at the UNGA Brazil's commitment not to pursue a nuclear-weapons program or conduct PNEs.[87] That same month, in a highly publicized event, Collor closed the purported nuclear testing site at Cachimbo. Symbolically shutting down the test

---

[81] For scholarly speculation about the possibility of Brazilian nuclearization, see: Myers (1984, 906); Hurrell (1986, 112).

[82] Lamazière and Jaguaribe (1992, 111).

[83] Kutchesfahani (2014, 28).

[84] Barletta (1997, 24). See also: Albright (1989, 19).

[85] See: Goldemberg and Feiveson (1994, 13).

[86] See: Barletta (1997, 27).

[87] See: President Collor de Mello, speech at the UN General Assembly, September 24, 1990, Presidential Library of Brazil. Available at: www.biblioteca. presidencia.gov.br/presidencia/ex-presidentes/fernando-collor/discursos/1990/ 88.pdf/view. Last accessed: April 29, 2016.

shaft, Collor declared: "These guys are crazy. They were really going to explode the bomb. This is absolutely true."[88] In an interview with the *Washington Post*, he added: "The important thing is that the shaft is being covered with concrete and that we are not going to enter into any nuclear adventure in Brazil."[89] To *Newsweek*, Collor described the shaft, adding that it "would be suitable for an explosion test of a nuclear artifact."[90] At the end of the 1990 Parliamentary Commission of Inquiry on nuclear activities, former president Figueiredo reportedly stated: "The Cachimbo air base could have been used for nuclear tests, but the government at the time [1984–1985] did not think about building a nuclear weapon."[91]

Most observers, however, believe that Collor exploited the Cachimbo "discovery" to score political points against the military, which he wanted to defund while firmly controlling it; and to demonstrate to his Argentinian counterpart that he was squarely in charge of the Brazilian program.[92] When the Cachimbo shafts were inspected, they were found unsuitable for a nuclear test. As a former official put it, "If anyone would have tried to test a nuclear bomb in there, they would have failed."[93] In sum, although some rudimentary preparations for a nuclear explosion may have been undertaken, there was never a political decision to detonate a nuclear device.

Collor also pushed on rapprochement with Argentina, initiating the deepest phase in the two countries' nuclear cooperation. During the early 1990s, Brasília and Buenos Aires coordinated their nuclear policies so as to allay concerns of a nuclear race between them and gain the economic and diplomatic benefits inherent in their integration in

---

[88] Quoted in Barletta (1997, 27).

[89] Quoted in Don Podesta, "Brazilian Calls for A-Test Ban: Leader to Change Nuclear Program," *The Washington Post*, September 20, 1990, p. A27.

[90] President Collor de Mello, interview with *Newsweek*, October 1990, Presidential Library of Brazil. Available at: www.biblioteca.presidencia.gov.br/ presidencia/ex-presidentes/fernando-collor/discursos/1990/100.pdf/view. Last accessed: April 29, 2016, our translation.

[91] Quoted in Malheiros (1993, 117), our translation.

[92] Speaking in 2010, Leonam dos Santos Guimarães, project coordinator at the Nuclear Propulsion Program of the Navy's Technological Center during the 1990s, concluded that "the [Cachimbo] hole was made to be discovered.... The explanation that the military wanted to explode a bomb and made a test hole doesn't stick." Quoted in Patti (2013b, 128), our translation.

[93] Quoted in Hibbs (2014).

the U.S.-led international order of the post–Cold War.[94] Before 1990 was over, Collor signed with Argentinian president Carlos Menem (1989–1999) the (Iguaçu) Declaration on the Common Nuclear Policy of Brazil and Argentina, renouncing nuclear tests, delineating terms for mutual inspections, establishing a framework for the implementation of IAEA safeguards, and pledging to ratify the Treaty of Tlatelolco.[95] The following year, Collor and Menem formally renounced PNEs and established a joint Agency for Accounting and Control of Nuclear Materials (ABACC), "a binational system of mutual inspections and verification of non-safeguarded nuclear installations between the two states, confirming their non-nuclear weapons status."[96] Both presidents also signed the so-called Quadripartite Agreement with the IAEA, accepting its inspections. One of the main drivers behind these agreements was international suspicion about the two countries' motives for developing nuclear technology. As Othon Pinheiro later remarked, Brazil signed a deal with Argentina given that "the whole world was saying that we wanted to develop the bomb because of our rivalry with Argentina. So, I was very much in favor of the treaty with Argentina that ended that business."[97]

In 1996, Brazil joined the Nuclear Suppliers Group (NSG), entering the club of acknowledged civilian nuclear powers.[98] The following

---

[94] See: Redick et al. (1994, 118); Reiss (1995, 60); Velazquez (2004); Patti (2013b, 37). Domingo Cavallo, Menem's minister of foreign affairs (1989–1991), named two key motivations behind Argentina's nuclear rapprochement with Brazil in the early 1990s. First, Menem understood that his country needed to improve relations with Washington and overcome obstacles to international economic integration, key among which was U.S. opposition to Argentina's nuclear program, in order to achieve faster economic development. This required joining the NPT regime, which in turn required coordination with Brazil. Second, Menem thought that the military used the specter of a "Brazil threat" as an argument to get funding for its industries – among them the nuclear program. Since these industries were the source of the military's economic power and, consequently, independence from political leadership, Menem wanted to curb them in order to increase civilian control over the military. This required dispelling the notion that Brazil was a threat. Source: Personal interview, New Haven, October 3, 2011.

[95] See: Goldemberg and Feiveson (1994, 10); Carasales (1995, 42); Oliveira (1996); Carasales (1999, 58).

[96] Kutchesfahani (2014, 24, 53–57). See also: Carasales (1995, 42–43); Barletta (1997, 26); Carasales (1999, 58); Patti (2012a, 228); Coutto (2014).

[97] Pinheiro da Silva (2010, 102–103), our translation.

[98] See: Patti (2012a, 236).

year, Brazil entered the NPT, completing its process of integration in the global nuclear-nonproliferation regime. In contrast with earlier decades, during which joining the NPT would have stymied nuclear development, by the 1990s Brazil "had developed an autonomous nuclear sector and mastered the main technologies in the area."[99] Therefore, at that moment, joining the NPT would not "undermine Brazil's ability to control the nuclear fuel cycle, which had been Brazil's strategic goal since the inception of its nuclear program, more than forty years earlier. To the contrary, entry into the NPT now ensured that Brazil would be able to keep its nuclear independence."[100]

Almost two decades after joining the NPT, Brazil has maintained the goals of increasing energy production from nuclear sources, achieving nuclear fuel independence, boosting its role as a nuclear fuel exporter, and developing a nuclear submarine propulsion system.[101] Furthermore, cooperation with Argentina remains a pillar of Brazil's nuclear policy. In August 2012, the two countries signed a new nuclear declaration boosting the ABACC safeguard system.[102] At the same time, Brazilian officials have maintained that nuclear weapons may become necessary in the future, should a security threat to the country's vast territory and waters materialize.[103]

U.S. Nonproliferation Efforts

Suspicious of the country's goals, the United States has, throughout Brazil's nuclear development, attempted to impede its progress. Under the civilian regime that ruled Brazil until the 1964 coup, Brazilian elites grew increasingly disappointed with Washington's lack of support for

---

[99] Ibid., 237. During a visit to Washington, Brazilian foreign minister Luis Felipe Lampreia (1995–2001) expressed the country's "unwavering commitment to the use of nuclear energy for exclusively peaceful purposes." "Remarks on Brazil's Accession to the NPT," September 18, 1998, Federation of American Scientists. Available at: www.fas.org/nuke/control/npt/news/98091823_llt.html. Last accessed: April 29, 2016.

[100] Patti (2012a, 18).

[101] See: Argüello (2011, 185); Kassenova (2014).

[102] See: Argüello (2011, 187).

[103] See: "José Alencar defende que Brasil tenha bomba atómica," *Estado de São Paulo*, September 24, 2009. Available at: http://politica.estadao.com.br/noticias/geral,jose-alencar-defende-que-brasil-tenha-bomba-atomica,440556. Last accessed: May 2, 2016.

their country's development and wider influence in Latin America.[104] In the nuclear realm, Washington's efforts to prevent Brazil from acquiring nuclear technology were perceived by Brazilian elites as attempts to ensure their country's subaltern status. As early as 1946, the passing of the (McMahon) Atomic Energy Act by the U.S. Congress restricted Brazilian access to U.S. nuclear technology and, in the eyes of the Brazilian leadership, extended the global U.S. industrial monopoly in the nuclear realm, limiting other countries' development potential.[105] Then, in 1954, Washington pressed Brazil to drop a deal with West Germany for the supply of uranium-enrichment centrifuges and sought the reversal of the "specific compensation" policy – according to which Brazilian exports of heavy minerals had to be rewarded with transfers of nuclear technology, not just hard currency – all the while encouraging Brazil's commitment to exclusive nuclear cooperation with the United States.[106]

During the first half of the 1960s, two developments led Washington to strengthen its nuclear nonproliferation efforts: the Cuban Missile Crisis of late 1962 and the Chinese nuclear test of 1964.[107] For Brazilian nuclear development, a tighter U.S. nonproliferation policy presented a substantial risk because the country's civilian program depended on U.S. supplies of nuclear fuel.[108] In the immediate aftermath of the 1964 military coup, the Castelo Branco administration sought to reinforce its ties with Washington in order to ensure continued access to nuclear materials and technology.[109] That attempt would soon prove fruitless.

---

[104] See: Hurrell (1986, 43).

[105] See: Patti (2012a, 33).

[106] See: Patti (2013a, 13); State Department Instruction CA-2553 to U.S. High Commissioner, Bonn, "Centrifuges for Brazil," October 16, 1954, in National Security Archive (NSA) Electronic Briefing Book (EBB) 518, "The Gas Centrifuge Secret: Origins of a U.S. Policy of Nuclear Denial, 1954–1960," Doc. 5.

[107] See: Motta (2010, 120). Washington was also deeply concerned about Brazilian president João Goulart's (1961–1964) left-leaning proclivities, leading President John F. Kennedy (1961–1963) to declare in December 1962 that the situation in Brazil "worried him more than that in Cuba." See: "Memorandum of Conversation," Washington, December 13, 1962, in *Foreign Relations of the United States (FRUS)*, 1961–1963, Vol. XII, *American Republics*, Doc. 52. For an excellent overview of U.S.-Brazil relations at the time of the Cuban Missile Crisis, see: Hershberg (2004a, 2004b).

[108] See: Motta (2010, 118).

[109] See: Hurrell (1986, 95).

During the Costa e Silva years, as Brazil prioritized acquisition of nuclear technology and opposition to emerging nonproliferation norms over its ties with the United States, U.S.-Brazilian relations on the nuclear front took a turn for the worse.[110] Brasília's opposition to the Tlatelolco and NPT agreements, its refusal to renounce PNEs, and its suspected nuclear rivalry with Argentina combined to generate considerable suspicion in Washington.[111]

This suspicion would lead to U.S. nonproliferation pressure when Brazil signed an agreement with U.S.-based Westinghouse in 1972 for the sale of a nuclear power plant. Given Brazil's opposition to the NPT, Washington pressed the company not to sell Brasília natural uranium heavy-water reactors, preferred by the Brazilian scientific community but deemed unsafe in terms of their proliferation potential.[112] Brazil ended up going for a light-water reactor from which "it is literally impossible to produce a bomb."[113]

Still, U.S. pressure on Brazil was limited by both governments' interest in opposing leftist regimes in South America.[114] A January 1971 "Country Analysis and Strategy Paper" (CASP) prepared by the U.S. embassy in Brasília argued that "[t]he fundamentally most important US interest in Brazil is the protection of US national security through the cooperation of Brazil as a hemispheric ally."[115] President Nixon (1969–1974) was keen on persuading President Médici that his administration was "the best friend Brazil has had in this office."[116] Brazilian officials reciprocated, noting that Washington was the "powerful partner" Brazil needed "to ensure that imminent revolutionary advances were effectively quashed in South America."[117]

Brazil's relations with the United States in the nuclear domain would worsen during the Geisel administration. The July 1974 revision of

---

[110] Ibid., 111.
[111] See: Barletta (1997, 1).
[112] See: Myers (1984, 885); Patti (2013b, 56, 115).
[113] Pinheiro da Silva (2010, 28), our translation.
[114] See: Harmer (2012, 666–670).
[115] Ibid., 667.
[116] "Conversation among President Nixon, the President's Assistant for National Security Affairs (Kissinger), and President's Assistant (Haldeman)," Washington, June 11, 1971, in *Foreign Relations of the United States* (*FRUS*), 1969–1976, Vol. E-10, *Documents on American Republics, 1969–1972*, Doc. 139.
[117] Harmer (2012, 668).

nuclear supply contracts by the U.S. Atomic Energy Commission (AEC) limited Brazil's trust in the ability to obtain nuclear fuel for its power plants from the United States.[118] At that time, Geisel was implementing his broader policy of *abertura* or "opening," aimed at boosting Brazil's ability to act autonomously from the United States by improving relations with Western European countries.[119] In part pushed by the AEC's new policy, Geisel started secret negotiations toward a vast nuclear agreement with Germany. Washington got word of the talks and reacted by applying considerable pressure on Bonn to require that its technology transfers be subject to safe-guards.[120] U.S. concerns focused on the possibility that Germany would provide Brazil with a reprocessing facility, from which plutonium could be extracted.[121] Furthermore, Washington pressed the FRG not to sell proven uranium-enrichment ultracentrifuge technology, leading Bonn to supply Brazil with experimental jet-nozzle enrichment technology, which would prove useless.[122] After the deal was concluded, U.S. officials continued to press their FRG counterparts to delay delivery of the agreed technologies to Brazil.[123] Making matters worse, the FRG-Brazil deal met with outspoken opposition in the United States. A *New York Times* editorial titled "Nuclear Madness" called it a "reckless move that could set off a nuclear arms race in Latin America, trigger the nuclear arming of a half-dozen nations elsewhere and endanger the security of the United States and the world as a whole."[124] Washington decided to reassess U.S. nuclear supplies to Brazil.[125] On the whole, U.S. pressures virtually guaranteed that Brazil would not be able to build the bomb using German technology.

Brazilian officials were flabbergasted with their ally. As the U.S. Embassy in Brasília reported back to Washington in late 1976, an official in the Brazilian Ministry of Mines and Energy declared to the

---

[118] See: Gall (1976, 8); Myers (1984, 885, 900).
[119] See: Spektor (2006, 57–69).
[120] See: Squassoni and Fite (2005, 16); Kutchesfahani (2014, 37).
[121] See: Gall (1976, 6); Camargo (2006, 15).
[122] See: Patti (2012a, 121–123). For an excellent account of the deal from the German perspective, see: Gray (2012).
[123] See: Patti (2012a, 123).
[124] Quoted in Gall (1976, 5).
[125] See: Patti (2012a, 137).

press: "The Americans, our allies, are behaving in a way worse than that of our common enemies, the Russians." The official continued:

Our nuclear program will continue, at least to the extent it depends on us, against all internal and external pressures. ... We do not want the atomic bomb. We want to be independent, to construct our future, and to prevent (the effects of) any future world petroleum and energy crisis. Brazil will not give way.[126]

Anticipating U.S. nonproliferation pressure, Brazilian leaders increasingly conducted their nuclear policy in secret. (In fact, according to the secretary-general of the CSN at the time, General Hugo Abreu, negotiations for the 1975 deal had already been conducted in secret in order to "avoid the expected pressures, especially from the United States."[127]) This secrecy strengthened Washington's suspicion that Brasília's nuclear intentions were not peaceful – thereby creating a vicious cycle connecting U.S. suspicions of proliferation and Brazilian secret nuclear development.

U.S. nonproliferation efforts would increase during the administration of President Jimmy Carter (1977–1981).[128] As President Carter remarked in a handwritten note he appended to a March 1977 memo sent by U.S. Secretary of State Cyrus Vance (1977–1980) on nuclear talks with Brazil: "We should pronounce a policy of no nuclear fuel to those who reprocess to see what we can do towards those who refuse to sign [the] NPT."[129] Besides implementing more stringent criteria for purchases of U.S. nuclear materials, the Carter administration pushed other supplier countries to do the same. One week after Carter's

---

[126] "U.S. Embassy Cable, Brazilian Public Reaction to US Nuclear Policies," November 19, 1976, Wilson Center Digital Archive, Brazilian Nuclear History.

[127] Abreu (1979, 44), our translation. On how a similar dynamic affected U.S. perceptions of Argentina's nuclear efforts, see: Hymans (2001, 153–154).

[128] For Brazilian concerns about Carter's harder line on nuclear matters at the outset of his administration, see: "Memorandum from Brazilian Foreign Minister Silveira to President Geisel on Jimmy Carter's 'Radical' Nuclear Stance," January 31, 1977, Wilson Center Digital Archive, Brazilian Nuclear History. For a detailed analysis of different types of threats and promises Washington might use to get Brazil to cease its nuclear cooperation with West Germany, as well as possible Brazilian reactions, see: "Memorandum from Brazilian Foreign Minister Silveira to President Geisel, US Threats and Promises and Brazilian Responses," February 25, 1977, Wilson Center Digital Archive, Brazilian Nuclear History.

[129] Quoted in Patti (2012a, 169). See also: Patti (2013b, 93).

inauguration in January 1977, Vice President Walter Mondale (1977–1981) was sent to West Germany in part to try to dissuade it from supplying nuclear technology to Brazil. His message was clear: the United States was "unalterably opposed" to this technology transfer.[130] The following July, then Deputy Secretary of State Warren Christopher (1977–1981) met with German Chancellor Helmut Schmidt (1974–1982) with the same goal.[131] Moreover, this period saw access to U.S. nuclear supplies and technology by non-NPT members such as Brazil severely limited by legislative measures in Washington – the Symington (1976) and Glenn (1977) amendments to the Foreign Assistance Act of 1961 as well as the Nuclear Nonproliferation Act (NNPA) of 1978. In practical terms, these measures meant that "contractual commitments to furnish fuel for the Angra I civilian power reactor, were made conditional of Brazilian acceptance of more extensive safeguards."[132]

Unsurprisingly, these developments engendered great skepticism in Brazil about the United States' reliability as a nuclear partner.[133] For Brazilian decisionmakers, there was little doubt that Washington was trying to sabotage their nuclear progress. Venturini, head of the CSN during the Figueiredo years, characterized U.S. policy as an effort to deny "Brazil the capacity to implement its own progress."[134]

As a result, U.S. nonproliferation efforts produced three unintended consequences. First, U.S. pressure is at least partly responsible for the secret nature of the PATN, created in 1979. According to Admiral Maximiano da Fonseca, minister of the navy at the time, the nascent Brazilian enrichment program needed to be secret because U.S. pressure was "terrible."[135] Overall, "PATN officials and documents stress the need to maintain secrecy due to international pressures, particularly from the United States."[136] At least in part, the leading role the military played in the Brazilian nuclear program and the secrecy that

---

[130] Patti (2012a, 159). That same month, in a letter to Brazilian Foreign Minister Azeredo da Silveira (1974–1979), Vance offered to guarantee the supply of fuel for Brazilian nuclear reactors purchased from the FRG, as long as no enrichment technologies would be transferred. This offer was not taken seriously in Brasília. See: Ibid., 160, 165.

[131] See: Coutto (2014, 10).

[132] Barletta (1997, 14).

[133] See: Redick (1978, 163–165); Barletta (1997, 14); Argüello (2011, 187).

[134] Barletta (1997, 25).

[135] "Testimony of Maximiano da Fonseca to Parliamentary Inquiry Commission," Senado Federal, 1990. Quoted in Malheiros (1996, 82), our translation.

[136] Barletta (1997, 20).

involved much of Brazil's nuclear development resulted from the country's determination to circumvent U.S. nonproliferation efforts.

Second, U.S. nonproliferation pressure also led to Brazil's persistent refusal to join the NPT during the 1970s and 1980s. Brazilian accession to the NPT could have happened much earlier if it were not for U.S. policies, which denied Brazil access to effective uranium enrichment technology. During a top-level advisory meeting in Brasília in February 1978, *before* the secret PATN was created, Foreign Minister Azeredo da Silveira (1974–1979) offered the view, supported by President Geisel, that "in the event that Brazil would been [sic] able to acquire that [ultracentrifuge uranium enrichment] technology, Brazil could sign the NPT, if that would represent the determinant condition for obtaining such a process."[137] As it was, Washington prevented Brasília from obtaining the centrifuges, so it would take another ten years for Brazil to master the nuclear fuel cycle and begin to move in the direction of joining the global nuclear-nonproliferation regime.

Finally, U.S. pressure led to nuclear cooperation between Brazil and Argentina starting in the late 1970s. In a way, "as U.S.-Brazilian relations worsened over nuclear issues, Argentine-Brazilian nuclear policy collaboration advanced."[138] As we saw, the two countries would over time develop a full-blown process of nuclear collaboration.[139] This rapprochement dampened U.S. suspicions about Brazil's nuclear goals.

---

[137] Patti (2012a, 193).

[138] Redick et al. (1994, 111).

[139] Coutto (2014, 12). Even when the United States tried to introduce a wedge between the two countries on nuclear matters, it found itself largely unable to do so. For example, when Secretary of State Vance visited Buenos Aires and then Brasília in November 1977, he tried to persuade the Argentinians to ratify Tlatelolco and accept full-scope safeguards in return for additional U.S. technological assistance. Then, in Brazil, Vance tried to inveigle Geisel with the specter of a U.S.-Argentina nuclear rapprochement, but Geisel replied that "the Brazilians were conscious of the Argentinean capability to build an atomic device, but that Buenos Aires was not perceived as a threat because of the cordial relations between the two countries" (quoted in Patti [2012a, 187–188]). At the end of a meeting with Azeredo da Silveira that took place before his meeting with President Geisel, Vance, apparently by accident, left behind a position paper titled "Brazil Scope Paper: Implications of the Argentine Visit," which stated that Washington's strategy would "consist of avoiding overt opposition to the German-Brazilian agreement while offering the provision of enriched fuel if the country relinquished technology transfer." See: Coutto (2014, 10). It is unclear what effect this document revealing a relatively soft U.S. position had in leading Brazilian leaders to resist Washington's pressure.

Still, given the secret military nature of Brazil's nuclear program and the country's refusal to join the NPT, these suspicions subsisted.[140] A 1985 Special National Intelligence Estimate (SNIE) concluded that "Brazil's determination to master the fuel cycle is reflective of its overall quest for major-nation status [and of its] wishes to develop the capabilities that would enable it to build nuclear weapons at some time in the future."[141] The following year, the Central Intelligence Agency (CIA) pointed out that it had "no indication that a political decision on the nuclear explosive option has been made nor any current outward indication that this is officially under discussion," but it nevertheless noted that as "Brazil approaches that technological threshold, an explosive and weapons option becomes real, not just theoretical."[142]

Certainly, U.S. nonproliferation pressure created incentives for Brazil to join the global nuclear-nonproliferation regime, contributing to the end of the secret component of Brazil's nuclear program – the PATN.[143] Once Brasília had achieved its core goal of mastering the nuclear fuel cycle and would no longer benefit from conducting its nuclear development effort in the context of a secret, unsafeguarded program, Brazil swiftly moved toward normalizing its nuclear policy, establishing itself as an autonomous threshold state within the global nuclear regime. Ultimately, U.S. efforts to deny Brazil access to nuclear technology were unsuccessful. The United States did not prevent Brazil from mastering the nuclear fuel cycle. Nor were U.S. nonproliferation efforts the cause of Brazil's nuclear forbearance. Brazil remained nonnuclear because its benign security environment undermined its willingness to nuclearize. As Admiral Maximiano da Fonseca put it during a 1990 congressional inquiry: "Building an atomic bomb here would be stupid. We have no threats."[144]

---

[140] See: Leventhal and Tanzer (1992); Kutchesfahani (2014, 27).

[141] Special National Intelligence Estimate, Memorandum to Holders, "Brazil's Changing Nuclear Goals: Motives and Constraints," December 1985, in National Security Archive (NSA) Electronic Briefing Book (EBB) 423, "China May Have Helped Pakistan Nuclear Weapons Design, Newly Declassified Intelligence Indicates," Doc. 6B, p. 3.

[142] Central Intelligence Agency, Directorate of Intelligence, "President Sarney and Brazil's Nuclear Policy," September 8, 1986, in NSA EBB 423, Doc. 6C, p. 6.

[143] See: Pinheiro da Silva (2010, 92–95).

[144] Quoted in Malheiros (1993, 118), our translation.

Alternative Explanations

Perhaps the most popular among existing accounts of the causes of Brazil's considerable nuclear ambitions is the view that Brazil's military nuclear program was motivated by its strategic rivalry with neighboring Argentina, which was also undertaking nuclear development at the time.[145] To be sure, that was the U.S. government's perspective, and it was largely responsible for the efforts Washington devoted to stymieing Brazil's nuclear development. Still, no top decisionmaker in Brazilian nuclear politics throughout the arc of its nuclear development favored the creation of a nuclear deterrent. The reason is simple: Brazil faced no security threat emanating from Argentina.

In fact, Argentina's nuclear program was peaceful in nature. As Jacques Hymans and others have established, "the weight of the evidence against the existence of an Argentine nuclear bomb program is overwhelming."[146] The U.S. intelligence community reached the same estimate in the mid-1980s.[147] In the postwar period, the most salient disagreement between the two countries was the long-standing dispute over hydric resources in the River Plate basin, which was ultimately settled in 1979.[148] During the following twelve years, Argentina and Brazil would sign no less than ten agreements and joint declarations on nuclear issues.[149] These agreements publicly affirmed the peaceful, energy-focused nature of the two countries' nuclear programs, allowed for reciprocal visits to each other's nuclear facilities, and coordinated the two countries' nuclear policies in terms of their gradual integration into the global nuclear-nonproliferation regime.[150] In light of such deep nuclear cooperation, the argument that the two Southern Cone powers were security rivals engaged in a nuclear race is hard to sustain.

Much of the suspicion about Brazil's nuclear motives was prompted by the discovery in the late 1980s of the secret PATN, run by the military. But this suspicion reveals "a lack of understanding of the

[145] See: Barletta (1997, 13).
[146] Hymans (2001, 159). See also: Hymans (2006, chapter 6).
[147] See: Special National Intelligence Estimate, "Brazil's Changing Nuclear Goals: Motives and Constraints," October 21, 1983, in NSA EBB 423, Doc. 6A, p. 2.
[148] See: Selcher (1985); Fajardo (2004).
[149] See: Kutchesfahani (2014, 55–56).
[150] Ibid., 53.

historical role of the military in Brazil's technical and scientific development."[151] CNEN director Rex Nazaré Alves, the official in charge of the PATN, insisted that "preoccupation with the Argentina program did *not* influence the PATN, and that the only military motivation involved was the Navy's interest in nuclear submarine propulsion."[152] Absent a security rivalry, the "motivating factor for the nuclear programs [in Brazil and Argentina] was principally the drive toward development, modernization, and industrialization, with the military element as important but secondary."[153]

A second security-based alternative explanation for Brazil's nuclear trajectory is T. V. Paul's argument that in the late 1980s the Southern Cone went "from a moderate- to a low-conflict zone," leading Brazil's leaders to see the nuclear program "as hampering their economic and security co-operation and as leading to a technological race with military implications."[154]

In our view, this argument overemphasizes the magnitude of the change in Brazilian nuclear policy that took place during the Collor presidency – as well as the magnitude of the transformation in Brazil's security environment in the late 1980s. Brazil always perceived its strategic situation to be one of abundant security, and therefore never pursued a nuclear weapon. The overall goal of Brazilian nuclear policy since the early 1950s was mastery of the fuel cycle. When Collor became president in 1990, this objective had been achieved, so the secret unsafeguarded PATN – which had yielded the greatest nuclear progress – could be brought to light, allowing for the country's integration in the global nuclear-nonproliferation regime. None of these steps took away Brazil's technological achievements; to the contrary, they turned the country into an established civilian nuclear power. So what Paul sees as a 180-degree turnaround from nuclear pursuit to forbearance in the early 1990s is in fact the result of a deeper underlying continuity in Brazil's nuclear goals.

A third alternative account of Brazil's nuclear trajectory is put forth by Etel Solingen, who argues that "[t]he pursuit of security simply does

---

[151] Wrobel (1996, 342–343). See also: Kutchesfahani (2014, 29).
[152] Barletta (1997, 14), emphasis added. For a reciprocal statement by Vice Admiral Carlos Castro Madero, president of the Argentinian National Atomic Energy Comission (CNEA, 1976–1983), see: Kutchesfahani (2014, 27–28).
[153] Redick et al. (1994, 110).
[154] Paul (2000, 100).

not tell us enough about differences across space nor changes over time."[155] To explain Brazil's obduracy in its nuclear development during the 1970s and early 1980s, and its replacement with a posture of regional and global integration in the late 1980s and 1990s, Solingen looks instead at the varying economic preferences of Brasília's ruling elites. In her view, Brazil's turn toward nuclear forbearance resulted from Collor's determination to liberalize the Brazilian economy and integrate it internationally. To achieve these goals, Collor had to shut down the nuclear program, which he essentially did during his first year in office.[156]

Like Paul, Solingen underplays the overall consistency of Brazilian nuclear policy. Furthermore, her focus on a well-defined policy shift fails to account for the initial phases of nuclear rapprochement with Argentina as well as for President Geisel's refusal in 1984 to test a nuclear device the following year – both of which took place before the country's transition to democracy.[157] As Solingen documents, Brazil's rulers prior to Collor "implemented a nationalist-populist mixture of domestic heterodoxy and anti-IMF policy."[158] Yet, they also took seminal steps in the rapprochement process with Argentina. In our view, this apparent contradiction results from Solingen's focus on the economic preferences of the ruling elites. If we focus instead on security goals, it becomes clear that Brazilian nuclear policy was consistent throughout the nuclear age, with the country's leaders pressing ahead toward the aim of mastering the nuclear fuel cycle while seeking better relations with Argentina so as to dispel the myth of a nuclear-arms race.

Finally, arguments about how supply-side restrictions on access to nuclear technology and materials condition a country's ability to build a nuclear weapon could be extended to account for Brazil's nuclear forbearance.[159] In the view of supply-side theorists, U.S. nonproliferation

---

[155] Solingen (1994, 129).

[156] See: Ibid., 161.

[157] Certainly Collor tried to portray the military – and, retroactively, the military regime of the 1970s and early 1980s – as the key driver behind the nuclear program. Yet, the leaders of the military dictatorship never pushed for the bomb and in 1984 declined to conduct a nuclear test. Furthermore, Sarney, the first civilian leader after the democratic transition, also did nothing to stop nuclear development until Brazil mastered the complete fuel cycle.

[158] Solingen (1994, 160).

[159] See: Fuhrmann (2009a, 2009b, 2012); Kroenig (2009a, 2009b, 2010).

policies that impose restrictions on other states' nuclear development are key in preventing them from going nuclear.

Yet, Brazil was able to circumvent decades of U.S. supply-side restrictions, developing its own indigenous program (the PATN) and purchasing nuclear materials from other non-NPT members. Analysts of Brazilian nuclear politics have little doubt of the country's ability to build nuclear weapons if it so wished, despite the limitations on Brazil's nuclear supplies imposed by successive U.S. administrations.[160] In fact, a 1983 U.S. SNIE stated flatly: "We do not believe that the United States can deter Brazil from pursuing its fundamental objective of mastery of the nuclear fuel cycle."[161] Since Brazil's nuclear effort was both indigenous and unsafeguarded, the report concluded that "it will be difficult for the United States – or any other nation – to have a major impact on its nuclear policies."[162]

Taking stock, Brazil faced no serious security threats and therefore did not possess the willingness to acquire nuclear weapons. Its substantial nuclear endeavors, which resulted in the country becoming an established civilian nuclear power with control over the entire fuel cycle by the late 1980s, resulted from the country's drive for political autonomy, economic development, and greater international status. Suspicious that Brazil wanted to build the bomb, the United States attempted to stymie its nuclear development. Still, Brazil managed to reach a position in which it had the opportunity to nuclearize if it so willed. In the end, Brasília opted for not building an atomic bomb. Even when combined, the nonsecurity factors driving Brazil's nuclear efforts proved insufficient to result in nuclear proliferation.

If Brazil's security environment were to worsen so as to give it the willingness to nuclearize, the country would be likely to have the opportunity to build the bomb. No regional rival has the power to deter it through preventive counterproliferation action. Given Brazil's strength, sticks-based attempts by the United States to coerce it into remaining nonnuclear would also likely fail. Therefore, in this scenario, the only way to ensure the maintenance of Brazil's nonnuclear status would be for the United States to implement a carrots-based

---

[160] See: Redick (1978, 171); Barletta (1997, 29n34).
[161] NSA EBB 423, Doc. 6A, p. 12.
[162] Ibid., 13.

nonproliferation policy, encompassing comprehensive security guarantees capable of removing Brazil's willingness to nuclearize.

Soviet Union

On August 29, 1949, the Union of Soviet Socialist Republics (USSR) ended a four-year U.S. nuclear monopoly by testing its own atomic device. Emerging from the Second World War as one of two superpowers and quickly entering a global geopolitical contest with the United States, the Soviet leadership felt threatened by its rival's unique nuclear capability. Therefore, since at least 1945, Moscow possessed the willingness to acquire nuclear weapons, indeed making nuclearization its top national priority.

Soviet conventional strength, combined with the limited capability of U.S. atomic forces during the nuclear monopoly period, gave Moscow the opportunity to build the bomb. Confident that Washington would not launch a preventive military strike, Soviet officials were quite open about their determination to acquire a nuclear deterrent. Therefore, throughout the nuclear-monopoly period, U.S. policymakers were aware the Soviets were developing their own nuclear weapons. Washington was also aware that Soviet acquisition would pose serious problems for U.S. strategic aims – particularly for the ability to deter Soviet aggression in Western Europe with a relatively light U.S. conventional force by threatening Moscow with nuclear retaliation. Yet, U.S. leaders knew that any effective preventive counterproliferation action would be exceedingly costly, leading them to countenance Soviet nuclearization.

Soviet Interest in Nuclear Weapons

Having witnessed the power of atomic bombs – and U.S. willingness to use them – during the last few days of the Second World War, the Soviet leadership understood the impact of nuclear weapons on the postwar balance of power. Soviet leader Joseph Stalin (1922–1953) was deeply affected by the atomic bombing of Japan, saying: "Hiroshima has shaken the whole world. The balance has been destroyed."[163]

---

[163] Quoted in Holloway (1994, 132).

The Soviet Reaction to the U.S. Nuclear Monopoly

Stalin's thinking about the U.S. nuclear monopoly consisted of two main points. First, he thought the bomb posed an immediate politico-diplomatic challenge to Soviet strategic aims in the postwar order. Stalin knew that U.S. atomic weapons curtailed the Soviet Union's geostrategic freedom of action and exposed it to nuclear blackmail, and he therefore worried about the diplomatic and psychological effect of the U.S. atomic monopoly.[164] As Craig and Radchenko write, "the fact that the United States had the bomb and the Soviet Union did not have it, weakened Stalin's bargaining position and his great-power claims."[165] In a November 1945 cable to Washington assessing the impact of the atomic bomb on Soviet policy, U.S. ambassador to Moscow W. Averell Harriman (1943–1946) noted that "suddenly the atomic bomb appeared and they recognized that it was an offset to the power of the Red Army. ... They could no longer be absolutely sure they could obtain their objectives without interference."[166] Along similar lines, the British ambassador to the Soviet Union reported on the mood among the Soviet leadership in Moscow in December 1945, writing: "then plump came the [U.S.] Atomic Bomb. At a blow the balance ... was rudely shaken. ... The three hundred [Soviet] divisions were shorn of much of their value."[167] The immediate danger of the bomb, in Stalin's view, was that the United States would become a revisionist power, behaving aggressively toward, and demanding concessions from, the Soviet Union.

Stalin's second reaction to U.S. nuclear acquisition was to think that it might endanger the Soviet Union in the future if Washington decided to produce large numbers of atomic weapons in short order. Stalin's urgency in developing its own nuclear bomb was therefore also aimed at staving off the possibility of a future nuclear threat to the survival of the Soviet state.[168] The Soviet leader understood that, "in a few years, the United States would have more – and more powerful – bombs, and it would be more willing to go to war and use them against the USSR."[169]

---

[164] See: Ibid., 132–133.
[165] Craig and Radchenko (2008, 97).
[166] Quoted in Holloway (1994, 154).
[167] Quoted in Gordin (2009, 62).
[168] See: Holloway (1994, 153, 171).
[169] Craig and Radchenko (2008, 110).

At the same time, Stalin downplayed the short-term military significance of the U.S. nuclear monopoly. Given the small size of the American nuclear arsenal, he was not concerned that the American bomb would pose an immediate military threat to the Soviet Union. As he told the *Sunday Times* correspondent in Moscow in an interview: "Atomic bombs are meant to frighten those with weak nerves, but they cannot decide the outcome of a war, since atomic bombs are quite insufficient for that."[170] Furthermore, he thought the U.S. arsenal would remain small in the near future; it would therefore be insufficient to inflict crippling destruction on the Soviet Union for some years to come. This led Stalin to downplay the immediate military threat posed by the U.S. nuclear monopoly.[171] In short, Washington's bomb posed an immediate political threat to Soviet geostrategic aims, and might well turn into a military threat in the foreseeable future.

The only way of limiting the political danger posed by even a nominal U.S. nuclear monopoly and eliminating the military risk posed by an eventual U.S. nuclear buildup was, Stalin thought, to develop a Soviet bomb. He was therefore determined to eliminate the U.S. nuclear monopoly as soon as possible. Although the Soviet nuclear project had started in 1942, after Hiroshima Stalin raised its status to "Problem Number One," devoting unlimited resources to the nuclear effort.[172] By April 1946, work on the project was going so well that the Soviet leadership expected to have an atomic bomb by the beginning of 1948.[173] As it turned out, the Soviets completed their nuclear development program in 1949, detonating their first nuclear device on August 29 that year.

The Public Character of Soviet Nuclear Development

Throughout the period of U.S. nuclear monopoly, the Soviet posture regarding its own nuclear program was remarkably defiant. For years before Soviet nuclear acquisition, the United States knew that

---

[170] Quoted in Holloway (1994, 171). According to Craig and Radchenko (2008, 109–110), there was also an undeniable element of propaganda in Stalin's attempts to underplay the role of the bomb, in order to undermine the perceived advantage enjoyed by the United States while its nuclear monopoly lasted.

[171] See: Craig and Radchenko (2008, 109–110).

[172] Ibid., 106. See also: Holloway (1994, 122).

[173] See: Craig and Radchenko (2008, 109).

Moscow was developing nuclear weapons. U.S. officials knew about Soviet espionage of the Manhattan Project since as early as 1942; and revelations of the Soviets' atomic espionage in the West in September 1945 and February 1946 had made that much clear to the American public.[174] As early as August 8, 1945, only two days after the United States dropped an atomic bomb on Hiroshima, Stalin mentioned his own ongoing nuclear program to Ambassador Harriman.[175] By August 1946, a Soviet observer to a U.S. nuclear test in the Bikini atoll declared to American journalists that

the Soviet government is planning some time to have a demonstration of the atomic bomb. ... I do not know whether we have an atomic bomb right now – perhaps we have, perhaps we have not. But I believe that very soon we will have everything you have in the United States. We have worked for many years on atomic energy in the Soviet Union. Russia has the raw material and the personnel.[176]

Upping the ante, Soviet foreign minister Vyacheslav Molotov (1939–1949, 1953–1956) told the UNGA in October that year that "one must not forget that for one side's atomic bombs the other side may find atomic bombs and something else."[177] By the following year, the Soviet leadership was hinting at the impending end of the U.S. nuclear monopoly. On November 6, 1947, during the ceremonies marking the thirtieth anniversary of the Soviet revolution, Molotov said that the United States "put their faith in the secret of the atomic bomb, although this secret has long ceased to be a secret."[178]

U.S. Counterproliferation Efforts

Stalin's openness about the existence of a Soviet nuclear program was possible because a preventive U.S. strike against the Soviet Union entailed tremendous costs, and was therefore highly unlikely. The United States, despite its nuclear monopoly, did not have the capability

---

[174] Ibid., 113.
[175] Ibid., 115.
[176] Quoted in ibid., 143.
[177] Quoted in ibid., 144.
[178] Quoted in Holloway (1994, 258).

to destroy the Soviet Union, or even to blunt its offensive capabilities in Europe, East Asia, and the Middle East.

For his part, Stalin went to great lengths to hide the location of Soviet nuclear facilities from American eyes, increasing the required magnitude of a putative U.S. counterproliferation strike. In contrast to its public acknowledgment of the existence of a Soviet nuclear program, the Soviet leadership was extremely guarded about the logistical details of its nuclear effort. Moscow went to great lengths to hide its nuclear facilities, in one extreme case, under a lake.[179] At the same time, the U.S. arsenal never grew much before Soviet nuclear acquisition. In the absence of a U.S. nuclear buildup, Soviet leaders continued throughout 1947 and 1948 to view the bomb as a political, not military, threat in the short term.[180] In other words, the small size of the U.S. nuclear arsenal denied Washington the ability to eradicate the Soviet nuclear program in one fell swoop using atomic weapons. In May 1949, analyzing the possibility of a covert U.S. attack against China – a much weaker target – Stalin wrote: "War is not advantageous to the imperialists. … The material conditions for an attack, for unleashing war, do not exist. The way matters stand now, America is less ready to attack than the U.S.S.R. to repulse an attack."[181] The Soviets estimated that a U.S.-launched preventive strike on their nuclear program was highly unlikely, as the Americans would know that Soviet conventional retaliation – possibly leading to general war – was inevitable, and were unprepared to bear such steep costs.

The Expected Effects of Soviet Nuclear Acquisition on U.S. Security

Stalin's calculation about the low likelihood of a U.S. preventive attack against the Soviet nuclear program – which mirrored U.S. President Harry S. Truman's (1945–1953) ultimate decision not to launch such an attack – explains the Soviet decision to develop the bomb out in the open. Stalin understood – as did Truman – that although Soviet efforts to develop a bomb were no secret, the United States would ultimately decide against launching a preventive strike on Soviet nuclear facilities. When compared with the eventual effect of Soviet nuclearization on the balance of power, the costs of a preventive U.S. strike against the

---

[179] See: Rhodes (1995, 287).
[180] See: Holloway (1994, 258).
[181] Quoted in ibid., 264.

Soviet program were too high for such an attack to be rational. Both Stalin's gamble and Truman's reluctance to launch a preventive strike can be accounted for by the cost of preventive war, which was greater than the effect of nuclearization on the balance of power.

No doubt, U.S. policymakers expected Soviet nuclear acquisition to have important effects on the balance of power. By ending the U.S. nuclear monopoly, a Soviet bomb would take away Washington's ability to defend its interests around the world with a relatively small nuclear arsenal and a clear inferiority in conventional forces in key theaters such as Western Europe. If the Soviets proceeded with a quick expansion of their own nuclear forces, a costly U.S. arms buildup would be necessary in order to maintain stability in great-power relations. Furthermore, as successive crises over Berlin would demonstrate, a Soviet nuclear capability was likely to embolden the leadership in the Kremlin, leading it to make ever growing demands on the United States, and thereby raising the specter of war. In sum, a Soviet bomb would challenge Washington's ability to defend the international status quo on the cheap.

Still, Soviet nuclear acquisition in 1949 did not dramatically change the balance of power. For superpowers, which possess the ability to inflict severe damage on rival states even without nuclear weapons, proliferation per se does not appreciably alter the balance of power. As Rosenberg writes,

[T]he Soviet atomic explosion, despite its political impact, did not immediately alter the world military situation. Intelligence estimates prepared after the Soviet test projected that the Soviet Union would not acquire a large enough stockpile or the necessary delivery systems to threaten the United States before 1951 at the earliest, and more probably 1953 or even 1955.[182]

The Expected Costs of a Hypothetical U.S. Counterproliferation Strike

Ultimately, none of the expected consequences of Soviet nuclearization appeared to be as dire as the likely outcome of a U.S. preventive

---

[182] Rosenberg (1979, 80). That the balance of power was not gravely affected by the Soviet acquisition of nuclear weapons is reflected in the fact that talk of preventive war against the USSR among American policymakers increased after Soviet acquisition, during the Korean War. See: Buhite and Hamel (1990, 376–377).

counterproliferation strike on the Soviet Union. Three reasons dictated that cost estimates for such an attack would be higher than the expected outcome of Soviet nuclear acquisition, making a preventive strike irrational.

To begin with, the quality of U.S. intelligence on the location of Soviet nuclear facilities was dismal. Soviet facilities were well hidden, and U.S. intelligence in the late 1940s (in the pre-satellite, pre-U-2 reconnaissance aircraft era) relied mostly on data obtained from German prisoners of war and maps from the German invasion of Russia in 1941 or even from the Tsarist period, well before the Soviet program grew on the ground.[183] In practice, the U.S. military was unable to compile a target set capable of guaranteeing the eradication of the Soviet nuclear program. Secretary of Defense James Forrestal (1947–1949) noted in his diary on July 8, 1947, that "[t]here is no knowledge, for example, of what progress Russia has made either in the field of actual assembly of the bomb or of the availability to them of the necessary materials."[184] As a result, any preventive strike would have to be large; in practice, indistinguishable from an attempt to destroy the Soviet state.

Second, such an exacting military goal was beyond the reach of U.S. nuclear forces. The U.S. nuclear arsenal was remarkably small throughout the monopoly period. As Rosenberg notes, in the early postwar era,

---

[183] On the difficulty of U.S. intelligence gathering on the Soviet nuclear program, see: Rosenberg (1982, 29); Gordin (2009, 66–71, 80–84). On Soviet efforts to hide nuclear facilities, see: Zaloga (1993, 50, 62, 68); Rhodes (1995, 287). Key facilities in the Soviet nuclear program prior to the 1949 test included: (i) the Kurchatov Institute in Moscow, where the first bomb was designed, and which included a research reactor that achieved a self-sustaining nuclear reaction in late 1946; (ii) the Chelyabinsk Mayak plant, in Ozyorsk (on the shore of the Irtyash Lake, in the Ural mountains region), which had five research reactors and a plutonium reprocessing plant, and where the first bomb was assembled from materials produced on site; and (iii) the Semipalatinsk test site in northeastern Kazakhstan, where the 1949 test was conducted. See: Henry S. Lowenhaupt, "On the Soviet Nuclear Scent," Fall 1967, in National Security Archive (NSA) Electronic Briefing Book (EBB) 286, "U.S. Intelligence and the Detection of the First Soviet Nuclear Test, September 1949," Doc. 2; Rachel Oswald, "Fifty Years after Above-Ground Blasts, a Sense of Calm at Kazakhstani Nuclear Site," *Global Security Newswire*, September 3, 2013. Available at: www.nti.org/gsn/article/fifty-years-after-blasts-kazakhstani-nuclear-site/. Last accessed: May 2, 2016.

[184] Quoted in Gordin (2009, 83).

[T]he most critical determinant in strategic and operational planning was capability. From 1945 through 1948, the vaunted era of American nuclear monopoly, the nation's stockpile [of nuclear weapons] and delivery capability were extremely limited. There were only two weapons in the stockpile at the end of 1945, nine in July 1946, thirteen in July 1947, and fifty in July 1948. None of these weapons was assembled.[185]

The Berlin crisis of 1948 led to an increase in the production of nuclear weapons. Still, by the time the Soviets tested their nuclear device, the U.S. arsenal consisted of fewer than two hundred bombs.[186] This limited number of nuclear devices, particularly when combined with a shortage of modified bombers able to drop them and crews trained to load and fly the airplanes, left the United States far from fulfilling the requirements for destroying a country as vast as the Soviet Union.[187] A 1945 air force study noted that in order to destroy the Soviet Union, the United States needed to be able successfully to deliver 466 atomic bombs to their targets.[188] By mid-1950, one year *after* the Soviet nuclear breakthrough, the U.S. arsenal totaled 298 bombs.[189] As David Holloway writes, "Soviet and American military planners agreed in 1949–1951 that the atomic air offensive would not win the war."[190] Indeed, according to Buhite and Hamel, U.S. "war plans consistently demanded more bombs than existed in the U.S. arsenals well into the 1950s."[191] The U.S. nuclear monopoly was, therefore, largely nominal. Any preventive strike would need to rely on conventional forces, entailing considerable casualties and a protracted war. In sum,

---

[185] Rosenberg (1983, 14).
[186] The most accurate estimate available puts the number at 169. See: Norris and Arkin (1993, 48); Norris and Arkin (1994, 58–59). Their figures supersede previous (inflated) estimates in Rosenberg (1982, 25–30). On the limiting effect of the small stockpile on U.S. war plans, see: Buhite and Hamel (1990, 383); Williamson Jr. and Rearden (1993, 107–111).
[187] See: Rosenberg (1982, 29).
[188] See: Rhodes (1995, 226). As Holloway notes, some in the armed forces thought these requirements to be too high and underestimate the destructive potential of nuclear weapons, but the basic point that the arsenal of the time was much below what was needed to deal a decisive blow to the Soviet Union was consensual. See: Holloway (1994, 230).
[189] See: Holloway (1994, 230).
[190] Ibid., 240.
[191] Buhite and Hamel (1990, 383).

the U.S. administration had no clear line of sight to a quick military victory over a prenuclear Soviet Union.

Third, and finally, without a quick victory in sight, a preventive strike would invite massive Soviet conventional retaliation. U.S. war plans were pessimistic in this respect. After the quick post–Second World War U.S. demobilization, the balance of conventional forces, especially in Europe, heavily favored the Soviets.[192] By mid-1946, the staff in charge of drafting the (failed) Baruch nuclear disarmament plan noted that "if we were to stop making bombs we would be almost defenseless and would certainly have only a modicum of military power with which to stand up to the U.S.S.R."[193] In December 1947, Secretary of Defense James Forrestal considered the "predominance of Russian land power in Europe and Asia" to be one of the "outstanding military factors in the world."[194] As John Lewis Gaddis notes, "one Pentagon estimate credited [the Soviet Union] with sufficient strength to overrun most of continental Europe, Turkey, Iran, Afghanistan, Manchuria, Korea, and North China."[195] The Harmon Committee report, a study of the consequences of eventual preventive action against the Soviet Union published in May 1949 – a mere four months before the Soviet nuclear test – concluded that even if a U.S. attack would go as planned, destroying seventy Soviet cities, this would not "bring about the capitulation, destroy the roots of Communism, or critically weaken the power of the Soviet leadership to dominate the people." In a characteristic understatement, the report continued, such an attack would "produce certain psychological and retaliatory reactions detrimental to the achievement of Allied war objectives and its destructive effects will complicate post-hostilities problems." Among these developments "detrimental to the achievement of Allied war objectives," the report highlighted the fact that "the capability of Soviet armed forces to advance rapidly into selected areas of Western Europe, the Middle East, and the Far East would not be seriously impaired."[196] In short, the near-certain Soviet

---

[192] See: Holloway (1994, 231); Rhodes (1995, 301); Gordin (2009, 26–27).

[193] Gordin (2009, 54). Estimates of the balance of forces in the European theater differ, but U.S. decisionmakers at the time took the Soviet ability to overrun Western Europe for granted. See: Evangelista (1982–1983); Rhodes (1995).

[194] Rhodes (1995, 313).

[195] Gaddis (1987, 109).

[196] All quotes of the Harmon Committee report come from Rosenberg (1979, 72–73).

retaliation against a U.S. preventive strike was likely to cause massive manpower, materiel, and territorial losses for the United States and its allies. A preventive strike on the Soviet nuclear program would virtually guarantee nothing less than all-out war with the Soviet Union.

Summing up, both the Soviet decision to make no secret of its attempt to develop nuclear weapons and the U.S. decision not to thwart such an attempt by military means can be explained by the cost of a preventive war against the Soviet Union, which was expected to be greater than the effect of Soviet nuclearization. The threat of preventive war therefore lacked credibility and the Soviet Union could advance with its nuclear development, becoming the second country to acquire the bomb.

Alternative Explanations

The conventional wisdom on the failure of U.S. counterproliferation efforts centers on two arguments. Some scholars attribute the U.S. decision not to attack the Soviet nuclear program to the poor quality of the information that Washington possessed about Soviet progress toward nuclear acquisition.[197] Granted, the United States was deeply uncertain about the timeline for completion of the Soviet program.[198] American intelligence consistently overestimated the time it would take for the Soviets to end the U.S. nuclear monopoly. U.S. decision-makers therefore never saw the Soviet bomb as imminent. To the contrary, intelligence reports pointed to a date for a Soviet nuclear test up to twenty years down the road. Eventually, a consensus emerged around a five-year estimate put forth by the scientific community. Truman publicly agreed with the scientists, but privately tended to lean toward longer, fifteen- to twenty-year estimates.[199] Curiously, the five-year figure remained unchanged, so that in practice the estimated date of the Soviet breakthrough kept being pushed back.[200] On July 1, 1949, less than three months before the Soviet test, Admiral Roscoe H. Hillenkoeter, Director of the CIA (1947–1950), reiterated his 1948 Estimate of the Status of the Russian Atomic Energy Project

---

[197] For a recent argument in this vein, see: Bas and Coe (2012).
[198] See: Goodman (2007).
[199] See: Gordin (2009, 78–80).
[200] Ibid., 66.

from one year earlier. It predicted that "the earliest date by which it is remotely possible that the U.S.S.R. may have completed its first atomic bomb is mid-1950, but the most probable date is believed to be mid-1953."[201] Ironically, an estimate published *after* the Soviet test – but before the United States found out about it – continued to point to a three-to-five-year window for Soviet acquisition.[202] To a large extent, this was due to U.S. ignorance of the Soviet capability to produce fissile material, and particularly of its natural uranium stocks. Unaware that the USSR possessed 40 percent of global uranium deposits, the United States, which went to great lengths to monopolize international control of the mineral, thought the Soviets would have another five to ten years of work ahead of them to produce the core for a nuclear bomb. In short, when the Soviet test took place, U.S. policymakers were caught by surprise.

According to proponents of the timeline argument as an explanation for the absence of a U.S. preventive strike, these lengthy estimates took pressure for preventive action off the U.S. administration. The Truman administration never felt urged to act against the Soviet program, because it never estimated Soviet acquisition to be imminent.[203] As Gordin writes, "[t]he first immediate effect of a lengthy estimate was to discourage a preemptive strike against the Soviet Union."[204]

Yet, this timeline explanation is unconvincing in two respects. First, the presumed length of the window of opportunity until Soviet acquisition did not necessarily lead to added prudence regarding potential counterproliferation strikes. Top U.S. decisionmakers knew the estimates were mere guesses. David Lilienthal, the chairman of the AEC (1946–1950), which controlled the U.S. arsenal in the early postwar years, noted that the intelligence estimates were "five percent information and ninety-five percent construction … [based on sources] so poor as to be actually merely arbitrary assumptions."[205] Criticizing the way government bureaucracies were using mere "guesstimates" to shape policy, Lilienthal commented:

---

[201] Quoted in Holloway (1994, 220).
[202] See: CIA Intelligence Memorandum 225, cited in CIA (1994, 319).
[203] For a detailed analysis of U.S. (and British) intelligence efforts around the Soviet nuclear program, see: Richelson (2006, 62–104); Goodman (2007, 7–35).
[204] Gordin (2009, 87).
[205] Quoted in Goodman (2007, 28).

[T]he thing that rather chills one's blood is to observe what is nothing less than lack of integrity in the way the agencies deal with the meager stuff they have. It is chiefly a matter of reasoning from our own American experience, guessing how much longer it will take Russia using our methods and based upon our problems of achieving weapons. But when this is put into a report, the reader, e.g. Congressional Committee, is given the impression, and deliberately, that behind the estimate lies specific knowledge, knowledge so important and delicate that its nature and sources cannot be disclosed.[206]

Given this level of uncertainty, at least some high-level decisionmakers reflected the view that a long estimate for Soviet completion should not necessarily lead to the postponement of a U.S. preventive strike. General Leslie Groves, who had headed the U.S. nuclear effort during the Second World War and remained the top military commander in charge of nuclear weapons once the war ended (1942–1948), himself estimated more than twenty years of American atomic monopoly, yet supported immediate preventive war. As early as October 1945, he wrote in a secret report of the Joint Chiefs of Staff (JCS) Joint Intelligence Committee, which was working on a first-strike plan against the Soviets:

If we were truly realistic instead of idealistic, as we appear to be, we would not permit any foreign power with which we are not firmly allied, and in which we do not have absolute confidence, to make or possess atomic weapons. If such a country started to make atomic weapons we would destroy its capacity to make them before it has progressed far enough to threaten us.[207]

In January 1946, Groves was more explicit, telling Congress that the United States "should consider a preventive attack against Soviet atomic research facilities."[208] The logic behind his reasoning was clear: the longer the United States waited, the harder it would be to destroy the Soviet nuclear program. This logic is borne out by the history of preventive attacks against nuclear programs: the "historical cases that have successfully delayed proliferation are those

---

[206] Quoted in Goodman (2007, 33).
[207] October 1945 Plan: JIC321/9 "Strategic Vulnerability of the U.S.S.R. to a Limited Air Attack," quoted in Rhodes (1995, 225).
[208] Quoted in Buhite and Hamel (1990, 374).

when the attacking state struck well before a nuclear threat was imminent."[209]

Second, this timeline explanation does not address the question of whether a preventive attack would have been rational in case U.S. policymakers had been aware of an imminent Soviet nuclear test. In other words, had U.S. intelligence estimates for the completion of the Soviet nuclear program been shorter, would it have been rational for Washington to launch a preventive attack against the USSR? Were Truman to have known that there was a clear and present danger of a Soviet nuclear breakthrough, he would likely have considered a preventive strike more seriously. Stalin, for his part, played a clever strategy. On the one hand, he portrayed Soviet nuclear aspirations as undeterrable, and often bragged about making quick progress on developing a nuclear capability. On the other hand, he did not give precise information about the location of his program or the precise stage of its development. (He did not even make a public announcement about the first Soviet nuclear test.) Such actions could have reduced the cost of a preventive strike or rallied public support in the United States for a more aggressive foreign policy.[210]

Still, the odds of Truman ordering such a hypothetical strike would remain low because of the underlying strategic situation, which made a preventive attack exceedingly costly. Journalist William Laurence hinted at this when he wrote:

The shorter we believe the time to be[,] the more likely we are to be overcome by fear, leading inevitably to a state of mind in which "hit-emfustest-with-themostest" would appear to be the only possible choice. On the other hand, the more time we have, or think we have, for *considered judgment*, the greater the chance reason may prevail.[211]

But the timeline explanation is silent on what the outcome of this "considered judgment" would be. It does not address the question of whether a preventive attack would be a reasonable option when contemplated with the benefit of time. If an attack would not have been rational anyway, then the overblown estimates of how much

---

[209] Kreps and Fuhrmann (2011, 161).
[210] See: Holloway (1994, 267).
[211] Quoted in Gordin (2009, 87), emphasis added.

time the Soviet effort would take to be completed cannot account for the absence of a U.S. preventive strike. The costs of such an attack were higher than the estimates of the effect of Soviet nuclear acquisition, making a preventive U.S. strike irrational even if Washington had been aware of the impending Soviet nuclearization. Therefore, the timeline explanation cannot account for U.S. acquiescence to Soviet nuclearization.

A second common explanation for the absence of a U.S. preventive strike on the Soviet program is based on moral reasons. In 1948, President Truman opposed the military's request for control of the nuclear arsenal, arguing that nuclear weapons' destructive power should place particular restrictions on their use.[212] One year after the Soviet test, Truman explained to reporters why an attack on the Soviet Union had not been undertaken, saying that preventive war "is the weapon of dictators, not of free democratic countries like the United States."[213] The moral explanation for the absence of preventive war is also supported by Truman's viewpoint as expressed in a July 1948 meeting with members of the AEC, the agency that controlled the U.S. nuclear arsenal. Many in the military wanted control to be transferred to the armed forces. Truman opposed this for fear of an unauthorized launch, saying:

I don't think we ought to use this thing unless we absolutely have to. It is a terrible thing to order the use of something like that ... that is so terribly destructive, destructive beyond anything we have ever had. You have got to understand that this isn't a military weapon. ... It is used to wipe out women and children and unarmed people, and not for military uses. So we have got to treat this differently from rifles and cannon and ordinary things like that. ... You have to understand that I have got to think about the effect of such a thing on international relations. This is not time to be juggling an atom bomb around.[214]

Two important reasons undermine the explanatory power of the moral explanation, however. First, as Buhite and Hamel show, "a great

---

[212] See: Rhodes (1995, 327).
[213] "Text of Truman's 'Report to Nation' on Korea War: Truman Speaking to the World Last Night," *The New York Times*, September 2, 1950, p. 4.
[214] Rhodes (1995, 327).

many Americans, some of them in the highest ranks of the government, in the nation's most prestigious universities, and among the country's leading journalists, at one time or another advocated attacking the Soviet Union before the Soviets could endanger the security of the United States."[215] Reflecting this pro-prevention mood, the military recommended as early as September 1945 that the United States "demonstrate its readiness and determination to take prompt and effective military action abroad to anticipate and prevent an attack on the United States."[216] In sum, many Americans, including those in positions of responsibility, thought that military prevention was a perfectly reasonable course of action. Moral reasons – including the need to assure the survivability of Western society, which most in Washington considered morally superior – could just as easily be harnessed in support of preventive action against the Soviet nuclear program.

In addition, and similarly to the timeline explanation, the moral justification for the absence of a preventive strike suffers from a second shortcoming: it fails to address the question of whether a preventive attack would have been rational. Moral reasoning was not the most important factor weighing against a U.S.-launched preventive strike on the Soviet Union.[217] U.S. inability to deliver a successful destructive blow to the Soviet homeland is likely to have played a more important role:

Limited American capabilities were probably a greater element behind the decision not to engage in preventive war. Postwar demobilization had severely weakened the world's most powerful military machine, and low levels of spending kept it in a weakened state into the 1950s.[218]

One plausible way of interpreting Truman's retrospective moral opposition to a preventive U.S. strike against Soviet nuclear facilities, therefore, is to view it as at least partially a consequence of the vast-scale military operation such an attack would have entailed, with millions of civilian victims. In other words, the magnitude of the death and

---

[215] Buhite and Hamel (1990, 367). See also: Williamson Jr. and Rearden (1993, 140).

[216] Quoted in Buhite and Hamel (1990, 373).

[217] See: Ibid., 367–384.

[218] Ibid., 382–383.

destruction required to forestall Soviet nuclear acquisition by military means exacerbated moral concerns about prevention.

To conclude, in the absence of intelligence that enabled the construction of a target set for the Soviet nuclear program, a successful surgical strike was unfeasible. A preventive strike thus required a nuclear arsenal capable of crippling the Soviet Union. Since the U.S. arsenal was far from possessing this capability, any strike in practice required large-scale conventional action. Alas, such an attack would lead to Soviet retaliation in areas – such as Western Europe – where the balance of power strongly favored the USSR, potentially granting it great territorial gains. A preventive strike would therefore lead to an outcome that was worse than the expected result of Soviet nuclear acquisition. An attack was simply too costly to be a viable option. This strategic logic, rather than considerations about U.S. estimates on the timeline of Soviet nuclearization or moral reasons, is at the basis of both Stalin's decision to be open about his nuclear efforts and Truman's decision not to use force to avoid the end of the U.S. nuclear monopoly.[219]

Iraq

The Iraqi nuclear program began with the founding of the Iraqi Atomic Energy Commission (IAEC) in 1956. In the early years of its nuclear development, Iraq perceived Israel and Iran as its most important adversaries. Since the 1991 Gulf War, however, Iraq also confronted the United States, an even more potent security threat. As a weak state facing multiple adversaries, Iraq had a high willingness to acquire nuclear weapons.

At the same time, Iraq lacked the opportunity to nuclearize, and was vulnerable to foreign pressure, most notably in the form of preventive strikes, sanctions, and, ultimately, a U.S.-led invasion in 2003. In September 1980, Iran attempted to destroy the Iraqi research nuclear reactor in Osirak, and Israel successfully did so in June 1981. Subsequently, Iraq dispersed its nuclear-weapons program in an attempt to elude international scrutiny. After the Iraqi invasion of Kuwait in August 1990, the United States led a coalition to liberate Iraq's neighbor. In the aftermath of the Gulf War, the international

---

[219] See: Ibid.; Williamson Jr. and Rearden (1993, 140–141).

community was surprised by the extent of the Iraqi program and imposed intrusive inspections and severe sanctions, backed by the threat of war – and by actual air strikes in 1998. Uncertain about Iraq's progress and fearing Iraqi nuclearization, the United States invaded Iraq in March 2003, deposing Saddam Hussein, who had been in power since 1979. As would become clear after the war, however, Iraqi nuclear development had successfully been halted years earlier.

Iraqi Interest in Nuclear Weapons

Iraq inaugurated its nuclear program with the founding of the IAEC in 1956, taking advantage of the U.S. Atoms for Peace program. In these early years of the Cold War, Iraq was an ally of the West, joining the United Kingdom and other countries in the region in the Baghdad Pact of 1955, an anticommunist alliance.[220]

Two years later, however, Iraq moved away from the West. On July 14, 1958, the monarchy fell to a coup and, the following March, Iraq withdrew from the Baghdad Pact. Soon, the Soviet Union offered technical assistance, training Iraqi scientists and, in 1962, supplying a research reactor for the Tuwaitha Atomic Center near Baghdad.[221] The Soviet-Iraqi rapprochement was formalized in April 1972 but the "entente" between the two countries fell short of a defensive pact, including only consultation and nonaggression clauses. This agreement would eventually be rescinded in September 1990, after the Iraqi invasion of Kuwait.

During the remainder of the Cold War, Western countries also offered some support to Iraq. France was eager to develop an independent grand strategy toward the Arab world and intent on securing an inflow of oil.[222] Starting in the late 1960s, Paris supplied Iraq with arms and technical assistance.[223] Other countries – such as Italy and Brazil in the late 1970s, and even the United States in the early

---

[220] The state of Iraq had emerged from the ashes of the Ottoman Empire in 1920, being placed under a British mandate. A monarchy was established in 1921 and the country became independent in 1932.

[221] See: Snyder (1983, 565), Solingen (2007, 143).

[222] See: Bozo (2013, 35).

[223] By 1982, Iraq represented close to 40 percent of France's overall arms sales. See: Bozo (2013, 36).

1980s – also offered technical assistance.[224] For Washington, Iraq could act as an important ally in the region following the Iranian Revolution of 1979. Yet, despite all this support, no country offered Baghdad a security guarantee. Throughout the duration of its nuclear-weapons program, Iraq was without a security sponsor.

The key figure behind the Iraqi nuclear-weapons program was Iraqi dictator Saddam Hussein, who perceived Israel, Iran, and, later, the United States as Iraq's main security threats. Iraq fought against Israel from the very first days of the Jewish state. Following the proclamation of the state of Israel in May 1948, Iraq led its invasion alongside Syria, and was joined by Lebanon, Transjordan, and Egypt. Israel prevailed on the battlefield and Iraq stopped fighting in July 1948, though it did not formally agree to the end of the war. In June 1967, Israel destroyed the Egyptian air force, fearing an impending attack by Nasser. In what became known as the Six-Day War, Iraq again fought Israel alongside Egypt, Jordan, and Syria, but its air force was also quickly destroyed and the Arab states were defeated.[225] Israel emerged stronger than ever, now controlling the Sinai Peninsula, the Gaza Strip, the West Bank, and the Golan Heights, and making further progress in its quest for the bomb.[226]

Iraq faced another potent threat in the east: Iran. In the early years of the Cold War, the two countries maintained friendly relations. They had settled their territorial dispute over the Shatt al-Arab, a joint waterway giving access to the Gulf, in 1937. In the agreement, Iran, militarily the more powerful of the two, granted control over most of the Shatt to Iraq. Furthermore, the two countries cooperated in efforts to contain communist expansion in the region as part of the Baghdad Pact of 1955. Yet, relations between the two countries soured after the fall of the monarchy in Baghdad and the subsequent rapprochement between Iraq and the Soviet Union.[227] Twice, in 1959–1960 and again in 1969, Iraq and Iran clashed over control of the Shatt. Starting in 1965, Iran allied with Israel in supporting Kurdish rebels against the Iraqi government.[228]

[224] See: Snyder (1983, 574); Solingen (2007, 143); Woods, Palkki, and Stout (2011, 19); Fuhrmann (2012, 112).
[225] See: Oren (2002).
[226] See our case study of Israel in Chapter 5.
[227] See: Karsh (1990, 262).
[228] See: Parsi (2007, 53).

In March 1975, Iran and Iraq settled their disputes in the Algiers Agreement. Taking advantage of its greater conventional capabilities, Iran obtained greater sovereignty over parts of the Shatt. In return, Tehran pledged to respect Iraq's territorial integrity – effectively ending its support for Kurdish rebels.

Yet, this thaw in relations was short-lived. Tensions between the two countries flared again after the Iranian Revolution of 1979. The Islamic Republic of Iran supported resistance by both the Shiite majority and the Kurdish population in the north against the secular Baathist state in Baghdad.[229] In September 1980, Saddam abrogated the 1975 agreement and launched a major offensive against Iran. The bloody conflict lasted until August 1988, when the two sides reached a ceasefire arranged by the UN.[230]

During the Iran-Iraq War (1980–1988), Baghdad received assistance from Washington.[231] Yet, the Iraqi regime was suspicious of U.S. intentions. Baghdad resented Washington's support for Israel as well as its reliance on the shah as its preferred regional ally in the 1970s.[232] In a speech in January 1980, Saddam declared that "U.S. imperialism has been trying for years to control the area."[233] Later that year, he called the United States "the arch-Satan."[234] Despite restoring diplomatic relations with the United States in 1984, Saddam declared in October 1985 that the Americans "are still conspiring bastards."[235] A year later, President Ronald Reagan (1981–1989) admitted that the United States had sold weapons to Iran, breaking its own arms embargo, in

---

[229] See: Karsh (1990, 265–266).

[230] See: Alan Cowell, "Cease-Fire Takes Effect in 8-Year Iran-Iraq War," *The New York Times*, August 21, 1988, p. A6.

[231] As Brands and Palkki (2012, 636–637) highlight, U.S. weapons sales were small, relative to Iraqi imports from other countries. Iraq purchased eighty-seven-times more arms from the Soviet Union, twenty-four-times more from China, and twenty-two-times more from France.

[232] See: Brands and Palkki (2012, 631–632).

[233] "President Addresses Army, Speaks on Iran, Afghanistan," Foreign Broadcast Information Service (FBIS) Daily Report, Middle East and North Africa, FBIS-MEA-80-005, January 8, 1980. See also: Brands and Palkki (2012, 630).

[234] "Text of President Husayn's 10 Nov Press Conference," Foreign Broadcast Information Service (FBIS) Daily Report, Middle East and Africa, FBIS-MEA-80–220, November 12, 1980. See also: Brands and Palkki (2012, 634).

[235] CRRC SH-SHTP-D-000-567, "Meeting between Saddam Hussein and Baath Party Officials," October 5, 1985, quoted in Brands and Palkki (2012, 626).

the hope of obtaining the release of U.S. hostages. Saddam perceived this measure as a "stab in the back."[236]

The Rationale for an Iraqi Nuclear Deterrent

During the early years of his rule, Saddam saw Israel and Iran as its main foreign threats, and believed that nuclear weapons could significantly improve Iraq's security vis-à-vis these adversaries.[237] With the peace treaty between Egypt and Israel in 1977, Baghdad had the opportunity to lead the Arab countries in their fight against, to use Saddam's rhetoric, "the Zionist entity."[238] Nuclear weapons could help reclaim the territories lost to Israel in the Six-Day War.[239] Three months after assuming the presidency of Iraq, Saddam declared:

The struggle against Israel will be arduous and prolonged. In its course, it is even feasible that Israel will attempt to use an atomic bomb against the Arabs. Consequently, it is incumbent upon the Arabs to prepare all the means necessary for victory.[240]

In Saddam's view, nuclear weapons could provide the means for such victory. In 1981, he explained the benefit of nuclear weapons as follows:

We have to have this protection for the Iraqi citizen so that he will not be disappointed and held hostage by the scientific advancement taking place in Iran or in the Zionist entity. Without such deterrence, the Arab nation will continue to be threatened by the Zionist entity and Iraq will remain threatened by the Zionist entity.[241]

---

[236] CRRC SH-SHTP-A-000-609, "Saddam Hussein's Meeting with Baath Party Cabinet Ministers," early 1987, quoted in Brands and Palkki (2012, 642).

[237] See: Nakdimon (1987, 91); Solingen (2007, 162); Brands and Palkki (2011a, 133–166; 2011b).

[238] Woods, Palkki, and Stout (2011, 77). See also: Nakdimon (1987, 137); Brands (2011, 504).

[239] See: Brands and Palkki (2011a, 133).

[240] Quoted in Nakdimon (1987, 106).

[241] Quoted in Woods, Palkki, and Stout (2011, 266); Brands and Palkki (2011b). There is some disagreement over Saddam's ranking of these threats. Solingen (2007, 147) claims that senior Iraqi officials saw Iran as a greater threat than Israel. Some evidence suggests a greater concern for Israel. In 1980, Saddam told his subordinates: "Our worst enemy is Zionism" (quoted in Brands and Palkki 2011b). That same year, state-run media in Iraq claimed that "[t]he Iranian people should not fear the Iraqi nuclear reactor, which is not intended to be used against Iran, but against the Zionist entity" (quoted in Grant 2002, 75).

According to a CIA analysis at the time, Saddam believed that Arabs "can have no security as long as Israel alone commands the nuclear threat."[242]

To master nuclear technology, Baghdad turned to foreign assistance. In 1972, Iraq obtained a commitment from French Premier Jacques Chirac for the sale of a nuclear reactor as well as uranium fuel.[243] The following year, Saddam Hussein, then vice president of Iraq, became president of the IAEC.[244] The nuclear project was an important venture for Saddam. Upon becoming president, he stated: "I am the Godfather of the IAEC and I love the IAEC."[245] In 1974, Saddam negotiated the purchase of two reactors from France – Tammuz-1 and Tammuz-2 – also known as Osirak and Isis.

Unsurprisingly, Iraq's nuclear program raised concerns abroad. On June 7, 1981, Israel launched a preventive strike against Osirak, successfully destroying the reactor.[246] This attack did not diminish Saddam's appetite for nuclear weapons, however. Much to the contrary. In July 1981, Saddam declared that the raid "will not stop the course of scientific and technical progress in Iraq. Rather, it is an additional strong stimulus to develop this course ... with even greater resources and more effective protection."[247]

Still, in 1981, the IAEC initiated an effort to produce fissile material using the method of electromagnetic isotope enrichment of uranium (or EMIS). This method offered important benefits: it was unlikely to be detected by international intelligence,[248] and it seemed relatively easy for Iraqi scientists to master.[249] In 1987, Iraq initiated a second major track in its nuclear program, pursuing gas centrifuge uranium enrichment technology under the leadership of Mahdi Obeidi. Starting that same year, Saddam's son-in-law, Hussein Kamel, took control of

---

[242] Central Intelligence Agency, Office of Political Analysis, Interagency Intelligence Assessment, "Implications of Israeli Attack on Iraq," July 1, 1981, p. 3. Available at: www.foia.cia.gov/sites/default/files/document_conversions/89801/DOC_0000211961.pdf. Last accessed: March 15, 2016.

[243] See: Snyder (1983, 570).

[244] See: Braut-Hegghammer (2011, 106).

[245] Quoted in Duelfer (2004, Vol. 1, 26).

[246] For a detailed account of the raid, see: Claire (2004).

[247] "President Hussein's Press Conference on Iraq's Internal, Arab, and International Policies," 1981, quoted in Braut-Hegghammer (2011, 116).

[248] See: Hymans (2012, 99).

[249] See: Albright (2002).

the weaponization effort, reorganizing the project under code name PC-3 in mid-1989.[250]

After the conclusion of the costly war with Iran, Iraq invaded Kuwait, an oil-rich country that had partly funded the war, in August 1990. The invasion was strongly opposed by the international community,[251] and the UN authorized the use of force if Iraq did not withdraw its forces from its neighbor's territory by January 15, 1991. Under great international pressure, Baghdad launched a crash program to complete its nuclear-weapons project. Iraq would divert the highly enriched uranium on its territory, at the time under IAEA safeguards, for the production of a bomb. The goal was to make enough fissile material for a bomb by the following spring,[252] yet progress remained slow and in the meantime Iraqi forces were quickly defeated.[253]

The United States launched Operation Desert Storm on January 16, 1991. On February 28, after all Iraqi forces had been evicted from Kuwait, a ceasefire was implemented. As a result of the war, Baghdad lost much of its military materiel.[254] Iraqi officials lamented their country's diplomatic isolation. In their view, such a full-scale assault by an international coalition would not have been possible if the Soviet Union were still a superpower. Tariq Aziz, Iraq's foreign minister (1983–1991) and deputy prime minister (1979–2003), asserted: "We don't have a patron anymore. ... If we still had the Soviets as our patron, none of this would have happened."[255]

---

[250] See: Braut-Hegghammer (2011, 123); Hymans (2012, 103).

[251] There is some scholarly debate on whether the U.S. ambassador to Iraq, April Glaspie (1988–1990), led Saddam to believe in July 1990 that Washington would consent to an Iraqi invasion of Kuwait (see, e.g.: Karsh [2002, 91–92]; Brands and Palkki [2012, 627]).

[252] See: Albright and Kelley (1995, 53).

[253] See: Gordon and Trainor (1995).

[254] On February 22, 1991, well into the air campaign against Iraqi forces but before the ground war started, Saddam accepted a plan to withdraw from Kuwait in twenty-one days. The U.S. administration, however, rejected it, demanding a seven-day withdrawal, which would force Saddam to leave behind his materiel, in particular armored vehicles. The ground war resulted from Saddam's rejection of this demand, which would leave him with little more power than a military defeat. Most Iraqi materiel deployed in Kuwait ended up being destroyed all the same. See: Pape (1996).

[255] Quoted in Thomas L. Friedman and Patrick E. Tyler. "From the First, U.S. Resolve to Fight," *The New York Times*, March 3, 1991. Available

A Dormant Nuclear-Weapons Program

In the aftermath of the Gulf War, Iraq was in a very precarious strategic situation, but the dream of a nuclear deterrent was still alive. In February 1992, Mahdi Obeidi was asked to report on the remaining potential of the centrifuge program. For Obeidi, the implication was clear: "to wait out the inspections process and try to build a bomb later, when the world was no longer watching."[256]

Yet, the inspections and sanctions regime would prove significantly stronger than Saddam had hoped. After the war, UNSC Resolution 687 required Iraq to dismantle its nuclear-weapons program and tasked the United Nations Special Commission (UNSCOM) to carry out inspections on Iraq's biological, chemical, and missile capabilities.[257] The international community was soon shocked to learn that it had missed most of Iraq's efforts to obtain the bomb.[258] As a result, Iraq would remain under international sanctions until the work of UNSCOM and the IAEA was completed.

Saddam resented the severity of the UN sanctions[259] and hoped he could revive his nuclear-weapons program if given the opportunity. In June 1995, he admitted to Baath party members, "I mean we do not have biological weapons ... but this is the truth. We do not have chemical weapons; this is true. We do not have the capability to produce nuclear [weapons]."[260] In early 1996, Saddam told the General

---

at www.nytimes.com/1991/03/03/world/after-war-reconstruction-path-war-bush-s-crucial-decisions-special-report-first.html. Last accessed: December 9, 2013.

[256] Obeidi and Pitzer (2004, 152).

[257] See: "United Nations Security Council Resolution 687 (1991)," S/RES/687 (1991), April 3, 1991. Available at: www.un.org/Depts/unmovic/documents/687.pdf. Last accessed: May 2, 2016; Wing and Simpson (2013, 9–40). For a discussion of tensions between UNSCOM and the IAEA, see: Harrer (2014).

[258] See: U.S. House of Representatives, Report of the Oversight and Investigations Subcommittee, Committee on Armed Services, "Intelligence Successes and Failures in Operations Desert Shield/Storm," p. 23. 103rd Congress, 1st Session, August 16, 1993. Available at: www.dtic.mil/dtic/tr/fulltext/u2/a338886.pdf. Last accessed: May 2, 2016.

[259] The Iraqi leadership was concerned with the impact of the sanctions on the legitimacy of the regime. The Iraqi vice president declared that sanctions undermined "the ability of the Iraqi citizen to tolerate the current situation." Quoted in Palkki and Smith (2012, 279). For an argument that sanctions strengthened Hussein's government, see: Mazaheri (2010).

[260] "Saddam Hussein Meeting with Ba'ath Party Members to Discuss the Results of the UN Inspectors' Mission to Look for WMDs," June 19, 1995, in Wilson Center Digital Archive, Saddam Hussein's Iraq.

Command of the Armed Forces: "But what can we do; thank God, anyway! There is nothing, do you think we would talk like this if we had any, and suffer from sanctions for six years if we had chemical, nuclear, and biological missiles?"[261]

Since the early 1990s, Saddam tried to circumvent UN sanctions.[262] In January 1993, the UNSC found Iraq to be in "material breach" of its obligations, leading to bombing raids of radar sites and suspected nuclear facilities by the United States, the United Kingdom, and France. In October 1994, Hussein attempted to pressure the international community to end the sanctions by sending troops to the Kuwaiti border. Yet, the UNSC responded forcefully and called for Iraq to cooperate with UNSCOM and withdraw its forces. Iraq soon complied with this demand.[263] Again the following year, Hussein threatened to end his cooperation with UNSCOM unless there was progress toward ending the sanctions.[264] Three years later, in August 1998, Hussein expelled the inspectors, only to reverse himself in mid-November under the threat of U.S. air strikes. Upon reentering Iraq, inspectors found that Hussein was once more impeding their work. On December 16, 1998, they were evacuated and Washington launched a military campaign against Iraq – Operation Desert Fox. A year later, in December 1999, a new commission, the United Nations Monitoring, Verification, and Inspection Commission (UNMOVIC), was tasked with disarming Iraq and verifying its compliance with nonproliferation obligations.

Looking back, Scott Ritter, a UN weapons inspector in Iraq between 1991 and 1998, concluded that the severity of international sanctions convinced Saddam to unilaterally destroy his program.[265] Yet, inspectors would not return to Iraq until November 2002. U.S. officials therefore wondered whether they had successfully halted Saddam's drive for the bomb, and worried that even a stalled Iraqi program could be revived in the future.

[261] "Saddam Hussein Meeting with the General Command of the Armed Forces Regarding Iraqi Development and Defense Theory," January 1996, in Wilson Center Digital Archive, Saddam Hussein's Iraq.
[262] See: Harrer (2014).
[263] See: Thompson (2010, 100).
[264] Ibid.
[265] See: Ritter (1999, 34).

Israeli and U.S. Counterproliferation Efforts

In the early 1970s, U.S. and Israeli policymakers attempted to check Iraqi power, allying with Iran to tie down Iraqi forces by supporting Kurdish rebels.[266] The shah terminated such assistance with the Algiers Agreement of 1975.[267] As the Iraqi nuclear program developed, it increasingly became the target of preventive efforts from its enemies.

Strikes, Sanctions, and More Strikes

Development of the Osirak reactor was initially hampered in 1979, when the French firm in charge of supplying the technology was attacked. France believed that Israel was responsible for this operation.[268] Then, in September 1980, two Iranian F-4s bombed Osirak.[269] The following June, as we saw, Israel successfully destroyed the reactor.

Israeli Prime Minister Menachem Begin (1977–1983) feared the prospect of Iraqi nuclearization and believed that the Osirak raid was his "chance to save the Jewish people."[270] Saddam himself seemed to agree that the attack was a setback to Iraqi nuclear ambitions: "Technically, they are right in all of their attempts to harm Iraq. ... They might hit Iraq with an atomic bomb someday if we reach a certain stage. And we are prepared, and if God allows it, we will be ready to face it."[271]

U.S. officials also grew increasingly worried about Iraqi nuclearization. In making the case for pushing Iraq out of Kuwait in September 1990, President George H. W. Bush spoke of U.S. commitments to prevent nuclear proliferation – as well as, more generally, aggression – in the region.[272] After the Gulf War, when Washington became fully aware of the extent of the Iraqi nuclear program, the United States imposed a stringent inspections and sanctions regime, pledging to "use force if Saddam threatens Iraq's neighbors or

---

[266] See: Milani (2010, 79–80).
[267] See: Parsi (2007, 55).
[268] See: Snyder (1983, 579).
[269] See: Woods, Palkki, and Stout (2011, 77).
[270] Quoted in Grant (2002, 75). See also: Nakdimon (1987, 159).
[271] Quoted in Brands and Palkki (2011a, 156).
[272] See: George Bush, "Address before a Joint Session of the Congress on the Persian Gulf Crisis and the Federal Budget Deficit," September 11, 1990.

coalition forces, reconstitutes or deploys WMD, or moves against the Kurds."[273] This led Saddam to worry about a Western preventive strike against his nuclear program,[274] and he ordered the Iraqi air force to prepare to repel an eventual sequel to the 1981 Israeli aerial strike on Osirak.[275]

Sanctions had a significant effect on the Iraqi economy. By 1993, per capita GDP had regressed to the level of the 1960s.[276] Iraqi imports were reduced by 86 percent between 1990 and 1996.[277] In 1996, Baghdad finally accepted the oil-for-food program that it had rejected in 1991. The international community also mustered a robust set of strikes against Iraqi capabilities. With Operation Desert Fox in December 1998, the United States launched 400 cruise missile strikes and 650 aircraft sorties over a handful of days.

The inspections and sanctions regime, boosted by the threat of force in case of noncompliance, was a key component in the counterproliferation efforts directed at Iraq.[278] Hans Blix, head of the IAEA from 1981 to 1997 and chairman of UNMOVIC from 2000 to 2003, concurred when he wrote in 2004 that the system of inspections, "backed up by military pressure and by sanctions that provided control of exports, did work and provided effective containment."[279] According to British intelligence, "while sanctions remain effective Iraq would not be able to produce a nuclear weapon."[280]

Online by Gerhard Peters and John T. Woolley, *The American Project.* Available at: www.presidency.ucsb.edu/ws/?pid=18820. Last accessed: March 9, 2016.

[273] U.S. Department of State, "Saddam Hussein's Iraq," September 1999, in National Security Archive (NSA) Electronic Briefing Book (EBB) 167: "Saddam's Iron Grip: Intelligence Reports on Saddam Hussein's Reign," Doc. 13, p. 22.

[274] See: Alan Cowell, "Iraq Chief, Boasting of Poison Gas, Warns of Disaster if Israelis Strike," *The New York Times*, April 3, 1990, p. A1.

[275] See: Woods (2008, 71–72). See also: Brands and Palkki (2012, 652).

[276] See: Palkki and Smith (2012, 280).

[277] See: Blix (2004, 56–57).

[278] See: Hahn (2012, 113–115).

[279] Blix (2004, 273).

[280] U.K. Joint Intelligence Committee, "Iraq's Weapons of Mass Destruction: The Assessment of the British Government," September 2002, in National Security Archive (NSA) Electronic Briefing Book (EBB) 80, "Iraq and Weapons of Mass Destruction," Doc. 11, pp. 26–27.

The 2003 U.S. Invasion of Iraq

Yet, the international community was concerned with Iraq's stated inability "to locate any additional documentation that might have indicated the extent of development of the nuclear weapon and associated technologies at the time of programme abandonment."[281] Reeling from the September 11, 2001, terrorist attacks against the United States, the administration of George W. Bush (2001–2009) built an argument for invading Iraq, in large part grounded on the risks of Iraqi nuclearization.[282] At his 2002 State of the Union Address, President Bush pledged not to "permit the world's most dangerous regimes to threaten us with the world's most destructive weapons."[283] He soon thereafter reiterated the argument: "Saddam Hussein must understand that if he does not disarm, for the sake of peace, we, along with others, will go disarm Saddam Hussein."[284] On February 5, 2003, in a highly publicized attempt to legitimize the invasion, Secretary of State Colin Powell made a presentation to UNSC titled "Iraq: Failing to Disarm." Powell argued that "possession of the world's most deadly weapons is the ultimate trump card," and the United States "will not and cannot run [the] risk for the American people" that he would "someday use these weapons at a time and place and in a manner of his choosing."[285] The day after Baghdad fell, in the absence of any immediate WMD findings on the ground, White House press secretary Ari Fleischer reiterated this argument: "[W]e have high confidence that they have weapons of mass destruction. *That* is what this war was about."[286]

---

[281] "Note by the Secretary-General," October 8, 1997 w/att: Letter dated October 6, 1997 from the Director General of the International Atomic Energy Agency to the Secretary General, in NSA EBB 80, Doc. 7, p. 9.

[282] Granted, a multiplicity of other arguments was introduced to justify the invasion, including Iraqi human-rights abuses and the need to democratize the Middle East. See: Tenet (2007, 301). But WMD played the central role in the U.S. administration's case for forcible regime change. See: Freedman (2004); Debs and Monteiro (2014).

[283] "President Delivers State of the Union Address," January 29, 2002, White House Archives. Available at: http://georgewbush-whitehouse.archives.gov/news/releases/2002/01/20020129-11.html. Last accessed: April 29, 2016.

[284] "Bush, Blair: Time Running out for Saddam," CNN.com, January 31, 2003. Available at: http://cnn.com/2003/US/01/31/sprj.irq.bush.blair.topics. Last accessed: April 9, 2010.

[285] Colin L. Powell, "Remarks to the United Nations Security Council," February 5, 2003, in NSA EBB 80, Doc. 27.

[286] "Press Briefing with Ari Fleischer," April 10, 2003, emphasis added. Online by Gerhard Peters and John T. Woolley, *The American Presidency Project.* Available at: www.presidency.ucsb.edu/ws/?pid=61071. Last accessed: May 2,

Iraqi nuclear acquisition was expected to have a large effect, essentially making Saddam immune to any externally driven efforts to depose him. The cost of war against a nonnuclear Iraq, in contrast, was expected to be relatively low. U.S. forces had easily prevailed in the 1991 Gulf War and dealt a serious blow to Iraqi military capabilities.

Supporting the most optimistic expectations of those who argued for the war, Baghdad fell a mere twenty-one days after the invasion was launched, and the major operations phase of the war ended six days later. Although fighting a defensive war in its own country against an expeditionary force, the Iraqi army lost all engagements with coalition forces and ended up suffering 9,200 fatalities – or more than 50 times the 172 lives lost by coalition forces.[287]

In assessing the benefit of an invasion, the September 11 attacks played a key role in heightening Washington's concerns. The Bush administration became particularly worried, based on contested intelligence, about the possibility of an Iraqi nuclear handoff to a terrorist group for use against U.S. targets.[288] As the then National Security Advisor Condoleeza Rice put it in her memoirs:

A policy-maker confronted with one assessment that says that Baghdad "could make a nuclear weapon within several months to a year" should it "acquire sufficient fissile material from abroad" and the ... alternative view that could not speak to timing is not likely to take the risks of accepting the latter, particularly after 9/11 and the specter of WMD terrorism. ... We'd failed to connect the dots on September 10 and had never imagined the use of civilian airliners as missiles against the World Trade Center and the

2016. Later, in the absence of WMD findings, Paul Wolfowitz, one of the architects of the war, claimed that there were four motivations behind the invasion: Iraq's WMD, its support for terrorism, the nexus between these two, and the regime's treatment of the Iraqi population. According to Wolfowitz, "for reasons that have a lot to do with the U.S. government bureaucracy we settled on the one issue [WMD] that everyone could agree on." Paul Wolfowitz, "Interview with Sam Tannenhaus." *Vanity Fair*, May 9, 2003. Available at: www.defense.gov/transcripts/transcript.aspx?transcriptid=2594. Last accessed: April 9, 2010.

[287] A U.S. Army study attributes the outcome of the war to "a synergistic interaction between advanced coalition technology and a major skill differential." Biddle et al. (2004, v).

[288] See: Rhodes (2010, 269).

Pentagon; that an unconstrained Saddam might aid a terrorist in an attack on the United States did not seem far-fetched.[289]

Enjoying a preponderance of power over Iraq, Washington set a high standard of evidence on Iraqi compliance, making peace harder to sustain. The invasion of Iraq represented the paradigmatic application of the "1 percent doctrine." This line of reasoning, attributed to Vice President Dick Cheney, suggests that in the post-9/11 security environment, the United States must deal with "low-probability, high-impact" events as if they were certain.[290]

Retrospectively, much has been made of intelligence failures. Clearly, once the Bush administration was convinced of the need for regime change, it mounted the most persuasive campaign to justify the invasion.[291] But the problem was that in order to change U.S. policy, intelligence reports would have to prove that Iraq *did not have and would not develop* WMD. Unfortunately, it is almost impossible for intelligence services to prove a negative. In fact, Western intelligence communities were determined not to miss the next threat and therefore took a more sanguine line regarding Iraq's WMD program. As Robert Jervis notes, "the belief that Iraq had active WMD programs was held by *all* intelligence services, even those of countries that opposed the war."[292] Based on the imperfect information the United States possessed about Iraq's WMD capabilities, "[a] responsible judgment could not have been that the programs had ceased."[293] "Furthermore," Jervis adds, "intelligence could not have said that Saddam would not resume pursuit of WMD at some point in the future."[294]

---

[289] Rice (2011, 169–170).

[290] See: Suskind (2006).

[291] In a meeting of the British cabinet in July 2002, the chief of British intelligence reported on a recent meeting with U.S. officials: "Military action was now seen as inevitable. Bush wanted to remove Saddam, through military action, justified by the conjunction of terrorism and WMD. But the intelligence and facts were being fixed around the policy." United Kingdom, Matthew Rycroft, Private Secretary to the Prime Minister, "Cabinet Minutes of Discussion, S 195/02," July 23, 2002, in National Security Archive (NSA) Electronic Briefing Book (EBB) 418, Doc. 4, p. 1.

[292] Jervis (2010, 134), Jervis's emphasis.

[293] Ibid., 155.

[294] Ibid., 126. Jervis convincingly dismisses the thesis that politicization was responsible for the intelligence failure on Iraq's WMD: "while alternatives [to the picture intelligence reports painted of Saddam's putative

Indeed, Scott Ritter warned in 1998 that "without effective monitoring, Iraq can in a very short period of time measured in months, reconstitute chemical and biological weapons, long-range ballistic missiles to deliver these weapons, and even certain aspects of their nuclear weaponization program."[295] In 2003, Hans Blix stated that UNMOVIC's reports "do not contend that weapons of mass destruction remain in Iraq, but nor do they exclude that possibility."[296]

In Washington, there was a broad political consensus that Saddam possessed, or intended to acquire, WMD.[297] Senator John Kerry (1985–2013) from Massachusetts, soon to become the Democratic presidential nominee, claimed that, "according to the CIA's report, all U.S. intelligence experts agree that Iraq is seeking nuclear weapons. There is little question that Saddam Hussein wants to develop nuclear weapons."[298]

Yet, all the Iraq Survey Group could find after the invasion was evidence that Saddam intended to revive such programs if and when sanctions were lifted. The group's final report states:

Saddam wanted to recreate Iraq's WMD capability – which was essentially destroyed in 1991 – after sanctions were removed. ... Saddam aspired to develop a nuclear capability – in an incremental fashion, irrespective of international pressure and the resulting economic risks – but he intended to focus on ballistic missile and tactical chemical warfare (CW) capabilities.[299]

The war was the final, deadly, manifestation of the strategic relationship between Saddam's Iraq and its adversaries, which prevailed in

WMD programs] should have been considered, doing so probably would not have changed the estimates." Jervis (2010, 128). For a dissenting opinion, see: Rovner (2010, chap. 7).

[295] Scott Ritter, "Interview with Elizabeth Farnsworth," *PBS News Hour*, August 31, 1998. See also: IISS (2002).

[296] Hans Blix, "An Update on Inspection," Presentation to the UNSC, January 27, 2003. Available at: www.un.org/Depts/unmovic/Bx27.htm. Last accessed: May 2, 2016.

[297] For a detailed counterfactual analysis of what an administration of 2000 Democratic presidential candidate Al Gore would have done that conclusively dispels the notion that war was caused by the Bush administration's idiosyncratic preferences, see: Harvey (2012).

[298] John Kerry, Congressional Record. October 9, 2002. Available at: www. freerepublic.com/focus/f-news/1240102/post. Last accessed: January 26, 2015.

[299] Duelfer (2004, 1). For a previous report on WMD findings in Iraq after the invasion, see: Kay (2004).

keeping it nonnuclear. As a weak state without a nuclear ally, Iraq possessed a strong willingness to acquire nuclear weapons but also lacked the opportunity to do so.

Alternative Explanations

In understanding the motivation behind Iraqi nuclear development and its eventual failure, some scholars have focused on domestic political factors. For example, Etel Solingen argues that "the nature of Saddam's regime was a main driver of nuclearization."[300] His strategy for domestic survival was to adopt an "inward-looking model," discounting the costs of international sanctions that would result from his attempt at nuclear acquisition.[301] Saddam pressed for nuclear weapons because they were "a means to endow his regime first, Iraq second, and the Arab world third, with prestige."[302]

We agree that Saddam was greatly concerned about his hold on Iraqi politics, and that a nuclear weapon could significantly improve his regime's standing. At the same time, the crucial feature of the Iraqi case is that nuclear weapons would improve Saddam's standing in the event of an interstate conflict – and Iraq experienced a great deal of conflict. As made clear by recently uncovered archival evidence, Saddam thought of the bomb as offering immunity against nuclear blackmail by Israel and Iran. Granted, targeting countries who were also the adversaries of other Arab states could be politically expedient for him, since Saddam profited from the secular ideology of the Baath party and its pan-Arab foreign policy. Nevertheless, the strategic interaction between Iraq and its foreign foes was a crucial determinant of Iraq's push for nuclear-weapons development.

Put differently, Iraqi domestic politics may have played a role in shaping Saddam's perception that an investment in nuclear weapons was productive. But the threat environment in which Iraq operated certainly mattered as well. Once a leader perceives the security environment to be threatening, he may "turn inward" and press for the bomb in the face of sanctions and international pressure. Yet, the main question of interest for us is whether a state that perceives an investment

[300] Solingen (2007, 153).
[301] See: Ibid., 156.
[302] Ibid., 162.

in nuclear weapons to be productive can successfully obtain the bomb. To answer this question, a consideration of the strategic interaction between Iraq and its adversaries is both necessary and sufficient.

Others would disagree with our contention. For example, Jacques Hymans argues that domestic politics was responsible for the slow progress of the Iraqi nuclear-weapons program. For Hymans, Iraq was doomed to fail in its attempt to acquire the bomb given the neo-patrimonial structure of Saddam's state apparatus.[303] The attack on Osirak did not slow down Iraqi efforts to produce the bomb. Instead it accelerated such efforts. The problem was that the program was mismanaged.[304] The Iraqi state exhibited a profound disregard for scientific expertise. Scientists were repressed and felt pressured to meet unreasonable targets. Contrary to the conventional wisdom, the Gulf War did not stop a nuclear-weapons program that was on the cusp of completion. Instead, Iraq was far from the bomb. When Iraq resumed its nuclear development after expelling the inspectors in 1998, its program was a shell of its erstwhile self.

Certainly, the Iraqi nuclear-weapons program was severely mismanaged. But that did not necessarily lead to its failure. Iraq was a weak state facing serious security threats. Baghdad therefore had the willingness to proliferate, and such willingness was further fueled by foreign attacks, such as the Israeli raid on Osirak. Yet, ultimately Iraq failed to proliferate because it did not have the opportunity to acquire the bomb. Hymans acknowledges that international pressure slowed down the Iraqi program and could have ultimately prevented its fruition. The French did not help rebuild the Osirak facilities.[305] In the 1980s, Iraq pursued its proliferation goals through the inefficient EMIS method because it wanted to avoid raising international suspicion.[306] According to Hymans, the Gulf War did not "cause" the end of the program, because the international community would have most certainly intervened otherwise: "It is far-fetched to assume that Iraq could have had even until 1992 to work on its nuclear weapons project

---

[303] See: Hymans (2012, chapter 3).
[304] For an argument that the destruction of Iraqi capabilities slowed down the program, see: Tamsett (2004). For arguments that the Osirak raid accelerated Iraqi efforts to obtain the bomb, see: Betts (2006), Reiter (2006), Braut-Hegghammer (2011).
[305] See: Hymans (2012, 96).
[306] Ibid., 99.

unperturbed by UN inspectors or American bombs."[307] Herein lies the importance of a strategic approach to nuclear proliferation. Domestic politics is an interesting perspective that enriches the account of the case, but it is not necessary to understand the ultimate failure of the Iraqi program.

One highly controversial chapter in Iraq's strategic interaction with the rest of the world remains the 2003 U.S.-led invasion.[308] Some scholars, such as David Lake, contend that this conflict cannot be understood within the existing rationalist framework for war.[309] According to this view, the mechanisms that form the core of the rationalist framework – information and commitment problems – are constant over time and space and cannot explain both the Iraq War and the absence of conflict against, for example, a nuclearizing North Korea. In the lead-up to the invasion, Lake argues, pathologies of decisionmaking played a central role. On the Iraqi side, Saddam underestimated U.S. resolve, continuing to send mixed signals with multiple audiences in mind.[310] On the American side, Washington miscalculated the cost of a war in Iraq and failed to acknowledge mounting evidence that Saddam had terminated its WMD program. For Lake, such actions require "a behavioral theory of war."[311]

Granted, information and commitment problems are fundamental features of the international system. In order to understand why they contributed to the 2003 invasion of Iraq, we need to appreciate why such problems were particularly salient in this case. Our theory can account for the U.S. decision to invade Iraq and not other targets, such as North Korea, and for the timing of such a decision. The effect of nuclear proliferation was significantly greater for Iraq than for North Korea relative to the cost of preventive war.[312] Thus, preventive war was more likely against Iraq than against North Korea. In addition, the U.S. administration became significantly more concerned about the ability of the intelligence community to detect security threats in

---

[307] Ibid., 118, emphasis added.
[308] See also: Debs and Monteiro (2014).
[309] See: Lake (2010–2011).
[310] For a discussion of possible reasons for Saddam's obstructionist behavior, see also: Hahn (2012, chapters 5 and 6).
[311] Lake (2010–2011, 10). See also: Lake and McKoy (2011–2012); Debs, Monteiro, and Lake (2013).
[312] See our case study of North Korea in Chapter 5.

a timely manner in the wake of the terrorist attacks of September 11, 2001. As a result, the likelihood of war increased thenceforth. Facing ambiguous evidence that Saddam had resumed its nuclear-weapons program, the Bush administration decided to invade Iraq and depose the Iraqi leader.

As would become clear after Saddam was deposed, the preventive war was mistaken. Saddam had not, in fact, resumed its WMD program. Still, this does not mean that the war eludes a rational theory.

On the American side, a rational decisionmaker could determine that, given the large expected consequences of Iraqi nuclear proliferation, even a small likelihood of proliferation could justify an invasion. Because of the difficulty of proving a negative, additional pieces of information might not sway the basic calculation away from the decision to go to war. Moreover, additional information about an existing nuclear-weapons program would not necessarily reassure Washington about Saddam's *future* intentions. The strategic benefit of war for Washington was to eliminate the possibility of current and future proliferation by removing Saddam from power. Were Washington confident about its ability to detect current and future attempts to proliferate, it could have simply used threats to deter Saddam from acquiring the bomb.[313]

On the Iraqi side, a complete understanding of Saddam's behavior would require a richer analysis than our theory allows for, but its main contours can nonetheless be based on a rational framework. Iraqi obstructionism could be due to Baghdad's frustration that Washington, as the preeminent power, would never be satisfied and continue pressing for further concessions. As Tariq Aziz declared in a revolutionary command council and regional command meeting in the early 1990s, and told Rolf Ekeus, UNSCOM director (1991–1997):

[E]ven if we implement and moved from 20% to 30% to 40% to 50% to 60% to 70% in implementation and there is no advancement from your [UNSCOM] side as if we did not implement anything ... you hit us in the past and now you are threatening us that you could attack us. So we do not

---

[313] With such perfect information, peace would have been "costless." For another view on costly peace as a cause of conflict, see: Coe (2012).

have any guarantee that you will not attack us again either if we implement or not implement because the motivations are political.[314]

Furthermore, Iraqi officials feared that additional intelligence could be used to prepare future strikes.[315]

At the same time, Baghdad may have hoped that Washington would stop short of regime change, given the costs of a possibly drawn-out invasion. In March 2002, Saddam downplayed the possibility of a U.S. invasion:

[I]n our assessment, the Americans will not strike, or maybe they will only strike military targets. They will not take an action to change the regime at this time and at least for a while because this requires considering their risks as far as the public opinion impact for attacking two Muslim countries. Bush's relation with his people regarding the conspiracy is currently excellent and he is hoping to strengthen his position in Congress, so his party needs to win the people support. Though, what he is saying [about regime change] requires much more time and there are indications that his popularity is starting to partially diminish.[316]

To obtain a more complete understanding of the benefit of a strong bargaining stance, we could incorporate the role of domestic politics and multiple audiences, which did seem to play a role.[317] Still, the key analytical step needed to understand the arc of Iraq's nuclear program – why Iraq had a high willingness to acquire nuclear weapons, why it was struck preventively, and why the war occurred after

---

[314] "SH-SHTP-A-000-850: Revolutionary Command Council and Regional Command Meeting about UN Inspections and Security Council Resolutions (February 29, 1992)," quoted in Hiroshima (2015, 38–39).

[315] See: Harrer (2014, 21, 176); Hiroshima (2015, 41).

[316] "SH-SPPC-D-000-304: Meeting between Iraqi President Saddam Hussein and Nijirfan Al-Barzani in 2002 Discussing the Possible Attack from the USA (14 March 2002)," quoted in Hiroshima (2015, 46). In an interview in June 2004, Saddam declared that it became clear to him four months before the invasion that the war was inevitable. "Saddam Hussein Conversation with FBI Agent George Piro," June 11, 2004, in NSA EBB 418, Doc. 10, p. 3.

[317] In an interview in June 2004, Saddam declared that the main reason why he did not allow the return of UN inspectors was the Iranian threat. See: NSA EBB 418, Doc. 10, p. 2. The Iraq Survey Group indeed concluded that Saddam wanted to impress upon Iran and possibly also Israel and his own people that he might have some WMD capabilities, while trying to persuade the United States that it had no active program. See: Duelfer (2004).

9/11 – is to understand its strategic predicament, which is the focus of our theory.

In short, Iraq remained nonnuclear because it was a weak state without a nuclear ally. Facing significant security threats in Israel, Iran, and later the United States, Iraq had a high willingness to acquire nuclear weapons, but it eventually failed to proliferate because it lacked the opportunity to do so. Faced with counterproliferation strikes, sanctions, and the threat of preventive war, Baghdad remained nonnuclear until 2003, when the United States invaded Iraq, deposing Saddam from power and giving a fateful end to his bid for the bomb.

In order to acquire nuclear weapons, Iraq's strategic environment would have to evolve in such a way that it would perceive a significant security benefit from nuclearizing and yet possess the opportunity to do so. Such a scenario currently appears highly unlikely. Iraq is weaker than its historical enemies, the United States, Israel, and Iran, and unlikely to find a nuclear sponsor willing to protect it against such possible threats. Iraq's relations with Iran and the United States are also likely to be better than under Saddam, lowering Iraqi willingness to nuclearize.

Iran

Until the Islamic Revolution of 1979, Iran was one of the United States' staunchest allies. As Secretary of State Henry Kissinger (1973–1977) said of Muhammad Riza Pahlavi, the Shah of Iran between 1941 and 1979: "The Shah is a tough, mean guy. But he is our real friend. He is the only one who would stand up to the Soviet Union."[318] With the Revolution, the government in Tehran was no longer a friend of the United States. After students seized the U.S. embassy in Tehran, a hostage crisis gripped both countries for more than a year. With diplomatic lines of communication cut off, relations remained adversarial, reaching their nadir during the presidency of George W. Bush, whose administration characterized Iran as part of an "Axis of Evil" and openly discussed the possibility of preemptive action and regime change.

---

[318] "Memorandum of Conversation," Washington, August 17, 1974, in *Foreign Relations of the United States (FRUS) 1969–1976*, Vol. XXXVII, *Energy Crisis, 1974–1980*, Doc. 2.

One of the main points of contention between the two countries since 2001 has been Iran's nuclear program. Iran's efforts to develop nuclear energy had in fact begun in the early 1970s, with U.S. assistance. At the time, Iran's chief security threat was Iraq, a neighboring state over which it enjoyed conventional superiority. Iran thus had the opportunity to proliferate, but its nuclear efforts were cut short by the Revolution. Since the inception of the Islamic Republic, however, Iran has faced a powerful group of enemies, including the United States and Israel. As a result, Tehran arguably has a high willingness to acquire nuclear weapons, so as to boost its bargaining power and deter future international attempts at regime change. Yet, because of its relative weakness, Tehran lacks the opportunity to proliferate. With Washington keeping all options "on the table" – a not-so-subtle hint at the possibility of preventive military action – Iran agreed in 2015 to a deal that limited its nuclear program and precluded its nuclearization for the foreseeable future.

Iranian Interest in Nuclear Weapons

Iran entered the atomic age as an ally of the United States, intent on cooperating with U.S. efforts to contain communism and using U.S. assistance to protect itself against the Soviet threat. Iran had a conflictual recent past with the Soviet Union, which eyed its oil resources, threatening its territorial integrity. In August 1941, Soviet and British forces invaded Iran, which had declared its neutrality in the Second World War, so as to ensure the safe delivery of war materiel to help Moscow repel the German invasion.[319] In January 1942, the Soviet Union and the United Kingdom signed a tripartite treaty with Iran through which they agreed to withdraw their troops within six months of the end of the war.[320] At the Tehran Conference of 1943, the Allied powers, including the United States, further stated their commitment to the independence, sovereignty, and territorial integrity of Iran.[321] Yet, in November 1944, Soviet pressure led to the resignation of Prime Minister Muhammad Sa'id (1944, 1948–1950). Sa'id had imposed a moratorium on negotiations for oil concessions until the end of the

---

[319] See: Ramazani (1975, 25–44); Lytle (1987, 9–10).
[320] See: Ramazani (1975, 45–53).
[321] Ibid., 66–67.

war, angering the Soviet Union, which hoped to exploit oil fields in northern Iran.[322] A year later, the Soviet Union supported rebellions by Azeri and Kurdish populations in Iran.[323] In January 1946, Tehran called upon the UN to help settle the dispute, in what was the first case brought to the attention of the UNSC, and after U.S. diplomatic pressure, Moscow finally agreed to withdraw its troops.[324]

Concerned that the government of Muhammad Musaddiq (1951–1953), which nationalized the Anglo-Iranian Oil Company in the spring of 1951, would fall into communist orbit, Washington approved covert operations to unseat him.[325] After Musaddiq's deposition, the shah told the U.S. ambassador that he "would always feel deeply indebted for this proof of genuine friendship."[326] Tehran would now tighten its alliance with Washington to protect itself against the Soviet Union. In October 1955, Iran signed the Baghdad Pact, joining Iraq, Pakistan, Turkey, and the United Kingdom in an effort to contain communism.[327] Washington supported this effort[328] but was not formally a signatory of the agreement, leaving Iran keen to obtain greater U.S. support against the Soviet Union.

As the Baghdad Pact began to teeter on the verge of collapse due to a coup in Iraq, Iran obtained increased assurances from Washington. In July 1958, the Iraqi monarchy fell to a coup, and in March 1959, the new government of General Abdul Karim Qasim (1958–1963) withdrew from the Baghdad Pact, which became the Central Treaty Organization (CENTO). Hoping to revive anticommunist efforts in the region, Washington publicly declared its support for the pact and, in

[322] Ibid., 98–99.
[323] Ibid., 114.
[324] Ibid., 127–143.
[325] See: Gavin (1999, 79).
[326] "The Ambassador in Iran (Henderson) to the Department of State," Tehran, August 23, 1953, 10 p.m., in *Foreign Relations of the United States (FRUS) 1952–1954*, Vol. X, *Iran, 1951–1954*, Doc. 353. See also: Rahnema (2015, 4–5).
[327] See the text of the treaty at: "Baghdad Pact; February 4, 1955," The Avalon Project, Yale University. Available at: http://avalon.law.yale.edu/20th_century/baghdad.asp. Last accessed: April 29, 2015.
[328] See: "Circular Telegram from the Department of State to Certain Diplomatic Missions," in *Foreign Relations of the United States (FRUS) 1955–1957*, Vol. XII, *Near East Region; Iran; Iraq*, Doc. 13; "United States Liaison with Baghdad Pact Organization," *Department of State Bulletin*, Vol. XXXIII, No. 857 (November 28, 1955), p. 895.

March 1959, concluded a bilateral defense agreement with Tehran.[329] The JCS recognized the importance of Iran for U.S. strategic objectives in the region, stating that "the basic problem in CENTO, both politically and militarily, is Iran." In their view, the country was "the soft spot in the CENTO defense line and one of the soft spots in the Free World's collective security system surrounding the periphery of the Soviet Bloc."[330]

While remaining tied to the Western bloc, Tehran also sought to reduce tensions with the Soviet Union.[331] Starting in late 1958, the shah started negotiating with Moscow for a mutual nonaggression pact.[332] In September 1962, Soviet first secretary Nikita Khrushchev (1953–1964) accepted the shah's pledge that Iran would not host foreign bases in its territory, marking the beginning of a rapprochement between the two countries.[333] Soon thereafter, Iran received economic assistance from Moscow[334] and, in early 1967, their cooperation extended to the military domain, with their first arms accord.[335] This thawing of relations allowed Iran to begin relocating troops previously stationed on the Soviet border.[336]

As tensions with the Soviet Union decreased, the shah reframed the argument for continued U.S. military assistance. As he explained to Richard M. Nixon in April 1967, Iran should get a free hand in becoming the Free World's regional policeman.[337] With the British

---

[329] See: Cohen (2005, 209, 213).

[330] See: "JCSM–449–60, Joint Chiefs of Staff Views on the Role of the United States in CENTO," undated, in *Foreign Relations of the United States (FRUS)*, 1958–1960, Vol. XII, *Near East Region; Iraq; Iran; Arabian Peninsula*, Doc. 93.

[331] In his 1961 memoirs, the shah reiterated that the Soviet Union represented the greatest threat to Iranian security: "In our experience it is the new imperialism – the new totalitarian imperialism – that the world's less-developed countries today have most to fear." Pahlavi (1961, 131).

[332] See: "Special National Intelligence Estimate SNIE 34-2-59, Consequences of a Soviet-Iranian Non-Aggression Pact," Washington, February 3, 1959, in *FRUS*, 1958–1960, Vol. XII, Doc. 265; "Editorial Note," *FRUS*, 1958–1960, Vol. XII, Doc. 267; Pahlavi (1961, 122).

[333] See: Chubin and Zabih (1974, 61–69); Alvandi (2014). The shah had first made such a pledge in his 1956 visit to Moscow (Pahlavi 1961, 120).

[334] See: Ramazani (1975, 330–338); "Intelligence Memorandum ER IM 72–79," Washington, May 1972, in *Foreign Relations of the United States (FRUS) 1969–1976*, Vol. E-4, *Documents on Iran and Iraq, 1969–1972*, Doc. 181.

[335] See: Ramazani (1975, 343); *FRUS*, 1969–1976, Vol. E-4, Doc. 181.

[336] See: Rubin (1980, 120).

[337] See: Milani (2011, 327).

withdrawal of forces from the Persian Gulf, completed in 1971, Tehran was the ally best positioned to support U.S. strategic interests in the region. The shah was not really concerned about "outright aggression by the Soviet Union." Such an act "would elicit a concerted Free World response" – a response that, in his view, represented "a satisfactory deterrent." Instead, he argued that "[t]he more probable and more logical threat was that of local and limited war." Accordingly, the shah "sought adequate strength to ward off any 'foolish aggressor.' "[338]

This "foolish aggressor" could be any of the Soviet-backed regimes with which Iran had tense relations in the region, in particular Egypt and Iraq. For some time, Egyptian President Gamal Abdel Nasser (1956–1970) threatened to dominate the Middle East. Egypt and Iran clashed indirectly during the Yemeni civil war, when the shah funded royalist forces against Egyptian and republican forces. Nasser's resounding defeat in the Six-Day War of 1967, however, was a severe blow to Egyptian capabilities and prestige, and relations with Cairo ultimately improved.[339] Under President Anwar Sadat (1970–1981), Egypt would further keep its distance from the Soviet Union.

Iraq proved to be a more persistent, albeit weaker, foe. The two countries fought over the control of the Shatt-al-Arab, a common waterway, with crises occurring in 1959–1960, 1961, and again in 1969.[340] Iran also supported the Iraqi Kurds in their fight against Baghdad, providing arms to guerrilla leader Mullah Mustapha Barzani.[341]

Thus, by the early 1970s, Iran's security environment did not warrant a strong willingness to obtain nuclear weapons. At the time, Iran had a rudimentary nuclear energy program. In March 1957, Iran had signed a civil nuclear cooperation agreement with the United States, taking advantage of President Eisenhower's Atoms for Peace program.[342] In November 1967, the Tehran research reactor, built with American assistance, had gone critical.[343]

---

[338] "Memorandum of Conversation," Washington, April 1, 1969, in *FRUS*, 1969–1976, Vol. E-4, Doc. 6. See also: Rubin (1980, 124–125).

[339] See: Chubin and Zabih (1974, 141–169); Ramazani (1975, 421–423).

[340] See: Chubin and Zabih (1974, 170–192).

[341] See: Parsi (2007, 52–58).

[342] See: "Agreement on Cooperation for Civil Uses of Atomic Energy between the United States and Iran," March 5, 1957, in Alexander and Nanes (1980, 290–295).

[343] See: Fuhrmann (2012, 82).

The Quest for Modernity and Energy Independence

Iran's investment in its nuclear program increased significantly in April 1974 with the founding of the Atomic Energy Organization of Iran (AEOI), led by Akbar Etemad (1974–1978). Iran was benefiting from increased oil revenue over a sustained period following the oil shock of 1973, generated by the Organization of the Petroleum Exporting Countries (OPEC). In 1960, Iranian petroleum exports stood at $600 million. They reached $5.6 billion in 1973 and $20.9 billion in 1974.[344] With such resources at his disposal, the shah planned to build an ambitious civilian nuclear program, officially preparing for the day when oil production would taper off:[345] the stated objective was to generate 23,000 megawatts (MWe) of nuclear power by 1994.[346]

To reach this goal, the shah concluded agreements with several Western nuclear powers. In 1974, Iran offered some $1 billion to build a gaseous diffusion plant in southern France, as part of the Eurodif consortium, with the right to purchase enriched uranium, and a promise for the future construction of facilities in Iran.[347] In 1975, the West German company Kraftwerk Union AG began construction of a nuclear power plant at Bushehr.[348] That same year, Iran and the United States reached a protocol agreement on a $12.5 billion deal, which included $6 billion for nuclear development.[349]

AEOI president Etemad was interested in making Iran "a knowledgeable customer"[350] on nuclear matters while ensuring a steady nuclear fuel supply.[351] A domestic reprocessing capability could serve these purposes, but it also posed inherent proliferation risks. To allay

---

[344] See: OPEC (2016).
[345] See: "Report of the NSSM 219 Working Group [,] Nuclear Cooperation Agreement with Iran," [April 1975], in National Security Archive (NSA), Electronic Briefing Book (EBB) 268, "U.S.-Iran Nuclear Negotiations in 1970s Featured Shah's Nationalism and U.S. Weapons Worries," Doc. 5a, p. 1.
[346] See: U.S. Embassy Tehran Airgram A-76 to State Department, "The Atomic Energy Organization of Iran," April 15, 1976, in NSA EBB 268, Doc. 14a, pp. 1, 5.
[347] See: Hamblin (2014, 1124).
[348] See: Patrikarakos (2012, 37).
[349] See: "Summary of Protocol," Washington, undated, in *Foreign Relations of the United States* (FRUS), 1969–1976, Vol. XXVII, *Iran; Iraq, 1973–1976*, Doc. 108.
[350] Quoted in Hamblin (2014, 1125).
[351] See: Tehran Embassy cable 7886 to State Department, "Nuclear Energy Discussions," August 3, 1976, in NSA EBB 268, Doc. 22, p. 2.

international concerns, Iran pledged that its program remained peaceful, signing the NPT in July 1968 and the IAEA Safeguards Agreement in May 1974. In addition, Iran opted for light-water reactors, which are least conducive to the production of nuclear weapons.[352]

Despite Tehran's cautious steps, any buildup in Iran's nuclear capabilities could serve as a foundation for a future nuclear-weapons program, and Iran could later revise its nuclear policy. In an interview with a French newspaper *Les Informations* in June 1974, the shah is reported to have said that Iran would "[c]ertainly" have nuclear weapons, "and sooner than is believed."[353] The Iranian government strongly denied the comments reported in the interview.[354] Yet, in another interview with *Le Monde*, the shah stated that "if in this region each little country tries to arm itself with armaments that are precarious, even elementary, but nuclear, then perhaps the national interests of any country at all would demand that it do the same."[355]

Concerned about the proliferation risks tied to the shah's nuclear program, Washington asked Iran to take a leadership role in accepting tighter safeguards than those contained in IAEA agreements,[356] and to accept a U.S. veto on national reprocessing.[357] Iran initially rejected these U.S. entreaties, which it perceived as discriminatory treatment.[358] But after twice rejecting a U.S. veto in 1975 and

[352] See: Poneman (1981, 575).
[353] Quoted in U.S. Embassy Paris cable 15305 to Department of State, "Interview with Shah," June 24, 1974, in NSA EBB 268, Doc. 1a, p. 2.
[354] See: U.S. Embassy Tehran cable 5192 to Department of State, "Shah's Alleged Statement on Nuclear Weapons," June 25, 1974, in NSA EBB 268, Doc. 1c, p. 2.
[355] Quoted in U.S. Embassy Paris cable 15445 to Department of State, "Further Remarks by Shah on Nuclear Weapons," June 25, 1974, in NSA EBB 268, Doc. 1d, p. 2.
[356] Memorandum to Secretary Kissinger from Alfred Atherton, Bureau of Near Eastern Affairs, and Nelson F. Sievering, Bureau of Oceans, International Environmental, and Scientific Affairs, "Nuclear Energy Agreement for Cooperation with Iran," December 6, 1974, in NSA EBB 268, Doc. 4, p. 5; State Department cable 254826 to Embassy Tehran, "Nuclear Agreement for Cooperation," October 25, 1975, in NSA EBB 268, Doc. 9a, p. 3.
[357] See: National Security Decision Memorandum 292, Washington, April 22, 1975, in *FRUS*, 1969–1976, XXVII, Doc. 115; "National Security Decision Memorandum 324," Washington, April 20, 1976, in *FRUS*, 1969–1976, XXVII, Doc. 173.
[358] See: NSA EBB 268, Doc. 5a, p. 5; NSA EBB 268, Doc. 22, p. 2.

1976,[359] in February 1977 Etemad relented, dropping his search for national reprocessing.[360] By then, it was clear that Washington would not budge on the issue. President Gerald Ford (1973–1977) had publicly rejected Iran's desire for national reprocessing[361] and President Jimmy Carter (1977–1981) had taken a strong stance against proliferation soon after his inauguration as U.S. president.[362] In May 1978, the State Department sent a draft agreement to Tehran, including the U.S. veto on reprocessing. Instead of reprocessing domestically, Washington proposed that Iran do its reprocessing in the United Kingdom, France, or any "another mutually agreed state," with the fabricated fuel to be returned "under conditions or arrangements which are deemed to be more proliferation resistant than those which currently exist."[363] As Iran worried that future U.S. deals with other countries might offer more generous terms on reprocessing, it was granted a "most-favored nation" status, "subject to US law which includes determination of no significant increase in the risk of proliferation associated with approvals for reprocessing."[364] This agreement, however, was never formally signed.[365] Increasing unrest was sweeping across Iran, and the shah fled the country in early 1979.

---

[359] See: NSA EBB 268, Doc. 9a, p. 1; U.S. Embassy Tehran cable 7485 to State Department, "Iranian Counterproposals for Atomic Energy Agreement," July 23, 1976, in NSA EBB 268, Doc. 21, Section 3, p. 4.

[360] See: U.S. Embassy Tehran Cable 1232 to State Department, "Nuclear Power: Comments of Head of Atomic Energy Organization of Iran (AEOI)," February 7, 1977, in NSA EBB 268, Doc. 25a, p. 1.

[361] See: Gerald R. Ford, "Statement on Nuclear Policy," October 28, 1976, *The American Presidency Project*. Available at: www.presidency.ucsb.edu/ws/?pid=6561. Last accessed: April 29, 2016.

[362] In his inaugural address, he spoke of starting in the coming year to move toward "our ultimate goal" of "the elimination of all nuclear weapons from this Earth." Jimmy Carter, "Inaugural Address," January 20, 1977, *The American Presidency Project*. Available at: www.presidency.ucsb.edu/ws/?pid=6575. Last accessed: April 29, 2016.

[363] State Department cable 125971 to Embassy Tehran, "U.S.-Iran Nuclear Cooperation Agreement," May 17, 1978, Confidential, in NSA EBB 268, Doc. 31a, Sec. 8, p. 3.

[364] Department of State cable 226045 to Embassy Canberra, "Provisions of US-Iranian Nuclear Agreement," September 6, 1978, in NSA EBB 268, Doc. 31b, p. 5.

[365] See: Burr (2009, 30).

Revolution and War

The Islamic Revolution led to a complete turnaround of U.S.-Iranian relations. The revolutionary leader, Ayatollah Ruhollah Khomeini (1979–1989), had long complained about the "poisonous culture of imperialism," which he saw as corrupting Muslim society.[366] Back in Tehran after a long exile, Khomeini denounced the United States as the "Great Satan" who had acted as a "tyrant" on the "oppressed" people of Iran.[367]

Tehran now saw the nuclear program as a white elephant – an expensive, ineffective endeavor that cultivated Iranian dependence on the West.[368] In 1979, the new head of the AEOI, Fereidun Sahabi (1979–1981), announced that he wanted to cancel the contract for the two reactors at Bushehr, citing "soaring costs which were never predicted when these agreements were first signed."[369] Continuing the nuclear program, he added, would require foreign assistance, "which again would bind us economically and industrially to those countries."[370] Iran soon became embroiled in legal disputes with West Germany and France, and the construction of nuclear reactors was halted.[371]

Acrimony with Western countries peaked when a group of students stormed the U.S. embassy in Tehran, holding more than fifty U.S. citizens hostage for 444 days. Two weeks earlier, President Carter had allowed the shah to enter the United States for medical treatment. Students vowed that they would not allow the United States to return the shah to power, as it did in 1953, and protested against the interim government of Mehdi Bazargan (1979), which they viewed as lacking "revolutionary decisiveness."[372]

Relations also deteriorated significantly with neighboring Iraq, turning into full-scale war when Saddam Hussein's troops invaded

---

[366] See the "Message to the Pilgrims," February 6, 1971, in Khomeini (1981, 195–199); quote at 195.

[367] Quoted in Ramazani (2013, 72).

[368] For an excellent account, see: Patrikarakos (2012, 90–101).

[369] Quoted in Branigin, William (1979), "Iran Set to Scrap $34 Billion Worth of Civilian Projects," *The Washington Post*, May 30, p. A22.

[370] Quoted in "Iran: AEO Chief Says Cancel," *Nuclear News*, July 1979, Vol. 22, No. 9, p. 72.

[371] See: Patrikarakos (2012, 97–98, 103–105).

[372] Bazargan was meeting with national security adviser Zbigniew Brzezinski (1977–1981) in Algiers at the time. See: Ramazani (2013, 42–45). See also: Pollack (2004, 153–155); Takeyh (2009, 39).

Iran on September 22, 1980. Baghdad had several grievances toward Tehran.[373] With the Algiers Agreement of March 1975, Iraq had reluctantly ceded part of its sovereignty over the Shatt-al-Arab, setting the border between the two countries at the median, deep-water line. Since the fall of the shah, Iran attempted to export the revolution; Iraq, with a majority Shiite population ruled by a Sunni dictator, was a prime target. On April 1, 1980, Iraqi deputy prime minister Tariq Aziz (1979–2003) escaped an assassination attempt by Shiite forces.[374] With Iran diplomatically isolated and reeling from purges in its military, Iraq believed that the time was ripe for an attack. Yet, the war dragged on for almost eight years, causing more than a million casualties and ending in a stalemate.

During the course of the Iran-Iraq War, Bushehr was targeted by Iraq on eight occasions, with the first attack taking place in March 1984. By then, Iran had resolved its dispute with Kraftwerk Union, but the German company refused to complete the reactors while the war was ongoing. That year, Iran set aside funds for their completion, and soon signed a secret agreement with China to train nuclear scientists.[375] In late 1986 or early 1987, Tehran communicated with the network of Pakistani scientist Abdul Qadeer ("A. Q.") Khan with the purpose of obtaining centrifuge technology.[376] Iran's steps in developing nuclear technology were still tentative, but they would accelerate in the 1990s.

After the (Cold) War: Crises and Accord
The end of the Cold War brought a new security outlook for Iran. In the Gulf War of 1990–1991, Saddam was soundly defeated by a U.S.-led coalition. While Iran could take some comfort in the neutralization of the Iraqi threat, the United States was now increasingly involved directly in the Middle East. Iranian relations with Israel also worsened.

For three decades, Iran and Israel had been engaged in a secret alliance.[377] As early as 1958, Israeli prime minister David Ben Gurion (1955–1963) told President Eisenhower about the benefit of an alliance with countries "on the outside perimeter of the Middle East,"

---

[373] See: Karsh (1987, 9–14); Karsh (2002, 7–9).
[374] See: Takeyh (2009, 83).
[375] See: Patrikarakos (2012, 104, 108, 135, 305).
[376] Ibid., 124.
[377] See: Parsi (2007).

including Iran, so as to balance against Israel's Arab neighbors.[378] Iran too benefited from the alliance, given its initial concerns about Soviet influence in the pan-Arab movement. The two countries collaborated in supporting the Kurdish rebellion in Iraq,[379] and this cooperation endured after the Islamic Revolution, given their common enmity with Iraq. In 1981, Iran assisted Israel in its successful raid against Osirak, the Iraqi nuclear reactor that Iranian forces had tried to destroy.[380] In turn, Israel supplied weapons to Iran in its war against Iraq, circumventing the arms embargo imposed by the United States. Notably, Israel acted as a key intermediary in the Iran-Contra affair, through which Washington sold weapons to Iran, in contravention of its own embargo, in an attempt to obtain the release of U.S. hostages.[381]

With Saddam's defeat, however, Israel came to see Iran as its primary threat, given its support for anti-Israeli terrorist groups such as Hezbollah. Prime Minister Yitzhak Rabin (1974–1977, 1992–1995) first made this case in late 1992. In an interview with France 3 television in October, he declared that "Iran is the greatest threat (to peace) and greatest problem in the Middle East ... because it seeks the nuclear option while holding a highly dangerous stance on extreme religious militantism."[382] Over time, this view grew increasingly popular in Israel.[383]

Throughout the 1990s, Iran made important progress in its nuclear program, deepening its cooperation with both China and Russia. In January 1990, Tehran and Beijing began discussions for a uranium conversion facility and signed a ten-year nuclear cooperation agreement, which included plans for the construction of a plutonium-production plant at the Isfahan Nuclear Technology Centre.[384] In January 1995, Russia agreed to complete the construction of the first reactor at Bushehr.[385]

---

[378] Quoted in Segev (1988, 36).
[379] See: Parsi (2007, 52–58).
[380] Ibid., 107.
[381] See: Segev (1988).
[382] Quoted in "Peres Says Iran Greatest Danger to Mideast," *Reuters News*, October 25, 1992. Available at: https://global.factiva.com/redir/default. aspx?P=sa&an=lba0000020011123doap024uz&cat=a&ep=ASE. Last accessed: April 28, 2016.
[383] See: Parsi (2007, 163).
[384] See: Patrikarakos (2012, 135).
[385] Ibid., 140.

Publicly, Iran has consistently claimed that it does not aim at building nuclear weapons. Its supreme leaders, Ayatollahs Khomeini and Sayyed Ali Khamenei (1989–), even declared that nuclear weapons are incompatible with Islam.[386] Instead, Iranian officials claimed that they were exercising their rights to the exploitation of the peaceful uses of nuclear energy, as guaranteed in Article IV of the NPT, which in their view includes the right to enrich uranium. As President Mahmoud Ahmadinejad (2005–2013) put it at the 2005 UNGA, "peaceful use of nuclear energy without possession of nuclear fuel cycle is an empty proposition."[387] Ahmadinejad argued that since Iran was not pursuing nuclear weapons, it should be allowed to enjoy its right to enrich uranium, asking: "Can nations be deprived of scientific and technological progress through the threat of use of force and based on mere allegations of possibility of military diversion?"[388]

By the turn of the millennium, therefore, the Iranian nuclear program was proceeding afoot while Iranian nuclear intentions remained ambiguous. At the same time, the threat of U.S. military action against Iran increased with the muscular foreign policy of President George

---

[386] See: Glenn Kessler, "Did Iran's Supreme Leader Issue a Fatwa against the Development of Nuclear Weapons?," *The Washington Post*, November 27, 2013. Available at: www.washingtonpost.com/news/fact-checker/wp/2013/11/27/did-irans-supreme-leader-issue-a-fatwa-against-the-development-of-nuclear-weapons/. Last accessed: April 28, 2016; Gareth Porter, "When the Ayatollah Said No to Nukes," *Foreign Policy*, October 16, 2014. Available at: http://foreignpolicy.com/2014/10/16/when-the-ayatollah-said-no-to-nukes/. Last accessed: April 28, 2016.

[387] Quoted in "Iranian President's UN Speech," *BBC News*, September 18, 2005. Available at: news.bbc.co.uk/2/hi/uk_news/politics/4257278.stm. Last accessed: July 23, 2016. Both Ahmadinejad's predecessor, reformist president Muhammad Khatami (1997–2005), and his opponent in the 2009 presidential election, Mir-Hossein Moussavi, also affirmed Iran's right to enrich uranium. For example, in 2005, Khatami claimed that uranium enrichment was "our clear right." Quoted in "Iran 'Will Stick to Nuclear Plan,'" *BBC News*, February 9, 2005. Available at: http://news.bbc.co.uk/2/hi/middle_east/4252019.stm. Last accessed: April 28, 2016. During the 2009 presidential election campaign, Mousavi said that "Tehran would not deviate from its nuclear programme if he was elected," according to Agence France Presse. "A right to have technology is different from deviating to weapons building," he added. "Mousavi Vows to change Iran's 'Extremist Image.'" Jay Deshmukh, *Agence France Presse*, April 6, 2009. Available at: https://global.factiva.com/redir/default.aspx?P=sa&an=AFPR000020090406e5460063k&cat=a&ep=ASE. Last accessed: April 28, 2016.

[388] "Address by H.E. Dr. Mahmood Ahmadinejad, President of the Islamic Republic of Iran, before the Sixtieth Session of the United Nations General

W. Bush. As evidenced by the March 2003 invasion of Iraq – another member of the "Axis of Evil" – Bush professed no hesitation about pressing for regime change.[389] This heightened risk of conflict increased the value of an Iranian nuclear deterrent.

Fear of U.S. or Israeli military action also justified Tehran's efforts to raise the cost of a preventive counterproliferation attack. Yet, by hoping to shield its program from outside intervention, Iran fueled doubts about its peaceful intentions and its nuclear program's averred civilian goals. Major nuclear facilities were hidden from the international community or uncovered only at a late stage. In August 2002, an Iranian opposition group, the People's Mujahedin of Iran, revealed the existence of a uranium-enrichment site at Natanz and a heavy-water plant at Arak.[390] The IAEA sent a team of inspectors to Iran and concluded that the country had not met its obligations under its safeguards agreement.[391] In September 2009, Iran sent a letter to the IAEA director general revealing the existence of a uranium-enrichment plant being built at Fordow, near the holy city of Qom. The IAEA again found Tehran in breach of its obligations under the safeguards agreement, noting that Iran should have disclosed this facility as soon as it had taken the decision to build it. "Iran's delay in submitting such information to the Agency," noted the November 2009 report, "does not contribute to the building of confidence."[392] The very size of the facility was difficult to rationalize. As President Barack Obama put it shortly after Iran's revelation in September 2009, "Iran has a right to peaceful nuclear power that meets the energy needs of its people. But

Assembly," September 17, 2005, United Nations, p. 8. Available at: www.un.org/webcast/ga/60/statements/iran050917eng.pdf. Last accessed: January 27, 2016.

[389] "President Delivers State of the Union Address," January 29, 2002, White House Archives. Available at: http://georgewbush-whitehouse.archives.gov/news/releases/2002/01/20020129-11.html. Last accessed: April 29, 2016.

[390] See: Patrikarakos (2012, 175–177).

[391] See: "Implementation of the NPT Safeguards Agreement in the Islamic Republic of Iran," IAEA, GOV/2003/40, June 6, 2003, p. 7. Available at: www.iaea.org/sites/default/files/gov2003-40.pdf. Last accessed: April 29, 2016.

[392] "Implementation of the NPT Safeguards Agreement and Relevant Provisions of Security Council Resolutions 1737 (2006), 1747 (2007), 1803 (2008) and 1835 (2008) in the Islamic Republic of Iran," IAEA, GOV/2009/74, November 16, 2009, p. 7. Available at: www.iaea.org/sites/default/files/gov2009-74.pdf. Last accessed: April 29, 2016.

the size and configuration of this facility is inconsistent with a peaceful program."[393]

During this time, Iran was also developing potential delivery mechanisms, such as the Shahab-III missile, based on North Korean designs. Work on the Shahab-III began in the early 1990s and, in 2002–2003, included attempts to integrate a new spherical payload, as the IAEA later found out.[394] While the U.S. intelligence community did not believe that Iran had an active nuclear-weapons program,[395] Washington was determined to avoid being presented with an Iranian nuclear bomb as a fait accompli. Ultimately, the United States was able to reach an agreement with Tehran to limit Iran's nuclear program: the JCPOA of July 14, 2015. How was Washington able to conclude this accord?

U. S. Nonproliferation and Counterproliferation Efforts

Washington first had to grapple with the possibility of an Iranian nuclear weapon in the 1970s. Initially, Kissinger viewed nuclear assistance as a bargaining chip in ensuring a steady flow of oil, paying little attention to the associated proliferation risks. According to the March 1975 protocol agreement, the United States would receive 500,000–750,000 barrels per day below OPEC prices. Elated, Kissinger declared: "I don't think they realize what they are doing. ... We may have broken OPEC."[396] In a 2005 interview with the *Washington Post*, Kissinger claimed that the nuclear deal with Iran was "a commercial

---

[393] "Statements by President Obama, French President Sarkozy, and British Prime Minister Brown on Iranian Nuclear Facility," September 25, 2009, White House. Available at: www.whitehouse.gov/the-press-office/2009/09/25/ statements-president-obama-french-president-sarkozy-and-british-prime-mi. Last accessed: April 29, 2016.

[394] See: "Final Assessment on Past and Present Outstanding Issues Regarding Iran's Nuclear Programme," IAEA, GOV/2015/68, December 2, 2015. Available at: www.iaea.org/sites/default/files/gov-2015–68.pdf. Last accessed: January 27, 2016.

[395] See: National Intelligence Estimate "Iran: Nuclear Intentions and Capabilities," National Intelligence Council, November 2007. Available at: www.dni.gov/files/documents/Newsroom/Reports%20and%20Pubs/ 20071203_release.pdf. Last accessed: January 28, 2016.

[396] "Memorandum of Conversation," Washington, March 4, 1975, in *FRUS*, 1969–1976, Vol. XXVII, Doc. 109.

transaction. We didn't address the question of them one day moving toward nuclear weapons."[397]

Divining the Shah's Intentions

Other U.S. officials did worry about Iran's nuclear ambitions. Building such a large program could be consistent with securing energy independence, but also with the desire to build a nuclear-weapons capability. In July 1975, U.S. deputy chief of mission Jack Miklos (1974–1978) stated that no Iranian official "has satisfactorily explained how Iran expects to absorb 23,000 MWe of additional power within the next twenty years." In his view, it was "possible" that Iran's interest in developing a nuclear program was "in part, motivated by the desire to preserve the option of developing nuclear weapons should the region's power balance shift toward the nuclear."[398] Not only could threats to the security of Iran become more severe, but developments within Iran could also contribute to its nuclearization. According to a memorandum from the Bureau of Near Eastern Affairs, "[a]n aggressive successor to the Shah might consider nuclear weapons the final item needed to establish Iran's complete military dominance of the region."[399]

To address these concerns, Washington sought a veto over Iranian reprocessing activities and, as we have seen, obtained one in the agreement of 1978. (Kissinger himself approved the policy of seeking a U.S. veto in reprocessing in late 1974, apparently reappraising the importance of nonproliferation goals.[400] In early 1977, he stated: "As an historian, I am convinced that some nuclear spread is extremely probable. As a policy-maker, I feel we should move heaven and earth. Even if we can buy only a decade its [*sic*] worth it to prevent it."[401])

---

[397] Quoted in Dafna Linzer, "Past Arguments Don't Square with Current Iran Policy," *The Washington Post*, March 27, 2005, p. A15.

[398] Tehran Embassy cable 5939 to State Department, "Multinational Nuclear Centers: Assessment of Iranian Attitudes toward Plutonium Reprocessing," July 17, 1975, in NSA EBB 268, Doc. 7, p. 2.

[399] Memorandum from Alfred L. Atherton Jr., Bureau of Near Eastern Affairs (NEA), to the secretary of state through Mr. Sisco, "Cooperation with Iran: Nuclear Energy," June 20, 1974, p. 4, in NSA EBB 268, Doc. 2, p. 4.

[400] See: NSA EBB 268, Doc. 4, p. 5.

[401] Memorandum of Conversation, "Secretary's Meeting with the General Advisory Committee on Arms Control and Disarmament," January 6, [1977], in NSA EBB 268, Doc. 24, pp. 6–7.

Coercive Threats against the Revolutionary Regime

Little more than a decade later, Iran had become an enemy of the United States, which was by then a preponderant power in the region, after the defeat of Saddam Hussein; and without a contest the most powerful state in the world, after the fall of the Soviet Union. In this novel geostrategic reality, the Clinton administration announced a new foreign policy for the Middle East, called "dual containment."[402] Washington would no longer support one privileged ally, as it did with the shah's Iran (which it supported as a regional policeman, in order to check Soviet influence in the region) or, later, with Iraq (which it supported during the 1980s in its war against a stronger Iran). Instead, Washington would contain both Iran and Iraq. In practice, this policy was quite aggressive against Saddam, including sanctions and air strikes against its regime.[403] Against Iran, the military option was not employed.[404] Nevertheless, Washington tried to restrict Tehran's access to nuclear technology through embargoes and diplomatic pressure on its potential suppliers.[405]

This U.S. strategy met with mixed success. In September 1995, China agreed to cancel its contract to supply Tehran with a pair of nuclear reactors.[406] Two years later, Beijing promised that it would offer no further assistance to the Iranian nuclear program.[407] Perhaps unsurprisingly, Russia proved less cooperative with Washington's aims. In May 1995, Russian president Boris Yeltsin (1991–1999) agreed to

---

[402] Martin Indyk, "The Clinton Administration's Approach to the Middle East," speech given at the Washington Institute for Near East Policy, May 18, 1993, The Washington Institute. Available at: www.washingtoninstitute.org/policy-analysis/view/the-clinton-administrations-approach-to-the-middle-east. Last accessed: April 29, 2016.

[403] See our case study of Iraq in this chapter.

[404] See: Pollack (2004, 263).

[405] See: "Iran Sanctions Act of 1996," August 5, 1996, Department of the Treasury. Available at: www.treasury.gov/resource-center/sanctions/Programs/Documents/isa_1996.pdf. Last accessed: January 28, 2016; "Iran Nonproliferation Act of 2000," March 14, 2000, U.S. Congress. Available at: www.congress.gov/106/plaws/publ178/PLAW-106publ178.pdf. Last accessed: January 28, 2016.

[406] See: Elaine Sciolino, "China Cancels a Sale to Iran, Pleasing U.S.," *The New York Times*, September 28, 1995, p. A1.

[407] See: John M. Broder, "Beijing to Halt Nuclear Deals with Iran," *The New York Times*, October 30, 1997, p. A1.

cancel the sale of gas centrifuges, but not the sale of two nuclear reactors;[408] Moscow still planned to complete the Bushehr nuclear plant.

The Bush administration put the military option squarely on the table, and there was much speculation that Iran would be Washington's next target after deposing Saddam. According to a senior British official: "Everyone wants to go to Baghdad. Real men want to go to Tehran."[409] The United States invaded Iraq on March 20, 2003, and declared victory over Saddam on May 1. With American power in the region reaching its apex, Tehran presented a proposal to the Swiss ambassador for a revision of U.S.-Iranian relations. Among other things, Iran pledged to put its nuclear program under intrusive international inspections and sign the Additional Protocol to the NPT.[410]

Yet, Washington did not respond to this proposal. According to Larry Wilkerson, chief of staff (2002–2005) of Secretary of State Colin Powell (2001–2005), hard-liners opposed any dialogue with Iran, saying "[w]e don't speak to evil."[411] European states picked up the initiative in negotiations. The foreign ministers of the United Kingdom, France, and Germany (the EU-3) concluded the Tehran Agreement with Iran in October 2003, whereby Iran voluntarily suspended its uranium enrichment and reprocessing activities, and pledged to sign the IAEA Additional Protocol.[412] But negotiations failed to produce a long-term settlement.

---

[408] See: "A Summit for the Season," *The New York Times*, May 11, 1995, p. A28; "Iran Relieved about Nuclear Sale," *The New York Times*, May 12, 1995, p. A8.

[409] Quoted in John Barry, "Beyond Baghdad: Expanding Target List," *Newsweek*, August 18, 2002. Available at: www.newsweek.com/beyond-baghdad-expanding-target-list-144099. Last accessed: April 28, 2016.

[410] For the text of the offer, see: Parsi (2007, 341–342). See also: Gareth Porter, "Burnt Offering," *The American Prospect*, May 21, 2006. Available at: http://prospect.org/article/burnt-offering. Last accessed: April 28, 2016; Glenn Kessler, "In 2003, U.S. Spurned Iran's Offer of Dialogue," *The Washington Post*, June 18, 2006. Available at: www.washingtonpost.com/wp-dyn/content/article/2006/06/17/AR2006061700727.html. Last accessed: April 28, 2016; Parsi (2012, 1–8).

[411] Quoted in Gordon Corera, "Iran's Gulf of Misunderstanding with U.S." *BBC News*, September 25, 2006. Available at: http://news.bbc.co.uk/2/hi/middle_east/5377914.stm. Last accessed: April 28, 2016.

[412] See: "Full text: Iran Declaration," October 21, 2003, *BBC News*. Available at: http://news.bbc.co.uk/2/hi/middle_east/3211036.stm. Last accessed: April 28, 2016. For the text of the interim Paris agreement, concluded in November 2004, see: "Communication Dated 26 November 2004 Received from the Permanent Representatives of France, Germany, the Islamic Republic of

In August 2005, Tehran announced that it had resumed its uranium enrichment,[413] and in April 2006, Iran enriched uranium to 3.5 percent, sufficient to power light-water reactors. "Iran has joined the nuclear countries of the world," claimed President Ahmadinejad.[414] Within two months, the United States was ready to enter into negotiations with Iran, but its demand that Iran suspend its uranium enrichment activities as a precondition to the talks was unacceptable to Tehran.[415] Failing to begin negotiations, the United States imposed sanctions against Iran for the next two and a half years, both unilaterally and through the UN.[416]

In its first months in office in 2009, the Obama administration conducted a review of U.S. foreign policy toward Iran, and decided to follow a "dual track" approach: prioritizing diplomacy and engagement without preconditions, while preparing for sanctions if Iran did not comply.[417] Fending off pressure from Congress and Israel for quick

Iran and the United Kingdom Concerning the Agreement Signed in Paris on 15 November 2004," IAEA, INFCIRC/637, November 26, 2004. Available at: www.iaea.org/sites/default/files/publications/documents/infcircs/2004/infcirc637.pdf. Last accessed: January 28, 2016.

[413] See: Thomas Fuller and Nazila Fathi, "U.N. Agency Urges Iran to Halt Its Nuclear Activity," *The New York Times*, August 12, 2005, p. A8.

[414] Quoted in Nazila Fathi, David E. Sanger, and William J. Broad, "Iran Reports Big Advance in Enrichment of Uranium," *The New York Times*, April 12, 2006, p. A1.

[415] See: Michael A. Fletcher and Glenn Kessler, "U.S. to Join Talks with Iran if Uranium Enrichment Stops," *The Washington Post*, June 1, 2006, p. A01; "Defiant Iran: A Moment of Truth for Russia and China," *The Washington Post*, July 12, 2006, p. A14.

[416] See: "United Nations Security Council Resolution 1696 (2006)," IAEA, S/RES/1696 (2006), July 31, 2006. Available at: www.iaea.org/sites/default/files/unsc_res1696-2006.pdf. Last accessed: January 28, 2016; "Iran Freedom Support Act," U.S. Public Law 109–293, September 30, 2006, Department of the Treasury. Available at: www.treasury.gov/resource-center/sanctions/Documents/pl109_293.pdf. Last accessed: January 28, 2016; "United Nations Security Council Resolution 1737 (2006)," IAEA, S/RES/1737 (2006), December 27, 2006. Available at: www.iaea.org/sites/default/files/unsc_res1696-2006.pdf. Last accessed: January 28, 2016; "United Nations Security Council Resolution 1747 (2007)," IAEA, S/RES/1747 (2007), March 24, 2007. Available at: www.iaea.org/sites/default/files/unsc_res1747-2007.pdf. Last accessed: January 28, 2016; "United Nations Security Council Resolution 1803 (2008)," IAEA, S/RES/1803 (2008), March 3, 2008. Available at: www.iaea.org/sites/default/files/unsc_res1803-2008.pdf. Last accessed: January 28, 2016; "United Nations Security Council Resolution 1835 (2008)," IAEA, S/RES/1835 (2008), September 27, 2008. Available at: www.iaea.org/sites/default/files/unsc_res1835-2008.pdf. Last accessed: January 28, 2016.

[417] See: Parsi (2012, 54).

action on additional sanctions, Obama saw a diplomatic opening in June when Iran asked the IAEA to purchase nuclear fuel for the Tehran Research Reactor. Washington proposed that the fuel be produced from Iran's own stockpile of low-enriched uranium (LEU), which Iran would send abroad for enrichment. Iranian assent would represent an important confidence-building measure: Tehran would be less concerned about relinquishing a stockpile of LEU if it did not intend to enrich it to nuclear-weapons grade.

Officials in the five permanent members of the UNSC and Germany (the P5+1) believed that they had an initial agreement with Iran in Geneva in early October, but Tehran delayed its final approval, missing a deadline imposed by the IAEA.[418] In late November, the IAEA referred Iran to the UN Security Council,[419] and the United States and the European Union prepared to impose sanctions on the country.[420]

Washington ratcheted up the pressure on Tehran with cyber warfare and threats of preventive action. In 2010, a software virus, Stuxnet, affected operations at the Natanz enrichment facility. Later it was revealed that the virus had been launched as a joint U.S.-Israeli

---

[418] See: Fitzpatrick (2010); Parsi (2012, 127–142).

[419] See: "Implementation of the NPT Safeguards Agreement and Relevant Provisions of Security Council resolutions 1737 (2006), 1747 (2007), 1803 (2008) and 1835 (2008) in the Islamic Republic of Iran." IAEA, GOV/ 2009/82, November 27, 2009. Available at: www.iaea.org/sites/default/files/ gov2009-82.pdf. Last accessed: January 28, 2016.

[420] Tehran did ultimately agree to the fuel swap in May 2010, in a joint declaration negotiated with Brazil and Turkey. But for the Obama administration, this "Tehran Declaration" came too late; in the interim, Iran had increased its stockpile of LEU and also started enriching uranium to 19.75 percent. Brazilian and Turkish officials were furious, since these factors were not described as deal breakers in an April 20 letter that Obama had sent to Brazil. See: Glenn Kessler, "Letter at Center of U.S.-Brazil Dispute over Iran Deal; Lula's Government Says Obama Note Was Used as Guide in Nuclear Talks," *The Washington Post*, May 28, 2010, p. A17. On the sanctions, see: United Nations Security Council, "Resolution 1929 (2010)," IAEA, S/RES/ 1929 (2010), June 9, 2010. Available at www.iaea.org/sites/default/files/unsc_ res1929-2010.pdf. Last accessed: January 28, 2016; "U.S. Comprehensive Iran Sanctions, Accountability, and Divestment Act of 2010," July 1, 2010, Department of the Treasury. Available at www.treasury.gov/resource-center/ sanctions/Documents/hr2194.pdf. Last accessed: January 28, 2016; Stephen Castle, "Europe Toughens Penalties on Iran for Nuclear Work," *The New York Times*, July 27, 2010, p. A7.

operation to disable Iranian centrifuges.[421] The United States and Israel also considered military options in preventing Iran from acquiring a nuclear bomb. Tel Aviv especially feared that its window of opportunity for striking the Iranian program preventively was closing.[422] Israel pressured its U.S. ally to state a clear red line for the Iranian program, backed up by the threat of war, and discussions of preventive strikes were especially heated in the run-up to the 2012 U.S. presidential election.[423] In his address at the UN in late September that year, Prime Minister Netanyahu physically drew a red line on the diagram of a bomb, claiming that Iran was getting closer to obtaining the necessary fuel and should be stopped by spring or early summer 2013 at the latest.[424] With greater conventional capabilities, Washington had a longer window of opportunity to consider preventive strikes against the Iranian program. In the end, neither state launched a preventive counterproliferation strike.

---

[421] See: David E. Sanger, "Obama Order Sped Up Wave of Cyber Attacks Against Iran," *The New York Times*, June 1, 2012, p. A1.

[422] For a 2007 study that is relatively optimistic of Israeli capabilities, see: Raas and Long (2007). Over time, views of Israeli capabilities to destroy Iranian nuclear facilities have become more skeptical. In December 2009, former military intelligence chief Aharon Ze'evi-Farkash (2002–2006) declared that "Israel cannot deal with the Iranian threat on its own. It can only take part in a course of action." Daniel Edelson, "Former MI Chief: Israel Can't Face Iran Alone," March 11, 2009. Available at www.ynetnews.com/articles/0,7340,L-3684838,00.html. Last accessed: February 2, 2016. In 2010 and 2011, Prime Minister Benjamin Netanyahu and Defense Minister Ehud Barak (1999–2001, 2007–2013) allegedly supported the idea of a strike but were overruled by other members of the government, concerned about the operational difficulties of such a mission. "Barak: Netanyahu Wanted to Strike Iran in 2010 and 2011, But Colleagues Blocked Him," *The Times of Israel*, August 21, 2015. Available at: www.timesofisrael.com/barak-netanyahu-wanted-to-strike-iran-in-2010-and-2011-but-colleagues-blocked-him/. Last accessed: April 28, 2016. In May 2011, Meir Dagan, the former leader of Mossad (2002–2011), said that a strike against Iran's nuclear facilities would be "a stupid idea," because it might not be successful and could trigger a long war. Isabel Kershner, "Ex-Mossad Chief Says Strike on Iran Would Be 'Stupid'," *The New York Times*, May 9, 2011, p. A8.

[423] See: Debs and Monteiro (2012); Kahl (2012); Kroenig (2012); Mark Landler and Helene Cooper, "Obama Rebuffs Netanyahu on Setting Limits on Iran's Nuclear Program," *The New York Times*, September 14, 2012, p. A7.

[424] Rick Gladstone and David E. Sanger, "Nod to Obama by Netanyahu on Iran Bomb: But He Tells U.N. That Time to Act is 2013," *The New York Times*, September 28, 2012, p. A1.

Efforts for a diplomatic solution were reignited in September 2013, when Obama and Iranian president Hassan Rouhani (2013–) spoke on the phone, the highest level conversation between the two countries since 1979.[425] Three months later, Iran and the P5+1 agreed on a Joint Plan of Action (JPOA), a temporary accord constraining Iran's nuclear program in exchange for partial sanctions relief.[426] In July 2015, a JCPOA was produced,[427] taking effect on January 16, 2016. In exchange for sanctions relief, Iran assented to important limitations on its nuclear program and agreed to intrusive inspections. For its uranium-enrichment program, Iran is allowed to operate only 5,060 first-generation centrifuges for ten years, and they must be confined to Natanz; it must keep its uranium enrichment to a low level of 3.67 percent for fifteen years; and it must reduce its stockpile of enriched uranium by 98 percent, to 300 kilograms, less than the amount required (at that level of enrichment) for a nuclear bomb. Together, these steps are expected to increase the amount of time that Iran needs to build a nuclear weapon, from two-to-three months to twelve months.[428] In sum, Iran has forfeited any short-run designs to nuclearize for the foreseeable future. Vulnerable to preventive counterproliferation action, Tehran acceded to halt its nuclear development.

[425] See: Jeff Mason and Louis Charbonneau, "Obama, Iran's Rouhani Hold Historic Phone Call," *Reuters*, September 28, 2013. Available at: www.reuters.com/article/us-un-assembly-iran-idUSBRE98Q16S20130928. Last accessed: April 28, 2016.

[426] See: "Communication Dated 27 November 2013 Received from the EU High Representative Concerning the Text of the Joint Plan of Action," IAEA, INFCIRC/855, November 27, 2013. Available at: www.iaea.org/sites/default/files/publications/documents/infcircs/2013/infcirc855.pdf. Last accessed: January 28, 2016.

[427] See: "Communication Dated 24 July 2015 Received from China, France, Germany, the Russian Federation, the United Kingdom, the United States of America (the E3/EU+3) and the Islamic Republic of Iran Concerning the Text of the Joint Comprehensive Plan of Action (JCPOA)," IAEA, INFCIRC/887, July 31, 2015. Available at: www.iaea.org/sites/default/files/infcirc887.pdf. Last accessed: January 28, 2016.

[428] See: Goldenberg et al. (2015, 12–13); Perkovich et al. (2015); Samore (2015). For arguments that the JCPOA produces a shorter break-out time, see: Alan J. Kuperman, "The Iran Deal's Fatal Flaw," *The New York Times*, June 23, 2015, p. A23; David Albright, Houston Wood, and Andrea Stricker, "Breakout Timelines under the Joint Comprehensive Plan of Action," August 18, 2015, *Institute for Science and International Security Report*; and discussion

Alternative Explanations

There is much scholarly debate on the Iranian nuclear program, beginning with its initial purpose under the shah and culminating with the JCPOA – whether Iran will comply with its obligations under the agreement, whether Washington obtained the best possible deal, and whether it should have opted for a diplomatic solution in the first place. Iran's nuclear program has been – and is likely to remain – one of the most hotly contested topics in nuclear politics.

Considering the early years of the program, some argue that the shah was motivated by a search for prestige and a sense of pride; and, as such, Iran's nuclear program represents a challenge for security-based explanations.[429] According to Jim Walsh, the shah "made his most earnest efforts to build a nuclear infrastructure at a time when relations with his chief protector, the United States, were arguably at their best and when the threat of a Soviet Union had receded."[430] Because the shah's motivations were not based on security concerns, this argument goes, U.S. assurances were unsuccessful in preventing his nuclear efforts.

While the shah certainly had ambitious goals for Iran's nuclear program, he had not yet made a decision to build nuclear weapons. In fact, the Iranian program was still in its early stages when the shah was deposed by the 1979 revolution – neither of the reactors at Bushehr had been completed. This ambiguity in the shah's nuclear purposes is quite consistent with our security-based approach. The threat from the Soviet Union had receded, and Iran enjoyed conventional superiority over its immediate adversaries, so the shah's willingness to acquire nuclear weapons was relatively low. Iran did not need nuclear weapons to remain the region's strongest power. Instead, the shah may have wanted to acquire the option to build nuclear weapons at a later date. The real question in evaluating U.S. nonproliferation policy is thus hypothetical: would the United States have been able to prevent Iran

---

in Graham Allison and Gary Samore, "The Iran Op-Ed's Fatal Flaw," July 2, 2015. Available at: http://iranmatters.belfercenter.org/blog/iran-op-eds-fatal-flaw. Last accessed: January 29, 2016; Alan J. Kuperman, "Misleading Spin on Centrifuges," July 6, 2015. Available at: http://iranmatters.belfercenter.org/blog/misleading-spin-centrifuges. Last accessed: January 29, 2016.

[429] See: Patrikarakos (2012, 29); Walsh (2012, 111).
[430] Walsh (2012, 111).

from obtaining nuclear weapons if the shah had wanted to obtain them later on? Here, a security-based explanation suggests that Washington's leverage would have been limited. Since Iran enjoyed conventional superiority over its potential regional enemies, it had the opportunity to proliferate on its own, and coercive measures would likely have failed.

Other scholars question the usefulness of a security-based explanation for explaining the nuclear behavior of the revolutionary regime. According to Etel Solingen, Iraq was the main security threat that could have motivated a search for nuclear weapons in Iran since the 1980s. Therefore, the persistence of the Iranian nuclear program after the 2003 overthrow of Saddam's regime can be better understood by focusing on the economic preferences of ruling elites: Iran's radical inward-looking leadership has shown great willingness to incur the opportunity costs of developing a nuclear deterrent.[431]

Still, there appears to be an important degree of continuity in Iran's nuclear development. The shah had nuclear ambitions. Even outward-looking President Khatami asserted that Iran had a right to enrich uranium. Iran advanced down the nuclear path despite the varying economic preferences of its elites over time. Furthermore, these preferences cannot account for why Iran has not successfully acquired a nuclear deterrent. To understand both Iranian nuclear development and its nuclear forbearance, our strategic security-based approach proves valuable. As a state with relatively weak conventional capabilities, Iran is likely to possess the willingness to nuclearize, but also to lack the opportunity to do so. Recent evidence, including the May 2003 offer for normalized relations, highlight Iran's concerns about U.S.-led attempts to promote regime change. Ultimately, as a state with weak conventional capabilities, Iran has been coerced to accept limits on its nuclear program, with Washington allowing all options to remain "on the table," and imposing a robust sanctions regime backed by the threat of military action.[432]

Finally, yet other scholars debate whether the United States should have tried to prevent Iran's nuclearization by reducing its security concerns, thus removing its willingness to develop nuclear weapons.

[431] See: Solingen (2007, 185–186).
[432] See: David E. Sanger, "Diplomacy and Sanctions, Yes. Left Unspoken on Iran? Sabotage," *The New York Times*, January 20, 2016, p. A8.

Writing in 2012, Trita Parsi argued that the "dual track" approach was doomed to fail, since the threat of military action undermines the level of trust needed to establish constructive negotiations. In his view, Obama was too quick to impose sanctions on Iran.[433]

Given Iran's disadvantage in conventional capabilities, a threatening U.S. approach could lead Tehran to see a significant benefit in acquiring nuclear weapons, even if that meant that war could break out. But by the same token, the United States enjoyed considerable leverage to obtain a deal limiting Iran's nuclear program, as it did in July 2015.[434] In the end, U.S. coercion worked.

Taking stock, in the early years of the nuclear program under the shah, Iran had a weak willingness to acquire nuclear weapons, given its advantage in conventional capabilities over its immediate threats. Since the Islamic revolution, relations with the United States and Israel have deteriorated. Given an unfavorable balance of power for Iran vis-à-vis these two threats, nuclear weapons would bring a significant security benefit. Tehran's willingness to build the bomb grew. By the same token, however, the international community has significant leverage to limit the Iranian program. In the summer of 2015, the United States was able to obtain a deal aimed at ensuring a long break-out time, with intrusive inspections, allowing for a response in case Iran decides to obtain a nuclear weapon.

The 2015 JCPOA goes a long way toward ensuring the maintenance of Iran's nonnuclear status for the next fifteen years. Past that point, Iran's nuclearization will again depend on the evolution of its strategic situation. Should its security rivals continue to be Israel and the United States, it is highly likely that Tehran will maintain its willingness to build the bomb but lack the opportunity to do so. Either through renewed coercive measures or through counterproliferation military action, Iran's adversaries are likely to be able to ensure the continuation of its nonnuclear status. According to our theory, Iranian nuclearization would only obtain in one of two hypothetical transformations in the country's strategic environment: greater conventional strength, or protection from an ally that is willing to deter aggression against Iranian territory but unwilling to extend sufficient security commitments to undermine Iranian willingness to nuclearize. Should

---

[433] See: Parsi (2012, 152, 235).
[434] On the challenges of coercive diplomacy, see: Jervis (2013).

Iran continue to be a relatively weak and unprotected state – or should it become protected by a reliable ally – its nuclearization will remain unlikely.

* * *

The four historical cases we analyzed in this chapter prompt several pertinent counterfactuals. To begin with, regarding the Brazilian case, the relevant counterfactual is a hypothetically highly threatened Brazil. In our view, in a highly threatening security environment, Brazil would have been willing to acquire nuclear weapons and, given its high relative power vis-à-vis any other state in its region, it would in all likelihood ultimately have proliferated. We therefore devoted considerable attention in the case to highlighting how Brazil did not perceive its security environment as highly threatening and how, in consequence, Brasília was never willing to acquire the bomb. Specifically, in contrast to the conventional view, Brazil did not think of Argentina as a security adversary. Rather, the relationship between the two states can be characterized as one of friendly rivalry, and there was much nuclear collaboration between the two.

Additionally, for each of the three other cases we analyzed – the Soviet Union, Iraq, and Iran – one should posit two relevant types of counterfactuals. In the first set of counterfactuals, we should think about what would have happened if none of these states had faced a high-level security threat. Our contention is that, as with Brazil, these other states would not have possessed the willingness to proliferate and, thus, would not have attempted to acquire the bomb.

The second set of relevant counterfactuals for these cases requires us to alter the relative power of the state developing nuclear weapons vis-à-vis its adversaries and see how this change would have altered their opportunity to go nuclear. In the case of the Soviet Union, we contend that Moscow would not have had the opportunity to acquire nuclear weapons had it possessed lower relative power. Specifically, had the United States not been convinced that launching a preventive attack would have been more costly than sustaining the effect of Soviet nuclear acquisition, Washington would in all likelihood have been able to coerce the Soviet Union into remaining nonnuclear by credibly threatening it with a preventive strike. Either Moscow would have internalized this threat, or it would have been subject to preventive military action. In contrast, the relevant counterfactual in the Iraqi and Iranian cases is to think of what would have happened if they had possessed sufficient relative power to impose high costs on their adversaries in case these launched a preventive counterproliferation strike. In our view, a relatively stronger Iraq or Iran would have had the opportunity to acquire the bomb and would have done so if the level of threat they faced remained high until they completed their nuclear development.

After having spent this chapter examining the role of threats and relative power in shaping the odds of nuclear acquisition by states that do not possess an alliance partner capable of protecting them, in the next two chapters we shift our focus to the dynamics that shape nuclear proliferation among states that benefit from security guarantees extended by a sponsor. Specifically, the next chapter looks at proliferation attempts by loose allies, whose patrons were only moderately committed to their security. Then, in Chapter 6, we will turn to cases of proliferation among close allies, which benefit from robust security guarantees.

5 | Loose Allies and Proliferation

In this chapter, we use eight case studies — of Sweden, China, Israel, India, South Africa, North Korea, Taiwan, and Pakistan – to delineate the dynamics of proliferation among states that are offered limited security assurances. As we saw in Chapter 2, the presence of a security sponsor dampens a state's willingness to proliferate and may, when the security guarantees offered by the sponsor are deemed credible, make it unwilling to pursue the bomb. At the same time, when a relatively weak country is offered even a modest security guarantee, it will be able to impose higher costs on any adversary that considers a preventive counterproliferation strike, thereby improving its opportunity to acquire nuclear weapons. Loose security alliances may thus provide a protégé with the opportunity to go nuclear while not undermining its willingness to do so. When this happens, the protégé will follow the second causal pathway to proliferation laid out in our theory.

We start with the case of Sweden, which, after spending the 1950s embodying the willingness to acquire nuclear weapons in order to ameliorate its security outlook and making considerable progress toward the bomb, inverted this path in the early 1960s and dropped its nuclear ambitions. The reason for this turnaround was a decrease in the level of threat faced by Sweden, concomitant with Stockholm's policy of stealthy rapprochement with NATO, which in effect placed Sweden under the U.S. nuclear umbrella, undermining the country's willingness to go nuclear.

We then turn to seven cases of states that maintained their willingness to proliferate: China, Israel, India, South Africa, North Korea, Taiwan, and Pakistan. These cases enable us to highlight the role of nonproliferation efforts by a loose ally in shaping the patterns of nuclear proliferation.

When protégés are relatively strong vis-à-vis their adversaries, they would have the opportunity to acquire nuclear weapons on their own, even if abandoned by their security sponsors. This means that, in order to be successful, their sponsors will have to concentrate their non-proliferation policies on taking away their protégé's willingness to acquire the bomb. But in the case of loose allies such as China, Israel, India, South Africa, and North Korea, the overlap of interests between sponsor and protégé was insufficient for the sponsor to be willing to extend security guarantees that were robust enough for the protégé to no longer be willing to go nuclear. As we will see, all these five protégés were willing to proliferate because they were unable to extract more robust security guarantees from their security sponsors. Given their ability to impose high costs on their adversaries in the event of a preventive counterproliferation strike, they also had the opportunity to go nuclear, and ended up acquiring the bomb.

In contrast, a weak state's opportunity to nuclearize is highly dependent on the protection of a security sponsor during its nuclear development period. In principle, the security sponsor can ensure that its weak protégé does not have the opportunity to proliferate by threatening it with abandonment. Such was the case of Taiwan, whose relative weakness vis-à-vis China allowed the United States to effectively coerce Taipei into maintaining its nonnuclear status despite receiving modest U.S. security guarantees.

In some circumstances, however, the security sponsor may prioritize other foreign policy goals over its nonproliferation concerns. When this happens, it may be willing to turn a blind eye to the protégé's nuclear efforts, allowing it to nuclearize while the protégé benefits from its protection. Such was the case with Pakistan. After the Soviet invasion of Afghanistan, Pakistan became a key ally in fighting the spread of communism, and the United States looked the other way as Islamabad developed a nuclear capability. Effectively, the United States provided Pakistan with an opportunity to proliferate.

Taken together, the six cases of nuclearization examined in this chapter illustrate the second strategic pathway to proliferation laid out by our theory: states that benefit from some protection from a security sponsor that, when combined with their own relative power, is sufficient to give them the opportunity to proliferate but at the same time is insufficient in its reliability to take away their willingness to build the bomb are likely to acquire nuclear weapons.

Sweden

At the outset of the Cold War, Sweden faced a threatening situation. Since its airspace lay in the flight path of both superpowers' strategic bombers and its territorial waters were instrumental for submarine warfare in the Atlantic, its geographic position made it an important target in case of a confrontation between the United States and the Soviet Union.[1] Furthermore, its commitment to a neutral foreign policy meant that it could not formally rely on security guarantees offered by a superpower sponsor in order to deter an attack. Swedish neutrality aimed at keeping the country out of a general war – or at least its opening phase. Given the stated U.S. policy of "massive retaliation," which meant that any war with the Soviet Union would involve nuclear weapons in its early phase, and the limited size of the Soviet nuclear arsenal, whether Sweden entered the war earlier or later was a matter of considerable importance.[2] A nuclear arsenal might thus help deter a direct Soviet nuclear attack on Swedish territory. Early in the postwar era, therefore, Sweden had the willingness to acquire nuclear weapons.

Stockholm initiated its nuclear program shortly after the end of the Second World War, with the Swedish military playing the key role behind the drive for nuclear weapons.[3] Until the early 1960s, the program advanced steadily, such that Sweden expected to be able to build a nuclear weapon by the mid-1960s.

Yet, by 1962, the Swedish military shifted its priorities away from building a nuclear deterrent and toward reinforcing its conventional defenses. Funding for the nuclear program was cut in 1964–1965, producing a rapid decline in the number of personnel and resources available to pursue Sweden's erstwhile nuclear ambitions.[4] Sweden no longer possessed the willingness to go nuclear and abandoned its goal of developing an independent arsenal.

---

[1] See: Wallin (1991, 360–361); Dalsjö (2014, 185).

[2] See: Dalsjö (2014, 179–180). Later, with the advent of a U.S. policy of flexible response and a larger Soviet nuclear arsenal capable of ensuring mutually assured destruction (MAD), staying out of the early phase of a U.S.-Soviet war lost its importance as a strategic goal, and Swedish neutrality would acquire a more idealistic character. Ibid., 193.

[3] For a review of the technical progress of the Swedish nuclear program, see: Jonter (2010a).

[4] See: Agrell (1990, 168); Wallin (1991, 365).

This reversal in Swedish nuclear policy was due to strategic considerations. Changes in the international environment from the early 1960s onward convinced decisionmakers in Stockholm that an attempt to acquire an independent nuclear force might actually undermine Swedish security. Instead, Sweden came to believe that great-power conflict was less likely and that it could effectively rely on the United States in an eventual conflict with the Soviet Union. Given these changes, nuclear weapons were no longer an investment that would produce benefits for Sweden's security outlook, leading Stockholm to drop its willingness to build the bomb and instead adopt a posture of nuclear forbearance.

Swedish Interest in Nuclear Weapons

Early in the Cold War, nuclear weapons appeared to be a sensible way of boosting Sweden's security outlook. Throughout the 1950s, both the United States and the Soviet Union were expanding their nuclear arsenals at a rapid pace. Several members of each superpower bloc were expected to acquire their own nuclear deterrent or receive deployments of nuclear weapons from their superpower sponsor.[5] The risk that a local conflict would escalate to the nuclear level was perceived to be high.

Furthermore, Sweden's experience in the Second World War still loomed large. Despite its neutrality during that conflict, its conventional defenses had conveyed an appearance of relative weakness. Once German forces invaded neighboring Denmark and Norway in April 1940, Sweden was cut off from the global arms market and seemed vulnerable.[6] In the view of Stockholm's leadership, this vulnerability mandated that Sweden be self-sufficient in providing for its security. As a later Swedish Defense Ministry report put it: "Our basic approach to security must be based on the fact that we are a small country with limited resources and our security may be endangered by the superpowers."[7]

Neutrality and Nuclear Development

If a war between members of the two superpower blocs broke out, Sweden would be highly vulnerable. As Swedish Supreme Commander

---

[5] See: ÖB-utredningarna 1957 (OB57) (1957, 284).
[6] See: Agrell (1990, 156); Wallin (1991, 361).
[7] Försvarsdepartementet (1968, 129), our translation.

General Nils Swedlund (1951–1961) would argue in his 1957 recommendations (known as OB57), "East and West have so many nuclear weapons that their use is not limited to particularly important objectives," and might therefore also target Swedish territory.[8] According to the Swedish military, Stockholm would have to disperse its troops to protect them against a possible nuclear attack.[9]

The enemy might be particularly tempted to use nuclear weapons if it knew that Sweden did not possess the capabilities necessary for nuclear retaliation. As Swedlund put it in OB57:

> The largest military risk to Sweden still seems to be that our country would be involved in a conflict between the major powers associated with Sweden's geographic location between the two power bloc's spheres of influence. ... A crucial component of Sweden's neutrality is the army's ability, through its strength, to deter an opponent from attack. The conclusion for us is that we must have a defense that is capable of defending against air and remote weapon attack and against an invasion. The enemy's ability and means to implement an attack against us are strongly affected by whether our defense is backed by nuclear weapons.[10]

A nuclear arsenal might therefore be useful in deterring the Soviet Union from targeting Sweden in the early phase of a war against the West – a key Swedish strategic goal, since the early phase of a U.S.-Soviet war was when an "apocalyptic rain of hydrogen bombs" was expected to land on European NATO members. Specifically, tactical nuclear weapons would improve Swedish defenses and deter possible attacks, allowing the country to sit out the war at least until "the Soviet Union had had its nuclear fangs removed."[11] As Swedlund put it in OB57: "there are strong reasons to believe that if the Swedish armed forces did not have nuclear weapons, it would increase rather than decrease the likelihood that an aggressor would use such a weapon against it."[12] He argued that "if we had nuclear weapons our possibilities for defense would increase considerably,"[13] adding that "if a small

---

[8] OB57 (1957, 282), our translation.
[9] See: Wallin (1991, 370).
[10] OB57 (1957, 287, 290), our translation.
[11] Dalsjö (2014, 189).
[12] OB57, quoted in Rublee (2009, 170–171).
[13] Quoted in Reiss (1988, 47).

nation lacks access to nuclear weapons and is not a party to an alliance which possesses them, it can become an open target for aggression."[14] In other words, Sweden needed nuclear weapons "in order to uphold its non-aligned policy."[15] By the mid-1950s, the development of an independent tactical nuclear arsenal was seen by the Swedish military as key to its ability to deter an attack on the country were a war between the two superpower blocs to break out.

By then, the Swedish nuclear program was well under way. In August 1945, the supreme commander of the Swedish Armed Forces had asked the National Defense Research Agency (FOA) to investigate what was known about nuclear weapons and to divert money for related design and research activities.[16] Until 1952, Sweden's nuclear program explored nuclear technology, concluding that a large-scale plutonium-producing reactor was needed in order to get the fissile material necessary for a weapon. That same year, the chief of the Swedish Air Force, Lieutenant General Bengt Nordenskiöld (1942–1954), became the first high-ranking Swedish military officer to state that Sweden should possess nuclear weapons.[17]

In July 1954, Sweden's first reactor, a one-megawatt research facility, went critical.[18] Two months later, the army engaged in large-scale maneuvers at Bergslagen aimed at testing its readiness for combat in a nuclear war.[19] At the same time, Swedlund officially recommended the development of a tactical nuclear device.[20] Sweden also took advantage of President Eisenhower's Atoms for Peace program. In January 1956, the country signed an agreement with the United States on civilian nuclear energy cooperation. In May 1957, the United States agreed to sell twenty-six tons of heavy water to Sweden.[21] By then, FOA had expanded its nuclear complex in Grindsjoen, south of Stockholm, by initiating construction of the Ågesta plutonium-producing research reactor (R3), located underground in a rock cave.[22] That same year, FOA stated that

[14] Quoted in Garris (1973, 191).
[15] Jonter (2010a, 68).
[16] See: Wallin (1991, 362); Jonter (2001, 21).
[17] See: Garris (1973, 190); Reiss (1988, 44); Wallin (1991, 368).
[18] See: Reiss (1988, 43).
[19] See: Garris (1973, 191).
[20] See: Agrell (1990, 160); Paul (2000, 87).
[21] See: Jonter (2012, 223–224).
[22] See: IAEA (2009); Presbo (2009).

Sweden could have the materials necessary to build an operational nuclear weapon by 1963–1964.[23] Yet, by then Stockholm would have reversed its nuclear course and dropped its willingness to build the bomb.

Prime Minister Tage Erlander (1946–1969) avoided political controversy by not taking a public stand for or against nuclear weapons while supporting the construction of the Ågesta dual-purpose reactor.[24] This political ambiguity, however, was not without costs. Supreme Commander Swedlund resigned in 1961 after failing to obtain unequivocal political support to build a nuclear weapon. The following year, as the Ågesta nuclear reactor came on line, the Swedish military – now under the leadership of Torsten Rapp (1961–1970) – pivoted its position and became opposed to the nuclear option.[25] The armed forces Supreme Commander's recommendations for that year (known as OB62) argued that defense priorities should be shifted from nuclear weapons to improvements in conventional forces.[26] In June 1963, Erlander informed U.S. ambassador J. Graham Parsons (1961–1967) that, although Sweden "had the possibility of developing its own weapons rather quickly and quite easily," it was interested in "a test ban agreement and full agreement with the US on avoiding proliferation of nuclear capability to other countries."[27] What led to this change in Sweden's nuclear course?

The Swedish Decision to Renounce Nuclear Weapons

If Sweden's acquisition of nuclear weapons could improve its defense, it could also be seen as dangerous for Sweden's potential adversaries. Swedish military leaders were aware of this risk. For this reason, they eschewed attempting to develop strategic nuclear weapons, focusing only on acquiring tactical devices. On this point, the military establishment reasoned as follows: "If Sweden acquires strategic nuclear weapons, this ... would completely transform our military-political position with incalculable consequences on the risk that we may be drawn into war. Such a solution of our defense is therefore not recommended."[28]

---

[23] See: Agrell (1990, 163).
[24] Ibid., 161–163.
[25] Ibid., 237 fn. 11; Wallin (1991, 372).
[26] See: Agrell (1990, 166–167).
[27] Cable #A-1166 from Stockholm to State, June 15, 1963, quoted in Cole (1997, 243).
[28] OB57 (1957, 291–292), our translation.

Even so, any nuclear weapon, tactical or strategic, could seriously affect the regional balance of power and invite a preventive strike. In 1955, Östen Undén, Sweden's foreign minister (1924–1926, 1945–1961), wrote in a memo to his government colleagues that "if Sweden managed to produce atomic bombs – which by their nature are highly offensive weapons – our territory would become a more dangerous neighbourhood as seen from the Soviet Union, as Sweden could become [sic] forced into a war because of pressure from western powers."[29]

Anticipating such important changes following Sweden's nuclearization, potential enemies might be tempted to strike preventively before Swedish nuclear acquisition. In the Swedish military's view, "in order to be certain that Sweden does not acquire nuclear weapons, an attacker might be tempted to use nuclear weapons against us without the risk of counteraction with the same weapon on our side."[30] The Swedish prime minister shared this view. In his memoirs, Erlander stated: "If we decided to construct our armed forces around the atomic bomb, we would face a pretty long period of adjustment during which our defense would be weakened."[31] During this period of vulnerability, an adversary could be tempted to strike. Erlander added:

The effectiveness of the atomic bomb was so great that even a superpower could worry about a small state in its near abroad possessing this weapon. In a situation of crisis, the superpower could feel obligated to exterminate such risks. Such a preventive war would never erupt owing to the possession of conventional weapons.[32]

Aware of these risks, Erlander hedged on the decision to acquire nuclear weapons. Eventually, the strategic situation changed, undermining arguments in favor of the bomb and facilitating a shift toward nuclear forbearance.

Starting in the early 1960s, Sweden's strategic outlook underwent a gradual transformation. The first of these changes in Sweden's strategic environment was the advent of assured retaliation between the superpowers and of mutually assured destruction (MAD) shortly

---

[29] Quoted in Wallin (1991, 377).
[30] OB57 (1957, 294), our translation.
[31] Erlander (1976, 83), our translation.
[32] Ibid., our translation.

thereafter. The deterrent value of large arsenals of intercontinental ballistic missiles (ICBMs) lowered the risk of general nuclear war and led to a renewed emphasis on conventional warfare and the development of a doctrine of limited war and flexible response in both Washington and Moscow. This decreased the likelihood that future conflict between the two superpowers would be fought with nuclear weapons – at least in its initial phase.[33] Since this was the only scenario in which Swedish nuclear weapons would be useful, the advent of assured retaliation between the superpowers diminished the significance of a Swedish nuclear-weapons capability, weakening the Swedish military's arguments in their favor.[34] Accordingly, the Swedish supreme commander's recommendations for 1965 (OB65) emphasized the importance of conventional forces in the context of a limited war between the superpowers in which nuclear weapons would not be employed.[35]

Second, prompted in part by the stalemate in their nuclear balance, the superpowers entered a period of détente that allowed for progress in negotiations to curtail nuclear proliferation, resulting in the Partial Nuclear Test Ban Treaty (PTBT) of 1963 and in reinvigorated discussions that resulted in the onset of the nonproliferation regime centered on the NPT a handful of years later. These developments suggested that the overall probability of proliferation would be low and that nuclear conflict in Europe would in all likelihood be limited to superpower conflict – which, as we have just seen, was now less likely. In this environment, the productivity of an investment in nuclear weapons decreased significantly. As a 1965 Defense Ministry report concluded, "[i]t is not in our country's security interests to acquire nuclear weapons."[36]

Assuming that the most likely conflicts that might break out in its vicinity would be great-power wars, Sweden's important strategic situation could serve as an asset, drawing in one superpower to help repel an eventual attack by the other. Indeed, the Swedish Parliamentary Commission of Defense concluded in February 1968: "If a major war in Europe occurs, Sweden represents an indispensable passage for

---

[33] See: Dalsjö (2014, 189).
[34] See: Garris (1973, 199); Agrell (1990, 168).
[35] See: Wallin (1991, 372).
[36] Försvarsdepartementet (1968, 139), our translation.

either side."[37] This meant that Sweden's strategic importance would invite a response by the other superpower:

The Party considering an attack on Sweden with or without the use of nuclear weapons must in this case also expect that nuclear weapons may be used against his operations even though Sweden does not have such weapons. ... The conclusion is that Sweden by and large is under the nuclear umbrella approximately in the same way that countries in our vicinity are, regardless which power bloc or great power sphere of interests they belong to.[38]

By emphasizing the likely response of any superpower bloc to an attack, this policy statement was truthful to Sweden's formal commitment to neutrality. Yet, underneath this public discourse of neutrality, Sweden assessed the risk of an attack by either bloc to be very different. Since the outset of the Cold War, Stockholm believed that the Soviet Union was its only plausible potential enemy. The 1948 communist coup in Czechoslovakia heightened Sweden's concerns over the threat posed by the Soviet Union.[39] Sweden even discussed the possibility of forming a Scandinavian Defense Pact with Norway and Denmark before they decided to join NATO.[40] In the absence of formal security guarantees from the Western bloc, nuclear weapons were seen as a way to deter or repel a Soviet invasion.[41] Consequently, Moscow made "implicit threats and warnings against a Swedish weapon."[42]

Official statements of neutrality were expected to reassure both superpowers of Sweden's limited aims. As the Ministry of Defense put it, "[t]he combination of a solid, reassuring foreign policy, and a strong defense should cause the great powers to respect our neutrality and our will and ability to resist aggression against us in a war."[43] To achieve this goal, Sweden should not appear to lean in favor of any of the blocs. Again, in the words of the Ministry of Defense, "[i]n a war, the warring parties must be certain that neither party can obtain

[37] Ibid., 132, our translation.
[38] Ibid., 138, quoted in Reiss (1988, 69).
[39] See: Reiss (1988, 38).
[40] Ibid., 38; Wallin (1991, 360); Gunnarsson et al. (1994, 9–10).
[41] See: Cole (1997, 236–237).
[42] Ibid., 247.
[43] Försvarsdepartementet (1968, 135), our translation.

an advantage by unjustly using Swedish territories."[44] Consistent with this goal, Sweden's official policy of neutrality was characterized by "non-participation in alliances in peacetime, aiming at neutrality in war."[45] As a result, Swedish neutrality precluded an alliance with the West or any direct coordination of wartime plans during peacetime.

Yet, Sweden's neutrality did not prevent it from making unilateral preparations to receive Western assistance. In a telling example, although cabinet minister Dag Hammarskjöld (1951–1953) told the British ambassador to Sweden in late 1951 that the Swedish defense minister's position was that even informal coordination of Swedish defense planning with the United Kingdom was inconceivable, he maintained that "it would be of use were Sweden to be privy to parts of the Western planning for the contingency of a Soviet invasion of Scandinavia. Sweden could then act 'autonomously' when drawing up and revising its own plans, while taking Western plans into consideration."[46]

Swedish preparations for receiving Western assistance in the event of a war were large in scale. From the late 1940s, Sweden had concluded that it could not withstand a sustained Soviet attack. It had also concluded that U.S. bombers would need to use Swedish airspace to reach industrial targets in the Soviet Union, likely leading to Soviet retaliation.[47] This led Swedish leaders to hope for "indirect" assistance from the Western powers in the form of air bombardments against Soviet airbases and the use of embarkation ports across the Baltic Sea, as well as provision of supplies to Swedish forces. Swedish leaders thought they could reasonably expect this kind of support despite their country's formal neutrality because they generally assumed that "lending such assistance was in the interests of the Western Powers themselves."[48] OB54 explicitly recommended that Swedish strategy "focus on creating conditions to be supported, in war, by states in whose interests it would be to assist us," identifying "Western strategic bombing" of invading Soviet forces as the most likely form of support.[49]

---

[44] Ibid., 136, our translation.
[45] Gunnarsson et al. (1994, 8).
[46] Ibid., 18–19.
[47] For evidence that Swedish military leaders were aware of this since at least around 1950, see: Dalsjö (2014, 185).
[48] Gunnarsson et al. (1994, 34).
[49] Ibid., 11.

Thereafter, Sweden made significant unilateral preparations for facilitating military assistance from the West, including personal military contacts; the establishment of secure means of communication with Denmark and Norway, which could then be connected with the NATO command and control system if war broke out; coordination of air operations and expansion of runways on the country's eastern coast, in order to allow NATO bombers to use them; coordination of air surveillance; and intelligence exchange. Such preparations were so extensive that in 1992 an official Commission on Neutrality Policy was set up to determine whether they had violated the principle of Swedish neutrality, and therefore domestic and international law. The commission concluded that not only were these measures compatible with Swedish neutrality, "it would have been irreconcilable with the responsibilities resting with Sweden's political and military leadership had no measures been taken to facilitate the reception of assistance from the Western great powers."[50] Put differently, Swedish political neutrality was compatible with – indeed required – actions that in effect ensured that the country's military would receive significant NATO assistance if an attack by the Soviet Union threatened its neutral status.

Therein lies a paradoxical conclusion: Swedish neutrality actually increased its overlap of interests with the Western bloc. Because Swedish foreign policy aims were limited, the scenarios under which Sweden was threatened would be those in which Western Europe more broadly was also threatened. In such scenarios, the United States had a strong incentive to assist Sweden, given the strategic importance of Western Europe – and of Swedish airspace and territorial waters – to its defense. Moreover, by the early 1960s, a direct confrontation between the superpowers was, though unlikely in itself, the most probable war scenario affecting Sweden. This was due to the fact that the rate of proliferation had fallen far below the most pessimistic estimates of the 1950s and that international negotiations allowed for a higher degree of confidence that this rate would remain low. Given this geostrategic situation and the sustained efforts undertaken by Swedish policymakers to secure U.S. support, by the early 1960s Sweden could effectively consider itself under the U.S. nuclear

[50] Ibid., 35.

umbrella, further obviating the need for an independent nuclear deterrent.[51]

U.S. Nonproliferation Efforts

Swedish confidence in American assistance was well-founded. According to the same report by the Swedish Commission on Neutrality Policy, there is compelling evidence that, despite the lack of any public guarantees of assistance, the United States appears "to have been fully intent on assisting Sweden."[52] The United States believed in the strategic importance of Sweden and eventually agreed with Swedish efforts to prepare for U.S. assistance. In January 1952, Washington adopted National Security Council Report 121 (NSC-121), stating that Scandinavia was "of strategic importance to the defense of Europe and to the security of the United States," so that it was "in the interest of the United States that the component parts, Norway, Denmark and Sweden, be in the best possible position to resist Soviet pressure or aggression." Washington should seek this goal while accepting Stockholm's preference for neutrality.[53] In April 1960, Washington adopted NSC-6006/1, which expressed the preference that Sweden renounce its nuclear ambitions and instead modernize its conventional defense forces so as to make them "compatible with and complementary to" the weapon systems of the NATO allies neighboring Sweden.[54] The report added that "[i]n the event of general war with Soviet Bloc," the United States would "be prepared to come to the assistance of Sweden as a part of a

[51] See: Cole (1997, 239–240). By 1968, the Swedish military establishment was quite satisfied, relative to its previous assessment in 1958, with its conventional capabilities and its ability to accept Western assistance, given the relatively low risk of conflict between East and West (Gunnarsson et al. 1994, 12).
[52] Gunnarsson et al. (1994, 35).
[53] "Memorandum by the Planning Board of the National Security Council to the National Security Council," Washington, January 8, 1952, in *Foreign Relations of the United States (FRUS)*, 1952–1954, Vol. VI, Part 2, *Western Europe and Canada*, Doc. 819.
[54] National Security Council Report, "NSC 6006/1: Statement of U.S. Policy Toward Scandinavia," April 6, 1960, in *Foreign Relations of the United States (FRUS)*, 1958–1960, Vol. VII, Part 2, *Western Europe*, Doc. 300. For more on the adoption of NSC-6006/1 and the contrast with NSC-121, see: Bruzelius (2008).

NATO or UN response to the aggression."[55] In effect, this turned the United States into Sweden's loose ally.

Given the limited security goals Stockholm pursued, the willingness to acquire nuclear weapons it demonstrated between 1945 and 1962 was driven exclusively by considerations about self-defense. As its strategic outlook evolved in the direction of a lower risk of Swedish involvement in a nuclear conflict, Sweden also moved closer to the Western bloc in its military preparations, if not in its political position. Taken together, these two developments led Swedish leaders to conclude by the early to mid-1960s that in no plausible scenario would an independent nuclear deterrent play a significant role in boosting the country's security. As T. V. Paul has noted before, in the strategic environment of the mid-1960s, "[n]uclear possession would have increased [Sweden's] insecurity, while making [its] neutrality policies less effective."[56]

Early in the postwar era, when they thought that tactical nuclear weapons might be part of a strong military force, Swedish leaders had worked toward nuclearization. As the fear of impending war in Europe decreased and the overlap between Swedish and U.S. interests increased, Swedish thinking changed. Convinced that in case of a Soviet attack Sweden would be under the nuclear umbrella of the United States and NATO, Swedish leaders no longer saw a security benefit in acquiring nuclear weapons.[57] Given the lower productivity of a Swedish investment in a nuclear deterrent in this new strategic environment, Stockholm lost its willingness to acquire atomic weapons, abandoning its nuclear ambitions. In a nutshell, when Sweden finally acquired the technical capability necessary for nuclearization, it no longer possessed the willingness to nuclearize.[58]

---

[55] *FRUS*, 1958–1960, Vol. VII, Part 2, Doc. 300. In November, the NSC added that U.S. intervention should be unilateral, not within NATO (ibid.). Thomas Jonter adds that in 1962 Washington adopted stronger language, saying that in such an eventuality "we should undertake to come to the assistance of Sweden as a part of NATO or UN response to the aggression." (Notice to holders of NSC 6006/1 by Bromley Smith, "Rescission of NSC 6oo6/1, U.S. Policy toward Scandinavia (Denmark, Norway and Sweden), dated April 6, 1960," May 2, 1962, RG 59, Records Relating to Department of State participation in the Operations Coordinating Board and the NSC, 1947–1963, Lot File 63 D 351, Box 99, NA, quoted in Jonter [2012, 234]).

[56] Paul (2000, 85).

[57] See: Reiss (1988, 69).

[58] See: Garris (1973, 203).

Alternative Explanations

The existing literature includes four alternative explanations of Swedish nuclear forbearance. First, proponents of the argument that supply-side restrictions are key to curtail nuclear proliferation might claim that Sweden's inability to nuclearize was the result of superpower efforts to avoid the development of a Swedish bomb. After all, both superpowers opposed Swedish nuclearization. Such restrictions, however, only mattered to the extent that they forced Stockholm to develop an indigenous nuclear program. Sweden was in an enviable position to complete such a program. It possessed large reserves of uranium, a well-developed industrial infrastructure, a reasonably well-developed scientific research capability,[59] and, throughout the 1950s, levels of per capita wealth that were amongst the highest in the world, nearly twice those of the rest of Europe.[60] The Swedish supreme commander asserted in OB57 that "with affordable human and financial effort we can produce atomic charges that can be adapted to domestically produced weapons carriers."[61] The following year, the ruling Swedish Social Democratic Party (*Sveriges Socialdemokratiska Arbetareparti*, or SAP) appointed a committee to study the issue of nuclear acquisition. Its report, issued in 1959, asserted that, given controls on sales of nuclear weapons and materials, the only road to nuclear acquisition would be domestic production, which it estimated for as soon as "the later part of the 1960s."[62] In short, superpower-imposed restrictions on Sweden's access to nuclear materials or technologies cannot explain nuclear forbearance.

Recent scholarship suggests a variation on this argument, whereby supply-side restrictions proved instrumental in determining Sweden's nuclear forbearance as a result of the Swedish decision to couple its nuclear-weapons program with its civilian program.[63] Indeed, Sweden's civilian nuclear program relied heavily on U.S. technology, giving Washington great leverage. By the time Stockholm had to decide whether to build the bomb, the United States could have exercised significant pressure over Stockholm, trying to coerce it to give up the nuclear option.[64]

---

[59] See: Wallin (1991, 362).
[60] See: Cole (1997, 245).
[61] OB57 (1957, 284), our translation.
[62] Sveriges Socialdemokratiska Arbetareparti (1960, 109), our translation.
[63] See: Jonter (2002); Holloway (2010); Jonter (2010b); Jonter (2012).
[64] See: Jonter (2010b, 3).

This account is largely compatible with ours. Until the early 1960s, Erlander had good reasons to postpone a decision to acquire nuclear weapons. To begin with, the Swedish program was not sufficiently advanced, and more work was required before nuclearization became a possibility. In addition, there was uncertainty about the potential value of a nuclear deterrent, given ongoing nuclear disarmament negotiations.[65] Thus, the decision to postpone nuclearization was partly due to Sweden's strategic situation, which eventually shifted toward a more benign security environment. Ultimately, changes in Sweden's strategic environment were sufficient to motivate its decision to terminate the nuclear-weapons program. Whether or not supply-side restrictions imposed by the United States after a hypothetical Swedish decision to build a nuclear bomb would have prevented it from doing so is a question we cannot settle with the available empirical evidence.

A second alternative account of the Swedish case claims that, although Sweden could absorb the financial cost of the nuclear-weapons program, it chose not to do so because of the domestic political consequences of acquiring nuclear weapons. Indeed, several authors point to Swedish domestic politics as the key variable determining the abandonment of Sweden's nuclear program.[66] In its public response to the Swedish armed forces supreme commander's recommendations contained in OB54, the government denied that it had any ambition of becoming the next state to acquire nuclear weapons.[67] Furthermore, according to Maria Rost Rublee, the mid-1960s shift against nuclear weapons was due to the role of the antinuclear faction of the SAP, which discredited the nuclear option in public debates.

It is undeniable that Swedish neutrality had a strong domestic-politics component, but the domestic-politics explanation suffers from several shortcomings. To begin with, the SAP – and, specifically, Prime Minister Erlander – ruled Sweden throughout the duration of its nuclear program, so the shift from a pronuclear to an antinuclear stance can hardly be explained through shifting domestic coalitions, the evolving preferences, or the different psychological profiles of successive Swedish leaders. Furthermore, recent research has highlighted the "small-state realism" motivation behind Swedish neutrality during

---

[65] See: Ibid., 10.
[66] See: Cole (1997); Rublee (2009).
[67] See: Garris (1973, 192).

the first phase of the Cold War, until the late 1960s.[68] In this period, neutrality stemmed from the strategic imperative to stay out of the earlier – and most devastating – phase of any U.S.-Soviet war. As Erlander told the Swedish Parliament in 1959, "neutrality policy means that we strive for the advantage of being able to avoid being immediately drawn into a future world war."[69] It was only in the early 1970s, when MAD lowered the value of joining NATO allies only late in the war, that neutrality acquired the "small-state idealism" overtones that scholars have come to associate with it.[70] So the neutrality policy itself stemmed at least in part from strategic imperatives. Finally, domestic politics did not alter the Swedish leadership's view of their country's strategic situation – and the possible effect of nuclear weapons on its security. Swedish policymakers assessed their main threat to come from the Soviet bloc. As we laid out earlier, Swedish neutrality did not prevent the government and military leadership from making unilateral preparations to receive U.S. protection in the event of a conflict. The challenge for Sweden was to keep these efforts secret and convince foreign audiences that it would not privilege any bloc in the event of a conflict. To meet this challenge, the Swedish government needed to dissimulate its actions in the domestic political arena. For example, when pressed on the issue in a 1959 parliamentary session, Prime Minister Erlander categorically ruled out preparations for, and consultations on, military cooperation with members of a great-power alliance. In reviewing the evidence more than three decades later, the Commission on Neutrality Policy concluded that the prime minister's statement "deliberately conveyed a [sic] erroneous picture of what had actually taken place."[71] In other words, while there may have been a popular preference for neutrality, such preference did not hinder the efforts of Swedish policymakers to improve the country's defenses in the event of a conflict. Likewise, while there may have existed a popular preference for maintaining the nonnuclear status of Sweden, this preference did not preclude significant advances in the Swedish nuclear program for as long as Stockholm thought that possession of a nuclear arsenal would improve the country's security. It therefore seems more

---

[68] See: Dalsjö (2014, 179).
[69] Quoted in ibid., 188.
[70] See: Ibid., 179–180.
[71] Gunnarsson et al. (1994, 36).

appropriate to say that, at least in this particular instance, domestic politics were subordinated to strategic considerations.[72]

A third alternative argument on the Swedish case maintains that there were strong international normative constraints against the acquisition of nuclear weapons. Indeed, Rublee argues that international norms against proliferation played a key role in producing Swedish nuclear forbearance: "Sweden's case is an excellent example of how the international social environment surrounding nuclear nonproliferation can have a real impact on state nuclear decision-making."[73] According to her, the high degree of trust in international treaties exhibited by the Stockholm leadership and its corresponding desire not to harm NPT negotiations led to Swedish nuclear forbearance.[74] Moreover, Rublee argues that only a strong commitment to international norms explains why Sweden signed the NPT in 1970 and abided by its commitments to forgo nuclear weapons, despite an increasing Soviet threat during the Cold War.[75]

This argument is not without problems, however. Swedish leaders took the decision to abandon their nuclear program well before the negotiations for the NPT were anywhere near completion. In fact, Wilhelm Agrell, in one of the most detailed studies of Swedish nuclear decisionmaking, argues that the NPT was important only inasmuch as it provided the SAP with a public justification to abandon its erstwhile-cherished nuclear program.[76] International factors seem to have played a role, but not in terms of a powerful norm that would trump strategic calculations. If proliferation were expected to be slow, perhaps due to international institutions, the strategic benefit of acquiring nuclear weapons would also be lower. Yet, there is evidence that Swedish policymakers were willing to reconsider the nuclear option, following an eventual change in the international strategic environment that would again make them more valuable. The previously mentioned 1959 SAP report asserts that "Sweden will not give up nuclear weapons due to ethical reasons, if other countries equip their forces with such weapons."[77] In 1965, the Swedish Ministry of Defense, while opposing

---

[72] See: Ibid., 36.
[73] Rublee (2009, 180).
[74] See: Ibid., 174.
[75] Ibid., 171.
[76] See: Agrell (1990, 169).
[77] Sveriges Socialdemokratiska Arbetareparti (1960, 110), our translation.

nuclearization, argued that "[i]f long-term developments would lead to nuclear weapons becoming a normal part of small nations' armed forces, the question of Swedish nuclear weapons could come again at this time."[78] Consistent with this position, while the Ågesta nuclear reactor was finally shut down in 1974, it has been preserved in a manner that would allow for its reactivation within a few months.[79] In this case, it seems more appropriate to say that the preference to abide by international norms was secondary vis-à-vis strategic considerations.

Finally, a fourth possible alternative to the argument we laid out in the preceding text would be that, though Sweden was capable of completing a nuclear-weapons program and could in principle afford to bring it to completion, the cost would be so high that it would entail significant cutbacks to other public projects. According to Paul M. Cole, there is a conventional wisdom that Sweden could not afford both a nuclear arsenal and its social welfare system.[80] This argument does not hold, however. Nuclear weapons were considered by the Swedish leadership to be cheaper than the equivalent conventional weaponry necessary to achieve the same deterrent effect.[81] Overall, nuclear weapons were expected to absorb only around 5 percent of the total defense budget for the period 1965–1975.[82] Furthermore, Sweden abandoned its nuclear program *after* having made the bulk of the necessary investments, namely, in its plutonium-producing reactor at Ågesta. There is no evidence that cost considerations factored into Sweden's nuclear forbearance.

To conclude, the main reasons for the development and abandonment of the Swedish nuclear-weapons program were strategic in nature. As a weak neutral state with no nuclear security sponsor, Sweden had a strong incentive to pursue nuclear weapons at the outset of the Cold War. Yet, Sweden also worried about the incentives of other states, in particular the Soviet Union, to resist Sweden's acquisition of nuclear weapons. By the early 1960s, changes in the international environment – the slowdown in the rate of proliferation, a reduction in

---

[78] Försvarsdepartementet (1968, 73–74), our translation.
[79] See: Steve Coll, "Neutral Sweden Quietly Keeps Nuclear Option Open," *The Washington Post*, November 25, 1994, pp. A1, A42.
[80] See: Cole (1997, 245–246).
[81] As concluded in OB57. See: Garris (1973, 196); Wallin (1991, 370).
[82] See: NWG, Kärnladdningsgruppen betänkande, p. C2, quoted in Cole (1997, 235).

tensions between the superpowers, and the evolution of international negotiations to limit the spread of nuclear weapons – reduced the perceived benefit of developing nuclear weapons, leading to the abandonment of the Swedish nuclear program for lack of willingness to nuclearize.

Given the abundant security in Sweden's strategic environment, it is difficult to envision conditions that would lead Stockholm to once again be willing to build a nuclear deterrent.

China

Victorious over the Nationalists in a bloody civil war, the Communist forces of Mao Zedong (Chairman of the Central Committee of the Chinese Communist Party [CCP], 1945–1976) founded the People's Republic of China (PRC) in October 1949. Fifteen years later, on October 16, 1964, China detonated its first atomic device at Lop Nur. Beijing's willingness to acquire a nuclear deterrent stemmed from the grave security threat posed by the United States, which could not be mitigated by the increasingly unreliable support China enjoyed from the Soviet Union.

During the 1950s, the PRC repeatedly clashed with the United States. In 1950–1953, it was involved in the Korean War, supporting Communist forces in the North against an international coalition led by the United States. In 1954–1955 and again in 1958, the PRC confronted the Republic of China (ROC, or Taiwan) and the United States across the Taiwan Strait. In all these crises, China faced a militarily superior enemy in the United States, whose deterrent efforts relied heavily on nuclear threats.

At the same time, China benefited from the support of its Communist brethren, the Soviet Union. In 1950, the two countries signed a security pact. Yet, over the course of the following decade, a rift deepened between the two allies. In part, the Soviet Union was concerned about China's recklessness in its attempts to capture Taiwan. The PRC, in turn, was concerned about what it described as Soviet "revisionism," or a lack of resolve in confronting the United States.

Against this strategic backdrop, Beijing decided to launch a nuclear-weapons program in September 1955. Moscow pledged to assist it, but these promises went largely unfulfilled until Soviet aid was terminated abruptly in the summer of 1960, further deepening the Sino-Soviet split. Nevertheless, China's nuclear development proceeded apace.

The United States – particularly under President John F. Kennedy (JFK, 1961–1963) – became especially worried about the consequences of a nuclear-armed China. Washington attempted to prevent China's nuclearization by negotiating the PTBT and considering a preventive strike. In late 1963 and early 1964, the U.S. government conducted a systematic analysis of preventive military options. Failing to obtain support from the Soviet Union for joint action, Washington concluded that the cost of a strike was greater than the effect of Chinese nuclearization. In the end, Chinese conventional strength and the modicum of support lent to it by the Soviet Union were enough to deter counterproliferation action by the United States, granting Beijing the opportunity to nuclearize.

Chinese Interest in Nuclear Weapons

Mao's views on grand strategy and warfare were not a priori conducive to a nuclear-weapons program. Mao articulated a strategy of "People's War," insisting on the importance of popular forces in warfare and downplaying the role of technology.[83] Analyzing the final stages of the Pacific War in early August 1945, Mao declared that the decisive factor in the imminent Japanese surrender was the entry of the Soviet Union into the war, not the U.S. nuclear attacks on Hiroshima and Nagasaki.[84] It is a "big mistake," he argued, to "believe that the atom bomb is all-powerful." Instead, he retorted: "Without the struggles waged by the people, atom bombs by themselves would be of no avail."[85]

Over the next decade, Mao experienced firsthand U.S. attempts to wield nuclear threats as tools of coercive diplomacy. Publicly, he consistently downplayed the importance of nuclear weapons. In August 1946, he famously described the atomic bomb as "a paper tiger."[86] At the same time, Mao also decided that the PRC too could use a nuclear deterrent. Summing up his strategic thinking, he stated in April

---

[83] See: Mao Zedong, "On Protracted War," May 1938, in Mao Zedong (1963, 260); Garver (1993, 258).

[84] See: Mao Zedong, "The Situation and Our Policy after the Victory in the War of Resistance against Japan," August 13, 1945, in Mao (1961, 11).

[85] Ibid., 21.

[86] Mao Zedong, "Talk with the American Correspondent Anna Louise Strong," August 1946, in ibid., 100.

1956: "In today's world, if we don't want to be bullied, we have to have this thing [the atomic bomb]."[87] Starting in 1959 the Chinese military defined its strategy as "People's War under modern conditions."[88]

The Birth of the U.S.-China Rivalry

If U.S.-China relations proved to be tense in the 1950s and 1960s, such a development was not foreordained, nor was it predictable in the mid-1940s. During the Second World War, Washington had opposed the Japanese invasion of China in an attempt to preserve the Open Door policy.[89] In December 1943 the United States signed the Cairo Declaration, agreeing that all territories that Japan had taken from China – including Manchuria, Formosa (Taiwan), and the Pescadores – should be returned to China.[90] The United States at the time supported the Nationalist forces of Chiang Kai-shek (1928–1975), whom it recognized as the legitimate government of China.[91] Yet, the Communists were keen to receive military assistance from Washington and even considered deeper economic ties with the United States. Mao told a U.S. military officer in December 1944 that he welcomed U.S. support in fighting the Japanese and that whether or not it was forthcoming, "we shall still be friends of the United States."[92] In March 1945, he explained that "China's greatest post-war need is economic development. She lacks the capitalistic foundation necessary to carry this out alone. ... America is not only the most suitable country to assist this economic development of China: she is also the only country fully able to participate."[93]

---

[87] "Talk by Mao Zedong at an Enlarged Meeting of the Chinese Communist Party Central Committee Politburo (excerpt)," April 25, 1956, in Wilson Center Digital Archive, Chinese Nuclear History.

[88] Lewis and Xue (1994, 212).

[89] See: Barnhart (1987).

[90] See: Bush (2004, 9–39).

[91] Interestingly, at the end of the Second World War, the Soviet Union also recognized the Nationalists rather than the Communists as forming the legitimate government of China. See: Tucker (2001, 14–15).

[92] "Memorandum of Conversation, by the Second Secretary of Embassy in China (Davies)," Chungking, November 17, 1944, in *Foreign Relations of the United States (FRUS)*, 1944, VI, *China*, Doc. 483, p. 730.

[93] Mao paraphrased by John S. Service, "Report by the Second Secretary of Embassy in China (Service)," Yenan, March 13, 1945, in *Foreign Relations of the United States (FRUS)*, 1945, Vol. VII, *The Far East, China*, Doc. 194, pp. 273–274.

After the ouster of the Japanese, the Nationalists and Communists were on the brink of civil war. In December 1945, President Harry Truman sent General George C. Marshall to China to mediate a cease-fire agreement; and in the coming months, Washington restrained the Nationalist government from attacking the Communists.[94] Ultimately, peace broke down in late March 1946 and pitted the two superpowers along the ideological lines of the emerging Cold War. Soviet troops completed their withdrawal from Manchuria in the spring of 1946, leaving the CCP in control. Washington signed a trade treaty with the Nationalist government in the fall of 1946,[95] and offered it close to $2 billion in aid between 1945 and 1949.[96] U.S. support of the Nationalists enraged Mao, who claimed in June 1949 that the United States "wanted to enslave the whole world; it supplied arms to help Chiang Kai-shek slaughter several million Chinese."[97] The CCP, therefore, would "lean to one side" and ally with the Soviet Union.[98]

In the first year of the conflict, the Nationalists seemed poised to win, but the tide of the civil war had turned in favor of the Communists by 1948. In April 1949, they captured the capital, Nanjing, and in May Chiang Kai-shek fled to Taiwan. As the Truman administration acknowledged in the China White Paper of August 5, the defeat of the Nationalist government was not due to the inadequacy of U.S. aid, but to the ineptitude of Chiang's government: "[t]he Nationalist armies did not have to be defeated; they disintegrated."[99]

By extension, the Truman administration anticipated the Nationalist government to crumble in Taiwan. As Secretary of State Dean Acheson (1949–1953) explained to the JCS in December 1949, the authorities in Taipei faced a great risk of "continual decay," given "a

---

[94] See: Westad (2003, 31–32).
[95] Ibid., 51, 86–87.
[96] Dean Acheson, "Letter of Transmittal," July 30, 1949, in U.S. Department of State, *United States Relations with China: With Special Reference to the Period 1944–1949* (Washington, D.C.: U.S. Government Printing Office, 1949), p. XIV.
[97] Mao Zedong, "On the People's Democratic Dictatorship," June 30, 1949, in Mao (1961), p. 414.
[98] Ibid., 415.
[99] Dean Acheson, "Letter of Transmittal," July 30, 1949, p. XIV.

hostile population, overrun by refugees," and a "corrupt government." A U.S. intervention could delay the fall of the Nationalists, but by doing so Washington would "have once more involved U.S. prestige in another failure for all to see; moreover, and of greater importance," Acheson added, it would provoke "the united Chinese hatred of foreigners."[100] Since Taiwan was not deemed to be of significant strategic importance, Acheson argued against direct intervention.[101] In NSC-48/2, the U.S. government ruled out a military defense of Taiwan,[102] a policy announced publicly by President Truman on January 5, 1950.[103]

Soon, however, Washington had to revise its security commitments in the region. On June 25, 1950, the North Korean troops of supreme leader Kim Il-sung (1948–1994) invaded the South, after Kim received the approval of Stalin and Mao.[104] President Truman announced that he would support South Korean leader Syngman Rhee (1948–1960). In addition, he sent the Seventh Fleet to the Taiwan Strait to "neutralize" the area, calling for international discussions to determine its political status.[105] In both the Korean and Taiwanese theaters, the PRC had suddenly become subject to U.S. nuclear threats. This exposure to nuclear coercion played an instrumental role in Beijing's decision to acquire nuclear weapons.

---

[100] "Memorandum of Conversation, by the Secretary of State," [Washington,] December 29, 1949, in *Foreign Relations of the United States (FRUS), 1949*, Vol. IX, *The Far East: China*, Doc. 490.

[101] See also: "Memorandum of Conversation, by the Secretary of State," Washington, January 5, 1950, in *Foreign Relations of the United States (FRUS), 1950*, Vol. VI, *East Asia and the Pacific*, Doc. 127.

[102] "Memorandum by the Executive Secretary of the National Security Council (Souers) to the National Security Council," Washington, December 30, 1949, in *Foreign Relations of the United States (FRUS), 1949*, Vol. VII, Part 2, *The Far East and Australia*, Doc. 386.

[103] "The President's News Conference," January 5, 1950, Harry S. Truman Library, Public Papers of the Presidents, Harry S. Truman, 1945–1953. Available at: www.trumanlibrary.org/publicpapers. Last accessed: May 1, 2016.

[104] See: Chen (2004, 104–105). Stalin and Mao were concerned with a possible US intervention in the conflict. The fact that Acheson omitted South Korea when publicly delineating the American defense perimeter in the Pacific seems to have played a role in their decision to endorse the invasion. See: Goncharov, Lewis, and Xue (1993, 101, 142); Chen and Yang (1998, 251); Zhihua (2000, 63). For Acheson's speech, see: Acheson (1950, 116).

[105] See: Accinelli (1996, 29–34).

Nuclear Coercion in the Korean War and Taiwan Strait Crises

U.S. intervention in Korea led to direct clashes with Chinese forces. On September 15, 1950, U.S./UN forces made an amphibious landing at Inchon, behind the DPRK forces. Two weeks later, on October 1, Kim formally asked for the PRC's entry into the Korean conflict.

The PRC leadership faced a difficult decision. Mao had warned Kim about the prospect of U.S. intervention.[106] Now the United States had entered the conflict, and some congressional leaders were pressing for the use of nuclear weapons.[107] Sending troops to support the DPRK presented a clear risk. PRC Marshall Lin Biao refused Mao's request to command Chinese forces in Korea. Officially citing poor health, he warned of the dangers in fighting U.S. forces. In a meeting of the Central Military Commission in early October, Lin declared: "The United States is highly modernized. In addition, it possesses the atomic bomb. I have no certainty of success [in fighting the U.S. army]. The central leadership should consider this with great care."[108] Mao remained steadfast in his desire to support the North Korean communists. On October 8, he ordered China's entry into the war,[109] and in mid-October the first Chinese "volunteer" troops secretly crossed the Yalu River into North Korea.

By the end of the year, Chinese troops had repelled U.S. forces out of northwest Korea. Condemning the entry of PRC forces in the conflict, President Truman publicly entertained the idea of using the atomic bomb. In a news conference on November 30, Truman declared that the United States "will take whatever steps are necessary to meet the military situation" and that such a measure "includes every weapon that we have." When asked if this included the atomic bomb, he responded that there "has always been active consideration of its use," though a press release later that day clarified that the president had not authorized the use of nuclear weapons.[110]

As the war dragged on, the prospect of nuclear use in Korea became more likely. In the winter of 1950–1951, Washington began testing atomic artillery, and tactical nuclear weapons were included in

[106] See: Chen (2004, 104–105).
[107] See: Ryan (1989, 26).
[108] Quoted in Goncharov et al. (1993, 167).
[109] See: Ibid., 184.
[110] "Editorial Note," in *Foreign Relations of the United States* (*FRUS*), 1950, Vol. VII, *Korea*, Doc. 902.

U.S. defense plans by 1952.[111] U.S. media reported on possible nuclear use in the Korean theater.[112] In the course of the conflict, the U.S. stockpile increased significantly, tripling between the summer of 1950 and the summer of 1953, to about 1,000 atomic weapons.[113]

The Eisenhower administration placed a greater reliance on atomic threats than did its predecessor, and wished to blur the distinction between nuclear and conventional weapons also in East Asia.[114] In late October 1952, the National Security Council (NSC) adopted NSC-162/2, which articulated the doctrine of massive retaliation.[115] To deter Communist aggression, the United States should develop and maintain a "strong military posture, with emphasis on the capability of inflicting massive retaliatory damage by offensive striking power." In this posture, nuclear weapons played a key role, and they should "be as available for use as other munitions."[116] In a meeting on March 31, 1953, President Eisenhower and Secretary of State John Foster Dulles (1953–1959) agreed that "somehow or other the tabu which surrounds the use of atomic weapons would have to be destroyed."[117]

To break the stalemate in negotiations for an armistice in Korea, the United States wished to signal to the PRC that it was willing to escalate the conflict. In a meeting in New Delhi on May 21, 1953, Dulles told Indian prime minister Jawaharlal Nehru (1947–1964) that "if armistice negotiations collapsed, the United States would probably make a stronger rather than a lesser military exertion," a message which he believed would be relayed to the PRC leadership.[118] On June 8, the PRC

---

[111] Calingaert (1988, 188–189).
[112] See: "Atomic Group Sees Lovett in Secret; Conference Spurs Speculation on Use of Nuclear Weapon on Enemy in Korea," *The New York Times*, October 11, 1951, p. 18; "Air Force Atoms," *Newsweek*, March 3, 1952, pp. 25–26.
[113] Calingaert (1988, 184).
[114] See: Jones (2008).
[115] For the famous public expression of the doctrine, see: "Text of Dulles' Statement on Foreign Policy of Eisenhower Administration," *The New York Times*, January 13, 1954, p. 2.
[116] "NSC 162/2: Report to the National Security Council by the Executive Secretary (Lay)," Washington, October 30, 1953, in *Foreign Relations of the United States (FRUS)*,1952–1954, Vol. II, Part 1, *National Security Affairs*, Doc. 100.
[117] "Memorandum of Conversation at a Special Meeting of the National Security Council," March 31, 1953, in *Foreign Relations of the United States (FRUS)*, 1952–1954, Vol. XV, Part 1, *Korea*, Doc. 427.
[118] "Memorandum of Conversation by the Secretary of State," New Delhi, May 21, 1953, 11:30 a.m., in *FRUS, 1952–1954*, Vol. XV, Part 1, Doc. 537.

accepted U.S. demands on the repatriation of prisoners of war, paving the way for the signature of an armistice, which took place on July 27. In retrospect, U.S. policymakers were convinced that nuclear threats played a crucial role in producing a truce in the Korean conflict.[119]

Soon, the PRC once again confronted Washington's nuclear power. U.S. intervention in the Strait in the summer of 1950 had forced Beijing to table plans to invade Taiwan.[120] Mao resented American intervention and rejected the argument that the status of Taiwan was undetermined, instead claiming that it was an internal affair. On September 3, 1954, the PRC began shelling the offshore island of Jinmen (Quemoy), controlled by Taiwan, initiating the First Taiwan Strait Crisis. U.S. policymakers condemned the attack and prepared for a response. According to Admiral Arthur W. Radford, Chairman of the JCS (1953–1957), if Washington decided to intervene in defense of the offshore islands, "it must be done with whatever force is necessary to achieve success, including the use of atomic weapons if necessary."[121] Secretary Dulles rejected Chiang's arguments that these islands were of crucial importance for the defense of Taiwan, which in his view depended on "the deterrent power represented by the massive retaliatory capacity of the United States."[122] Dulles believed that deterrence could be further strengthened with the formalization of the alliance between Washington and Taipei, and some deliberately "fuzzy" language about the territories included in the defense agreement. On December 2, the United States and Taiwan concluded a Mutual Defense Treaty. On January 29, 1955, Congress passed the Formosa Resolution, giving the president authority to use force to defend Formosa (Taiwan), the Pescadores, as well as unnamed "related positions and territories."[123]

---

[119] See: Dulles's interview with *Life* in January 1956 (Shepley 1956, 77). For a critical assessment, see: Foot (1988–1989).

[120] See: Whiting (1968, 62–64); Zhang (1992, 73).

[121] "Memorandum of Conversation of the Joint Chiefs of Staff (Radford) to the Secretary of Defense (Wilson)," Washington, September 11, 1954, in *Foreign Relations of the United States (FRUS)*, 1952–1954, Vol. XIV, Part 1, *Japan and Korea*, Doc. 291.

[122] "Memorandum of Discussion at the 221st Meeting of the National Security Council," Washington, November 2, 1954, in *FRUS*, 1952–1954, Vol. XIV, Part 1, Doc. 375.

[123] Elie Abel, "President Signs Formosa Measure; Sees Peace Guard," *The New York Times*, Jan. 30, 1955, p. 1.

In the midst of the Taiwan crisis, the PRC made the decision to launch a nuclear-weapons program. At a meeting of the Central Secretariat on January 15, 1955, Mao declared: "During the past years we have been busy doing other things, and there was not enough time for us to pay attention to this matter [of nuclear] weapons. Sooner or later, we would have had to pay attention to it. Now, it is time for us to pay attention to it."[124]

At the same time, the PRC leadership condemned U.S. atomic coercion. Premier Zhou Enlai (1949–1976) accused Washington of "publicly gearing up for atomic war," and "conventionalizing" nuclear weapons.[125] Mao declared that the Americans "have occupied our Taiwan and the Taiwan Straits and are contemplating an atomic war." However, he added, Washington "cannot annihilate the Chinese people with its small stack of atom bombs." In a conflict against American planes and bombs, "China with its millet plus rifles is sure to emerge the victor."[126]

The Eisenhower administration, for its part, remained convinced that nuclear coercion was Washington's most effective strategy. On March 6, 1955, Secretary Dulles met with the president after a trip to Asia, where he attended the inaugural meeting of the South East Asian Treaty Organization (SEATO) in Bangkok. Dulles opined that the United States needed to be more active in the defense of Quemoy and Matsu and that "this would require the use of atomic missiles." Eisenhower declared that he "thoroughly agreed" and asked Dulles to present nuclear weapons in his upcoming news conference as "interchangeable" with conventional weaponry.[127] In his address of March 8, Secretary Dulles suggested that in a general war, China would have to confront U.S. forces equipped with "new and powerful weapons" of great precision, which would spare civilian casualties.[128] Eisenhower

---

[124] Quoted in Lewis and Xue (1988, 39).

[125] Quoted in Tan Wenrui, "Oppose the US preparation for Atomic War" *Renmin Ribao* [*People's Daily*], January 16, 1955, p. 2, our translation.

[126] Mao Zedong, "The Chinese People Cannot Be Cowed by the Atom Bomb," January 28, 1955, in Mao (1977), pp. 152–153.

[127] "Memorandum of Conversation between the President and the Secretary of State," Washington, March 6, 1955, in *Foreign Relations of the United States* (*FRUS*), 1955–1957, Vol. II, *China*, Doc. 141.

[128] John Foster Dulles, "Report from Asia, Delivered on March 8," *Department of State Bulletin*, Vol. XXXII, No. 821, March 21, 1955, 459–464, quote at 459.

reinforced the same message in a press conference on March 16, where he explained that if nuclear weapons could be used exclusively on military targets, he saw "no reason why they shouldn't be used just exactly as you would use a bullet or anything else."[129]

Zhou accused the United States of "continu[ing] to create tension in the Taiwan area" and rejected any attempt to treat nuclear weapons as conventional.[130] At the same time, he stated that China did not want war and was willing to enter into negotiations with Washington.[131] On May 1, the PRC stopped shelling Quemoy and Matsu, ending the First Taiwan Strait Crisis, and ambassadorial-level talks were set up in August 1 to manage future relations between the two countries.[132]

This crisis fueled the PRC's interest in possessing a nuclear force. In April 1956, Mao concluded that the acquisition of nuclear weapons and delivery systems should take greater priority than conventional weaponry.[133] Beijing soon faced an even stronger possibility of U.S. nuclear use starting in May 1957, when Washington began to station Matador missiles on Taiwan.[134] Moreover, U.S.-China negotiations had stalled.[135] On the status of Taiwan, Washington pressed

---

[129] Eisenhower (1959a, 332).

[130] "Speech by Premier Chou En-lai," April 19, 1955, in *Bandung: Texts of Selected Speeches and Final Communique of the Asian-African Conference, Bandung, Indonesia, April 18–24, 1955* (New York: Far East Reporter, 1955), 22.

[131] "Premier Chou En-lai's Report on Bandung to the Standing Committee of the National People's Congress, People's Republic of China," May 16, 1955, in *Bandung: Texts of Selected Speeches and Final Communique of the Asian-African Conference, Bandung, Indonesia, April 18–24, 1955* (New York: Far East Reporter, 1955), 57; "Telegram from the Ambassador in Indonesia (Cumming) to the Department of State," Jakarta, April 23, 1955, 10 p.m., in *FRUS*, 1955–1957, Vol. II, Doc. 216.

[132] See: Ross and Jiang (2001); Tucker (2001, 96).

[133] See: Zhang (1992, 232). Later, the "Guidelines for Developing Nuclear Weapons," approved at a conference of the Central Military Commission held between May and July 1958, instructed that "[a]ny other projects for our country's reconstruction will have to take second place to the development of nuclear weapons" (quoted in Lewis and Xue 1988, 70).

[134] See: "Telegram from Ambassador U. Alexis Johnson to the Department of State," Geneva, May 15, 1957, 1 p.m., in *Foreign Relations of the United States (FRUS), 1955–1957*, Vol. III, *China*, Doc. 251.

[135] See: "Agreed Announcement of the Ambassadors of the United States of America and the People's Republic of China," Geneva, September 10, 1955, 5 p.m., in *FRUS, 1955–1957*, Vol. III, Doc. 53; Barnett (1977, 187); Goldstein (2001, 207).

for a peaceful resolution of the conflict, while Beijing insisted that it remained an internal matter.[136] Ambassadorial-level talks were suspended in December 1957.

On August 23, 1958, PRC forces once again began shelling Quemoy and Matsu, opening the Second Taiwan Strait Crisis. Until then, U.S. policy had been vague about defense commitments to the offshore islands, hoping that the PRC could be deterred by American ambiguity. Facing Chinese provocations, the Eisenhower administration debated the risks of escalation. Previous analyses had argued that Washington might succeed in "localizing" (i.e., limiting) a conflict in the Strait even if it used tactical nuclear weapons, given Soviet interest in avoiding a general war. On September 4, Dulles and President Eisenhower converged on a forceful response.[137] In a press release that day, Dulles explained that the security of Taiwan was increasingly tied with the defense of Quemoy and Matsu, and that the United States reserved the right to use force to defend the offshore islands under the Formosa resolution.[138] Nevertheless, recognizing the precarious situation of these islands, Washington publicly questioned Chiang Kai-shek's policy of stationing significant troops there.[139] On October 23, Dulles and Chiang issued a joint communiqué, reaffirming their alliance, while insisting that it was defensive in nature.[140] The crisis abated and war was averted.

Mao rejoiced at the U.S. decision to tie the defense of the offshore islands to the security of Formosa. Doing so, Washington had slipped a "noose" around its own neck, which Beijing could tighten whenever expedient.[141] Such a development would also make it harder to pursue

---

[136] See: "Telegram from the Acting Secretary of State to Ambassador U. Alexis Johnson, at Geneva," Washington, September 27, 1955, 10:36 a.m., and "Telegram from Ambassador U. Alexist Johnson to the Department of State," Geneva, October 5, 1955, 4 p.m., both in *FRUS, 1955–1957*, Vol. III, Docs. 65, 69.

[137] See: "Memorandum of Conference with President Eisenhower," Newport, Rhode Island, September 4, 1958, 10:30 a.m., in *Foreign Relations of the United States (FRUS), 1958–1960*, Vol. XIX, *China*, Doc. 66.

[138] See: "White House Press Release," Newport, Rhode Island, September 4, 1958, in *FRUS, 1958–1960*, Vol. XIX, Doc. 68.

[139] See: "Editorial Note," in *FRUS, 1958–1960*, Vol. XIX, Doc. 143; Eisenhower (1959b, 715).

[140] See: "Joint Communiqué," Taipei, October 23, 1958, in *FRUS, 1958–1960*, Vol. XIX, Doc. 209.

[141] See: Li (2001, 159–167). For their part, U.S. policymakers again perceived the termination of the crisis as evidence that a firm stand deterred the PRC.

a "two-China" policy, since the offshore islands were so much closer to the mainland than to Taiwan.[142] Yet, if Mao viewed the crisis as a diplomatic success, it contributed to the deterioration of the PRC's relations with its ally, the Soviet Union. Beijing had left Moscow in the dark about its plans to attack the islands.[143] Furthermore, Beijing's rhetoric downplaying the deterrent effect of U.S. nuclear forces was viewed as cavalier in Moscow.[144] In a meeting with Soviet minister of foreign affairs Andrei Gromyko (1957–1985) during the crisis, Mao reportedly asked the Soviet Union to respond to a U.S. attack with "everything you've got." Gromyko was "flabbergasted."[145] Though Khrushchev defended the PRC during the crisis, threatening Eisenhower with retaliation,[146] Mao's reckless behavior strained relations between the two countries. In fact, concerns over the reliability of the alliance with the Soviet Union would become another motivation for Chinese acquisition of the bomb. These concerns would prove well-founded, as the Sino-Soviet alliance would soon begin to fray.

The Sino-Soviet Alliance and Its Split
In the early years of the Sino-Soviet alliance, Washington perceived the two countries as a bloc. Reacting to Mao's decision to "lean to one side" and ally with the Soviet Union in June 1949, Acheson declared that Beijing had chosen its "subservience" to Moscow.[147] Two years later, Dulles declared that the PRC was "a puppet regime" of the Soviet Union.[148]

During the early 1950s, the PRC was confident in Soviet guarantees and enthusiastic about Soviet technical assistance for its nuclear-weapons

See: "Draft Statement Prepared in the Department of State," Washington, undated, and "Editorial Note," both in *FRUS*, 1958–1960, Vol. XIX, Docs. 267, 274.

[142] Quemoy is a small archipelago in close proximity to Xiamen, in the PRC, and around 170 miles from Taiwan. The Matsu Islands are a minor archipelago more than 100 miles from Taiwan and around ten miles from the PRC.

[143] See: Goldstein (2000, 82).

[144] See: Lewis and Xue (1988, 60).

[145] Gromyko (1989, 251). This claim is disputed. See: Li (2001, 161).

[146] See: "Telegram from the Embassy in the Soviet Union to the Department of State," Moscow, September 7, 1958, 9 p.m., and "Telegram from the Embassy in the Soviet Union to the Departmment of State," Moscow, September 19, 1958, 8 p.m., both in *FRUS*, 1958–1960, Vol. XIX, Docs. 74, 110.

[147] Acheson (1949, XIV).

[148] Quoted in Chang (1990, 83). See also: Tucker (2001, 66).

program. In January 15, 1955, when discussing the Chinese nuclear program, Mao announced that because "the Soviet Union is giving us assistance, we must achieve success!"[149] Over the following three years, the two countries concluded six agreements on nuclear research, uranium mining, and enrichment.[150] In October 1957, they signed the New Defense Technology Agreement, whereby Moscow agreed to provide Beijing with "a sample nuclear weapon" as well as assistance on missile technology.[151] By mid-July 1960, there were about 1,400 Soviet experts working in China on economic, cultural, and military programs.[152]

Despite its solid appearance, the Sino-Soviet alliance showed ominous signs of possible disagreement already at the time of their security agreement of February 1950. Moscow was reluctant to agree on a pledge to offer "all means at its disposal" in the event of an invasion of China. This Soviet concern most likely originated from Moscow's reluctance to use its nascent nuclear capability and thereby escalate the conflict.[153] Symptomatically, as the PRC prepared to enter the Korean War in October 1950, Stalin refused to commit troops to the conflict, saying that this would risk a Third World War with the United States. Instead, he offered only military assistance to the PRC.[154] As early as 1954, upon returning from a visit to Beijing, Khrushchev told his comrades: "Conflict with China is inevitable."[155]

At the same time, Soviet assistance raised growing suspicions in Beijing. By the late 1950s, competition for leadership of the international communist movement and diverging views on core security interests had led to a widening gap between the PRC and the USSR.[156]

---

[149] Quoted in Lewis and Xue (1988, 39). Later that month, Zhou Enlai declared that "with Soviet help," the PRC could "catch up" and "master atomic energy." See: "Address by Zhou Enlai at the Plenary Session of the Fourth Meeting of the State Council (Excerpt)," January 31, 1955, in Wilson Center Digital Archive, Chinese Nuclear History.

[150] Liu and Liu (2009, 71–73).

[151] Taubman (2003, 389). See also: Kramer (1995–1996, 175); Pleshakov (1998, 232).

[152] See: "Letter, Khrushchev to the Central Committee of the Socialist Unity Party of Germany, Regarding Soviet Specialists in China," July 18, 1960, in Wilson Center Digital Archive, Sino-Soviet Split, 1960–1984; "The Leaders of the CPSU Are the Greatest Splitters of Our Time," *Peking Review*, Vol. 7, no. 1 (February 7, 1964), 9.

[153] See: Goncharov et al. (1993, 118).

[154] Ibid., 189–190, 195.

[155] Quoted in Taubman (2003, 337).

[156] On the Sino-Soviet split, see: Barnett (1977, 32–33); Kramer (1995–1996); Westad (1998); Radchenko (2009, 2010); Li and Xia (2014).

Mao took umbrage at Khrushchev's efforts to distance himself from Stalin.[157] As he declared unambiguously during his visit to Moscow in November 1957, Khrushchev was proposing a "revisionist" foreign policy that was too conciliatory toward the West.[158] Khrushchev also did not endear himself to PRC leaders when, in the spring of 1958, he informed Zhou Enlai that the Soviet Union intended to pursue disarmament agreements with Western nuclear powers.[159] The following summer, Moscow offered to build (and control) a long-wave radio station on the Chinese coast and build a joint Sino-Soviet submarine flotilla. Mao feared that Moscow would attempt to control China's defense and foreign policy and opposed both ideas vehemently, giving Khrushchev a smackdown during his visit to Beijing to sell the projects.[160] Later, the Chinese leadership roundly criticized Khrushchev's handling of the Cuban Missile Crisis. On October 31, 1962, the Chinese embassy declared that "Khrushchev's reconciliation and submission to American imperialism constitutes a fiasco in the diplomatic struggle of the Soviet Union. Its influence on future development is bound to be extremely negative."[161] In the CCP's view, Khrushchev's retreat "was an unprecedented humiliation to the socialist countries."[162] At around the same time, China's border conflict with India escalated to a full-scale war, and Beijing was irate at Soviet behavior – namely, the sale of military aircraft to India – which it blamed at least in part for Delhi's "stubbornness and [its] unwillingness to solve problems through peaceful means."[163]

---

[157] See: Barnett (1977, 32–33).

[158] See: Garver (1993, 130); Chen (2001, 71); Tucker (2001, 145).

[159] See: Jersild (2013); Garver (1993, 130); Chen (2001, 71); Tucker (2001, 145).

[160] See: Christensen (1996, 209–210); Chen (2001, 74); Taubman (2003, 389–390).

[161] Chinese Embassy in Moscow, "Khrushchev's Reconciliation with the United States on the Question of the Cuban Missile Crisis," October 31, 1962, in "The Global Cuban Missile Crisis at 50: New Evidence from behind the Iron, Bamboo, and Sugarcane Curtains, and Beyond," Doc. 20, p. 88, edited by James G. Hershberg and Christian F. Ostermann, translated by Zhang Qian, Cold War International History Project Bulletin, Issues 17–18 (October 2012).

[162] "The CCP CC Circular on the Current Situation of Cuba's Anti-American Struggle," December 4, 1962, in Guangxi Autonomous Region Archives, 1/31/166, pp. 3–4, quoted in Li and Xia (2014, 44).

[163] "Minutes of Conversation between Chinese Deputy Director of the Department of Soviet and European Affairs Yu Zhan and Charge d'Affaires of the Soviet Union Nikolai Mesyatsev on the Sino-Indian Boundary Issue," December 12, 1962, in Wilson Center Digital Archive, Sino-Soviet Split, 1960–1984. See also: Radchenko (2009, 29).

In the course of this widening split between the PRC and the Soviet Union, Moscow withdrew its support for the Chinese nuclear-weapons program. In March 1958, the Soviet Union decided not to send a prototype of the atomic bomb to China.[164] Later that year, the PRC leadership issued new guidelines for its nuclear-weapons program, declaring that it should proceed without trying to "imitate other countries."[165] Reacting to growing Chinese criticism of Soviet policy, in June 1959 the Soviet leader annulled the agreement he had signed two years before to provide China with the technology necessary to build a nuclear weapon.[166] Aware that this measure might lead China to doubt Moscow's protection, boosting Beijing's willingness to build its own nuclear arsenal, Khrushchev took pains to emphasize the importance of the Soviet nuclear umbrella for protecting Chinese territory.[167] But relations continued to deteriorate. Ending nuclear cooperation, in July 1960, Khrushchev ordered all advisors and experts in the PRC to return to the Soviet Union.[168] Estimates of the role of Soviet help in speeding up Chinese nuclear development vary widely. In the most extensive analysis of Moscow's support for Beijing's nuclear ambition, Liu and Liu conclude:

China could have built its first atomic bomb by 1964 or 1965 if it had independently started research on producing nuclear material in 1956, instead of relying on Soviet technology transfer; however, this would have required mobilization of more scientists, technicians, and workers from other agencies, with consequent effects on education, employment, and manufacturing.[169]

During the early 1960s, the rhetorical dispute between Beijing and Moscow only grew louder over time. In an interview published in the *Washington Post* in December 1963, PRC vice premier Chen Yi (1954–1972) declared that the "Soviet protection is worth nothing to us."[170]

---

[164] See: Lewis and Xue (1988, 60–61).
[165] Quoted in ibid., 70.
[166] See: Pantsov and Levine (2007, 467).
[167] See: Jersild (2013).
[168] "Note, the Soviet Embassy in Beijing to the Ministry of Foreign Affairs of the People's Republic of China," July 18, 1960, Wilson Center Digital Archive, Sino-Soviet Split, 1960–1984.
[169] Liu and Liu (2009, 100).
[170] Department of State Circular CA-43 to U.S. Embassy in Thailand et al., "Status of Program to Influence World Opinion with Respect to a Chinese Communist Nuclear Detonation," July 20, 1964, in National Security Archive

In February 1964, a Chinese editorial in the *People's Daily* questioned Khrushchev's leadership, accusing him of being "the greatest splitter" in the international communist movement.[171] By July, Mao warned that the security of China's northern border with the Soviet Union, was just as concerning as the security of the south, where the Vietnam War was raging, admonishing his Politburo colleagues: "don't just pay attention to imperialism and not to revisionism."[172]

In part, Beijing's disagreements with Moscow had their roots in the Chinese nuclear program. When in the summer of 1962 the U.S. government presented Moscow with the idea of limiting or banning nuclear tests, the Soviet leadership agreed to start the talks that would ultimately lead to the PTBT of 1963.[173] When Moscow notified Beijing of these negotiations, the PRC reacted by stating that it "resolutely opposes the U.S. proposals because they are mainly spearheaded against China ... and attempt to sow dissension between China and the Soviet Union." Furthermore, Chinese officials warned their Soviet counterparts that "the Soviet Union had no right to assume legal 'responsibilities on behalf of China.'"[174] Soon thereafter, Beijing decided to schedule its first nuclear test for late 1964 or early 1965.[175] As Li and Xia conclude, "[f]or Chinese leaders, the push for nuclear nonproliferation amounted to 'collusion between Khrushchev and the United States to prevent us from doing atomic research.'"[176]

As the Chinese nuclear-weapons program was coming to completion, the Sino-Soviet split was so severe that Washington tried to elicit Moscow's support for military action aimed at preventing the Chinese

(NSA) Electronic Briefing Book (EBB) 38, "The United States and the Chinese Nuclear Program, 1960–1964," Doc. 14, p. 6.

[171] "The Leaders of the CPSU Are the Greatest Splitters of Our Time," *Peking Review*, Vol. 7, no. 1 (February 7, 1964), 5–21.

[172] Quoted in Wang (2007, 149). Between October 15, 1964 and March 1969, Beijing claimed that a total of 4,189 incidents occurred on the Sino-Soviet border (see: Robinson 1981, 268). In March 1969, the dispute erupted into a full-scale conflict, which lasted until September that year.

[173] See: Li and Xia (2014, 45).

[174] Ibid., quoting Zhou Wenqi and Chu Lianghe, eds., *Teshu er fuzha de keti – Gongchanguoji, Sulian he Zhongguogongchandang guanxi biannianshi* [A Special and Complicated Topic: Annals of Relations between the Comintern, the Soviet Union, and the Chinese Communist Party] (Wuhan: Hubei Renmin Chubanshe, 1993), 527–528.

[175] See: Li and Xia (2014, 45).

[176] Ibid., 45–46, quoting Zhou and Chu, eds., *Teshu er fuzha de keti*, 532.

from acquiring the bomb. Ultimately, the Americans were unsuccessful in their counterproliferation attempt. In September 1963, the PRC had a draft design of an atomic weapon. By the spring of 1964, the nuclear fuel processing plant at Subei had produced sufficient enriched uranium for a bomb.[177] On October 16, 1964, the Chinese detonated their first nuclear weapon. What explains this failure of U.S. counterproliferation?

U.S. Counterproliferation Efforts

Washington was keenly interested in monitoring the Chinese nuclear-weapons program from its inception. In January 1956, a National Intelligence Estimate (NIE) declared that Beijing's nuclear research capability was "primitive," but that with Soviet assistance "the Chinese Communists could in a short time achieve the capability to use nuclear weapons."[178] By April 1961, the Department of State concluded that given recent intelligence assessments, "it is no longer a question of whether Peiping is engaged in a nuclear weapons program, but only of when a detonation may be expected."[179]

President John F. Kennedy was especially concerned about the prospects of facing a nuclear-armed China, and so were many in his administration. In November 1962, National Security Adviser McGeorge Bundy (1961–1966) wrote to Kennedy that "[a] Red China nuclear presence is the greatest single threat to the status quo over the next few years."[180] In a meeting with CIA director John A. McCone (1961–1965) in January 1963, Bundy declared that according to Kennedy, the development of a nuclear capability in the PRC was "probably the

---

[177] See: Lewis and Xue (1988, 162).

[178] "National Intelligence Estimate 13–56," Washington, January 5, 1956, in *FRUS, 1955–1957*, Vol. III, Doc. 126.

[179] Memorandum from John M. Steeves, Bureau of Far Eastern Affairs, to Roger Hilsman, Director, Bureau of Intelligence and Research, "National Intelligence Estimate on Implications of Chinese Communist Nuclear Capability," April 12, 1961, in NSA EBB 38, Doc. 2, p. 1. The memorandum refers to National Intelligence Estimate NIE 13–60 of December 6, 1960 ("National Intelligence Estimate 13–60," Washington, December 6, 1960, in *FRUS, 1958–1960*, Vol. XIX, Doc. 362).

[180] "Memorandum from the President's Special Assistant for National Security Affairs (Bundy) to President Kennedy," Washington, November 8, 1962, in *Foreign Relations of the United States (FRUS), 1961–1963*, Vol. VII, *Arms Control and Disarmament*, Doc. 243.

most serious problem facing the world today. ... [N]uclear weapons in the hands of the Chinese Communists would so upset the world political scene it would be intolerable to the United States and to the West."[181]

In an attempt to prevent the PRC from developing a nuclear capability, the Kennedy administration devised a two-pronged approach. To begin with, the United States pressed for restrictions on nuclear testing – the PTBT was signed in Moscow in August 1963 and went into effect on October 10, 1963. Additionally, Washington considered the option of a preventive attack on the PRC's nuclear facilities.

Discussing PTBT negotiations with the Soviets in January 1963, Kennedy explained that their "primary purpose" was "to halt or delay the development of an atomic capability by the Chinese Communists."[182] By then, the Sino-Soviet split was so severe that Moscow seemed open to the idea of reaching an agreement on the treaty. Then assistant secretary of state for far eastern affairs, Averell Harriman (1961–1963), shared the president's concerns about a PRC nuclear capability, and believed that the Soviets would be willing to collaborate in pursuit of this goal. In his view, Moscow believed that "with such an agreement" – the PTBT – "together we could compel China to stop nuclear development, threatening to take out the facilities if necessary."[183]

At the same time, Kennedy publicly hinted at the possibility of using force to convince states that rejected a test ban treaty to forego their

[181] "Editorial Note," in *Foreign Relations of the United States (FRUS)*, 1961–1963, Vol. XXII, *Northeast Asia*, Doc. 162. In a press conference in August 1963, Kennedy declared that the situation in which the PRC could find itself in the 1970s "of weak countries around it, 700 million people, a Stalinist internal regime, and nuclear powers, and a government determined on war as a means of bringing about its ultimate success, as potentially a more dangerous situation than any we faced since the end of the Second War." By comparison, he added, "the Russians pursued in most cases their ambitions with some caution." "The President's News Conference," August 1, 1963, The American Presidency Project, Public Papers of the Presidents, John F. Kennedy. Available at: www.presidency.ucsb.edu/ws/index.php?pid=9366. Last accessed: May 1, 2016.

[182] "Record of the 508th Meeting of the National Security Council," Washington, January 22, 1963, in *Foreign Relations of the United States (FRUS)*, 1961–1963, Vol. VIII, *National Security Policy*, Doc. 125.

[183] "Editorial Note," in *FRUS*, 1961–1963, Vol. XXII, Doc. 164. See also: "Memorandum of Conversation," New York, September 25, 1962, 1:15 p.m., in *FRUS*, 1961–1963, Vol. VII, Doc. 331.

nuclear ambitions. In a press conference in Bonn on June 24, 1963, he stated that "it is proposed in the treaty that those who sign the treaty would use *all the influence that they had in their possession* to persuade others not to grasp the nuclear nettle."[184]

The Soviets were indeed willing to consider a PTBT, but would not countenance the use of force against the Chinese nuclear-weapons program. In a lunch with the Soviet ambassador Anatoly Dobrynin (1962–1986) in May 1963, Bundy commented that the "nuclear posture" of the PRC was a matter of "real common interest" and offered to have a "quite private and serious exchange of views" on the topic. Dobrynin declined the invitation.[185] Two months later, Harriman traveled to Moscow to finalize PTBT negotiations. Kennedy had instructed him to sound out Khrushchev's interest in joint military action against the Chinese program: "You should try to elicit Khrushchev's view of means of limiting or preventing Chinese nuclear development and his willingness either to take Soviet action or to accept US action aimed in this direction." The Soviet leader, however, "tried to give the impression of not being greatly concerned" about a Chinese nuclear-weapons capability.[186]

In fact, for all the concern about a PRC nuclear capability, U.S. intelligence reports were mixed about its effects.[187] A systematic cost-benefit analysis of possible counterproliferation strikes was needed. On October 15, 1963, a staffer in the Policy Planning Group, Robert Johnson, produced one such analysis: a report entitled "A Chinese

---

[184] "The President's News Conference at the Foreign Ministry in Bonn," June 24, 1963, The Presidency Project, Public Papers of the President, John F. Kennedy. Available at: www.presidency.ucsb.edu/ws/index.php?pid=9297. Last accessed: May 1, 2016, emphasis added. See also: Chang (1990, 240–241).

[185] McGeorge Bundy, "Memorandum of Conversation with Ambassador Dobrynin, at lunch," May 17, 1963, in NSA EBB 38, Doc. 7.

[186] "Editorial Note," in *FRUS*, 1961–1963, Vol. XXII, Doc. 180. See also: *FRUS*, 1961–1963, Vol. VII, Doc. 331.

[187] See: "Military Implications of a Communist Chinese Nuclear Capability," Study Memorandum No. 14 by General John B. Cary, August 31, 1962, in National Security Archive (NSA) Electronic Briefing Book (EBB) 488, "China's First Nuclear Test – 50th Anniversary," Doc. 4-B; Acting Deputy Assistant Director National Estimates, Central Intelligence Agency, to U.S. Intelligence Board, Special National Intelligence Estimate 13-6-62 Central Intelligence Agency, "Communist China's Nuclear Weapons Program," December 14, 1962, in NSA EBB 488, Doc. 5-B.

Communist Nuclear Detonation and Nuclear Capability."[188] The report argued that the impact of the PRC's nuclearization would be limited to deterring "some levels of U.S. attack upon the mainland."[189] It added that Beijing would probably not be emboldened by its nuclearization. In April 1964, Johnson completed another study, this time evaluating the policy options available to the United States in trying to prevent the PRC's nuclearization.[190] He concluded that "the significance of such a capability is not such as to justify the undertaking of actions which would involve great political costs or high military risks."[191] It is unlikely that Washington would have identified all the facilities in the PRC program that should be targeted, and a relatively large campaign would be needed to destroy the facilities "permanently." In short, the most thorough cost-benefit analysis conducted inside the U.S. government on the rationality of a preventive counter-proliferation strike on the Chinese nuclear program concluded against it for the reasons specified in our theory.

On September 15, 1964, a meeting between the president's main advisors, McCone, Bundy, Secretary of State Dean Rusk (1961–1969), and Secretary of Defense Robert McNamara (1961–1968) took place at the State Department. They had previously received a copy of the Johnson report[192] and during the meeting reached a consensus against unilateral military action. Nevertheless, they could still explore a joint action with the Soviet Union.[193] Ten days later, Bundy met with Dobrynin in Washington and indicated that the United States was

---

[188] Robert H. Johnson, State Department Policy Planning Council, "A Chinese Communist Nuclear Detonation and Nuclear Capability: Major Conclusions and Key Issues," October 15, 1963, in NSA EBB 38, Doc. 10. This was a condensed, 100-page version of a 200-page-long report completed in June. See: Burr and Richelson (2000–2001, 76).

[189] Ibid., p. 1.

[190] "Paper Prepared in the Policy Planning Council," Washington, April 14, 1964, in *Foreign Relations of the United States (FRUS)*, 1964–1968, Vol. XXX, *China*, Doc. 25.

[191] Ibid.

[192] Walt Rostow, Policy Planning Staff, U.S. Department of State, to McGeorge Bundy, "The Bases for Direct Action against Chinese Communist Nuclear Facilities," April 22, 1964, April 14, 1964, in NSA EBB 488, Doc. 16.

[193] "Memorandum for the Record," Washington, September 15, 1954, in *FRUS*, 1964–1968, Vol. XXX, Doc. 49. See also: Burr and Richelson (2000–2001, 87); Goldstein (2003, 751).

ready for a "private and serious talk" on a possible joint course of action with the Soviet Union regarding the Chinese nuclear-weapons program. As he had done earlier, Dobrynin minimized the importance of a Chinese nuclear capability and, when hearing of disagreements between Washington and Beijing, "gently remarked on the continued existence of the treaty between the USSR and the ChiComs."[194] The last avenue for forceful action against the Chinese nuclear-weapons program was thus shut. Having realized that the effect of Chinese nuclear acquisition would likely be smaller than the cost of a unilateral preventive counterproliferation strike, and aware of Moscow's loose support for Beijing's regime, Washington could not but relent in its effort to keep the PRC from obtaining the bomb. Within a month, Beijing became a nuclear power.

Alternative Explanations

There is a broad scholarly consensus on the crucial role that security threats originating in the United States played in driving China's willingness to acquire nuclear weapons. According to the classic account by John Lewis and Xue Litai, Chinese leaders initiated the nuclear-weapons program "under duress" and "resolved to stand firm in the face of the American 'blackmail.'"[195] We agree with this assessment. The security threat presented by the United States, an enemy with superior military capabilities, is sufficient to explain China's willingness to obtain nuclear weapons in the absence of a reliably ally.

A second factor deemed important by some scholars is Chinese nationalism.[196] According to Lewis and Xue, in a counterfactual world where China did not confront the United States over Taiwan, the PRC may have still pursued nuclear weapons: "the revolutionary elite under Mao Zedong came to power in 1949 with beliefs that may well have led to the nuclear weapons decision even without the unbroken chain of crises." Put differently, "[t]he decision to acquire a nuclear arsenal rested on fundamental national interests as much as on the

---

[194] "Memorandum of Conversation," Washington, September 25, 1964, 1–3:30 p.m., in *FRUS, 1964–1968*, Vol. XXX, Doc. 54.

[195] Lewis and Xue (1988, 11, 15). See also: Zhang (1992, 221); Foot (1995, 172); Goldstein (2000, 111); Yeaw, Erickson, and Chase (2012, 55).

[196] See: Lewis and Xue (1988, 35); Foot (1995, 172); Hymans (2012, 134–135).

immediate security threat."[197] In a related thesis, Jacques Hymans describes a country's interest in nuclear weapons as irrational. Only leaders of a certain psychological profile, i.e., oppositional nationalist leaders, pursue nuclear weapons.[198] Mao represents a stereotypical case of an oppositional nationalist leader, imbued with an "emotional" drive to match his rivals. Though Hymans concedes that U.S. nuclear threats were the "immediate spark" for the decision to acquire nuclear weapons, he argues that this decision was born of a "national identity impulsion."[199]

Mao was by all accounts a deeply nationalist leader, but it is difficult to view the role of Chinese nationalism as separate from China's security outlook. PRC leaders believed that Taiwan represented Chinese territory, which should be returned to Beijing's control. As a result, the pursuit of nationalist interests is, at least in this case, inextricably linked to the search for security. Including nationalism, therefore, does not add much explanatory power to our understanding of the causes of Chinese nuclear acquisition. China's strong interest in nuclear weapons can easily be understood given the disadvantageous balance of power with its security rival, the United States.

The economic preferences of Beijing's ruling coalition constitute a third possible impetus behind the Chinese nuclear-weapons program.[200] Yet, here also, it is difficult to see the lack of international integration of the Chinese economy as being independent from China's security situation. China was not a major trading partner with the United States and its allies because of the economic sanctions imposed by Washington.[201] In turn, the sanctions were imposed to oppose the Communist regime and its support for the North Korean invasion in the Korean War. Moreover, it is difficult to view the PRC leadership as "inward-looking" in the broad sense of the term, given its staunch desire to spread the Communist revolution abroad. A focus on China's security situation is instead a better way of accounting for its interest in nuclear weapons.

Turning to China's opportunity to acquire nuclear weapons, there are different accounts of how Beijing managed to succeed in

---

[197] Lewis and Xue (1988, 35).
[198] See: Hymans (2006).
[199] Hymans (2012, 134–135).
[200] This explanation would be compatible with Solingen (1994, 2007).
[201] See: Zhao (2010).

its nuclearization. A first perspective, consistent with the supply-side approach to the study of nuclear proliferation, is that China successfully nuclearized because of Soviet assistance. As Matthew Fuhrmann and Matthew Kroenig each document, states receiving technical assistance are more likely to obtain nuclear weapons.[202] China received assistance from the Soviet Union between 1958 and 1960 – assistance that, the argument goes, would prove crucial in its nuclearization.

Still, it is difficult to attribute China's success to Soviet assistance. Technical progress on the Chinese nuclear-weapons program resulted mainly from domestic Chinese scientific and industrial efforts rather than from Soviet assistance, which was limited, lower than promised, and quite short in its duration. In fact, Mao derided Soviet assistance in 1967, declaring with great irony that Chinese "guided missiles and nuclear weapons have had great achievements, and it is the result of Khrushchev's 'help.' He pulled out his experts and forced us to go it alone. We must give him a badge of merit that weighs one ton."[203] A retrospective analysis of Soviet assistance supports this assessment.[204] Ultimately, China's atomic bomb is better understood as resulting from the inadequacy of Soviet support. Chinese interest in nuclear weapons was fueled by doubts over Soviet security guarantees, and hardened with the termination of Soviet nuclear technical assistance.

Finally, recent scholarship attributes China's opportunity to acquire a nuclear arsenal to President Lyndon B. Johnson's (1963–1969) views on nuclear proliferation, which purportedly led to Washington's decision not to strike Beijing's nuclear-weapons program.[205] Whereas President Kennedy worried about the general consequences of nuclear proliferation, and feared the prospect of a Chinese bomb, this argument goes, President Johnson was more sanguine about the consequences of the PRC's nuclearization. Yet, the difficulty in making such a causal claim is that President Kennedy never saw Robert Johnson's cost-benefit analysis of a counterproliferation strike, which was only concluded in April 1964. As William Burr and Jeffrey Richelson document, this cost-benefit analysis played a key role in convincing President Johnson's cabinet that a strike was not a viable option.[206]

---

[202] See: Fuhrmann (2009, 2012); Kroenig (2009, 2010).
[203] Mao, "Comments after Hearing the Report from the xxxx [*sic*] Conference," July 7, 1967, in Mao (1967–1969, 318).
[204] See: Liu and Liu (2009).
[205] See: Whitlark (2013).
[206] See: Burr and Richelson (2000–2001).

It is impossible to know whether President Kennedy would have ordered a strike had he seen the Johnson study. In contrast, our focus on the costs and benefits of a strike is sufficient to explain Washington's decision not to strike the PRC program, granting China the opportunity to nuclearize.

In sum, China's nuclearization can be accounted for by looking at the strategic interaction between Beijing; its key adversary, the United States; and its faltering ally, the Soviet Union. Whereas other perspectives enrich our historical view of Chinese nuclear efforts, our strategic theory sheds light on the security causes of Beijing's willingness and opportunity to build a nuclear deterrent.

Israel

Despite maintaining a policy of nuclear ambiguity to this day, Israel is widely thought to have assembled its first nuclear device between 1966 and 1967, under the threat of war with its Arab neighbors.

Following its independence in 1948, Israel faced a hostile security environment, with a coalition of adversaries that vastly outmatched its own capabilities. Furthermore, despite relatively friendly relations with both superpowers, Israel had no reliable ally committed to securing its survival. Therefore, Israel possessed the willingness to build nuclear weapons.

Initially, Israeli military forces were supplied by Czechoslovakia while Egypt, its most formidable adversary, relied on Western weapons. In 1955, however, the Soviets authorized a large arms deal supplying Czech weapons to Egypt, cooling relations between the Eastern bloc and the Jewish state and pushing Israel closer to the West. Shortly thereafter, however, Israel would realize the limits of U.S. assistance in the context of the 1956 Suez Crisis. During this episode, France and the United Kingdom joined Israel in a secret ploy to recapture the Suez Canal, which Egyptian president Gamal Abdel Nasser had recently nationalized. The Soviet Union reacted to this joint military action by threatening nuclear retaliation against all three. While President Eisenhower publicly pledged to retaliate against attacks on London or Paris, he did not offer such pledges on Israel's behalf.

The United States cared about supporting Israel, but not to the detriment of its relations with Arab states. Washington feared that were it to extend strong public support for Israel, the Soviet Union would be drawn further into the region, offering similar guarantees to Israel's

Arab neighbors. Additionally, U.S. policymakers wanted to maintain warm relations with the Arab world, in order to secure access to oil and keep open the possibility of a U.S.-Arab anti-Soviet alliance. Therefore, Washington implemented a limited carrots-based nonproliferation approach toward its loose ally. While privately giving Israel its first security guarantee in 1957, Eisenhower – as well as Kennedy and Johnson after him – turned down Israeli requests to make this guarantee public and official. Overall, then, U.S. ability to deter Israeli nuclearization was hampered by Washington's determination to maintain good relations with Arab states, which led it to eschew a formal commitment to the security of Israel.[207]

Aware of the security benefit that Israel would extract from nuclear acquisition, Israel's enemies, especially Nasser, were concerned about the Israeli nuclear-weapons program, and preventive considerations may have factored into Egypt's strategic calculus prior to the 1967 Six-Day War. Yet, Israel had the ability to defend itself and protect its nuclear program, and in the end ensure the opportunity to nuclearize.

Likewise, the United States preferred Israel to remain nonnuclear. When U.S. intelligence uncovered evidence of an Israeli nuclear program, and realizing that its carrots-based approach to nonproliferation was failing, Washington asked Jerusalem for guarantees that the program was not of a military nature. Kennedy, in particular, demanded that U.S. inspectors be granted access to Israel's nuclear facilities. Yet, the inspections on the Israeli nuclear-weapons program were not particularly intrusive. The looseness of U.S. security guarantees (itself determined by broader U.S. strategic interests in the Middle East) limited the pressure Washington could place on Israel in the context of a sticks-based nonproliferation effort. Since Washington's contribution to Israeli security was modest, so was its ability to coerce Israel through a sticks-based approach. If anything, by providing its loose ally with advanced conventional weapons, the United States contributed to ensuring Israel's opportunity to proliferate, helping it prevail in the Six-Day War.

Israeli Interest in Nuclear Weapons

Having proclaimed independence on May 14, 1948, Israel faced a security environment opposed to its existence and a coalition of

---

[207] See: Kogan (2013a, 194).

adversaries that vastly outmatched its own capabilities. Relative to its Arab rivals, Israel faced a three-hundred-to-one territorial disadvantage, a fifteen-to-one population disadvantage, and a three-to-one military materiel disadvantage.[208] Immediately after its independence, Israel had to repel a joint invasion by Egyptian, Iraqi, Jordanian, Lebanese, and Syrian forces. Israel prevailed in this conflict, yet the threat persisted, and Israel's geographic position, encircled by enemies with revisionist goals, represented a significant security concern. "The Israeli philosophy of peace," as a late-1960s NSC memo put it, "is that Israel must be so strong that the Arabs will realize they have no prospect whatsoever of winning back their lands by force."[209] Ultimately, nuclear weapons proved to be a key element of this strategic posture.

Early Nuclear Development in the 1950s
Soon after its independence, Israel discovered significant uranium deposits in the Negev region.[210] In 1952, an Israeli Atomic Energy Commission (IAEC) was set up as part of the Department of Defense.[211] Three years later, Israel took advantage of President Eisenhower's Atoms for Peace program, obtaining U.S. aid for the construction of a one-megawatt (MW) research reactor,[212] and for the training of dozens of Israeli nuclear scientists.[213]

There were limits to U.S. assistance in the nuclear realm, however. In August 1955, the head of the IAEC asked the United States for sophisticated nuclear technology, which could produce "new elements such as plutonium," only to be rebuffed by his American counterpart.[214] At the same time, Israel's security situation was deteriorating. In September 1955, Egypt announced a military arms deal with Czechoslovakia, significantly boosting its conventional power.[215] The next month, Egypt

---

[208] See: Peres (1970, 12–14); Bass (2003, 188).
[209] "Memorandum from Harold H. Saunders of the National Security Council Staff to the Assistant Secretary of State for Near Eastern and South Asian Affairs (Battle)," Washington, May 21, 1968, in *Foreign Relations of the United States (FRUS)*, 1964–1968, Vol. XX, *Arab-Israeli Dispute, 1967–68*, Doc. 179.
[210] See: Evron (1994, 1).
[211] Ibid., 2.
[212] See: Paul (2000, 137).
[213] See: Rabinowitz (2014, 75).
[214] Quoted in Kroenig (2010, 69–70).
[215] See: Crosbie (1974, 10); Cohen (1998, 49); Bass (2003, 40).

and Syria signed a military alliance, threatening Israel with Soviet arms both from the north and south.[216]

Given the severity of the security threats it faced and the reluctance with which the United States offered its assistance in nuclear matters, Israel turned to France, which became its largest supplier of weapons.[217] In September 1956, Paris agreed to aid in the development of an Israeli nuclear reactor and a plutonium reprocessing plant.[218] A month later, Israel and France expanded their partnership by signing the Protocol of Sèvres, together with the United Kingdom.[219] This document laid the basis for a joint attack against their common enemy, Egypt. Reacting to Nasser's nationalization of the Suez Canal in 1956, France, Israel, and the United Kingdom devised a secret ploy to recapture it. On October 29, Israel invaded the Sinai, followed a week later by British and French landings around the Canal.[220]

The plan quickly went awry, however. The Soviet Union threatened military action and nuclear retaliation against Israel and its Western backers. In a not-so-veiled nuclear threat, Moscow accused Israel of "playing with the fate of peace, with the fate of its own people, in a criminal and irresponsible manner ... which will place a question [mark] upon the very existence of Israel as a State."[221] In response, Eisenhower publicly pledged to retaliate against Soviet attacks on London or Paris, while withholding similar pledges in the eventuality of a Soviet attack on Israel and singling out the Jewish state for sharp criticism, warning that it "risked UN opprobrium, Soviet attack, and the termination of all U.S. aid."[222] To decisionmakers in Jerusalem, Suez provided ample evidence that Washington was not willing to guarantee Israel's survival unconditionally.[223]

---

[216] See: Crosbie (1974, 60–61).

[217] See: Kroenig (2010, 71, 88).

[218] See: Evron (1994, 2); Bass (2003, 190); Kroenig (2010, 72–73); Lin (2012, 103); (2014, 74–75).

[219] See: Kyle (2011, 328).

[220] See: Bass (2003, 42–44); Kyle (2011, 328).

[221] Bulganin to Ben-Gurion, November 5, 1956, in "Exchange of Letters – Bulganin – Ben-Gurion – 5 and 8 November 1956." Available at: http://mfa.gov.il/MFA/ForeignPolicy/MFADocuments/Yearbook1/Pages/7%20Exchange%20of%20Letters-%20Bulganin-%20Ben-Gurion-%205%20and.aspx. Last accessed: April 28, 2016.

[222] Bass (2003, 44).

[223] See: Little (1993, 563).

The Failed Quest for Robust U.S. Security Guarantees

On the heels of the Suez crisis, Israel continued to seek security guarantees while renewing its efforts to acquire the bomb. In early 1957, President Eisenhower unveiled his "doctrine" for the Middle East, advocating arms sales, military assistance, and foreign aid to friendly states in the region, including Israel.[224] In May, the U.S. president gave Israel its first private security guarantee, stating that American policy "embraced the preservation of the state of Israel."[225] Six months later, Eisenhower reiterated his support, telling Israeli prime minister Ben-Gurion that he "should have no doubt of deep U.S. interests in [the] preservation [of the] integrity and independence of Israel."[226] Along similar lines, Secretary of State John Foster Dulles assured Ben-Gurion in August 1958 that "[t]he United States is committed to Israel's existence and would fight for her should an attack by the Soviet Union compel her to do so."[227] By the late 1950s, then, the United States was acting privately as Israel's nuclear ally.

Yet, being private, U.S. security guarantees had limited deterrent effect. Furthermore, these guarantees did not cover all security interests Israel considered vital. When Eisenhower unveiled his doctrine, he pressured Israel to pull out of Gaza and all Egyptian territory seized in 1956, threatening to support UN sanctions.[228] He also refused to offer a public security guarantee to Israel. In October 1957, Ben-Gurion requested military hardware and argued that Washington's "NATO commitment should be extended to the Middle East."[229] By mid-November, Dulles declined, telling Ben-Gurion that "we have made quite clear to the Soviet Union our deep interest in the maintenance of independence and integrity of all the states in the Near East, including Israel."[230]

Washington's reluctant assurances could not satisfy Israel's security needs, prompting in Jerusalem a renewed effort toward nuclear

---

[224] See: Bass (2003, 45–46).

[225] Quoted in Little (1993, 565).

[226] Quoted in ibid.

[227] Alteras (1993, 312), quoting Haggai Eshed, *Mossad shel Ish Ehad: Reuven Shiloah – Avi Ha-Modyin Ha-Israeli* [One Man's Mossad: Reuven Shihloah, father of the Israeli intelligence Service] (Tel Aviv: Edonim, 1988), 272.

[228] See: Little (1993, 563–564).

[229] Bergus, "Israel," October 28, 1957, quoted in ibid., 565.

[230] Quoted in ibid.

acquisition. In 1958, construction of the Dimona reactor began in the northern part of the Negev Desert.[231] The same year, Israel established its armament development authority, RAFAEL, tasking it with overseeing its nuclear-weapons development.[232] A year later, Israel acquired twenty-two tons of heavy water from Norway, officially for peaceful purposes.[233] Dimona would soon become a complex that hosted facilities for uranium purification, enrichment, and conversion, as well as nuclear fuel fabrication and reprocessing. The first reactor became critical in 1963, producing the plutonium used in the Israeli bomb. A nearby uranium mine allowed for the end of Israeli uranium imports by 1965. This complex was therefore crucial to the country's nuclear efforts; it included fortified underground facilities and was aggressively defended by the Israeli military.[234]

As the nuclear program developed, Israeli leaders publicly acknowledged that they saw great benefit in acquiring the bomb. In 1961, Prime Minister David Ben-Gurion told the Canadian prime minister that "if the Arab threat continued to grow ... Israel might as a matter of self-defense be required to develop nuclear-weapons capability."[235] That same year, an Israeli official told his State Department counterparts that Israel faced a "grim security situation" since it was "surrounded by fanatically hostile Arab neighbors. In this situation Israel naturally looked to whatever means it could find for protecting itself."[236]

Then, in early 1963, Israel's security outlook worsened with unrest in Jordan; coups in Iraq and Syria; and a joint Egyptian, Iraqi, and Syrian declaration vowing to liberate Palestine.[237] Shortly thereafter, Ben-Gurion renewed his request for a formal U.S. security pledge. According to him, Israel needed to have access to nuclear capabilities. In order "to ensure that another Holocaust would not be inflicted

---

[231] See: "Memorandum from Secretary of State Rusk to President Kennedy," Washington, January 30, 1961, in *Foreign Relations of the United States (FRUS), 1961–1963*, Vol. XVII, *Near East, 1961–1962*, Doc. 5.

[232] See: Narang (2014, 182).

[233] See: Richelson (2006, 240).

[234] See: Spector and Smith (1990, 172–174).

[235] Quoted in Bass (2003, 200).

[236] "Memorandum of Conversation," May 16, 1961, in National Security Archive (NSA), *Israel and the Bomb*, The First American Visit to Dimona, Doc. 11, p. 2.

[237] See: Little (1993, 569); Bass (2003, 211–212).

on the Jewish people, Israel must be able to threaten a potential perpe-
trator with annihilation."[238] Kennedy, however, was unwilling to offer
any public security guarantees backed by the U.S. nuclear deterrent,
and instead asked for assurances that Israel's program had peaceful
purposes.

This exchange continued with successive administrations. Given
Washington's reluctance to offer a formal alliance commitment,
Israeli defense officials wondered about "the ability of the U.S. to
act promptly in support of Israel."[239] In April 1965, Prime Minister
Levi Eshkol (1963–1969) told the U.S. ambassador that "the Israeli
Government could not foreswear nuclear weapon development in the
absence of binding security guarantees" from the United States.[240]

Starting with the Kennedy administration, Israel accepted U.S.
inspections at Dimona, but made sure that U.S. scientists would not find
evidence of a military program. In 1963, Israel purchased nearly 100
tons of unsafeguarded uranium from Argentina,[241] and in December of
that year, the Dimona reactor reached criticality. Soon the U.S. intelligence community began to realize the progress Israel was making in
its nuclear-weapons program. In January 1964, a CIA memo concluded
that Israel now had the capability "to redirect the program in the future
toward achievement of a small nuclear weapons capability, should they
so decide."[242] By early 1965, a State Department memorandum judged
that this decision had already been taken, noting that all "indications
are toward Israeli acquisition of a nuclear capability," which would be
reached within a few years.[243] By 1966, the U.S. intelligence community concluded that Israel had begun plutonium separation and could

---

[238] Quoted in Bass (2003, 213).
[239] "Memorandum of Conversation," Washington, March 4, 1964, 3 p.m., in
Foreign Relations of the United States (FRUS), 1964–1968, Vol. XVIII, *Arab-
Israeli Dispute, 1964–67*, Doc. 23.
[240] "Telegram from the Embassy in Israel to the Department of State," Tel Aviv,
April 23, 1965, in Ibid., Doc. 210, note 3.
[241] "Memorandum from the Under Secretary of State (Katzenbach) to President
Johnson," Washington, May 1, 1967, in Ibid., Doc. 415.
[242] "Memorandum from the Department of State's Executive Secretary (Read)
to the President's Special Assistant for National Security Affairs (Bundy),"
Washington, February 11, 1964, in ibid., Doc. 12, note 7.
[243] "Memorandum from the Director of the Office of Near Eastern Affairs
(Davies) to the Assistant Secretary of State for Near Eastern and South Asian
Affairs (Talbot)," Washington, March 5, 1965, in ibid., Doc. 178.

just be "weeks away" from a nuclear device.[244] As U.S. secretary of state Dean Rusk put it in a meeting with Israeli foreign minister Abba Eban (1966–1974) in February that year, Israel's nuclear program was reaching "a precarious situation somewhat akin to eight months of pregnancy."[245]

Sometime during the following twelve months, in 1966 or 1967, Israel is believed to have acquired a nuclear capability.[246] In early November 1966, it successfully carried out a test of "special significance," which could have been the detonation of an ultralow yield, subcritical nuclear device, or the test of a nuclear prototype without fissile material.[247] Some argue that Israel made this capability operational in June 1967 during the Six-Day War.[248] President Johnson learned of Israel's nuclear status in the summer of 1968, though he instructed his CIA director not to "tell anyone else, even Dean Rusk and Robert McNamara."[249] The news had begun to spread by the time Richard Nixon took office in 1969, and later that year the U.S. inspection regime ended. Why did U.S. efforts to prevent Israeli nuclearization fail?

U.S. Nonproliferation Efforts

The Eisenhower administration articulated a foreign policy for the Middle East that, in its view, would correct the excessive pro-Israeli bias of his Democratic predecessor. Arab states were important strategic partners and, in order to gain their trust, a serious rebalancing of U.S. policy was in order. When Secretary Dulles met Israeli prime minister Ben-Gurion in Tel-Aviv, he shared his "conviction that without [the] goodwill and confidence of [the] Arabs, the United States would not be able to play [a] useful role in [the] area."[250] In June 1953,

---

[244] Cover note to "Telegram from Department of State to Embassy in Tel Aviv," February 23, 1967, in NSA, *Israel and the Bomb*, Miscellaneous Documents, Doc. 3.

[245] "Memorandum of Conversation," Washington, February 9, 1966, 4:30 p.m., in *FRUS*, 1964–1968, Vol. XVIII, Doc. 269.

[246] See: Cohen (1996, 209); Richelson (2006, 242); Cohen (2007).

[247] See: Munya M. Mardor, *Rafael* [in Hebrew] (Tel Abib: Misrad Habitachon, 1981), quoted in Cohen (1996, 232).

[248] See: Cohen (1996, 208).

[249] "Editorial Note," in *FRUS*, 1964–1968, Vol. XX, Doc. 130.

[250] Quoted in Ben-Zvi (1998, 32–33).

Assistant Secretary Henry Byroade (1952–1955) told then Israeli ambassador Abba Eban (1950–1959):

[i]f only Israel and Arab relations were concerned, the problem would be relatively easier. What is at stake, however, is the possible loss of all Western influence in the Middle East, including oil, airfields, etc. *The decline in influence has resulted ... from Western support of Israel, and we are quite concerned about it.*[251]

Pressing the point further, Dulles explained to Israeli foreign minister Moshe Sharrett (1948–1956) in October 1955 that "any unilateral action in Israel's favor would be liable to aid Soviet expansion among the Arab states."[252]

Limited U.S. Security Guarantees
In practice, this meant that the Eisenhower administration refused to make public its security guarantees to Israel. Furthermore, Washington supplied arms to both Israel and its Arab neighbors, without appearing to privilege either side.[253] In a press conference in October 1955, Dulles reacted to the news of an Egyptian-Czech arms deal, which so worried the Israelis, by expressing hope that it would be possible to avoid "participating in what might become an arms race."[254] In 1960, when Ben-Gurion asked for increased military aid, Eisenhower "questioned the desirability of the U.S. becoming the arsenal for Israel," instead urging Ben-Gurion to "look to the U.K., France, and West Germany" for help.[255]

While U.S. unwillingness to extend robust security guarantees to Israel might have been expected to prompt Jerusalem to pursue the nuclear

---

[251] Quoted in ibid., 33, Ben-Zvi's emphasis.
[252] Dulles's remarks to Sharrett on October 30, 1955, quoted in ibid., 34.
[253] See: Alteras (1993, 37–38, 109).
[254] Dana Adams Schmidt, "U.S. Tells Soviet Arab Arms Deal Is Hurting Amity: Dulles Says He Gave Molotov Views on the Middle East at Recent Parley Here," *The New York Times*, Oct. 5, 1955, pp. 1, 8, quote at p. 8. The Eisenhower administration even blamed the previous administration for the Czech-Egyptian arms deal, as Truman had tried to "meet the wishes of the Zionists in this country." Steven L. Spiegel, *The Other Arab-Israeli Conflict: Making America's Middle East Policy* (Chicago: University of Chicago Press, 1985), quoted in Bass (2003, 41).
[255] Quoted in Little (1993, 567).

option, Washington was not ready to embrace the possibility of a nuclear Israel. Once the United States suspected that the Israeli nuclear program included a military component, it requested assurances from Jerusalem that it was not pursuing the bomb. If Israel were developing the bomb, Washington could be suspected of aiding and abetting it. This could be detrimental to U.S. influence in the region: Egypt could turn to the Soviets for military assistance or close the Suez Canal, and Arab states as a whole could cut off oil supplies.[256] As Rusk later put it to the Senate Foreign Relations Committee in June 1963: "We just can't imagine anything more disastrous from our point of view than if Israel were to explode a nuclear device.... I can't think of anything that would drive the Arab world more tumultuously into the arms of the Soviet."[257] A NIE from that same month reached a similar conclusion: "Acquisition of nuclear weapons by Israel would add greatly to Arab hostility toward the West. The US ... would receive much of the blame.... It would probably then become much more difficult for the US to maintain the delicate complex of its interests in the Middle East."[258]

In the summer of 1960, Israeli officials explained that the nuclear facilities at Dimona were a "textile plant." Three months later, they claimed that Dimona was a "metallurgical research installation."[259] In December 1960, CIA and AEC experts believed that the Israeli nuclear program must have a military component.[260] The Israeli and French ambassadors were summoned to the White House, and both pledged that the program was peaceful.[261]

---

[256] See: "Memorandum from Secretary of State Rusk to President Johnson," Washington, January 16, 1964, in *FRUS*, 1964–1968, Vol. XVIII, Doc. 9; Aronson (2000, 89); Bass (2003, 195, 202).

[257] Quoted in Little (1993, 572).

[258] "National Intelligence Estimate Number 4–63, 'Likelihood and Consequences of a Proliferation of Nuclear Weapons Systems,'" June 23, 1963, p. 13, in Wilson Center Digital Archive, Israeli Nuclear History.

[259] "Memorandum for the President," March 30, 1961, in NSA, *Israel and the Bomb*, The First American Visit to Dimona, Doc. 6, p. 1.

[260] See: "Memorandum of Discussion at the 407th Meeting of the National Security Council," December 8, 1960, in *Foreign Relations of the United States (FRUS), 1958–1960*, Vol. XIII, *Arab-Israeli Dispute; United Arab Republic; North Africa*, Doc. 177. For a series of documents on what the Eisenhower administration knew and how it chose to avoid a confrontation with Israel over Dimona, see: "The U.S. Discovery of Israel's Secret Nuclear Project," National Security Archive (NSA) Electronic Briefing Book (EBB) 510, "The U.S. Discovery of Israel's Secret Nuclear Project."

[261] See: "Telegram from the Department of State to the Embassy in Israel," Washington, December 9, 1960, 10 p.m., in *FRUS*, 1958–1960, Vol. XIII,

That same year, a State Department report, written before the news of Israel's nuclearization had spread, assessed the quality of U.S. inspections as follows:

Our "visits" to Dimona have shed virtually no light on the role that site may play in a weapons program. Israel has been hyper-sensitive to any initiative on the part of our teams ... so that the teams have felt circumscribed in what they could do and ask.... Since the visits are arranged far in advance, Israel has every opportunity for concealment. [As a result,] Israel might very well now have a nuclear bomb.[273]

While Washington was lenient toward Israeli nuclear development, it remained convinced that Israel would be able to defend itself conventionally, and therefore it continued to refuse Jerusalem an explicit, public security guarantee. In April 1963, Ben-Gurion sent a seven-page letter to President Kennedy, responding to an Arab proclamation to liberate Palestine, complaining about Western assistance to Egypt, and asking for a joint guarantee by the United States and the USSR for the territorial integrity of all Middle Eastern states.[274] Kennedy asked for an assessment of the military balance in the Middle East, and received word that "Israel will probably retain its overall military superiority vis-à-vis the Arab states for the next several years."[275] On May 4, Kennedy turned down Ben-Gurion's request, reassuring the Israeli leader that "we have Israel's problems very much in mind" and "we are watching closely current developments in Arab world."[276] In October, Kennedy insisted that "the existing informal arrangements meet Israel's needs" and a formal guarantee "would contribute little to deterrence."[277]

U.S. confidence in Israeli conventional capabilities persisted over time. In May 1964, the JCS deemed Israel "able to maintain quite a

---

[273] "Briefing Book – Visit of Mrs. Golda Meir," September 19, 1969, in NSA EBB 189, Doc. 21.

[274] See: "Memorandum From the Department of State Executive Secretary (Brubeck) to the President's Special Assistant for National Security Affairs (Bundy)," Washington, April 27, 1963, in *FRUS*, 1961–1963, Vol. XVIII, Doc. 220; Cohen (1998, 120).

[275] Quoted in Cohen (1998, 120).

[276] Quoted in ibid., 121.

[277] *FRUS*, 1961–1963, Vol. XVIII, Doc. 332.

deterrent edge for the foreseeable future."[278] In May 1967, the State Department contended that Israel had "a safe margin of superiority over any combination of Arab forces likely to attack it and can be expected to maintain that position for at least the next five years."[279]

Certainly, there were some concerns that Israel's enemies would want to strike preventively against the country's nuclear-weapons program. On a few occasions, starting as early as December 1960, Nasser declared that the development of an Israeli nuclear weapon would constitute a casus belli.[280] Over the past few years, scholars have vigorously debated the extent to which the Egyptians were preparing a preventive strike in the lead-up to the Six-Day War, and whether the Soviets had played a role in encouraging them.[281] From our perspective, the crucial point is that there was a significant security shift that would result from Israeli nuclearization, but Israel was sufficiently strong to repel an eventual preventive strike. Particularly given Washington's loose support for Israel, the United States need not fear entrapment resulting from a putative preventive strike against Israel's nuclear program. Furthermore, it was highly unlikely that Israel would use its nuclear capability to pursue revisionist goals, so Israeli nuclearization would not result in heightened odds of conflict in the Middle East. Consequently, U.S. nonproliferation pressures were weak, and Israel successfully acquired the bomb. If anything, Washington may have increased Israel's opportunity to proliferate, given that its sales of conventional weapons, such as the HAWK missiles in 1962 and the Skyhawk jet bombers in 1966, boosted Israeli deterrent capabilities.[282]

In sum, the United States applied minimal pressure on Israel over the need to thoroughly inspect its nuclear facilities. Because its support for Israel was quite limited, Washington did not face a serious risk

---

[278] "Memorandum from Robert W. Komer of the National Security Council Staff to President Johnson," Washington, May 28, 1964, in *FRUS*, 1964–1968, Vol. XVIII, Doc. 63. See also: *FRUS*, 1964–1968, Vol. XVIII, Doc. 9.

[279] *FRUS*, 1964–1968, XVIII, Doc. 415.

[280] See: Cohen (1996, 192, 197); Cohen (1998, 175, 244); National Intelligence Estimate No. 35–61, "The Outlook for Israel," October 5, 1961, in NSA EBB 547, Doc. 11A; *FRUS*, 1964–1968, XVIII, Doc. 12; "Telegram from the Department of State to the Embassy in Israel," Washington, March 19, 1964, 3:10 p.m., in ibid., Doc. 31.

[281] See: Ginor and Remez (2007). For critical perspectives, see: Gat (2005); Golan (2006, 2008); Popp (2006); Ro'i and Morozov (2008).

[282] See: Little (1993, 568–569).

of entrapment as a result of the Israeli nuclear program. Furthermore, Washington concluded that Tel-Aviv would have a conventional advantage in an eventual conflict with its Arab enemies and would therefore be able to prevail in such a conflict even before its eventual nuclear acquisition and without direct U.S. involvement in the fighting. Israel's survival could therefore be ensured with minimal U.S. involvement, allowing for the maintenance of good U.S. relations with Arab states. From Washington's perspective, this meant that little geopolitical capital should be devoted to preventing Israeli nuclearization.

Alternative Explanations

The claim that Israel acquired nuclear weapons because of grave security threats that were not satisfactorily mitigated by American security guarantees is the object of a broad consensus in the literature.[283] Nonetheless, there are a few points of disagreement among different scholars working on Israeli nuclear history. Specifically, the literature includes four arguments that can be seen as alternatives to ours.

A first alternative account comes from Etel Solingen, whose account of Israeli nuclear acquisition focuses on domestic political dynamics in the country.[284] Solingen acknowledges that security motivations dominated Israel's decision to acquire nuclear weapons. At the same time, she finds several shortcomings to existing security-based explanations, which focus exclusively on balance of power considerations. First, Solingen claims that security-based arguments ignore how Israel's security concerns were strongly influenced by history, for example, by the memory of the horrors of the Holocaust. Second, balance of power considerations produce indeterminate results on key questions about Israel's nuclear decisions, as evidenced by the strong disagreements among scholars on the benefit of nuclear weapons for a state's defense. Would Israel benefit from nuclear weapons? Why was Israel not reassured by the United States? Why was it not coerced by the United States, given that, according to Solingen, President Kennedy applied "unrelenting pressure" on Ben-Gurion and Eshkol?[285] Why did Israel hide its nuclear deterrent? In response to these shortcomings in the

---

[283] See: Crosbie (1974, 13); Cohen (1998, 10); Paul (2000, 140).
[284] See: Solingen (2007).
[285] Ibid., 191.

security-based literature on Israeli nuclearization, Solingen argues that external and domestic reasons best explain the path of "ambiguous nuclearization" chosen by Israel.[286] Ambiguity helped prevent the ire of American and European allies, and helped prevent domestic pressures in enemy states to build their own nuclear deterrent.

We agree with Solingen's assessment of the existing literature, but not with her prescription for how to overcome its shortcomings. Standard security-based explanations of Israeli nuclearization no doubt have important limitations. As a result, Solingen decides to move away from security and explore other motives for nuclear acquisition.

In contrast, we believe the solution lies in advancing a more refined security-based argument on the Israeli nuclear-weapons program; one that encompasses the motivations of decisionmakers in all the major states with something at stake in Israel's nuclear status. Given that, as Solingen agrees, Israeli leaders were especially motivated by security concerns in their pursuit of the bomb, this seems to be the most fruitful approach to the question of Israeli nuclear acquisition.

Clearly, Israel perceived the likelihood of conflict with its Arab neighbors to be high, an assessment reinforced by the weight of history. Yet, this is insufficient to explain Israel's acquisition of nuclear weapons. While Israel perceived the benefit of an investment in nuclear weapons to be high, Israel's enemies were concerned with the consequences of Israel's nuclearization, and Israel's loose ally, the United States, was concerned about regional instability and growing Soviet encroachment in the Middle East. Moreover, given that nuclearization is a costly investment with delayed returns, enemies and allies had a fairly long window of opportunity to prevent Israel from going nuclear.

Yet, why were enemy threats and allied assurances unsuccessful in pursuing this goal? This question is not well answered in the extant literature, either by standard security-based scholarship or by the alternative approach put forth by Solingen. Her account helps us understand *the form* of Israel's nuclearization – i.e., nuclear ambiguity – but not the fact that Israel was able successfully to develop a nuclear capability.[287]

---

[286] Ibid., 193.
[287] We agree that Israel opted for nuclear ambiguity because it did not want to embarrass its American ally. This was the basis for the so-called Nixon-Meir agreement of 1969, according to which Israel committed not to publicize (e.g.,

We provide a novel security-based answer to this question. Israel was sufficiently strong to fend off preventive attacks and thereby possessed the opportunity to acquire nuclear weapons. At the same time, the United States was not available to implement the measures necessary to take away Israel's willingness to nuclearize, which would entail additional security guarantees: Washington did not want to antagonize Arab states, whose support was important in getting access to oil, airfields, and so forth. Believing that Israel would prevail in a conflict against its regional adversaries either on its own or with limited U.S. assistance, Washington did not fear escalation and applied minimal pressure on Israel to terminate its program. Contrary to Solingen's claim, and as documented in the preceding text, the United States never really imposed harsh inspections on the Israeli nuclear-weapons program. In July 1963, after receiving Kennedy's letter demanding that U.S. inspectors be allowed to visit Dimona, Eshkol is reported to have said: "What am I frightened of? His man will come, and he will actually be told that he can visit [Dimona] and go anywhere he wishes but when he wants a door opened at some place or another then [Emmanuel] Prat [who headed operations at the Dimona site] will tell him, 'Not that.' "[288] If anything, U.S. lenience and its assistance through sales of conventional weapons actually helped Israeli nuclearization by boosting its capabilities and helping Israel fend off preventive attacks.

A second alternative argument about Israeli nuclear acquisition claims that the United States failed to prevent it because it chose the wrong policy instrument – sales of conventional weapons – overestimating its effectiveness. Indeed, some argue that Johnson believed that Prime Minister Eshkol "could be induced by the promise of American arms to open up Dimona to the International Atomic Energy Agency."[289] The Johnson administration may have hoped that the sale of conventional weapons would satisfy Israel's security needs, slowing down and perhaps obviating the need for a nuclear deterrent.[290]

---

by testing) its nuclear capability while the United States pledged to tolerate and even shield it from attack. See: Cohen (2005); Karpin (2006); Cohen (2008); Cohen and Miller (2010). For a recent account of this and similar agreements between the United States and its other loose allies – e.g., South Africa and Pakistan – see: Rabinowitz (2014).

[288] Quoted in Karpin (2006, 237).

[289] Hersh (1991, 132).

[290] See: Little (1993, 578, 580); Levey (2004, 275); Shalom (2005, 74); Aronson (2009, 120); Lin (2012, 159).

Perhaps most forcefully, Shlomo Aronson declares that the conventional arms sales agreement of 1965 between the United States and Israel was concluded "obviously in order to prevent Israel from adopting a nuclear deterrent posture."[291]

Certainly, the United States on some occasions used the sale of conventional weapons to request inspections at Dimona, pressure Israel not to go nuclear, and obtain guarantees that the Skyhawk bombers it was selling to Israel would not ever be nuclear armed.[292] At the same time, the United States was aware that the sale of conventional weapons might not prevent Israel from trying to acquire the bomb. Faced with mounting evidence of Israeli intent to nuclearize, Washington decoupled the sale of conventional weapons from its demands for inspections at Dimona and did not threaten to withdraw the Skyhawk deal.[293]

More generally, were not responsible for the U.S. failure to prevent Israeli nuclearization. The United States was simply not available to remove Israeli willingness to acquire nuclear weapons – something it could only have done by extending more robust security guarantees to the Jewish state. In fact, during the JFK administration, the Israeli leadership put the United States on notice that it would want a public security guarantee in exchange for nuclear forbearance.[294] Given the importance of maintaining good relations with Arab states, and U.S. assessments that Israel would prevail in a conflict, such a public guarantee was too high a price to pay to guarantee the maintenance of Israel's nonnuclear status.

A third alternative argument on the causes of Israeli nuclear acquisition blames U.S. domestic politics for the weak diplomatic pressure applied by Washington.[295] According to this argument, a pro-Israel lobby in the United States limited the nonproliferation pressure Washington could exert over its protégé.

We agree that domestic political considerations may have played a role in U.S. foreign policy. For example, the Eisenhower administration blamed domestic political considerations for the fact that the United States had until then heavily favored Israel. But as early as May

---

[291] Aronson (2009, 120). See also: Levey (2004, 275); Shalom (2005, 74); Lin (2012, 159).

[292] See: Little (1993, 568–569, 576); Levey (2004, 273, 275).

[293] See: Gazit (2000, 421–422); Levey (2004, 273); Shalom (2005, 74, 87).

[294] See: Little (1993, 572).

[295] See: Levey (2004, 271–272); Shalom (2005, 92).

1953, Dulles explained to Ben-Gurion that "the new administration ... was elected by [an] overwhelming vote of the American people as a whole and [it] neither owes that type of political debt to any segment nor [does it] believe in building power by cultivating particular segments of [the] population."[296] This meant that the United States would respond to the Israeli nuclear-weapons program by prioritizing strategic considerations, working for the safety of Israel while maintaining good relations with Arab states. This fundamental principle continued into the Kennedy and Johnson administrations. If anything, the harshest rhetoric came from the president who had won election by the slightest margin and most needed the vote of Jewish Americans – JFK. In practice, as we showed in the preceding text, even his demands for inspections were weak. We don't think that this is evidence of an all-powerful Israeli lobby in U.S. domestic politics. After all, the United States objected to Israel's venture in the Suez Canal and refused Israeli requests for a public security guarantee. Security motivations are sufficient to explain U.S. foreign policy toward Israel during the run-up to Israel's nuclear acquisition in the mid- to late-1960s. The security assurances that Israel was seeking from Washington were too costly, given that the United States wished to maintain good relations with Arab states. Furthermore, Washington was convinced that Israel could prevail in a conflict, and didn't seriously risk entrapping the United States in a fight for Israel's survival. The United States could thus achieve its foreign policy goals with private assurances and the sale of conventional weapons, and its fears of escalation were too weak to warrant intrusive inspections.

Finally, a fourth alternative view on the causes of Israeli nuclear acquisition is the supply-side argument put forth by Matthew Kroenig. He argues that the United States more vigorously opposed Israeli nuclearization than, for example, France, which actively aided the Israeli nuclear program, because the United States, as opposed to France, was capable of projecting power over the Middle East, and would therefore have seen a greater reduction in its influence should Israel become nuclear.[297] Although this is an interesting thesis, it is unable to account for Israeli nuclear proliferation. Supply-side arguments may explain which state is more likely to provide assistance, but they do not explain when

---

[296] Quoted in Ben-Zvi (1998, 32–33).
[297] See: Kroenig (2010).

a given power-projecting state is willing, or able, to limit proliferation by withholding sensitive nuclear assistance. Ultimately, the United States was unable to prevent Israeli nuclearization, even though it demanded inspections on the Israeli program, pressured France not to provide sensitive assistance, and offered Israel modest security guarantees. Our theory addresses this shortcoming, accounting for the failure of U.S. nonproliferation efforts in the Israeli case. Israel successfully nuclearized because it perceived U.S. security guarantees to be unreliable, was sufficiently strong to thwart preventive attacks, and was subjected to minimal U.S. nonproliferation pressure.

In sum, Israeli nuclearization was driven by the security dynamics captured by our theory. Facing a security environment that threatened its survival, and lacking a reliable security sponsor, Israel was willing to develop a nuclear weapon. Having sufficient relative power to defend itself and its nuclear facilities – and enjoying military support from the United States during the Six-Day War – it had the opportunity to cross the nuclear threshold.

India

In May 1974, India detonated a nuclear device, dubbing it a "peaceful nuclear explosion." Although New Delhi did not weaponize its nuclear program after this initial test, it invested in delivery capabilities and by the late 1980s was capable of quickly assembling nuclear devices. Two days after Pakistan tested intermediate range ballistic missiles in April 1998, Prime Minister Atal Bihari Vajpayee (1996, 1998–2004) approved a second round of nuclear tests, performed the following May. India's nuclear capability, already well known, was now unequivocal.

India had gained independence on August 15, 1947, in the partition of the British Indian Empire that also created Pakistan. Under the leadership of Prime Minister Jawaharlal Nehru (1947–1964), India pursued an autonomous foreign policy, becoming one of the leaders of the Non-Aligned Movement (NAM). Initially, for Nehru, India's security environment was relatively safe, despite tensions with Pakistan, a smaller and weaker neighbor. It was only with the 1954 incorporation of Tibet by the PRC that India's leader started entertaining concerns about a security threat from the PRC.[298]

---

[298] See: Raghavan (2010).

Then, in 1962, border skirmishes with the PRC escalated to a full-scale war, and Chinese forces advanced deep into Indian territory. Two years later, Beijing detonated its first atomic device. On each occasion, Indian security concerns spiked and New Delhi turned to the international community, and the United States in particular, for security assurances. While moving to normalize relations with the PRC in the early 1970s – with Islamabad's assistance – the United States opted for a "tilt" toward Pakistan. India responded by concluding a treaty of friendship with the Soviet Union, but doubted the long-term reliability of Moscow's assurances. Over time, calls in favor of building an autonomous nuclear deterrent grew louder in Indian political circles. The rising security threat posed by China gave India the willingness to nuclearize.

India's case poses some difficulties when it comes to identifying the origins of its opportunity to nuclearize. Certainly, China was a far stronger state than India in the mid-1970s, and so, if measured by the distribution of conventional power, India should not have had the opportunity to cross the nuclear threshold in 1974. Yet, it is doubtful whether Beijing possessed the intelligence and targeting capabilities to deny India the ability to build its nuclear device. Furthermore, India did not weaponize its nuclear effort then. It was not until the 1980s that it had the capability to rapidly assemble nuclear weapons. By then, relations with China had improved and India's main adversary was Pakistan, which was considerably weaker.[299]

For the United States, efforts to prevent Indian nuclearization were complicated by broader strategic considerations. Given that India was not a protégé of the United States, Washington possessed scant coercive leverage over it, so a sticks-based nonproliferation approach was out of the question. Furthermore, Washington was uncertain about New Delhi's intentions to develop a nuclear deterrent, and calculated that implementing a carrots-based nonproliferation approach by offering security assurances to a nonaligned country would have far-reaching consequences for its commitments around the world. In the end, Washington was unable to undermine India's willingness to proliferate.

Indian Interest in Nuclear Weapons

India's quest for the mastery of nuclear energy began with the creation of the Indian Atomic Energy Commission (IAEC) led by physicist

---

[299] For an overview of Indo-Pakistani relations, see: Cohen (2013).

Homi J. Bhabha (1948–1966) in 1948.[300] In a January 1950 meeting with Frédéric Joliot-Curie, the French high commissioner for atomic energy (1945–1950), Nehru declared that "India's interest in atomic energy is solely for its peaceful uses,"[301] a statement the Indian prime minister would repeat on multiple occasions over the years.[302] Joliot-Curie, in turn, explained how atomic bombs could be used for constructive purposes, "removing small mountains and diverting the courses of rivers."[303] India and France concluded a nuclear cooperation agreement a year later.[304]

The Indian government further institutionalized its nuclear program in 1954 with the creation of the Department of Atomic Energy, with Bhabha as its secretary.[305] India relied heavily on foreign assistance to develop its program. On August 4, 1956, the Apsara research reactor, built with British assistance, went critical.[306] Four years later, on July 10, 1960, the Canadian-Indian Reactor, U.S. (also known as CIRUS) became critical. It had been built in Trombay, outside of Mumbai, with Canada providing technological assistance and the United States providing heavy water.[307]

---

[300] See the historical note from Homi Bhabha in "Historical Note on Tata Institute of Fundamental Research," January 1, 1954, in Wilson Center Digital Archive, Indian Nuclear History. The IAEC was created by the Atomic Energy Act of August 15, 1948, replacing the Atomic Energy Research Committee (AERC), which had been set up in 1946. See: Chakma (2004, 45).

[301] "Minutes of a Special Meeting of the Indian Atomic Energy Commission," January 16, 1950, in Wilson Center Digital Archive, Indian Nuclear History.

[302] In January 1958, Nehru declared: "We have the technical know-how for manufacturing the atom bomb. We can do it in three to four years if we divert sufficient resources in that direction. But, we have given the world an assurance that we shall never do so. We shall never use our knowledge of nuclear science for purposes of war." Quoted in Mirchandani (1968, 231). On May 18, 1964, less than two weeks before his death, Nehru reiterated his pledge, stating, "We are determined not to use weapons for war purposes. We do not make atom bombs. I do not think we will" (Quoted in ibid., 23).

[303] "Minutes of a Special Meeting of the Indian Atomic Energy Commission," January 16, 1950, in Wilson Center Digital Archive, Indian Nuclear History.

[304] See: "Letter from the French Foreign Ministry to the UK Embassy in Paris on the Franco-Indian Reactor Agreement," August 24, 1951, in Wilson Center Digital Archive, Indian Nuclear History. See also: Sarkar (2015b).

[305] See: Abraham (1998, 75).

[306] See: Lavoy (1997, 236); Abraham (1998, 35).

[307] See: Lavoy (1997, 245); Abraham (1998, 121); Donaghy (2007); Touhey (2007). In addition, India concluded an agreement with Sweden in 1961.

As it developed a peaceful nuclear program, India initially perceived itself to be in a relatively safe environment. The only security threat came from Pakistan, which fought for control over the Kashmir region from the time of independence. Yet, Pakistan possessed significantly weaker military capabilities, and India retained most of Kashmir in the war of 1947. As Nehru explained in March 1956: "So far as the external danger to India is concerned – the only possible danger is from Pakistan. There is no other danger – not even the remotest danger."[308] Two years earlier, India had recognized the PRC's sovereignty over Tibet, and the two countries agreed on principles of "peaceful co-existence," including mutual nonaggression and respect for each other's sovereignty and territorial integrity.[309]

Within this context, New Delhi eschewed any alliance with a superpower, which would not provide a clear security benefit, would reduce the independence of India's foreign policy, and would raise the risk of entrapment. As Nehru stated in September 1946, when he articulated the principle of nonalignment: "We propose as far as possible to keep away from the power politics of groups, aligned with one another, which have led in the past to world wars and which may again lead to disaster on an even vaster scale."[310]

Under the surface, however, Nehru's optimism about China's intentions had by the mid-1950s given way to a more somber view. In 1954 China declined India's wish to proclaim a newly agreed bilateral treaty on the topic of Tibet valid for twenty-five years. Instead, Beijing insisted on restricting the treaty's duration to eight years, arising suspicion in New Delhi.[311] As Nehru put it at the time, "No country has any

---

See: Office of Scientific Intelligence, Central Intelligence Agency, "Swedish Assistance to the Indian Nuclear Power Program," May 1964, in National Security Archive (NSA) Electronic Briefing Book (EBB) 187, "U.S. Intelligence and the Indian Bomb," Doc. 4, p. 36.

[308] Quoted in Lavoy (1997, 115).

[309] See: "Agreement between the Republic of India and the People's Republic of China on Trade and Intercourse between the Tibet Region of China and India." April 29, 1954, in Wilson Center Digital Archive, Foundations of Chinese Foreign Policy. See also: "China's Initiation of the Five Principles of Peaceful Co-Existence," Ministry of Foreign Affairs of the People's Republic of China. Available at: www.fmprc.gov.cn/mfa_eng/ziliao_665539/3602_665543/3604_665547/t18053.shtml. Last accessed: May 1, 2016.

[310] Quoted in McGarr (2013, 44). See also: Chakma (2004, 43).

[311] See: Raghavan (2010, 240–242); Ray (2011, 244–245).

deep faith in the policies of another country, more especially in regard to a country which tends to expand."[312]

The Sino-Indian War and the Chinese Nuclear Test

India was thus not taken entirely by surprise when the PRC started a war against it in the fall of 1962. On October 20, Beijing launched a massive attack on the Sino-Indian border and within two days PRC units were deep in Indian territory. On the 25th, Nehru admitted that India had been "getting out of touch with the modern world [and] ... living in an artificial atmosphere of our own creation."[313] The next day, Nehru felt that he had "no choice" but to "somewhat affect" the Indian policy of nonalignment.[314] On November 19, he told the Indian Parliament that he had requested massive military assistance from the West.[315] Secretly, Nehru asked for *direct* military intervention, in the form of an air war against China.[316] Discussions over Western military assistance became moot when the PRC announced a unilateral cease-fire on November 20. Nevertheless, the following July, India and the United States concluded an Air Defense agreement, which provided for joint consultation in the event of an attack by the PRC against India.[317]

Nehru passed away on May 27, 1964; and on June 9, Lal Bahadur Shastri became prime minister (1964–1966). Shastri reiterated India's commitment to the peaceful uses of nuclear energy,[318] but soon faced alarming security developments. On October 16, the PRC tested a nuclear device. As Shastri explained, India was now "confronted with a nuclear menace in Asia, something new for this peace-loving continent."[319] Publicly, Shastri maintained his opposition to nuclear weapons,[320] yet he also approved preparations for the explosion of

---

[312] Quoted in Raghavan (2010, 241).

[313] Quoted in McGarr (2013, 153).

[314] Quoted in ibid., 157.

[315] Cited in Thomas F. Brady, "Chinese Drive into India, Imperiling Assam Plains; Nehru Asks More U.S. Aid," *The New York Times*, November 20, 1962, p. 1.

[316] When Nehru's secret request was revealed in March 1965 by a member of India's upper house of Parliament, a scandal ensued. See: Sarkar (2015a, 936).

[317] See: "Telegram from the Embassy in India to the Department of State," New Delhi, July 10, 1963, 8 p.m., in *Foreign Relations of the United States* (FRUS), 1961–1963, Vol. XIX, *South Asia*, Doc. 307.

[318] See his October 7, 1964 statement quoted in Lavoy (1997, 304).

[319] Quoted in ibid., 303.

[320] See: Ibid., 324–325.

a nuclear device with the Study of Nuclear Explosions for Peaceful Purposes (SNEPP) program in November 1964.[321] Although the program emphasized the peaceful applications of nuclear devices, it opened the door to the development of nuclear weapons. In December, Shastri declared that India would seek to obtain guarantees of protection from other existing nuclear powers against a possible attack by the PRC.[322] At the same time, Indian policymakers hinted at how, if such efforts failed, India could get a nuclear device. In February 1965, Indian ambassador to the United States, Braj Kumar Nehru (1961–1968), declared that "[t]he need of India, as of other nonnuclear powers, is security against nuclear attack. This can be provided either by an independent deterrent or through the combined and collective security offered by all the present nuclear powers and we are waiting for an answer."[323]

Another security shock soon occurred along the northwestern frontier with Pakistan. Between April and June 1965, the two countries fought over the control of the Rann of Kutch, an area straddling the Indo-Pakistani border, agreeing on June 30 to a ceasefire and the withdrawal of their forces to mutually agreed positions.[324] In early August, however, fighting resumed when Pakistan invaded Kashmir and the conflict escalated to a full-scale war.[325] During the conflict, China threatened to open a second front, claiming Indian violations of its territory.[326] In response, India sought assistance from the United States in the event of a Chinese attack.[327] Fortunately, fighting subsided after Pakistan accepted a UN-proposed ceasefire on September 22, and the two belligerent countries formally agreed to a return to the status quo ante in a conference mediated by the Soviets between January 4 and 10, 1966.[328]

---

[321] See: Perkovich (1999, 82–83).
[322] See: Noorani (1967, 491); Chakma (2004, 72).
[323] Quoted in "State Department Telegram for Governor Harriman from the Secretary," February 27, 1965, in National Security Archive (NSA) Electronic Briefing Book (EBB) 6, "India and Pakistan – On the Nuclear Threshold," Doc. 7, p. 4. See also: Noorani (1967, 495).
[324] See: McGarr (2013, 301, 309).
[325] Ibid., 314.
[326] See: Noorani (1967, 494–495); McGarr (2013, 329).
[327] See: "Telegram from the Department of State to the Embassy in India," Washington, September 17, 1965, 6:13 p.m., in *Foreign Relations of the United States (FRUS)*, 1964–1968, Vol. XXV, *South Asia*, Doc. 208.
[328] See: McGarr (2013, 331, 340).

This second war over Kashmir boosted pressure for the acquisition of an independent Indian nuclear deterrent. On the same day Pakistan accepted the ceasefire, eighty-five members of the Indian Parliament signed a statement that "India's survival both as a nation and as a democracy, in the face of the collusion between China and Pakistan, casts a clear and imperative duty on the Government to take an immediate decision to develop our nuclear weapons."[329] In a session in the Upper House of Parliament on November 16, Shastri reiterated India's commitment to nonproliferation, but stated that if the PRC were to develop its nuclear power and delivery capabilities, "then we will certainly have to consider as to what we have to do."[330]

Both Shastri and Bhabha passed away in January 1966. Indira Gandhi (1966–1977, 1980–1984) became prime minister and appointed Vikram Sarabhai as the second chair of the IAEC (1966–1971). Both new leaders reiterated India's long-standing commitment to the peaceful uses of nuclear energy, and in fact initially curtailed efforts to prepare for a peaceful nuclear explosion.[331] Like her predecessor, Gandhi focused on obtaining security assurances from the superpowers in order to counter a possible threat from the PRC. In April 1967, she sent a senior official, Laxmi Kant Jha, to Moscow and Washington to discuss possible security guarantees. In his meeting with Defense Secretary Robert McNamara, Jha declared that "the psychological effects of the Chinese nuclear program make the credibility of assurances essential, to deter both Indian expenditure and Chinese attack."[332] As Gandhi herself explained to French president Charles de Gaulle (1959–1969), the military threat from the PRC made it difficult for India to pursue the development of atomic energy solely for peaceful purposes; any nonproliferation regime should be nondiscriminatory.[333] The PRC was indeed making quick progress on

[329] Quoted in Mirchandani (1968, 39). See also: Director of Central Intelligence, "SNIE 31-1-65, *India's Nuclear Weapons Policy*," October 21, 1965, in NSA EBB 187, Doc. 9, p.3.

[330] Quoted in Office of Scientific Intelligence, Central Intelligence Agency, "The Indian Nuclear Weapons Program and Delivery Capabilities," December 1965, in NSA EBB 187, Doc. 10, p. 10.

[331] See: Chengappa (2000, 98); Kapur (2001, 139); Chakma (2004, 89).

[332] Memorandum of Conversation from the Office of the Assistant Secretary of Defense, "Meeting between the Secretary of Defense and Mr. L. K. Jha, Tuesday, 18 April at 10 a.m.," April 25, 1967, in NSA EBB 6, Doc. 15, p. 1.

[333] See: Sarkar (2015a, 944). See also her statement in a session of Parliament in favor of a nondiscriminatory nonproliferation regime: "Rajya

its nuclear program, detonating its first hydrogen bomb on June 17, 1967. On December 11, Gandhi declared in Parliament that India does "not deem it proper at this time to go in for atomic bombs."[334]

Thus, while India had a long-standing commitment to the peaceful uses of nuclear energy, it was concerned about possible security threats emanating from Beijing and opened the door to a revision of its nuclear policy, should its search for assurances fail. Ultimately, this search failed, leading to India's nuclearization.

U.S. Nonproliferation Efforts

The U.S. intelligence community began seriously considering the time needed for India to construct an atomic device in the early 1960s. On June 29, 1961, the State Department asked its embassies to collect information on the Indian nuclear program and on New Delhi's possible interest in nuclear weapons.[335] At the time, a year after the CIRUS reactor went critical, Bhabha was confidently telling journalists that India could produce an atomic bomb in two years if it so desired.[336] U.S. officials agreed that the time needed to construct a weapon was short, but they were less optimistic than Bhabha, concluding in June 1963 that it would take India four to five years to build an atomic device from the moment New Delhi made a decision to do so.[337]

U.S. officials believed that India would eventually have the motivation to acquire nuclear weapons. On October 31, 1963, a Policy Planning Paper assessing the effect of the PRC's possible acquisition of a nuclear deterrent concluded that "[o]ver the long term it may be very difficult for India, despite the test ban, to forego a nuclear capability indefinitely when its principal enemy possesses such a capability."[338]

Sabha Debate on the Non-Proliferation Treaty," November 21, 1967, in Wilson Center Digital Archive, Indian Nuclear History.

[334] Quoted in Touhey (2007, 29).
[335] See: State Department Instruction: "Indian Capability and Likelihood to Produce Atomic Energy," June 29, 1961, in NSA EBB 6, Doc. 1.
[336] See: Central Intelligence Agency, *India's Potential to Build a Nuclear Weapon*," July 1988, in NSA EBB 187, Doc. 34, p. 1.
[337] See: "National Intelligence Estimate Number 4–63, 'Likelihood and Consequences of a Proliferation of Nuclear Weapons Systems,'" June 23, 1963, in Wilson Center Digital Archive, Indian Nuclear History, p. 7.
[338] U.S. Department of State Policy Planning Council, "Policy Planning Statement on a Chinese Communist Nuclear Detonation and Nuclear Capability," October 15, 1963, in NSA EBB 488, Doc. 12, p. 50.

During the Sino-Indian war of 1962, the Kennedy administration was sympathetic to Indian requests for military assistance, but asked in return for Indian mobilization of military resources, assistance in containing the PRC, and even renunciation of the principle of non-alignment.[339] Such a proposition was problematic for Nehru, who wished to maintain the independence of Indian foreign policy and avoid entrapment in disputes between the superpowers.

After the PRC's nuclear test of October 16, 1964, President Johnson offered India general security assurances, and vowed for continuity in U.S. defense commitments. "The United States reaffirms its defense commitments in Asia," he stated, claiming that "[t]his explosion comes as no surprise to the United States Government" and "has been fully taken into account in planning our own defense program and our own nuclear capability."[340] Two days later, in a televised address, the president again minimized the meaning of the PRC's nuclear test, stating that "the nations that do not seek national nuclear weapons can be sure that if they need our strong support against some threat of nuclear blackmail, they will have it."[341]

U.S. officials surmised that existing levels of support might not be sufficient to prevent India's proliferation. According to an NIE of October 21, 1964, "[i]t is conceivable that the Indians would decide not to develop nuclear weapons if they were able to obtain unequivocal assurances from the US or the USSR to come to India's assistance in case of nuclear attack from Communist China." Yet, such an outcome was unlikely: the Indians were not "optimistic that assurances which they considered adequate could be obtained."[342] In sum, the report concluded, "the chances are better than even that India will decide to develop nuclear weapons within the next few years."[343]

---

[339] See: McGarr (2013, 169).

[340] "Statement by the President on the First Chinese Nuclear Device," October 16, 1964, The American Presidency Project, Lyndon B. Johnson, 1963–1964: Book II. Available at: www.presidency.ucsb.edu/ws/?pid=26615. Last accessed: May 1, 2016.

[341] "Radio and Television Report to the American People on Recent Events in Russia, China, and Great Britain," October 18, 1964, The American Presidency Project, Lyndon B. Johnson, 1963–1964: Book II. Available at: www.presidency.ucsb.edu/ws/?pid=26627. Last accessed: May 1, 2016.

[342] National Intelligence Estimate Number 4-2-64, "Prospects for a Proliferation of Nuclear Weapons over the Next Decade," October 21, 1964, p. 9, in Wilson Center Digital Archive, Indian Nuclear History.

[343] Ibid., p. 1.

Many voices in Washington argued against stronger commitments to India. For the JCS, it was "most important that no actions be taken that could alienate US allies, especially Pakistan."[344] Ambassador-at-large Llewellyn Thompson (1962–1967) laid out the broader implications of stronger guarantees:

India will undoubtedly wish to remain a nonaligned country, which I should think would exclude any formal United States guarantee which, in any event, would have serious disadvantages for us and which would probably result in our having to give similar guarantees to a large number of other countries.[345]

The Indian program continued to progress and Indian policymakers inched closer to a decision to develop nuclear weapons. In June 1966, the State Department suggested that "a decision point is likely to be reached within a few years and, unless there is some new development, India almost certainly will go nuclear."[346] Nevertheless, the following month, Rusk advised the president not to take any dramatic step to prevent India's nuclearization, as the administration had been "unable to devise anything dramatic which would not cost us more than any anticipated gain."[347] Jha and Sarabhai's commitment-seeking trip to Washington in April 1967 was unsuccessful. The United States eventually rejected the Soviet proposal for joint security guarantees to India which, as National Security Advisor Walt W. Rostow (1966–1969) argued, would commit the United States to reject the first-use of nuclear weapons and would thus be unacceptable given defense commitments in Vietnam and North Korea, in particular.[348]

Washington was attempting to dissuade India from nuclearization because of the financial costs involved.[349] An NIE of January 1966

---

[344] Memorandum for the Secretary of Defense, "The Indian Nuclear Problem: Proposed Course of Action," October 23, 1964, in NSA EBB 6, Doc. 2, p. 2.

[345] Memorandum from the State Department, Ambassador at Large, "Indian Nuclear Weapons Capability," January 30, 1965, in NSA EBB 6, Doc. 6, p. 1.

[346] State Department Memorandum for the President, "NSC Meeting, June 9, 1966," June 7, 1966, in NSA EBB 6, Doc. 10, p. 4.

[347] Quoted in Abraham (1998, 127); Sarkar (2015a, 940).

[348] See: Sarkar (2015a, 944).

[349] See: "State Department Telegram Regarding Estimated Cost of Indian Nuclear Weapon Program," May 24, 1966, in NSA EBB 6, Doc. 9, p. 1; State

opined that "[a]ny Indian leader would be reluctant to disregard US pressures against proliferation, particularly at a time when India is so dependent on the US to help alleviate India's critical food situation."[350] To conduct a nuclear test in the near future, the report added, India would use the plutonium from the CIRUS reactor, which according to the agreement with Canada should be used for peaceful purposes.[351] U.S. and Canadian officials made sure to communicate to Indian officials that, in their view, there was no distinction between a "peaceful nuclear explosion" and a nuclear-weapons test, raising the potential negative repercussions of performing a PNE.[352] Dissatisfied with such a weak U.S. response, India soon abandoned its search for stronger security guarantees and rejected the NPT, keeping open the option of obtaining a nuclear deterrent.[353]

The Nixon Administration and the "Tilt"

From India's perspective, Washington's foreign policy took a more adversarial turn in 1971. In late March, Pakistani president Yahya Khan (1969–1971) began a violent crackdown in East Pakistan against the Awami League, a Bangladeshi nationalist movement which had won a majority of seats in the previous parliamentary elections. U.S. consul general in Dhaka Archer Blood (1970–1971) decried the repression as "a genocide" and denounced U.S. inaction.[354]

Department Memorandum for the President, "NSC Meeting, June 9, 1966," June 7, 1966, in NSA EBB 6, Doc. 10, p. 5.

[350] "National Intelligence Estimate, NIE 4–66, 'The Likelihood of Further Nuclear Proliferation,'" January 20, 1966, p. 8, in Wilson Center Digital Archive, Indian Nuclear History.

[351] See: Ibid., pp. 7–8. See also: Director of Central Intelligence, "SNIE 31-1-65, *India's Nuclear Weapons Policy*," October 21, 1965, in NSA EBB 187, Doc. 9, p. 6.

[352] See: Sarkar (2015a, 944); State Department cable 40378 to U.S. Embassy, Ottawa, "Indian Nuclear Intentions," March 9, 1972, in National Security Archive (NSA) Electronic Briefing Book (EBB) 367, "The Nixon Administration and the Indian Nuclear Program, 1972–1974," Doc. 6, pp. 3–4; State Department cable 50634 to U.S. Embassy Canada, "Indian Nuclear Intentions," March 24, 1972, in NSA EBB 367, Doc. 8, p. 2.

[353] See: "Rajya Sabha Q&A on the Non-Proliferation Treaty Draft," May 2, 1968; and "Rajya Sabha Q&A on India's Position Regarding the Acquisition of a Nuclear Umbrella from Friendly Nuclear Powers," March 20, 1969, both in Wilson Center Digital Archive, Indian Nuclear History.

[354] U.S. Consulate (Dacca) Cable, "Dissent from U.S. Policy Toward East Pakistan," April 6, 1971, in National Security Archive (NSA) Electronic

Nixon insisted on an accommodative stance toward Pakistan, approving Kissinger's policy recommendations against U.S. action and adding a handwritten note: "To all hands: Don't squeeze Yahya at this time."[355] Yahya had been acting as a secret liaison between Washington and Beijing to open direct talks.[356] The day before Kissinger's policy recommendation, he had conveyed to Washington Zhou Enlai's message that Beijing would welcome the visit of a high-level envoy,[357] and the following July, Kissinger would secretly fly out of Pakistan to reach Beijing.

As a result of the repression in East Pakistan, a heavy flow of refugees entered India, and the State Department warned in May that the conflict could degenerate into a war between the two states.[358] Nixon wished to avoid any international intervention. Not only did he feel a personal debt toward Yahya for his assistance in establishing contacts with the PRC,[359] but his administration also feared potentially deleterious consequences on the prospect of improved relations with the PRC. For years, Beijing had insisted that relations with the United States could be normalized only if Washington recognized Taiwan as Chinese territory; and that the United States did not have a right to

Briefing Book (EBB) 79, "The Tilt: The U.S. and the South Asian Crisis of 1971," Doc. 8, p. 2. For a history of the crisis and detailed account of U.S. policy, see: Bass (2013).

[355] Memorandum for the President, "Policy Options Toward Pakistan," April 28, 1971, in NSA EBB 79, Doc. 9, p. 6.

[356] See: "Memorandum from Lindsey Grant and Hal Saunders of the National Security Council Staff to the President's Assistant for National Security Affairs (Kissinger)," Washington, August 21, 1969, "Memorandum of Conversation," Washington, August 28, 1969, "Memorandum from the President's Assistant for National Security Affairs (Kissinger) to President Nixon," Washington, October 16, 1969, and "Memorandum from the President's Assistant for National Security Affairs (Kissinger) to President Nixon," Washington, February 23, 1970, all in *Foreign Relations of the United States* (*FRUS*), 1969–1976, Vol. XVII, *China, 1969–1972*, Docs. 26, 28, 39, 70; National Security Archive (NSA) Electronic Briefing Book (EBB) 66, "The Beijing-Washington Back-Channel and Henry Kissinger's Secret Trip to China."

[357] See: "Message from Zhou Enlai to Nixon, 21 April 1971, rec'd 27 April 1971, Responding to Nixon's 16 December 1970 Message," in NSA EBB 66, Doc. 17.

[358] See: Department of State, Memorandum for the President, "Possible India-Pakistan War," May 26, 1971, NSA EBB 79, Doc. 12.

[359] On August 7, Nixon thanked Yahya, stating: "Those who want a more peaceful world in the generation to come will forever be in your debt." "Handwritten Letter from President Nixon to President Yahya," August 7, 1971, in NSA EBB 79, Doc. 20, p. 2.

interfere in the domestic affairs of another sovereign state.[360] In an NSC Senior Review Group meeting on August 11, Nixon stated:

We will not measure our relationship with the [Pakistani] government in terms of what it has done in East Pakistan. By that criterion, we would cut off relations with every Communist government in the world because of the slaughter that has taken place in the Communist countries.[361]

In his memo to Nixon on August 18, Kissinger explicitly linked the conflict in East Pakistan to possible concerns on the PRC's part: "At this stage in our stance toward China, a US effort to split off part of Pakistan in the name of self-determination would have implications for Taiwan and Tibet in Peking's eyes."[362] Two days earlier, Kissinger had conveyed U.S. policy to the PRC's ambassador in Paris, explaining that the administration viewed the conflict as a domestic affair of Pakistan, and would threaten to cut off all economic aid to India if New Delhi initiated military action.[363]

News of the Sino-American rapprochement in mid-July raised concerns in New Delhi about American willingness to provide a nuclear umbrella against the PRC, raising "the spectre of Sino-US and Pakistani alignment."[364] On August 9, India moved closer to the Soviet Union when the two countries signed a treaty of peace, friendship, and cooperation, which provided for mutual consultation in the event of an attack by a third party.[365] The same day, Gandhi sent a letter to

---

[360] See the case studies of China and Taiwan in this chapter and Anderson, Debs, and Monteiro (2015).

[361] "Memorandum for the Record," August 11, 1971, in NSA EBB 79, Doc. 21, p. 4.

[362] Memorandum for the President, "Implications of the Situation in South Asia," August 18, 1971, in NSA EBB 79, Doc. 24, p. 3.

[363] See: Memorandum for the President, "My August 16 Meeting with the Chinese Ambassador in Paris," August 16, 1971, in NSA EBB 79, Doc. 23, pp. 6–7.

[364] Hilali (2005, 40). See also: State Department Bureau of Intelligence and Research Intelligence Note, "India to Go Nuclear?," January 14, 1972, in NSA EBB 367, Doc. 2, p. 3.

[365] See: "The Treaty of Peace, Friendship and Cooperation between the Union of Soviet Socialist Republics and the Republic of India," *The Current Digest of the Russian Press*, Vol. 23, No. 32, September 7, 1971, p. 5. For U.S. reactions, see: "Memorandum from Acting Secretary of State Irwin to President Nixon," New York, Washington, August 9, 1971, in *Foreign Relations of the United States (FRUS)*, 1969–76, Vol. XI, *South Asia Crisis, 1971*, Doc. 116.

Nixon, criticizing U.S. inaction in finding a political settlement in East Pakistan.[366]

The Indo-Soviet agreement fell short of a tight alliance treaty, however. Whereas Moscow wanted to secure India's support in its growing rivalry with China and was keen to bring India into the fold, New Delhi was mainly interested in stopping the flow of Soviet weapons to Pakistan. In fact, Gandhi rejected a "Brezhnev doctrine" of collective security for Asia and was keen on retaining "the central tenet of non-alignment: the need to avoid being ensnared in military alliances."[367] For New Delhi, the solution to the Chinese threat could not rely exclusively on Moscow's support.

U.S. intelligence officials shared this evaluation, believing that the Indo-Soviet Treaty served to alleviate Indian security concerns, albeit only partially. A SNIE of August 1972 suggested:

the closer connection forged with the USSR (as signaled in the August 1971 Treaty of Friendship) has temporarily enhanced India's sense of security with respect to the Chinese. Indian fears that even a small inventory of nuclear bombs could, in time of crisis, trigger off a pre-emptive Chinese attack has almost certainly been eased by recent demonstrations of Soviet support.

Yet, the treaty would not be sufficient to allay India's long-term security concerns. The report added:

The durability of the Soviet guarantee, however, is undoubtedly open to question in New Delhi. Moreover, New Delhi clearly believes it has lost any hope of a US nuclear umbrella against China. The fear of becoming further dependent on the Soviet Union for its ultimate security against China and the need to hedge against possible depreciation of the present Soviet guarantee would be two powerful motives in favor of an early nuclear decision.[368]

The 1971 war between India and Pakistan officially started on December 3. Nixon was furious. That day, Kissinger declared in the Washington Special Action Group meeting: "I am getting hell every

---

[366] See: Department of State, Cable, "Letter from Prime Minister Gandhi," August 14, 1971, in NSA EBB 79, Doc. 22.
[367] Raghavan (2013, 112).
[368] "Special National Intelligence Estimate 31'72," Washington, August 3, 1972, in *Foreign Relations of the United States (FRUS)*, 1969–1976, Vol. E-7, *Documents on South Asia, 1969–1972*, Doc. 298, pp. 7–8.

half-hour from the President that we are not being tough enough on India. ... He wants to tilt in favor of Pakistan."[369] Nixon insisted on applying economic pressure on India by withholding credit and food aid. The administration presented India as the aggressor in the conflict, dispatching the Seventh Fleet to the Bay of Bengal in support of Pakistan, and illegally transferring fighter planes to Pakistani territory.[370] Within two weeks, the war was over. Pakistan forces had been thoroughly defeated in East Pakistan. Their surrender led to the creation of an independent Bangladesh.

The events of 1971 – not only Nixon's tilt toward Pakistan but also his opening to China – prompted India to speed up its nuclear development.[371] In the fall of 1972, Indira Gandhi gave the final formal approval for a nuclear test.[372] On May 18, 1974, India tested a nuclear explosive device at Pokhran in the Rajasthan desert. The test, codenamed "Smiling Buddha," used plutonium from the CIRUS reactor and was declared to be a "peaceful nuclear explosion."[373]

Although the next nuclear tests would not come until 1998, India would use this interregnum to develop its delivery capabilities. In late 1982, Indira Gandhi approved a program to develop a fighter aircraft capable of delivering atomic bombs.[374] The following year, India launched a ballistic missile program.[375] By 1988, New Delhi was able to quickly assemble nuclear weapons.[376] On May 22, 1989, India fired

---

[369] National Security Council, "Notes, Anderson Papers Material," January 6, 1972, in NSA EBB 79, Doc. 45, p. 2.

[370] See: "Background Briefing with Henry Kissinger," December 7, 1971, United States Embassy (New Delhi) Cable, "*U.S. Public Position on Road to War*," December 8, 1971, Memcon, "Huang Ha, T'ang Wen-sheng, Shih Yen-hua, Alexander Haig, Winston Lord," December 12, 1971, Department of State, "Situation Report #4, *Situation in India-Pakistan as of 0700 hours (EST)*," December 14, 1971, Central Intelligence Agency, Intelligence Memorandum, "*India-Pakistan Situation Report (As of 1200 EST)*," December 16, 1971, United States Embassy (Tehran), Cable, "F-5 Aircraft to Pakistan," December 29, 1971, all in NSA EBB 79, Docs. 30, 31, 36, 38, 42, 44.

[371] See: Ganguly and Hagerty (2005, 44–45).

[372] There is some uncertainty and debate around the date of the decision. Perkovich (1999, 172) says that it was made in September 1972. See also: Kapur (2001, 165); Chakma (2004, 85).

[373] See: Central Intelligence Agency, "The 18 May 1974 Indian Nuclear Test," September 1974, in NSA EBB 187, Doc. 24.

[374] See: Chengappa (2000, 284).

[375] See: Chellaney (1994, 168); Kampani (2014b, 94).

[376] See: Perkovich (1999, 293).

its first nuclear-capable Intermediate-Range Ballistic Missile (IRBM), the Agni.[377]

In 1995, Washington applied generalized diplomatic pressure for the permanent extension of the NPT and the completion of the Comprehensive Nuclear-Test-Ban Treaty (CTBT). Without clear progress on the nuclear disarmament of nuclear-weapon states, domestic pressure grew in India to perform a nuclear test, but the test was called off after U.S. insistence.[378]

Atal Bihari Vajpayee of the nationalist Bharatiya Janata Party (BJP) came to office on May 16, 1996, intent on performing a nuclear test, but fell after losing a vote of confidence. Back in office in March 19, 1998, Vajpayee approved nuclear tests on April 8, two days after Pakistan test-fired its own IRBMs. This second round of tests, called Operation Shakti (or Pokhran II), consisted of five detonations carried out on May 11 and May 13. Later in the month, Vajpayee declared that "the onus of India's nuclear tests [is] on the nuclear haves who had over the decades stubbornly refused to negotiate any treaty to dismantle the nuclear weapon stockpiles." According to him, in the preceding decades, "a gradual deterioration of our security environment [had] occurred as a result of nuclear/missile proliferation."[379] Although the tests took the international community by surprise, India's nuclear capability had long been known.

Alternative Explanations

The existing scholarship includes multiple explanations for India's nuclearization. In part, this results from India's unique route to nuclearization, which represents a challenge for any analysis. Some scholars set India's nuclear acquisition when it performed the peaceful nuclear explosion of 1974,[380] others when it prepared at least two dozen

---

[377] See: Spector and Smith (1990, 74).
[378] See: Rabinowitz (2014, 169).
[379] Quoted in Paul (1998, 7).
[380] See: Wohlstetter (1978); Duncan (1989); Lavoy (1997); Abraham (1998); Thesis, U.S. Joint Military Intelligence College, "From Independence to the Bomb: India's Nuclear Motivations, 1945–1974," August 2000, in Wilson Center Digital Archive, Indian Nuclear History; Anderson (2010); Szalontai (2011).

nuclear weapons for quick assembly in the late 1980s,[381] and yet others when it performed the Pokhran II / Shakti tests of 1998.[382]

On the whole, many scholars focus on security explanations to account for India's first test of 1974.[383] Some emphasize the role of the threat from a nuclear-armed China,[384] and New Delhi's failure to secure superpower guarantees from both the United States and the USSR to confront this threat.[385]

Still, this view has become less prominent of late. Other scholars consider the lag between, on the one hand, the war with China (1962) and Beijing's first nuclear test (1964) and, on the other hand, the peaceful nuclear explosion of 1974, to be too long for this explanation to hold.[386] Still others question why India nuclearized despite signing a security treaty with the Soviet Union in 1971.[387] At the time of the 1974 explosion, Scott Sagan points out, senior defense and diplomatic officials in India were unaware of Gandhi's decision to perform a test, and the country was unprepared to deal with Canada's decision to terminate nuclear assistance in reaction to the test. Increasingly, India is cited as a challenge for a security-based explanation of proliferation, and one of the main reasons for moving away from such a framework.

Instead, for some scholars domestic considerations appear more sensible, given the government's sagging popularity at the time of the 1974 test.[388] India's economic situation at the time was dire, and

---

[381] See: Kampani (2014a, 81, 84).

[382] See: Paul (1998); Perkovich (1999); Chengappa (2000); Conley (2001); Kapur (2001); Hymans (2002; 2006); Bajpai (2003). Some scholars characterize India's situation in the 1980s as nuclear hedging or keeping the nuclear option open. See: Subrahmanyam (1987); Spector and Smith (1990); Thakur and Thayer (1992); Chellaney (1994); Paul (1998); Perkovich (1999); Chengappa (2000); Kapur (2001). Finally, some scholars offer accounts of the 1974 PNE as well as the 1998 tests. See: Subrahmanyam (1998); Ganguly (1999); Paul (2000); Bajpai (2003); Kennedy (2011).

[383] See: Ganguly and Hagerty (2005, 44–45).

[384] See: Wohlstetter (1978, 59); Duncan (1989, 55); Spector and Smith (1990, 63); Thakur and Thayer (1992, 137–138); Chellaney (1994, 169); Subrahmanyam (1998, 32); Paul (2000, 127); Bajpai (2003, 51); Chakma (2004, 88).

[385] See: Wohlstetter (1978, 63–64); Ganguly (1999, 158–159); Kennedy (2011).

[386] See: Abraham (1998, 16).

[387] See: Szalontai (2011, 5); Kampani, et al. (2012, 183–184, 186).

[388] See: Sagan (1996–1997, 65–68). See also: Chengappa (2000, 207); Anderson (2010, 479–480).

a test might demonstrate the government's competence and leadership.[389] George Perkovich, author of a seminal account of India's nuclear program, agrees that the nuclear test bolstered Indira Gandhi's domestic political situation and helped consolidate her hold on power. "Domestic factors," he states, "including moral and political norms, have been more significant in determining India's nuclear policy."[390] Nuclear technology was seen as a sign of modernity that conferred prestige upon nuclear-weapons states.[391] Moreover, domestic politics may help explain differences between the PNE of 1974 and the tests of 1998. According to Jacques Hymans, the psychological makeup of leaders differed in 1974 and 1998. In 1998, the country was ruled by an oppositional nationalist government, the BJP, which was more likely to favor weaponization of the nuclear program.[392]

To be sure, India's unique trajectory toward building the bomb challenges simple categorizations of nuclear-capable states, leading to two separate questions: Why did India become nuclear-capable? What explains the timing of India's nuclear tests? It might appear in retrospect that Indira Gandhi performed the test of 1974 to boost her popularity. But Gandhi herself questioned that logic: "How could it have been political? There were no elections coming up. ... It would have been useful for elections. But we did not have any."[393] In fact, the U.S. intelligence community, unaware that Gandhi had approved the PNE, argued in January 1974 that domestic political conditions militated *against* a test.[394] Given challenging economic conditions, and uncertain benefits of peaceful nuclear explosions, a majority of Indians would disapprove of an expensive PNE and prefer greater attention to productive economic investments. Within a month of the test, U.S. officials noticed that the initial burst in popularity had receded, giving place to growing disillusionment with the government in the face of unclear

---

[389] See: Anderson (2010, 479–488).
[390] Perkovich (1999, 6).
[391] See: Subrahmanyam (1987, 4); Thakur and Thayer (1992, 138); Abraham (1998, 28, 149); U.S. Joint Military Intelligence College (2000, 15); Szalontai (2011, 6–7).
[392] See: Hymans (2002, 144; 2006, 200).
[393] Quoted in Chakma (2004, pp. 89–90).
[394] See: "Telegram 943 from the Embassy in India to the Department of State," January 19, 1974, in *Foreign Relations of the United States (FRUS), 1969–1976*, Vol. E-8, *Documents on South Asia, 1973–1976*, Doc. 156.

economic applications for PNEs.[395] Indeed, India's plans for the peaceful exploitation of nuclear explosions were vague.[396] The decision to call the test a "peaceful nuclear explosion" can easily be understood as pressing the argument that India abided by the terms of the agreement with Canada, so as to increase the chances that such cooperation would thenceforth continue.[397]

We agree that the timing of nuclear tests may be driven at least in part by domestic considerations. But the overall arch of India's nuclearization was driven by security concerns. The domestic politics account of the 1974 Indian test at best accounts for its timing, not for the consistent push toward weaponization that India pursued for decades. Rather than predicting the timing of a test when India was already nuclear capable, or the label that it would assign to an explosion, we focus on understanding why India became nuclear-capable in the first place.

Security considerations, starting with the Sino-Indian war and the PRC's nuclear test, were important elements in favor of nuclearization. The long delay between these security triggers and India's first nuclear test can be attributed to two factors. The first is the investment needed to develop nuclear technology, compounded by leadership changes at the IAEC. Homi Bhabha was arguably more favorable to the development of nuclear weapons than his successor Vikram Sarabhai. Thus, Bhabha's death in 1966 probably delayed the program, while Sarabhai's passing in 1971 probably accelerated it.[398] The second factor is India's consideration of security guarantees by the superpowers as a plausible alternative to an autonomous nuclear deterrent. Immediately after the PRC's nuclear test, U.S. officials offered India security guarantees. Admittedly, these were vague, and India sought to strengthen them. But it was only with the 1971 Nixon rapprochement with the PRC and his tilt toward Pakistan that same year that U.S. guarantees became

---

[395] See: Bureau of Intelligence and Research, Intelligence Note: "India: Uncertainty over Nuclear Policy," June 13, 1974, in NSA EBB 6, Doc. 19, p. 1.
[396] See: Lavoy (1997, 401).
[397] As early as October 1965, US intelligence officials predicted that, should India perform a test, it would label it a "peaceful nuclear explosion" for this reason. See: Director of Central Intelligence, "SNIE 31-1-65, *India's Nuclear Weapons Policy*," October 21, 1965, in NSA EBB 187, Doc. 9, pp. 6–7.
[398] See: Abraham (1998, 135, 140).

highly questionable, leading India to move toward an autonomous deterrent.

Indian officials explained that there were two motivations in their search for an autonomous deterrent: security and prestige. In his April 1967 meeting with McNamara, when India sought assurances from Washington, Jha explained that there were "two major obstacles to Indian acceptance" of the NPT. "One is the security problem vis-à-vis China; the other is the fact that India has developed nuclear technology which contributes to Indian confidence and prestige, but which appears threatened by serious curtailment if India adheres to NPT."[399] In that same meeting, Sarabhai explained that "if disarmament is not to be the next step, then India is reluctant to give up the option of building the bomb." Without disarmament, China would remain nuclear. As Jha clarified, "even if China signs the NPT, this provides no control over further Chinese nuclear weapons development. India's security problem thus remains."[400] As such, security motivations appear sufficient to explain India's reluctance to forgo the nuclear option.

Traditional security explanations face an important challenge in accounting for the effect of security guarantees on proliferation. Our theory clarifies this effect, explaining how alliances affect both a state's willingness and its opportunity to proliferate. Our theory can also offer some guidelines on India's circuitous path to nuclearization. In the 1960s and 1970s, India perceived China as a threat. Given China's success in the 1962 war, its advantage in conventional weaponry, and a budding nuclear arsenal, the effect of India's nuclearization vis-à-vis China was relatively large. In that sense, New Delhi had an incentive to downplay the progress that it was making in its nuclear program, lest it provoke an aggressive reaction from Beijing. In the 1990s, when immediate security concerns centered on the nuclear program and aggressive posture of Pakistan, a weaker enemy, the effect of India's nuclearization was smaller, leading to weaker concerns about possible preventive action from adversaries.

---

[399] Memorandum of Conversation from the Office of the Assistant Secretary of Defense: "Meeting between the Secretary of Defense and Mr. L. K. Jha, Tuesday, 18 April at 10 a.m.," April 25, 1967, in NSA EBB 6, Doc. 15, p. 2.
[400] Ibid., p. 3.

In sum, India nuclearized due to security concerns, triggered first by a war with China and the PRC's nuclear test. Soviet security guarantees increased New Delhi's opportunity to proliferate but did not undermine its willingness to acquire nuclear weapons. Intent on pursuing an autonomous foreign policy, New Delhi detonated a nuclear device in 1974 and, over the ensuing decades, built up a deliverable nuclear arsenal.

South Africa

In 1979, South Africa assembled its first nuclear devices and throughout the 1980s viewed nuclear weapons as a diplomatic tool to elicit U.S. support. When the communist threat abated with the end of the Cold War, Pretoria decided to dismantle its nuclear arsenal. In July 1991, South Africa joined the NPT and in March 1993 President Frederik Willem ("F. W.") de Klerk (1989–1994) announced the end of South Africa's nuclear-weapons program. South Africa thus became the first and, to date, only state to renounce the possession of a nuclear deterrent and reverse its nuclear status.

South Africa emerged from the Second World War as a key member of the Western bloc, given its staunch anticommunism and its vast uranium ore reserves. Three decades later, after a 1974 coup in Portugal led to the independence of its colonies, among them Angola and Mozambique, South Africa's security concerns were heightened. The power vacuum left in these neighboring countries was filled by leftist insurgents, African nationalist regimes, and, most importantly, Soviet and Cuban influence. The United States, however, preferred to keep some distance vis-à-vis the apartheid regime in Pretoria. When in late 1975, as conflict raged in Angola, Washington's covert support for South Africa became public, U.S. assistance quickly ended, and Pretoria realized that it could not rely on U.S. security assurances.

Facing a growing communist threat in its region and enjoying limited U.S. support, South Africa had the willingness to nuclearize. Nuclear weapons could be used to deter enemies and also elicit support from Washington, which would prefer to avoid escalation of a regional conflict to the nuclear level. At the same time, South Africa possessed the opportunity to proliferate. The country was significantly stronger than its immediate enemies in the region, and a counterproliferation strike was unlikely to materialize.

The United States attempted to prevent South Africa's nuclear acquisition by deploying a sticks-based nonproliferation policy. In reaction to Pretoria's refusal to accede to the NPT, Washington ceased all nuclear aid in 1976. International pressure mounted in the ensuing years, with South Africa's ejection from the IAEA board of directors, a 1977 UN resolution banning the sale of conventional arms to Pretoria, and congressional measures taken during the Carter administration with the goal of keeping South Africa nonnuclear. Yet, such coercive efforts were ineffective. South Africa deepened its ties with other suppliers of nuclear technology, most notably Israel, but also France. In the end, given its relative strength vis-à-vis its adversaries, Pretoria had the opportunity to build the bomb.

South African Interest in Nuclear Weapons

A dominion of the British Commonwealth, South Africa entered the Cold War as an ally of the United States. In 1944–1945, a U.S. survey concluded that South Africa possessed the largest unexploited reserves of uranium in the world.[401] For the Truman administration, controlling access to uranium and preventing the Soviet Union from tapping into such sources was of paramount importance. In 1950, South Africa concluded an agreement with the United States and the United Kingdom for the sale of uranium over the following ten years, making Pretoria one of the world's largest uranium producers.[402]

The Apartheid Regime's Early Nuclear Development

South African leaders believed that nuclear technology could provide an efficient route to meet their energy needs.[403] In March 1949, the newly elected National Party government established the Atomic Energy Board (AEB) to explore the peaceful purposes of nuclear energy.[404] South Africa endorsed President Eisenhower's plan to share

---

[401] See: Borstelmann (1993, 50).
[402] Ibid., 163. See also: Pabian (1995, 2); Fig (1999, 78).
[403] See: Fuhrmann (2012, 158).
[404] See: van Wyk (2007a, 1); Fuhrmann (2012, 158). The board replaced the Uranium Research Committee formed after the Second World War. See: van Wyk (2013, 3).

nuclear technology and develop its peaceful applications, as articulated in his "Atoms for Peace" speech of December 1953. In fact, Pretoria soon took advantage of the program. In July 1957, it reached a bilateral agreement with Washington that included a secret addendum allowing South African scientists to be trained in the United States.[405] Pretoria then launched a program for Atomic Energy Research and Development, with the goal of reprocessing its own uranium.[406] South Africa's project to refine uranium was made public in April 1960.[407] With assistance from the United States, the country completed the construction of its first nuclear research reactor, the South African Fundamental Atomic Research Installation 1 (SAFARI-1), at Pelindaba, near Pretoria, by 1965.[408]

South African nuclear ambitions remained peaceful, but there were incipient security concerns. The international community was growing increasingly critical of the apartheid regime. In 1962, the UN called for punitive measures, eventually leading to an arms embargo in August 1963.[409] That same year, South African strategists started conceiving of the colonial and minority-ruled territories to its north as a "cordon sanitaire," a buffer against the radical left.[410] At the time, Prime Minister Hendrik Verwoerd (1958–1966) said that South Africa must repel any "African national-communist invasion" and "hold vast and enormously rich South Africa as a last redoubt of

---

[405] See: Fig (1999, 80); van Wyk (2010a, 563).

[406] See: van Wyk (2009, 57). For a debate in South African policy circles on pursuing nuclear energy, see: A. J. A. Roux, Director of Atomic Energy Research Programme, "Proposed Atomic Energy Research and Development Programme for South Africa," January, 1958, in Wilson Center Digital Archive, South African Nuclear History; and Letter, S. M. Naude, "South African Atomic Energy Research Programme," May 20, 1958, in Wilson Center Digital Archive, South African Nuclear History.

[407] See: "Proposed Press Release, Information Regarding Activities in Atomic Energy in South Africa," April 5, 1960, p. 1, in Wilson Center Digital Archive, South African Nuclear History; Letter, South African Department of Foreign Affairs, "Informing the United States of South Africa's Intent to Request Nuclear Materials," March 30, 1960, in Wilson Center Digital Archive, South African Nuclear History; and South Africa Department of Foreign Affairs, "Proposed Application to United States for Assistance in Meeting Costs of Research Reactor in Western Province," May 4, 1960, in Wilson Center Digital Archive, South African Nuclear History.

[408] See: van Wyk (2010a, 563).

[409] See: van Wyk (2013, 6–7).

[410] Daniel (2009, 37).

Christianity and Western civilization against a reversal to primitiveness and chaos."[411]

By 1966, there were stronger voices in favor of an aggressive foreign policy. The government of Balthazar Johannes ("John") Vorster (1966–1978) worried that black liberation movements, such as the African National Congress (ANC) and the South-West African People's Organization (SWAPO), could threaten the regime's survival if they benefited from the support of Communist powers.[412] His defense minister, Pieter Willem ("P. W.") Botha (1966–1981), believed that South Africa could play a crucial role in stemming the tide against international communism.[413]

Yet, South Africa worried that Washington did not share its security priorities. In a 1963 memo, the South African ambassador voiced the concern that the United States "recently omitted the oceans of Southern Africa from its waters of great strategic importance." He added that "[f]rom South Africa's understanding, the US seems to be willing to accept the risk of passing the control of the South West African coastline facing the Atlantic Ocean to a neutral country."[414]

Pretoria now took steps to hedge in the direction of a nuclear-weapons capability. It refused to sign the NPT when it came into effect in March 1970. In July that year, Vorster declared in Parliament that his government had developed a "unique" method to enrich uranium.[415] Later in 1970, Pretoria began construction of a uranium enrichment plant, named the "Y plant," at Valindaba.[416] Around the same time, South African nuclear scientists wished to visit nuclear-weapons testing sites in the United States.[417] The Vorster government commissioned

---

[411] Quoted in van Wyk (2013, 7).

[412] See: Miller (2013a, 7).

[413] See: Daniel (2009, 38).

[414] Letter, South African Ambassador to the United States, "Regarding Armed Forces Attache's Report," April 11, 1963, pp. 1–3, in Wilson Center Digital Archive, South African Nuclear History. See also: Letter, South African Ambassador to the United States, Taswell, "United States Defence Policy," March 31, 1967, in Wilson Center Digital Archive, South African Nuclear History.

[415] See: Reiss (1995, 33).

[416] See: Rabinowitz (2014, 109–110).

[417] Though at this point the United States admitted that it did not have evidence that South Africa intended to produce nuclear weapons. See: U.S. Department of State, "Memorandum from Martin Jacobs to Mr. Nelson on South African Nuclear Scientist's Visit US Nuclear Testing Facilities," August 25, 1970, p. 1, in

studies on the feasibility of a nuclear-weapons program in 1971.[418]
Between 1972 and 1973, South Africa's AEB investigated the possibility of producing a gun-type nuclear device, designing and constructing a scale model.[419]

The Consequences of the Portuguese Revolution for South Africa's Security

South Africa's security concerns worsened in the mid-1970s, when the regime feared the prospect of a communist "total onslaught."[420] In April 1974, the "carnation revolution" overthrew the Portuguese Estado Novo regime of Marcelo Caetano (1968–1974). The fall of the dictatorship, and Portugal's withdrawal from its former colonies, removed Pretoria's "cordon sanitaire," leaving a power vacuum that communist forces were eager to fill.[421] In Mozambique, the Front for the Liberation of Mozambique ("Frelimo") consolidated power in 1975, after defeating forces financed by Rhodesia and South Africa. Angola also descended into civil war, with the communist People's Movement for the Liberation of Angola (MPLA) pitted against the National Union for the Total Independence of Angola (UNITA) and the National Liberation Front of Angola (FNLA). South Africa offered its support to UNITA and FNLA, first through regular meetings with their leaders in early 1975, and soon through military and economic assistance.[422] In July 1975, Botha ordered South African troops to secure key hydroelectric installations on the South-West African border with Angola.[423] In October, with support from the United States, South Africa sent troops to Angola to assist UNITA and FNLA forces.[424] The conflict escalated when, to aid the MPLA, Cuba sent thousands of soldiers, a commitment that peaked at 50,000 troops.[425] Moscow also supported

---

Wilson Center Digital Archive, South African Nuclear History. See also: van Wyk (2009, 63).

[418] See: Reiss (1995, 8); van Wyk (2010a, 563).
[419] See: van Wyk (2009, 60).
[420] See: Miller (2013a).
[421] See: Barber and Barratt (1990, 253–255); Saunders and Onslow (2010); Miller (2012).
[422] See: Miller (2013a, 11–12).
[423] Ibid., 21–22.
[424] On the role played by the United States in the South African decision to intervene in Angola, see: Miller (2013a, 2013b); Saunders (2013).
[425] See: Stumpf (1995–1996, 4); Gleijeses (2013).

the communist forces, sending economic aid, armaments, and military advisors.[426]

The fall of the Estado Novo regime in Lisbon exacerbated security concerns in South Africa both because it suggested a more immediate foreign threat and also because it highlighted the unreliability of U.S. assurances. A month after Caetano's fall, in May 1974, South Africa successfully tested a prototype using nonnuclear explosives.[427] The AEB reported to Prime Minister Vorster that it was capable of producing a nuclear weapon, and Vorster authorized the construction of a test site at the Vastrap military base in the Kalahari Desert.[428]

At this time, U.S. foreign policy was a clear source of concern for South Africa. When Washington's covert support for the South African effort in Angola became public in December 1975, Congress passed the Clark Amendment, demanding the Ford administration to suspend all aid to South Africa in the Angolan conflict. The abrupt end to Washington's support was seen in Pretoria as an act of betrayal.[429] Botha later stated that South Africa had been "ruthlessly left in the lurch" in Angola.[430] This feeling of betrayal was an important factor that led to the acceleration of South Africa's nuclear-weapons program.[431]

In early 1976, South Africa withdrew from Angola in defeat. In June, riots in Soweto posed a domestic threat to the apartheid regime. For some strategists, there was a link between foreign and domestic threats. The emerging African nationalist regimes in neighboring states could provide a safe haven for liberation movements in South Africa, deepening South Africa's fears of a global, Soviet-driven antiapartheid campaign.[432] As a former South African Defense Force (SADF) officer put it years later, many domestic liberation movements were seen "as part and parcel of the Soviet onslaught against the 'civilised/free/democratic' Western world."[433]

---

[426] For Fidel Castro's account of his involvement in Angola, and a critical analysis, see: Shubin (2009).

[427] See: van Wyk (2009, 60).

[428] See: Reiss (1995, 8).

[429] See: Harris et al. (2004, 463); Du Preez and Matteig (2010, 307).

[430] Quoted in Gleijeses (2013, 29).

[431] See: Daniel (2009, 43).

[432] Ibid., 45.

[433] Quoted in Daniel (2009, 35).

In response to this heightened level of security threat, South Africa
significantly increased its defense expenditures in the latter half of the
1970s.[434] In 1977, a Defense White Paper articulated a "Total National
Strategy," making the case that South Africa should double the size of
its armed forces, triple the defense budget, and initiate "an intensified
commitment to developing nuclear weapons."[435]

The international community was becoming increasingly aware
of South Africa's effort to acquire a nuclear deterrent. Washington
learned that South Africa planned to produce and export highly
enriched uranium (HEU). In 1977, a CIA analysis of the Y plant at
Valindaba estimated that South Africa could produce enough highly
enriched uranium "to make several nuclear devices per year."[436] In
July of the same year, the Soviet Union discovered the nuclear-weapon
test site in the Kalahari Desert, approaching Washington to prevent a
South African test.[437] The United States threatened South Africa that
any further progress toward the development of a nuclear capability
"would have the most serious consequences for all aspects of our relations."[438] The test was averted.

Nevertheless, South Africa would continue making progress in developing a nuclear capability. In early 1978, the Y Plant started producing
HEU.[439] In April that year, Vorster approved the country's first clear

[434] See: Miller (2012, 184–185).
[435] See: Reiss (1995, 9).
[436] Quoted in Central Intelligence Agency, Directorate of Central Intelligence,
Office of Scientific Intelligence, "South African Uranium Enrichment
Program," August 1977, in NSA EBB 423, Doc. 9A, p. i. Earlier U.S.
intelligence reports, in July 1974 and September 1976, doubted South
Africa's ability to produce nuclear weapons. See: Office of Scientific
Intelligence, Central Intelligence Agency, "South Africa Not Currently in
Position to Produce Nuclear Weapons," July 22, 1974, and Office of Scientific
Intelligence, Central Intelligence Agency, "South Africa Again Rumored to Be
Working on Nuclear Weapons," September 13, 1976, in National Security
Archive (NSA) Electronic Briefing Book (EBB) 181, "U.S. Intelligence and the
South African Bomb," Docs. 7 and 14.
[437] See: Warren Christopher to William Hyland, "Response to Soviet Message
on South Africa," August 10, 1977, in National Security Archive (NSA)
Electronic Briefing Book (EBB) 451, "Proliferation Watch: U.S. Intelligence
Assessments of Potential Nuclear Powers, 1977–2001," Doc. 1A.
[438] Letter, US Ambassador Bowlder to South African Foreign Minister Botha,
August 18, 1977, p. 1, in Wilson Center Digital Archive, South African
Nuclear History.
[439] See: Reiss (1995, 8).

enunciation of a nuclear-military strategy,[440] and in October the components of the country's first nuclear device are believed to have been completed.[441] That month, P. W. Botha became prime minister (1978–1984), and in July of the following year, South Africa decided to build a small nuclear arsenal to serve as a "credible deterrent capability."[442] In November 1979, South Africa constructed its first nuclear device.[443] Why did U.S. efforts to prevent South Africa's nuclearization fail?

U.S. Nonproliferation Efforts

In the early years of the Cold War, Washington sought to secure the global supply of uranium, both to limit nuclear proliferation by other states and to prepare for a possible conflict with the Soviet Union.[444] According to an NSC report of the late 1940s, "the cardinal principle [of U.S. policy] … has been to increase our raw materials position and to deprive the Soviets of supplies from outside the USSR."[445] Along with the United Kingdom, the United States set up the Common Development Agency (CDA) and agreed in 1950 to purchase South Africa's abundant uranium.

The Ambivalent U.S.-South African Alliance

Together with Pretoria's strong anticommunist posture, the need to control South Africa's uranium supplies led Washington to tolerate the abhorrent racial politics of the apartheid regime. Yet, already during the Truman administration, Washington started to take some distance away from Pretoria, such that "South Africa evolved during the Truman years from minor member of the victorious Allied of World War II to a status approaching that of international pariah."[446] Washington was concerned that racial discrimination by the United States and by U.S. allies could bolster the Soviet Union's world influence.[447] Still, Washington would continue its alliance with Pretoria,

---

[440] Ibid., 33.
[441] Ibid., 9.
[442] Liberman (2001, 53).
[443] See: Reiss (1995, 8).
[444] See: Borstelmann (1993, 92, 129).
[445] Quoted in ibid., 92.
[446] Ibid., 3.
[447] See: Ibid., 143.

focusing on areas of common interest. Early in the Kennedy adminis-tration, Secretary of State Dean Rusk noted:

There are numerous fields in which our two countries can continue to col-laborate closely and fruitfully to our mutual benefit ... especially in the areas of common defence against threats emanating from the communist bloc ... in the fields of missile activity and space exploration, atomic energy, and in the entire range of scientific, technical and research activities.[448]

Pretoria's virulent anticommunism was also appreciated by the Johnson administration.[449] In 1967, the United States and South Africa agreed to a ten-year extension of their nuclear deal, subject to IAEA safeguards. The United States was not insistent on obtaining guaran-tees of the peaceful nature of South Africa's nuclear program.[450] By December 1968, the chief of staff of the SADF, General Henry James Martin (1967–1968), claimed that South Africa was ready to make "its own nuclear weapons," but his government denied the allegation, and Washington accepted Pretoria's assurances.[451] Until the early 1970s, there were no concerns in the United States that the South African nuclear program would have a military component.[452] The test of a prototype in May 1974 was done in utmost secrecy. The following fall, a U.S. NIE determined that South Africa was unlikely to develop a nuclear-weapons program in the 1970s.[453]

Yet, South Africa's continued refusal to sign the NPT, and its deci-sion to produce and export HEU, led to increased tension in its rela-tions with Washington. In early 1975, the Ford administration stopped supplying the SAFARI-1 reactor, cutting all ties with the South African nuclear program by 1976.[454] In 1977, South Africa was ejected from the board of directors of the IAEA.[455] That same year, Washington

---

[448] Quoted in van Wyk (2009, 57–58).
[449] See: Miller (2012, 190).
[450] See: van Wyk (2007a, 2); Rabinowitz (2014, 109).
[451] Quoted in Rabinowitz (2014, 109).
[452] See: van Wyk (2009, 58) and South African Department of Foreign Affairs, "Nuclear Proliferation Problem," March 18, 1967, p. 2, in Wilson Center Digital Archive, South African Nuclear History.
[453] See: Director of Central Intelligence, Memorandum, "*Prospects for Further Proliferation of Nuclear Weapons*," September 4, 1974, in NSA EBB 181, Doc. 8. See also: van Wyk (2009, 63).
[454] See: Bissell (1982, 115); Pabian (1995, 2).
[455] See: Reiss (1995, 9).

helped pass UNSC Resolution 418, which banned the sale of conventional weapons to South Africa,[456] and pursued its efforts to prevent a nuclear test and obtain Pretoria's adherence to the NPT.[457]

These measures were counterproductive. If anything, they strengthened Pretoria's willingness to acquire nuclear weapons: "[t]here was a feeling [in Pretoria] of being embattled all around. *There was a sense of terrible isolation, a sense of having to stand up to the whole world. This feeling of being alone and left in the lurch, soon turned into a bitter and pervasive determination.*"[458] This determination was channeled into the nuclear-weapon program. According to Waldo Stumpf, the former head of the South African AEC (1990–2001),[459] UNSC Resolution 418 "reinforced the perception that the country had no alternative but to develop a nuclear weapon capability to counter external threats." This factor, he continues, "was probably most compelling to government officials at the time."[460] The U.S. NNPA of 1978, which further restricted Pretoria's access to nuclear technology, only served to harden this resolve.

Ineffective U.S. Supply-Side Efforts

The effectiveness of Washington's supply-side restrictions was limited because Pretoria had the opportunity to proliferate: South Africa was sufficiently powerful to deter counterproliferation strikes from its direct enemies on its own and could turn to other suppliers of nuclear technology to further its ambitions.

For one thing, Pretoria enjoyed a clear preponderance of power over its immediate neighbors. In 1975, South Africa's GDP was over ten times that of Angola.[461] Moreover, by the late 1970s the Soviet Union "lacked logistical support capabilities for deploying large ground

---

[456] Full text available at: "United Nations Security Council Resolution 418 (1977)." Available at: www.un.org/en/ga/search/view_doc.asp?symbol=S/RES/418(1977). Last accessed: August 28, 2013. See also: Reiss (1995, 33).

[457] See: Warren Christopher to William Hyland, "Response to Soviet Message on South Africa," August 10, 1977.

[458] Steyn et al. (2003, 50), Steyn et al.'s emphasis.

[459] The AEB was merged with other government bodies to become the AEC in 1985.

[460] Stumpf (1995–1996, 4).

[461] Angola's GDP in 1975 was approximately $3.1 billion while South Africa's was roughly $36.9 billion (measured in current U.S. dollars). See: United Nations Data (2013).

forces in southern Africa."[462] In 1976, Moscow requested American
assistance in ending South Africa's nuclear program, proposing a joint
counterproliferation strike on the Valindaba nuclear facility, which
was key to Pretoria's nuclear effort. Washington, keen not to alienate
its ally in the Southern Africa region, rejected the proposal.[463] In 1977,
Moscow again requested U.S. assistance, this time to close the recently-
discovered testing site in the Kalahari.[464] Under pressure, Pretoria did
close the site, but it nevertheless acquired a nuclear capability two
years later.

Given that it possessed both the willingness and the opportunity
to acquire nuclear weapons, Pretoria circumvented U.S. attempts to
restrict the supply of sensitive materials by approaching other suppliers. After Washington cancelled the sale of commercial reactors in
1976, South Africa turned to France.[465] Furthermore, Pretoria came
to develop a deep alliance with Israel.[466] Officials in Pretoria and Tel
Aviv believed that they were facing similar strategic threats, and would
benefit from military cooperation. In a surprisingly candid assessment,
Israeli major general Avraham Tamir stated:

In the same way that we would describe the existential dangers facing Israel
due to the Soviet Union's involvement and control over Arab states, they
also talked about the Soviet footholds around South Africa. Their conclusion was identical to ours: to defend against these dangers it was necessary
to develop an extremely potent offensive capability, including nuclear capability. Obviously we had deep cooperation with them in all spheres.[467]

Cooperation between South Africa and Israel in the nuclear sphere was
indeed extensive. Generally, Pretoria wanted minimal controls over its
exports of uranium.[468] In early 1965, the two reached an agreement

---

[462] Liberman (2001, 59).
[463] See: Albright (1994, 42).
[464] See: Reiss (1995, 10).
[465] See: Rabinowitz (2014, 111).
[466] See: Polakow-Suransky (2011).
[467] Quoted in Liberman (2004, 10).
[468] See: "Letter from South African Ambassador A. G. Dunn to South African
Department for Foreign Affairs Official M. I. Botha on the Sale of Uranium
to Israel," July 20, 1960, in Wilson Center Digital Archive, South African
Nuclear History; and "Memorandum from Deputy Chair, South African
Atomic Energy Board, T. E. W. Schumann Regarding 2 June 1961 Paris

on the sale of this key material for Israel's own nuclear program.[469] On March 31, 1975, they held secret talks about the sale of Jericho missiles to South Africa, concluding a deal that may have included nuclear technology.[470] Around 1977, South Africa is believed to have obtained thirty grams of tritium (a nuclear-yield-boosting element) from Israel, in exchange for fifty tons of uranium.[471] Some also suspect that the two countries cooperated on an unconfirmed nuclear test that took place in September 1979, when a U.S. Vela satellite surveying an area of the South Atlantic detected a "double-peaked" signature, generally associated with a nuclear detonation.[472]

Faced with possible abandonment by the United States, South Africa constructed its first nuclear device by November 1979, completed its second bomb in 1982, and by the end of the 1980s was developing a second-generation, implosion-type design.[473]

Limited Post-Nuclearization U.S. Support and South Africa's Nuclear Reversal

Strategically, and given how fears of abandonment by the United States were a major motivation for nuclear acquisition, Pretoria opted for using its nuclear deterrent as a catalyst for American intervention in case of an eventual conflict. Threats to use nuclear weapons would work as a form of blackmail to keep the United States involved, out of fear of South African escalation.[474] According to Botha, nuclear weapons could act in this way as a "diplomatic weapon."[475] In his view,

Meeting on Bilateral Safeguards," May 29, 1961, in Wilson Center Digital Archive, South African Nuclear History.
[469] See: "Draft Agreement between South Africa and Israel on the Application of Safeguards to the Sale of Uranium," February 1, 1965, p. 1, in Wilson Center Digital Archive, South African Nuclear History.
[470] See: "Minutes of Second Israel-South Africa (ISSA) Meeting," March 31, 1975, in Wilson Center Digital Archive, South African Nuclear History. See also: Harris et al. (2004, 461); Liberman (2004, 4).
[471] See: Liberman (2004, 7); van Wyk (2009, 73).
[472] See: Reiss (1995, 9). While some believed that this was a South African test, most of the available evidence suggests that this was an Israeli test that South Africa may have merely observed. See: Reiss (1995, 11); Stumpf (1995–1996, 5); van Wyk (2009, 76).
[473] See: Pabian (1995, 12); Reiss (1995, 11).
[474] See: van Wyk (2007b), Goodson (2012); Purkitt and Burgess (2012, 37–52); Narang (2014).
[475] Quoted in Liberman (2001, 59).

"[o]nce we set this thing off, the Yanks will come running."[476] In sum, the primary purpose of South Africa's nuclear acquisition was to elicit U.S. security assistance in the event of a crisis.[477]

By the mid-1980s, it appeared unlikely that Pretoria would succeed in obtaining U.S. support. In October 1986, the U.S. Congress overturned President Ronald Reagan's (1981–1989) veto to pass a stringent set of sanctions, the Comprehensive Anti-Apartheid Act.[478] At the same time, South Africa's strategic environment was taking a turn for the worse. In late 1987, Cuba sent 15,000 more troops to Angola,[479] and in June of the following year Cuban leader Fidel Castro (1959–2008) issued veiled threats to send tank brigades into territory occupied by Pretoria in South-West Africa.[480]

The moment seemed ripe for using nuclear weapons in order to elicit U.S. support. In late 1988, Botha ordered the abandoned site in the Kalahari Desert to be revisited, apparently in preparation for a nuclear test.[481] As a South African counterintelligence officer later admitted: "Of course we knew the satellites would see the whole thing."[482] For this officer, the reopening of the facility "gave the West and the Soviets a hell of a fright," and consequently "the West began to put pressure on the Soviets to get the Cubans to withdraw from Angola."[483] Botha's gamble thus appeared to pay off, and negotiations for a ceasefire in Angola were concluded by August 1988. In December, South Africa, Angola, and Cuba agreed on a timetable for

---

[476] Ibid., 60. This strategy, called "catalytic deterrence," would follow three steps in the escalation of an eventual conflict. On the first step, South Africa would maintain ambiguity about its nuclear arsenal. If a significant threat emerged, then on the second step Pretoria would reveal its nuclear capabilities *to the United States*, so as to elicit U.S. support in order to forestall nuclear use. If this attempt failed, South Africa would in a third step reveal its nuclear arsenal to its adversary, so as to deter an attack. See: Reiss (1995, 15); Goodson (2012, 213).

[477] See: Bissell (1982, 104); Narang (2014); Rabinowitz (2014). Not all South African officials believed that the strategy could work. For a dissenting view, see: Botha (2008, 11).

[478] See: Baker (1989, 5, 44–47).

[479] See: Pabian (1995, 8).

[480] See: Reiss (1995, 14).

[481] At the time, Botha was state president. In 1984, the position of prime minister was replaced with the formerly ceremonial position of state president following constitutional reforms.

[482] Hamann (2001, 168).

[483] Ibid. See also: Narang (2014, 213); Rabinowitz (2014, 127–130).

the withdrawal of forces from South-West Africa, which would gain independence as the Republic of Namibia in 1990.[484]

With this reduction of tensions, South Africa moved toward the dismantlement of its nuclear-weapons program. In July 1988, the apartheid government approached the United Kingdom, the United States, and the Soviet Union on the possibility of renouncing its nuclear arsenal and joining the NPT as a nonnuclear state.[485] The following year, F. W. de Klerk replaced Botha as president of South Africa, after the latter suffered a stroke, and proceeded to dismantle the nuclear-weapons program. The Kalahari test site was completely abandoned and South Africa's uranium enrichment facility was formally shut down. In 1991, South Africa joined the NPT as a nonnuclear state. As de Klerk would put it two years later, South Africa had been interested in

a limited nuclear deterrent capability ... [as a result of the] Soviet expansionist threat in Southern Africa, as well as prevailing uncertainty concerning the designs of the Warsaw Pact members. The buildup of the Cuban forces in Angola reinforced the perception that a deterrent was necessary.[486]

Given the marked improvement in Pretoria's security environment brought about by the end of the Cold War and the demise of the Soviet Union, "a nuclear deterrent had become, not only superfluous, but in fact an obstacle to the development of South Africa's international relations."[487] The security concerns that fueled South Africa's willingness to acquire nuclear weapons had ceased to exist; with them, the South African nuclear arsenal would soon vanish.[488]

Alternative Explanations

It is generally accepted that South Africa's perception of an intense security threat, coupled with international isolation, were key drivers for its nuclear-weapons program.[489] Despite this consensus, some

[484] See: Reiss (1995, 14).
[485] See: van Wyk (2010b, 62).
[486] Quoted in Liberman (2001, 59).
[487] Quoted in Pabian (1995, 10).
[488] Some scholars suggest that domestic political considerations also played a role in South Africa's decision. We discuss this argument in the following text.
[489] See: De Villiers et al. (1993); Pabian (1995); Reiss (1995); Stumpf (1995–1996); Liberman (2001); Steyn et al. (2003).

scholars question the usefulness of a rational cost-benefit analysis focused on the security dimension for understanding South Africa's decision to acquire the bomb. These critics raise three points.

First, some argue that South Africa's threat perception was unjustified. According to Peter Liberman, South Africa "did not face the kind of nuclear coercion or conventional invasion threats commonly thought to trigger nuclear weapons programs." Aggression by the Soviet Union, direct or indirect, was a remote possibility, and "nuclear weapons would have provided only a limited remedy to this threat, even had it materialized."[490] Policymakers and analysts were puzzled by South Africa's perception that it would derive security benefits from nuclear weapons. Fidel Castro did admit, years after the end of the war in Angola, that the possibility of a nuclear attack by South Africa affected its troop deployments.[491] Yet, in the same breath he questioned the advisability of a South African nuclear attack: "The right of the matter was whether they would decide to drop it or not. Who were they going to use the weapon against? Against us? Inside South Africa?"[492] A CIA assessment of April 1981 concurred:

It is difficult to see a near term military usefulness to nuclear weapons except in the most extreme, and unlikely, circumstances. The principal threat to South Africa is likely to remain black urban insurrection and guerillas operating in border areas, for which nuclear explosives would be useless.[493]

---

[490] Liberman (2001, 46).

[491] Recalling Cuba's involvement in Angola, Fidel Castro declared in 1995 that "South Africa had become a nuclear power by then. And we knew it. We even deployed our forces in such a way that we were taking into account that South Africa had nuclear warheads." "Excerpt from Fidel Castro's address to Abyssinian Baptist Church in Harlem," October 23, 1995, Hartford Web Publishing, World History Archives. Available at www.hartford-hwp.com/ archives/43b/022.html. Last accessed: May 1, 2016. See also: Scholtz (2013, 383). Jorge Risquet, top Cuban negotiator for the peace settlement, admitted in his visit to South Africa in 2010 that the possibility that South Africa could deliver nuclear weapons by means of its artillery constrained Cuba "from embarking on plans to cross the northern border of Namibia." Academic Peace Orchestra Middle East (2013, 15).

[492] "Excerpt from Fidel Castro's address to Abyssinian Baptist Church in Harlem," October 23, 1995, Hartford Web Publishing, World History Archives. Available at www.hartford-hwp.com/archives/43b/022.html. Last accessed: May 1, 2016. See also: Scholtz (2013, 383).

[493] Special Assistant for Nuclear Proliferation Intelligence, National Foreign Assessment Center, Central Intelligence Agency, to Resource Management

Some of these critics acknowledge that nuclear weapons eventually brought security benefits to South Africa, but as a catalyst for U.S. intervention, not as a military deterrent per se, and that this diplomatic rationale for the bomb was made post hoc. So, prior to 1979, the South African government had no plausible rationale for building the bomb.[494] In other words, "Pretoria's anxiety was misplaced."[495] According to this line of criticism, approaches based on psychology, organizational structures, and domestic politics – such as Jacques Hymans's work – are better at capturing South Africa's strategic thinking.[496]

These are valuable points, but it is important to clarify what our rational security-based explanation seeks to achieve. A rational account seeks to elucidate how a strategic interaction between decisionmakers, with their own preferences and beliefs, produces a certain outcome. A rational theory does not explain, let alone justify, the underlying beliefs and preferences of decisionmakers. The fundamental political principle of the apartheid regime was morally repugnant. Even cost-benefit analyses were couched in racist terms. For example, Dr. Andries Visser of the AEB stated in 1965 that "we should have the bomb to prevent aggression from loud mouthed Afro-Asiatic states."[497]

Yet, incorporating these preferences of decisionmakers in Pretoria into a rationalist framework elucidates some key aspects of the South African experience. South Africa enjoyed conventional superiority over its immediate enemies, which meant that the effect of its nuclearization on the balance of power would be relatively small. One might stop here and conclude that its nuclearization would not be rational. Still, the security benefit of nuclear weapons also depended on the perception of the level of foreign threat. South African policymakers were persistently anticommunist. They identified the Soviet Union as

Staff, Office of Program Assessment et al., "Request for Review of Draft Paper on the Security Dimension of Non-Proliferation," April 9, 1981, in National Security Archive (NSA) Electronic Briefing Book (EBB) 377, "New Documents Spotlight Reagan-era Tensions over Pakistani Nuclear Program," Doc. 5, p. 41.

[494] See: Goodson (2012, 213).
[495] Purkitt and Burgess (2012, 40). See also: Burgess and Purkitt (2005).
[496] See: Hymans (2006).
[497] Quoted in Rabinowitz (2014, 109).

a security threat in the early 1960s, and pressed for a more aggressive anticommunist policy from the mid-1960s onward.[498] A belief that future conflict was highly likely could make an investment in nuclear weapons greatly productive.

A second line of criticism comes from scholars who question the initial security motivations for South Africa's nuclear-weapons program. As discussed in the preceding text, Pretoria first looked at the possibility of acquiring nuclear weapons before the fall of the Caetano regime in Portugal. According to Anna-Mart Van Wyk, this suggests that, although Pretoria's threat perceptions were further strengthened by the fall of the Portuguese dictatorship in 1974, Pretoria's drive to nuclearize "came from the sense of prestige, a technological 'can-do' mentality and a strong sense of Afrikaner nationalism."[499]

We do not disagree that South Africa's nuclear program may have included a prestige dimension. Our contention is that security dynamics, however, are both necessary and sufficient to account for Pretoria's acquisition of a nuclear arsenal. The decision to develop a nuclear-weapons capability was taken no sooner than 1974, and analysts generally agree that the fall of the Caetano regime in Portugal provided a significant boost to the South African nuclear-weapons program.[500] Indeed, van Wyk agrees that this was a "watershed" moment for decisionmakers in Pretoria, who:

believed that as a result of the mentioned events [Portugal's loss of its colonies after the fall of the Caetano regime], a Soviet-orchestrated assault in Southern Africa was inevitable, and that because of South Africa's increasing international isolation, they could not depend on outside assistance in the

---

[498] According to Scholtz (2013), the General Staff first identified communism and the Soviet Union as a security threat in a 1960 analysis. See: Ibid., 34.

[499] See: van Wyk (2010a, 563). See also: Barber and Barratt (1990, 238–243); McNamee (2005).

[500] Unfortunately, many of the documents pertaining to the program were destroyed when South Africa dismantled it. Goodson (2012, 213) estimates that nearly 12,000 technical and policy documents were destroyed. See also: Fig (1999, 75). A 1983 U.S. intelligence report claims that "South Africa formally launched a weapons program in 1973," but provides little accompanying evidence. See: Du Preez and Matteig (2010, 309). According to Wing and Simpson (2013, 75), the earliest date for the initiation of the nuclear-weapons program was 1974, as later claimed by F. W. de Klerk. According to Waldo Stumpf, the decision was taken in 1977 and formalized in 1978.

event of an attack. In addition, they regarded all radical Black Nationalist liberation movements as totally under the control of the Soviet Union and Cuba, which meant that they needed a suitable deterrent against a perceived communist onslaught.[501]

Because it feared a "total onslaught" of communism, with the backing of Soviet and Cuban forces, South Africa possessed the willingness to proliferate. Because it possessed conventional superiority, South Africa had the opportunity to proliferate. It was thus very likely that – despite the efforts of its adversaries and allies to stop it – Pretoria would acquire nuclear weapons, as it did in 1979.

A final line of criticism is put forth by scholars who agree that South Africa's nuclearization appeared inevitable in the late 1970s, but attribute this outcome to Washington's cooperation with the South African nuclear program.[502] The difficulty faced by this argument is that when Washington restricted its assistance, South Africa turned to other suppliers, in particular France and Israel. South Africa's conventional superiority, combined with the limited coercive leverage yielded by limited U.S. support, led U.S. policymakers to worry about the effectiveness of threats and sanctions to stop the nuclear-weapons program. Instead, they realized that their most effective nonproliferation tool would be to boost the scope and reliability of U.S. security assurances – something they were unwilling to do. This is well supported by the historical evidence. Intelligence reports were doubtful about U.S. success in preventing proliferation in the critical summer of 1977. In August, a report from the Director of Central Intelligence concluded that there may be flexibility in the timing of a test, but "[w]e see no credible threat from the West which would be sufficient to deter the South African government from carrying out a test; indeed, threats would, in our judgment, be more likely to harden South African determination."[503] The following month, the Special Projects Division of the Lawrence Livermore Laboratory concluded that "there are few levers that can be used against South Africa to prevent it from exploding a nuclear device if it should so choose. ... A reduction of their perception

---

[501] van Wyk (2010a, 563).
[502] See: Fig (1999); van Wyk (2009); Fuhrmann (2012, 158–160).
[503] Director of Central Intelligence, Interagency Assessment, "South Africa: Policy Considerations Regarding a Nuclear Test," August 18, 1977, in NSA EBB 181, Doc. 18, p. i.

of threat is likely to be the only sure way of guaranteeing that South Africa will not eventually explode a nuclear device."[504] South Africa proliferated because it perceived a significant security threat and was relatively powerful, thus possessing both the willingness and the opportunity to do so despite U.S. efforts to avert its nuclearization.

Our security-based framework also offers a simple explanation for Pretoria's decision to forgo nuclear weapons. With the end of the Cold War, the communist threat receded and Pretoria dismantled its arsenal, seeing increased benefits in joining the international community as a nonnuclear state. Some point instead to the importance of domestic politics, and the apartheid government's reluctance to cede nuclear weapons to an ANC government.[505] Yet, this claim is speculative. Van Wyk forcefully concluded in 2010 that there was "no evidence to back the suggestion that the de Klerk government did not wish to risk seeing a potentially radical Black Nationalist government in South Africa armed with nuclear weapons."[506]

It is not clear what would have been the domestic political logic leading to nuclear forbearance. Some scholars argue instead that concerns about an ANC government possessing nuclear weapons were prompted by the possibility of a handoff to other states or foreign nonstate actors, such as Cuba, Libya, Iran, and the Palestine Liberation Organization (PLO), to "pay off old political debts."[507] To prevent such proliferation, the United States applied a high level of pressure on Pretoria, starting in 1987.[508] South Africa ultimately decided it would

---

[504] Special Projects Division, Lawrence Livermore Laboratory, "South Africa: Motivations and Capabilities for Nuclear Proliferation," September 1977, in NSA EBB 451, Doc. 1B, pp. 11–12.

[505] See: Albright and Hibbs (1993, 33); Pabian (1995, 10); Reiss (1995, 20–21).

[506] van Wyk (2010b, 69). See also: Liberman (2001, 85).

[507] Pabian (1995, 10). In doing so, South Africa may have been allaying concerns of its Western allies, including Israel. See: Botha (2008, 12); Polakow-Suransky (2010, 220).

[508] See: Burgess, Purkitt, and Liberman (2002, 187). Burgess and Purkitt even claim that "De Klerk and his associates decided to dismantle South Africa's nuclear weapons program to placate the United States. They understood U.S. fears that nuclear weapons would fall into the hands of the ANC, especially after de Klerk initiated the transition from apartheid to majority rule in the second half of 1989." Burgess, Purkitt, and Liberman (2002, 190). See also: Burgess (2006, 523). The importance of U.S. pressure, however, is disputed. See: Burgess, Purkitt, and Liberman (2002, 192–193); Du Preez and Matteig (2010, 319–320).

be better off if it were to dismantle its nuclear arsenal. But, given the lower level of threat that Pretoria faced by then, domestic motivations are unnecessary to account for this outcome. South Africa's nuclear forbearance can be explained based solely on international security concerns.

In sum, a focus on South Africa's strategic environment – its inter-actions with adversaries and allies – accounts for the central steps in Pretoria's nuclear decisionmaking. Were South Africa to, once again, feel threatened by any of its weak neighbors to the point at which an investment in nuclear weapons might once again be productive, Pretoria would, once again, have the opportunity to build the bomb. Therefore, Washington's ability to keep a threatened South Africa non-nuclear would require it to implement a carrots-based nonprolifera-tion approach, consisting of credible security guarantees.

North Korea

The Democratic People's Republic of Korea (DPRK) – a. k. a. North Korea – tested its first nuclear weapon in October 2006, and con-ducted three subsequent tests in May 2009, February 2013, and January 2016. Facing a declining balance of conventional power vis-à-vis the Republic of Korea (ROK) in the South and its backer, the United States, and unable to obtain robust security guarantees in the post–Cold War, North Korea perceived a nuclear deterrent to yield a significant security benefit. Therefore, Pyongyang had the willingness to nuclearize.

Korea emerged from the Second World War as a divided nation. In August 1945, the Soviet Union and the United States split the pen-insula, previously occupied by Japan (1910–1945), at the 38th par-allel.[509] Attempts to transition to a single political entity failed, and in the summer of 1948 the DPRK and ROK were founded. Both claimed to represent all of Korea. The DPRK was intent on reunit-ing Korea and launched an invasion of the South in June 1950. The invasion triggered a forceful response from the United States, which led an international coalition. The Korean War ended in a stalemate, with the Demilitarized Zone (DMZ) becoming the de facto border

[509] See: Cumings (1997, 186–187).

between the North and the South; no definitive peace settlement has yet been achieved.

In 1961, the DPRK obtained security guarantees from both the USSR and its neighboring PRC. Yet, these did not assuage Pyongyang's security concerns; it remained opposed by the significant U.S. military presence in the South and uncertain about the support that it could receive from either Moscow or Beijing in case armed hostilities would resume. With Soviet assistance, the DPRK began a nuclear program in the 1960s, progressing slowly in its nuclear development.

After the end of the Cold War, Pyongyang accelerated its nuclear-weapons program, trigerring concerns in Washington. In turn, these resulted in the October 1994 Agreed Framework between the United States and the DPRK, whereby Pyongyang agreed to freeze its nuclear-weapons program in exchange for U.S. economic inducements. Delays in the provision of U.S. aid and DPRK obstruction of IAEA inspections led to the collapse of the agreement in late 2002. The DPRK withdrew from the NPT the following January. Three years later, Pyongyang conducted its first nuclear test.

Washington was unsuccessful in deterring the DPRK's nuclear program because threats of counterproliferation military action lacked credibility. The South Korean capital, Seoul, located only thirty-five miles from the DMZ, could be severely damaged by a conventional attack from DPRK artillery forces, raising the cost of a putative counterproliferation strike, and undermining U.S. attempts to prevent Pyongyang from crossing the nuclear threshold. Ultimately, North Korea's conventional strength warranted it the opportunity to nuclearize.

North Korean Interest in Nuclear Weapons

From its inception, the DPRK was intent on using force to reunite Korea. In 1950, Kim Il-sung, the North's premier (1948–1972, and president from 1972 to 1994), convinced Stalin and Mao to approve an invasion of the South. The United States, Kim argued, was unlikely to intervene in a conflict. After all, Secretary of State Dean Acheson had famously omitted Korea from the essential defense perimeter of the United States in the Pacific.[510]

---

[510] See: Goncharov, Lewis, and Xue (1993, 101, 142). For Acheson's speech, see: Acheson (1950, 116).

North Korean troops invaded the South on June 25, 1950. Immediately, President Harry Truman denounced the attack and committed U.S. forces to repel the invasion.[511] Later in the year, Truman invoked the "Trading with the Enemy Act" of 1917 to end all economic interactions with the DPRK. On September 15, 1950, the United States led a UN coalition in an amphibious landing at Incheon, behind DPRK forces. The tide was turning against North Korea. On September 29 and October 1, Kim requested direct assistance from, respectively, the Soviet Union and China.[512]

For the remainder of the conflict, Kim found himself in a difficult position. U.S. forces represented a prodigious security threat. To mitigate it, the DPRK could rely on foreign assistance, but risked losing its autonomous decisionmaking power. In the end, the Soviet Union provided most of the weapons to fight the conflict and China most of the manpower – by early 1952, there were three times as many Chinese as there were North Korean soldiers on the peninsula.[513] According to an Eastern European ambassador, once China entered the war, Beijing "put Kim Il-Sung in the bunker and told him to keep quiet."[514] During the conflict, the Americans on several occasions brandished the threat of a nuclear attack, and such threats may have played a role in convincing the Chinese to end the hostilities.[515]

The U.S.-South Korean Threat and North Korea's Nuclear Development

Though the fighting ended with the July 1953 armistice, the DPRK continued for decades to find itself in a grave strategic situation: intent on reuniting Korea on its own terms, opposed by American military power, and uncertain about its allies' support.

The United States first deployed nuclear weapons on South Korean territory in January 1958; between 1960 and 1964 it expanded its nuclear forces on the peninsula. By 1967, Washington had an arsenal of about

---

[511] See: "Statement by the President on the Situation in Korea," June 27, 1950, Harry S. Truman Library, Public Papers of the Presidents, Harry S. Truman, 1945–1953. Available at: http://www.trumanlibrary.org/publicpapers. Last accessed: May 1, 2016.

[512] See: Stueck (1995, 98).

[513] Ibid., 270.

[514] Quoted in Pollack (2011, 33).

[515] See our case study of China in this chapter.

950 nuclear warheads in the South.[516] Pyongyang resented the U.S. military presence in South Korea, and in particular the American deployment of nuclear weapons. In August 1962, DPRK foreign minister Pak Seong-cheol (1959–1970) told Soviet ambassador Vasily Moskovsky:

> The Americans hold on to Taiwan, to South Korea and South Vietnam, blackmail the people with their nuclear weapons, and, with their help, rule on these continents and do not intend to leave. Their possession of nuclear weapons, and the lack thereof in our hands, objectively helps them, therefore, to eternalize their rule.[517]

Since the end of the Second World War, North Korea was well positioned to develop a nuclear industry. Secret nuclear facilities had been set up by the Japanese in Yongbyon during their occupation, and uranium deposits had been mined as early as 1946.[518] Ten years later, the DPRK participated in the founding of the Joint Institute for Nuclear Research in Dubna, outside Moscow,[519] and signed a nuclear cooperation agreement with the USSR.[520] In April 1958, the DPRK ambassador to the USSR formally requested Soviet assistance in a peaceful nuclear program,[521] and the following year Pyongyang signed another nuclear cooperation agreement with the USSR and a first agreement with the PRC.[522] By the early 1960s, the DPRK had begun developing the Yongbyon Nuclear Research Complex, with the USSR providing a reactor and low-enriched uranium.[523] Pyongyang hoped to obtain its own nuclear weapons by enlisting Soviet assistance.

---

[516] See: Norris, Arkin, and Burr (1999, 30); Norris, Kristensen, and Handler (2003, 74).
[517] "Conversation between Soviet Ambassador in North Korea Vasily Moskovsky and North Korean Foreign Minister Pak Seong-cheol," August 24, 1962, in Wilson Center Digital Archive, North Korean Nuclear History.
[518] See: Pollack (2011, 44, 50).
[519] See: CIA, "North Korea: Potential for Nuclear Weapon Development," September 1986, in National Security Archive (NSA) Electronic Briefing Book (EBB) 87, "North Korea and Nuclear Weapons: The Declassified U.S. Record," Doc. 7, p. 17.
[520] See: Richelson (2006, 332); Szalontai and Radchenko (2006, 3).
[521] See: "From the Journal of Gromyko, Record of a Conversation with Ambassador Ri Sin-Pal of the Democratic People's Republic of Korea" April 28, 1958, in Wilson Center Digital Archive, North Korean Nuclear History.
[522] See: Richelson (2006, 332).
[523] See: Wing and Simpson (2013, 44).

Questioning Soviet and Chinese Support

At the same time, North Korea sought security assistance from its Soviet and Chinese allies. On July 6, 1961, Pyongyang concluded a defense pact with the USSR and, five days later, signed a treaty with the PRC. Each of these agreements stipulated that if either country in the alliance found itself in a state of war, "the other Contracting Party shall immediately extend military and other assistance with all the means at its disposal."[524] Despite these strongly worded guarantees, Pyongyang doubted the reliability of its security sponsors. The North Korean leadership had been suspicious of de-Stalinization efforts by the first secretary of the Communist Party of the Soviet Union, Nikita Khrushchev.[525] Moreover, the Cuban Missile Crisis of October 1962 heightened the DPRK's concerns about the steadfastness of Soviet guarantees. Kim felt that Khrushchev had betrayed Cuba's interests in de-escalating the crisis, and had imposed his will on its smaller ally.[526] As a result of Soviet actions in the crisis, first Deputy Prime Minister Kim Il (1959–1966) explained in January 1965 that the DPRK felt it "could not count that the Soviet government would keep the obligations related to the defense of Korea it assumed in the Treaty of Friendship, Cooperation and Mutual Assistance."[527] Consequently, the DPRK was "compelled to keep an army of 700,000 and a police force of 200,000."[528]

Indeed, concerns about Soviet guarantees, and Moscow's refusal to grant Pyongyang military aid in December 1962, induced the DPRK to invest greatly in its own defense capabilities. At the fifth plenum of the party, the leadership approved an "equal emphasis policy," calling

---

[524] Treaty of Friendship, Co-operation and Mutual Assistance with the Soviet Union (July 6, 1961). See also: The Treaty of Friendship, Co-operation and Mutual Assistance with the PRC (July 11, 1961). Both at: Institute for Advanced Studies on Asia, University of Tokyo, "The World and Japan" Database. Available at: www.ioc.u-tokyo.ac.jp/~worldjpn/documents/indices/docs/index-ENG.html. Last accessed: May 1, 2016.

[525] See: Cha (2012, 321).

[526] See: Szalontai (2006, 191); Person (2012, 121–122).

[527] "Record of a Conversation with the Soviet Ambassador in the DPRK Comrade V. P. Moskovsky about the Negotiations between the Soviet Delegation, Led by the USSR Council of Ministers Chairman Kosygin, and the Governing Body of the Korean Workers Party, 16 February 1965," Czech Foreign Ministry Archive, in Person (2012, 122).

[528] Report, Embassy of Hungary in North Korea to the Hungarian Foreign Minister, January 8, 1965, in Person (2012, 122).

for balanced investments in heavy industry and defense capabilities.[529] This defense strategy was part of an overall philosophy of national independence and self-reliance, known as "juche" (alternatively, *chuch'e*), which was fully implemented in the mid-1960s.[530]

The 1970s witnessed a decrease in the DPRK's confidence in Chinese security guarantees as well. Breaking the news of the Sino-American rapprochement, the Chinese leadership argued that such a development presented a new opportunity: the DPRK could now press U.S. forces out of the peninsula and reunify the nation.[531] Yet, the rapprochement also meant that Beijing had a stake in the stability of the peninsula, as it valued its improved relations with Washington.[532] In his meeting with national security adviser Henry Kissinger (1969–1975) in June 1972, Zhou Enlai expressed a strong interest in the peaceful re-unification of Korea. As Chairman Mao had previously stated, China would not go to war against the United States, nor threaten Japan or Korea.[533] In the eyes of Pyongyang, Beijing's decision to press for peaceful reunification was a sign of weakness.[534]

In fact, Beijing ultimately confronted Pyongyang over its attempts to destabilize the South Korean leadership through forceful means. North Korean agents launched multiple assassination attempts against South Korean presidents: against Park Chung-hee (1962–1979) in January 1968, June 1970, and August 1974; and against Chun Doo-hwan (1980–1988) in Gabon in 1982, and in Rangoon (Burma) in 1983.[535] China's leader Deng Xiaoping (1978–1992) saw the Rangoon bombing "as a personal affront."[536] In November 1985, he insisted with Kim that "[a]ll international problems may only be resolved through talks."[537]

Faced with decreasing levels of Chinese support, starting in the mid-1980s the DPRK worked to improve relations with the USSR. In

---

[529] See: Ibid., 122.
[530] See: Cumings (1997, 403).
[531] See: Xia and Shen (2014, 1092–1093).
[532] See: Brazinsky (2011). On more recent PRC-DPRK relations, see: Lee (1998); Glaser, Snyder, and Park (2008).
[533] As reported by Chou Enlai in "Memorandum of Conversation," Beijing, June 22, 1972, 3:58–6:35 p.m., in *FRUS*, 1969–1976, Vol. XVII, Doc. 233.
[534] See: Xia and Shen (2014, 1101–1102).
[535] See: Cha (2012, 54–57).
[536] See: Pollack (2011, 90).
[537] Quoted in Radchenko (2011, 191).

March 1984, the Soviet deputy foreign minister felt that there was a change in the tone of the DPRK's foreign policy.[538] In January 1986, the Soviet minister of foreign affairs, Eduard Shevardnadze (1985–1990, 1991), visited Pyongyang and concluded that "the Korean comrades now really do need support" because "South Korea is armed to its teeth and has large military bases."[539]

Yet, the DPRK leadership remained suspicious of its allies' attempts to defuse tensions in the region, engage South Korea, and promote political and economic reforms. As the Chinese ambassador in Pyongyang told his Mongolian counterpart in June 1987: "Taiwan is ahead of us on many economic indicators. But South Korea is even better than Taiwan, its economy is good. It has become necessary for us to try to become closer to them. The people will follow the good side of life." Likewise, the Soviet leader Mikhail Gorbachev (1985–1991) declared in a speech in September 1988 that "in the context of a general amelioration of the situation on the Korean peninsula, opportunities can also be opened up for arranging economic ties with South Korea."[540] Two years later, Shevardnadze visited Pyongyang and announced that the Soviet Union would establish diplomatic relations with South Korea the following January. Kim Il-sung was incensed and refused to meet with him. In his place, DPRK foreign minister Kim Yong-nam (1983–1998) declared that the Soviet recognition of the South marked the end of the security alliance. Without a security umbrella, North Korea would now seek its own nuclear weapons.[541]

A nuclear weapon could act as the ultimate deterrent given the DPRK's ageing conventional capabilities. Since the 1970s, the quality of North Korea's armed forces has steadily declined relative to the South.[542] As Michael O'Hanlon puts it, "[a]bout half of North Korea's major weapons are of roughly 1960s design; the other half are even older."[543] Since the end of the Cold War, Pyongyang made significant progress on its nuclear-weapons program and eventually crossed the nuclear threshold. What measures did Washington implement to

---

[538] See: Ibid., 192.
[539] Quoted in ibid., 193.
[540] Ibid., 199.
[541] See: Ibid., 203–204. The security alliance from the Soviet Union/Russia formally lapsed in September 1996.
[542] See: Kang (2003, 306).
[543] O'Hanlon (1998, 142). See also: Cha (2012, 216).

attempt to prevent North Korean nuclearization and why they did ultimately prove unsuccessful?

U.S. Counterproliferation Efforts

Until the late 1980s, the U.S. intelligence community remained positively unimpressed with the DPRK's nuclearization efforts. In May 1963, a memo from the Bureau of Intelligence and Research assessed that North Korea was "unlikely to develop an independent nuclear weapons capability," adding that "the few North Koreans who have participated in the Dubna Joint Institute for Nuclear Research in the USSR lack sufficient technological and material support to promote a meaningful nuclear program."[544] Twenty years later, the CIA reached the same conclusion: there was "no basis for believing that the North Koreans have either the facilities or the materials necessary to develop and test nuclear weapons."[545]

Washington did not reach this conclusion as a result of misinformation; in fact the CIA kept a close eye on the development of the DPRK's program. Between 1966 and 1972, Washington took satellite images of Yongbyon on thirty-six occasions.[546] In July 1982, the CIA first documented the construction of the 5 MW reactor in the Yongbyon Nuclear Research Center.[547]

With the discovery in January 1985 of a reactor that could be used to produce plutonium, however, Washington's concerns increased. "North Korean motives and intentions are unclear," a State Department briefing paper concluded.[548] The United States worked to prevent states from supplying the DPRK with sensitive material. In December of the same year, the Soviet Union induced the DPRK to sign the NPT in exchange for four light-water reactors

---

[544] Memorandum from George C. Denney Jr., Bureau of Intelligence and Research, to Secretary of State, "Probable Consequences of a Chinese Communist Nuclear Detonation," May 6, 1963, in NSA EBB 488, Doc. 9, p. 9.

[545] CIA, "A 10-Year Projection of Possible Events of Nuclear Proliferation Concern," May 1983, in NSA EBB 87, Doc. 2, p. 5.

[546] See: Richelson (2006, 346).

[547] See: [CIA], "North Korea: Nuclear Reactor," July 9, 1982, in NSA EBB 87, Doc. 1, p. 1.

[548] Department of State Briefing Paper, ca. January 5, 1985, in NSA EBB 87, Doc. 5, p. 1.

(LWRs).[549] Despite its adherence to the NPT, the DPRK delayed the completion of a safeguards inspection agreement with the IAEA, eventually missing an extended deadline of December 1988. As a CIA report had noted the previous May, "[w]e have no evidence that North Korea is pursuing a nuclear weapon option, but we cannot rule out that possibility."[550] Meanwhile, construction at Yongbyon was expanding rapidly,[551] including, by 1989, what appeared to be a reprocessing facility.[552] In 1991, a State Department memo saw the DPRK's acquisition of nuclear weapons as a distinct possibility, though not until the middle of the decade. To prevent this development, the memo called for imminent international efforts that would include the PRC and would aim at reducing tensions in the region.[553]

In principle, the U.S. government insisted that there could be no quid pro quo in exchange for the DPRK's compliance with its non-proliferation obligations.[554] Yet, in September 1991, Washington announced that it would withdraw its nuclear weapons from the Korean Peninsula, a key demand of the DPRK.[555] The following January, Pyongyang signed the IAEA safeguards agreement,[556] and the same month the DPRK and the ROK signed a joint declaration on the denuclearization of the peninsula, whereby each country pledged not to "test, manufacture, produce, receive, possess, store, deploy or use nuclear weapons."[557]

In April 1992, the DPRK announced that it would allow IAEA inspections at three facilities: the 5 MW reactor at Yongbyon as well as two previously undisclosed facilities under construction, a 50 MW

---

[549] See: Montgomery and Mount (2014, 379).

[550] CIA, "North Korea's Expanding Nuclear Efforts," May 3, 1988, in NSA EBB 87, Doc. 10, p. 2.

[551] See: CIA, "North Korea: Nuclear Program of Proliferation Concern," March 22, 1989, in NSA EBB 87, Doc. 13, p. 1.

[552] See: Richelson (2006, 357).

[553] See: Department of State, "Talking Points Paper for Under Secretary of State Bartholomew's China Trip," ca. May 30, 1991, in NSA EBB 87, Doc. 15, p. 1.

[554] Ibid.

[555] See: Kristensen (2002, 57).

[556] See: Richelson (2006, 517); Cha (2012, 250).

[557] Text of the treaty available at: "Joint Declaration on the Denuclearization of the Korean Peninsula," Entry into Force February 19, 1992, Federation of American Scientists. Available at: http://fas.org/news/dprk/1992/920219-D4129.htm. Last accessed: May 1, 2016.

plant at Yongbyon and a 200 MW reactor at Taechon. In May, the DPRK presented an initial report of its nuclear program, admitting that it had produced plutonium. During the inspectors' visit, Pyongyang offered to abandon reprocessing in exchange for assistance in building new LWRs.[558]

The Mid-1990s Crises Leading to the Agreed Framework

Suspicions over North Korea's previous nuclear activities quickly emerged and jeopardized relations with the international community. In July, the IAEA concluded that the DPRK had under reported its plutonium reprocessing activities.[559] The IAEA wished to get access to two sites suspected of containing nuclear waste. The DPRK demurred, saying that these facilities were under military control and irrelevant to its nuclear activities; granting access to these sites would be an infringement on its sovereignty. In February 1993, the IAEA gave the DPRK a month to accede to its request. Tensions further escalated on March 8 when the United States and the ROK conducted a joint military exercise, Team Spirit. Four days after the beginning of this exercise, the DPRK announced that it would withdraw from the NPT within three months, asking the United States to remove its "nuclear threats" and the IAEA its "unjust conduct."[560]

---

[558] See: David E. Sanger, "North Korea Plan on Fueling A-Bomb May Be Confirmed," *The New York Times*, June 15, 1992, pp. A1, A6. The DPRK's representative in Geneva repeated this offer in June 1992. See: Sigal (1998, 210).

[559] See: "Report by the Director General of the International Atomic Energy Agency on Behalf of the Board of Governors to All Members of the Agency on the Non-Compliance of the Democratic People's Republic of Korea with the Agreement between the IAEA and the Democratic People's Republic of Korea for the Application of Safeguards in Connection with the Treaty on the Non-Proliferation of Nuclear Weapons (INFCIRC/403) and on the Agency's Inability to Verify the Non-Diversion of Material Required to be Safeguarded," IAEA, INFCIRC/419, April 8, 1993. Available at: www.iaea. org/sites/default/files/publications/documents/infcircs/1993/infcirc419.pdf. Last accessed: March 2, 2016; IAEA, "The DPRK's Violation of Its NPT Safeguards Agreement with the IAEA," 1997, in NSA EBB 87, Doc. 18, pp. 1–2; Richelson (2006, 517).

[560] "Letter Dated 12 March 1993 from the Permanent Representative of the Democratic People's Republic of Korea to the United Nations Addressed to the President of the Security Council," UNSC, S/25405, 12 March 1993. Available at: https://documents.un.org/prod/ods.nsf/home.xsp. Last accessed: May 1, 2016. See also: Sigal (1998, 49–50).

In June, Washington and Pyongyang came to an agreement to defuse the tension. Pyongyang would suspend its withdrawal from the NPT in exchange for a negative security assurance (i.e., a commitment not to attack North Korea) from the United States.[561]

Underpinning Washington's concessions was the expectation that a military conflict with the DPRK would be costly. Seoul, the ROK's capital, is only approximately thirty-five miles from the DPRK's border. A preventive counterproliferation strike on North Korea would no doubt trigger a response across the border, which could lead to a great many casualties and much physical destruction. In the fall of 1993, General Gary Luck, the commander of U.S. forces in Korea (1993–1996), visited Washington and explained that "the United States would win another war fought on the Korean peninsula. The real issue was cost." Simulations supported the prediction that U.S. and ROK forces would prevail while suffering an estimated 300,000–750,000 casualties in military personnel.[562] The following April, the ROK minister of defense Rhee Byong-tae (1993–1994) explained that "during the Korean War, there were two million casualties, with ten million family separations. A war now would be 100 times worse, and South Korean nation-building would be turned into ashes." His U.S. counterpart, Defense Secretary William Perry (1994–1997), responded by stating U.S. policy: "(1) we will not initiate war; (2) we will not provoke a war; but (3) we should not invite a war by being weak. Therefore, deterrence is very, very important, and our readiness is very, very important."[563] Ultimately, Washington found it challenging to deter the DPRK's nuclearization given the prohibitive cost of launching a counterproliferation strike.

In December 1993, the DPRK and the United States agreed that Pyongyang would attempt to assure the continuity of inspections, with details to be left to the IAEA.[564] But the two sides soon disagreed over the details of these inspections, with Pyongyang rejecting full access to its facilities. At the same time, South Korea threatened to resume the Team Spirit exercises unless the North consented to

[561] See: Sigal (1998, 64); Lee (2002, 169–170).
[562] See: Wit, Poneman, and Gallucci (2004, 102).
[563] Cable, Seoul 0331 to Secretary of State, April 21, 1994, in National Security Archive (NSA) Electronic Briefing Book (EBB) 474, "The United States and the Two Koreas, Part II: 1969–2010," Doc. 1, p. 9.
[564] See: Sigal (1998, 98).

full inspections.[565] Under the threat of UN sanctions, a DPRK official stated in March 1994: "It does not matter what sanctions are applied against us. We are ready to respond with an eye for an eye and a war for a war. ... Seoul is not very far from here. If a war breaks out, Seoul will turn into a sea of fire."[566] In May, the DPRK pulled fuel rods from its research reactor without the presence of IAEA inspectors, opening the possibility that they would be reprocessed for use in a nuclear weapon. On June 13, the DPRK announced that it would withdraw from the IAEA.[567] In response, Washington suggested at the UNSC the imposition of sanctions on North Korea. Pyongyang answered that sanctions would represent an act of war.[568]

Aware of the high cost of a possible war with the DPRK, ROK president Kim Young-sam (1993–1998) pressed for calm, telling President Bill Clinton (1993–2001) on June 16:

The Korean peninsula must never become a battlefield. If war breaks out, a large number of servicemen and civilians would be killed both in the South and in the North; the economy would be totally devastated; and foreign capital would fly away. You [President Clinton] might be able to bomb [the North] from the air, but then North Korea would immediately start firing artillery shells against major cities in South Korea. An uncountable number of people got killed in the Korean War, but the modern weaponry is much stronger. No war is acceptable.[569]

That same day, former president Jimmy Carter (1977–1981) traveled to Pyongyang, opening the way for the Agreed Framework concluded in October.[570] North Korea, now led by Kim Jong-il (1994–2011), who had replaced his father after his passing on July 8, agreed to freeze and eventually dismantle its nuclear-weapons program. In exchange, the United States would grant it economic inducements as well as supply it with two LWRs to provide for North Korea's energy needs, under the

---

[565] Ibid., p. 102.
[566] Quoted in John Burton, "N Korea's 'Sea of Fire' Threat Shakes Seoul," *The Financial Times*, March 22, 1994, p. 6.
[567] See: IAEA, "The DPRK's Violation of its NPT Safeguards Agreement with the IAEA," 1997, in NSA EBB 87, Doc. 18, p. 2.
[568] Ibid. See also: Cable, Seoul 0331 to Secretary of State, April 21, 1994, in NSA EBB 474, Doc. 1, p. 6.
[569] Quoted in Michishita (2003, 58).
[570] See: Kang (2006, 27).

auspices of the Korean Peninsula Energy Development Organization (KEDO), initially a joint venture with South Korea and Japan. The two countries also agreed to work toward the normalization of diplomatic relations, which had never been established since the founding of the DPRK.[571]

The Framework Agreement promised to open the door to the stabilization of the Korean Peninsula. A January 1996 U.S. government report was optimistic about the agreement's implementation, though concerned about "less than full DPRK cooperation with IAEA activities" and U.S. difficulties in obtaining congressional approval for financing its side of the deal.[572] By April 1997, the IAEA complained that "the DPRK was still not in full compliance with its safeguards agreement."[573] In late 1997 and early 1998, U.S. intelligence discovered activity in Kumchang-ri, an underground site, which could be intended either for a nuclear reactor or a plutonium reprocessing unit.[574]

Under pressure from Congress, President Clinton commissioned his former secretary of defense William Perry to review the administration's Korea policy in November 1998. Washington and Seoul prepared a multipronged approach to meet the proliferation challenge raised by the DPRK's nuclear activities.[575] Washington requested access to the Kumchang-ri. This was a risky decision, since the intelligence was not definitive, and insisting on inspections could further worsen relations with Pyongyang. ROK president Kim Dae-jung (1998–2003) attempted to defuse tensions on the peninsula by increasing economic interactions with the North, announcing his "sunshine policy" soon after taking office. In July 1999, the United States and the ROK issued a joint statement against the testing of long-range missiles, and Seoul agreed to lend $3.2 billion to fund the construction of LWRs in North Korea.[576]

---

[571] The full text of the agreement is in International Atomic Energy Agency, "Agreed Framework of 21 October 1994 between the United States of America and the Democratic People's Republic of Korea," November 2, 1994, in NSA EBB 87, Doc. 17.

[572] State Department Memorandum, "U.S. Policy Toward North Korea: Next Steps," ca. January 1996, in NSA EBB 474, Doc. 11, pp. 1–2.

[573] Cable U.S. Mission Vienna to Secretary of State, "Subject: GAO Teleconference with IAEA on DPRK Issues," April 16, 1997, in NSA EBB 474, Doc. 14, p. 2.

[574] See: Richelson (2006, 527–528); Hymans (2012).

[575] See: Higgins (2000a).

[576] See: Higgins (2000b, 280).

The DPRK also made concessions, albeit partial ones. In exchange for food aid, Pyongyang granted access to Kumchang-ri in March 1999.[577] U.S. inspectors concluded that there was no evidence of nuclear activity at the site.[578] At the same time, North Korea objected to any linkage between financial assistance and missile development, arguing that this connection was "threatening the entire agreement."[579]

Washington's room for maneuver was slim. On September 15, 1999, Perry presented his report to Congress. In his view, "deterrence of war on the Korean Peninsula is stable on both sides." Neither side would be willing to trigger an armed conflict given the expected cost of war. "It is likely that hundreds of thousands of persons – U.S., ROK, and DPRK – military and civilian – would perish, and millions of refugees would be created. ... [T]he prospect of such a destructive war is a powerful deterrent to precipitous U.S. or allied action."[580] In October 2000, Washington and Pyongyang issued a joint communiqué, pledging to "build mutual confidence," and North Korea agreed to refrain from testing long-range missiles while bilateral talks continued.[581]

From Bush's Axis of Evil to Pyongyang's Nuclear Tests

The arrival of George W. Bush to the presidency led to a shift in U.S.-DPRK relations. According to the Bush administration, engagement – centered on the Agreed Framework and Seoul's sunshine policy – had proven ineffective.[582] As President Bush put it, the Agreed Framework had created a pattern in which Kim Jong-il "throws his food on the

---

[577] See: John M. Goshko, "North Korea to Allow U.S. Inspections; Suspected Nuclear Site Due First Visit in May," *The Washington Post*, 17 May 1999, p. A01.

[578] See: Steven Mufson, "N. Korean Site Passes a Test; U.S. Finds No Evidence of Nuclear Weapons Development," *The Washington Post*, May 29, 1999, p. A24. Later, Gary Samore, senior director for nonproliferation at the national security council (1996–2000), admitted that turning Kumchang-ri into a major issue was "the biggest mistake I made in my career as a civil servant." Quoted in Chinoy (2008, 14).

[579] Higgins (2000b, 281).

[580] William J. Perry, "Review of United States Policy toward North Korea: Findings and Recommendations," October 12, 1999, in NSA EBB 87, Doc. 20, p. 4.

[581] Quoted in Lee (2002, 183).

[582] There was some disagreement within the administration. Secretary of State Colin Powell was in favor of engagement with North Korea. See: Chinoy (2008).

floor, and all the adults run to gather it up and put it back on the table. He waits a little while and throws his food on the floor again."[583] For Bush, the sunshine policy also seemed to emerge from a position of weakness on the ROK's part. In her memoir, Condoleezza Rice, who served as President Bush's national security advisor (2001–2005) and later as secretary of state (2005–2009), declared: "One sensed that Kim Dae-jung simply wanted to avoid conflict with Kim Jong-il at almost any cost."[584] Before the ROK president's first visit to Washington in March 2001, the Bush administration decided to move away from the Agreed Framework.

In 2001 and 2002, the United States and the DPRK complained about each other's compliance with the agreement. In June 2001, Washington asked Pyongyang to adopt a less threatening conventional posture; the DPRK responded that the Agreed Framework should be implemented "as agreed upon," and complained about delays in U.S. funding for LWRs.[585] In his State of the Union address in January 2002, President Bush reflected on the new threats facing the United States since the terrorist attacks of September 11, 2001, and included North Korea as a member of the "axis of evil," a regime "arming with missiles and weapons of mass destruction, while starving its citizens."[586] In the summer of 2002, the CIA became suspicious that the DPRK had been purchasing parts for a possible uranium enrichment program starting in late 1997 and 1998, with increased contacts between Pyongyang and Pakistani scientist A. Q. Khan.[587]

Washington confronted Pyongyang over its alleged transgressions of the Agreed Framework. In October 2002, James Kelly, U.S. assistant secretary of state for East Asian and Pacific affairs (2001–2005), accused Pyongyang of conducting a secret enrichment program – a

---

[583] Quoted in Rice (2011, 158).
[584] Ibid., 35.
[585] See: Cha and Kang (2003, 139); Pollack (2003, 24).
[586] "President Delivers State of the Union Address," January 29, 2002, White House Archives. Available at: http://georgewbush-whitehouse.archives.gov/news/releases/2002/01/20020129-11.html. Last accessed: May 1, 2016.
[587] See: Chinoy (2008, 87–96). See also: Braun and Chyba (2004, 12, 25); Albright (2010, 160); Buszynski (2013, 31). In his 2006 memoir, General Pervez Musharraf, who ruled over Pakistan between 1999 and 2008, declared that A. Q. Khan had over the years transferred "nearly two dozen P-1 and P-II centrifuges to North Korea." Musharraf (2006, 296).

charge that Pyongyang did not deny.[588] For its part, the CIA issued a report saying that it possessed "clear evidence" that the DPRK had been developing such a program for the last two years.[589] In November, KEDO announced that it would suspend its supply of heavy fuel oil to North Korea.[590] Tensions soon escalated. In December, National Security Presidential Directive 23 was leaked to the press, accusing the DPRK of pursuing WMD and long-range missiles, and explaining U.S. intentions to act preemptively to avert such threats.[591] In January 2003, the DPRK again announced that it would withdraw from the NPT.[592]

The DPRK's nuclear program then showed clear signs of progress. U.S. satellites obtained unmistakable evidence that the DPRK had begun reprocessing in the spring of 2003.[593] In August, the CIA concluded that the DPRK's program had produced one or two simple nuclear weapons and did not need to perform a nuclear test to validate its design.[594] A team of U.S. visitors, including Siegfried Hecker, former director of the Los Alamos National Laboratories (1986–1997), toured Yongbyon in January 2004 and concluded that North Korea was capable of producing weapons-grade plutonium.[595] In April, U.S. intelligence assessed that the DPRK now possessed an arsenal of eight nuclear bombs.[596]

Diplomacy eventually produced a preliminary accord. Multilateral negotiations, which began in April 2003 as the Three-Party Talks,

---

[588] See: Norris et al. (2003, 75); Chinoy (2008, 117–126).

[589] CIA, Untitled, November 2002, in NSA EBB 87, Doc. 22, p. 1.

[590] See: Lee and Moon (2003, 137); Pollack (2003, 41); Chinoy (2008, 140–141).

[591] See: "National Security Presidential Directive/NSPD-23, SUBJECT: National Policy on Ballistic Missile Defense," December 16, 2002, Federation of American Scientists. Available at: http://fas.org/irp/offdocs/nspd/nspd-23.htm. Last accessed: May 1, 2016; Bill Gertz, "Bush Case on Defense Plan Cites N. Korea," *The Washington Times*, May 27, 2003. Available at: www.washingtontimes.com/news/2003/may/27/20030527-124651-5190r/. Last accessed: May 28, 2016; Chinoy (2008, 147).

[592] See: Norris and Kristensen (2005, 65).

[593] See: Richelson (2006, 532–533); Chinoy (2008, 174).

[594] See: Pollack and Reiss (2004, 278).

[595] See: Siegfried S. Hecker, "Senate Committee on Foreign Relations Hearing on 'Visit to the Yongbyon Nuclear Scientific Research Center in North Korea,'" January 21, 2004, Federation of American Scientists. Available at: http://fas.org/irp/congress/2004_hr/012104hecker.pdf. Last accessed: May 1, 2016; Chinoy (2008, 198–201).

[596] See: Richelson (2006, 534–535).

hosted by the PRC, were extended to Six-Party Talks in August, including South Korea, Japan, and Russia.[597] These talks produced the historic agreement of September 2004, whereby North Korea would abandon its nuclear-weapons program and return to the NPT, with Washington offering a negative security assurance, allowing the two states to normalize their relations and coexist peacefully.[598]

However, further talks stalled over Pyongyang's connection with Banco Delta Asia, a Macau-based bank believed to help North Korea in money laundering.[599] In July 2006, the DPRK performed missile tests, and the following October Pyongyang conducted an underground nuclear test.

Ultimately, the new tone presented by the Bush administration notwithstanding, the strategic situation remained the same: any war with the DPRK would be very costly, undermining the effectiveness of threats aimed at deterring North Korea's nuclearization.[600] As Secretary of State Rice herself acknowledged: "The military option against Pyongyang was not a good one; it was fraught with unintended consequences and the near-certainty of significant damage to Seoul. Kim Jong-il maintains missile batteries whose projectiles can reach South Korea's capital city in a very short period of time."[601]

The 2006 nuclear test results were less than convincing. In May 2009, Pyongyang conducted another nuclear test, a month after testing a new long-range missile, the Taepodong-2. In February 2013, Kim Jong-un, who succeeded his father in December 2011, ordered a third nuclear test. In January 2016, North Korea announced that it had successfully tested a hydrogen bomb; a claim doubted by many international observers. Yet, it was now clear that the DPRK had entered the nuclear club.

Alternative Explanations

Many analysts agree that North Korea's interest in nuclear weapons stemmed from security concerns. North Korea unquestionably faced

[597] See: Chinoy (2008, 170).
[598] Ibid., 249–251. See also: Kim (2009, 92); Pinkston (2009); Haggard and Noland (2012).
[599] See: Chinoy (2008, 256–257, 264–265, 313–314).
[600] For different views on the merits of sanctions and engagement, see: Sigal (1998); Cha and Kang (2003); Chinoy (2008); Haggard and Noland (2015).
[601] Rice (2011, 712).

powerful enemies in the United States and South Korea, and received only weak guarantees from the Soviet Union and China.[602]

Despite these strong security motivations, some scholars question the usefulness of a security framework for understanding North Korea's nuclearization. For example, Etel Solingen notes the following problems with a security approach: North Korea's program made progress in the 1960s, when U.S. foreign policy was least threatening; the North's security demands (that the United States withdraw its tactical nuclear weapons from the peninsula and that South Korea renounce a nuclear-weapons program) were met in the early 1990s; North Korea did not lack a nuclear guarantee – in fact it was allied with two nuclear powers, China and Russia.[603] According to Solingen, the failure of China and the Soviet Union/Russia to prevent North Korea's nuclearization "compel[s] the need to explain why alliances and hegemonic coercion fail to prevent nuclearization in some cases but not others." Departing from the security model, Solingen argues that North Korea nuclearized because of the preferences of its ruling coalition. As an inward-looking state, the Kim regime was impervious to foreign coercion.[604]

To begin with, it is important to recognize that North Korea occupied a precarious security situation. No peace treaty was signed at the conclusion of the Korean War, and there were good reasons for Pyongyang to prepare for a possible resumption of hostilities. With the end of the Cold War, North Korea lost any prospect of protection from the Soviet Union. The trajectory of economic and technological developments continued to favor North Korea's enemies. As a result, Pyongyang could certainly see a benefit in complementing its declining conventional capabilities with a nuclear deterrent, no matter what assurances it might receive from Beijing and Moscow – or from Washington.

If a security approach accounts for Pyongyang's interest in nuclear weapons, we agree with Solingen that a compelling explanation should also account for the failure of nonproliferation measures in the North Korean case. We propose such a theory, focusing on the strategic

---

[602] See: Lee (2009, 163); Olsen (2009, 143); Pollack (2011, 83–85); Park (2012, 213).

[603] See: Solingen (2007, 120).

[604] Solingen (2007, 121). See also: Snyder (2009); Nincic (2012).

interaction between the DPRK, its enemies, and its allies. Starting with North Korea's allies, China and the Soviet Union/Russia could not successfully coerce North Korea to give up its nuclear-weapons program.[605] Their concerns that the DPRK's often reckless foreign policy might entrap them in an unwanted conflict led them not to extend reliable security guarantees to Pyongyang. This limited the leverage that Beijing and Moscow had over their protégé's nuclear decision-making, and they ultimately failed in removing the DPRK's willingness to nuclearize. Washington, for its part, was also limited in its ability to deter North Korea's nuclearization. Given Pyongyang's ability to inflict severe damage on Seoul, the cost of a preventive U.S. counter-proliferation attack would have been high. This undermined the credibility of U.S. threats to use force. As a result, North Korea had the opportunity to proliferate.

The strategic approach we put forth is thus sufficient to explain North Korea's successful nuclearization. A focus on the preferences of the DPRK's ruling coalition is certainly enlightening, but it is difficult to argue that the economic preferences of the Kim regime caused its decision to pursue nuclear weapons. Instead, North Korea's preferences in the economic and security realms constituted two dimensions of the same worldview. More appropriately, North Korea's self-reliance derived from its security choices and foreign policy priorities. North Korea was cut off from trade with the United States when President Truman invoked the "Trading with the Enemy Act" in response to its invasion of the South in 1950.[606] Also, as historian Bruce Cumings states, North Korea chose to be less reliant on its Soviet and Chinese patrons as it grew frustrated with their support. The previously mentioned concept of juche

first emerged in 1955 as Pyongyang drew away from Moscow, and then appeared full-blown in the mid-sixties as Kim sought a stance independent of both Moscow and Beijing. One can find uses of the term *chuch'e* before 1955 in North and South, but no one would notice, were it not for its later prominence.[607]

---

[605] In addition, Pyongyang could successfully undermine international sanctions. See: Park and Lee (2008, 269).

[606] The Act was lifted by President Bush in June 2008, though note that the DPRK remains under a battery of U.S. and UN sanctions. See: Haggard and Noland (2012); Reynolds and Wan (2012).

[607] Cumings (1997, 403).

A second alternative account of North Korea's interest in nuclear weapons focuses on the psychology of its leadership, as articulated in the work of Jacques Hymans.[608] The Kim dynasty represents a paradigmatic case of an oppositional nationalist leadership, which is, according to Hymans, the most likely to forego rational cost-benefit analyses and pursue nuclear weapons.[609]

Certainly, nuclear weapons promise a security benefit only if a decisionmaker believes that future conflicts are likely. Yet, it is difficult to determine whether such beliefs are objectively warranted or derive from psychological biases. On the one hand, the North Korean leadership has seemed mired in the confrontation between communism and "imperialism." As Victor Cha puts it, "[t]he Cold War was integral to South Korean history, but for North Korea, the Cold War is not only its past, it is also its present and future."[610] On the other hand, historical legacies and facts on the ground suggest that there are objectively unresolved points of contention: the North Korean leadership initiated the Korean War with the goal of reunifying the two Koreas; the conflict ended without a peace treaty; and the South is an economic powerhouse backed by the military might of the United States. So a perception of acute security threat on the part of the DPRK's leadership is certainly supported by the country's security environment. (Furthermore, any analysis of the North Korean leadership's psychological profile is bound to face difficulties, given the lack of available data.[611]) Rather than debate the source of a leader's beliefs, we focus on explaining whether, based on its security environment, a country is likely to develop the willingness to acquire nuclear weapons and, if so, also likely to possess the opportunity to build them. In the case of North Korea, an investment in nuclear-weapons technology was warranted, given the country's lack of reliable foreign support and its downward economic, technological, and military trajectory vis-à-vis its adversaries. Given these adversaries' evaluation that a preventive counterproliferation strike would be more costly than the likely consequences of North Korea's nuclear acquisition, Pyongyang was able to successfully complete its nuclear program.

---

[608] See: Hymans (2008). See also: Kim (2009).
[609] See: Hymans (2006).
[610] Cha (2012, 20–21).
[611] See: Kim (2009, 81).

Finally, yet other scholars point to the importance of prestige considerations to account for North Korea's interest in nuclear weapons.[612] Interestingly, prestige considerations are here assigned to one of the most isolated regimes in the world. As such, nuclear weapons could bestow prestige upon the regime in its relation to other *domestic* actors, boosting its support basis and possibly preventing military coups. Given a history of conflict with South Korea over the unification of the peninsula, and the different development trajectories between the North and the South, nuclearization could be used domestically as a success story for the North Korean regime. In that sense, for the North Korean regime the atomic bomb brings domestic political benefits insofar as it bolsters the belief that the regime could stand up to external threats. As a result, in the North Korean case the prestige benefit of nuclear weapons is ultimately tightly linked to its foreign security benefit, and it is not clear that prestige considerations significantly add to the predictive power of a theory. More generally, and as we saw in the case of Brazil, a quest for international prestige is insufficient to prompt a country to acquire the bomb.

Taking stock, our strategic theory of proliferation accounts for North Korea's nuclearization. Pyongyang's security concerns vis-à-vis the South and the United States, combined with the absence of a reliable ally since at least the end of the Cold War, account for North Korea's willingness to proliferate. Its ability to inflict high costs on its adversaries using conventional weaponry deterred counterproliferation military action, granting North Korea the opportunity to become, as of this date, the latest state to have built the bomb.

Taiwan

Twice since defeated Nationalist forces took refuge there in 1949, the island of Taiwan (officially, the Republic of China, or ROC) has possessed an active nuclear program with a military component. Yet, Taiwan remains a nonnuclear state.

Since the creation of the PRC in 1949, Taiwan has faced an existential threat from its much stronger neighbor. To counter this threat, Taiwanese leaders initially relied on an alliance with the United States.

---

[612] See: Szalontai and Radchenko (2006, 9); Byman and Lind (2010, 63); Cha (2012, 304).

The two countries signed a Mutual Defense Treaty in 1954, and the United States intervened on behalf of Taiwan in two crises with the PRC over control of different islands in the Taiwan Strait during the 1950s. Starting in the mid-1960s, however, Taiwan's security outlook worsened further with the October 1964 Chinese nuclear test. Complicating matters, Taiwan soon came to doubt the reliability of U.S. guarantees. By the late 1960s and 1970s, the Nixon Doctrine (also known as the Guam Doctrine) and U.S.-China rapprochement meant that U.S. commitments to Taiwan were drastically reduced, starting with the withdrawal of U.S. naval destroyers in 1969, of nuclear weapons by 1974, and of troops by 1978. Taiwan was increasingly isolated. The country was eventually ousted from the UN in October 1971, when the PRC was recognized as China's legitimate representative. This decline in U.S. support left Taipei in a difficult strategic situation. As the Taiwanese leader told the Assistant Secretary of State for East Asian and Pacific affairs Richard Holbrooke (1977–1981) in 1977, "the U.S. and [the] ROC are as close as lips and teeth, when the lips are gone, the teeth feel cold."[613]

Dwindling U.S. security support in the face of a much stronger PRC gave Taiwan the willingness to build the bomb. Yet, the United States staunchly opposed Taiwanese nuclearization. Despite Taipei's signing of the NPT in 1968 and its ratification in 1970, Washington suspected that Taiwan's nuclear program had military objectives. Given that Taiwan faced a much stronger PRC, it would have been very costly for Washington to implement a carrots-based nonproliferation policy and try to remove Taiwan's willingness to acquire nuclear weapons by boosting support for its protégé. This would have required substantial additional security commitments and force deployments to the island. Such a high degree of support, however, was not warranted by the level of U.S. interest in fighting on behalf of Taiwan, which was somewhat limited. Therefore, the easier way to prevent Taiwan from acquiring nuclear weapons was to ensure that U.S. protection did not give Taipei an opportunity to acquire nuclear weapons. With this goal in mind, Washington deployed a sticks-based nonproliferation policy, pressuring Taipei by demanding

---

[613] "Telegram from the Embassy in the Republic of China to the Department of State," Taipei, August 27, 1977, in *Foreign Relations of the United States* (*FRUS*), 1977–1980, Vol. XIII, *China*, Doc. 54.

intrusive inspections and threatening to terminate the entire security relationship if Taiwan insisted on a nuclear-weapons program. Giving in to U.S. pressure, Taiwan placed its nuclear ambitions on hold in April 1977.

This coercive U.S. effort to stymie Taiwan's opportunity to proliferate did not undermine its willingness to acquire nuclear weapons, however. In 1978–1979, Washington replaced the Mutual Defense Treaty with the Taiwan Relations Act, offering to sell conventional weaponry but falling short of committing to defend Taiwan in the case of an attack from China. This decline in U.S. commitments would lead Taipei to revive its nuclear program. In 1987, the ROC began building a facility for the extraction of plutonium from spent fuel rods. Again, the United States resorted to a sticks-based nonproliferation policy, threatening to terminate its defense relationship with Taiwan. This coercive effort successfully pushed Taipei into stopping its nuclear-weapons program. In the end, the United States prevented proliferation by ensuring that the ROC did not have the opportunity to build the bomb.

Taiwanese Interest in Nuclear Weapons

Ever since they retreated to Taiwan in May 1949, Chinese Nationalists perceived the PRC as a significant security threat, with a population that was nearly thirty times its own and with more than twenty times its military expenditure, on average, through the 1960s and 1970s.[614]

To counter this threat, Taiwan counted on the support of its American ally. In 1954–1955 and again in the 1958, the PRC shelled islands in the Taiwan Strait, initiating two crises. On both occasions, the United States intervened to protect its ally. In the midst of the First Taiwan Strait Crisis, in December 1954, Washington and Taipei formalized their security cooperation with the signature of a Mutual Defense Treaty.

Taiwan's Reaction to the PRC's Nuclear Test of 1964
For the following decade, Washington was able to ensure the security of its protégé while achieving its nonproliferation goals. Given U.S.

---

[614] See: Singer (1987).

commitments, Taiwan felt sufficiently secure against the PRC and thus did not attempt to acquire its own nuclear weapons. This situation would change in October 1964. With its successful nuclear test, the PRC took American and Taiwanese officials by surprise. As late as April that year, ROC president Chiang Kai-shek (1949–1975) confided to Secretary of State Dean Rusk that "he did not believe that the Communists would be able to explode a nuclear device in the next three to five years."[615] Surprised by the Chinese test, Chiang became extremely concerned. He argued that in Asia as a whole the "psychological reaction was enormous and far reaching" and that it "could not be overestimated."[616] The test ostensibly encouraged Chiang to consider his own nuclear deterrent. As a CIA analysis later put it, Chiang likely "felt an urgent need to counter the new potential for nuclear blackmail from Peking."[617]

Until then, the Taiwanese nuclear program had been peaceful. Taiwan was an early participant in President Eisenhower's Atoms for Peace program, having signed an agreement to cooperate with the United States on the peaceful uses of nuclear energy in 1955.[618] That same year, Taipei created the Atomic Energy Council and the Atomic Power Research Commission, both committed to the peaceful applications of nuclear technology.[619] In 1956, Taiwan completed its first nuclear reactor at National Tsinghua University.[620] The following year, two Chinese scientists working in the United States shared the Nobel Prize in physics for the first time, inspiring many students in Taiwan to study nuclear physics.[621] By the late 1970s, Taiwan had sent more than a thousand scientists to the United States for training in nuclear science and technology.[622]

---

[615] "Memorandum of Conversation," Taipei, April 16, 1964, 9:30–10:30 p.m., in *FRUS*, 1964–1968, Vol. XXX, Doc. 27.

[616] "Telegram from the Embassy in Republic of China to the Department of State," Taipei, October 19, 1964, 11 p.m., in *FRUS*, 1964–1968, Vol. XXX, Doc. 59.

[617] Special National Intelligence Estimate 43-1-72, "Taipei's Capabilities and Intentions Regarding Nuclear Weapons Development," 16 (?)November 1972, in National Security Archive (NSA) Electronic Briefing Book (EBB) 221, "U.S. Opposed Taiwanese Bomb during 1970s," Doc. 1A, 4.

[618] See: Bullard and Yuan (2010, 184).

[619] See: Wang (2008, 412).

[620] See: Mitchell (2004, 296). The reactor would reach criticality five years later.

[621] See: Wang (2008, 413).

[622] See: Cooper (1979, 291).

The PRC's nuclear test of 1964 triggered an upsurge of interest in the military dimension of the nuclear program. In 1965, Chiang Kai-shek founded the Chung-Shan Science Institute (CSSI), tasking it with exploring the military applications of nuclear technology.[623] In early 1966, Taiwan initiated negotiations for the purchase of a 50 MW nuclear reactor from West Germany.[624] In April, Taiwanese officials asked for advice from the IAEA on the placement of a 200 MW reactor, to be built by a "consortium," which, according to an IAEA official, "no doubt included the GRC [Government of the Republic of China] military."[625] The following year, the Ministry of Defense launched a $140 million nuclear program ("Hsin Chu"), administered by the CSSI and a newly constituted Institute of Nuclear Energy Research (INER).[626]

During this period, the PRC's nuclear-weapons program was developing at a brisk pace. In October 1966, Beijing successfully tested its first nuclear-tipped missile, with sufficient range to reach Taipei from the mainland.[627] In June 1967, Beijing tested its first hydrogen bomb, reaching this milestone before the French. Overall, in the three years after its first nuclear test, the PRC conducted seven nuclear tests, ranging from 12 kilotons to 3.3 megatons.[628]

Taiwan's Reaction to the Nixon Doctrine

Taiwan's security concerns were further exacerbated by the trajectory of U.S. policy in East Asia. With the announcement of the Nixon

---

[623] CSSI was funded by Taiwan's Ministry of National Defense. See: NSA EBB 221, Doc. 1A, p. 2.

[624] See: U.S. Embassy Bonn, Cable 3000, "German Nuclear Reactor for Taiwan," March 25, 1966, in National Security Archive (NSA) Electronic Briefing Book (EBB) 20, "New Archival Evidence on Taiwanese 'Nuclear Intentions,' 1966–1976," Doc. 3.

[625] U.S. Embassy Taipei, Airgram 813, "GRC Request to IAEA Team for Advice on Location of Reactor for Possible Use by Military Research Institute," April 8, 1966, in NSA EBB 20, Doc. 5, p. 2.

[626] See: Albright and Gay (1998, 55); Hersman and Peters (2006, 543).

[627] See: "Telegram from the Embassy in the Republic of China to the Department of State," Taipei, November 3, 1966; and "Special National Intelligence Estimate, 13-8-66," Washington, November 3, 1966, both in *FRUS*, 1964–1968, Vol. XXX, Docs. 196 and 198.

[628] See: "Nuclear Weapons Tests," May 27, 2000, Federation of American Scientists. Available at: www.fas.org/nuke/guide/china/nuke/tests.htm. Last accessed: May 1, 2016.

Doctrine in July 1969, Washington sought to reduce its commitments abroad, asking its allies to do more for their own defense. In late 1969, Washington withdrew two destroyers that had patrolled the Taiwan Strait since the late fifties.[629] National security advisor Henry Kissinger conveyed to President Nixon that Chiang "was by no means pleased" with that decision. The Taiwanese leader was worried that "'gaps' will be created which will tempt the Communists to attack."[630] In late 1970, Washington announced that it would shrink its Military Assistance Program to Taiwan. Unsurprisingly, this decision had a startling effect on Taipei. In a conversation with the U.S. ambassador, Chiang Ching-kuo (son of Chiang Kai-shek, at the time vice premier of the ROC, who would become its president between 1978 and 1988) confided that his government "could not see how the U.S. action, particularly as to the manner in which it was carried out, could be reconciled with the requirements of alliance and friendship." He added that "confidence in US consistency and dependability had been seriously diluted in all sectors of his government."[631] Over the course of the following decade, Washington removed all U.S. troops from Taiwan, decreasing from a high of 9,000 troops stationed on the island in 1971 to virtually nil by the end of 1978.[632] In the nuclear realm, Washington also withdrew its

---

[629] See: Solingen (2007, 153); "Telegram from the Department of State to the Embassy in the Republic of China and Commander, U.S. Taiwan Defense Command," Washington, September 23, 1969, in *FRUS*, 1969–1976, Vol. XVII, Doc. 34.

[630] "Memorandum from the President's Assistant for National Security Affairs (Kissinger), to President Nixon," Washington, December 9, 1969, in *FRUS*, 1969–1976, Vol. XVII, Doc. 50.

[631] "Telegram from the Embassy in the Republic of China to the Department of State," Taipei, October 22, 1970, in *FRUS*, 1969–1976, Vol. XVII, Doc. 92. See also: "Memorandum of Conversation," Washington, October 25, 1970, 3:20 p.m., in *FRUS*, 1969–1976, Vol. XVII, Doc. 93.

[632] See: "Memorandum from Phil Odeen of the National Security Council Staff to the President's Assistant for National Security Affairs (Kissinger)," Washington, March 29, 1972, and "Memorandum from John H. Holdridge of the National Security Council Staff to the President's Assistant for National Security Affairs (Kissinger)," Washington, November 3, 1972, both in *FRUS*, 1969–1976, Vol. XVII, Docs. 216 and 264; "National Security Decision Memorandum 339," Washington, September 20, 1976, in *Foreign Relations of the United States (FRUS)*, 1969–1976, Vol. XVIII, *China, 1973–1976*, Doc. 156; "Memorandum from Zbigniew Brzezinski, Richard Gardner, and Henry Owen to President-Elect Carter," Washington, November 3, 1976, "Summary of Conclusions of a Policy Review Committee Meeting," Washington, June 27, 1977, 3–4:30 p.m., and "Memorandum from the President's Assistant for National Security Affairs

commitments, reducing in half its nuclear arsenal deployed in Taiwan in 1972, and removing it entirely by 1974.[633]

To make matters worse from Taipei's perspective, not only was Washington decreasing its commitments to the security of the ROC, it was doing so as part of a broader effort to improve relations with Beijing. During July 9–11, 1971, Kissinger made a secret visit to China, and on July 15 Nixon announced that he planned to visit Beijing the following year. Without delay, the ROC ambassador "lodged strong protest and expressed profound regret."[634] Chiang Kai-shek later called the upcoming visit "especially hurtful to his government."[635] In October 1971, the UN recognized the PRC as the legitimate representative of China, leading to the ROC's expulsion from the organization.[636] In a meeting with U.S. officials shortly thereafter, Taiwan's vice minister foresaw "the rapidly increasing besiegement and eventual strangulation of the GRC unless drastic change is undertaken immediately."[637] After Nixon's actual visit to China in February 1972, the ROC ambassador told Kissinger that the people of Taiwan "now have the impression the Republic of China is a non-nation."[638] U.S.-China rapprochement could eventually lead to the normalization of relations between Washington and Beijing, a development that, as Chiang later told Kissinger, would "virtually mean negation of the existence of the Republic of China."[639] Taiwan's very survival seemed to be at stake.

(Brzezinski) to Secretary of Defense Brown," Washington, May 12, 1978, in *FRUS*, 1977–1980, Vol. XIII, Docs. 1, 34, and 103.

[633] See: "Memorandum of Conversation," New York, April 12, 1972, 5:15–6:40 p.m., in *FRUS*, 1969–1976, Vol., XVII, Doc. 220; Solingen (2007, p. 103).

[634] "Telegram from the Department of State to the Embassy in the Republic of China," Washington, July 16, 1971, in *FRUS*, 1969–1976, Vol. XVII, Doc. 145.

[635] "Memorandum from John H. Holdridge of the National Security Council Staff to the President's Assistant for National Security Affairs (Kissinger)," Washington, November 5, 1971, *FRUS*, 1969–1976, Vol. XVII, Doc. 170,

[636] See: Mitchell (2004, 295); "Editorial Note," in *FRUS*, 1969–1976, Vol. XVII, Doc. 167.

[637] "Telegram from the Embassy in the Republic of China to the Department of State," Taipei, November 30, 1971, in *FRUS*, 1969–1976, Vol. XVII, Doc. 174.

[638] "Memorandum of Conversation," Washington, March 1, 1972, 12:30 p.m., in *FRUS*, 1969–1976, Vol. XVII, Doc. 205.

[639] "Letter from President Ford to Republic of China Premier Jiang Jingguo," Washington, January 24, 1976, in *FRUS*, 1969–1976, Vol. XVIII, Doc. 141.

Taiwanese Nuclear Development in the 1970s

Publicly, Taiwan pledged to maintain its nonnuclear status. It signed the NPT in 1968, ratified it in 1970, and the same year began talks with the IAEA for a safeguards agreement on its nuclear facilities.[640] Yet, the Taiwanese nuclear program continued to expand. In 1969, Taiwan bought a 40 MW heavy-water research reactor from Canada, which arrived in early 1972 and became operational the following year.[641] Through the early seventies, Taiwan obtained nearly one hundred metric tons of uranium from South Africa and entered into nuclear cooperation agreements with both France and West Germany.[642]

U.S. intelligence officials had suspected that the Taiwanese nuclear program had a military component since at least June 1966.[643] According to the CIA, the purchase of the Canadian reactor was an indication that Taiwan's "interests extend beyond nuclear power and other peaceful-use applications."[644] Furthermore, Taiwan sought to acquire from West Germany a reprocessing plant that, American intelligence concluded, "might be used to manufacture nuclear weapons."[645] In a SNIE from 1972, U.S. officials expressed concern that "the generation of electric power is not the only serious interest that the GRC has in the nuclear field."[646] In February 1973, U.S. officials learned from their British counterparts about a possible nuclear-weapons-related site in the north of Taiwan.[647]

---

[640] See: Albright and Gay (1998, 58).

[641] See: State Department Memorandum of Conversation, "ROC Nuclear Intentions," April 5, 1973, with Intelligence and Research (INR) report on "Nuclear Weapons Intentions of the Republic of China" attached, in NSA EBB 20, Doc. 23; Mitchell (2004, 298).

[642] See: Albright and Gay (1998, 57); Hersman and Peters (2006, 544); Kroenig (2010, 105). For an assessment of Taiwanese capabilities in the early 1970s, see: Quester (1974).

[643] See: US Embassy Taipei, Airgram 1037, "Indications GRC Continues to Pursue Atomic Weaponry," June 20, 1966, in NSA EBB 20, Doc. 8, p. 1. Washington obtained its first satellite photograph of Taiwanese nuclear facilities in September 1965. See: Richelson (2006, 262).

[644] NSA EBB 221, Doc. 1A, pp. 2–3. See also: Mitchell (2004, 298).

[645] Memorandum from Leo J. Moser, Office of Republic of China Affairs, to Assistant Secretary for East Asian and Pacific Affairs (Marshall Green), "Nuclear Materials Reprocessing Plant for ROC," December 14, 1972, in NSA EBB 20, Doc. 13.

[646] NSA EBB 221, Doc. 1A, p. 2.

[647] See: State Department Memorandum of Conversation, "Nuclear Programs in Republic of China," February 9, 1973, in NSA EBB 20, Doc. 19.

By the fall of 1974, there was little doubt in Washington that Taiwan sought its own nuclear deterrent. According to the CIA, "Taipei conducts its small nuclear program with a weapon option clearly in mind, and it will be in a position to fabricate a nuclear device after five years or so."[648] Taiwan was indeed making quick progress, producing fifteen kilograms of weapons-grade plutonium – more than enough for one weapon – by the end of 1975.[649] In 1976, further evidence of a military program surfaced, with missing fuel rods, and the discovery of a non civilian nuclear infrastructure by IAEA inspectors.[650] The Taiwanese leadership offered assurances about the peaceful nature of its nuclear program. Yet, by September, U.S. officials concluded that a "formal démarche" was necessary to convey the American position that "no reprocessing shall take place on Taiwan."[651] U.S. actions succeeded in preventing Taiwan from acquiring nuclear weapons, which to this day remains nonnuclear.

U.S. Nonproliferation Efforts

In February 1949, as Chinese Nationalists were retreating to Taiwan, the JCS concluded that the island's strategic importance was "great" but not "vital" to U.S. national security, and they argued against an intervention to defend it. The Joint Chiefs asserted that "the current disparity between our military strength and our many global obligations makes it inadvisable to undertake the employment of armed forces in Formosa."[652] In December, NSC-48/2 ruled out a military defense of Taiwan,[653] a policy announced by President Truman on January 5, 1950.[654]

---

[648] Director of Central Intelligence, Memorandum, "Prospects for Further Proliferation of Nuclear Weapons," September 4, 1974, in NSA EBB 181, Doc. 8, p. 4. Other branches of the U.S. government agreed with this assessment. See: "Study Prepared by the Ad Hoc Interdepartmental Regional Group for East Asia and the Pacific," Washington, November 12, 1974, in *FRUS*, 1969–1976, Vol. XVIII, Doc. 90.

[649] See: Albright and Gay (1998, 57).

[650] Ibid., 58. See also: Mitchell (2004, 299).

[651] State Department cable 91733 to Embassy Taiwan, "ROC's Nuclear Intentions," September 4, 1976, in NSA EBB 221, Doc. 6A, 1.

[652] "Note by the Executive Secretary of the National Security Council (Souers) to the Council," [Washington,] February 11, 1949, in *FRUS*, 1949, Vol. IX, Doc. 314. For an analysis, see: Zhang (1992, 49); Christensen (1996, 106).

[653] See: *FRUS*, 1949, Vol. VII, Part 2, Doc. 386.

[654] See: "The President's News Conference," January 5, 1950, Harry S. Truman Library, Public Papers of the Presidents, Harry S. Truman, 1945–1953.

The Korean War

The onset of the Korean War soon thereafter led Washington to reeval-
uate its position. On June 27, 1950, Truman declared that communism
had revealed its intention to "use armed invasion and war" to "conquer
independent nations."[655] Taiwan had just been a Japanese colony and
Washington acknowledged during the Second World War that it should
be returned to China. Yet, if China were in civil war, there was some
ambiguity about "which China" should take control over Taiwan.
With Communist aggression in Korea, Truman now doubted that disputes over sovereignty on the island would be resolved peacefully. The
president argued that the status of Taiwan was undetermined, and any
attempt to settle the matter should await the restoration of stability in
the region and be subject to international consideration. In this speech,
Truman laid out the legal justification for U.S. intervention. To defend
the island, he ordered the Seventh Fleet to the Taiwan Strait.

For the next twenty years, Washington sought to deter the PRC from
invading Taiwan while minimizing its costs as well as any risks of entrapment. Already in the spring and summer of 1949, Chiang Kai-shek had
endorsed the idea of a "Pacific Union," a multilateral alliance system
that would serve as the equivalent of the newly constituted NATO for
the Pacific, proposed by Philippine president Elpidio Quirino (1948–
1953).[656] Washington rejected the idea, instead favoring a nonmilitary
alliance with the Philippines, and excluding Taiwan.[657] During the
Korean War, Washington wished to limit the conflict to the Peninsula,
rejecting the entry of Nationalist troops.[658] In April 1953, an NSC
meeting discussed, in the words of Eisenhower, the "real trouble and
danger that Chiang Kai-shek might go on the warpath."[659] U.S. officials

---

Available at: www.trumanlibrary.org/publicpapers. Last accessed: May 1,
   2016.
[655] "Memorandum of Conversation, by the Ambassador at Large (Jessup),"
   [Washington,] June 27, 1950, 11:30 a.m., in *FRUS*, 1950, Vol. VII, Doc. 116.
[656] Chiang was joined by Syngman Rhee of South Korea. See: Cha (2009–2010,
   178).
[657] See: Mabon (1988, 157).
[658] See: "Memorandum by the Assistant Secretary of State for Far Eastern Affairs
   (Allison) to John Foster Dulles," [Washington,] December 24, 1952, in *FRUS*,
   1952–1954, Vol. XIV, Part 1, Doc. 63.
[659] "Memorandum of Discussion at the 139th Meeting of the National Security
   Council," Washington, April 8, 1953, in *FRUS*, 1952–1954, Vol. XIV, Part 1,
   Doc. 93.

wanted assurance that Chiang "will not use the new equipment we give him [F-84 Thunderjet aircraft] against the China mainland without our prior consent."[660]

In two crises during the Eisenhower administration, Beijing tested Washington's commitment to the defense of Taipei. In both the First and Second Taiwan Strait crises – in 1954–1955 and 1958 – Washington used the threat of military intervention and its superior capabilities to successfully deter the People's Republic from invading Taiwan. The Eisenhower administration at the time relied on a doctrine of massive retaliation, pledging to use nuclear weapons to meet Communist attacks. To boost this deterrent, Eisenhower deployed the first nuclear-armed missiles on Taiwan in May 1957.[661]

U.S. officials offered a security guarantee to Taiwan during the First Taiwan Strait Crisis. Yet, they also insisted on the importance of avoiding entrapment. In November 1954, Dulles explained to Eisenhower that the Mutual Defense Treaty "stakes out unqualifiedly our interest in Formosa and the Pescadores and does so on a basis which will not enable the Chinese Nationalists to involve us in a war with Communist China."[662] When tensions flared again over the Taiwan Strait in 1958, Washington warned the Nationalists that an escalation of the conflict would be "fatal to their own interests;" it could "lead to large-scale, possibly nuclear conflict" with a "catastrophic impact" on Taiwan.[663]

Through the early 1960s, the United States continued successfully to deter the PRC at relatively low cost. Despite the PRC's advantage in the East Asian theater, Washington enjoyed a significant overall advantage in conventional forces and could threaten nuclear escalation to prevent Beijing's aggression against the ROC.[664] Total U.S. spending

[660] "Memorandum by the Deputy Under Secretary of State (Matthews) to the Secretary of State," [Washington,] March 31, 1953, in *FRUS, 1952–1954*, Vol. XIV, Part 1, Doc. 88. See also: Accinelli (1996, 118).

[661] See: *FRUS, 1955–1957*, Vol. III, Doc. 251.

[662] "Memorandum by the Secretary of State to the President," in *FRUS, 1952–1954*, Vol. XIV, Part 1, Doc. 403. See also: Pruessen (2001, 88–89).

[663] "Telegram from the Department of State to the Embassy in the Republic of China," Washington, September 25, 1958, 5:38 p.m., in *FRUS, 1958–1960*, Vol. XIX, Doc. 128. For the Dulles-Chiang Communiqué of October 1958, and its interpretation as an effort to restrain Chiang from undertaking offensive military operations against the mainland, see: *FRUS, 1958–1960*, Vol. XIX, Doc. 209; Barnett (1977, 236); Tucker (2001, 129–130).

[664] By traditional measures, the United States was nearly twice as powerful as China between 1960 and 1964. See: Singer (1987).

on Taiwan in the form of military and economic aid was small, no greater than the cost of maintaining a single division on U.S. soil. As Nancy Tucker put it, "it seemed a bargain."[665] In the mid-1960s, however, this fragile equilibrium became increasingly strained.

Washington's Response to the PRC's Nuclear Test

In October 1964, the PRC successfully conducted its first nuclear test. Taiwan's security concerns immediately spiked, fueled in part by Washington's past actions. When assistant secretary of state for far eastern affairs William Bundy (1964–1969) met with Chiang the following month, he surmised that the Taiwanese leader's "coolness reflects to some degree [a] sense of personal affront over ... [a] general feeling of personal neglect over long period of time." The problem was that this "crotchety old man," in Bundy's words, still had "the power to make decisions that can affect our interests seriously."[666]

In the short term, Washington attempted to reassure the Taiwanese leader. In December 1964, President Johnson wrote to Chiang that "the American people regard their Mutual Defense Treaty with the Republic of China as one of their basic international commitments." He added: "I believe that the continuing strength of our alliance will deter the Chinese Communists from any thought of a nuclear attack on Taiwan."[667] Yet, the Taipei leadership remained concerned about the threat from the PRC. For Chiang, the test meant that the island "could be wiped out in one attack. ... An attack on Taiwan would leave the island desolated and U.S. retaliation would be too late."[668] In March and April 1965, Chiang insisted with the American ambassador that the U.S. nuclear deterrent would not be effective against the PRC.[669]

---

[665] Tucker (2009, 15).

[666] "Telegram from the Embassy in the Republic of China to the Department of State," Taipei, November 3, 1966, in *FRUS*, 1964–1968, Vol. XXX, Doc. 196.

[667] "Telegram from the Department of State to the Embassy in the Republic of China," Washington, December 21, 1964, 9:52 a.m., in *FRUS*, 1964–1968, Vol. XXX, Doc. 74.

[668] US Embassy, Taipei, cable number 347 to Department of State, October 24, 1964, in NSA EBB 38, Doc. 20, pp. 1–2.

[669] See: "Telegram from the Embassy in the Republic of China to the Department of State," Taipei, March 23, 1965, 4 p.m., and "Airgram from the Embassy in the Republic of China to the Department of State," Taipei, April 14, 1965, both in *FRUS*, 1964–1968, Vol. XXX, Docs. 81 and 82.

During this period, U.S. officials were, on the whole, skeptical about the PRC's ability to attack Taiwan, given the costs of such an operation.[670] The problem for Washington was that, given its commitment to Taiwan, it too would pay a high cost in the event of a war between the PRC and the ROC. Chiang himself put it plainly in 1969. He complained about the "inadequacy of US military aid in view of ChiCom threat" and "expressed doubt whether GRC in present circumstances could hold out more than 3 days against full ChiCom attack on Taiwan." Chiang also "observed that if there is a military crisis in this area and ROC is unable [to] fulfill its defensive role, [the] US inevitably would become deeply involved."[671] From Taipei's perspective, the solution was, of course, for Washington to increase its military support for the ROC.

The Sino-American Rapprochement and Beyond

As it turns out, Nixon actually decided to reduce its commitments to Taiwan. The president had long understood the risks of confrontation with a nuclear China. In his trip to Asia a few months after the PRC's nuclear test, Nixon shared his vision for a rapprochement with China with several members of his entourage. In Taipei, he told U.S. diplomat Arthur W. Himmel Jr. that the Nationalists would never reclaim the homeland and it was time for Washington to improve relations with the PRC.[672] Two years later, Nixon published an article in *Foreign Affairs* explaining the risks of a nuclear confrontation between the United States and China, and arguing for bringing China back into the family of nations.[673]

With Nixon's arrival in office, conditions appeared ripe for a rapprochement.[674] In March 1969, Moscow and Beijing were engaged in

---

[670] See: "Memorandum from Secretary of State Vance to President Carter," Washington, April 15, 1977, and "National Intelligence Analytical Memorandum 43-1-77," Washington, July 26, 1977, both in *FRUS*, 1977–1980, Vol. XIII, Docs. 26 and 38. See also: "Paper Prepared in the Central Intelligence Agency," Washington, June 1976, in *FRUS*, 1969–1976, Vol. XVIII, Doc. 148.

[671] "Telegram from the Embassy in the Republic of China to the Department of State," Taipei, August 8, 1969, in *FRUS*, 1969–1976, Vol. XVII, Doc. 22.

[672] Cited in Tucker (2009, 35).

[673] See: Nixon (1967).

[674] Previous administrations had also explored the possibility of an improvement in relations with the PRC, but conditions were not favorable for such a

overt border clashes. The widening Sino-Soviet rift offered an opportunity to split the communist camp and check Soviet expansionism.[675] Furthermore, Washington hoped to enlist Chinese support in a resolution of the war in Vietnam.[676] In light of these great potential strategic benefits of China's realignment, Taiwan began to appear expendable.

In order to facilitate a rapprochement with Beijing, Washington was keen to avoid potential entrapment in a conflict with the PRC over Taiwan.[677] With this goal in mind, Kissinger and Nixon made key concessions on the legal basis of U.S. involvement in Taiwan and on military commitments to the defense of the island.[678] While in China in February 1972, Nixon told PRC premier Zhou Enlai that the United States would no longer adhere to the position that the status of Taiwan is undetermined: "Principle one. There is one China, and Taiwan is a part of China. There will be no more statements made – if I can control our bureaucracy – to the effect that the status of Taiwan is undetermined." Washington would draw down its forces in Taiwan and would "not support any military attempts by the Government of Taiwan to resort to a military return to the Mainland." The administration would

---

development. For example, in December 1963, Roger Hilsman, assistant secretary for far eastern affairs (1963–1964), declared that the United States adopted an "open door" policy in improving relations. In July 1966, President Lyndon B. Johnson called for improved relations with the PRC in a nationally televised address. Yet, the complexity of negotiations over Taiwan, and later the Cultural Revolution in China, sapped the prospects of a rapprochement. See: Roger Hilsman, "United States Policy toward Communist China," Address Made before the Commonwealth Club at San Francisco, California, Dec. 13, 1963, in *The Department of State Bulletin*, Vol. L, No. 1280, January 6, 1964, pp. 11–17; Lyndon B. Johnson, "Speech on U.S. Foreign Policy in Asia," July 12, 1966, Miller Center, University of Virginia. Available at: http://millercenter.org/president/lbjohnson/speeches/speech-4038. Last accessed: May 1, 2016. See also: Tucker (2012).

[675] On the Sino-Soviet split, see: Barnett (1977, 32–33); Westad (1998); Radchenko (2010). On U.S. perceptions of the split, see: Tucker (2001, 146).

[676] Needless to say, U.S. officials also feared that the Vietnam War could escalate to a direct confrontation with the PRC, and carefully planned military operations to avoid such clashes. See: Schulzinger (2001).

[677] We expand on the claim that the PRC's nuclearization contributed to U.S. concessions on Taiwan in our work with Nicholas Anderson. See: Anderson, Debs, and Monteiro (2015).

[678] Kissinger initially downplayed the importance of concessions to the PRC on Taiwan in his memoirs. See: Kissinger (1979, 685, 705, 1080). With archival evidence of the private conversations with PRC officials in 1971 and 1972

also "seek the normalization of relations with the People's Republic."[679] In their joint communiqué, Nixon added, the United States and the PRC should "find language which will meet your need yet does not stir up the animals so much that they gang up on Taiwan and thereby torpedo our initiative."[680] Conspicuously, Washington failed to demand a pledge for a peaceful resolution of the Taiwan question as a precondition for the improvement in relations.[681]

Coercing Taipei to Halt Its Nuclear Development

Understandably, the rapprochement between Washington and Beijing raised doubts in Taipei about the reliability of U.S. security guarantees and led Taiwan to consider acquiring an independent nuclear deterrent. Washington was well aware of this risk. As a 1972 NIE pointed out:

> While the nuclear umbrella of the US is still implied by the Mutual Defense Treaty, some on Taiwan may be questioning how long they can count on allout US support. In this perspective, a nuclear weapons option may be seen by the GRC as one of the few feasible deterrents to communist attack in an uncertain future.[682]

According to a National Security Studies Memorandum two years later, the "inhibitions which have kept the ROC in line could be swept aside by a ROC calculation that a nuclear capability was required as an effective substitute for the vanishing U.S. security commitment."[683] In fact, this same study predicted that in a direct conflict between PRC and ROC forces, the PRC would prevail.

recently surfacing, we now know that the United States made significant concessions to the PRC on Taiwan, a key factor contributing to the rapprochement. See: Ross (1995, 1–2); Mann (1999, 15–16); Goldstein (2001, 237); Romberg (2003, 21, 41); Bush (2004, 5, 176); Accinelli (2007, 12); Tucker (2009, 42, 44).

[679] Memorandum of Conversation, Tuesday, February 22, 1972, 2:10 p.m.-6:00 p.m., in National Security Archive (NSA) Electronic Briefing Book (EBB) 106, "Nixon's Trip to China," Doc. 1, pp. 5–6.

[680] Memorandum of Conversation, Tuesday, February 22, 1972, 2:10 p.m.–6:00 p.m., in NSA EBB 106, Doc. 1, pp. 6–7.

[681] See the text of the Shanghai communiqué in "Joint Statement Following Discussions with Leaders of the People's Republic of China," in *FRUS*, 1969–1976, Vol. XVII, Doc. 203.

[682] NSA EBB 221, Doc. 1A, p. 4.

[683] *FRUS*, 1969–1976, Vol. XVIII, Doc. 90.

A Taiwanese nuclear-weapons program would increase the risks of entrapment for the United States, however, and was therefore antithetical to U.S. interests. Since the beginning of secret negotiations between U.S. and PRC officials in August 1955, Beijing made it clear that it was willing to use force to implement its one-China policy and reunify with Taiwan.[684] In its view, the reunification of Taiwan with the mainland was a domestic matter and Beijing could not renounce the use of force as a matter of sovereignty. On December 4, 1975, then vice-premier Deng Xiaoping (1974–1976) declared to President Ford: "We do not believe in peaceful transition" due to the presence of "a huge bunch of counterrevolutionaries over there."[685] The development of a nuclear-weapons capability in Taiwan would certainly complicate Beijing's plans for eventual reunification, and could reasonably become a casus belli.

Washington wanted to avoid a costly conflict with the PRC over a Taiwanese nuclear-weapons program and sought assurances from Taipei that its nuclear program had solely peaceful purposes. As early as November 1973, U.S. officials had warned their ROC counterparts that the United States "would be compelled to react should [the] ROC move from consideration of nuclear weapons program to actual implementation."[686] In the fall of 1976, U.S. officials again confronted the ROC over its nuclear ambitions. During the previous summer, U.S. embassies in Europe had reported ROC interest in purchasing a reprocessing plant, and the IAEA raised concerns that the

[684] For an analysis of U.S.-PRC negotiations in Geneva and Warsaw, see: Ross and Jiang (2001).
[685] "Memorandum of Conversation," Beijing, December 4, 1975, 10:05–11:47 a.m., in *FRUS*, 1969–1976, Vol. XVIII, Doc. 137. Chinese officials repeated similar comments to the Carter administration in February and August 1977. See: "Memorandum of Conversation," Washington, February 8, 1977, 10 a.m., and "Memorandum of Conversation," Beijing, August 24, 1977, 9:30 a.m.–12:20 p.m., in *FRUS*, 1977–1980, Vol. XIII, Docs. 5 and 49. Certainly, PRC leaders made overtures for a peaceful resolution of the conflict with Taiwan. Such measures include Mao's speech of May 1960; the "Message to Compatriots" in January 1979; the "Nine-Point" proposal of September 1981; Deng's own proposal for a "one country, two systems" solution in June 1983; and Jiang Zemin's (1993–2003) "Eight Points" speech of January 1995. Yet, PRC leaders consistently refused to renounce the use of force as a matter of principle.
[686] State Department cable 223116 to U.S. Embassy Taiwan, "Atomic Energy Study Team Visit to Taiwan," November 14, 1973, in NSA EBB 221, Doc. 3A, p. 2.

ROC was secretly engaging in reprocessing activities.[687] In September, U.S. ambassador Leonard Unger (1974–1979) met with the ROC premier to make him "fully aware of the possible drastic consequences in store should the GROC persist in its cover efforts to develop a pilot plant reprocessing capability."[688] Chiang reassured Unger that all research related to reprocessing would be terminated. The ROC also publicly pledged that it had "no intention whatsoever" to develop nuclear weapons or purchase equipment for reprocessing activities.[689]

Yet, doubts remained about Taipei's nuclear intentions.[690] Making matters worse, given U.S. support for Taipei's civilian nuclear program, Beijing made it clear that it would view Washington as complicit in the development of a Taiwanese nuclear-weapons capability. For example, in a meeting with an Australian official in October 1976, a Chinese diplomat "accused the US of assisting Taiwan's nuclear weapons program and said that the PRC would hold the US responsible in the event that Taiwan acquired nuclear weapons."[691] Intent on coercing Taiwan to remain nonnuclear, Washington continued to draw down its commitment to Taiwan. On September 20, 1976, the Ford administration approved NSC-339, which pledged to reduce its commitment to Taiwan to less than 1,400 Department of Defense personnel by the end of the year.[692]

---

[687] See: U.S. Embassy Netherlands Cable 8502 to State Department, "Nuclear Fuel Processing Plant," July 7, 1976, U.S. Mission IAEA Cable 6195 to State Department, "Fuel Reprocessing Pilot Plant in Taiwan," August 19, 1976, and U.S. Embassy Belgium cable 8149 to State Department, "Nuclear Processing in ROC," August 20, 1976, all in NSA EBB 221, Docs. 4A, 4D, 4E.

[688] U.S. Embassy Taiwan cable 6272 to State Department, "ROC's Nuclear Intentions: Conversation with Premier Chiang Ching-kuo," September 15, 1976, in NSA EBB 221, Doc. 7A.

[689] U.S. Embassy Taiwan cable 6272 to State Department, "ROC's Nuclear Intentions: Conversation with Premier Chiang Ching-kuo," September 15, 1976, and U.S. Embassy Taiwan cable 6301 to State Department, "ROC's Nuclear Intentions," September 17, 1976, both in NSA EBB 221, Docs. 7A, 7B.

[690] For the U.S. embassy's assessment, see: U.S. Embassy Taiwan cable 8654 to State Department, "U.S. Nuclear Team Visit," December 30, 1976, in NSA EBB 221, Doc. 10A.

[691] Memorandum from Burton Levin, Office of Republic of China Affairs, to Oscar Armstrong, Deputy Assistant Secretary for East Asian Affairs, "PRCLO Comment on Taiwan Nuclear Development," October 12, 1976, in NSA EBB 20, Doc. 29, p. 1.

[692] See: *FRUS*, 1969–1976, Vol. XVIII, Doc. 156.

The Carter administration maintained this effort at reducing tensions with the PRC while coercing Taiwan to stop its nuclear-weapons program. In February 1977, National Security Advisor Zbigniew Brzezinski (1977–1981) wrote to President Carter that "the ROC, in the absence of U.S. steps, will have the capacity to detonate a nuclear device in the next two to four years," adding that "the situation requires far-reaching action."[693] In March, Washington warned Taipei that "unless the ROC's nuclear program is significantly modified to eliminate all proliferation risks, we will not be able to continue cooperation on peaceful nuclear energy matters. Other important relationships between us will also suffer."[694] Two weeks later, the ROC sent an official response, accepting U.S. demands to terminate its nuclear-weapons program.[695] In May, Taiwanese officials were unusually cooperative with U.S. inspectors,[696] who confirmed the termination of the Taiwanese program.[697] Specifically, the Taipei government agreed to close down the Taiwan Research Reactor (TRR) "pending mutual agreement concerning the disposition of spent fuel, adequate safeguard measures, and an acceptable research program."[698] The following December, Washington presented to Taipei the terms under which

[693] "Memorandum from Michel Oksenberg of the National Security Council Staff to the President's Assistant for National Security Affairs (Brzezinski)," Washington, February 16, 1966, in *FRUS*, 1977–1980, Vol. XIII, Doc. 12.

[694] State Department cable 67316 to Embassy Taiwan, "Nuclear Representation to the ROC," March 26, 1977, in NSA EBB 221, Doc. 13A, p. 3. Already in September 1976, U.S. ambassador to the ROC Leonard Unger had invoked the Symington Amendment, which required Washington to terminate economic and military assistance to any country engaged in reprocessing and proliferation activity. See: NSA EBB 221, Doc. 6A, pp. 3–4. Unger now was stressing the "very stro[ng] emphasis placed by the new Carter administration on" nuclear-weapons proliferation. U.S. Embassy Taiwan cable 1354 to State Department (repeated by Department to White House), March 11, 1977, in NSA EBB 221, Doc. 11B, p. 1. For similar conversations in January and February 1977, see: U.S. Embassy Taiwan cable 332 to State Department, "US Nuclear Team Visit to ROC – Calls," January 19, 1977, in NSA EBB 221, Doc. 10E, p. 2; and *FRUS*, 1977–1980, Vol. XIII, Doc. 11.

[695] See: "Editorial Note," in *FRUS*, 1977–1980, Vol. XIII, Doc. 23.

[696] See: U.S. Embassy Taiwan cable 3158 to State Department, "U.S. Technical Team Visit," May 31, 1977, in NSA EBB 221, Doc. 16A, p. 2.

[697] See: "Proposed Talking Points for Joe Hayes Briefing of the NRC on the ROC Nuclear Program," with "Talking Points" Attached, n.d. [circa September 1978], in NSA EBB 221, Doc. 22, p. 6.

[698] State Department telegram 305274 to U.S. Embassy Taipei, "The Taiwan Research Reactor," December 22, 1977, in National Security Archive

it would allow restarting the TRR, including a provision for shipment of "all spent fuel" to a site of its choosing and the continuation of "unlimited access [by U.S. inspectors] to all ROC nuclear facilities on a continuing basis."[699]

Managing Taipei's Remaining Willingness to Build the Bomb

This coercive U.S. approach to deny Taiwan the opportunity to proliferate did not eliminate Taipei's willingness to acquire a nuclear arsenal, however. In June 1977, a State Department cable cautioned that the "underlying security fears of the ROC ... will continue to exist as our own role and policies in Asia develop and change, and our 'protection' becomes increasingly less credible."[700] Then, in the summer of 1978, while meeting with Taiwanese scientists, U.S. scientists uncovered work in laser uranium enrichment technology, with considerable proliferation potential. This led Secretary of State Cyrus Vance to send a threatening letter to President Chiang, warning him that such research "has raised the most serious doubts within the U.S. government as to whether it could continue nuclear exports to the ROC."[701] In September 1978, a cable from the Embassy in Taipei continued to warn that "[g]iven the ROC's strategic/political vulnerability, the temptations to examine the possibility of acquiring a nuclear weapons capacity have to be assumed."[702]

Taiwan's vulnerabilities in fact increased as Washington completed the normalization process with the PRC. On December 15, 1978, Carter announced that the United States would normalize relations with the PRC beginning in the new year.[703] On December 23, he

(NSA) Electronic Briefing Book (EBB) 541, "Nuclear Weapons on Okinawa Declassified December 2015," Doc. 2A, p. 1.

[699] Ibid.

[700] U.S. Embassy Taiwan cable 3310 to State Department, "U.S. Technical Team Visit," June 6, 1977, in NSA EBB 221, Doc. 16B, p. 3.

[701] State Department telegram 225046 to U.S. Embassy Taipei, "Follow-Up to Nuclear Team Visit: Demarche to President Chiang," September 5, 1978, in NSA EBB 541, Doc. 2B, p. 2.

[702] U.S. Embassy Taiwan cable 6351 to State Department, "Proposed Assignment of U.S. Nuclear Scientists to ROC," September 18, 1978, in NSA EBB 221, Doc. 21E, p. 2.

[703] See: Wang (2008, 414); "Backchannel Message from Secretary of State Vance and the President's Assistant for National Security Affairs (Brzezinski) to the Ambassador to the Republic of China (Unger)," in *FRUS*, 1977–1980, Vol. XIII, Doc. 171.

announced the termination of the Mutual Defense Treaty, effective on January 1, 1980.[704] Remarkably, Chiang Ching-kuo was notified of Carter's decision to normalize relations with the PRC only seven hours before the president's public address. To no one's surprise, the Taiwanese president reportedly took the news "very badly and predicted the gravest consequences."[705]

U.S. support for Taiwan now consisted solely of sales of conventional weapons; and even this issue was a matter of debate between Washington and Beijing.[706] In April 1979, Congress passed the Taiwan Relations Act, whereby the United States pledged "to provide Taiwan with arms of a defensive character" and to "maintain the capacity of the United States to resist any resort to force or other forms of coercion that would jeopardize the security" of Taiwan.[707] The Act, however, remained quite vague about Washington's response to an attack on Taiwan.[708] PRC leaders, for their part, opposed continued U.S. arms sales to Taiwan.

President Ronald Reagan came to office in early 1981 intent on offering greater support for Taiwan and adopting a stronger stance against the PRC.[709] In particular, Reagan wished to link a reduction in arms sales to Taiwan with a commitment by the PRC to the peaceful resolution of the conflict. Yet, PRC leaders rejected this quid pro quo, as they had consistently done until then, claiming that this was a question of national sovereignty, reunification being a domestic matter. In the Arms Sales Communiqué of August 1982, Washington further decreased its support for Taiwan, reaffirming its commitment to a "one China" policy, its desire not to infringe on Chinese sovereignty,

---

[704] See: "Telegram from the Department of State to the Embassy in the Republic of China," Washington, December 23, 1978, in *FRUS*, 1977–1980, Vol. XIII, Doc. 180.

[705] "Backchannel Message from the Ambassador to the Republic of China (Unger) to Secretary of State Vance and the President's Assistant for National Security Affairs (Brzezinski)," Taipei, December 15, 1978, in *FRUS*, 1977–1980, Vol. XIII, Doc. 173.

[706] Negotiations for the normalization of U.S.-PRC relations almost fell apart on this issue in December 1978. PRC leaders claimed that Washington had agreed to end all future arms sales to Taiwan; U.S. negotiators claimed that they had simply agreed to a one-year moratorium, while the Mutual Defense Treaty lapsed. See: Romberg (2003, 76–101); Tucker (2009, 101–107).

[707] "Editorial Note," in *FRUS*, 1977–1980, Vol. XIII, Doc. 235.

[708] See: Wang (2008, 409).

[709] See: Romberg (2003, 118–150); Tucker (2009, 127–168).

and its intention "to reduce gradually its sales of arms to Taiwan, leading over a period of time to a final resolution."[710]

Squelching Taiwan's Brief 1980s Reawakening

News of a reactivated Taiwanese nuclear-weapons program came in December 1987, when the deputy director of the INER, working as a spy for the CIA, defected to the United States. The official provided evidence of Taiwan's attempt to build a hot cell facility, which could be used for plutonium extraction, and of Taiwanese efforts to develop a nuclear bomb.[711] In response, President Reagan sent a letter to Chiang Ching-kuo that, in effect, said "we know what you're doing and, if you value the defense relationship, you've got to stop it."[712] In February 1988, the ROC agreed to dismantle the facility, close down its largest civilian research reactor, and allow further IAEA inspections.[713]

Since that date, there has been little reported activity that could be imputed to a Taiwanese nuclear-weapons program. In 1995–1996, after the Taiwanese president Lee Teng-hui (1988–2000) was allowed to deliver a highly visible speech at Cornell University during which he defended the Taiwanese democracy as a "model" for China, the ROC and the PRC came again to the brink of war.[714] Yet, even under those circumstances, Lee pledged that Taiwan would not pursue nuclear weapons.[715]

In sum, Taiwan initiated a nuclear program because of concerns about the reliability of U.S. security guarantees in the face of a security threat posed by the PRC, and terminated its program as a result

---

[710] For the text of the Arms Sales Communiqué, see: Romberg (2003, 242–244). For Reagan's private message to the Taiwanese leadership, i.e., the "Six Assurances," see: ibid., 134–137. See also: Tucker (2009, 148–152). For Reagan's public statement of conditionality to Republican party candidates in October 1982, and the PRC's rejection of such conditionality, see: Hearings before the Subcommittee on Separation of Powers of the Committee on the Judiciary, United States Senate, Ninety-Seventh Congress, Second Session, on Taiwan Communiqué and Separation of Powers, September 17 and 27, 1982 (U.S. Government Printing Office: Washington, 1983), 123–124.

[711] See: Mitchell (2004, 300); Richelson (2006, 367–368).

[712] Then deputy national security advisor John Negroponte, quoted in Kogan (2013b, 42).

[713] See: Albright and Gay (1998, 59); Richelson (2006, 368).

[714] For a good account of the crisis, see: Tucker (2009, 213–230).

[715] See: Christie Su, "President Says No to Nuclear Arms," *The Free China Journal*, August 4, 1995, vol. 12, No. 29, p. 1.

of U.S. coercive measures. Given the severity of the security threat from the PRC, which still maintains the stated goal of reuniting with Taiwan,[716] U.S. assurances needed to be extensive in order to satiate the ROC's willingness to acquire nuclear weapons. Alas for Taipei, Washington was keen on improving relations with the PRC, which strenuously opposed Taiwanese nuclearization. Moreover, Washington feared entrapment, and wanted to impress upon Taipei that the alliance would not offer the opportunity to proliferate. Taiwan was left with little choice. As an NSC memorandum put it in February 1971, the United States is "largely responsible for the very existence" of the ROC.[717] Taiwanese officials themselves understood the severity of their predicament. In February 1977, ROC vice minister Frederick Chien (1975–1979) agreed with Ambassador Unger that any decision to move toward nuclear weapons would be "suicidal."[718]

Alternative Explanations

There is general agreement that Taiwan initiated a nuclear program because, faced with a threatening PRC, Taipei had concerns about the reliability of U.S. security guarantees.[719] Furthermore, most analysts agree that the alliance with the United States played an important role in Taiwan's nuclear forbearance. The precise mechanism through which the alliance mattered is a subject of debate, however.[720]

One plausible alternative explanation for the fact that Taiwan remained nonnuclear is that U.S. arms sales essentially satiated Taiwan's interest in nuclear weapons.[721] U.S. policymakers themselves presented such an argument to PRC leaders when justifying their policy. In September 1978, President Carter explained that U.S. arms sales to Taiwan would continue after the normalization of

[716] See: Myers and Zhang (2006, 112).
[717] "Draft Response to National Security Council Study Memorandum 106," Washington, February 16, 1971, in *FRUS, 1969–1976*, Vol. XVII, Doc. 105.
[718] "Telegram from the Embassy in the Republic of China to the Department of State," Taipei, February 16, 1977, in *FRUS, 1977–1980*, Vol. XIII, Doc. 11.
[719] See: Dunn (1982); Frankel (1993); Albright and Gay (1998); Solingen (1994; 2007).
[720] See: Dunn (1982); Albright and Gay (1998); Levite (2002–2003); Mitchell (2004); Hersman and Peters (2006).
[721] For an argument about the nonproliferation effect of arms sales, see: Lin (2012).

relations between the United States and the PRC. "I would hate to see Taiwan turn to other sources or even to develop dangerous weapons that would be threatening to you," Carter told PRC diplomat Ch'ai Tse-min, adding: "As you know, the people of Taiwan have the scientific development of atomic weapons, and we feel some relations with us are important to prevent this dangerous development."[722]

Yet, there are good reasons to be skeptical of such arguments. Continued U.S. arms sales to Taiwan were driven by two other motives unrelated to Washington's desire to deter Taipei's nuclearization. To begin with, the United States had an interest in boosting the viability of the ROC in order to keep the PRC contained within the first island chain. Arms sales held the promise of achieving this goal while minimizing Washington's risk of entrapment as well as Beijing's opposition. Additionally, arms sales were driven by domestic political considerations in the United States. U.S. leaders repeatedly referred to "political realities" in domestic politics as the source of "difficult issues" in the normalization process.[723] Accordingly, PRC leaders rejected Washington's claim about the nonproliferation benefit of arms sales. In December 1978, PRC representative Han Nien-lung told Leonard Woodcock, Chief of the Liaison Office in China (1977–1979):

[a]s regards the U.S. assertion that such a move [arms sales] is meant to prevent the Chiang clique from obtaining nuclear weapons, we must point out first that the U.S. side should stand by its own promise and refrain from letting the Chiang clique make or acquire such weapons.[724]

In other words, PRC officials understood that U.S. success in preventing Taiwanese nuclearization required Washington to implement a coercive sticks-based nonproliferation approach.

Indeed, a global analysis of U.S.-ROC relations suggests that security assurances and conventional arms sales – all part of a carrots-based

---

[722] "Memorandum of Conversation," Washington, September 19, 1978, 11:35 a.m.–12:12 p.m., in *FRUS*, 1977–1980, Vol. XIII, Doc. 135.

[723] Ibid. See also Nixon's statements, quoted in the preceding text, in Memorandum of Conversation, Tuesday, February 22, 1972, 2:10 p.m.–6:00 p.m., in NSA EBB 106, Doc. 1, pp. 6–7.

[724] "Backchannel Message from the Chief of the Liaison Office in China (Woodcock) to Secretary of State Vance and the President's Assistant for National Security Affairs (Brzezinski)," Beijing, December 4, 1978, in *FRUS*, 1977–1980, Vol. XIII, Doc. 159.

approach to nonproliferation – did not ensure Taiwan's nonnuclear status. U.S. commitments to Taiwan, as we saw, declined since the beginning of the U.S. rapprochement with the PRC. Taiwanese leaders were concerned about U.S. assurances, demanded advanced U.S. weapons to counter the quantitative advantage of the PRC,[725] and, even though they obtained them, *nevertheless maintained their program until the late 1980s*. At that point, even President Reagan, avowedly a friend of Taiwan, decided to coerce the island into remaining nonnuclear.

Even among the scholars who point to the role of coercion, there is disagreement about the causes of this nonproliferation success. To begin with, Etel Solingen concedes that Washington "weighed heavily" in Taiwan's decision to renounce nuclear weapons. Still, because U.S. efforts have failed to induce other countries to renounce nuclear weapons, Solingen claims that "[s]uch variability in responses to U.S. coercion compels us to delve into domestic factors that might have influenced Taiwan's choice to comply where others stood firm."[726] In her view, Taiwan renounced the nuclear option because of the preferences of its ruling coalition. Despite their interest in nuclear weapons, Taiwanese leaders overall put a higher priority on export-oriented growth, and this required the country to maintain good relations with its U.S. ally.

The fact that Taiwanese leaders were susceptible to U.S. pressure, while leaders in some other countries were not, does not require an explanation based on domestic political factors. True, such an approach can bring fresh insights on the causes of nuclear forbearance, and a complete account of the case would necessarily include a broader description of the preferences of Taiwanese elites. Nevertheless, Taiwan's nuclear forbearance can be accounted for solely on the basis of its security environment, which included a much stronger adversary, the PRC, and an ally, the United States, which although lukewarm in its commitments was the only available security sponsor that could give the ROC a chance of surviving. U.S. officials were mindful of Taiwan's dependence. During the Second Taiwan Strait Crisis in 1958, Secretary Dulles noted: "It is today widely assumed that the

---

[725] See the statement of the representative of Taiwan's Defense Ministry in September 1981, quoted in Tucker (2009, 141).

[726] Solingen (2007, 104). See also: Solingen (1994).

GRC has only a limited life expectancy."[727] U.S. assistant secretary of state Walter Robertson (1953–1959) told ROC ambassador George Yeh (1958–1961) at the time that Taiwan "must work with us. It will be ten times harder for [the] Republic of China [to] maintain its position if it loses United States support."[728] This strategic context, and the dire PRC threat, is sufficient to explain the effectiveness of U.S. coercive measures.

Another alternative approach to account for the U.S. coercive success would be to focus on domestic political considerations in the United States. Nicholas Miller argues that since the late 1970s, congressional legislation has made the threat of U.S. sanctions credible, ultimately leading a state like Taiwan to stop its nuclear-weapons program.[729] According to him, the only states that initiated programs after 1976 are inward-looking states, against which the threat of sanctions is ineffective. In Miller's account, U.S. policymakers estimated that Taiwan was pursuing nuclear weapons in 1972. Yet, until 1976 they did not propose sanctions, instead focusing on limiting the supply of nuclear materials. The threat of U.S. sanctions then succeeded in August 1977, when nonproliferation congressional legislation (which had been passed in June 1976) came into effect. In Miller's words, though evidence of uranium enrichment and plutonium reprocessing resurfaced in 1978 and 1987–1988, "there is no indication that Taiwan ever made the political decision to pursue nuclear weapons again post-1977."[730] In this view, the threat of renewed sanctions ensured Taiwan's nonnuclear status.

While enlightening, this argument is not without problems. First, congressional legislation was not the only relevant development of the mid-1970s. This was also the period during which the Taiwanese nuclear-weapons program accelerated due to the Nixon Doctrine and the Sino-American rapprochement. Contrary to Miller's claims, it was only in 1974 that U.S. intelligence definitively concluded that the Taiwanese were pursuing a military nuclear

---

[727] "Talking Paper Prepared by Secretary of State Dulles," Taipei, October 21, 1958, in *FRUS*, 1958–1960, Vol. XIX, Doc. 196.

[728] "Telegram from the Department of State to the Embassy in the Republic of China," Washington, September 21, 1958, 3:32 p.m., in *FRUS*, 1958–1960, Vol. XIX, Doc. 116.

[729] See: Miller (2014).

[730] Ibid., 933.

option.[731] U.S. officials obtained assurances from the Taiwanese leadership about the peaceful nature of the program, and when there was mounting evidence that the ROC did not live up to its commitment, a coercive approach became necessary. The State Department memo that made the case for a formal démarche with the ROC asserted: "Our most compelling reason for approaching the ROC at this stage is conclusive evidence that it is continuing its clandestine efforts to acquire reprocessing technology and equipment from Comprimo [a Dutch firm] notwithstanding your May 27 approach to the premier."[732] So it was at this time that U.S. coercive pressure became necessary for nonproliferation. It is not the case, therefore, that U.S. officials were consistently applying pressure on Taiwan since an earlier period and that pressure had failed in the absence of congressional legislation supporting it.

Second, the analytic decision to treat congressional legislation as an independent nonproliferation force is questionable. Given that the Taiwanese program accelerated in the 1970s, there were good strategic reasons for Congress to step up its nonproliferation role alongside the executive branch. U.S. politicians had an interest in avoiding entrapment and bolstering the nonproliferation regime, given mounting concerns about U.S. allies inching closer to the bomb. Rather than an independent nonproliferation force, congressional legislation was largely shaped by the same strategic reasons that compelled the executive branch to increase its nonproliferation pressure on Taiwan.

---

[731] The earlier CIA estimate, on which Miller relies, was somewhat careful in its conclusion. In its view, Taiwan had a "serious interest" in military options, but rather than having a definitive plan for military applications, it may instead seek to "keep its weapons option open." NSA EBB 221, Doc. 1A, pp. 2, 4–5. In April 1973, the U.S. Bureau of Intelligence and Research (INR) still doubted the presence of a nuclear-weapons program. "The Republic of China's intentions regarding the development of nuclear weapons have been far from clear." At this point, the analysts were "inclined to believe that no organized program for the production of nuclear weapons has been authorized or initiated by the ROC." State Department Memorandum Conversation, "ROC Nuclear Intentions," April 5, 1973, with Intelligence and Research (INR) Report on "Nuclear Weapons Intentions of the Republic of China" attached, pp. 1–2. The assessment of Taiwan's nuclear intentions was more definitive in the study by the director of central intelligence in the fall of 1974, quoted in the preceding text.

[732] NSA EBB 221, Doc. 6A, p. 2.

Third, the effectiveness of U.S. pressure in the late 1970s and early 1980s varied across cases, even when congressional legislation supporting sanctions was in place. While the United States pursued its nonproliferation goals aggressively in the case of Taiwan, the executive in Washington opted for applying only mild nonproliferation pressure on Pakistan and turned a blind eye to Islamabad's nuclear development, *despite existing Congressional legislation* – the Pressler Amendment – ultimately tolerating its nuclear acquisition in 1990.[733] Thus, congressional legislation, domestic political preferences, and intra-U.S. government dynamics, more broadly, are neither necessary *nor sufficient* to explain variations in the effectiveness of U.S. nonproliferation efforts.

Finally, it is not entirely clear that U.S. nonproliferation efforts vis-à-vis Taiwan "succeeded" in 1977. After all, the Taiwanese were still researching enrichment technology in 1978.[734] Furthermore, Taipei's nuclear-weapons program reemerged in 1987, when Chiang Ching-kuo authorized the construction of a hot cell facility that posed proliferation risks.[735]

To understand both Taiwan's interest in nuclear weapons and the success of U.S. nonproliferation tools, we need to look at the overall strategic interaction between the United States, Taiwan, and the PRC. Taiwan was a weak state with an unreliable ally. Therefore, its interest in nuclear weapons was strong. At the same time, this weakness meant that the United States could effectively prevent Taiwan from acquiring nuclear weapons with the threat to cut ties. This is why, to this day, Taiwan remains nonnuclear.

A third alternative account of Taiwanese nuclear forbearance attributes the effectiveness of U.S. nonproliferation pressures to the format of their alliance. As Victor Cha has argued, bilateral agreements allow the United States to have greater control over an ally, reducing its risk of entrapment.[736] Extending Cha's argument, one could say that the United States succeeded in preventing proliferation in Taiwan because the bilateral format of their alliance boosted the credibility of Washington's coercive threats of abandonment if the ROC continued its nuclear development.

---

[733] See our case study of Pakistan in this chapter.
[734] See: NSA EBB 541, Doc. 2B.
[735] See: Richelson (2006, 367).
[736] See: Cha (2009–2010).

We agree that bilateral alliances allow Washington to better tailor its foreign policy toward each of its protégés. Yet, the United States adopted different nonproliferation strategies with other allies in the region, notably South Korea and Japan, with whom it also had bilateral agreements.[737] To understand this variation in U.S. nonproliferation strategy, we need to understand the differences in the strategic environments faced by these different U.S. allies. Taiwan was considerably weaker vis-à-vis its adversary, the PRC, than either South Korea or Japan were vis-à-vis theirs. This meant that the United States would have to make deeper security commitments to take away the ROC's willingness to proliferate. Unwilling to extend these commitments and fearing entrapment in a PRC-ROC conflict, Washington opted for implementing a nonproliferation strategy aimed at removing Taipei's opportunity to nuclearize. This strategy ultimately proved effective because Taiwan's relative weakness left it vulnerable to Washington's threats of abandonment, even when the level of protection offered by the United States was relatively low.

Finally, in a related alternative account, Eugene Kogan argues that the basis of U.S. success was "coercion by technology denial" – i.e., the threat of sanctioning nuclear technological supply, not the threat of security abandonment, which he labels "punishment."[738] In support of this view, Kogan shows how the Taiwanese "apparently never stopped seeking a capability to separate weapons-grade plutonium, calling into question the efficacy of the coercion by punishment threats [i.e., abandonment] the U.S. had made over the years."[739] Although we agree that Taiwanese nuclear forbearance was the result of U.S. nonproliferation efforts, we think that Kogan's argument is based on a false dichotomy between technological denial and security abandonment as nonproliferation strategies. U.S. coercive tools were inextricably linked, and U.S. measures to deny nuclear technology to Taiwan were effective precisely *because they came from Taiwan's sole security*

---

[737] In Taiwan, the United States significantly reduced its commitments in the 1960s and 1970s. Since then, U.S. commitments amount to a vague security guarantee and arms sales. In South Korea, U.S. commitments fluctuated but remain significant. Likewise, the United States still possesses a sizable military presence in Japan. See our case studies of South Korea and Japan in Chapter 6.

[738] See: Kogan (2013b).

[739] Ibid., 26.

sponsor.[740] Put differently, the real dichotomy is not between different coercive tools to remove Taiwan's opportunity to nuclearize, but between approaches aimed at removing either the opportunity (sticks) or the willingness (carrots) to proliferate. Taiwan was a weak state, with potentially great willingness to proliferate. The United States was not willing to cover such security needs, concerned about the risk of entrapment in a conflict with the PRC, with which it wanted to improve its relations. Instead, Washington sought to guarantee that Taiwan would remain nonnuclear by ensuring that it did not have the opportunity to proliferate. As such, the fact that Taiwan maintained an interest in nuclear weapons is not very puzzling: the United States offered minimal security guarantees, which did not assuage Taiwan's willingness to proliferate.

More broadly, the view that Taiwan refrained from proliferating because it did not want to lose the security guarantees offered by the United States is incomplete.[741] It is implicitly based on the claim that U.S. nonproliferation efforts "took away" Taiwan's opportunity to proliferate. But Taiwan's weakness vis-à-vis the PRC meant that Taipei would not have had the opportunity to proliferate if abandoned by the United States. So it is not the case that Washington "removed" Taiwan's opportunity to acquire a nuclear weapon. Rather, the United States ensured that its security relationship did not offer Taiwan an opportunity to proliferate. This explains why Washington was successful in its nonproliferation effort vis-à-vis Taiwan even if the security guarantees it extended to Taipei were actually quite weak.

In sum, despite great willingness to acquire nuclear weapons in order to deter its far more powerful neighbor, China, Taiwan has lacked the opportunity to build the bomb. Its weakness leaves it vulnerable to Chinese preventive action, the specter of which gives Washington great incentive to deter Taiwanese proliferation. As the ROC's sole ally, and despite its limited support, Washington also has powerful coercive leverage. Were the United States to abandon Taiwan, Taipei would be left vulnerable to Chinese military force, and therefore even less able

---

[740] For evidence that Taiwan did not take U.S. threats seriously until the security relationship was at stake, see: Roger Sullivan to Assistant Secretary of State for Far East and Pacific Affairs Arthur W. Hummel Jr., "Nuclear Study Group Visit to Taiwan," October 29, 1973, in NSA EBB 221, Doc. 2B, p. 3.

[741] See: Dunn (1982, 57); Frankel (1993); Mitchell (2004, 309); Bullard and Yuan (2010, 189).

to build a nuclear deterrent. Consequently, the United States has so far been successful in applying a sticks-based nonproliferation policy, coercing Taipei to abandon its nuclear ambitions.

In order to be able to nuclearize, Taiwan would need U.S. protection against Chinese preventive action and U.S. acquiescence toward its nuclear ambitions. Given the potential that Taiwanese nuclear development would have for prompting a Chinese counterproliferation strike, these two conditions are unlikely to be present at the same time. In all likelihood, either Washington will abandon Taiwan, or it will lend it military support but coerce Taiwan into maintaining its non-nuclear status. Either way, Taiwan is likely to continue to lack the opportunity to nuclearize

Pakistan

Pakistan became a nuclear-capable state in the late 1980s and performed its first nuclear tests in 1998. Since its independence in 1947, Pakistan's foreign policy has been directed toward countering India, its stronger neighbor and adversary.[742] Given this clear threat to the country's survival, the Pakistani government possessed the willingness to develop nuclear weapons unless it could enjoy the reliable protection of a powerful ally.

Initially, Pakistan sought to meet its security needs through an alliance with the United States, which offered it security guarantees and supplied it with conventional weapons. During the 1965 and 1971 Indo-Pakistan wars, however, America's support fell far short of Pakistan's expectations, generating serious doubts about the reliability of U.S. protection. Clearly, U.S. commitments to Pakistan's security were insufficient to undermine Islamabad's willingness to nuclearize.

Starting in 1972, Pakistan pressed forward with an independent nuclear-weapons program. Washington did not always approve of Pakistan's nuclear effort, and at times attempted to hinder its progress. Fortunately for Islamabad, the 1979 Soviet invasion of neighboring Afghanistan turned Pakistan into a crucial U.S. ally. From that moment on, Washington dropped its sticks-based attempt to stymie Pakistan's nuclear effort. In exchange for Pakistani help in the Afghan

---

[742] For an overview of Indo-Pakistani relations, see: Cohen (2013).

anti-Soviet struggle of the 1980s, Washington resumed military aid and agreed to turn a blind eye toward the Pakistani nuclear-weapons program. Furthermore, Washington also played a role in deterring Indian preventive military action against the Pakistani nuclear program by sharing intelligence assessments on New Delhi's calculations with its protégé. In light of past U.S. unreliability, however, this temporary support was insufficient to represent an effective carrots-based nonproliferation effort. With U.S. support, Pakistan had the opportunity to become a nuclear state.

Pakistani Interest in Nuclear Weapons

Since it became independent, Pakistan has viewed India as its main foreign threat. In August 1947, the British Indian Empire was divided along religious lines, with the Dominion of Pakistan as the Muslim-majority state and the Union of India as the Hindu-majority state, leading to massive population transfers that entailed great bloodshed, and a death toll estimated in the hundreds of thousands. Partition left another legacy that would haunt Indo-Pakistan relations: the disputed status of the state of Kashmir. With the Indian Independence Act of 1947, princely states were given the option of joining Pakistan, India, or remaining independent. The Maharaja of Jammu and Kashmir, a Hindu ruling over a Muslim-majority state, decided to join the Union of India. Over the years, Pakistan and India have fought three wars over the control of Kashmir – in 1947, 1965, and 1999 – and the issue remains a source of great tension to this day. With each conflict, Pakistan was reminded of the power imbalance that favored its adversary. Indeed, India was a formidable threat. Compared with Pakistan, it was more than four times larger, five times more populous, and it possessed ten times as much manufacturing capability.[743] Ultimately, the intensity of conflict with India and the magnitude of this power imbalance deepened Pakistan's determination to acquire nuclear weapons.

Harnessing U.S. Support to Counter the Indian Threat
Soon after independence, Pakistan decided to address its security needs by developing an alliance with the United States. The two countries

[743] See: McGarr (2013, 18).

signed multiple security agreements, including the Mutual Security and Assistance Agreement of May 1954, SEATO in September 1954, the 1955 Baghdad Pact (later renamed CENTO), and the Pakistan-United States Bilateral Agreement of Cooperation in March 1959. Although SEATO was aimed at deterring communist aggression and did not provide for U.S. support to Pakistan in case of an attack by India, the 1959 Pact was not specifically anticommunist. Instead, the treaty pledged that "[i]n case of aggression" against Pakistan, the United States "will take such appropriate action, including the use of armed forces, as may be mutually agreed upon," so as to "assist" Pakistan "at its request."[744] Ultimately, what the United States and Pakistan could mutually agree upon would be a point of contention.

In the early period of the U.S.-Pakistani security relationship, though, U.S. security commitments appeared solid. Washington supplied Pakistan with conventional weapons, making Pakistan the largest recipient of U.S. military aid between 1954 and 1965 – a total of $1.5 billion.[745] Pakistani leaders at the time were convinced that the West "would provide Pakistan the security it needed against perceived Indian threats."[746] Such was the degree of alignment between the two countries that, by the late 1950s, Pakistan "gained the dubious distinction of being America's 'most allied ally' in Asia."[747]

Collaboration with the United States also extended to the nuclear realm. Taking advantage of President Eisenhower's Atoms for Peace program, Pakistan signed a nuclear cooperation agreement with the United States in August 1955.[748] Within a year, the Pakistani Atomic Energy Commission (PAEC) was established, and a research lab was set up in Karachi in 1957.[749] The United States also helped in the creation of the Pakistan Institute of Nuclear Science and Technology (PINSTECH): a U.S. firm built the Pakistan Atomic Research Reactor

---

[744] "U.S. Signs Agreements of Cooperation with Turkey, Iran, and Pakistan," in *Department of State Bulletin*, March 23, 1959, Vol. XL, No. 1030, pp. 416–418, quote at p. 417. See also: Bhutto (1969, 46); Sattar (2007, 46–50).

[745] See: Ibid., 59; Lin (2012, 205); McGarr (2013, 297).

[746] Ahmed (1999, 181). See also: Ahmed and Cortright (1998a, 90); Cheema (1987, 121).

[747] Hilali (2005, 37).

[748] See: Armstrong and Trento (2007, 20).

[749] See: Khan (2012, 28).

(PARR-1), to be supplied with HEU from the United States. In December 1965, PARR-1 achieved a self-sustaining reaction.[750]

Throughout the 1950s and 1960s, the Pakistani nuclear program appears to have been restricted to civilian purposes. Muhammad Ayub Khan, president of Pakistan (1958–1969), dismissed the call for a military component to the nuclear program made by his foreign minister, Zulfikar Ali Bhutto (1963–1966). Ayub Khan saw little benefit in an autonomous deterrent, and was concerned about its financial and diplomatic costs, since he foresaw that a nuclear-weapons program would have a deleterious effect on U.S.-Pakistani relations.[751] Khan therefore rejected the idea of an autonomous nuclear deterrent, due to "his confidence in the United States as a strategic ally" and his belief that "in the case of war between Pakistan and India, Washington would guarantee Islamabad's security."[752] Furthermore, in Khan's view: "If Pakistan wanted nuclear weapons, it could get them 'off the shelf' from Western allies."[753]

Such enthusiasm about American support would not endure, however. When tensions between India and China started escalating in 1959, Washington decided to increase its aid to New Delhi. As Bhutto remarked in 1969, there was "a growing sense of uneasiness" in the early 1960s "as the balance tilted each day more in India's favor."[754] U.S. officials understood Islamabad's concerns and tried to reassure Pakistani leaders. Secretary of Defense Robert McNamara acknowledged "that military assistance to India had 'deeply troubled' Pakistan but felt that, 'it is important to the entire free world, including Pakistan, that India be able to defend itself against Communist Chinese aggression.'"[755] The bases of this budding rift in U.S.-Pakistani relations were differences between the two partners in their interests and threat perceptions:

Despite its anticommunist orientation, Pakistan remained at heart concerned about the threat from India rather than any menace from the communists. In contrast, the United States saw the security accord as directed

[750] Ibid., 57.
[751] See: Hussain (1998, 32); Khan (2012, 63).
[752] Ahmed and Cortright (1998a, 90).
[753] Quoted in ibid., 90.
[754] Bhutto (1969, 74).
[755] Ibid., 69.

strictly against the communist threat and was wary of becoming entangled in Pakistan's dispute with India.[756]

These different interests would be brought into bold relief during the Sino-Indian war of 1962.[757] Weeks into the fighting, and despite its leadership in the NAM, India requested substantial military aid from the United States, stunning Western officials.[758] Secretly, Indian prime minister Jawaharlal Nehru also sent a request to Kennedy for a direct and immediate intervention, namely, by waging an air war against China.[759] By the time the war ended on November 21, a U.S. aircraft carrier was en route to the Bay of Bengal.[760]

Although Washington's support fell far short of India's request, the possibility of U.S. military aid to India generated outrage in Pakistan, which was displayed by public protests and Khan's threat to "cultivate closer Sino-Pakistani ties."[761] Khan urged Washington to take this opportunity to force India into a settlement on Kashmir, but Washington was reluctant to upset its budding strategic partnership with New Delhi.[762] Making matters worse, in an attempt to counter China's growing influence, Kennedy boosted aid to India for 1963–1964 to $100 million.[763]

By the time President Johnson came to office in Washington, U.S.-Pakistan relations were decidedly frayed. They would only get worse. When Bhutto visited the United States for President Kennedy's funeral, President Johnson made him wait four days before seeing him, and then proceeded to "excoriate" him "for his country's ongoing flirtations with Communist China."[764] Early the following year, Johnson approved a five-year military aid program for India and Pakistan, of $50–60 million annually for each.[765] In early 1965, President Khan visited China and the USSR in quick succession, prompting angered reactions in Washington.[766] On April 16, President Johnson unilaterally announced

---

[756] Sattar (2007, 61).
[757] See: Kux (2001, 84).
[758] See: McGarr (2013, 159, 168).
[759] Ibid., 168.
[760] See: NSA EBB 6, Doc. 7, p. 5.
[761] McGarr (2013, 160).
[762] Ibid., 174–175.
[763] See: Sattar (2007, 83).
[764] McGarr (2013, 282). See also: Ibid., 283.
[765] Ibid., 289–290.
[766] See: Sattar (2007, 83–85).

that Khan's visit to the United States, planned for later that month, would be postponed.[767]

The 1965 and 1971 Wars and the Limits of U.S. Support

The question for Pakistan was, of course, whether it could rely on Washington's support in case of a direct clash with India. The first test of U.S. intentions came with the Second Kashmir War of 1965. In August, Pakistan sent thousands of guerrilla fighters into Kashmir to incite a Muslim uprising.[768] The ensuing war lasted only seventeen days, and Washington remained neutral throughout. When India counterattacked in the Punjab in early September, Washington rejected the Pakistani governement's invocation of the two countries' mutual defense agreement, pointing out that the U.S. obligation to come to Pakistan's assistance were limited to "aggression by a communist state."[769] Pakistani officials became "fully aware of the fact that the long-nourished American equalizer was not available in a local crisis."[770] Foreign Minister Bhutto forcefully decried the lack of U.S. support, telling a U.S. envoy that Washington's posture "would mean that Pak[istani]-U.S. relations could not be the same again. ... [T]he decision [was] not an act of an ally and not even that of a neutral."[771] After the end of the war, Washington imposed an arms embargo on both countries, which fell disproportionately on Pakistan, since it was more dependent on U.S. military supplies.[772] The "American equalizer" could not be counted on in a crisis.[773] For Bhutto and other high-level Pakistani officials, the war had demonstrated the need for a nuclear deterrent.[774]

U.S.-Pakistan relations would improve once President Richard Nixon took office in January 1969. Nixon was keen on improving relations with the PRC.[775] Pakistan could help open the door in Beijing,

[767] Ibid., 85.
[768] See: Ganguly and Hagerty (2005, 30); Armstrong and Trento (2007, 27).
[769] Sattar (2007, 58). See also: McGarr (2013, 326).
[770] Thornton (1970, 352).
[771] Quoted in Kux (2001, 162).
[772] See: National Security Council Memorandum for Henry Kissinger, "Jordanian Transfer of F-104s to Pakistan," December 7, 1971, in NSA EBB 79, Doc. 29. See also: Cheema (1987, 123); Ahmed (1999, 182); McGarr (2013, 324–326).
[773] Hilali (2005, 17).
[774] See: Ganguly and Hagerty (2005, 45).
[775] See our case studies of China and Taiwan in this chapter.

and soon Islamabad agreed to Nixon's request to broker secret Sino-American talks.[776] This led to the so-called Nixon "tilt" toward Pakistan and away from India. When in March 1971 East Pakistan declared independence, the military government of President Yahya Khan in Islamabad ordered a brutal crackdown, leading millions of Bengalis to flee to India.[777] Nixon and national security advisor Henry Kissinger, leery of jeopardizing their efforts to normalize relations with China, opted for maintaining U.S. aid to Pakistan, with the president scribbling on a memorandum discussing U.S. policy options: "To all hands: Don't squeeze Yahya at this time."[778] In May, Nixon told Pakistani officials that "Yahya is a good friend." Seemingly in response to the genocide-like repression in the East, Nixon noted that he "could understand the anguish of the decisions which [Yahya] had to make," adding that the United States "would not do anything to complicate the situation for President Yahya or to embarrass him."[779] Over the next few months, the U.S. government avoided ruffling Pakistani feathers for fear of imperiling Kissinger's secret trip to China, planned for July.[780] Any pressure for the self-determination of East Pakistan could not only undermine Pakistan's willingness to play the role of intermediary between Washington and Beijing, it might also, as Kissinger suggested, "have implications for Taiwan and Tibet in Peking's eyes," making Chinese leaders ill-disposed toward the United States.[781]

The limits of Nixon's "tilt" would soon be exposed, however. When India intervened in the conflict, another Indo-Pakistan war ensued,

---

[776] See: Sattar (2007, 108).

[777] See: U.S. Consulate (Dacca) Cable, "Extent of Casualties in Dacca," March 31, 1971, in NSA EBB 79, Doc. 5. See also: Hagerty (1998, 70); Bass (2013).

[778] NSA EBB 79, Doc. 9.

[779] Memcon, "The President, M. M. Ahmad, Agha Hilaly, and Harold H. Saunders," May 10, 1971, (4:45–5:20 p.m.), in NSA EBB 79, Doc. 11. For a detailed and highly critical account of U.S. policy during this crisis, see: Bass (2013).

[780] See: Department of States, Cable, "Indo-Pakistan Situation," July 15, 1971, Memorandum for the Presidents File, "President's Meeting with Ambassador Joseph Farland," July 28, 1971, "Handwritten Letter from President Nixon to President Yahya," August 7, 1971, and "Memorandum for the Record: The President, Henry Kissinger, John Irwin, Thomas Moorer, Robert Cushman, Maurice Williams, Joseph Sisco, Armistead Seldon, and Hardold Saunders," August 11, 1971, all in NSA EBB 79, Docs. 17, 18, 20, and 21.

[781] Memorandum for the President, "Implications of the Situation in South Asia," August 18, 1971, in NSA EBB 79, Doc. 24, p. 3.

beginning December 3, 1971. The Indian Army conclusively defeated Pakistani forces in the East, leading to their surrender two weeks later. Eventually, East Pakistan seceded and became Bangladesh. The war was disastrous for Pakistan, and a painful illustration of India's conventional superiority.[782] Furthermore, Washington once again eschewed the kind of direct support that Pakistan hoped for based on the 1959 Agreement.[783] Instead, U.S. intervention consisted of the deployment of the Seventh Fleet into the Bay of Bengal, which, although traumatic for India, was perceived as merely symbolic in Islamabad. Moreover, Pakistan felt hindered in its war fighting ability by the U.S. arms embargo.[784] To make matters worse for Pakistan, in August 1971, India signed a Treaty of Friendship with the Soviet Union. As its powerful rival was now allied with a hostile superpower, Pakistan's own superpower alliance failed to bring the anticipated benefits.

All in all, the 1971 war led to growing support in Pakistan for a foreign policy reorientation away from Washington.[785] After the U.S. arms embargo of 1965, Pakistan had turned to the PRC for military assistance.[786] Now, the option for an independent nuclear deterrent gained momentum.

On December 20, 1971, three days after the end of the war, Bhutto was named president (1971–1973). Bhutto had long pressed for the development of a nuclear capability. In 1966, he had famously stated that if India makes the atomic bomb, "even if Pakistanis have to eat grass, we will make the bomb."[787] Bhutto's rationale was clear: if Pakistan is not able to acquire sufficient conventional weaponry to deter India, it must focus on developing a nuclear deterrent.[788] In the aftermath of the 1971 defeat, this logic was virtually unquestionable. As Vipin Narang puts it, "[t]he genesis of the Pakistani nuclear weapons program after the 1971 war provides deep insight into its ultimate

---

[782] See: Hilali (2005, 41).

[783] See: Sattar (2007, 50).

[784] See: Ganguly and Hagerty (2005, 35).

[785] See: Bhutto (1969, 86); Cheema (1987, 125); Ahmed and Cortright (1998b, 9, 10); Armstrong and Trento (2007, 28).

[786] See: Khan (2012, 81). It is also possible that Bhutto requested assistance from China for the development of nuclear capability when he met with Zhou Enlai in March 1965. Perkovich (2008, 62).

[787] Quoted in Ahmed (1999, 183).

[788] See: Bleek (2010a, 203–204).

aim: to avoid another massive conventional defeat at the hands of the Indians."[789]

In January 1972, Bhutto met with top officials to discuss a nuclear-weapons program. He replaced the reticent head of the PAEC and ordered his scientists to produce a bomb within the next three years.[790] The infrastructure for a nuclear-weapons program was thin. Pakistan had one reactor, the recently built Canadian Deuterium (CANDU) reactor at the Karachi Nuclear Power Plant (KANUPP).[791] Financial resources were scarce and, compounding the problem, the inflow of materials and technology from the West was limited. Yet, Bhutto was determined to obtain a nuclear deterrent. To this purpose, he gained financial assistance from Iran, Libya, and Saudi Arabia.[792] In March 1974, a Directorate of Technical Development (DTD) was set up within the PAEC to coordinate all activities for the military nuclear-weapons program.[793]

India's Smiling Buddha Nuclear Test

India's progress on the development of a nuclear capability provided an added catalyst for Pakistan's willingness to build a nuclear weapon. When New Delhi successfully conducted a nuclear test in May 1974, security concerns in Pakistan spiked. The following month, a report from the U.S. embassy in Islamabad stated that India's test "has created profound shock in Pakistan, has greatly exacerbated chronic feeling[s] of insecurity, and has led to all-out GOP [Government of Pakistan] efforts to seek urgent security guarantees and arms aid from major powers."[794] Bhutto, by then prime minister of Pakistan (1973–1977), himself reacted to the test in strong terms: "Let me make it clear that we are determined not to be intimidated by this threat. I give a solemn pledge to all our countrymen that we will never let Pakistan be a victim of nuclear blackmail."[795]

---

[789] Narang (2014, 56).
[790] See: Khan (2012, 85, 89, 91); Rabinowitz (2014, 139).
[791] See: Khan (2012, 54). KANUPP went critical in August 1971. Ibid., 55.
[792] See: Armstrong and Trento (2007, 35–36).
[793] See: Khan (2012, 177).
[794] "Telegram 5623 from the Embassy in Pakistan to the Department of State," Islamabad, June 12, 1974, in *FRUS*, 1969–1976, Vol. E-8, Doc. 167, p. 1. See also: Mission to NATO, "Assessment of Indian Nuclear Test," June 5, 1974, in NSA EBB 6, Doc. 18.
[795] Quoted in Khan (2012, 118).

The Indian test significantly increased the importance that Pakistan assigned to its nuclear program. Pakistani leaders were clear to the United States that, given the Indian threat, insufficient security commitments from Washington prompted their nuclear development. For example, in an October 1974 interview with the *New York Times*, Bhutto claimed that "[i]f we are satisfied with our security requirements in conventional armaments, ... we would not hazard our economic future and promote an economic and social upheaval by diverting vast resources for a nuclear program."[796] According to a December 1975 CIA memorandum, "Bhutto stated publicly in late 1974 that Pakistan would explode a nuclear device if denied the help it sought in strengthening its conventional military capabilities."[797] Acquiring the bomb became a national security imperative.[798]

In October 1974, Pakistan reached an agreement with France for the construction of a plutonium-reprocessing plant.[799] Later that year, Bhutto met with A. Q. Khan, a metallurgical engineer living in the Netherlands at the time, and eventually placed him in charge of an effort to produce a nuclear weapon using the uranium-enrichment method.[800] Two years later, Bhutto called for the construction of multiple test sites, in the Ras Koh area and the Kharan desert.[801] There are also some indications that Pakistan signed an agreement with China in May 1976 whereby the PRC agreed to provide Pakistan with nuclear assistance.[802] In September 1976, Pakistan started construction of a uranium-enrichment plant at Kahuta.[803]

By then, the United States was growing suspicious of a possible military component to the Pakistani nuclear program, especially given the deal with the French to supply a plutonium-reprocessing plant. Prior to Bhutto's 1975 visit to the United States, the State Department

---

[796] Bernard Weinraub, "Pakistani Presses U.S. for Arms," *The New York Times*, October 14, 1974, p. 10.
[797] Memorandum to Holders, Special National Intelligence Estimate, "Prospects for Further Proliferation of Nuclear Weapons," SNIE 4-1-74, December 18, 1975, in National Security Archive (NSA) Electronic Briefing Book (EBB) 333, "The United States and Pakistan's Quest for the Bomb," Doc. 1.
[798] See: Marwah (1981, 170); Sheikh (1994, 195); Hagerty (1998, 74); Hilali (2005, 37); Bleek (2010a, 201); Khan (2012, 126).
[799] See: Armstrong and Trento (2007, 43); Khan (2012, 131).
[800] See: Perkovich (2008, 65).
[801] See: Rabinowitz (2014, 140).
[802] See: Khan (2012, 171).
[803] See: Hussain (1998, 34–35); Armstrong and Trento (2007, 59).

warned Secretary Kissinger that "[t]he [government of Pakistan] is trying to develop an independent nuclear fuel cycle and the technical
skills that would make the nuclear explosion option feasible."[804] Why
did Washington fail to stymie Pakistan's nuclear development?

U.S. Nonproliferation Efforts

Since the beginning of the Cold War, the primary goal of U.S. foreign policy in South Asia was to counter the spread of communism.
Because of its virulent anticommunist government, Pakistan became
an attractive strategic partner.[805] Yet, the basis for this strategic alliance was fragile. India, as a populous democracy, was a more natural
partner for the United States, if it were not for the Indian leadership's
steadfast commitment to neutrality.[806] Therefore, despite its support of
Pakistan, Washington entertained the hope of maintaining good relations with India. From the beginning, the United States made clear
that its military aid to Pakistan was not intended for a conflict with
India.[807] U.S. officials understood the difficulty of maintaining good
relations with Pakistan and India at the same time. In 1962, President
Kennedy recognized that "everything we give to India adversely affects
the balance of power with Pakistan, which is a much smaller country.
So we are dealing with a very, very complicated problem, because the
hostility between them is so deep."[808]

Limited Coercive Leverage during the 1970s

The tensions inherent in pursuing friendly relations with both Pakistan
and its key adversary conditioned U.S. nonproliferation efforts. After
the 1965 Kashmir War, the United States imposed an arms embargo on
both Pakistan and India. Then, in the early 1970s, Washington gradually reduced its exports of HEU to Pakistan and, after the Indian test of
1974, cut off all nuclear assistance and pressed its allies to restrict sensitive transfers while insisting on safeguards against proliferation.[809]

---

[804] Quoted in Kux (2001, 219).
[805] See: Cheema (1987, 120, 122); Harrison (1987, 136).
[806] See: Bhutto (1969, 43). Also see: Armstrong and Trento (2007, 20).
[807] See: Bhutto (1969, 69).
[808] Kennedy (1963).
[809] See: Khan (2012, 96).

This duality of U.S. interests limited the coercive leverage that Washington possessed over Islamabad in the nuclear realm. U.S. non-proliferation efforts would be made more effective if Pakistan had more to lose by upsetting the United States. In part driven by such concerns, in early 1975 President Gerald Ford lifted the arms-sales embargo to Pakistan and India, a measure that disproportionally benefited the relatively weaker Pakistani side.[810] Still, U.S. conventional weaponry support remained quite modest. Secretary of State Kissinger recognized this when, in a State Department meeting in 1976 to discuss Pakistan's attempt to purchase a French reprocessing plant, he admitted to having "some sympathy for Bhutto in this. We are doing nothing to help him on conventional arms, we are going ahead and selling nuclear fuel to India even after they exploded a bomb and then for this little project we are coming down on him like a ton of bricks."[811]

Consequently, U.S. intelligence analysts estimated that resumption of U.S. conventional weaponry sales "may have reduced Pakistan's motivation to develop nuclear weapons, but we believe that it did not remove it."[812] In fact, Washington's intelligence community now estimated that "the Pakistanis could develop a device *as early as 1978*."[813] The administration was not alone in Washington in its attempt to stymie Pakistan's nuclear effort. Congressional legislation was also actively pursuing nonproliferation goals, conditioning U.S. actions vis-à-vis Islamabad. In 1976, the Symington Amendment was adopted, suspending most assistance to any country transferring nuclear equipment, material, or technology, unless they do so under IAEA safeguards. The following year, Congress passed the Glenn Amendment to prohibit any assistance to a country that attempts to acquire reprocessing technology or test a nuclear device.

If anything, the Carter administration, elected in part on a nonproliferation platform, decreased support for Pakistan. Invoking the Glenn Amendment, Carter cut off aid and imposed sanctions on Islamabad

---

[810] See: NSA EBB 333, Doc. 1.

[811] "Memorandum of Conversation," Washington, July 9, 1976, 4 p.m., in *FRUS, 1969–1976*, Vol. E-8, Doc. 231, p. 3. In a remarkably candid comment betraying the unreliability of U.S. support for Pakistan, Kissinger added: "There is no question that we can break Pakistan's back because they have made the mistake of allying themselves with us." Ibid., p. 11.

[812] NSA EBB 333, Doc. 1, p. 8.

[813] Ibid., emphasis in the original.

in September 1977.[814] The following month, a Department of State memo described U.S. leverage in Islamabad as "distinctly limited."[815] In 1978, the United States passed the NNPA, restricting the transfer of civilian nuclear technology to nonnuclear-weapon states and threatening sanctions against any country seeking to obtain unsafeguarded technology. At this time, a CIA "Pakistan Nuclear Study" made clear the vast commitments to Pakistan's security that the United States would have to make in order to remove the country's willingness to build the bomb: "On various occasions Pakistanis have stated that an Indian nuclear advantage could be offset by stronger conventional forces. ... Pakistan has drawn up an extensive shopping list, but even if it were able to obtain most of these items, they would be insufficient to alter the military balance in Pakistan's favor."[816] It was clear that short of a robust and reliable security guarantee similar to that given to U.S. NATO allies – which Washington was unwilling to extend – Pakistan would maintain its willingness to build a nuclear bomb.

Bhutto was unseated as president in a coup in July 1977 by General Mohammed Zia ul-Haq (1977–1988) and executed two years later.[817] Yet, Pakistani interest in nuclear weapons did not abate. In June 1978, the PAEC succeeded in separating Uranium-235 from Uranium-238.[818] Early the following year, U.S. deputy secretary of state Warren Christopher visited Pakistan to obtain assurances that the Pakistani program remained peaceful. Zia vowed that the program was peaceful but rejected safeguards and did not rule out the possibility of "peaceful nuclear tests."[819] The following month, the United States imposed additional sanctions on Pakistan, invoking the Symington Amendment.[820] U.S. sanctions did not remove Pakistani interest in nuclear weapons,

---

[814] See: Hussain (1998, 34); Ahmed (1999, 186); Rabinowitz (2014, 141).

[815] Alfred L. Atherton and George S. Vest thru: Mr. Christopher, Mr. Habib, Mrs. Benson, to the Secretary, "The Nuclear Reprocessing Issue with Pakistan and France: Whether to Resume Aid to Pakistan," October 18, 1977, in NSA EBB 333, Doc. 4, p. 6.

[816] Central Intelligence Agency, "Pakistan Nuclear Study," April 26, 1978, in NSA EBB 333, Doc. 5, pp. 8–9.

[817] Bhutto accused the United States of threatening to replace him because of his commitment to an independent nuclear deterrent. Ahmed (1999, 185).

[818] See: Khan (2012, 155).

[819] Ibid., 209.

[820] See: Ahmed (1999, 186); Armstrong and Trento (2007, 80); Khan (2012, 209).

however. In July 1979, Zia declared: "We shall eat crumbs but we will not allow our national interest to be compromised."[821] By September 1979, concerns about a Pakistani nuclear test were particularly high in Washington.[822]

Through the late 1970s, Washington was at best lukewarm toward Islamabad. In order for Pakistan to drop its nuclear ambitions, the United States would need "to rebuild our relationship to a point where the Pakistanis will perceive it to be disadvantageous to their national interests to risk a severance of the US tie by pursuing a nuclear explosive option."[823] Absent a higher level of support, U.S. nonproliferation efforts were ineffective. As U.S. ambassador to Pakistan Arthur W. Hummel Jr. (1977–1981) concluded in a cable to Washington:

We lack the leverage to force Pakistan out of the nuclear business. Conventional carrots of the magnitude we can muster are insufficient to induce Pakistan to forego what it sees (erroneously in our view) as its only option to achieve security against an Indian threat.[824]

Washington's leverage over Islamabad was so limited that in 1979 Pakistan refused U.S. inspections of its nuclear facilities,[825] despite unambiguous threats that U.S. aid would be suspended.[826] At that time, the United States estimated that Pakistan would take "at least 3–5 years to produce a device."[827] In sum, given the serious security threat posed by India and the lack of reliable U.S. security guarantees, Pakistan had the willingness to build a nuclear weapon and was

[821] Quoted in Armstrong and Trento (2007, 85).
[822] See: Rabinowitz (2014, 143).
[823] Harold Saunders and Anthony Lake through Mr. Newsom and Mrs. Benson to the Secretary, "PRC Meeting, November 30, 1978 – Pakistan," in NSA EBB 333, Doc. 20, p. 4.
[824] U.S. Embassy Islamabad cable 2655 to State Department, "Pakistan's Nuclear Program: Hard Choices," March 5, 1979, in NSA EBB 333, Doc. 27, p. 3.
[825] See: U.S. Embassy Islamabad cable 2413 to State Department, "Pakistan Nuclear Program: Technical Team Visit," February 27, 1979, in NSA EBB 333, Doc. 25.
[826] See: U.S. Embassy Islamabad cable 2769 to State Department, "Nuclear Aspects of DepSec Visit Discussed with UK and French Ambassadors," March 7, 1979, in NSA EBB 333, Doc. 26A, p. 2.
[827] Department of State cable 22212 to Embassy New Delhi, "Ad Hoc Scientific Committee and Related Topics," January 27, 1979, in NSA EBB 333, Doc. 24, p. 2.

getting closer to that goal. At the same time, given Pakistan's weakness vis-à-vis India, the country might lack the opportunity to cross the nuclear threshold.

Turning a Blind Eye in the 1980s

Fortunately for Pakistan, Washington would soon have a good reason to bolster its relationship with Islamabad, opening a window of opportunity for Pakistan's nuclearization: the Soviet invasion of Afghanistan in December 1979. Pakistan now became a crucial U.S. ally in the region, especially given the fall of the shah in Iran earlier that year and his replacement with a government hostile to the United States.[828] The Carter administration, which until then championed nonproliferation, would soon begin to prioritize other foreign policy goals, quickly preparing legislation to resume military assistance to Pakistan.[829] National security advisor Zbigniew Brzezinski hoped that Pakistan could help turn Afghanistan into a "Soviet Vietnam."[830] In his January 4, 1980 speech on Afghanistan, President Carter also announced his intention to provide economic and military assistance to Pakistan.[831] Days later, Secretary of Defense Harold Brown (1977–1981), meeting with Chinese leader Deng Xiaoping in Beijing, made clear the change in U.S. priorities: "Our big problem with Pakistan was their attempts to get a nuclear program. Although we still object to their doing so, we will now set that aside for the time being and concentrate on strengthening Pakistan against potential Soviet action."[832] The United States was determined to provide equipment and aid to the mujahideen in order to thwart Soviet plans in Afghanistan – a goal that, according to Brzezinski, "will require a review of our policy toward Pakistan, more guarantees to it, more arms aid, and, alas, a decision that our security policy toward Pakistan cannot be dictated by our nonproliferation

---

[828] See: Hilali (2005, 18).
[829] See: Subramaniam (1987, 143).
[830] Armstrong and Trento (2007, 186).
[831] See: Jimmy Carter, "Speech on Afghanistan," January 4, 1980, Miller Center, University of Virginia. Available at: http://millercenter.org/president/carter/speeches/speech-3403. Last accessed: May 1, 2016. See also: Hilali (2005, 68).
[832] Secretary of Defense Harold Brown to Ambassador-at-Large Gerard C. Smith, January 31, 1980, enclosing excerpts from memoranda of conversations with Geng Biao and Deng Xiaoping, January 7 and 8, 1980, in NSA EBB 377, Doc. 3, p. 3.

policy."[833] This shift in U.S. priorities would prove crucial for Pakistan's opportunity to nuclearize.

The Reagan administration proceeded in the same vein. Aware that Islamabad's view of U.S.-Pakistan relations "is replete with instances of American failure, lack of will, and anti-Pakistani biases," and that suspicions about the reliability of U.S. support "continue to be a major factor in Pakistani perceptions of US aid," Reagan substantially increased U.S. aid.[834] From Washington's perspective, the rationale for doing this was "to give Pakistan confidence in our commitment to its security and provide us reciprocal benefits in terms of our regional interests," namely, opposition to the Soviet intervention in Afghanistan.[835] In April 1981, Reagan and Zia came to an agreement for a vast package of military assistance: $3.2 billion total for the period from 1982 to 1987.[836] Before the year ended, the U.S. Congress allowed the president to waive the Symington Amendment when dealing with Pakistan.[837] By 1982, Pakistan was already the fourth largest recipient of U.S. aid.[838] In return for military assistance, and for U.S. support in fighting the Soviets in Afghanistan, Pakistan pledged not to conduct a nuclear test.[839] Washington implicitly agreed with its nuclearization as long as it was not made public.

Pakistan took this opportunity to speed up its nuclear development. Between 1980 and 1998, when it eventually conducted its first nuclear test, Islamabad spent approximately $1 billion on the PAEC.[840] In March 1983, Pakistan conducted a first cold test – i.e., a test that does not produce a nuclear yield.[841]

U.S. officials were well aware of renewed Pakistani efforts to develop the bomb. In June 1983, a State Department memo concluded

---

[833] Quoted in Armstrong and Trento (2007, 90–91).
[834] Bureau of Intelligence and Research, U.S. Department of State, "Pakistan and the US: Seeking Ways to Improve Relations," March 23, 1981, in NSA EBB 377, Doc. 4, p. 3.
[835] Memorandum from Assistant Secretary-Designate Nicholas Veliotes to Deputy Secretary of State William Clark, March 7, 1981, quoted in Kux (2001, 257). See also: Narang (2014, 72).
[836] See: Khan (2012, 214); Rabinowitz (2014, 145–148).
[837] See: Hagerty (1998, 80); Ganguly and Hagerty (2005, 52).
[838] See: Kux (2001, 266).
[839] See: Rabinowitz (2014, 7–8).
[840] See: Mian (1998, 50).
[841] See: Khan (2012, 189).

Loose Allies and Proliferation

that there was "unambiguous evidence that Pakistan was actively pursuing a nuclear weapons program," with assistance from the PRC.[842] Yet, the U.S. administration placed a higher priority on fighting the Soviets and "Washington turned the pressure off."[843] As Secretary of State George Shultz (1982–1989) remarked to President Reagan: "We must remember that without Zia's support, the Afghan resistance, key to making the Soviets pay a heavy price for their Afghan adventure, is effectively dead."[844] When Zia visited Washington in December 1982, Reagan laid out a series of red lines in nuclear development that might jeopardize U.S. aid.[845] These red lines, however, when combined with lax enforcement on Washington's part, allowed Pakistan ample space for moving down the pathway toward nuclear acquisition. Throughout the following years, facing mounting evidence that Pakistan was "pursuing both the reprocessing and uranium enrichment routes," U.S. officials would issue repeated warnings, but ultimately accept Zia's denial of any military ambitions in the nuclear realm, and take no punitive action.[846]

As Pakistan progressed toward nuclear acquisition, Washington was increasingly forced to choose which foreign policy goals to prioritize when dealing with Islamabad. As an NSC memo prepared during the process of drafting a letter from President Reagan to President Zia put it in August 1984:

Recent progress in Pakistan's uranium enrichment program may, however, soon create a situation in which we could not rule out the possibility that Pakistan was taking all of the steps required to assemble a nuclear device, or even to stockpile nuclear weapons. We would then confront a stark choice

---

[842] State Department Briefing Paper, "The Pakistani Nuclear Program," June 23, 1983, in NSA EBB 6, Doc. 22, p. 1.

[843] Sattar (2007, 160).

[844] Quoted in Armstrong and Trento (2007, 116).

[845] See: Arnold Kanter, Acting Assistant Secretary of State for Politico-Military Affairs, and Richard Murphy, Assistant Secretary of State for Near East and South Asian Affairs, to Under Secretary of State for Political Affairs Michael Armacost, "Memo on Pakistan Nuclear Issue for the NSC," August 24, 1984, with enclosure, "Responding to Pakistan's Continuing Efforts to Acquire Nuclear Explosives," in National Security Archive (NSA) Electronic Briefing Book (EBB) 531, "The United States and the Pakistani Bomb, 1984–1985: President Reagan, General Zia, Nazir Ahmed Vaid, and Seymour Hersh," Doc. 4, p. 2.

[846] NSA EBB 6, Doc. 22, p. 1. See also: NSA EBB 531, Doc. 4, enclosure, p. 2.

between (1) acquiescing in Pakistan's nuclear activities and thus incurring almost certain Congressional action against our security assistance to Pakistan, the possibility of an Indian preventive strike against the Pakistani nuclear facilities, and seriously undermining the credibility of our global non-proliferation policy or (2) terminating the U.S.-Pakistani security relationship, thereby imperiling the Afghan resistance to Soviet occupation, doing grave and long-term harm to our political and security interests in Southwest Asia and with China, and convincing Pakistan it had nothing further to loose [*sic*] by building nuclear weapons or even conducting a nuclear test. Either outcome would constitute a serious foreign policy defeat.[847]

In the end, Reagan's letter to Zia dated September 12, 1984 did not include any explicit nuclear red lines, reflecting Washington's decision to prioritize the need to maintain Pakistani support for the anti-Soviet fight in Afghanistan over U.S. nonproliferation aims.[848] This same ranking of priorities was also evident in the talking points prepared for Ambassador Deane Hinton's (1983–1986) delivery of the letter, which included a note on how Washington remained "fully committed to supporting you in our common effort" in Afghanistan, while omitting any reference to penalties that Pakistan might incur if it insisted in its nuclear development.[849]

Proliferation concerns also grew stronger in the U.S. Congress, where there was serious disagreement with the administration's approach toward Pakistan. In December 1982, Senator John Glenn (D-Ohio, 1974–1999) pressed the administration to attest that the F-16s sold to Pakistan would not be used for the delivery of nuclear weapons.[850] In August 1985, the Pressler Amendment was adopted, requiring the president to certify before Congress that Pakistan did not possess nuclear weapons, for otherwise it would face economic and military sanctions. Intended as a nonproliferation tool, the Pressler

---

[847] Ibid. See also: National Security Council, Memorandum from Shirin Tahir-Kheli to Robert Oakley, "Dealing with Pakistan's Nuclear Program: A U.S. Strategy," July 23, 1987, in National Security Archive (NSA) Electronic Briefing Book (EBB) 446, "Pakistan's Illegal Nuclear Procurement Exposed in 1987," Doc. 9, p. 3.

[848] See: President Reagan to General Zia, September 12, 1984, in NSA EBB 531, Doc. 7A.

[849] "Talking Points for Use in Delivering Letter to General Zia," n.d., in NSA EBB 531, Doc. 7B.

[850] See: Subramaniam (1987, 149).

Amendment actually had the opposite effect. By defining a red line – possession of an explosive nuclear device – the Amendment allowed Pakistan to get to a point at which it was "a 'turn screw' away from the manufacture of a bomb" while skirting U.S. pressure.[851] An NSA memo on Pakistani nuclear violations written two years later would lay the responsibility for Pakistan's opportunity to proliferate squarely on Washington's prioritizing the conflict in Afghanistan over its non-proliferation goals: "[t]he assumption in Islamabad is that Afghan policy considerations have expanded the tolerance level in the U.S. of Pak[istani] transgressions vis-à-vis the nuclear red lines."[852]

President Reagan complied with the Pressler Amendment, certifying every subsequent year that Pakistan remained a nonnuclear-weapons state.[853] Still, only days after he first did so in 1986, U.S. intelligence reports indicated that "Pakistan had tested a triggering device for a nuclear weapon and had enriched uranium to weapons grade."[854] Islamabad was reaching the nuclear threshold, and Zia himself boasted in March 1987 that "Pakistan has the capability of building the bomb."[855] By the end of that year, U.S. intelligence had concluded that "Pakistan had produced enough fissionable weapons-grade uranium for four to six atomic bombs."[856] Reflecting Pakistani nuclear progress, in his 1989 testimony just before leaving office, President Reagan stayed close to the letter of the law while warning about future developments:

The statutory standard as legislated by Congress is whether Pakistan possesses a nuclear explosive device, not whether Pakistan is attempting to develop or has developed various relevant capabilities. ... Congress should be

---

[851] NSA EBB 446, Doc. 9, p. 2.

[852] Ibid., p. 1.

[853] For the 1987 certification, see: President Reagan to Speaker of the House, December 17, 1987, enclosing presidential determination, in NSA EBB 446, Doc. 24.

[854] Kux (2001, 284). See also: Bob Woodward, "Pakistani Atom Weapon Reported Near," *The Washington Post*, November 4, 1986, p. A1; Narang (2014, 62).

[855] Quoted in William R. Doerner and Ross H. Munro, "Pakistan Knocking at the Nuclear Door: A Key Ally Confirms That His Scientists Can Build the Bomb," *Time*, March 30, 1987. Available at: www.time.com/time/magazine/article/0,9171,963894,00.html. Last accessed: May 2, 2016. See also: Hagerty (1998, 123); Narang (2009–2010, 42); Narang (2014, 59–60).

[856] See: Narang (2014, 60).

aware that as Pakistan's nuclear capabilities grow, and if evidence about its activities continues to accumulate, this process of annual certification ... may be difficult or impossible to make with any degree of certainty.[857]

In its first year in office, the administration of George H. W. Bush (1989–1993) continued this certification despite having been warned by the CIA that "Islamabad had taken the final step toward a nuclear device."[858] Pakistan was, with a high probability, already a nuclear state.

Then, in 1989, Soviet forces withdrew from Afghanistan. Reacting to this geostrategic transformation, in 1990 President Bush refused to certify that Pakistan was nonnuclear, cutting all economic and military aid to the country. Pakistan was once again reminded of the consequences of shifting geostrategic priorities in Washington. Relations between the two countries had long been "an excellent example of an opportunistic relationship between two unequal powers."[859] By the time Washington withdrew its protection, however, "Pakistan had evolved into a de facto nuclear weapon state."[860] Islamabad possessed the ability to build a nuclear weapon on short notice, and missile technology that was likely capable of delivering them.[861]

U.S. Support and India's Preventive Calculus
The 1980s were "the first time the United States had provided an unequivocal guarantee of protection against a possible attack by India and its Communist allies."[862] This unequivocal U.S. support – though unreliable in the long term – contributed to giving Pakistan the opportunity to nuclearize by helping to deter preventive counterproliferation action on India's part.

Concerned about the progress of the Pakistani nuclear-weapons program, India considered striking Pakistan's Kahuta uranium

---

[857] Reagan's certification and accompanying letter to House Speaker Jim Wright (D-Texas, 1987–1989), quoted in David B. Ottaway, "Pakistan May Lose U.S. Aid: 'No Atom Bomb' Certification Is Unlikely," *The Washington Post*, January 28, 1989, p. A1.

[858] Hilali (2005, 233).

[859] Ibid., 187.

[860] Hagerty (1998, 132).

[861] See: Ibid., 126.

[862] Hilali (2005, 187).

enrichment facility preventively on a few occasions since the late 1970s.[863] A Department of State memo from early 1979 discussed the matter explicitly, noting that Indian prime minister Morarji Desai (1977–1979) might order "an Indian preemptive strike at Pakistan's nuclear facilities, perhaps marked by a renewed conflict over Kashmir or some other non-nuclear issue."[864] Ominously, Desai told the U.S. ambassador later that year that "if he discovered that Pakistan was ready to test a bomb or if it exploded one, he would act at on[c]e 'to smash it,'" adding that "he had recently assured" Pakistani foreign secretary Sardar Shah Nawaz (1977–1980) that "if Pakistan tries any tricks, we will smash you."[865]

These preventive calculations continued through the early 1980s. A 1982 report by the Hungarian embassy in New Delhi (based on information relayed by the Soviet ambassador to India) stated that "there is a quite widely held opinion" in the Indian military that Pakistani nuclear facilities "should be bombed" in a manner similar to the one used by Israel to destroy Iraq's nuclear reactor the previous year.[866] The report estimated that "India has a year to make a decision" and made it clear where Pakistan's opportunity to proliferate originated: "Conditions for this [development of the atomic bomb at a rapid pace] are provided by the United States, but China also gives assistance."[867]

The U.S. government was well aware of the possibility of Indian preventive counterproliferation action. Still, in 1982, Secretary Shultz noted to President Reagan that "India or Israel may decide to launch a preventive strike at Pak[istan's] nuclear facilities, but we have no indications that military action is likely in the near term."[868] India's

---

[863] See: Ganguly and Hagerty (2005, 46); Fuhrmann and Kreps (2010, 837).

[864] Anthony Lake, Harold Saunders, and Thomas Pickering through Mr. Newsom and Mrs. Benson to the Deputy Secretary, "PRC Paper on South Asia," enclosing Interagency Working Group Paper, "South Asian Nuclear and Security Problems, Analysis of Possible Elements in a U.S. Strategy," March, 23, 1979, in NSA EBB 333, Doc. 32A, Tab A, p. 2.

[865] U.S. embassy New Delhi cable 9979, "India and the Pakistan Nuclear Problem," June 7, 1979, in NSA EBB 333, Doc. 35B, p. 2.

[866] "Report, Embassy of Hungary in India to the Hungarian Foreign Ministry," January 19, 1982, in Wilson Center Digital Archive, Indian Nuclear History.

[867] Ibid.

[868] Secretary of State George Shultz to President Reagan, "How Do We Make Use of the Zia Visit to Protect Our Strategic Interests in the Face of Pakistan's

consideration of a preventive strike was corroborated by a December 1982 front-page article in the *Washington Post* quoting U.S. intelligence officials as saying that, the previous year, Indian military planners had presented the New Delhi government with plans to destroy Pakistan's nuclear facilities.[869] In 1984, the CIA noted that "a preemptive military strike by India is a near-term possibility."[870] U.S. intelligence assessments pointed out that "India will probably feel compelled at some point to take military action to prevent Pakistan from acquiring nuclear weapons," noting that such an attack "on Pakistan's nuclear facilities would almost certainly touch off a wider Indian-Pakistan conflict."[871]

Yet, India never carried out these plans. The United States arguably played a role in deterring an Indian attack.[872] The U.S. military aid packages of 1981 and 1986 boosted Pakistani conventional defenses, raising the cost of an eventual preventive war.[873] The United States also helped Pakistan by warning its ally of an impending Indian attack on Kahuta in 1984.[874] For example, Ambassador Hinton's talking points in advance of delivering Reagan's letter to Zia included that, in Washington's judgment, "it is likely that at some point India will take military action to pre-empt your nuclear program."[875] As a result of such warnings, the Pakistani Air Force stepped up its defenses and prepared to strike back at the Indian nuclear facilities at Trombay.[876] In October, the *Washington Post* reported that, according to U.S. sources, and prompted by concerns about a preventive strike, "some Pakistani

---

Nuclear Weapons Activities," November 26, 1982, in NSA EBB 377, Doc. 16, p. 2.

[869] See: Milton R. Benjamin, 1982, "India Said to Eye Raid on Pakistan's A-Plants," *The Washington Post*, December 20, pp. A1, A17.

[870] Memorandum from David W. McManis, National Intelligence Officer for Warning to Director of Central Intelligence, Deputy Director of Central Intelligence, "Monthly Warning and Forecast Meetings for July 1984," August 6, 1984, in NSA EBB 531, Doc. 3, p. 1.

[871] NSA EBB 531, Doc. 4, enclosure, p. 2.

[872] See: Kumaraswamy (2010, 230). According to some sources, Washington even threatened to come to the defense of Pakistan in a conflict. See: Kharnad (2002, 349–350).

[873] See: Reiss (1991, 48).

[874] See: Kharnad (2002, 348); Ganguly and Hagerty (2005, 57–58); Levy and Scott-Clark (2007, 103–105).

[875] NSA EBB 531, Doc. 7B, p. 3.

[876] See: Ibid., 105.

nuclear facilities have been moved underground."[877] Eventually, Indian prime minister Indira Gandhi backed down and in December 1985 India and Pakistan agreed not to launch preventive counterproliferation strikes against each other.[878]

Washington was aware of the role that U.S. politico-military support for Pakistan had in deterring New Delhi from launching a preventive counterproliferation strike. When discussing U.S. policy options, opponents of an "explicit Presidential endorsement of [an] additional 'Red Line'" argued that this option presented considerable danger, by making public an irrevocable commitment to terminate U.S. assistance if Islamabad proceeded undeterred in its nuclear pursuit. Among the consequences of such a commitment, critics pointed out, "a U.S. decision to halt securi[ty] assistance would be seen by India as confirmation of an imminent Pakistani nuclear threat, and could convince the Indians to undertake an immediate preemptive attack."[879]

Despite the 1985 Indo-Pakistan agreement ruling out preventive counterproliferation action against each other, the possibility of an Indian military strike against the Pakistani nuclear program reemerged during Rajiv Gandhi's tenure (1984–1989), in the context of the crisis surrounding Operation Brasstacks in 1986–1987.[880] Reacting to a large-scale Indian military exercise, Pakistan massed considerable forces along the Indo-Pakistan border. At the peak of the crisis, Indian officials again discussed an attack on Pakistan's Kahuta nuclear facility.[881] This dangerous situation led to a flurry of diplomatic activity involving U.S. mediation, ultimately defusing the crisis. Washington worried that escalation would prompt Pakistan to complete assemblage of its warheads, which, given the Pressler Amendment, would force the U.S. government to impose sanctions on Pakistan, in turn decreasing Islamabad's cooperation on Afghanistan, and undermining

---

[877] Don Oberdorfer, "Pakistan Concerned about Attack on Atomic Plants: Possible Assault by India Regarded as 'Serious Threat,' Foreign Minister Says," *The Washington Post*, October 12, 1984, p. A28.

[878] See: Hagerty (1998, 87); Ganguly and Hagerty (2005, 61).

[879] NSA EBB 531, Doc. 4, enclosure, p. 5.

[880] See: Bajpai et al. (1995); Ganguly and Hagerty (2005, 73–76).

[881] See: Narang (2014, 63). Around the same time, Pakistani nuclear scientist A. Q. Khan reportedly declared to an Indian journalist that Pakistan possessed a nuclear-weapons capability. See: Hagerty (1998, 103). Pakistan claimed that the report was a hoax, the purpose of which "was to sabotage the follow-on U.S. aid program for Pakistan." Ibid., 103.

U.S. interests in that theater.[882] Overall, the crisis led Pakistan to speed up its nuclear development – when the country was already only "two screwdriver turns" away from having the bomb.[883]

The 1998 Nuclear Tests

The world would have to wait more than a decade for visible confirmation of Pakistan's nuclear status. In May 1998, a month after the BJP acceded to power, India performed a series of nuclear tests. The Indian tests put Pakistan in a quandary. Were Islamabad to reciprocate by testing its own nuclear weapons, it would face U.S. sanctions. Were it not to respond to the Indian tests, however, its security might be imperiled and its status diminished. Before making a decision, Prime Minister Nawaz Sharif (1990–1993, 1997–1999, 2013–) told President Bill Clinton that Pakistan "needed a US security guarantee against India to hold off from testing."[884] When the U.S. president declined such a guarantee – and despite Clinton's offer to resume sales of conventional weaponry to Islamabad – Sharif ordered a series of six nuclear tests in the Chagai Hills of Baluchisthan between May 28 and May 30.[885] While the Islamabad government faced strong public pressure in favor of a test, its security rationale was also unquestionable: "Pakistan had to demonstrate that it, too, possessed weapons capability. Past experience underlined apprehensions that India might again exploit the power imbalance to blackmail and browbeat Pakistan."[886] Pakistan's nuclear status, which had long ceased to be a secret, was now plainly confirmed.

Alternative Explanations

The conventional wisdom holds that Pakistan obtained nuclear weapons for security reasons. Pakistan had an enduring dispute over the status

---

[882] See: Narang (2014, 62).

[883] Ibid., 59. See also: Hagerty (1998, 118).

[884] Kux (2001, 346), citing interviews with U.S. officials.

[885] On Clinton's offer, see: Tim Weiner, "Nuclear Anxiety: In Washington; After an Anguished Phone Call, Clinton Penalizes the Pakistanis," *The New York Times*, May 29, 1998. Available at: www.nytimes.com/1998/05/29/world/ nuclear-anxiety-washington-after-anguished-phone-call-clinton-penalizes. html. Last accessed: May 2, 2016. On the tests, see: Paul (2000, 133); Armstrong and Trento (2007, 175); Ahmed (2010, 177).

[886] Sattar (2007, 201).

of Kashmir with its conventionally stronger neighbor, India, and real-ized that its security sponsor, the United States, was not reliable. T. V. Paul puts it most succinctly: Pakistan "is situated in a high-conflict zone, has an active, protracted conflict with a more powerful neighbor, has weak or unreliable support, and has a security-first approach in its national strategy." Therefore, Paul concludes, Pakistan "is a powerful candidate for nuclear acquisition."[887]

This perspective is valuable but incomplete. The factors listed by Paul help us understand why Pakistan had a high willingness to acquire nuclear weapons.[888] Yet, to understand how Pakistan actually acquired nuclear weapons, we must ask how Pakistan obtained the opportunity to proliferate. As a weak state, Pakistan saw a great secu-rity benefit in acquiring nuclear weapons. At the same time, Pakistan's adversary, India, had a strong incentive to prevent Pakistan's nucle-arization. To account for Pakistan's successful nuclear acquisition, we need to understand the role played by its alliance with the United States, which provided Islamabad with the opportunity to proliferate, by granting it protection against a preventive strike.

An alternative view would posit that Pakistan successfully prolifer-ated because Washington applied the wrong nonproliferation policy tools. According to this line of reasoning, the United States miscal-culated in hoping that a carrots-based nonproliferation approach including security assurances and the sale of conventional weapons would be sufficient to meet Pakistan's security needs, guaranteeing the maintenance of its nonnuclear status. Indeed, there is some evidence that Washington hoped that the sale of conventional weapons would alleviate Pakistan's security concerns and thereby undermine its will-ingness to go nuclear. For example, the Ford administration lifted the arms embargo in February 1975, after evidence of Pakistani progress toward the bomb. Likewise, the Reagan administration argued that military assistance could keep Pakistan away from the bomb. In the

---

[887] Paul (2000, 137). See also: Riedel (2013, 196).
[888] Other considerations could supplement this security benefit for nuclear weapons, such as the benefit of nuclear weapons for Pakistan's "national identity." For scholars who agree that nuclear weapons presented a high security benefit and also affected Pakistan's own identity conception, see: Khan (2012); Rabinowitz (2014).

summer of 1981, responding to criticism of the Reagan administration's military aid to Pakistan, James Buckley, undersecretary of state for security assistance, science, and technology (1981–1982), laid out the logic of this U.S. nonproliferation approach, which aimed at removing Islamabad's willingness to acquire the bomb: "In place of the ineffective sanctions on Pakistan's nuclear program imposed by the past Administration, we hope to address through conventional means the sources of insecurity that prompt a nation like Pakistan to seek a nuclear capability in the first place."[889] Likewise, Feroz Hassan Khan describes the main features of the arrangement between Reagan and Zia as follows: "(1) U.S. security assurances, (2) Pakistani sovereignty, (3) covert intelligence cooperation, (4) Pakistan's assurances of the peaceful use of nuclear technology."[890] This suggests that Washington was misled into thinking that there was a quid pro quo where Pakistan would not develop a nuclear weapon in exchange for U.S. security assurances.

The problem with this alternative view is that the United States was simply not willing to offer the level of commitment that would have met Pakistan's security needs and remove its willingness to acquire the bomb. Furthermore, as historian Or Rabinowitz convincingly argues, the goal of the Reagan-Zia agreement was, from the U.S. perspective, to prevent a nuclear *test*, which would embarrass the administration in Washington and jeopardize its efforts to contain the Soviet Union in Afghanistan.[891] In 1981, Robert McFarlane, counselor at the State Department (1981–1982), met with Zia concerning "Pakistan's security concerns vis-à-vis India and its nuclear program."[892] McFarlane's instructions were to "try and make the most compelling case about how we would not tolerate a Pakistani defeat at the hand of India without spelling out what we were not prepared to do. We were not prepared to deploy forces and so our

---

[889] James L. Buckley, "Letter to the Editor: Why the U.S. Must Strengthen Pakistan," July 25, 1981, *The New York Times*, August 5, 1981, p. A22. See also: Reiss (1993, 1110).

[890] Khan (2012, 214).

[891] See: Rabinowitz (2014).

[892] Rabinowitz interview with Robert McFarlane, June 2013, Washington, DC, quoted in ibid., 147–148.

leverage, apart from willingness to maintain a modest armed force in Pakistan, was not persuasive."[893] McFarlane understood the predicament, noting that "all the diplomatic fluff ... never quite changes the fact that if you are not going to be physically there then nothing else would really matter. If you are not going to commit to coming into a conflict and have soldiers on the ground this does not have a meaning."[894] In response to McFarlane's vague assurances, Zia replied: "we have little choice but to match their [the Indians'] capabilities."[895] To be sure, Zia added, "we understand your country's sensitivities and we will not embarrass you."[896] Reflecting on the exchange, McFarlane would later say:

> Zia knew he had to have something to say to American officials, and what he had to say was that "we have not committed to a nuclear weapon" but at the end of the day it was really that "we are not going to embarrass you" which implicitly meant – we are really going to go forward with the nuclear program.[897]

When asked whether Zia was pledging not to embarrass the United States by refraining from a nuclear *test*, McFarlane responded: "Right."[898] In other words, Washington knew that its security commitments to Pakistan were insufficient to deter its nuclear acquisition.

Other scholars argue instead that there was nothing that Washington could have done to prevent Pakistan's nuclearization. According to George Perkovich: "No form of security guarantee or military

---

[893] Transcript of interview held on June 2013, Washington, DC, Or Rabinowitz private collection.
[894] Ibid.
[895] Rabinowitz interview with Robert McFarlane, June 2013, Washington, DC, quoted in Rabinowitz (2014, 148).
[896] Ibid.
[897] Ibid.
[898] Ibid. Later, when preparing for the December 1982 Zia visit to Washington, Secretary of State George Shultz, while noting the "overwhelming evidence that Zia has been breaking his assurances" not to build the bomb, agreed that the core of the informal agreement between the two countries was about nuclear *testing*, not acquisition per se. In Shultz's words: "Last year we received assurances from Zia that Pakistan would not manufacture nuclear weapons, not transfer sensitive nuclear technology, and not 'embarrass' us on the nuclear issue while we are providing aid. (We both understood this clearly

alliance by the United States would have kept Pakistan from seeking nuclear weapons."[899] Pakistan would inevitably nuclearize because its "obsession with India is so great that it would not willingly have abandoned its demand to acquire nuclear weapons to match or surpass India's nuclear capability."[900]

We agree that Pakistan's willingness to acquire nuclear weapons was high. As a weak state expecting a high likelihood of future conflict, Pakistan perceived the security benefit of nuclear weapons to be high. Therefore, it would have been very costly for Washington to remove Islamabad's willingness to develop nuclear weapons, and Washington was simply not ready to bear such a burden. Nevertheless, it is possible to prevent proliferation by an ally without removing its willingness to obtain nuclear weapons.[901] In fact, given Pakistan's strategic situation – namely, its weakness vis-à-vis India – the optimal nonproliferation strategy for the United States would have been to deny Pakistan the opportunity to proliferate. This would have required the United States to make its security support conditional on Islamabad stopping its nuclear program, threatening abandonment if Pakistan remained on its trajectory toward building a bomb. Washington, however, decided not to do so, because it gave higher priority to other foreign policy goals – namely, enlisting Pakistani support in the fight against the Soviets in Afghanistan. By providing a modicum of support for Pakistan without doing enough to remove its willingness to nuclearize, Washington placed Islamabad in a situation in which it had the opportunity to proliferate.

In sum, facing a serious security threat from India and enjoying limited support from the United States, Pakistan had the willingness to develop nuclear weapons. When the Soviet invasion of Afghanistan led Washington to prioritize other security goals and turn a blind eye to Pakistani nuclear efforts, Islamabad took the opportunity granted by stronger U.S. protection to nuclearize in the 1980s. As foreign minister of Pakistan Abdul Sattar (1999–2002) concluded, "Pakistan's

---

to mean that Pakistan would not test a nuclear device; it was left ambiguous as to what it meant short of a test.)" NSA EBB 377, Doc. 16, p. 2.

[899] Perkovich (2008, 77).

[900] Ibid., 83.

[901] See the case study of Taiwan in this chapter, as well as our case study of West Germany in Chapter 6.

sole motivation for the response to Indian [1998] tests was security, which was, in fact, the rationale for its pursuit of the nuclear
option."[902]

* * *

The relevant counterfactuals for these eight cases we just examined
concern the two factors on which we have focused our analysis in
this chapter: their relative power and their ally's unwillingness to offer
them reliable security guarantees.

Starting with a counterfactual analysis of the role of relative
power in these cases, how would they look if the state's power
changed while everything else remained the same? To begin with,
a hypothetical strong Sweden would still not have acquired nuclear
weapons, given that its rapprochement with NATO undermined its
willingness to go nuclear. China, India, North Korea, South Africa,
and, to a lesser extent, Israel, were able on their own to impose
significant costs on any adversary that would launch a counterproliferation strike. (Israel depended in part on U.S. support to do so.)
Had their relative power been lower and everything else remained
equal (i.e., their security guarantees from their security sponsors
remained weak), they would, in all likelihood, not have proliferated.
They would have been coerced into remaining nonnuclear by their
adversaries, internalizing their lack of opportunity to nuclearize; or
they would have ended up being targeted preventively by their adversaries; or they would have been deterred from proliferating by
their sponsors – which, given their counterfactual weakness, would
have had a greater ability to remove their opportunity to nuclearize
by threatening abandonment. In contrast, a counterfactually strong
Taiwan would have been better able to acquire the bomb, given its
ability to deter a counterproliferation strike from China and the
willingness to nuclearize that resulted from its lack of robust U.S.
security guarantees in the face of a threatening PRC. Finally, a counterfactually strong Pakistan would not have needed U.S. protection
to develop nuclear weapons. It would have proceeded unimpeded to
its nuclearization goal, just as the Soviet Union, as we analyzed in
the previous chapter.

---

[902] Sattar (2007, 202).

How would these cases have looked if we kept relative power constant, but counterfactually removed their ally's loose support? Sweden would likely not have proliferated. It would have been willing to acquire nuclear weapons, as it did in the early phases of the Cold War, but it would have probably lacked the opportunity to proliferate: either it would have been struck preventively by the Soviet Union or it would have internalized the threat of preventive war and terminated its nuclear program. China, India, North Korea, South Africa, and, to a lesser extent, Israel would all have nuclearized if they possessed no security sponsor. Their ability to impose relatively high costs on their adversaries in the case of a preventive counterproliferation strike made them good candidates for nuclearization even in the absence of a security sponsor. Not so with Taiwan, whose relative weakness vis-à-vis the PRC made it unlikely to go nuclear in the absence of U.S. support. In fact, it was the possibility of bringing about this counterfactual situation that made the U.S.'s sticks-based nonproliferation effort successful. Likewise, Pakistan's relative weakness vis-à-vis India made it unlikely that it would have had the opportunity to go nuclear had it not enjoyed temporary protection from the United States during the 1980s.

At the other end of the spectrum, how would each of these cases have played out if power remained constant but their security sponsors had been close allies, willing to extend them robust security guarantees? In our view, were these states to have received reliable security guarantees from a security sponsor, they would have lost the willingness to nuclearize as long as their security goals remained largely restricted to the protection of their territory. They would therefore have likely remained nonnuclear.

But it is important to question whether, at least in the cases of Taiwan and Pakistan, close U.S. protection might have had an impact on the extent of their security goals. It is entirely plausible that, were Taiwan and Pakistan to receive reliable extensive U.S. protection, they would have been more likely to have seen in nuclear weapons a tool to promote their broader security goals, such as, in the case of Taiwan, the reconquest of mainland China or, in the case of Pakistan, the annexation of Indian-controlled Kashmir. If we contemplate this possibility, then close U.S. protection would nonetheless have led them to pursue nuclear weapons in order to achieve these broader goals. In this case, and as we show in the following chapter, their ultimate nuclear status would depend on U.S. nonproliferation efforts, which, in turn, would depend on Washington's fear of entrapment as a result of their nuclear acquisition.

Having looked at proliferation dynamics among states that possess only a loose security alliance, we now turn to the dynamics shaping nuclear acquisition among countries that possessed a reliable, close security sponsor.

6 | *Close Allies and Proliferation*

In this chapter, we use four case studies – of Japan, South Korea, West Germany, and France – to analyze the dynamics of proliferation among states that are offered robust security assurances. Like the loose allies analyzed in the previous chapter, close allies can follow the second causal pathway to proliferation. They will do so when security alliances provide them with the opportunity to go nuclear without satisfying their willingness to acquire nuclear weapons. Because of the high level of support that they receive from their security sponsor, close allies may not have the willingness to proliferate. The high level of support that they receive from their sponsor suggests that the overlap of preferences between the two states is high, and that the sponsor is likely to come to its protégé's defense in a conflict. Yet, by the same token, close allies have a greater opportunity to proliferate. If the protégé doubts the reliability of the sponsor's support, either because it is expected to decrease over time or because it does not cover all of the protégé's security interests, the protégé retains the willingness to proliferate, and may indeed go nuclear.

We start with the case of Japan, which considered nuclear acquisition briefly during 1967–1970 but, given the robustness and reliability of U.S. security guarantees, never possessed the willingness necessary to actually explore the nuclear option.

We then turn to three cases of states that considered nuclear weapons more seriously: South Korea, West Germany, and France. These cases help us highlight the effectiveness of different nonproliferation tools in ensuring nuclear forbearance.

Facing possible proliferation by a relatively strong protégé, a sticks-based approach, with the goal of taking away its opportunity to proliferate through conditional threats of abandonment, is unlikely to work. Relatively strong protégés would have the opportunity to proliferate on their own. Instead, the most effective nonproliferation tool will in all likelihood be a carrots-based approach, with the goal of taking away the protégé's willingness to go nuclear.

Such was the case with South Korea. Seoul began considering nuclear weapons as a result of the Nixon Doctrine, when Washington announced that it would curtail its security commitments to East Asia and demanded that its allies take greater responsibility in their own defense. Sitting on the front line of conflict with the communist world, and doubting the reliability of U.S. commitments, South Korea began exploring the nuclear option. Worried about the consequences of a nuclear South Korea, the United States first coerced Seoul by making threats of abandonment. Then, in the early 1980s, Washington realized that Seoul still possessed the willingness to go nuclear and that rising relative power vis-à-vis the North might give South Korea the opportunity to nuclearize. As a result, Washington boosted its security commitments to its protégé, removing Seoul's willingness to proliferate and ensuring the end of its nuclear efforts to this day.

When, in contrast, the protégé considering proliferation is relatively weak, then a security sponsor may resort to a sticks-based approach to nonproliferation centered on threats of abandonment. Unlike in the case of a strong protégé, the effectiveness of this approach is made possible by the protégé's weakness, which guarantees that it will not have the ability to proliferate in the absence of support from the sponsor. Whether the sponsor is willing to apply a stern sticks-based approach to proliferation depends on the consequences of its protégé's nuclearization. The sponsor will exert serious effort in preventing proliferation only if it fears entrapment as a result of its protégé's nuclearization.

To illustrate these dynamics, we look at the cases of West Germany and France. Bonn developed an interest in nuclear weapons as a result of its concerns over the reliability of U.S. guarantees. Washington could retreat into a "Fortress America" that would exclude its European allies. Alternatively, Washington could actively attempt to repel a Soviet invasion, but in the process generate massive West German casualties. Initially, Washington pursued a carrots-based nonproliferation approach, fostering a nuclear-sharing agreement within NATO. This approach failed as the result of vehement opposition by other U.S. allies in Europe as well as the Soviets. The serious concerns expressed by the Soviets led U.S. decisionmakers to fear entrapment should West Germany attempt to acquire nuclear weapons. Thenceforth, Washington turned to a sticks-based approach, coercing

Bonn to forfeit its nuclear ambitions and colluding with the Soviet Union in creating a nonproliferation regime that stemmed from their common interest in keeping West Germany nonnuclear. Given its relative weakness vis-à-vis the Soviet Union, Bonn was susceptible to U.S. threats of abandonment, and it ultimately relented in its attempt to acquire nuclear weapons.

We then turn to our final case, France. In addition to concerns over the reliability of U.S. assurances of protection of the French mainland, which mirrored those any other Western European country may have felt, the French feared that Washington would not protect their broader security interests. Paris was intent on extending its influence in North Africa, the Middle East, and Southeast Asia. These security interests were not covered by the United States, however; a reality made clear to them in the 1954 Dien Bien Phu and 1956 Suez crises. At the same time, France's nuclearization was not a serious concern for Moscow, which in turn meant it did not increase the odds of U.S. entrapment in a conflict over French nuclear development. Less concerned about the consequences of a French nuclear weapon, Washington acquiesced to French nuclear proliferation.

Overall, these four cases illustrate the dynamics at play in the second causal pathway to proliferation: a state protected by a security sponsor will acquire the bomb only when it doubts the reliability of its sponsor's support while benefiting from it during its pursuit of the nuclear option. When its protégé is strong, a security sponsor can best prevent proliferation through a carrots-based approach, removing its willingness to proliferate. In contrast, a sticks-based approach is most useful if the protégé is weak, as it would not have the opportunity to proliferate on its own. Whether the sponsor is willing to expend political capital in pressuring the protégé to remain nonnuclear depends on the likelihood that its nuclearization would entrap the sponsor. The greater the sponsor's fear of entrapment, the more willing it is to exert effort in preventing proliferation.

Japan

Despite possessing one of the largest and most advanced civilian nuclear programs in the world, Japan has eschewed nuclear acquisition. Enjoying reliable U.S. security guarantees, Tokyo's government lacks the willingness to build a nuclear deterrent.

After an ambitious plan to dominate East Asia in the Second World War, Japan encountered defeat and suffered the atomic attacks on Hiroshima and Nagasaki on August 6 and 9, 1945 – to this day, the only instances of nuclear weapons being used in wartime. Japan formally renounced war in its new constitution of 1947, and soon adopted a foreign policy relying on U.S. guarantees to meet its security needs, known as the "Yoshida Doctrine," after Prime Minister Yoshida Shigeru (1946–1947, 1948–1954). In 1967, Japan further formalized its renunciation of nuclear weapons with the so-called three nonnuclear principles, stating that the country would not produce, possess, or introduce nuclear weapons on its territory. In short, Japan renounced nuclear weapons because it concluded that nuclearization would not significantly improve its security. To the contrary, an autonomous deterrent would suggest the revival of Japan's militaristic past, causing concerns among enemies and allies and ultimately undermining Japan's security.

Given Tokyo's resolute opposition to nuclear weapons, Washington has not needed to expend much effort to prevent Japan's nuclearization. In fact, throughout the duration of the alliance, the United States actually enjoined Japan to spend more on its defense and has, at times, even gently encouraged nuclear proliferation. U.S. assurances have so far proven sufficient to meet Japan's security needs, even as North Korea has nuclearized and islands disputes with the PRC have intensified.

Japanese Interest in Nuclear Weapons

During the Second World War, Japan developed a small nuclear program.[1] The war concluded in defeat, however, and marked the end of Japan's expansionist policy. Since the late nineteenth century, Japan had acquired foreign territories, including Taiwan after the first Sino-Japanese War (1894–1895), Korea after the Russo-Japanese war of 1904–1905,[2] and Manchuria after the invasion of September 1931.[3]

---

[1] See: Campbell and Sunohara (2004, 220).
[2] In the Treaty of Portsmouth at the conclusion of the Russo-Japanese war in 1905, Russia recognized Japan's predominant interest in Korea, which Japan formally annexed with the Japan-Korea Treaty of 1910.
[3] See: Barnhart (1987, 27–33).

Japan hoped to build a sphere of influence, the "Greater East Asia Co-Prosperity Sphere," aiming to absorb Australia, Borneo, Burma, India, Indochina, Malaya, New Zealand, the Dutch East Indies, and Thailand.[4] With the long and costly second Sino-Japanese war, begun in 1937, Japan's plans were thwarted, eventually leading to war with the United States and the Soviet Union, and the atomic attacks on Hiroshima and Nagasaki in August 1945. From then on, Japanese enemies, allies, and even its public sought to avoid a repetition of Japan's militaristic past.

From the Second World War to the Late 1960s: The Yoshida Doctrine

Japan's new constitution of May 1947, adopted under U.S. occupation, marked the country's renunciation of war:

the Japanese people forever renounce war as a sovereign right of the nation and the threat or use of force as means of settling international disputes.

In order to accomplish the aim of the preceding paragraph, land, sea, and air forces, as well as other war potential, will never be maintained. The right of belligerency of the state will not be recognized.[5]

In the eyes of Yoshida Shigeru, the prime minister at the time, Japan could achieve "security without armaments." By choosing to renounce the capabilities necessary to issue military threats, Japan could reassure foreign countries of its peaceful intentions. As Yoshida stated in the Japanese Parliament in November 1949, "the very absence of armaments is a guarantee of the security and happiness of our people, and will gain for us the confidence of the world."[6] In his negotiations to end the occupation, the prime minister developed a strategy, dubbed the Yoshida Doctrine, whereby Japan would focus on maximizing economic growth, relying on U.S. security guarantees and allowing for American bases to remain on its soil.[7] This arrangement was formalized in San Francisco in September 1951. A peace treaty

---

[4] See: Iriye (1987, 131); LaFeber (1997, 192–193); Monteiro and Debs (2015).

[5] See the text of the Constitution at: "The Constitution of Japan," November 3, 1946, Prime Minister of Japan. Available at: http://japan.kantei.go.jp/constitution_and_government_of_japan/constitution_e.html. Last accessed: May 1, 2016.

[6] See: Dower (1979, 382).

[7] See: Schaller (1985, 256); Pyle (1988, 454).

reinstated Japan's sovereignty over its territory,[8] and a security treaty with the United States allowed for American forces to remain "in and about Japan" to deter attacks and maintain peace in the Far East. The security treaty was meant to be a "provisional arrangement," to be renewed at a later date, and called for Japan to increase its own defense spending.[9]

Thenceforth, Japan focused on maximizing economic growth, and its development plan would rely on nuclear power to meet its energy needs. With the Atomic Energy Basic Act of December 1955, the government set up the Japan Atomic Energy Commission (JAEC) to coordinate the country's efforts in nuclear development, insisting on the peaceful nature of its program.[10] In 1957, the IAEA began monitoring Japan's nuclear activities.[11]

Less than ten years after the horrors of Hiroshima and Nagasaki, Japan once again became keenly aware of the dangers of nuclear weapons. On March 1, 1954, a Japanese fishing boat, the *Lucky Dragon*, received radioactive fallout from an American hydrogen bomb test at the Bikini atoll. Though it stood outside the danger zone, some eighty-five miles away from the test, the boat was affected due to strong winds and a bomb yield greater than expected. All twenty-three crew members were hospitalized, and one eventually died from complications.[12] The accident fueled popular discontent with U.S. extended deterrence, but Japanese leaders remained committed to the Yoshida Doctrine, and to the protection offered by the United States.

Tokyo's efforts to provide for its own defense in fact lagged behind Washington's expectations.[13] A week after the *Lucky Dragon* accident,

---

[8] See the text of the treaty at: "Treaty of Peace with Japan," September 8, 1951, UN Treaty Collection. Available at: https://treaties.un.org/doc/Publication/UNTS/Volume%20136/volume-136-I-1832-English.pdf. Last accessed: May 1, 2016. See also: Van Sant, Mauch, and Sugita (2007, xxvii).

[9] See the text of the treaty at: "Security Treaty between the United States and Japan," September 8, 1951, The Avalon Project, Yale University. Available at: http://avalon.law.yale.edu/20th_century/japan001.asp. Last accessed: May 1, 2016. See also: Gallicio (2001, 120).

[10] See: "Atomic Energy Basic Act," December 19, 1955, Japanese Law Translation, Ministry of Justice of Japan. Available at: www.japaneselawtranslation.go.jp/law/detail/?id=2233&vm=02&re=02. Last accessed: May 1, 2016; Takubo (2008, 72).

[11] See: Campbell and Sunohara (2004, 220); Hughes (2009, 108).

[12] See: Buckley (1992, 58–61); Kusunoki (2008, 37); Rublee (2009, 56).

[13] See: Schaller (1985, 293); Buckley (1992, 50, 56–57).

the two countries signed the Mutual Defense Assistance Agreement, whereby Japan agreed to take greater responsibility in its security by increasing its "defensive strength."[14] Yet, Tokyo committed to raise no more than 165,000 troops, about half the level expected by Washington.[15] Japan would rely mainly on U.S. forces for its protection.

U.S. bases could serve as a deterrent against foreign aggression, but because they were also important tools of U.S. power projection in the region, they raised fears that Japan would be entrapped in conflicts over issues that did not directly affect its security. During discussions for the Peace Treaty in the spring of 1950, the State Department predicted that the Japanese would take a keen interest in whether U.S. bases on their territory would be used "for Far Eastern defensive purposes or for the purpose of offensive operations against the Soviets in the event war should break out in Europe."[16] In the spring of 1958, the Soviet Union warned that the introduction of U.S. nuclear weapons in Japan would "menace the peace and security of the Far East." Khrushchev also declared that Japan would not be the target of a nuclear attack as long as its territory did not serve as a base for aggression against the Soviet Union.[17] In June of that same year, the Japanese foreign minister informed the American ambassador in Japan that Tokyo was ready to negotiate a revision to the 1951 security treaty, with a focus on "full consultation and agreement" between the two governments on the "deployment of US forces and their equipment (i.e., nuclears) in Japan" as well as on the "use of US forces based in Japan in hostilities elsewhere in Asia."[18]

The two countries reached an agreement in January 1960 for a revised security treaty. The Treaty of Mutual Cooperation and Security stated that in the event of an attack on Japanese territory, each country "would act to meet the common danger in accordance with its constitutional provisions and processes." The agreement also reaffirmed that

---

[14] For the text of the agreement, see: "Mutual Defense Assistance Agreement between Japan and the United States," March 8, 1954, U.S. Embassy, Tokyo, Japan. Available at: http://japan2.usembassy.gov/pdfs/wwwf-mdao-mdaa1954.pdf. Last accessed: May 1, 2016.

[15] See: Buckley (1992, 56–57); Gallicio (2001, 121).

[16] "Memorandum of Conversation, by the Special Assistant Secretary (Howard)," [Washington,] April 25, 1950, in *FRUS*, 1950, Vol. VI, Doc. 708.

[17] Quoted and cited in Buckley (1992, 71).

[18] "Telegram from the Embassy in Japan to the Department of State," Tokyo, June 5, 1958, in *Foreign Relations of the United States (FRUS)*, 1958–1960, Vol. XVIII, *Japan; Korea*, Doc. 15.

Japan granted basing rights to the United States so as to contribute to "the security of Japan and the maintenance of international peace and security in the Far East."[19] As such, the treaty did not alter Japanese reliance on U.S. force, nor did it affect the decisionmaking process for their use. In fact, in a separate secret agreement, Tokyo consented that it would not need to be consulted for the passage of nuclear weapons through U.S. bases in Japanese soil.[20] Furthermore, the agreement exempted the Ryukyu Islands – the largest of which is Okinawa – from military limitations in this secret treaty, allowing the United States to continue storing nuclear weapons there without consulting Japan.[21]

Over the following decade, Washington relied heavily on its bases in Japan to conduct operations in Indochina. The escalation of the Vietnam War led to fears of entrapment in Japan. In March 1965, Washington began the sustained bombing of North Vietnam in Operation Rolling Thunder.[22] The large majority of supplies for U.S. troops came from Okinawa. Later that year, U.S. admiral Grant Sharp, commander of the Pacific forces (1964–1968), claimed that "without Okinawa we couldn't continue fighting the Vietnam War."[23] Reporting on popular concerns about Japan's alliance with the United States, the U.S. ambassador in Japan Edwin O. Reischauer (1961–1966) wrote to the State Department in May that the bombing in North Vietnam produced an "adverse Japanese reaction" that "appear[ed] to be fundamentally a result of fear that Japan might become involved in the war if it further escalates."[24]

---

[19] See the text of the treaty at: "Treaty of Mutual Cooperation and Security between Japan and the United States of America," January 19, 1960, Ministry of Foreign Affairs of Japan. Available at: www.mofa.go.jp/region/n-america/us/q&a/ref/1.html. Last accessed: May 1, 2016.

[20] See: Gallicio (2001, 104); Kusunoki (2008, 38). On the secret transit agreement, see: "Okinawa Calendar of Documents," n.d., in NSA EBB 541, Doc. 1.

[21] See: Gallicio (2001, 126).

[22] See the description of the Operation by the Joint Chiefs of Staff in "Memorandum from the Joint Chiefs of Staff to Secretary of Defense McNamara," Washington, February 11, 1965, in *Foreign Relations of the United States (FRUS)*, 1964–1968, Vol. II, *Vietnam, January–June 1965*, Doc. 109.

[23] Quoted in Schaller (1997, 196).

[24] "Telegram from the Embassy in Japan to the Department of State," Tokyo, May 19, 1965, in *Foreign Relations of the United States (FRUS)*, 1964–1968, Vol. XXIX, Part 2, *Japan*, Doc. 46.

The mid-1960s brought about another important development in the region: the PRC tested a nuclear weapon in October 1964, producing a sharply critical reaction in Japan, especially in the press.[25] Prime Minister Sato Eisaku (1964–1972) even hinted at the possibility that Japan may also go nuclear. In late December 1964, he told ambassador Reischauer that "if other fellow had nuclears it was only common sense to have them oneself." Japanese public opinion, currently opposed to an autonomous nuclear defense, would have to be "educated" on this matter.[26] Yet, Sato seemed content with a restatement of U.S. assurances. The following month, President Lyndon Johnson declared that "since Japan possesses no nuclear weapons, and we have them, if Japan needs our nuclear deterrent for its defense, the United States would stand by its commitment and provide that defense." Driving the point home, Johnson stated that "Japan need not give even a second thought to the dependability of its American ally. If Japan is attacked, the United States will contribute to its defense." Sato reassured Johnson that "although he could see why it might be argued that if China has nuclear weapons, Japan should also, this was not Japan's policy." There was no need for an autonomous deterrent: "Due to U.S. commitments under the U.S.-Japan Security Treaty," Sato concluded, "the Chinese Communist nuclear explosion had not had [a] great impact in Japan."[27]

By the late 1960s, therefore, Japan remained committed to the Yoshida Doctrine, and further formalized its renunciation of nuclear weapons. In mid-November 1967, Sato met with Secretary of Defense Robert McNamara and President Johnson, stating that "Japan's whole security was based on its security arrangement with the U.S. The Japanese were well protected by the U.S. nuclear umbrella and Japan had no intention to make nuclear weapons."[28]

[25] See: Lindsay Grant memorandum to Assistant Secretary of State for Far Eastern Affairs, William Bundy, "Policy Implications of Far Eastern Reactions to CCNE," October 23, 1964, in NSA EBB 488, Doc. 24, p. 8.
[26] "Telegram from the Embassy in Japan to the Department of State," Tokyo, December 29, 1964, 6 p.m., in *FRUS*, 1964–1968, Vol. XXIX, Part 2, Doc. 37.
[27] "Memorandum of Conversation," Washington, January 12, 1965, 12:15 p.m., in *FRUS*, 1964–1968, Vol. XXIX, Part 2, Doc. 42.
[28] "Memorandum of Conversation," Washington, November 14, 1967, 5:05–6:15 p.m., and "Memorandum of Conversation," Washington, November 15, 1967, 5:23–6:59 p.m., in *FRUS*, 1964–1968, Vol. XXIX, Part 2, Docs. 104, 106.

The next month, Sato enunciated his "three nonnuclear principles," whereby Japan committed not to produce, possess, or introduce nuclear weapons on its territory.[29] In February 1968, Sato expanded his nonnuclear principles into "four pillars" of Japan's nonnuclear policy: the first pillar consisting of the three preexisting nonnuclear principles, to which Sato added reliance on the U.S. nuclear umbrella, promotion of worldwide disarmament, and development of nuclear energy for peaceful purposes. As such, Sato clarified that the U.S. nuclear umbrella was the backbone of Japan's renunciation of nuclear weapons.[30]

From the late 1960s: The Search for Reassurances

Notably, Sato had reaffirmed Japan's commitment to a nonnuclear policy and reliance on U.S. security guarantees without having done a detailed cost-benefit analysis of a Japanese nuclear deterrent.

Still, Sato eventually commissioned such a study from the Cabinet Information Research Office; it became known as the 1968–1970 Internal Report, as it was published in two parts, in September 1968 and January 1970.[31] Soon after President Johnson's assurances and Sato's enunciation of the four pillars, changes in U.S. foreign policy triggered concerns in Tokyo of U.S. abandonment, prompting the need for a closer look at the pros and cons of nuclear development. On March 31, 1968, Johnson announced that he would unilaterally de-escalate the Vietnam War, restricting the bombing of the North and the number of troops to be sent to the conflict, and that he would not seek reelection. Operation Rolling Thunder was terminated in October. The U.S. ambassador to Japan, U. Alexis Johnson (1966–1969), reported from Tokyo that the president's speech had "been widely misinterpreted ... as admission of defeat and reversal of U.S. policy on Vietnam, foreshadowing U.S. withdrawal from Asia" and the possible normalization of relations with the People's Republic of China.[32] Such normalization between Washington and Beijing was not yet in the offing. But Washington was hoping to reduce its defense spending in the region.

[29] See: Pyle (1988, 455).
[30] Ibid. See also: Green and Furukawa (2008, 350).
[31] See: Kase (2001, 55–59).
[32] "Editorial Note," in *FRUS*, 1964–1968, Vol. XXIX, Part 2, Doc. 119.

President Johnson's successor, Richard Nixon, announced in Guam in July 1969 what became known as the Nixon Doctrine: that the United States would expect its allies in Asia to shoulder a greater share of the region's security needs. The following November, Nixon and Sato agreed that Okinawa should revert to Japan, though Washington would continue to operate military bases on the island.[33]

The prospect of a decline in U.S. military expenditures strengthened the case for greater defense spending in Japan. In January 1970, a new director general came to the Japanese Defense Agency (JDA), Nakasone Yasuhiro (1970–1972), who was intent on a more autonomous defense posture for Japan.[34] That same month, the final results of the 1968–1970 internal report became available. The impact of the report on decisionmakers in Tokyo is unclear, but its perspective was consistent with the thrust of Japanese foreign policy:[35] it argued against an autonomous nuclear deterrent. The first part of the study, released in September 1968, analyzed the technical, economic, and organizational issues related to nuclearization. The second part, released in January 1970, focused on the strategic, political, and diplomatic dimensions. The report concluded that although a nuclear-weapons program was costly, Tokyo possessed the scientific know-how to bring it to completion. The argument against such a program was strategic. Explicitly comparing Japan to France, the report concluded that the atomic bomb would create much greater security concerns among Japan's enemies and allies than France's nuclear weapon had. In addition, Japan's high population density would make it vulnerable to a nuclear attack. As such, nuclear weapons could be counterproductive. Japan's security would be ensured as long as enemies believed that they would face U.S. retaliation, and the report recommended continued reliance on Washington's nuclear umbrella.[36] Nakasone was ultimately unsuccessful in his attempt to promote a more independent defense policy. In February 1970, Japan agreed to sign the NPT.

---

[33] See: Buckley (1992, 115–122); Green (1995, 54). On the negotiations to maintain U.S. nuclear weapons in Okinawa after the base reverted to Japan, see: NSA EBB 541, Doc. 1.
[34] See: Green (1995, 55); Hoey (2012, 58).
[35] See: Kase (2001, 56).
[36] Ibid., 59, 62–63.

The next year, concerns of abandonment again increased when Washington abruptly announced its desire to normalize relations with Beijing, in what Japan would call the "Nixon Shock."[37] National Security Advisor Henry Kissinger visited Beijing on July 9–11, 1971, and on the 15th President Nixon announced that he, too, would soon visit Beijing.[38] Japan was alerted only minutes before the president's address.[39] On the 20th, Japanese Ambassador Ushiba Nobuhiko (1970–1973) met with U. Alexis Johnson, by then the U.S. Undersecretary of State for Political Affairs (1969–1973), and explained the concerns raised by the rapprochement: "Sato had over the years based his policy on the Yoshida tradition of close collaboration with the US in foreign policy, especially in the China issue," Ushiba explained, yet "the charge would now be made that the US had pulled the rug out from under this policy by making this dramatic move on China policy, not only without consulting but even without any substantial prior notice to the Japanese government."[40] In January 1972, Sato and Nixon met at the president's California estate in San Clemente. The prime minister reiterated the goals of Japanese foreign policy. Japan "finds it difficult to convince anyone that it is not going militaristic, which is considered to be inevitable in view of Japan's great economic power." The country, in his view, "should not seek to become a military power, and should seek to play a larger economic role within that context."[41] Japan had committed to the three nonnuclear principles, and thus "must rely on

---

[37] It was also called "Asakai's Nightmare," in reference to Asakai Koichiro, Japanese ambassador to the United States (1957–1963), who reportedly dreamed that he would wake up to an announcement that Washington had recognized Beijing without warning Tokyo. See: Barnett (1977, 113); Schaller (2001, 367); Pan (2007).

[38] Text of the address available at: "Remarks to the Nation Announcing the Acceptance of an Invitation to Visit the People's Republic of China," July 15, 1971, The American Presidency Project, Public Papers of the Presidents, Richard Nixon, 1971. Available at: www.presidency.ucsb.edu/ws/index. php?pid=3079. Last accessed: May 1, 2016.

[39] See: Schaller (2001, 375).

[40] U.S. Department of State, Undersecretary for Political Affairs, "Conversation with Japanese Ambassador Ushiba; Include Memorandum for the Record," July 20, 1971, p. 1, in Digital National Security Archive (DNSA), "Japan and the United States, 1960–1976."

[41] U.S. Office of the White House, "Meeting with Eisaku Sato, Japanese Prime Minister," January 6, 1972, p. 5, in DNSA, "Japan and the U.S., 1960–1976."

the United States nuclear umbrella under the Mutual Security Treaty," adding that "in defense it has no other recourse except to the United States nuclear umbrella."[42]

In sum, Japanese decisionmakers concluded that the Nixon Doctrine and the U.S.-China rapprochement did not constitute sufficient change in Japan's security environment to warrant an autonomous nuclear deterrent. After all, they considered the Soviet Union, rather than the PRC, as their main security threat.[43] Sato's successor, Prime Minister Tanaka Kakuei (1972–1974), quickly normalized relations with Beijing in September 1972.[44] During his visit to the United States the following July, Tanaka reported on a meeting with Zhou Enlai and stressed that "as long as Japan does not possess nuclear weapons China would not entertain aggressive intentions against Japan, and since Japan has no aggressive intentions toward China," Tanaka concluded, "there is no danger of war."[45] In 1976, the JDA, which would later become the Ministry of Defense, started formulating a long-term National Defense Program Outline (NDPO), underpinned by the fact that there was no immediate military threat and that the alliance with the United States was the basic bloc of regional security in East Asia.[46] The Japanese cabinet set a limit of defense-related expenditure at 1 percent of GNP.[47]

Tokyo followed with apprehension developments over the following decades, especially on the Korean Peninsula. In his election campaign, Jimmy Carter, objecting to South Korea's human rights record, vowed to remove U.S. troops and tactical nuclear weapons from the country. In May 1977, the Japanese foreign minister told Secretary of Defense Harold

[42] Ibid., pp. 6–7.
[43] See: Schaller (1997, 247); "Memorandum from the President's Special Assistant (Rostow) to President Johnson," Washington, March 1, 1967, in *FRUS*, Vol. XXIX, Part 2, Doc. 84; U.S. National Security Council, "Meeting between Henry Kissinger and Prime Minister Tanaka," August 19, 1972, p. 18, in DNSA, "Japan and the U.S., 1960–1976."
[44] See: Schaller (2001, 386, 477).
[45] U.S. Office of the White House, "Meeting of President Nixon and Prime Minister Tanaka," July 31, 1973, p. 8, in DNSA, "Japan and the U.S., 1960–1976." See also: U.S. Embassy, "Fifth Security Consultative Group Meeting," August 20, 1973, p. 2, in DNSA, "Japan and the U.S., 1960–1976." See also: Barnett (1977, 112–117).
[46] See: Green (1995, 75).
[47] Ibid., 77. This resolution formalized a practice that had been in place in the 1960s. See: Pyle (1988, 456).

Brown (1977–1981) that he viewed the "presence of ground troops in Korea as [a] valuable contribution to [the] deterrence of war on [the] Peninsula." Therefore, the withdrawal of U.S. troops from South Korea would make Japan "uneasy."[48] That spring, the Carter administration decided to delay the withdrawal of its troops from South Korea, which was never carried out, to the satisfaction of Japanese policymakers.[49]

The threat of communism receded with the end of the Cold War when Japan's main security threat, the Soviet Union, disintegrated. In the discussions for the indefinite extension of the NPT in 1995, the JDA again considered the possibility of a Japanese nuclear deterrent. The report concluded, in line with the logic of the 1968–1970 Internal Report, that Japan's security would actually be undermined by the acquisition of a nuclear deterrent, given regional repercussions of Japanese militarization.[50]

Since the end of the Cold War, recurrent crises in the Korean Peninsula and North Korea's acquisition of nuclear weapons have raised concerns in Tokyo. After Pyongyang's October 2006 nuclear test, Prime Minister Shinzo Abe (2006–2007, 2012–) endorsed harsh sanctions against North Korea while reaffirming the country's adherence to the three nonnuclear principles.[51] Yet, other officials in the ruling Liberal Democratic Party (LDP), including the foreign minister, suggested the importance of a debate on the utility of nuclear weapons.[52] President George W. Bush expressed his concerns about the regional repercussions of an autonomous Japanese nuclear arsenal, and the United States quickly reasserted its commitment to the security of its allies in the region.[53] Secretary of State Condoleezza Rice

[48] U.S. Embassy in Japan, "Brown/Habib Consultations with Japanese Foreign Office," May 28, 1977, p. 7, in Digital National Security Archive (DNSA), "Japan and the United States, Part II, 1977–1992." In September 1973, Japanese defense minister Yamanaka had warned that "[i]f the entire peninsula is communized, Japan would then be in the front line of free nations in Asia." See: U.S. Department of Defense, Deputy Assistant Secretary for East Asia and Pacific Affairs, "Meeting of William Clements and Defense Minister Yamanaka," September 16, 1973, p. 3, in DNSA, "Japan and the U.S. II, 1977–1992."

[49] See: U.S. Department of Defense, "Brown-Yamashita Visit," August 16, 1979, p. 1, in DNSA, "Japan and the U.S. II, 1977–1992."

[50] See: L. Hughes (2007, 78); Green and Furukawa (2008, 353).

[51] See: Hughes and Krauss (2007, 163–164).

[52] See: C. Hughes (2007, 77); Mochizuki (2007, 303). See also: Rublee (2009, 76).

[53] See: C. Hughes (2007, 78, 89).

reassured Tokyo that "Japan's security is the United States' security."[54] President Barack Obama offered similar assurances after the 2009, 2013, and 2016 North Korean nuclear tests.[55]

In addition, the rise of China could create long-term challenges, and there have already been clashes between the two countries over the control of Senkaku/Diaoyu islands since April 2012. Nevertheless, Tokyo has remained steadfast in its commitment to nuclear forbearance and has continued to rely on Washington to meet its security needs. In turn, the United States has sought to reaffirm its commitment to the stability of the region with its "pivot" or rebalancing to Asia, announced in late 2011.[56] So far, concerns about the risks of Japanese militarization, combined with a relatively mild security environment and strong alliance commitments from the United States, have kept Tokyo from acquiring nuclear weapons.

There is much discussion about how long, given Japan's latent nuclear capability, would it take the country to build a deliverable nuclear weapon. Although the popular press often features estimates that Tokyo would be able nuclearize in less than six months, more conservative analysis estimates Japan's nuclear breakout period to be between three and five years.[57]

U.S. Nonproliferation Efforts

Since Tokyo saw no value in acquiring nuclear weapons as long as U.S. security guarantees were forthcoming, additional U.S. nonproliferation efforts were unnecessary to keep Japan nonnuclear. From the early years of the Yoshida Doctrine until the late 1960s, Japan resolutely relied on assurances from the United States to meet its security needs. U.S. officials expected that economic growth would eventually increase Japan's appetite for a more independent defense policy and a more robust military capability, and grew frustrated when such expectations failed to materialize. In the fall of 1961, a paper from the Department of State concluded that "[Japan's] recovery since 1945 has been most impressive in the economic sphere and least impressive in

[54] Quoted in ibid., p. 89.
[55] See: Samuels and Schoff (2013, 244–245).
[56] See: Clinton (2011).
[57] See: Lewis (2006).

the military field."[58] A year later, the JCS chairman, General Maxwell Taylor (1962–1964), complained of the "continued apathy of the Japanese toward the requirements of their own self defense."[59] Richard Nixon, in laying out his vision for the future of Asia in his famous *Foreign Affairs* article of October 1967, stated that it was "simply not realistic to expect a nation moving into the first rank of major powers to be totally dependent for its own security on another nation, however close the ties."[60] Social scientists, too, shared this belief, speculating that Japan would one day demand its own nuclear weapons. In an oft-quoted book, Herman Kahn stated that "if annual growth rates continue at about current levels … most Japanese will almost inevitably feel that Japan has the right and duty to achieve full superpower status and that this means possessing a substantial nuclear establishment."[61] Instead, Japan has officially renounced nuclear weapons.

As Washington prepared for a rapprochement with the PRC, Nixon and Kissinger in fact *encouraged* Tokyo to consider the nuclear option. If Washington could raise the specter of a militaristic Japan, then it could convince Beijing that a continued American presence in East Asia was also in the PRC's interest.[62] In fact, Chinese leaders in the early 1970s were concerned about a more autonomous Japanese defense policy. In April 1970, Zhou Enlai and North Korean leader Kim Il-sung declared that "Japanese militarism has revived and has become a dangerous force of aggression in Asia."[63]

In his meeting with Sato in January 1972, Nixon declared that he "understood the difficult position in which Japan finds itself: as the third strongest economic power in the world Japan must still depend on a commitment by another country, the United States, for its defense."

---

[58] "Department of State Guidelines Paper," Washington, undated, in *FRUS*, 1961–1963, Vol. XXII, Doc. 354.

[59] "Editorial Note," in *FRUS*, 1961–1963, Vol. XXII, Doc. 356. See also: "Department of State Policy Paper," Washington, June 26, 1964, and "Memorandum from the Assistant Secretary of State for Far Eastern Affairs (Bundy) to the Deputy Under Secretary for Political Affairs (Thompson)," Washington, August 20, 1965, both in *FRUS*, 1964–1968, Vol. XXIX, Pt. 2, Docs. 15, 58; Schaller (1997, 196).

[60] Nixon (1967, 121).

[61] Kahn (1970, 165).

[62] See: Schaller (2001, 369, 377–378); Tucker (2001, 253, 257, 281, 313, 344); Pan (2007, 141).

[63] Quoted in Schaller (2001, 377).

Recognizing the "major political problem in Japan" of relying on the U.S. nuclear deterrent, he thought the country faced "an unacceptable choice: either Japan develops its own deterrent power however unpalatable vis-à-vis its neighbors, who are armed with nuclear weapons, or it comes to an accommodation with them."[64]

Then, in his meeting with Zhou Enlai in February 1972, Nixon declared that although the PRC asked the United States to withdraw from Japan, doing so would not be in Beijing's best interest: "The U.S. can get out of Japanese waters, but others will fish there. And both China and the U.S. have had very difficult experiences with Japanese militarism." A revival of Japanese militarism could very well result from Washington's withdrawal, the president continued, speculating that the "Japanese, with their enormously productive economy, their great natural drive and their memories of the war they lost, could well turn toward building their own defenses in the event that the U.S. guarantee were removed." The best solution would be for Washington to remain in Asia, and Japan in particular, so that its voice would be heard.[65]

Washington would not be able to use this strategy of attempting to intimidate China with the specter of Japanese military resurgence for much longer, however. Soon, Japan persisted in its nuclear forbearance and normalized relations with Beijing. During his trip to China in February 1973, Kissinger noted that the Chinese "clearly consider Japan as an incipient ally."[66]

From then on, discussions about a possible Japanese nuclear arsenal has resurfaced after changes in the security environment, and Washington has responded with renewed security guarantees. Given the relatively low level of threat, and the security concerns that

[64] U.S. Office of the White House, "Meeting with Eisaku Sato, Japanese Prime Minister," January 6, 1972, p.6, in DNSA, "Japan and the U.S., 1960–1976."

[65] Memorandum of Conversation, 22 February 1972, 2:10p.m.–6:10p.m., in NSA EBB 106, Doc. 1, p. 12. Winston Lord, member of the NSC (1969–1973), declared that Washington would use the fear of Japanese militarism to enlist Chinese support, in particular for the resolution of hostilities in the Vietnam War: "We said that if you want us as a balancing force in Asia, and particularly against the Soviet Union, as well as a restraint on Japan, you should support us. If the Japanese felt insecure, they might feel a need to remilitarize and develop nuclear weapons." Tucker (2001, 344).

[66] Quoted in Schaller (2001, 387). On improved relations between Japan and the PRC, see also: Barnett (1977, 112–117).

an independent arsenal would trigger in the region, Tokyo has maintained its commitment to renounce nuclear weapons.

Alternative Explanations

Scholars typically argue that Japan's nuclear forbearance is overdetermined. The horrors of Hiroshima and Nagasaki fueled a "nuclear allergy" toward the atomic bomb. Furthermore, Japan relied on an alliance with the United States to provide its security needs, and Japanese opposition to nuclear weapons was enshrined in its domestic laws and fundamental principles. Thus, many scholars refer to a combination of security and domestic political factors to explain Japan's nuclear forbearance.[67] Scholarly debates revolve around the relative importance of such factors.

One argument, put forth by Etel Solingen, is that U.S. security guarantees are insufficient to explain Japan's decisions. "In an anarchic world with no fool-proof security guarantees," she asks, "why would a major power relinquish the ultimate guarantee?"[68] In her view, the most important factor explaining Japan's nuclear forbearance was the economic growth model chosen by its ruling coalition, which placed an emphasis on international trade.[69] The alliance with the United States was chosen to facilitate the pursuit of such an economic strategy.[70] Attempting to acquire nuclear weapons would jeopardize this model of economic openness, given adverse international reactions to nuclear proliferation.

We agree that economic and security policies are interconnected, but it is difficult to claim that economic priorities determined Japan's security policy. The alliance with the United States stemmed directly from the fact that Japan was occupied by U.S. forces in the aftermath of the Second World War. Furthermore, given the consequences of Japan's expansionism in the late nineteenth and early twentieth centuries, there were serious concerns about the regional repercussions of an autonomous Japanese defense policy. Tokyo was content to meet its security needs under a U.S. umbrella, which did not raise the specter of an expansionist Japan. There were thus good security reasons for Japan to

---

[67] See: Campbell and Sunohara (2004); Hughes (2004); L. Hughes (2007); Solingen (2007); Kusunoki (2008); Hughes (2009); Rublee (2009); Tatsumi (2012).
[68] Solingen (2007, 59). See also: Solingen (2010, 134).
[69] See: Solingen (2007, 71).
[70] Ibid., 74.

forgo the nuclear option, and it is not clear that a focus on the economic preferences of its ruling coalition adds much explanatory power.[71]

Another argument, put forth by Maria Rublee, emphasizes the importance of normative concerns in explaining Japan's nuclear decision.[72] In her view, while U.S. security guarantees were "likely necessary," they were "not sufficient."[73] Rublee argues that Japanese decisionmakers consistently found that an atomic weapon "would weaken their security." Yet, she continues, "this was not due to becoming a nuclear target (I found no record of this being a particular concern …) but rather because a nuclear weapons program would disrupt regional and international relations."[74] In Rublee's view, Japanese elites decided against a nuclear option because they "grew to accept the international and domestic norm against nuclear acquisition."[75]

We agree that Japan was not dissuaded from acquiring nuclear weapons for fear of preventive strikes. Given U.S. security guarantees, a (Soviet or Chinese) attack on Japan would have been very costly indeed. Instead, a reasonable concern was that the acquisition of nuclear weapons would ultimately undermine Japan's security, given neighboring states' fears of Japanese expansionism. A security approach is sufficient to explain this calculation. Moreover, although there was some domestic political opposition to nuclear weapons, it did not necessarily operate as an independent factor toward nuclear forbearance. The horrors of Hiroshima and Nagasaki could fuel a "nuclear allergy," but they also underpinned the logic that Japanese rearmament could actually undermine the country's security, as Prime Minister Yoshida frequently stated.

Other scholars have previously emphasized the importance of security factors to explain Japanese nuclear forbearance.[76] We essentially

[71] For example, Ayako Kusunoki argues that both domestic politics and security explanations mattered, and while one could argue that domestic requirements outweighed strategic considerations, "[t]he basis of this non-nuclear policy was Japan's dependence on the U.S. nuclear deterrent." Kusunoki (2008, 50).

[72] See: Rublee (2009, 2010).

[73] Rublee (2009, 89).

[74] Ibid., 87.

[75] Ibid., 54. For another account of Japanese nuclear forbearance based on domestic political preferences and the number of veto players, see: Hymans (2011).

[76] See: Frankel (1993, 47–48); Paul (2000, 52–57). See also: Levite (2002–2003, 71–73, 79–80); Lanoszka (2013). For an analysis of Japanese security "production" as a function of the threat environment, see: Anderson (2016).

agree with these security-based explanations, and only differ in our comparative evaluation of the Japanese case. Paul argues that during the Cold War, Japanese forbearance resulted from the same mechanism as Germany's nonnuclear status: "anticipated negative responses by neighbours, allies, and adversaries constitute a significant disincentive that helps explain Japan's non-nuclear policy."[77] In Paul's view, renewed U.S. commitment to Japanese security since the end of the Cold War "continues to limit Japan's offensive capabilities and military operations in the region."[78]

This argument portrays U.S. nonproliferation efforts toward Japan as more coercive than they actually were. Japan did not perceive the acquisition of nuclear weapons to be productive. Instead of being "limited" from acquiring nuclear weapons, Tokyo has instead decided to forgo the nuclear option of its own volition, sometimes even against Washington's prodding. In contrast, West Germany was concerned about U.S. security guarantees. Perceiving nuclear weapons to provide a security benefit, Bonn pursued the nuclear option, producing Soviet concerns, which in turn led Washington to apply coercive threats to keep West Germany nonnuclear.[79] It is important to understand the mechanism through which alliances produce nonproliferation, so as to better assess the effectiveness of different nonproliferation tools and the conditions under which proliferation concerns can reemerge. Whereas in the West German case the United States acted to remove Bonn's opportunity to nuclearize, in the Japanese case Washington did not need to do so, since its security guarantees had removed Tokyo's willingness to go nuclear.

In sum, Japan has refrained from acquiring nuclear weapons because it concluded that an autonomous nuclear deterrent would undermine its security. Tokyo worried about the regional consequences of its nuclear acquisition, perceived the level of threat to be relatively low, and relied on U.S. security guarantees for its defense. By now, Japan certainly possesses the capacity to build nuclear weapons, given its mastery of the nuclear fuel cycle and the large quantity of plutonium that it has amassed: according to a prominent expert, the country has enough plutonium for 1,000 nuclear weapons. Whether Japan remains

---

[77] Paul (2000, 53).
[78] Ibid., 54.
[79] See our case study of West Germany in this chapter.

nonnuclear therefore depends for the most part on its perception of the level of threat and the reliability of U.S. security guarantees.[80] Should China continue to rise and pose ever greater levels of threat to Japan's security, and should the United States decrease the reliability of its protection over the Japanese territory, Tokyo would develop the willingness to build a nuclear deterrent. But given Japanese weakness vis-à-vis China, Washington would likely be able to implement a sticks-based nonproliferation approach successfully, denying Japan the opportunity to build the bomb.

South Korea

Despite having possessed a nuclear program during the first half of the 1970s, and a long-standing rivalry with North Korea, which nuclearized in the 2000s, South Korea has never built a nuclear deterrent. Instead, Seoul was first denied the opportunity to nuclearize by U.S. coercive pressure and then lost the willingness to build the bomb due to the reassurances offered by its American ally.

Since the conclusion of the Korean War in 1953, South Korea faced a significant security threat: North Korea. To meet this threat, Seoul relied heavily on the United States. As the war ended, the two countries signed a Mutual Defense Treaty. In 1957, Washington created the U.S. Forces Korea, deploying troops as well as tactical nuclear weapons to the Korean Peninsula.

South Korean concerns about the reliability of U.S. guarantees spiked in 1969, when newly elected President Richard Nixon announced the Guam Doctrine. This plan aimed at limiting American military entanglement in Asia and encouraging allies to take greater control over their own security, and it led to the withdrawal of one-third of the U.S. troops (around 20,000) stationed in South Korea. Fearing abandonment, President Park Chung-hee initiated a nuclear-weapons program. In response, Washington deployed a sticks-based nonproliferation effort, applying significant nonproliferation pressure on Seoul, eventually leading South Korea to ratify the NPT on April 23, 1975 and terminate its nuclear program in December that year.

[80] For a discussion of possible future scenarios of Japanese nuclearization, see: Monten and Provost (2005); Samuels and Schoff (2013).

Such a coercive U.S. nonproliferation effort did not undermine South Korea's willingness to acquire nuclear weapons, however. Park tied the abandonment of the nuclear-weapons program to the provision of more robust U.S. assurances. South Korean concerns were heightened again in early 1977, when President Jimmy Carter, critical of Park's repressive policies, proposed to cut military aid to South Korea, withdraw American ground troops from the peninsula, and remove 1,000 tactical nuclear weapons from the country. Again, Park demonstrated his willingness to acquire nuclear weapons; and again U.S. officials were concerned about a resumption of the South Korean nuclear-weapons program. Ultimately, in 1981, the Reagan administration opted for a carrots-based nonproliferation policy toward Seoul, making a renewed commitment to the defense of South Korea, and convincing South Korean president Chun Doo-hwan to renounce nuclear weapons.

Since then, South Korea's security concerns have fluctuated over time. The four North Korean nuclear tests of October 2006, May 2009, February 2013, and January 2016 have raised concerns abroad about South Korean nuclearization. Given its relative strength vis-à-vis the North, South Korea might have the opportunity to go nuclear, but the high level of support it receives from the United States undermines its willingness to acquire nuclear weapons. Washington can therefore continue to deter South Korean nuclearization with a renewed commitment to its defense, and it seems willing to do so, making it unlikely that South Korea will acquire nuclear weapons in the foreseeable future.

South Korean Interest in Nuclear Weapons

Korea emerged from Japanese occupation at the end of the Second World War as a divided country, with the Soviet Union occupying the northern part of the country and the United States controlling the area south of the 38th parallel. Both North and South became independent states in August and September 1948 as, respectively, the Democratic People's Republic of Korea (DPRK) and the Republic of Korea (ROK). In the spring of 1950, DPRK leader Kim Il-sung invaded the ROK, hoping to reunify the country by force. The conflict lasted three years and caused significant human toll. Estimates vary, with some claiming that as many as three million Koreans – about 10 percent of the combined population of the DPRK and ROK – were killed, wounded, or missing.[81]

Even after the conclusion of hostilities, North Korea remained an important threat to the South. To counter it, South Korea relied on U.S. support. In October 1953, the two countries signed a Mutual Defense Treaty, whereby Washington publicly committed itself to deterring North Korea.[82] The U.S. troop presence decreased after the end of the Korean War, but a sizable contingent of around 60,000 remained on the peninsula throughout the 1950s.[83] In January 1958, Washington also deployed tactical nuclear weapons to Korea.[84]

Furthermore, the United States provided economic assistance to the South and supported Seoul's efforts to develop nuclear energy for civilian purposes. In 1955, the two countries signed a bilateral treaty for the transfer of civilian nuclear technology.[85] South Korea took a series of steps to assure others that its nuclear intentions remained peaceful. In 1957, it joined the IAEA.[86] Two years later, the ROK established the Korea Atomic Energy Research Institute (KAERI) to oversee nuclear energy research.[87] In 1964, Seoul ratified the PTBT.[88]

Wavering U.S. Support

In the late 1960s, however, two developments led to heightened security concerns in Seoul. First, North Korea's foreign policy became increasingly aggressive. In 1968, a thirty-one-member commando team attempted to assassinate President Park in a raid on his official residence, the Blue House. The same year, North Korea captured a U.S. intelligence ship, the *U.S.S. Pueblo*, triggering a crisis that lasted nearly a year.[89]

Second, the United States announced a reduction of its commitments to East Asia. On July 25, 1969, President Nixon declared a new doctrine

---

[81] See: Oberdorfer (1997, 10).
[82] See: Pollack and Reiss (2004, 266).
[83] See: Kane (2006).
[84] See: Choi and Park (2009, 375).
[85] See: Snyder (2010, 160).
[86] See: Pollack and Reiss (2004, 258).
[87] See: Snyder (2010, 160).
[88] See: Siler (1998, 58).
[89] See: Fischer (2007).

while visiting the Western Pacific island of Guam, whereby regional allies were expected to do more to contribute to their security. A year later, the United States announced that it would pull out 20,000 troops from the demilitarized zone (DMZ) dividing North and South Korea.

President Park was shocked at this announcement. He had actually supported the Guam Doctrine publicly when he met with President Nixon in August 1969.[90] Park was convinced that if South Korea continued to support the U.S. war effort in Vietnam, American troops would remain on the Korean Peninsula, and he would be consulted before any pullback of U.S. commitments to the ROK's security.[91] In Park's view, as reported by his aide Kim Seong-jin, the implementation of the Nixon doctrine in the form of important troop withdrawals was "a message to the Korean people that we won't rescue you if the North invades again."[92]

A Turn toward Nuclear Arms

Soon, Park was calling for a "self-reliant national defense" for South Korea,[93] which, although centered on more robust conventional capabilities, also involved the development of a "super weapon."[94] In 1970, he set up a military nuclear program controlled by the Agency for Defense Development (ADD).[95] KAERI was tasked with acquiring reprocessing capabilities[96] and a Weapons Exploitation Committee was secretly established, which was responsible for the procurement and production of nuclear weapons.[97]

In July 1971, over Park's objections, the United States withdrew the Seventh Infantry Division from South Korea.[98] The following November, Park met with Oh Won-cheol, a senior staff member responsible for the development of defense-related industries, saying:

Our national security is vulnerable because of the uncertainty surrounding continued U.S. military presence on the Korean Peninsula. To become secure

[90] See: Lee (2006, 67).
[91] Ibid. See also: Kim (2011, 51).
[92] Quoted in Oberdorfer (1997, 13).
[93] Quoted in Choi and Park (2009, 384).
[94] Quoted in Hong (2011, 483).
[95] See: Pollack and Reiss (2004, 262).
[96] See: Snyder (2010, 161).
[97] Ibid., 161.
[98] See: Hong (2011, 488).

and independent, we need to free ourselves from dependence on U.S. military protection.... Can we develop nuclear weapons?[99]

The next year, Park ordered Oh Won-cheol to secure the necessary technology for a nuclear deterrent.[100] Between 1971 and 1974, South Korea reached agreements with France, Belgium, and Canada for the purchase of nuclear fuel, a laboratory, and a reprocessing facility.[101] In February 1973 President Park signed the "Basic Plan for Developing Ballistic Missiles."[102] Later that year, the ADD estimated that a nuclear-weapons program would take six to ten years to complete, costing about $1.5–2 billion.[103]

Developments in Vietnam during the first half of the 1970s reinforced Park's sense of the value of nuclear weapons. The withdrawal of U.S. forces in 1973, the fall of Saigon in 1975, and the revolutionary victory in Cambodia that same year, all contributed to his view that "South Korea could be another South Vietnam" by emboldening Kim Il-sung to attempt an attack on the South.[104] South Korea then embarked on a dedicated nuclear-weapons program codenamed Project 890.[105] By late 1974 and early 1975, there were few doubts in U.S. policy circles that Seoul was seeking to acquire nuclear weapons.[106] Washington had to respond.

U.S. Nonproliferation Efforts

In the early years of the Cold War, Washington and Seoul had a shared interest in stopping the spread of communism. Yet, there were serious doubts in Washington about the wisdom of its commitment to the Korean Peninsula. The JCS declared on September 26, 1947 that the United States had "little strategic interest in maintaining the present troops and bases in Korea."[107] By June 1949, President Truman had

---

[99] Quoted in ibid., 483.
[100] See: Choi (2014).
[101] See: Kim (2001, 64).
[102] See: Hong (2011, 494).
[103] See: Pollack and Reiss (2004, 262); Hong (2011, 491).
[104] Choi (2014, 73).
[105] See: Central Intelligence Agency (1978, 7).
[106] See: U.S. Department of State Cable, "ROK Plans to Develop Nuclear Weapons and Missiles," December 11, 1974, in Wilson Center Digital Archive, South Korean Nuclear History. Kim (2001, 59).
[107] Quoted in Lee (2006, 24).

removed all U.S. troops from the ROK, except for a 495-strong advisory group.[108]

This decreased U.S. military presence on the Korean Peninsula was arguably one of the factors that facilitated Kim Il-sung's attempt to invade the ROK in the spring of 1950.[109] In the course of the conflict, doubts remained about the importance of the ROK for U.S. strategic interests. Secretary of State Dean Acheson claimed that the United States was fighting "the wrong nation" and "the second team," and should focus its efforts on the real enemy, the Soviet Union.[110] The Army Chief of Staff, General J. Lawton Collins (1949–1953), added that "Korea was not worth a nickel."[111]

At the same time, Washington valued the role that its protégé in the Korean Peninsula could play in deterring the spread of communism. Therefore, the United States committed vast human and material resources to defending South Korea during the war and offered Seoul security guarantees through the Mutual Defense Treaty. After the war, whenever Seoul manifested concerns about the reliability of U.S. security guarantees, American officials would reassure their South Korean interlocutors. During a visit to the ROK in 1966, Vice President Hubert H. Humphrey (1965–1969) declared that "as long as there is one American soldier on … the demarcation line, the whole and entire power of the United States of America is committed to the defense of Korea."[112] Two years later, Secretary of State Dean Rusk highlighted his country's efforts in defending South Korea, instructing the U.S. embassy in Seoul to quell South Korean concerns:

We have invested over 33,000 battle deaths, 20,000 non-battle deaths, and over 100,000 wounded in the security of an independent Republic of Korea. We have maintained large forces in that country for 17 years. We have invested over six billion dollars (almost half the total Marshall Plan) in economic and military assistance. … You should find ways to make it clear that Korean suspicion against this record is simply incomprehensible to the American people.[113]

---

[108] See: Ibid., 24–25.
[109] Ibid., 25–26.
[110] Quoted in ibid., 31.
[111] Ibid.
[112] Ibid., 55.
[113] Ibid., 59.

The Nixon Doctrine, when announced in 1969, thus came as a great surprise, posing a serious challenge for South Korean security and, therefore, for U.S. nonproliferation goals. If U.S. interest in the defense of the ROK were to be measured by the number of troops on the peninsula and the presence of U.S. troops along the line of demarcation, then serious security concerns were bound to emerge when Washington announced that it would pull out 20,000 troops from South Korea, leaving the ROK alone in defending the DMZ.

According to Nixon, the United States was committed to the defense of South Korea; the issue for him was that U.S. commitments to Seoul were too high and too costly. When he tasked his administration in November 1969 to draw up plans for troop withdrawals, he claimed that his intention was "to maintain the air and sea presence [in Korea] at whatever level is necessary for the kind of retaliatory strike which we have planned." This presence, in his mind, required cutting "the number of Americans there in half."[114] Unsurprisingly, Seoul perceived these actions as a partial allied abandonment, casting doubt on the reliability of U.S. commitments, and boosting the perceived benefits of developing nuclear weapons.

Korean Nuclear Efforts Revealed
Washington first learned about the ROK nuclear-weapons program in late 1974 and saw great proliferation risk in the reprocessing plant that its protégé sought to purchase from France. In early March 1975, the U.S. embassy in Seoul argued for a "more explicit course," claiming "there was no need to pussy-foot" because the South Koreans were "serious, tough customers bent in this case on a potentially harmful cause."[115] Later that month, Kissinger approached the French, attempting to get them to cancel the agreement.[116] In April, South Korea agreed to ratify the NPT, under U.S. pressure.

[114] Quoted in Stueck (2011, 23).
[115] U.S. Department of State Cable, "ROK Plans to Develop Nuclear Weapons and Missiles," March 12, 1975, in Wilson Center Digital Archive, South Korean Nuclear History.
[116] "Nuclear Suppliers Conference," March 26, 1975, in Digital National Security Archive (DNSA), "The Kissinger Transcripts: A Verbatim Record of U.S. Diplomacy, 1969–77," KT01550. Some claim that Kissinger threatened to terminate security ties with South Korea and withdraw all U.S. troops if Seoul continued to pursue a nuclear weapon. See: Paul (2000, 123); Hayes (1992, 24); Hersman and Peters (2006, 541). We were unable to find direct evidence that such a conversation took place.

Despite ratifying the NPT, Seoul remained deeply concerned about its security, indicating a willingness to acquire nuclear weapons. Park made clear that his adherence to nonproliferation goals was contingent on U.S. security guarantees. In an interview with *The Washington Post* on June 26, 1975, he reportedly said that "South Korea would do everything in its power to defend its own security – including development of nuclear weapons if necessary – if the U.S. nuclear umbrella were withdrawn."[117] Consequently, U.S. officials regularly reiterated their commitment to the defense of the ROK. In June 1975, Secretary of Defense James Schlesinger (1973–1975) testified in Congress that Washington would consider a nuclear attack in response to an eventual North Korean invasion of the South.[118] In July, a U.S. NSC memorandum recognized that it was increasingly difficult to ignore "the intimate relationship between the ROK's nuclear weapons plan and our security commitment there."[119]

While attempting to undermine South Korea's willingness to nuclearize by reassuring it of U.S. security commitments, Washington also applied coercive tools in an attempt to take away South Korea's opportunity to develop nuclear weapons. Specifically, U.S. officials made clear to their ROK counterparts that U.S. security assurances were conditional on the maintenance of Seoul's nonnuclear status. In August 1976, Schlesinger visited South Korea and stated bluntly that "the only thing that could undermine the political relationship between the U.S. and the ROK would be the Korean effort to acquire its own nuclear weapons."[120] Washington insisted on the cancellation of the agreement with France for the purchase of a reprocessing plant. In September, assistant secretary of state for East Asian and Pacific affairs, Philip Habib (1974–1976), traveled to South Korea to stress the "major importance" of South Korean plans for reprocessing, "urging cancellation" of the agreement with the French.[121] In December, the U.S. ambassador

[117] Don Oberdorfer, "Park: Seoul Target of North," *The Washington Post*, June 27, 1975, pp. A1, A32, quote at p. A32.
[118] See: Kim (2001, 64); Lin (2012, 178).
[119] U.S. National Security Council Memorandum, "Approach to South Korea on Reprocessing," July 8, 1975, in Wilson Center Digital Archive, South Korean Nuclear History.
[120] "Memorandum of Conversation," Seoul, August 27, 1975, in *Foreign Relations of the United States (FRUS), 1969–1976*, Vol. E-12, *Documents on East and Southeast Asia, 1973–1976*, Doc. 272.
[121] U.S. Department of State Cable, "ROK Nuclear Reprocessing," September 8, 1975, in Wilson Center Digital Archive, South Korean Nuclear History.

warned the South Korean deputy prime minister of the "very adverse implications" of the deal.[122] In his cable to Washington later that day, the ambassador argued that the United States "must make indelibly clear that far more than our nuclear support is at stake here, that if ROKs proceed as they have indicated to date [the] whole range of security and political relationships between [the] US and ROK will be affected."[123] Just days later, he asked his South Korean interlocutors

whether Korea [was] prepared [to] jeopardize … [its] vital partnership with [the] U.S., not only in nuclear and scientific areas but in broad political and security areas. [The] ROKG [ROK government] had to weigh [the] advantages of this kind of support and cooperation which [the] USG [US government] could provide against [the] French option.[124]

U.S. pressures were bearing fruit and there was some indication that South Korean officials were reconsidering the deal with the French. In January 1976, Kissinger confided to one of his assistants: "I think it's safe to say we've delivered the knock-out blow."[125] The following week, South Korea cancelled its agreement with France.[126]

While pursuing the nuclear option, South Korea also maintained an interest in modernizing its conventional forces. In January 1976, Seoul launched a five-year, $5 billion "improvement program" to build its conventional military.[127] Washington used its conventional assistance to South Korean forces to put additional pressure on its ally to give up its nuclear program entirely. In May 1976, the United States decided to cut its military aid in half.[128] In August 1976, South Korea agreed to discuss additional IAEA safeguards on its program,[129] and

[122] U.S. Department of State Cable, "ROK Nuclear Reprocessing (I)," December 10, 1975, in Wilson Center Digital Archive, South Korean Nuclear History.

[123] U.S. Department of State Cable, "ROK Nuclear Reprocessing (II)," December 10, 1975, in Wilson Center Digital Archive, South Korean Nuclear History.

[124] U.S. Department of State Cable, "ROK Nuclear Reprocessing," December 16, 1975, in Wilson Center Digital Archive, South Korean Nuclear History.

[125] "Middle East; ROK Nuclear Reactor," January 24, 1976, DNSA, "Kissinger Transcripts," KT01884.

[126] See: Central Intelligence Agency (1978, i); Park (1998, 109).

[127] See: Kim (2001, 64).

[128] Ibid.

[129] See: "IAEA/U.S./ROK Safeguards Suspension Protocol," August 18, 1976, in Digital National Security Archive (DNSA), "The United States and the Two Koreas, Part II, 1969–2010," KO00215.

in December 1976 Park terminated South Korea's nuclear-weapons program.[130] The CIA concluded that Park wanted to avoid U.S. pressures, which would befall South Korea if there were evidence of a nuclear-weapons program. Park and top South Korean officials agreed that "the weapons program was a major irritant in the relations with the United States,"[131] and was thus "intolerable."[132]

Lingering Korean Nuclear Interest

Despite having shut down its nuclear program as a result of U.S. efforts to remove Seoul's opportunity to nuclearize, South Korea nevertheless maintained the willingness to go nuclear. Park remained doubtful of U.S. guarantees, and hoped to build the foundations for an eventual resumption of nuclear activities. In November 1976, he told Oh Won-cheol to continue pursuing the development of a nuclear industry: "Acquire the capability, but in a manner not inviting foreign pressure."[133] U.S. officials understood the importance of boosting security commitments in order to undermine South Korea's willingness to acquire nuclear weapons. An undated Department of Defense document from the mid-to-late 1970s pointed out:

The Koreans are somewhat paranoid, but not without reason. Their security situation is precarious. Two of the major powers of the area, the USSR and the PRC, have contiguous borders with the North and are allied with Kim Il-sung. On the other hand, South Korea's only reliable ally, the U.S., is 10,000 miles away and [there are] increasing Korean doubts about our constancy.... It is therefore necessary to hold their hands frequently.[134]

[130] See: Central Intelligence Agency (1978).

[131] Ibid., 7.

[132] Ibid., 13, 16–17. In 1981, a State Department cable concurred with this intelligence assessment, stating that Korea had "cancelled its nuclear explosives development program in order not to impair its security relationship with the U.S." "Korean Nuclear Technology Acquisition," September 25, 1981, DNSA, "U.S. and the Two Koreas II, 1969–2010," KO00382. In 1977, Washington was also able to stop a plutonium deal between the ROK and Canada. See: Siler (1998, 70).

[133] Quoted in Kim (2001, 67).

[134] "Study Prepared by the Office of International Security Affairs in the Department of Defense," Washington, undated, in *FRUS*, 1969–1976, Vol. E-12, Doc. 274.

South Korean security concerns would soon be reignited after Jimmy Carter's arrival to the White House. President Carter was highly critical of Park's human rights record and decided to cut military aid and remove U.S. troops and tactical nuclear weapons from the peninsula.[135]

As a result, President Park once again considered the possibility of developing nuclear weapons[136] and a missile capability.[137] Carter then announced on March 9, 1977, that he would delay the withdrawal plans until 1982, essentially defanging the threat, given the uncertainty regarding the presidential election of 1979, which he would ultimately lose to Ronald Reagan. Eventually, following new assessments of North Korean forces produced in January 1979, which suggested a stronger threat against South Korea than initially anticipated, Carter suspended his plans for troop withdrawal until further review.[138] This suspension did not assuage security concerns in the ROK, however. Nor would Seoul feel hampered by its obligations under the NPT. South Korea's foreign minister Park Dong-jin (1975–1980) declared on June 30, 1977:

We have signed the Non-proliferation Treaty and thus ... our basic position is that we do not intend to develop nuclear weapons by ourselves. But if it is necessary for national security interests and people's safety, it is possible for Korea as a sovereign state to make its own judgment on the matter.[139]

U.S. intelligence assessments concurred that Washington's security commitments were a key factor in the ROK's considerations of the nuclear option. In 1978, a CIA report concluded that "[t]he most important factors in Korea's calculations regarding nuclear weapons will ... be successive reassessments of the US security commitment, the threat posed by North Korea, and Seoul's success in building its

---

[135] See: Paul (2000, 121); Snyder (2010, 161).
[136] See: Paul (2000, 123); Kim (2001, 67).
[137] See: Hong (2011, 494–495).
[138] See: Kim (2001, 67); Kim (2011, 55).
[139] Park Dong-jin responding to questions in the Foreign Affairs Committee of the National Assembly, as reported by the Korea Times, cited in Kim (2001, 68).

conventional arms strength."[140] Troop presence would be an important measure of U.S. commitment, yet for any troop level,

> South Korea will continue to questions whether the United States would employ nuclear weapons on its behalf. Waning confidence in the US nuclear umbrella, particularly if accompanied by a decline of US influence in Seoul, would strengthen the hand of those who want to pursue a nuclear weapons option.[141]

In short, South Korea's willingness to acquire nuclear weapons remained, and given the country's rising power vis-à-vis the North, it would be increasingly difficult to ensure the continuation of its non-nuclear status by issuing threats of abandonment. Therefore, South Korean nuclear forbearance would ultimately require renewed U.S. security commitments. Park's assassination in October 1979 and the arrival in power in Washington of President Ronald Reagan paved the way for a possible change in South Korea's nuclear policy. In 1981, the Reagan administration promised to restore and reaffirm Washington's long-standing security commitment to South Korea if the country would terminate its nuclear ambitions in the military realm. U.S. secretary of state Alexander Haig (1981–1982) told ROK president Chun Doo-hwan that "[a] first priority for America is to reestablish confidence in our security relationships."[142] Haig also told ROK foreign minister Lho Shin-yong (1980–1982) that Washington would keep its "nuclear weapons in Korea, although … it was important for the ROK to continue cooperating with our nonproliferation policy."[143] Chun was persuaded to focus on the civilian uses of nuclear energy, terminating all funding for the ADD.[144]

During the 1980s and 1990s, South Korea benefited from a nuclear umbrella extended by the United States as well as from increased diplomatic activity with North Korea. In December 1991, the ROK and

---

[140] Central Intelligence Agency (1978, 18).

[141] Ibid.

[142] "ROK President Chun's Meeting with the Secretary at the State Department," February 6, 1981, in DNSA, "U.S. and the Two Koreas II, 1969–2010," KO00369.

[143] "Korea President Chun's Visit – The Secretary's Meeting at Blair House," February 5, 1981, in DNSA, "U.S. and the Two Koreas II," KO00366.

[144] See: Snyder (2010, 162, 168).

the DPRK signed the "Basic Agreement," which planned for improved military relations and the phased reduction and eventual elimination of WMD from the peninsula.[145] The next month, the two countries signed the "Joint Declaration of Denuclearization of the Korean Peninsula,"[146] in which they pledged not to "manufacture or produce, deploy, store, or use nuclear weapons or to possess reprocessing and enrichment facilities."[147] North Korea also reached an agreement with the United States in 1994, the Agreed Framework, creating hopes of reduced tensions on the peninsula and an end to the DPRK's nuclear-weapons program.[148] Before the decade was over, Kim Dae-jung launched the "sunshine policy," offering economic and humanitarian aid to the DPRK in a renewed effort to reach reconciliation with the North.

North Korea, however, maintained its nuclear development, and by the early 2000s tensions increased again on the peninsula. The Bush administration, on the heels of the terrorist attacks of September 11, 2001, adopted a harder stance against (among others) North Korea, branding the regime a member of an "Axis of Evil" in January 2002.[149] The same year, Washington and Pyongyang abandoned the Agreed Framework, alongside the United States accusing North Korea of secretly enriching uranium.[150] In response to these renewed tensions, ROK president Roh Moo-hyun (2003–2008) made the case when reaching office in 2003 for "self-reliant national defense capabilities within the next ten years." Yet, he maintained his country's pledge to remain nonnuclear, focusing exclusively on building conventional forces.[151] In February 2004, South Korea ratified the IAEA's Additional Protocol on safeguards.[152] When evidence surfaced in August 2004 of a KAERI study on the construction of a reprocessing plant,[153] the government quickly reassured the international community that such were "isolated, laboratory-scale scientific experiments conducted at the

---

[145] See: Choi and Park (2009, 379).
[146] Ibid.
[147] Paul (2000, 123).
[148] See: Cumings (2001); Choi and Park (2009, 378).
[149] See: Kristensen (2002); Lee (2011).
[150] See: Lee and Moon (2003, 137); Pollack (2003, 41).
[151] Quoted in Choi and Park (2009, 391).
[152] See: Snyder (2010, 163).
[153] See: Pinkston (2004).

initiative of a small number of scientists. The Republic of Korea does not have nuclear weapons programs nor any programs for enrichment or reprocessing."[154]

Since then, increased nuclear activities in the North have raised concerns about a possible South Korean nuclear-weapons program. The first North Korean nuclear test of October 2006 was largely seen as a failure and was followed by other tests in May 2009, February 2013, and January 2016. In response, the United States has reiterated its pledges to defend South Korea; and South Korean willingness to acquire nuclear weapons has remained low. Eleven days after the first North Korean test, the term "extended nuclear deterrence" was for the first time added to the Joint Communiqué issued by South Korea and the United States at the end of their Security Consultative Meetings.[155] Given South Korea's military capabilities, the limited aims of its foreign policy, and the firm commitment of the United States to its defense, it remains unlikely that South Korea will develop its own nuclear weapons.

Alternative Explanations

Although it is generally accepted that security concerns triggered South Korean interest in nuclear weapons,[156] the literature is divided on the causes of Seoul's nuclear forbearance.

Etel Solingen argues that international economic factors led South Korea to abandon its efforts to acquire the bomb. Seoul's ruling coalition valued the benefits of integration in the international economy and was particularly sensitive to the cost and possible sanctions attached to a clandestine nuclear-weapons program. Furthermore, domestic political factors played an important role in guaranteeing the maintenance of South Korea's nonnuclear status – a role that Solingen considers "plausibly far more important than U.S. preferences on the matter."[157]

Although Solingen's argument has the benefit of incorporating economic and domestic politics dimensions into nuclear decisionmaking,

---

[154] Ibid.
[155] See: Choi and Park (2009, 392); Snyder (2010, 158).
[156] See: Cha (2001, 91); Kim (2001, 72); Lee (2006, 2); Choi and Park (2009, 385); Snyder (2010, 161); Hong (2011, 503–504); Yang (2011, 10).
[157] Solingen (2007, 98).

it underplays the role that security played in Seoul's economic choices – and in its ultimate commitment to remaining nonnuclear. To begin with, the transformative developmental character of the South Korean regime derives in part from "the heightened need for foreign exchange and war materiel induced by national insecurity."[158] Furthermore, South Korean economic priorities were themselves predicated on U.S. security commitments. With the United States assuming an important role in the defense of South Korea, Seoul's ruling coalition could focus on export-led growth. Without U.S. support, which had a fundamental security dimension, it would be much more difficult for South Korea to pursue its integrationist economic development strategy. Moreover, democracy no doubt allowed for multiple viewpoints to be represented in government, some more hawkish and some more dovish. But this variety is insufficient to explain the fact that South Korea's interest in nuclear weapons has remained weak over the past few decades, despite the North's nuclearization. Without an understanding of security relations with the United States, it is difficult to see why dovish forces prevailed. An account of Seoul's nuclear forbearance must therefore be built around the role played by U.S. security commitments. Had it not been for the Nixon Doctrine and the threats of abandonment it contained, it is unlikely that South Korea would have explored nuclear weapons in the first place.[159] Ultimately, the strategic dependence on the United States – strengthened by renewed U.S. strategic commitments – is sufficient to explain South Korea's nuclear forbearance. Seoul considered nuclear weapons when U.S. support wavered, and renounced them when Washington reasserted its commitment to the ROK's security.

Among existing approaches that, like ours, place a higher priority on U.S. nonproliferation efforts, opinions differ on the source of their effectiveness. Some insist that coercive measures stopped the South Korean program.[160] For example, Alexander Lanoszka argues that the South Korean program ended quickly and definitively because of the high economic dependence of South Korea and the bilateral structure of its alliance with the United States.[161]

[158] Doner et al. (2005, 328).
[159] See: Choi and Park (2009).
[160] See: Engelhardt (1996); Drezner (1999); Hong (2011, 507); Kogan (2013a); Lanoszka (2013); Miller (2014a).
[161] See: Lanoszka (2013).

This perspective is valuable but incomplete. The South Korean nuclear program ended quickly in the mid-1970s, but South Korean interest in nuclear weapons lingered and continued causing headaches for subsequent U.S. administrations. At this point, Washington did more than apply coercive tools; it also renewed its security commitments to South Korea. Additionally, in order to understand the success of U.S. nonproliferation efforts, the best starting point is not the alliance structure but the balance of power between a potential proliferator and its enemy. The United States had bilateral alliances with South Korea, Taiwan, and Pakistan, and yet interacted differently with these three states when evidence surfaced about their nuclear ambitions. Taiwan and Pakistan were weaker vis-à-vis their enemies, and would therefore hardly have had the opportunity to proliferate if abandoned by the United States.[162] The most effective nonproliferation strategy in these cases was to remove the opportunity for proliferation, a strategy that the United States was willing to implement in the case of Taiwan, but not in the case of Pakistan, as it prioritized other foreign policy goals in its relationship with Islamabad. South Korea was a stronger country relative to its adversary.[163] Shocked by the Nixon Doctrine, and until then reliant on the United States for its defense, South Korea asked for time to build up its own defenses. In June 1970, a senior aide to President Park stated that it could do more for its defense, adding: "But we need time. By 1975 we will be superior to North Korea in every respect and will be able to take care of ourselves."[164] A relatively stronger country has a greater opportunity to proliferate. Ultimately, the most effective nonproliferation strategy for the United States included not only coercive tools but also, crucially, security assurances, which took away Seoul's willingness to proliferate. The ROK's nonnuclear status depends on U.S. willingness to continue to uphold such commitments.

In the end, South Korean foreign policy succeeded in that it obtained enhanced U.S. security commitments. In light of this, some have

---

[162] See our case studies of Taiwan and Pakistan in Chapter 5.

[163] On the evolution of the military balance of power between North and South Korea, see: Heeseok Park, "The Claim That South Korea Surpassed North Korea Militarily Is Unreal," *Chosun Ilbo*, September 6, 2013. Available at: http://news.chosun.com/site/data/html_dir/2013/09/06/2013090602680.html. Last accessed: May 12, 2014.

[164] Philip Shabecoff, "Seoul Protests U.S. Plan for Withdrawal," *The New York Times*, June 17, 1970, p. 16.

argued that the goal of the South Korean nuclear-weapons program was actually not to build a nuclear weapon but to develop a breakout capability and coerce the United States into making additional security commitments. Lyong Choi argues that in the mid-1970s, South Korean leadership "considered its nascent nuclear programme a trump card in negotiations with the US; Park needed to prevent additional reductions of US troops from his country."[165] This claim only makes sense if South Korea could credibly threaten its ally with acquiring an independent nuclear arsenal. So the two possibilities – Seoul wanting a nuclear arsenal or using its nuclear program as a bargaining chip – are difficult to disentangle empirically: the latter aim requires a credible threat of pursuing the former goal. This means that had Washington not used its leverage – through both sticks *and carrots* – South Korean plans to nuclearize would likely have gone ahead. When U.S. security commitments weakened, Park developed the program with the prospect of producing a nuclear weapon. It was only after Washington applied coercion that Park shifted his goal to acquiring a breakout capability, developing an autonomous defense industry,[166] and reducing the time needed to produce a bomb.[167] Ultimately, the United States had to provide additional guarantees in order to undermine South Korea's willingness to acquire nuclear weapons, so that the outcome of the South Korean program may have been an increased U.S. security commitment. Yet, this outcome is understandable given South Korea's relative strength. Seoul's willingness to acquire nuclear weapons could be satisfied with a renewal of U.S. commitments. Washington's nonproliferation efforts were successful because they entailed the right mix of threats and assurances,[168] with Washington's military presence and security guarantees obviating the need for an autonomous nuclear deterrent, which Washington vehemently opposed.[169] Our argument offers a unified framework that explains why this particular mix of threats and assurances was effective vis-à-vis South Korea. The stronger a potential proliferator is, the more limited is the ability of a nuclear ally to take away its opportunity to proliferate. Instead, the

---

[165] Choi (2014, 81). See also: Siler (1998).
[166] See: Easley (2007).
[167] See: Park (1998).
[168] See: Paul (2000).
[169] Ibid. See also: Kim (2001); Pinkston (2004); Kim (2011); Yang (2011); Snyder and Lee (2012, 164, 168); Bleek and Lorber (2013, 18).

ally should meet the potential proliferator's security needs, eliminating its willingness to acquire nuclear weapons.

Our argument has implications for future U.S. nonproliferation efforts vis-à-vis South Korea. Some scholars argue that because South Korea's relative power is increasing, the importance of U.S. foreign policy in ensuring the nonnuclear status of South Korea will decrease. For example, Scott Snyder states that "the alliance/security factor may no longer be the decisive variable in shaping South Korean nuclear choices, as it so clearly was in South Korea under Park Chung-hee's leadership during the 1970s."[170] We differ on this point. We agree that as South Korea becomes stronger, it will have a greater opportunity to proliferate, and it will be more difficult for the United States to use coercive tools to ensure South Korea's nuclear forbearance. Yet, this does not eliminate the U.S. role in preventing South Korea's nuclearization; it simply changes the strategy that the United States should implement. As South Korea becomes stronger, it will have a greater opportunity to proliferate, but it will also have a diminished willingness to proliferate. The optimal U.S. nonproliferation strategy in this case would place an even greater emphasis on security commitments, aiming to remove South Korea's willingness to proliferate. To ensure the nonnuclear status of a relatively powerful ally facing a grave threat, Washington must commit decisively to its security.

Summing up, South Korea's nonnuclear status can be accounted for by looking at the country's strategic environment. Taken alone, the security threat posed by North Korea would be sufficient to give Seoul the willingness to build nuclear weapons. At the same time, Seoul enjoys reliable guarantees of protection provided by the United States. Therefore, South Korea has not been willing to build the bomb. Should the United States continue to offer reliable security guarantees, it is highly unlikely that South Korea would become a nuclear-weapons state.

West Germany

Despite having developed a large-scale nuclear energy program while being a frontline state in the Cold War, the Federal Republic of Germany (FRG, or West Germany) remained nonnuclear. Its nuclear

---

[170] Snyder (2010, 172).

forbearance is the result of intense coercive effort by the United States, which implemented a sticks-based approach toward its protégé, demanding that it abandon its nuclear ambitions and forcing it to remain nonnuclear. Washington possessed great coercive leverage over Bonn because West Germany was remarkably weak vis-à-vis its main adversary, the Soviet Union – a weakness that would make Bonn vulnerable to Soviet preventive counterproliferation action should Washington abandon West Germany.

After its recognition as a fully sovereign state in 1955, West Germany faced a much stronger enemy in the Soviet Union. Given Soviet conventional preponderance in Central Europe, Bonn essentially relied on U.S. security assurances for its survival. For its part, the United States perceived West Germany as central to maintaining control over one of the most important areas of the globe: Western Europe. Given its geographical proximity to Soviet territory, its economic potential, and its symbolic value, Germany would become one of the key theaters over which the Cold War would be fought. In the aftermath of the successful launch of Sputnik in October 1957, however, U.S. military action to protect its Western European allies threatened to prompt a Soviet nuclear attack on the U.S. homeland. This new strategic reality led U.S. NATO allies to question Washington's commitment to the defense of Western Europe. Would the United States be willing to risk an all-out nuclear war in order to protect them? Would it trade New York for Paris, London, or West Berlin?

Even before acquiring full sovereignty, West Germany pledged to remain nonnuclear. Soon, though, it became interested in acquiring nuclear weapons. The great reliance of the Eisenhower administration on nuclear retaliation, the heavy potential for casualties associated with this doctrine, and the evolution of Soviet retaliatory capabilities, all raised doubts about the credibility of U.S. deterrent threats issued against the Soviet Union. These doubts, in turn, gave West Germany the willingness to build an independent nuclear deterrent. In 1957–1958, Bonn negotiated with France and Italy the start of a nuclear-weapons program. Before bearing any fruit, however, this program would be opposed by the United States and cancelled by French president Charles de Gaulle. Still, West Germany's willingness to acquire nuclear weapons did not dwindle and would continue to generate great concern in Washington over the following decade.

Under President Kennedy, the United States announced a shift in its strategy to deter Soviet aggression. With "flexible response," Washington now promised to repel a putative Soviet conventional attack on Western Europe by using conventional means and only gradually escalating the ladder of nuclear responses. This approach was meant to bolster the credibility of U.S. threats against the Soviet Union. Furthermore, the United States proposed to centralize decisionmaking within its allied bloc, and Kennedy suggested the implementation of a multilateral nuclear force (the MLF), an Eisenhower-era concept aimed at integrating existing European (i.e., British and French) nuclear arsenals within NATO. Specifically, the MLF would be a sea-based force armed with U.S. nuclear warheads and operated by international NATO crews under the joint control of NATO allies under a U.S. veto. This approach was initially maintained under President Johnson, with U.S. officials hoping that this carrots-based nonproliferation approach and the shared control of nuclear weapons offered by the MLF would undermine West Germany's willingness to develop nuclear weapons. Both the Soviet Union and other European U.S. allies, however, having fought Germany in two world wars, were concerned that the MLF would serve as a route to proliferation and, specifically, to an independent German ability to issue nuclear threats. Safeguards for a U.S. veto over the use of MLF nuclear weapons might fail, and West Germany might also acquire useful information from its participation in the MLF to develop its own nuclear weapons. Since the prospect of German nuclear acquisition increased the likelihood of Soviet military action, the MLF also heightened the risk of U.S. entrapment in a European conflict.

Based on these concerns, the United States gradually turned away from its MLF-centric carrots-based nonproliferation policy between 1964 and 1966. Instead of trying to prevent West German nuclearization by sharing control over NATO nuclear weapons, thereby removing German willingness to proliferate, Washington would now try to implement a sticks-based nonproliferation effort aimed at preventing West German nuclearization by removing its protégé's opportunity to proliferate. With that goal in mind, the United States completed the agreement for the NPT with the Soviet Union, whereby nuclear powers agreed (among other things) to renounce nuclear sharing, and nonnuclear-weapons states agreed to forego any attempt to acquire their own nuclear arsenal. As a consequence of this U.S. policy, West Germany faced a stark choice. It could pursue its own nuclear deterrent without the support of the United States and risk Soviet preventive action. Or it could curtail its nuclear ambitions and rely on the U.S. nuclear deterrent for its survival. Bonn relented and ultimately gave up its nuclear ambitions for lack of an opportunity to proliferate.

West German Interest in Nuclear Weapons

Upon its creation as a state and subsequent accession to NATO, West Germany decided to renounce nuclear weapons at the London and Paris conferences of 1954. West German chancellor Konrad Adenauer (1949–1963) did not see this pledge as permanent, however. Rather, Adenauer claimed, this commitment to remain nonnuclear was only valid *rebus sic stantibus* – as long as circumstances remained the same.[171]

Soon, Bonn's strategic circumstances changed. West Germany realized the heavy cost it would pay in an eventual conflict between NATO and the Soviet Union. The Carte Blanche war games of 1955 estimated the number of German citizens killed or injured in such a conflict at five million.[172] Furthermore, when the Radford Plan for the reduction of U.S. forces in Europe was leaked in July 1956, West Germany learned of American intentions to withdraw 800,000 troops from the continent and rely even more heavily on nuclear weapons.[173]

These developments caused great alarm in Bonn. Adenauer declared to the press that he opposed a policy where "America is a fortress for itself, because that would mean that we would be outside that fortress."[174] He wrote to Secretary Dulles on July 22, 1956, that as a result of the Radford plan,

Europe, including Germany, has lost its confidence in the United States' reliability. These plans are regarded as clear evidence that the United States does

---

[171] See: "Memorandum of Conversation," Bonn, June 22, 1962, 11:30 a.m., in *Foreign Relations of the United States (FRUS)*, 1961–1963, Vol. XIII, *Western Europe and Canada*, Doc. 145; Schwarz (1992, 297); Schwarz (1997, 123); Granieri (2004, 83).

[172] See: Boutwell (1990, 18).

[173] See: Schwarz (1997, 235).

[174] Quoted in Granieri (2004, 88).

not feel itself to be strong enough to keep up the pace with the Soviet Union. The political consequences will appear very soon, unless the United States emphatically dissociates itself from these plans.[175]

To the U.S. secretary of the air force, visiting Bonn in September 1956, Adenauer stated that "[i]t is no exaggeration to say that NATO is finished."[176]

The Eisenhower administration's efforts to distance itself from the Radford plan did not reassure Adenauer. Concerns over the credibility of U.S. deterrent threats against the Soviet Union – and over their heavy reliance on nuclear weapons – led to a change in Bonn's nuclear policy. In September 1956, Adenauer declared that "Germany cannot remain a nuclear protectorate."[177] Consequently, he vowed to acquire "the most modern weapons" for West Germany.[178] The following month, Franz Josef Strauss was named minister of defense (1956–1962), and both committed to acquiring nuclear weapons.[179]

Bonn's government first sought to obtain nuclear weapons by taking advantage of international arrangements. Capitalizing on the American strategy of greater reliance on nuclear weapons, they argued that NATO divisions should be armed with such weapons.[180] The German Parliament even claimed that nuclear weapons were

---

[175] Quoted in Schwarz (1997, 235).
[176] Ibid., 236.
[177] Ibid., 239–240. See also: Granieri (2004, 99).
[178] Quoted in Boutwell (1990, 19).
[179] For the ongoing debate on Strauss's exact nuclear intentions, see: Ahonen (1995). Bonn's policy agenda in the 1950s also included a vigorous effort to reunify the country, which led it to deny diplomatic recognition to East Germany as an independent state. There is, however, little evidence to support the claim that West German leaders wanted nuclear weapons in order to pursue this reunification agenda. The Soviet arsenal would always be vastly superior, so the coercive potential of an eventual West German arsenal would be questionable. Furthermore, the same treaties of 1954–1955 that had turned West Germany into a quasi-sovereign state and made it a NATO member had also committed other NATO members, including the United States, to Bonn's preferred policy of peaceful national unification. From that moment onward, Adenauer's approach was to insist that the West must not move toward détente with Moscow before the Soviets agree to take steps toward German unification, a quid pro quo that the Kennedy administration would abandon, reversing its logic and trying instead to make progress on the German question by pursuing détente with Moscow.
[180] See: Kelleher (1975, 49); Schwarz (1997, 219).

necessary "to fulfill the obligations assumed by the Federal Republic within the NATO framework."[181] Furthermore, both Adenauer and Strauss thought of using EURATOM, the European Atomic Energy Community founded in 1958, to help in the production of nuclear weapons.[182]

West Germany's security concerns were heightened by the successful launch of Sputnik by the Soviet Union in October 1957. The credibility of U.S. security assurances was undermined by Moscow's ability to target American cities with nuclear forces – an ability that Moscow was now expected to acquire soon. As a result, Bonn shifted toward a more aggressive route in pursuit of nuclear weapons. Adenauer stated bluntly: "We must produce them."[183] West Germany held bilateral talks with France and, in November 1957, signed a "protocol for the joint research and production of modern weapons" with both the French and Italian governments, aimed at the development of a nuclear program: the so-called F-I-G treaty, after the initials of the three participant countries' names.[184] Negotiators working on the F-I-G agreement conceived of it not "as an alternative to NATO but rather as a tool to improve their own country's standing inside the alliance."[185] As Strauss put it in the context of the F-I-G negotiations, unless nuclear disarmament came about, "the possession of atomic warheads by all strategically exposed states, like Germany, France, and Italy, was unavoidable."[186] The United States, upon which the security of the F-I-G countries largely relied, was expected to support the program. Therefore information about the protocol was relayed to Washington. Eventually, French decisionmakers showed reluctance in sharing their budding nuclear capability with Germany, particularly given that such cooperation was expected to prompt a strong Soviet reaction.[187] Moreover, the program was criticized by the United States

[181] Quoted in Kelleher (1975, 113). See also: Mackby and Slocombe (2004, 185).
[182] See: Schwarz (1997, 239–240); Granieri (2004, 99).
[183] Quoted in Schwarz (1997, 319).
[184] See: "Protocole entre le Ministre de la Défense nationale et des Forces Armées de la République francaise, le Ministre de la Défense de la République fédérale allemande, le Ministre de la Défense de la République italienne," November 28, 1957, in Imprimerie nationale (1991, Document 380, 762–763). See also: Nuti (1998); Sheetz (2002); Nuti (2007, 161–163).
[185] Nuti (1998, 73).
[186] Quoted in Sheetz (2002, 285).
[187] See: Nuti (1998, 90–91); Sheetz (2002, 301).

and the United Kingdom. In the summer of 1958, shortly after becoming French prime minister (1958–1959), de Gaulle suspended it.[188]

Though West Germany's joint nuclear program was dropped after
such a short period, Bonn's willingness to acquire nuclear weapons
did not dwindle. In October 1960, Adenauer demanded assurances
from Washington that nuclear weapons would remain stationed in
Europe. Without these weapons, German troops would be "cattle for
slaughter."[189] When in May 1961 Kennedy proposed in a speech at
the Canadian Parliament to place several U.S. nuclear-armed submarines under NATO command, West Germany was the only country to
echo these remarks.[190] In June 1962, in a meeting with Secretary of
State Dean Rusk, Adenauer shared his concern that "the possibility
might arise" where a U.S. president "would be incapable of taking a
decision on the use of nuclear weapons." For Adenauer, "the military
aspect, rather than prestige and political aspects, was all important
since a matter of survival was involved."[191] In December 1962, when
offered the option of shared control over NATO nuclear weapons
through the MLF, Adenauer considered rejecting it in favor of renewed
direct Franco-German nuclear cooperation.[192] Soon, however, West
Germany saw the MLF as the best way to obtain control over nuclear weapons. After endorsing the MLF proposal in January 1963,
Adenauer stated: "We must arrange within NATO so that a decision
can be taken to use atomic weapons even before the [U.S.] President
is heard from."[193]

Precisely because of the proliferation risk that it presented, the
MLF met with strong opposition from the Soviet Union and significant suspicion among other U.S. allies.[194] West Germany proposed
to implement it as a bilateral agreement with the United States, if
necessary.[195] Yet, the MLF was dropped for good in late 1965, early

---

[188] See: Nuti (1998, 97).
[189] Quoted in Schwarz (1997, 481).
[190] See: Barbier (2012, 289–290).
[191] *FRUS*, 1961–1963, Vol. XIII, Doc. 145.
[192] See: Granieri (2004, 165).
[193] Quoted in Mackby and Slocombe (2004, 191).
[194] On the lack of enthusiasm for the MLF among European allies,
      see: "Memorandum from the President's Special Assistant for National
      Security Affairs (Bundy) to President Kennedy," in *FRUS*, 1961–1963, Vol.
      XIII, Doc. 201.
[195] See: Kelleher (1975, 248); Barbier (2012, 298).

1966.[196] From that point on, the United States and the Soviet Union made considerable progress in drafting the foundations for a nonproliferation treaty, the NPT, which they signed on July 1, 1968, along with sixty-two other countries. Under Chancellor Willy Brandt (1969–1974), who put forth a foreign policy of *Ostpolitik* – aimed at the normalization of relations with East Germany – Bonn signed the NPT on November 28, 1969, and entered a period of better relations with the Soviet Union, leading to the signature of the Treaty of Moscow in 1970.[197] Why did West Germany conduct this 180-degree turn in its nuclear policy, from determined nuclear pursuit to unquestioned nuclear forbearance? Bonn's nuclear turnaround resulted from its lack of opportunity to obtain nuclear weapons, which, in turn, was the product of significant U.S. pressure and the risk of a Soviet preventive strike in the absence of U.S. support.[198]

U.S. Nonproliferation Efforts

U.S. policy toward West Germany's nuclear aspirations went through four distinct phases until the late 1960s. The first two correspond, respectively, to the Eisenhower and Kennedy administrations. The third and fourth took place under the Johnson administration, which first supported the MLF but eventually dropped it in favor of cooperation with the Soviet Union in the creation of a nonproliferation regime, in the process coercing West Germany to remain nonnuclear.

[196] Kelleher (1975, 254) argues that the MLF was effectively killed in December 1964 when President Johnson put it on hold. Bundy (1988, 494) argues that the MLF was dropped at end of 1965. Costigliola (1994, 180) argues that it "faded away" in 1966. Küntzel (1995, 54) claims that it ended in November 1966, with the resignation of Ludwig Erhard's government.

[197] West Germany later ratified the NPT, in 1975. When it was reunited, Germany reiterated its renunciation of nuclear weapons and in 1994 voted to extend the NPT indefinitely.

[198] Of course, West German elites were not unanimously in favor of nuclear acquisition. On the diversity of positions on the nuclear question among German decisionmakers, see: Gray (2009); Schneider (2014). Nevertheless, the role played by U.S. nonproliferation efforts in coercing Bonn into reversing its nuclear ambitions, detailed in the following section, is undeniable. During the relevant period, the key West German leaders were actively pronuclear.

The Eisenhower Administration

U.S. grand strategy, and U.S. attitudes toward nuclear proliferation, evolved significantly since the birth of West Germany. President Eisenhower, facing a conventionally superior Soviet Union in Europe, developed the doctrine of massive retaliation, promising to respond to any attack by Soviet forces with the massive use of U.S. nuclear weapons. On the question of nuclear proliferation, Eisenhower believed that the best way to contain it was to share civilian nuclear technology with other countries while demanding that they not use it for military goals. He articulated this vision with his Atoms for Peace speech, delivered at the UNGA on December 8, 1953.

This approach raised two challenges. The first was that the threat of massive retaliation might not be deemed credible either by the Soviet Union or by the U.S. allies it was meant to protect. The second was that potential proliferators, such as West Germany, might take advantage of U.S. cooperation with their civilian nuclear programs to move closer to the acquisition of nuclear weapons – a development that might create intra-NATO tensions and prompt a Soviet reaction.

For Eisenhower, U.S. threats of massive retaliation against the Soviet Union were credible. He "expressed surprise" when Secretary Dulles questioned U.S. willingness to start a Third World War in order to defend West Berlin.[199] Yet, even if Eisenhower believed that U.S. threats to defend Berlin were credible, he also thought that a state like West Germany would eventually develop its own nuclear weapons and share the burden of defending Western Europe.[200] Ironically, nuclear sharing could be seen both as a nonproliferation tool – the intended aim of Eisenhower's Atoms for Peace vision – and as an efficient means of assistance to countries that would inevitably become nuclear powers. Eisenhower stated that it was inefficient for "[a]llies to command talent and money in solving problems that their friends have already solved – all because of artificial barriers to sharing."[201] During his administration, the Atomic Energy Act of 1946, which restricted the transfer of nuclear technology, was loosened. In 1954, the Act permitted NATO allies to access information on the "external characteristics of nuclear weapons" and to train in their use. By 1958, the Act was

---

[199] Quoted in Trachtenberg (1999, 256).
[200] See: Ibid., 261–262.
[201] Quoted in Nye (1987, 167).

revised to allow for the transfer of fissionable materials and of sensitive information to NATO allies.[202] Two years later, in February 1960, Eisenhower went as far as supporting an increase in European control of nuclear weapons, stating, "we should not deny to our allies ... what your potential enemy already has."[203]

Other American policymakers also believed that nuclear proliferation was inevitable, and encouraged U.S. nuclear sharing with its Western European allies. In July 1957, Secretary Dulles explained that "Italy, Germany, and the Netherlands cannot be held back forever from producing nuclear weapons when so many other countries are working on it."[204] Dulles proposed to establish Western European nuclear stockpiles for NATO members' access. In January 1960, supreme allied commander, General Lauris Norstad (1956–1963), supported the idea of NATO becoming the fourth nuclear power, alongside the United States, the Soviet Union, and the United Kingdom.[205] That year, the administration developed the concept of the MLF. This proposal was presented to NATO in December, right before President John F. Kennedy took office.[206]

The Kennedy Administration
Kennedy put forth a different vision for U.S. nuclear policy.[207] To prevent further proliferation, he pushed for a nuclear-test ban agreement, which materialized in the PTBT of 1963. He also laid the foundations for what would eventually become the NPT when his secretary of state, Dean Rusk, participated in the disarmament conference of Geneva in March 1963. This conference was the first attempt to implement the Irish Resolution of 1961, aiming at limiting the transfer of nuclear technology, which had been adopted unanimously by the UNGA.[208]

In terms of U.S. nuclear strategy, Kennedy adopted a policy of "flexible response," promising to initiate a U.S. response to an

---

[202] See: Ibid.
[203] Quoted in Kelleher (1975, 139).
[204] Quoted in Küntzel (1995, 14).
[205] See: Kelleher (1975, 139).
[206] On the origins of the MLF, see: Seaborg (1987, 86); Bunn (1992, 64); Granieri (2004, 164–165); Brands (2007, 393–394).
[207] See: Trachtenberg (1999, 283–285).
[208] See: Bunn (1992, 65–66).

eventual Soviet conventional attack on Western Europe by relying mostly on conventional weapons, and only gradually exercising U.S. nuclear options – in sharp contrast with Eisenhower's policy of threatening the Soviets with massive nuclear retaliation. Flexible response, which required centralized decisionmaking in order to control the escalation process, was seen as a way to improve the credibility of U.S. threats of nuclear retaliation while decreasing the risk of nuclear war. As Kennedy explained on July 25, 1961: "We intend to have a wider choice than humiliation or all-out nuclear action."[209] Secretary of Defense Robert McNamara discussed the strategy of flexible response in a NATO ministerial meeting in May 1962, saying that "our principal military objectives, in the event of a nuclear war stemming from a major attack on the Alliance, should be the destruction of the enemy's military forces while attempting to preserve the fabric as well as the integrity of allied society." McNamara pushed for

> the Alliance to engage in a controlled and flexible nuclear response in the event that deterrence could fail.... There must not be competing and conflicting strategies in the conduct of nuclear war.... [I]t is essential that we centralize the decision to use our nuclear weapons to the greatest extent possible.[210]

In practice, however, the policies of the Kennedy administration retained some important points of continuity with those of its predecessor. Searching for a cost-effective strategy to deter the Soviets, Kennedy opposed the conventional buildup that flexible response would have required. He also attempted to reduce the number of troops deployed on West German territory.[211]

In an attempt to centralize NATO nuclear decisionmaking and integrate the U.S., French, and British nuclear arsenals, Kennedy also endorsed the MLF.[212] This proposal to integrate NATO nuclear forces was seen as a way to satiate West German appetite for an independent nuclear arsenal,[213] or even for a joint Franco-German arsenal, the

---

[209] Quoted in Bundy (1988, 377).
[210] Quoted in Schwartz (1983, 157, 159).
[211] See: Gavin (2012, 42–43).
[212] See: Granieri (2004, 164–165); Barbier (2012, 286–297).
[213] See: Brands (2007, 393–394).

specter of which remained from the aborted attempt at nuclear collaboration between Bonn and Paris in the late 1950s.[214]

But Moscow was not prepared to accept a Western nuclear-sharing agreement that would include the FRG. In fact, it is difficult to overstate Soviet concerns about a nuclear West Germany during the late Eisenhower years and throughout the Kennedy years. German decisionmakers had not attempted to disguise their nuclear ambitions from Moscow. For example, in 1957, during talks with the Soviet ambassador to Bonn, Andrei Smirnov (1956–1966), Adenauer failed to deny that West Germany might become a nuclear power. His foreign minister Heinrich von Brentano (1955–1961), also present, added: "If England and other powers have atomic weapons, why should the FRG not have them?"[215] This sort of German posturing was a cause of great Soviet discomfort. In April 1958, Bonn passed a resolution opening the door to nuclear armament. Immediately, Soviet Premier Khrushchev sent his chief adviser Anastas Mikoyan to Bonn to warn Adenauer that the USSR would not countenance German nuclearization and would push for the Rapacki Plan for the denuclearization of Central Europe, which Poland had presented at the United Nations the previous year.[216] By November 1958, U.S. ambassador to Moscow Llewellyn Thompson (1957–1962) informed Washington that "Khrushchev is a man in a hurry and considers that time is against him ... in relation to atomic arming of West Germany."[217] There is strong evidence that Khrushchev engineered the Berlin crises of 1958–1962 to pressure the United States to keep West Germany nonnuclear.[218] In July 1962, at the UN's Eighteen Nation Disarmament Conference, the Soviet representative stated that nonproliferation "cannot be discussed in an abstract fashion. It is primarily the question of the spread of nuclear weapons to

---

[214] See: Seaborg (1987, 86).
[215] Smirnov's conversation report to Moscow, quoted in Zubok (2000, 288).
[216] See: Ibid.
[217] Thompson to Dulles, November 18, 1958, quoted in Troyanovsky (2000, 217–218).
[218] According to Joseph S. Nye Jr., Khrushchev believed "Berlin was a 'blister' that he could step on to make the Americans feel pain. He could trade stability in the status of Berlin for Western assurances that the Federal Republic of Germany would not get nuclear weapons." Nye (1987, 169). According to Marc Trachtenberg, "The German nuclear question ... lay at the heart of Soviet policy during the Berlin Crisis." Trachtenberg (1999, 253).

West Germany."[219] When the Soviet Union agreed to the PTBT, Soviet deputy foreign minister Vasilii Kuznetsov (1955–1977) declared that "[t]he main goal of the Soviet Union is, to begin with, to bind West Germany's hands, to prevent it from obtaining nuclear weapons."[220]

Despite being a step in the right direction, the PTBT did not assuage Soviet concerns about Bonn's nuclear ambitions. Before signing the treaty, the Kremlin was skeptical about the effect that it would have on West German nuclearization. When John McCloy, president Kennedy's disarmament policy chief (1961–1963), visited Moscow to discuss the test ban treaty in July 1961, "Khrushchev continually raised the issue of German nuclear weapons." At the time, the Soviets "derided the Test Ban as a nonproliferation instrument, arguing that Germany would get weapons by transfer from the United States, not by testing its own."[221]

Against this background, the MLF represented a great danger for Moscow. When Kennedy described it to the Soviets, Khrushchev was amazed by Kennedy's "attempt to convince me that neither the multinational nor multilateral nuclear forces being planned for NATO will increase the danger of the spreading of nuclear weapons." For Khrushchev, the MLF was "a crack" in nonproliferation efforts, and "once such a crack exists there will be found fingers which in this fashion will find their way to the control panels of these weapons."[222]

While the Irish Resolution adopted by the UNGA in 1961 was a step in the right direction, the Soviets quickly voiced their concerns that the restrictions on nuclear sharing that it envisioned were too loose, and the United States would end up arming a "revanchist" West Germany.[223] Negotiations in Geneva between the Soviets and the Americans showed little progress as the United States held on to the concept of the MLF.

The Johnson Administration, 1963–1965: The MLF and Its Demise
The attempt to avoid West German proliferation by promoting the MLF was initially continued by the Lyndon B. Johnson administration.

---

[219] Quoted in Nye (1987, 169).
[220] "Discussion between Soviet Marshal V. V. Kuznetsov and the SED Politburo," October 14, 1963, in Wilson Center Digital Archive, Warsaw Pact.
[221] Nye (1987, 169).
[222] "Message from Chairman Khrushchev to President Kennedy," Moscow, undated, in *Foreign Relations of the United States* (*FRUS*), 1961–1963, Vol. VI, *Kennedy-Khrushchev Exchanges*, Doc. 98.
[223] Quoted in Bunn (1992, 66).

Adrian Fisher, the deputy director of the U.S. Arms Control and Disarmament Agency (ACDA, 1961–1969), wrote in a memo to Secretary Rusk that the MLF "was intended to support our nonproliferation policy in the [*sic*] light of the growing nuclear ambitions of the Federal Republic."[224] Rusk agreed, and in a press conference he stated that the MLF was "some protection against the further spread of nuclear weapons on a national basis."[225] In 1965, U.S. undersecretary of state George Ball (1961–1966) warned President Johnson that the MLF was the only way "to prevent Germany from becoming once more the prey of its own Teutonic fantasies."[226]

Yet, others doubted the success of such a policy of extending control over NATO nuclear forces to Bonn in order to tame its appetite for an independent nuclear arsenal. In October 1964, recently elected British prime minister Harold Wilson (1964–1970, 1974–1976) famously objected to the MLF in the following terms: "If you have a boy and wish to sublimate his sex appetite, it is unwise to take him to a strip-tease show."[227] In late 1964, Johnson appointed the so-called Gilpatric Committee (named after its chairman, former deputy secretary of defense Roswell Gilpatric [1961–1964]) to review U.S. nuclear nonproliferation policy. The committee's report advocated for a greater emphasis on nonproliferation efforts, providing a conceptual framework for a policy change.[228] Among its recommendations, made in early 1965, the committee advocated for de-emphasizing nuclear-sharing agreements with NATO allies and argued for greater cooperation with the Soviet Union to prevent further nuclear proliferation, implicitly criticizing the MLF. Perhaps even more importantly, at this same time the Soviets made clear to U.S. leaders their belief that the MLF presented a great proliferation risk, specifically in what concerned West Germany. Maintaining its deep concern about the possibility of Bonn acquiring nuclear weapons, Moscow opposed the MLF in the strongest terms. So did West Germany's NATO allies. The possibility of German nuclearization threatened to break up the Western alliance, and to expose the FRG to Soviet military action.

---

[224] Quoted in Seaborg (1987, 131).
[225] Quoted in Bunn (1992, 68–69).
[226] Quoted in Maddock (2010, 256).
[227] Quoted in Kelleher (1975, 252).
[228] See: Brands (2006).

All of this led the Johnson administration to grow increasingly skeptical of the MLF.[229] By early November 1964, National Security Advisor McGeorge Bundy "expressed doubts to Johnson about the MLF, reminding him that the idea had always been conceived of 'as a means, and not an end in itself.' If the end was to keep West Germany from building its own nuclear weapons, perhaps they should rethink the means to achieve it."[230] Later that month, Bundy advocated that the administration "now arrange to let the MLF sink out of sight" and suggested asking "the President for authority to work toward a future in which the MLF does not come into existence."[231] In December, a leak to the press suggested that the Johnson administration had placed the MLF plan on hold, when a self-imposed deadline to reach an agreement about it within NATO had passed.[232] Those U.S. allies in Europe that had been at best lukewarm to the MLF were growing increasingly critical of the proposal.[233] In 1965, de Gaulle told the Soviet minister of foreign affairs Andrei Gromyko that he wanted West Germany to remain nonnuclear, and that he opposed West German participation in a European integrated force.[234]

In time, the Americans realized that they could more easily make progress with the Soviets on a nonproliferation treaty if they dropped the MLF. After meeting with Soviet ambassador to the United States Anatoly Dobrynin in October 1965, Bundy reported that Washington "may well be able to make some money with Moscow if we tell them privately before we sink it [the MLF] publicly."[235] Meeting with West German chancellor Ludwig Erhard (1963–1966) in December 1965, President Johnson conveyed the concerns raised by the MLF among other European allies and questioned the benefits of the proposal. Johnson

---

[229] See: Wenger (2004, 29).
[230] Brands (2006, 92), citing "NATO Nuclear Policy," November 8, 1964. See also: Ibid.,103.
[231] "Memorandum from the President's Special Assistant for National Security Affairs (Bundy) to the Undersecretary of State (Ball)," in *Foreign Relations of the United States (FRUS), 1964–1968*, Vol. XIII, *Western Europe Region*, Doc. 52.
[232] See: Kelleher (1975, 254); Granieri (2004, 199).
[233] See: Seaborg (1987, 92); Granieri (2004, 204); Maddock (2010, 255).
[234] See: Mackby and Slocombe (2004, 195). De Gaulle would later declare: "The MLF is dead. It is I who killed it." Quoted in Maddock (2010, 255).
[235] "Memorandum of Conversation between the President's Special Assistant for National Security Affairs (Mr. Bundy) and the Soviet Ambassador (Dobrynin)," Washington, November 24, 1965, 1–3 p.m., in *FRUS*, 1964–1968, Vol. XIII, Doc. 111.

claimed that he "personally was not obsessed by any fears about the German people or their attitudes. But he could also understand how the English, for instance, might feel differently."[236] He added that he "could not understand why the Germans would want to buy something that the United States had already paid for, when Wilson and Erhard and President Johnson all trusted each other."[237] From here on, the Johnson administration turned away from a "hardware" solution to satisfy the German willingness to nuclearize (code for nuclear sharing) and would instead uphold a "software" approach to the German nuclear program, which would entangle West Germany in a web of institutional arrangements – including the offer of a permanent seat to West Germany at the newly constituted Nuclear Planning Group (NPG) in late 1966 – that guaranteed the maintenance of its nonnuclear status.[238]

This about-face resulted from the Johnson administration's understanding that the odds of U.S. entrapment in a conflict with the Soviet Union would increase if it shared control of nuclear weapons with West Germany. The United States was committed to the defense of Western Europe, with large troop and nuclear-weapon deployments on the continent, and in West Germany in particular. Soviet concerns about German nuclearization could trigger a very costly conflict for the United States. Instead of diluting West German willingness to acquire nuclear weapons by sharing control over U.S. nuclear forces with Bonn, the United States pivoted to a strategy of removing West German opportunity to proliferate by colluding with the Soviet Union in the creation of the nonproliferation regime, while threatening to abandon West Germany if it insisted on its nuclear ambitions.

The Soviet Union had a similar view of the reasons behind U.S. support for the NPT. According to an April 1968 memorandum of conversation between the Hungarian delegate to the UN and his Soviet counterpart, and his Soviet counterpart: "The treaty *is directed against the FRG*, [whose] nuclear weapons would definitely evoke the danger of World War III."[239]

---

[236] "Memorandum of Conversation," Washington, December 20, 1965, 11:30 a.m., in *FRUS*, 1964–1968, Vol. XIII, Doc. 119.

[237] Ibid.

[238] See: Priest (2007).

[239] "Memorandum, Permanent Mission of Hungary to the UN to the Hungarian Foreign Ministry," April 12, 1968, in Wilson Center Digital Archive, Indian Nuclear History.

The Johnson Administration, 1965–1970:
The NPT and Germany's Nuclear Forbearance

In Washington, early 1966 saw increased congressional pressure for progress on a nonproliferation treaty.[240] Johnson instructed his administration officials to revise plans for nuclear coordination within NATO in ways that would make them more acceptable to the Soviets.[241] In July, he publicly expressed his willingness to come to an agreement with Moscow on nuclear nonproliferation. In August, he appointed Fisher – an opponent of the MLF – to lead negotiations with the Soviets in Geneva.[242] Fisher was given much latitude in his negotiations and by the end of September he had come to an agreement with his Soviet counterpart. To allay Soviet concerns that West Germany might gain control over nuclear weapons, the NPT would impose broad restrictions on the transfer of nuclear technology, not only to individual states but to groups of states as well.[243] The United States and the Soviet Union were agreeing to split the world into nuclear-weapons states and nonnuclear-weapons states. Nuclear-weapons states would promise neither to transfer nuclear explosive devices to nonnuclear-weapons states nor to assist them in their efforts to acquire the atomic bomb. They would also commit to their own eventual denuclearization. Reciprocally, nonnuclear-weapons states would pledge to remain nonnuclear.[244]

Consistent with their earlier declarations, the Soviets remained deeply concerned with the prospect of West Germany acquiring nuclear weapons. In January 1966, Soviet chairman of the council of ministers Alexei Kosygin (1964–1980) complained that NATO members seemed to be debating "how and to what extent to satisfy the growing nuclear demands of West Germany."[245] He stated that the Soviet Union would be "forced to take all measures which it, along with its allies and friends, would consider necessary for securing

---

[240] See: Seaborg (1987, 180); Bunn (1992, 73); Maddock (2010, 261).
[241] See: Bunn (1992, 74).
[242] Ibid., 73. See also: Brands (2006, 86).
[243] See: Seaborg (1987, 190–195).
[244] For more on the role of U.S.-Soviet collusion in the formation of the NPT, see: Swango (2009); Coe and Vaynman (2015).
[245] "Message from Chairman Kosygin to President Johnson," in *Foreign Relations of the United States (FRUS), 1964–1968*, Vol. XI, *Arms Control and Disarmament*, Doc. 108.

peace in Europe" in the event that West Germany "got access to nuclear weapons" in any form.[246] In September 1966, the chief Soviet delegate at the General Conference of the IAEA told his American counterpart that "the USSR's main concern was West Germany."[247] Along similar lines, a Soviet representative declared during NPT negotiations: "We primarily designed the whole treaty to close all doors and windows on the possibility of the Federal Republic of Germany having nuclear weapons."[248] The Soviets were willing to consider a range of actions to ensure that West Germany would sign the treaty. At a press conference in London in February 1967, Kosygin reiterated his threat publicly. He declared that West Germany would "have to join the agreement on nonproliferation whether it wants to or not," adding that the Soviet Union would "not allow the Federal Republic of Germany to have nuclear weapons and we will take all measures to prevent it getting nuclear weapons. We say it with utter resolution."[249]

Aware of Moscow's preferences, Washington understood that West German nuclearization entailed a high risk of U.S. entrapment. In 1967, Fisher explained that "[i]f the decision to develop their [West Germany's] own nuclear weapons were to be made, we would probably have an international crisis which would make the ten days preceding October 27, 1962 [the peak day of the Cuban Missile Crisis] look like ten relaxed days indeed."[250] As a result, it was of the utmost importance for the United States to be successful in convincing West Germany to forfeit its nuclear ambitions. For Undersecretary of State George Ball, a "non-proliferation agreement without a German signature will not be worth anything."[251]

Given the risks of entrapment, the United States considered the possibility of withdrawing its support to West Germany were Bonn to appear obdurate in its nuclear ambitions. U.S. ambassador to West Germany George McGhee (1963–1968) told Secretary Rusk that West Germany should reassure East European countries of its foreign ambitions, renouncing nuclear weapons and at least accepting

---

[246] Ibid.
[247] As recounted in Seaborg (1987, 283).
[248] Quoted in Küntzel (1995, 20).
[249] Quoted in Seaborg (1987, 359).
[250] Quoted in Küntzel (1995, 19–20).
[251] Quoted in Maddock (2010, 256).

the Oder-Neisse line. If Bonn attempted to acquire a nuclear capability, the United States "would withdraw our forces and support for Germany first," the other NATO allies "would dissociate themselves from Germany," and the Soviets would "make such efforts the subject of a preemptive attack." Ultimately, McGhee was convinced, West Germany could not acquire a national nuclear capability. This was not due to the technical requirement, "but because neither the Soviets – or her allies including us, would permit her to do it."[252] National security advisor Walt Rostow conveyed this message directly to Rainer Barzel, parliamentary leader of the West German Christian Union parties (CDU/CSU, 1964–1973) who was visiting Washington in February 1968: "If you would not sign [the NPT] and decided to defend yourself with your own nuclear weapons, you would (a) tear apart the Alliance [and] (b) face a very difficult period during which you might well be destroyed."[253]

Understanding its potential effects on West German opportunity to nuclearize, Bonn strongly opposed progress in U.S.-Soviet nonproliferation negotiations. For the West German government, the United States was committing West Germany to a nonnuclear status without any concessions on German reunification. Throughout the negotiations between the Soviets and the Americans, West Germany sought to obtain concessions on German reunification in exchange for nuclear forbearance – a goal in which it was ultimately rebuffed.[254] When these efforts failed, the NPT sent German officials into a paroxysm. In January 1967, in a lunch with Henry Kissinger (a White House consultant at the time), then finance minister Strauss called the treaty a "super-Yalta," adding that "the behavior of the United States reminded him of an acute alcoholic who was telling non-drinkers that if they took

---

[252] "Letter from the Ambassador to Germany (McGhee) to Secretary of State Rusk," Bonn, August 25, 1966, in *Foreign Relations of the United States (FRUS), 1964–1968*, Vol. XV, *Germany and Berlin*, Doc. 163.

[253] "Memorandum of Conversation," Washington, February 23, 1968, 5 p.m., in *FRUS, 1964–1968*, Vol. XV, Doc. 248.

[254] In July 1965, the United States declined to link a nonproliferation agreement with German reunification. Bunn (1992, 281). In July 1966, Erhard asked for concessions on German reunification in exchange for his support of the MLF. Brands (2007, 418). A working paper of the CSU concluded that Germans "could not expect from the Americans either 'an active reunification policy or the necessary strengthening of the European component of Atlantic defense.'" Quoted in Granieri (2004, 210).

one small drink they would be sentenced to death."[255] Also present, Adenauer considered that

President Johnson was proposing a hegemonial relation with the Soviet Union against the whole rest of the world. The two great "haves" are trying to divide up the world against all the "have-nots." ... It was outrageous that the United States was even considering making a treaty which would, for all eternity, inflict a discriminatory status on the Federal Republic.[256]

The following month, West German chancellor Kurt Kiesinger (1966–1969) denounced the NPT as an act of superpower "atomic complicity."[257] He later went as far as declaring that the treaty was "part of a superpower conspiracy to split and denuclearize Germany forever."[258] Strauss called the NPT "a new Versailles, and one of cosmic dimensions." Adenauer called it a "Morgenthau Plan raised to the power of two" and a "death warrant" for West Germany.[259] In April 1967, Chancellor Kiesinger confided to de Gaulle that he would not sign the NPT; he hoped for the support of the French in fighting the treaty. Furthermore, he told U.S. Vice President Hubert Humphrey that the NPT constituted "the most difficult problem that has emerged in a long time" between the United States and Germany.[260] In sum, Moscow, Washington, and Bonn all understood that one of the key goals of the NPT was the maintenance of West Germany's nonnuclear status.

---

[255] Quoted in Ferguson (2015, 715).

[256] Ibid. On the same occasion, Adenauer was clear on the effect NPT negotiations had on the reliability of U.S. commitments to the defense of West Germany by saying: "I no longer believe that you will protect us. Your actions over recent years have made clear that to you détente is more important than anything else. I do not believe that any American president will risk nuclear war for Berlin; the only thing that is saving us is that the Soviets cannot be sure of this." Ibid., 715.

[257] Quoted in Küntzel (1995, 96).

[258] Quoted in Maddock (2010, 276).

[259] Quoted in Küntzel (1995, 90). The Treaty of Versailles imposed heavy reparations on Germany after the First World War. The Morgenthau Plan, drafted during the Second World War and never implemented, aimed at the postwar destruction of sufficient German industrial capacity to ensure that the country would never again be able to fight. See also: Mackby and Slocombe (2004, 180, 196–197).

[260] Quoted in Gavin (2012, 97). According to Walt W. Rostow, national security advisor to the president (1966–1969), West German officials' attitudes

Unfortunately for Bonn, its strategic environment did not offer much of a choice. Washington's shift to a policy of collusion with the Soviet Union in pursuit of a global nonproliferation agreement, aimed at ensuring that West Germany did not have the opportunity to proliferate, put the FRG between a rock and a hard place. It could attempt to develop a nuclear arsenal but run the risk of being abandoned by the United States and other NATO allies and subsequently attacked by the Soviets before it acquired nuclear weapons; or it could continue to rely on the U.S. nuclear deterrent for its survival but abandon its nuclear ambitions. Understanding the risks that West Germany would incur if it were abandoned by the United States, Bonn renounced nuclear weapons and signed the NPT on November 28, 1969.[261] It forfeited its nuclear ambitions not for lack of willingness, but because U.S. nonproliferation efforts conducted under the shadow of Soviet power had removed any opportunity to nuclearize.

Alternative Explanations

The arc of West German nuclear intentions has attracted insufficient attention from political scientists.[262] This is especially surprising given the importance of the West German program in shaping the nonproliferation regime, by catalyzing efforts for both the PTBT and the NPT. That said, we identify three broad alternative explanations for West Germany's nuclear forbearance in the existing literature.

---

toward the NPT ranged from "total hostility" to "grudging acceptance." "Memorandum from the President's Special Assistant (Rostow) to President Johnson," Washington, November 7, 1967, in *FRUS, 1964–1968*, Vol. XI, Doc. 215.

[261] Having withdrawn the MLF option from the table and obtained a German pledge to remain nonnuclear, the United States could be relatively patient with Bonn's initial resistance to signing the NPT, which was now a *fait accompli*. See: Coe and Vaynman (2015, Appendix 2, p. 5). Washington understood that an open disagreement with West Germany over the NPT would only benefit the Soviets by weakening the Western bloc, and therefore opted for a low level of direct pressure over Bonn on this particular matter.

[262] Seminal statistical studies of proliferation conclude that West Germany never had a nuclear-weapons program. See: Singh and Way (2004); Jo and Gartzke (2007). A more recent survey concludes that West Germany had a nuclear-weapons program only in 1957–1958, during its negotiations with France and Italy. See: Sagan (2011). For a recent in-depth analysis of the West German nuclear-weapons program, see: Gerzhoy (2015).

The first is that West Germany renounced nuclear weapons because of normative concerns. According to Maria Rublee, "early German nuclear forbearance can best be seen as social conformity." Germany did not want to be seen as "an aggressive, militaristic neighbor."[263]

Certainly, the international community was concerned with possible German resurgence fueled by nuclear acquisition. Yet, normative concerns do not appear to have been a strong impediment on Bonn's elite decisionmaking, and nuclear forbearance can be explained without any appeal to them. Adenauer made it clear to the international community that his pledge to renounce nuclear weapons was contingent on strategic circumstances.[264] West German politicians after him also qualified their pledge to renounce nuclear weapons. In his meeting with President Johnson in December 1965, Chancellor Erhard declared that it was "impossible to assume that Germany will go forever without a nuclear deterrent."[265] The trajectory of West Germany's interest in nuclear weapons is therefore best explained by an analysis of its security environment – and a focus on U.S. nonproliferation efforts.

A second alternative explanation is that West Germany renounced nuclear weapons because they did not present any real security benefit. For example, according to McGeorge Bundy, West Germany understood the negative effects that a nuclear-weapons program would have on its allies and enemies, but the most important factor explaining nuclear forbearance is the fact that "the Germans themselves did not want the bomb."[266] To support this point of view, one could point to Chancellor Erhard's conversation with Henry Kissinger, then professor at Harvard, in January 1966. According to Kissinger, Erhard confided that "the last thing he wanted was for Germany to own nuclear weapons." Yet, he could not be known "as the man who had rejected a nuclear option for Germany when it was in effect offered to him."[267] At most, one could argue, West Germany wanted to have a voice in

---

[263] Rublee (2009, 197).
[264] See the meeting between Adenauer and de Gaulle in July 1960. Schwarz (1997, 462). Policymakers at the time and historians since then agree that Adenauer's pledge to renounce nuclear weapons was "anything but his last word on the subject." Ibid., 124. See also: Küntzel (1995, xvi); Bundy (1988, 498).
[265] *FRUS*, 1964–1968, Vol. XIII, Doc. 119.
[266] Bundy (1988, 504).
[267] Quoted in Maddock (2010, 260).

collective nuclear matters. Thus, when Bonn was offered a seat at the NPG in late 1966, it had achieved its objective and no longer needed to seek a nuclear deterrent.[268]

The problem with this argument is that it misses the ample existing evidence that West German politicians saw security benefits in controlling nuclear weapons. Erhard himself elaborated on such security benefits. In January 1965, discussing the deployment of Soviet MRBMs, he argued that "we desire to be defended with the same weapons as threaten us," adding that West Germans were ready to "carry our share of burdens and responsibilities" since "we feel threatened perhaps more than any other country in Europe."[269] In July 1965, the West German government stated that "though it was not seeking to acquire nuclear weapons, it could not bind itself never to do so until its interests were secured."[270]

By the time Erhard spoke with Kissinger, the MLF proposal had already suffered multiple setbacks. According to historian Ronald Granieri, the chancellor "began to rewrite history" when he described the motives behind his support for the MLF.[271] Erhard's decision to accept a permanent seat on the NPG is also telling. In his meeting with President Johnson in September 1966, he argued: "Nobody was expecting a 'hardware solution' *any longer*."[272] In our view, West Germany was left without alternatives and realized that, given its lack of opportunity to acquire nuclear weapons, it was in its best interest to renounce them formally.

A third alternative argument is that West Germany renounced nuclear weapons because of its dependence on the United States.[273] This argument is compatible with ours but incomplete in two respects. Certainly, the historical record supports the claim that West Germany saw a great benefit in U.S. security guarantees. Yet, in order to understand the causal effect of an alliance with the United States, we must think about the prospects of nuclear acquisition *absent that alliance*.

---

[268] On different German domestic positions on the nuclear issue during this period, see: Schneider (2014).

[269] "Telegram from the Embassy in Germany to the Department of State," Bonn, January 15, 1965, 9 p.m., in *FRUS*, 1964–1968, Vol. XIII, Doc. 69.

[270] Quoted in Seaborg (1987, 157).

[271] Granieri (2004, 202).

[272] "Memorandum of Conversation," Washington, September 26, 1966, 11 a.m., in *FRUS*, 1964–1968, Vol. XIII, Doc. 207, emphasis added.

[273] See: Paul (2000, chapter 3); Gerzhoy (2015).

West Germany was a weak state vis-à-vis the Soviet Union. Without the United States, it would have had a great deal of willingness to acquire nuclear weapons, but little opportunity to do so. Without the United States, West Germany would have been highly unlikely to acquire nuclear weapons. Therefore, dependency on the United States only explains German nuclear forbearance if contextualized by Germany's intrinsic weakness. Bonn's low relative power vis-à-vis Moscow was the source of Washington's coercive leverage over German nuclear aspirations.

Furthermore, dependency on an ally does not per se account for Germany's decision to forbear nuclearization. After all, France, which was equally dependent on U.S. security commitments to guarantee its security vis-à-vis the Soviet Union, ended up acquiring the bomb. Accounting for German forbearance, therefore, requires uncovering the rationale behind U.S. coercive nonproliferation pressure, which was much higher than in the French case. As we demonstrated in the preceding text, Washington's staunch opposition to German nuclear acquisition was itself a strategic response to Moscow's misgivings about Bonn's nuclear ambitions. The causal mechanism leading to nuclear forbearance encompasses the strategic interactions between Germany, its allies, and also its adversary, the Soviet Union.

To conclude, West German interest in nuclear weapons and its eventual nuclear forbearance are best explained by a strategic approach. West Germany became interested in nuclear weapons when it doubted the reliability of U.S. security assurances. Facing a much stronger enemy in the Soviet Union, Bonn could see a great security benefit in acquiring nuclear weapons. In order to undermine West Germany's strong willingness to proliferate, Washington considered sharing with its European allies the control of a NATO multilateral nuclear force. The Soviet Union, however, strongly opposed this move, which it feared would ultimately result in Bonn gaining autonomous control over nuclear weapons. In light of Moscow's objections, Washington faced a great risk of entrapment in trying to satisfy Bonn's willingness to acquire nuclear weapons. Eventually, the United States shifted strategy and coerced West Germany into renouncing the nuclear option, making sure that Bonn did not have the opportunity to proliferate. Facing great U.S. pressure, and unable to face the Soviet threat without U.S. protection, West Germany decided to forgo the nuclear option.

France

Possessing broad security interests, France came out of the Second World War enjoying U.S. protection. During the 1950s, however, Paris grew increasingly skeptical of Washington's security guarantees, both in what concerned the continued protection of the French mainland territory and, especially, in what concerned the pursuit of broader French security interests. Therefore, Paris became willing to build a nuclear deterrent. Given that its mainland territory was protected by U.S. nuclear forces, Paris also had the opportunity to nuclearize. In 1960, France tested its first nuclear weapon.

The Second World War, in which France suffered a quick and humiliating defeat at the hands of Nazi Germany in 1940 and was subsequently occupied by German forces, raised questions about the power, status, and security of France. Yet, France emerged from the war officially as one of its victors, retaining its colonies around the world. The postwar order presented its own challenges, namely, the prospect of a resurgent Germany and the threat of a powerful Soviet Union. Moscow possessed an advantage in conventional forces on the European continent and could limit French influence around the world. Both these threats were mitigated by French participation in NATO, which allowed Paris to benefit from U.S. security pledges in case of eventual German revisionism or a Soviet attack on the French homeland.

Nonetheless, U.S. security guarantees were not sufficiently reliable to dispel French willingness to acquire nuclear weapons. With the "New Look" of 1954, Washington promised to meet a Soviet attack with massive nuclear retaliation, thereby boosting the value of an atomic deterrent. Yet, the credibility of U.S. guarantees was soon severely questioned as a result of the Soviet launch of Sputnik in October 1957. In addition, Paris concluded that the overlap between its security interests and those of the United States was imperfect. The traumatic defeat at Dien Bien Phu in 1954 and the retreat in the Suez Crisis of 1956 made Paris acutely aware of the limits of American protection. In response, the French nuclear program, which had been initiated in 1945, accelerated in the mid-1950s, ultimately resulting in the French nuclear test of February 1960.

While remaining unable to offer reliable extended security guarantees that would remove French willingness to acquire nuclear weapons, the presence of the United States helped provide France with an opportunity to proliferate. With the creation of NATO, the United States pledged to defend the French homeland, and a preventive attack by the Soviet Union on Western Europe could thus escalate into a nuclear Third World War. From the Soviet perspective, the effect of French nuclearization on the balance of power between the two blocs did not warrant the costs inherent in attempting to avert it by force. The threat of preventive war by the Soviet Union was therefore not credible. Similarly, because the effect of French nuclearization was relatively small, U.S. fear of entrapment resulting from a French attempt to acquire nuclear weapons was relatively weak. The United States applied minimal pressure on France to stop its program, essentially acquiescing to French nuclearization. In sum, France had both the opportunity and the willingness to acquire nuclear weapons, because U.S. protection was sufficient to deter a preventive attack but insufficient to meet France's security interests.

French Interest in Nuclear Weapons

Immediately following the Second World War, French strategic concerns were focused on Germany.[274] Given the trauma of the two world wars, France cared about preventing a resurgence of German power. This security concern, however, did not warrant a strong commitment to the acquisition of nuclear weapons. With Germany under occupation and a U.S. nuclear monopoly after the Second World War, General Charles de Gaulle did not foresee the need to restart French nuclear-weapons research after its interruption in 1940. Instead, he merely promised that the government would keep the nuclear option on the table.[275]

The Early Years, 1945–1954
On October 18, 1945, as president of the provisional government, de Gaulle (1944–1946) created the *Commissariat à l'Énergie Atomique* (CEA). While the CEA was legally set up to oversee both the civilian and military applications of nuclear energy, it was initially committed to the peaceful uses of nuclear energy.[276] During the discussions over the international control of nuclear weapons at the UN in June 1946,

---

[274] See: Soutou (2012).
[275] See: Hymans (2006, 87–89).
[276] See: Vaïsse (1992); Mongin (1997); Bendjebbar (2000).

French ambassador Alexandre Parodi (1946–1949) claimed that the French nuclear program was purely for civilian uses.[277] Until the early 1950s, the French nuclear program progressed slowly because of the perception in Paris that "France's defense needs in Europe were being adequately fulfilled by the Brussels Pact [of mutual defense with Belgium, Britain, Luxemburg, and the Netherlands] and NATO."[278]

Soon, however, rising tensions made the nuclear option more attractive. To begin with, Paris had to reconcile its desire for a weak Germany with its need to deter a new, more serious threat: potential Soviet aggression in Western Europe. As a German newspaper put it at the time, "The French want a German Army that is at one and the same time bigger than the Russian Army and smaller than the French Army."[279] A stronger FRG, though it would help deter a Soviet attack, could undermine the relative power of France within NATO, with Paris fearing that West Germany would become America's "privileged ally" in Europe.[280] During the first half of the 1950s, France consistently attempted to preclude German rearmament by proposing the creation of a European army in lieu of West German accession into NATO.

By 1954, however, it was clear that this effort had failed. Ironically, the dream of the European Defense Community (EDC) had collapsed as a result of the French Parliament's refusal to ratify the treaty.[281] In response, the United States floated rumors of rearming Germany and excluding France from Western Europe's defense perimeter.[282] This forced Paris to accept German entry into NATO by 1955.[283] During

---

[277] See: Mongin (1997, 56). The scientific leadership at the CEA was also opposed to a military program. In March 1950, the high commissioner of the CEA, Frédéric Joliot-Curie, signed the Stockholm Appeal calling for a ban on nuclear weapons. Ibid., 113. Joliot-Curie, a member of the French Communist Party, declared at the party congress the following month that "[n]ever will progressive scientists and Communist scientists contribute one iota of their science to war against the Soviet Union." Goldschmidt (1990, 346). Such declarations went too far, however, causing a stir in the French and American media and leading to Joliot-Curie's firing at the end of April.

[278] Kohl (1971, 30).

[279] Grosser (1963, 554).

[280] See: Heuser (1998, 111).

[281] See: Hymans (2006, 92).

[282] See: Goldstein (2000, 190).

[283] See: Grosser (1963, 554).

this same period, Paris was increasingly worried about its strategic dependency on Washington. As the eruption of the Korean War – and, later, East-West crises over Berlin and Taiwan – made clear, it was possible that France would be brought into a war by the United States over goals about which it cared little. This risk of entrapment could only be alleviated by turning France into an independent international actor, a goal that would benefit from Paris acquiring its own nuclear arsenal. At the same time, France felt "abandonment anxiety" vis-à-vis the United States.[284] In particular, Paris feared it could not rely on U.S. nuclear guarantees, especially for the pursuit of its broader global interests. This fear of abandonment would eventually prove crucial in accelerating the French nuclear-weapons program after 1954.

Acceleration of the Nuclear-Weapons Program, 1954–1960

In January 1954, U.S. secretary of state John Foster Dulles announced a new strategy for NATO, the New Look, which promised massive atomic retaliation in response to a hypothetical Soviet invasion of Western Europe. Such a policy decreased the value of French conventional forces and boosted the argument that only nuclearization would reinstate France to the club of major powers.[285] In a note to French prime minister Pierre Mendès France (1954–1955) later that year, diplomat Jean-Marc Boegner explained that "national independence, and the autonomy of our diplomacy, on which the survival of the French union depends to a large extent, requires France to pursue its own efforts in the development of military applications of nuclear energy."[286] In addition, the New Look policy inspired a new concept of deterrence, in which nuclear weapons could effectively deter a conventionally superior state. This concept of deterrence was relayed to the French establishment when Pierre Gallois, a French representative at the NATO New Approach Group, presented this thesis to Prime Minister Guy Mollet (1956–1957) and to General de Gaulle in the spring of 1956.[287]

---

[284] See: Goldstein (2000, 143–145).
[285] See: Soutou (1989, 319); Mongin (1997, 310). For a dissenting view, see: Hymans (2006, 95).
[286] Quoted in Soutou (1989, 320).
[287] See: Mongin (1997, 404–408, 418–420). Other early proponents of the bomb included General André Beaufre and Colonel Charles Ailleret. Ibid., 246–274. See also: Tertrais (2004). For de Gaulle's perspective on deterrence of the strong by the weak, see: Peyrefitte (1994, 289–290, 342).

French interest in nuclear weapons was further enhanced when the credibility of the New Look came into question in October 1957. The successful launch of Sputnik demonstrated that the Soviets could place a nuclear warhead on the U.S. mainland. This led to a thorough reevaluation of U.S. and NATO nuclear strategy. Policymakers on both sides of the Atlantic reached the same conclusion: the United States could no longer start a nuclear war in response to conventional Soviet aggression in Europe. As de Gaulle later put it to President Eisenhower, "as the Soviet Union develops the capability to strike the cities of North America, one of your successors ... will be unwilling to go to nuclear war for anything short of a nuclear strike against North America."[288] De Gaulle repeated the same point to President Kennedy. In his view, "the United States would use nuclear weapons only if its own territory was directly threatened."[289] But while the U.S. response called for boosting the conventional component of its deterrent strategy, in Paris, de Gaulle believed that "Europe had to develop an independent nuclear deterrent."[290]

Whereas these broad developments affected all European states, they had a relatively stronger effect on France, which defined its core interests quite broadly. In contrast to other European NATO members, French interests overlapped less with those of the United States. France possessed important security goals that the United States did not share, and therefore was not willing to protect. Specifically, two crises contributed to deepening perceptions among top French policymakers and military leaders that dependency on U.S. support would undermine France's ability to protect its global interests.

The first of these crises was the culmination of the Indochina War against Viet Minh resistance forces. In the aftermath of the Japanese withdrawal at the end of the Second World War, French forces had reoccupied Indochina. Soon, however, the Viet Minh launched an armed attempt to liberate it from colonial rule. During the late 1940s, the French fought a rural insurgency. But once Chinese communist forces reached the Vietnamese border, the conflict approximated a conventional war. Ultimately, the French suffered a decisive defeat at Dien Bien Phu. A postwar provisional agreement divided Indochina – now

---

[288] Quoted in Walters (1978, 491).
[289] Paraphrased in Gallois (1976, 17).
[290] Gordon (1993, 48).

Vietnam – in two, with the Viet Minh controlling the north and pro-Western forces controlling the south.

For Paris, victory in Indochina was necessary to establish a reputation for toughness with independence movements in other French colonies.[291] This perception reflected "not only the French government's desire to tap overseas territories to augment the limited resources of its homeland, but also sensitivity to the political legacy of the country's humiliating defeat early in World War II."[292]

Critically, during the battle of Dien Bien Phu in the spring of 1954, French troops requested American air support to counter the unexpectedly powerful Viet Minh reaction.[293] The United States agreed on the critical importance of Indochina in the global fight against communism, and in fact had heavily supported the French war effort through military and economic aid since 1950.[294] At the same time, Washington did not want to get directly involved in a colonial war, and wanted to share the burden of such an intervention with its allies. The United States insisted on a multilateral endeavor, the "United Action," and demanded a French pledge for the independence of the Associated States of Indochina. Negotiations stalled. Washington could not secure London's support, and Eisenhower again refused a unilateral intervention. French forces soon surrendered at Dien Bien Phu.

Lack of U.S. support in the final battle of the Indochina War led to deep skepticism among French leaders about the advantages of an alliance with the United States. Furthermore, the French defeat in Indochina exemplified the possibility that the communist threat would manifest itself through a series of independence movements rather than as an all-out assault on Western Europe. This meant that nuclear weapons were needed both to support diplomatic actions deterring these movements and to ensure the security of the French mainland if French conventional military capabilities were to be forced to deploy and fight overseas.[295] Indeed, in September, the French military establishment concluded that it was necessary to obtain nuclear weapons in

---

[291] See: Goldstein (2000, 185).
[292] Ibid.
[293] See: Herring and Immerman (1984); Kaplan et al. (1990); Logevall (2012).
[294] See: Lawrence (2005).
[295] Nuclear weapons could be included in war plans at the tactical level. In fact, they were part of U.S. plans for a possible intervention, codenamed Operation Vulture. In early 1954, a study group in the Pentagon concluded

order to have "a certain autonomy" on defense issues as well as a "real influence in the development of joint plans."[296]

Consequently, the French nuclear program accelerated in the aftermath of the Indochina debacle. Before the year was over, French premier Mendès France made the key decision to advance toward building an atomic bomb.[297] On December 26, 1954, he convened a meeting at the Quai d'Orsay with all the relevant policymakers, about forty in total, to discuss the possibility of a nuclear-weapons program. Mendès France approved such a program, and two days later a new division was created within the CEA, the Bureau d'Etudes Générales, to pursue the military applications of nuclear energy.[298] The French nuclear program was now clearly geared toward building the bomb.

Developments in the mid to late 1950s only reinforced growing French skepticism toward U.S. security guarantees. In the summer of 1956, Washington again undermined Paris's pursuit of its foreign-policy aims. On July 26, Egyptian president Nasser announced the nationalization of the Suez Canal. France and Britain hatched a plan to recapture it, with the collaboration of Israel. France was especially keen to attack Nasser given his support for insurgents in Algeria. On October 29, Israeli land forces invaded the Sinai, followed by British and French parachute landings around the Canal.[299]

This intervention was met with strong opposition. On October 31, the United States presented a resolution at the UN condemning it. This resolution was blocked at the Security Council by vetoes from France and the United Kingdom, but it passed in the General Assembly, which condemned the intervention by a vote of 64 to 5. On November 5, the Soviet Union threatened a possible attack on London and Paris. The same day, the United States began to apply economic pressure on Great Britain. First, Washington attacked the pound and, the next day, it informed London that it would withhold an International Monetary

---

that three atomic bombs would be sufficient to defeat the Viet Minh forces at Dien Bien Phu. See: Logevall (2012, 499).

[296] Quoted in Duval and Mongin (1993, 30); Mongin (1997, 251), our translation. See also: Kohl (1971, 32–33).

[297] See: Soutou (1989).

[298] Ibid., 324–326. See also: Mongin (1997, 328–334). The program was meant to remain secret. Years later, Mendès France minimized his role in the French nuclear-weapons program. See: Soutou (1989).

[299] See: Bass (2003, 42–44).

Fund (IMF) loan until Britain withdrew from the area. London capitulated under U.S. pressure and France was forced to follow suit.[300] The operation ended with the ignominious withdrawal of their forces.

Even more so than Dien Bien Phu two years earlier, the Suez Crisis highlighted crucial differences between French and U.S. interests. In Vietnam, Washington had at least agreed that Indochina should not fall to communism, in fact offering significant aid to the French war effort. In the case of Suez, however, the Eisenhower administration hoped to maintain good relations with Nasser's Egypt and feared further Soviet encroachment in the region.

Thus, the crisis exemplified the lack of credibility of U.S. guarantees that French decisionmakers had feared would become apparent when their broader interests were at stake.[301] Raymond Aron, one of the foremost French public intellectuals of the era, argued that Suez "did a great deal to convince our leaders that nuclear armament was indispensible to France."[302] De Gaulle would later tell Eisenhower that the Suez Crisis was one of his main motivations for approving an atomic test, as it showed "that the United States did not always regard as its vital interests what some of its allies regarded as their vital interests."[303] Suez also shifted public preferences in favor of the bomb.[304]

In November and December 1956, the government of Guy Mollet intensified efforts to prepare for a nuclear test.[305] In a secret decree,

---

[300] See: Kunz (1991); Kirshner (1997).

[301] Washington did respond to the Soviet threat by saying that it would retaliate against any nuclear attack on Britain or France. There was good reason to doubt the Soviet threat, however, and U.S. coercive pressure on its allies was real. For the French, interested in an active foreign policy around the world, it was important to influence collective decisionmaking within the Alliance and, if possible, to develop an independent foreign policy.

[302] Quoted in Kelly (1960, 297). See also: Goldstein (2000, 163–167).

[303] Paraphrased in Walters (1978, 490). Immediately after the Suez Crisis, de Gaulle concluded that "American nuclear power does not necessarily and immediately meet all the eventualities concerning France and Europe." Quoted in Kohl (1971, 191).

[304] See: Mongin (1997, 442). According to a January 1960 CIA assessment, "French public acquiescence in a national nuclear weapons program stems from the Suez fiasco." Office of Current Intelligence, Central Intelligence Agency, "The French Nuclear Energy Program," January 28, 1960, in National Security Archive (NSA) Electronic Briefing Book (EBB) 184, "U.S. Intelligence and the French Nuclear Weapons Program," Doc. 12.

[305] See: Mongin (1997, 436–438).

he created the *Comité des Applications Militaires de l'Énergie Atomique*, a small committee of high-level officials responsible for coordinating the nuclear-weapons program between the CEA and the Defense Ministry. The French nuclear program was making substantial progress in 1957–1958, culminating in April 1958 with a decision by Félix Gaillard, then prime minister (1957–1958), to test a nuclear device by the first trimester of 1960.[306] During that period, France briefly considered developing nuclear weapons jointly with Italy and West Germany, sharing the cost of a program and allowing for a continental voice within NATO.[307] (The accord came to be known as the F-I-G treaty, after the name of the three signatories.) On January 17, 1957, the French and West German defense ministers agreed to an ambitious program of military cooperation. In November, they concluded an agreement with the Italian defense minister and extended their collaboration to the nuclear realm.[308] The following April, the three defense ministers met again, agreeing to proceed with the construction of an isotope separation facility in France.[309] This cooperation was short-lived, however. Paris was reluctant to share its emerging nuclear capability with Bonn. Soon after becoming prime minister in the summer of 1958, de Gaulle suspended the agreement.[310]

De Gaulle was called to power as the Fourth Republic was disintegrating over violence in Algeria. With Washington publicly supporting national independence movements, France felt diplomatically isolated.[311] Its possessions in North Africa, the Mediterranean, and the DOM-TOM (overseas departments and territories) were considered vital interests, integral to the "metaphysical survival" of the nation.[312] Washington, however, considered that French overseas operations "seriously weakened the [NATO] alliance."[313] The United States therefore

---

[306] Interestingly, Gaillard signed this decree on April 22 and dated it as of April 11, four days before the fall of his government. See: Barbier (1990, 111–112); Mongin (1997, 453).

[307] See: Soutou (1993, 1996); Nuti (1998); Sheetz (2002).

[308] See: *Documents diplomatiques français*, 1957, tome 2, document 380 (Paris: Imprimerie nationale, 1991); Soutou (1993, 1, 7–8).

[309] See: Soutou (1993, 1, 10).

[310] See: Peyrefitte (1994, 346); Nuti (1998); Sheetz (2002, 301).

[311] See: Kohl (1971, 36).

[312] Heuser (1998, 97–98).

[313] Grosser (1963, 558).

offered to protect only the French mainland from unprovoked attack, undermining French goals in Africa.[314]

The French Fifth Republic, instituted in the fall of 1958, was from the outset determined to renounce dependency on the United States – and to do so publicly.[315] De Gaulle established a new set of guidelines for French security policy, which would last until the late 1980s:

maintain the ideal of autonomy of decision, defend the theoretical independence of the *force de frappe* [the French independent nuclear strike force], avoid any new or explicit commitments to third-country security, refuse participation in any sort of integrated military command structure, manufacture and procure the vast majority of French weapons in France, and claim for France an exceptional status and special global role.[316]

For de Gaulle, nuclear weapons were an instrument of French self-determination, a means "to exist by ourselves and, in case of drama, to choose our direction by ourselves."[317] Nuclear weapons were "the only effective way of ensuring [France's] territorial integrity and political independence."[318] In 1959, France withdrew its Mediterranean Fleet from NATO's military structure, and on February 13, 1960, the country tested its first nuclear weapon at its *Centre Saharien d'Expérimentations Militaires* (CSEM), located in Reggane, in the Sahara desert.[319] The Soviet Union regretted the test, while the United States considered it an embarrassment.[320] Why did the superpowers fail in preventing French nuclear proliferation?

U.S. Nonproliferation Efforts

U.S. efforts to stop proliferation were relatively modest in the early stages of the Cold War. In June 1946, the U.S. Congress enacted legislation to limit nuclear sharing with allies, with the passage of the

---

[314] See: Ibid.
[315] See: Goldstein (2000, 147).
[316] Gordon (1993, xv).
[317] Tertrais (2004, 58).
[318] Quoted in Goldstein (2000, 181).
[319] See: Kelly (1960, 284). Up to the mid-1960s, the French nuclear program was based at the CSEM in Reggane, comprising enrichment and bomb assembly facilities.
[320] Ibid.

Atomic Energy Act. During the Eisenhower administration, however, Washington relaxed its nuclear-sharing policy. In December 1953, Eisenhower delivered his Atoms for Peace speech at the UNGA, announcing that the United States would share nuclear technology for civilian purposes. In addition, Eisenhower favored greater collaboration with U.S. allies on military nuclear technology. In an NSC meeting in October 1957, he "urged with great forcefulness the vital necessity of a fuller exchange of scientific information bearing on military matters between ourselves and our NATO allies."[321] As he later explained in another NSC meeting, it was "silly" for the United States to deny nuclear weapons to its allies, when the common enemy already possessed them.[322] In June 1958, the Atomic Energy Act was loosened, and Washington started offering technical assistance to the British, who had acquired their first nuclear weapon four years earlier.

Paris, however, did not receive technical assistance from the United States on nuclear matters during the 1950s.[323] In March 1957, when hearing about French requests to obtain uranium from British sources, Dulles responded that Washington was "not disposed to assist the French in a weapons program."[324] Secretary of State Christian Herter (1959–1961) declared that the United States could not offer any assistance until France performed its first atomic explosion.[325] De Gaulle resented the U.S. administration's legal arguments based on the McMahon Act and objected to Washington's decision to "keep her secrets."[326] As negotiations deteriorated, Washington took an even harsher position. When de Gaulle declared in December 1959 that France would soon conduct an atomic explosion, Herter responded that the detonation of a nuclear

---

[321] "Memorandum of Discussion at the 340th Meeting of the National Security Council," Washington, October 17, 1957, in *Foreign Relations of the United States (FRUS), 1955–1957*, Vol. XXVII, *Western Europe and Canada*, Doc. 54.

[322] *FRUS 1958–1960*, Vol. VII, Part 2, Doc. 128. For an analysis of Eisenhower's motivations, see: Trachtenberg (1999, 261–262).

[323] For U.S. assistance starting in the Nixon administration, see: Ullman (1989); Trachtenberg (2011).

[324] Memorandum of Conversation between John Foster Dulles and Selwyn Lloyd, "Atomic Energy Items: (1) French Request (2) Test Limitation," March 23, 1957, in Wilson Center Digital Archive, French Nuclear History.

[325] "Memorandum of Conversation," Paris, May 1, 1959, 3:30 p.m., in *FRUS, 1958–1960*, Vol. VII, Part 2, Doc. 109.

[326] "Letter from President de Gaulle to President Eisenhower," Paris, May 25, 1959, in ibid., Doc. 117. See also: Vaïsse (1991, 418).

device would not automatically entitle France to nuclear assistance from the United States. In fact, "what we might be able to do with France in this general area would be determined in the last analysis by the general impression in our Congress concerning the extent to which France was playing a cooperative role in NATO."[327]

By then, France was hardly a cooperative NATO ally. Negotiations between Paris and Washington had deteriorated significantly over France's proposed amendment to the structure of the alliance. In de Gaulle's view, NATO did not adequately serve France's security interests. In September 1958, he proposed a reorganization of its structure.[328] Just as its partners had security interests beyond the North Atlantic, as exemplified in the Lebanon crisis of July 1958 and the Second Taiwan Strait Crisis, so did France. As a result, de Gaulle proposed the creation of a tripartite organ – including Britain, France, and the United States – for coordinating global security policy. Eisenhower rejected de Gaulle's idea, declaring: "We cannot afford to adopt any system which would give to our other allies, or other free world countries, the impression that basic decisions affecting their own vital interests are being made without their participation."[329] De Gaulle's advisor Jean-Marc Boegner told the U.S. embassy in Paris that there was "little logic" to this argument, as "the way it is now the United States takes decisions affecting other countries on a unilateral basis, or sometimes … on a bilateral basis with the United Kingdom."[330] The French ambassador predicted that Paris would soon possess an atomic capability and that, if a tripartite consultation failed, France had "no interest in NATO in its present form."[331] Paris rejected any deployment of nuclear weapons on its territory and soon conducted its own atomic test.[332] Within the next decade, France withdrew from NATO's integrated command. Clearly, the alliance was seen in Paris as inadequate to protect French interests.

---

[327] "Editorial Note," in FRUS, 1958–1960, Vol. VII, Part 2, Doc. 152.
[328] See: "Letter from President de Gaulle to President Eisenhower," Paris, September 17, 1958, in ibid., Doc. 45.
[329] "Letter from President Eisenhower to President de Gaulle," October 20, 1958, in ibid., Doc. 63.
[330] "Memorandum of Conversation," Paris, October 28, 1958, in ibid., Doc. 66.
[331] "Memorandum of Conversation," December 4, 1958, in ibid., Doc. 77.
[332] See: "Memorandum from Secretary of Defense Gates to President Eisenhower," December 17, 1959, in ibid., Doc. 149.

In evaluating U.S. nonproliferation efforts, it is important to understand how the two Cold War superpowers perceived the consequences of French nuclear acquisition. The French were convinced that nuclear weapons would significantly improve their ability to pursue their extensive goals. At the same time, policymakers in Washington and Moscow did not really believe that the pursuit of such goals entailed great escalatory potential, and were therefore unlikely to entrap the superpowers into a conflict they did not desire. As politicians in both Paris and Moscow were aware, French nuclearization did not increase the overall threat faced by the Soviets. It merely complicated Moscow's calculus when its actions impacted the French interests that were not shared by Washington. Put differently, the effect of French nuclearization on the balance of power was relatively low.

In contrast, a Soviet counterproliferation attack on France would be extremely costly, risking a nuclear exchange between the superpowers. Thus, Moscow chose an accommodating posture toward French nuclear ambitions. Soviet premier Nikita Khrushchev played up the role of the *force de frappe* as France's "instrument of blackmail" over NATO, a source of discord within the Western bloc, and a symbol of France's "anti-Americanism."[333] He would later tell the French: "Your atomic force ... is made to annoy the Americans."[334] Given the minor consequences of French nuclearization for Soviet interests, and the high cost of a preventive counterproliferation attack against France, Moscow did not attempt to thwart France's nuclear efforts.[335]

Absent great concerns from Moscow or the likely prospect of being entrapped in a conflict because of French nuclearization, Washington applied minimal pressure to stymie Paris's efforts to acquire the bomb. The last round of negotiations on the NATO structure shouldn't necessarily be seen as a nonproliferation failure. As de Gaulle later admitted, he knew that he was asking too much in his September 1958 memo; he was simply looking for an excuse to withdraw from NATO's integrated command.[336] Given France's strategic situation,

---

[333] Gordon (1993, 41).
[334] Quoted in Heuser (1998, 119–120).
[335] See: Gordon (1993, 60).
[336] "I was asking for the moon," he confided to Alain Peyrefitte. Peyrefitte (1994, 352), our translation.

French nuclearization efforts did not warrant strong coercive efforts on the part of Washington.

In sum, France possessed the willingness to acquire nuclear weapons because of the unreliability of U.S. security guarantees, particularly in what concerned the imperfect overlap between French and American security interests. At the same time, France had the opportunity to proliferate because the effect of its nuclear acquisition was small relative to the cost of a preventive counterproliferation war launched by the Soviets. Because there was little escalatory potential tied to France's pursuit of nuclear weapons, U.S. concerns about French nuclearization were relatively weak, and U.S. pressure to stop French proliferation was overall timid.

Alternative Explanations

Existing work on the French nuclear-weapons program typically eschews security motivations,[337] instead focusing on two reasons for its proliferation: France's quest for prestige in the international system and the psychological predispositions of French elites.

The most common explanation of French nuclear acquisition is that France sought a nuclear arsenal to boost its worldwide prestige. Beatrice Heuser, for example, argues that the *force de frappe* was a means to express France's claim to be a world power and participate in the decisions shaping global politics.[338] Along similar lines, both Philip Gordon and Scott Sagan argue that during de Gaulle's administration, French nuclear weapons were a symbol of independence rather than a serious improvement to the defense of Europe.[339]

Such an explanation, based on motivations of prestige, typically emphasizes the role of Charles de Gaulle in France's nuclearization. It is important to note, however, that the key decisions leading

---

[337] For an exception, see: Tertrais (2004).

[338] See: Heuser (1998, 100–101).

[339] See: Gordon (1993, 39–40); Sagan (1996–1997, 77–80). In practical terms, the limitations of the initial French nuclear force in the early 1960s were clear. The French Mirage bomber force was vulnerable to a preemptive Soviet first strike. Even if the French planes got off the ground, they would have difficulty evading Soviet air defenses. See: Gordon (1993, 41). Moreover, without a sea-based deterrent or sufficient territorial depth, France lacked the second-strike capability necessary to make deterrence more credible. Ibid.

to the French atomic bomb – including the decisions to develop a military component to the nuclear program and the decision to test a device – had already been taken before de Gaulle came into office.

Certainly, de Gaulle used a different approach in managing French international affairs, and went further than his predecessors in pressing for French autonomy. In the Fourth Republic, most French decisionmakers were interested in developing a nuclear arsenal that would be integrated into NATO forces.[340] De Gaulle, in contrast, withdrew all French forces from NATO's integrated command in 1966.[341]

Yet, the key benefit of nuclear weapons was that they would allow France to pursue a broader set of security goals, one that the United States refused to support. Indeed, all key policymakers of the late 1950s concluded that nuclear weapons served the national interest.[342] French leaders of the Fourth Republic approached negotiations over international institutions, such as the EDC and EURATOM, with the express goal of avoiding any limit on the country's ability to develop nuclear weapons. In fact, such concerns were largely responsible for the French Parliament's refusal to ratify the EDC project in August 1954.[343] When thinking about integrating French nuclear forces within NATO, Fourth Republic leaders hoped for a greater degree of autonomy and a stronger bargaining position in collective decisionmaking. In this sense, there were important elements of continuity in the policy of the Fourth and Fifth Republics.[344]

A second problem with attributing causal power to French desire for greater international prestige is that any state should presumably prefer to have greater prestige. The pursuit of prestige, in and of itself, does not constitute a necessary or sufficient condition for nuclear acquisition.[345] Instead, the unique attractiveness that the

---

[340] For a discussion of debates within the French cabinet on the importance of obtaining U.S. consent for the F-I-G accord, see: Soutou (1993, 5).

[341] See: Bozo (2001).

[342] See: Mongin (1997, 456–457).

[343] See: Soutou (1996, 14); Bendjebbar (2000, 168, 171). For a skeptical view, see: Mongin (1997, 297). On the Euratom, see: Duval and Mongin (1993, 37); Mongin (1997, 397–413); Bendjebbar (2000, 215–216).

[344] Note that, before de Gaulle, Mendès France had proposed to establish a tripartite leadership within NATO, composed of the French, the British, and the Americans. See: Soutou (1996, 33). Also, Gaillard had proposed to extend NATO beyond Europe, so as to include areas of strategic importance to France. Ibid., 103.

[345] See our case study of Brazil in Chapter 4.

nuclear option presented to French policymakers resulted from France's strategic situation. In the aftermath of the Second World War, French politicians often spoke of recovering the country's prestige and reaffirming France's role as a major voice in world affairs. Nuclear weapons were mentioned as providing a "ticket" to the great-power club. As Premier Mendès France reportedly claimed, "if you do not have the Bomb you are nothing in international negotiations."[346] Acting as a great power meant that France would have a stronger bargaining position to defend the totality of French interests, including its interests abroad. Put differently, the prestige accruing from an independent nuclear force was especially attractive for France because it allowed for the pursuit of broad security interests for which it did not possess the support of the United States, its superpower ally.

A more recent alternative explanation for French nuclearization, put forth by Jacques Hymans, is based on the psychology of French leaders and the perception of their country's standing vis-à-vis Germany. In his view, nuclear decisions were not made to meet the Russian threat, since they were made at the height of U.S. credibility.[347] Instead, the French developed the bomb to meet the German challenge. The French "Europeans" had an "oppositional subaltern" conception vis-à-vis Germany and did not want to acquire the bomb. The French "nationalists," such as Pierre Mendès France and Charles de Gaulle, in contrast, had an "oppositional nationalist" conception toward Germany and pressed for the bomb.

This argument presents two important difficulties. First, despite the multiple changes in government, there was, as we just saw, a remarkable continuity in nuclear policymaking, starting with the first steps toward a military component in late 1954.[348] Even a "European" policymaker such as Guy Mollet made important decisions to press the nuclear program forward. As such, a focus on the psychological preferences of individual leaders appears inadequate.

A "nationalist" policy gained traction and was able to harness the resources necessary to produce a nuclear deterrent because of France's strategic environment. The military program started out of concerns

---

[346] See: Tertrais (2004, 54).
[347] See: Hymans (2006, 86). See also: Pelopidas (2015).
[348] See: Mongin (1997, 458).

about the imperfect overlap between the interests of France and those of the United States, beginning with the experience at Dien Bien Phu and later reinforced at Suez. Certainly, Sputnik presented a substantial blow to U.S. guarantees for the defense of Europe. Even before Sputnik, however, Paris had realized that it might need to enter into conflicts where the United States was not willing to offer its support. Because of concerns about the imperfect overlap between French and American interests, nuclear weapons appeared highly beneficial, leading Paris to overcome the willingness constraint on proliferation. At the same time, the presence of a U.S. commitment to defend the French homeland from an unprovoked Soviet strike meant that the effect of French nuclearization would, for the Soviets, be smaller than the cost of a preventive counterproliferation war, allowing Paris to overcome the opportunity constraint on nuclear acquisition. Combined, these two strategic dynamics explain why pronuclear nationalists carried the day in France.

Second, France's interest in an autonomous nuclear deterrent dictated its policy toward Germany, not the other way around. Determined to strengthen Europe's hand on NATO defense plans, France briefly considered a joint nuclear program with the Germans, resulting in the F-I-G treaty. When de Gaulle suspended this agreement, he did not do so out of fear that a nuclear Germany could hurt France – which would presumably also acquire nuclear weapons as a result of this joint effort. Rather, the problem with Franco-German nuclear cooperation was, from Paris's perspective, Soviet opposition to a German bomb, which could lead Moscow to start a new war. As de Gaulle later explained, "A German nuclear arsenal was the last *casus belli* left in the world, or one of the very last few."[349] Clearly, France's nuclear program was not driven by fears of German resurgence.

To conclude, France pursued and eventually acquired nuclear weapons because it possessed expansive security goals that its superpower ally, the United States, was unwilling to protect. The painful experiences of Dien Bien Phu and Suez drove this point home. Since the interests that France was determined to pursue did not threaten key Soviet security goals, and since the United States guaranteed to protect the French homeland, French nuclearization was unlikely to trigger a Soviet preventive strike. As a result, threats of preventive war by the

---

[349] Peyrefitte (1994, 345), our translation.

Soviet Union lacked credibility, and U.S. pressure against French proliferation was weak. Under American protection, France became the fourth nation to acquire nuclear weapons.

* * *

The relevant counterfactuals vary among the countries just studied. A first one, focusing on the presence of a security sponsor, applies to all four cases. Had any of these states faced the same level of threat and possessed the same relative power while having no security guarantees from a patron such as the United States, nuclear acquisition would have been likely only in the cases of Japan and perhaps South Korea, since these were the two states that possessed higher relative power vis-à-vis their adversaries and would therefore have had the opportunity to go nuclear. (Assuming that Japan would have armed itself conventionally too in a way commensurate with its latent capabilities.) West Germany and France, both weak countries vis-à-vis their adversary, the Soviet Union, would have probably lacked the opportunity to build the bomb.

Two additional counterfactuals apply to the Japanese, South Korean, and West German cases. To begin with, focusing on the extent of their security goals, had any of these countries possessed broader aims that would have been better pursued in the presence of a nuclear arsenal, their odds of nuclear acquisition would have also depended on the entrapment potential that their nuclear ambitions would pose for Washington. It is likely that in all these cases, this would have deepened Washington's opposition to their nuclear ambitions, so the outcome would likely have been similar in all three cases: nuclear forbearance.

Furthermore, focusing on their relative power, had Japan or South Korea been weaker vis-à-vis their enemies and nonetheless attempted to build the bomb, we would have probably witnessed U.S. efforts to remove their opportunity to nuclearize, by insisting that they remain nonnuclear in order to keep U.S. security guarantees. The United States could thus have reduced security commitments to these countries, just as it did with Taiwan, in order to obtain their nuclear forbearance. Conversely, had Germany been stronger vis-à-vis the Soviet Union, then Washington would have probably not led efforts to deny it the opportunity to proliferate. Such efforts would have been ineffective anyway, and Soviet threats of preventive action would not have been credible in the first place. Instead, we would have seen

U.S. efforts center on removing its willingness to go nuclear. Given that the United States was already extending sizeable commitments to West Germany, its counterfactual relative strength vis-à-vis the Soviet Union would likely have resulted in unimpeded nuclear acquisition.

Finally, the French case invokes two additional relevant counterfactuals.[350] For starters, focusing on the extent of its security goals, had France possessed no aims beyond its territorial integrity that were better pursued in the presence of a nuclear arsenal, Paris would not have had the willingness to acquire nuclear weapons as long as it benefited from robust and reliable U.S. security guarantees of protection of the French homeland. Furthermore, focusing on the entrapment potential that French nuclearization posed for the United States, it would have been highly unlikely that Washington would have allowed Paris to obtain the bomb if such entrapment concerns were high. Instead, we would have witnessed U.S. nonproliferation efforts aimed at making sure that France would not have the opportunity to go nuclear.

---

[350] In the case of France, a counterfactual that would increase its relative power vis-à-vis the Soviet Union while keeping all other aspects of the case constant would not be relevant, given that the low degree of concern about French nuclearization exhibited by Moscow makes French ability to impose costs in case of a preventive strike moot. Note that this does not deny the analytic power of our strategic approach in this case. Rather, it highlights how in cases of protégés that are well protected prior to their nuclear acquisition, the effect of their nuclearization is relatively small, and may therefore lead their adversary to eschew any preventive considerations.

7 | Conclusion

In this concluding chapter, we summarize our central arguments, highlight the strategic forces behind the historical patterns of proliferation, introduce our interpretation of the role of the NPT regime in shaping them, discuss the implications of our argument for the study of nuclear proliferation and for U.S. efforts to deter the spread of nuclear weapons, and lay out our views on the future of proliferation.

Key Elements of Our Argument

This book has introduced a security-based theory of nuclear proliferation focusing on the strategic interaction between a state, its enemies, and allies. By analyzing these interactions, we conclude that only two types of states acquire the bomb: powerful but highly threatened countries; and weaker countries that are protected by an ally they deem unreliable, either because it is unlikely to remain protective of their territory in the long-term or because it is not supportive of their broader security goals. The empirical rarity of these strategic situations is responsible for the relatively low number of states – ten, or slightly over 5 percent of the total number of independent countries in the world – that have acquired the bomb during the first seventy years of the nuclear age.

The vast majority of states do not possess the willingness or the opportunity necessary to acquire nuclear weapons. Many, perhaps most nonnuclear states, do not possess the willingness to nuclearize because their strategic environment does not present serious threats to their security. Others face serious threats but their willingness to build nuclear weapons is undermined by reliable allied security guarantees. Finally, some states have the willingness to nuclearize but lack the opportunity to do so because they are too weak and unprotected to deter preventive military action against their nascent nuclear program prior to crossing the nuclear threshold. One way or another, the strategic logic of nuclear proliferation leads most states to remain nonnuclear.

Our argument calls into question the view that nuclear weapons are the "weapons of the underdogs."[1] Nuclear possession would certainly present great security advantages for weak states. Yet, the weak cannot get them. The reason is simple: although the weak, when threatened, have the willingness to nuclearize, they rarely have the opportunity to build the bomb. The very weakness that makes nuclear weapons so enticing also makes the state vulnerable to preventive military action and, therefore, also to the "softer" tools of coercive diplomacy. Consequently, only the powerful – or those that enjoy their protection – have the opportunity to cross the nuclear threshold.

The theoretical arguments we put forth in this book can be summarized in a series of ten staccato theses:

1. The spread of nuclear weapons is determined by the strategic interaction that takes place during the period leading up to the state's nuclear acquisition or abandonment between the potential proliferator, its adversaries, and, when present, its allies.
2. This interaction is centered on three strategic variables:
   a. The level of security threat faced by the potential proliferator;
   b. The relative power of the potential proliferator vis-à-vis its adversaries;
   c. The reliability and robustness of allied commitments to the security of the potential proliferator.
3. The security benefit of proliferation increases with the level of threat faced by the potential proliferator and decreases with its relative conventional power and with the robustness and reliability of allied commitments to its defense.
4. When the security benefit of proliferation is greater than the cost of a nuclear program, the potential proliferator will have the willingness to nuclearize.
   a. When, on the contrary, the security benefit of proliferation is smaller than the cost of a nuclear program, the potential proliferator will opt for nuclear forbearance.
5. The cost of preventive war increases with the relative power of the potential proliferator vis-à-vis its adversaries, and with the robustness of allied commitments to its defense.

[1] O'Neill (2000, 191).

6. When the cost of preventive war is greater than the security benefit of nuclear acquisition, the potential proliferator will have the opportunity to nuclearize.
   a. When, on the contrary, the cost of preventive war is lower than the security benefit of nuclear acquisition, either the potential proliferator opts for nuclear forbearance, or it will be targeted by preventive military counterproliferation action.
7. Proliferation occurs when the potential proliferator has both the willingness and the opportunity to nuclearize.
   a. These two conditions are necessary and sufficient for proliferation to occur.
   b. Other proliferation drivers, such as prestige, economic incentives, domestic politics, and so on, are unnecessary and insufficient to lead the potential proliferator to nuclearize.
8. Adversaries of the potential proliferator have one essential tool at their disposal with which they can attempt to deter the spread of nuclear weapons: the threat of preventive counterproliferation military action.
   a. The efficacy of other counterproliferation tools available to the potential proliferator's adversaries – such as sanctions – depends on the credibility of threats of preventive counterproliferation military action.
9. Allies of the potential proliferator have two essential tools at their disposal with which they can attempt to deter the spread of nuclear weapons:
   a. Extending more robust security guarantees to the potential proliferator in a carrots-based nonproliferation policy;
      i. The effectiveness of carrots-based nonproliferation policies increases as the ability of the potential proliferator to ensure it has the opportunity to nuclearize on its own increases and the breadth of the potential proliferator's security interests decreases.
   b. Threatening the potential proliferator with abandonment in a sticks-based nonproliferation policy;
      i. The effectiveness of sticks-based nonproliferation policies increases as the ability of the potential proliferator to ensure it has the opportunity to proliferate on its own decreases.

10. These strategic conditions result in two distinct pathways to nu-
    clear proliferation:
    a. A state that faces a high level of threat to its security and has
        high relative power vis-à-vis its adversaries while not enjoy-
        ing reliable allied commitments to its security has both the
        willingness and the opportunity to nuclearize;
    b. A state that faces a high level of threat to the security of its
        homeland and enjoys allied security guarantees of protection
        of its homeland that are sufficient to make the cost of pre-
        ventive war greater than the security benefit of proliferation
        and yet are not reliable (either because the state doubts this
        protection will remain in the long-term or because this pro-
        tection does not cover the state's broader security interests)
        has both the willingness and the opportunity to nuclearize.

Our theory makes clear the centrality of security threats in shaping the patterns of nuclear proliferation. On the one hand, the more
serious the security threats a state faces, the higher its willingness
to acquire a nuclear deterrent. On the other hand, dire threats to
a state's security tend to emanate from powerful adversaries, and
powerful adversaries can use military action to deny the state its opportunity to build a nuclear arsenal. These countervailing effects of
threats on proliferation account for why not all threatened states end
up acquiring nuclear weapons. Security threats lead some states to
build the bomb, but prevent others from doing so. Specifically, only
powerful or protected states will have the opportunity to cross the
nuclear threshold when threatened. Either way, our theory exposes
the centrality of relations between adversaries to the process of nuclear proliferation.

At the same time, our theory highlights the crucial role of alliances
in shaping the spread of nuclear weapons. Whenever a serious security
threat emanating from an adversary gives a state the willingness to
nuclearize, whether it will do so or not depends on the potential proliferator's relations with its allies. The presence of a reliable ally that
covers all of the potential proliferator's threatened security goals will
undermine its willingness to build the bomb. It is only the presence
of an unreliable ally that nevertheless protects the territory of the potential proliferator in the near future that gives the potential proliferator both the willingness and the opportunity to nuclearize. All in all,
alliances are a powerful force both deterring and enabling the spread

of nuclear weapons, depending on the strategic circumstances of each particular case.

The Strategic Logic behind the History of Proliferation

Historically, the strategic logic of proliferation brings into bold relief the paramount role in shaping proliferation patterns played by what is perhaps the single most consequential strategic decision of the nuclear age: the United States' choice to remain deeply involved in the world in the aftermath of the Second World War through a vast network of alliances and security commitments.[2] During the Cold War, U.S. commitments protected numerous allies against the Soviet threat – and furthered U.S. interests in containing Soviet influence. In doing so, the U.S.-led system of Cold War alliances dampened proliferation considerably. As we have shown in the empirical chapters of this book, states such as Sweden, Japan, and South Korea would have been highly likely to proliferate in the absence of U.S. protection. In fact, nuclear weapons spread mostly among countries that were unable to get more reliable U.S. security guarantees, such as Israel, India, South Africa, and Pakistan. Were Washington more willing to extend reliable guarantees to the security of these states too, they would have been unlikely to build the bomb.

Since the end of the Cold War, the global network of U.S. alliances continues to play a key role in preventing the spread of nuclear weapons. To begin with, U.S. allies, enjoying the protection of the most powerful state in history, are less likely to possess the willingness to nuclearize. Furthermore, those who oppose U.S. interests are less likely to find protection against preventive counterproliferation military action by the United States or its allies. Taken together, these two dynamics account for the slower pace of nuclear proliferation we have witnessed since the collapse of the Soviet Union. At their core is the global network of U.S. security commitments.

The world would therefore have been very different – and so would the historical patterns of nuclear proliferation – if Washington had decided to do in 1945 what it had done in 1918, when the First World War ended: eschew extending guarantees of protection to friendly states around the globe.[3] Assuming that Moscow would have remained highly militarized in the absence of U.S. alliances, Soviet power virtually

---

[2] See: Fearon (2013).
[3] See: Cohrs (2008).

ensured that none of its adversaries would have had the opportunity to build a nuclear arsenal in the absence of U.S. protection. But after the demise of the Soviet Union, a world without extensive U.S. security guarantees would have been highly likely to lead to the faster spread of nuclear weapons. Lacking U.S. protection, additional states would have been willing to build the bomb in order to deter threats from their regional adversaries. The most powerful among these states would have been likely to nuclearize. Over the past quarter century, therefore, U.S. involvement in global security affairs has played an important role in deterring additional nuclear proliferation.[4]

At the same time, the vast network of U.S. alliances has granted Washington considerable additional leverage over its protégés. U.S. decisionmakers have worked hard to deter nuclear acquisition among U.S. allies, ensuring that their security would remain dependent on U.S. protection – and that they would, therefore, remain amenable to U.S. foreign-policy goals. In this sense, our theory undermines a view of alliances as tools of power aggregation. If the foremost purposes of alliances were to maximize the combined military capabilities of its members in order to deter aggression, then we would have expected the United States to allow, indeed encourage, its allies to build the bomb. Instead, U.S. behavior during the nuclear age reveals how alliances are often tools with which security sponsors seek to control the behavior of their own protégés. U.S. leaders repeatedly sought to maintain the nonnuclear status of their junior alliance partners. In exchange for Washington's protection, U.S. protégés were asked to remain vulnerable to the security threats they faced by keeping their nonnuclear status.

Beyond limiting the spread of nuclear weapons, U.S. nonproliferation efforts may also have advantages in dampening the level of interstate conflict and the odds of nuclear escalation. Washington usually requires its alliance partners to behave in a nonaggressive manner toward their adversaries. Therefore, to the extent that nuclear acquisition by a U.S. protégé would lower its reliance on U.S. security

---

[4] It is of course quite possible that the reverse is also true: concerns with the spread of nuclear weapons may have contributed to U.S. willingness to extend guarantees of protection to numerous countries around the world. Although this dynamic may have contributed to a greater number of security alliances, it does not alter the key predictions of our theory about their role in shaping the patterns of proliferation.

guarantees, it might also allow for more reckless behavior toward its adversaries. Furthermore, since the United States enjoys a considerable preponderance in conventional military capabilities, it can mitigate most threats to its protégés using conventional weaponry. Were these protégés to be forced to face their adversaries on their own, they would be more likely to escalate to nuclear use in case of a conflict. For these two reasons, the U.S. nuclear umbrella likely reduces the incidence of both war involving its protégés and of nuclear use.

The Role of the Nuclear-Nonproliferation Regime

While our theory focuses on strategic variables, other factors have also shaped the spread of nuclear weapons. They do so, however, by altering the strategic interactions on which we focus. For example, there is a widespread belief that the nuclear-nonproliferation regime centered on the NPT has deterred the spread of nuclear weapons. As nonproliferation norms spread, the argument goes, states became less likely to seek nuclearization.

We agree that the NPT has had an important effect in deterring proliferation. We do not, however, believe that this effect relates to normative compliance dynamics. Instead, in our view the NPT has played an important role in the proliferation process by making it more difficult for states to develop nuclear weapons undetected. In effect, no state has ever acquired nuclear weapons while being a party to the NPT. Six of the ten states that have developed nuclear weapons (China, France, South Africa, the Soviet Union, United Kingdom, and United States) did so before joining the NPT; three others (India, Israel, and Pakistan) never joined the treaty; and North Korea withdrew from the treaty in 2003, three years before its first nuclear test. Given the level of surveillance of nuclear activity occurring in NPT member states – particularly after the treaty's Additional Protocol was adopted in 1997 – it would be difficult for a state to build the bomb while remaining within the nonproliferation regime. At the same time, states can exit the NPT in order to develop the bomb; or they can remain outside the NPT, as the previously mentioned three nuclear powers do. Therefore, the nonproliferation regime on the spread of nuclear weapons functions as a trigger-warning about nuclear development.

A refusal to join the NPT can stem from many different concerns, with sovereignty and a perception that the two-tiered nuclear system at the core of nonproliferation regime is unfair being among the most prevalent. Still, refusal to enter the NPT – or a decision to exit it – would prompt concerns about nuclearization, leading the preventive dynamics at the core of our theory to come into play, and allowing the potential proliferator's adversaries and allies to attempt to coerce it into eschewing its nuclear ambitions. This logic arguably played an important role in the maintenance of the nonnuclear status of several countries that at one point or another were engaged in nuclear development, including, most recently, Iran.

Additionally, the NPT has a second-order strategic effect on the spread of nuclear weapons. By making it harder for its member states to build nuclear weapons undetected, the nonproliferation regime lowers the need that states have to engage in nuclear development out of fear for the surprise nuclearization of an adversary. Thus, the NPT has an important role in coordinating expectations about the slow pace of proliferation, reinforcing deterrent barriers to the spread of nuclear weapons.

The crucial role played by the NPT, alongside nuclear detection and surveillance technologies deployed by many states to monitor the nuclear activities of others, only becomes evident when we understand the centrality of preventive dynamics (by adversaries) and coercive diplomacy (by allies) in stymieing the spread of nuclear weapons. Our theory makes clear why and how detection of nuclear development prior to nuclearization is crucial to avoid the spread of nuclear weapons. The only way that a weak and unprotected state might be able to nuclearize would be by remaining unsuspected of nuclear development until it can present its nuclear acquisition as a fait accompli.[5] Nuclearization "by stealth" would therefore deny the empirical implications of our theory. But it is exceedingly unlikely that a state would be able to acquire a functioning nuclear device without any of its adversaries or allies suspecting that this is happening and attempting to prevent this outcome.

---

[5] Note that remaining undetected is not sufficient for stealthy nuclearization in the sense that preventive dynamics are triggered as soon as other states suspect that the potential proliferator is involved in nuclear development. In fact, as we have argued elsewhere, these dynamics can lead to mistaken preventive wars against states that were *not* detected as involved in nuclear activity, merely suspected of doing so, as was the case of Iraq in the run-up to the 2003 U.S.-led invasion. See: Debs and Monteiro (2014).

The problem with stealthy nuclearization is different: if an adversary does not know where a potential proliferator's nuclear facilities are located, the cost of an effective preventive military strike increases, as stopping the potential proliferator's nuclear ambitions would require controlling its entire territory or replacing its regime with a friendlier one. (This was arguably the logic that led to the invasion of Iraq in 2003, despite the fact that Iraq's nuclear activities had ended more than a decade earlier.) Likewise with the possibility of a state acquiring a functioning nuclear weapon from an ally, a possibility that has been discussed in connection with the hypothetical sale of a nuclear device by Pakistan to Saudi Arabia.[6] Although discussion of such a possibility would indicate that the adversaries and allies of the state that is contemplating the purchase of a nuclear weapon are aware that this transaction might occur, their ability to deter nuclearization through the purchase of a nuclear weapon is more limited than it would be were the state to attempt nuclear development by investing in a physical nuclear program, which can be targeted in a military operation short of full-scale war. Still, given the robust surveillance and detection apparatuses controlled by the IAEA and the United States, the efforts of other states around the world to monitor the nuclear activities of their adversaries, and the robust inspections regime of the NPT, the overall prospects of stealthy nuclearization – either through nuclear development or nuclear purchase – are exceedingly slim.[7] In all likelihood, the spread of nuclear weapons will continue to be shaped by the strategic logic on which our theory focuses.

Implications for the Study of Nuclear Proliferation

Although we contend that strategic dynamics revolving around security concerns are sufficient to account for the decision to build – or forfeit – nuclear weapons, we agree that a complete account of the dynamics of nuclear proliferation must take into consideration other nonsecurity variables. In fact, several extant contributions to the study of proliferation can be incorporated in our framework in a symbiotic relationship. A strategic theory such as ours can be enriched

---

[6] See: Kahl et al. (2013).
[7] See: Department of Defense (2014).

by bringing into its framework additional variables that have been explored in the literature. At the same time, existing theories of proliferation could be refined by taking into account the strategic dynamics highlighted by our theory.

For example, Etel Solingen's work on the role that the economic orientation of ruling elites plays in the proliferation process can easily be incorporated into our framework. Solingen's argument is that elites who want to integrate their country in the global economy are more likely to forbear nuclear weapons and those who do not ("inward-looking" elites) are more likely to pursue the bomb.[8] While we focus on the expected security costs and benefits of nuclear acquisition – and contend that these security factors are sufficient to explain a country's nuclear acquisition or forbearance – a more complete picture of the proliferation process would benefit from incorporating the economic costs on which Solingen's work centers, which could add to the overall cost of a nuclear program, undermining a state's willingness to nuclearize. Reciprocally, further work on the role of economic preferences in conditioning the spread of nuclear weapons should incorporate strategic interaction in its logic: as Solingen acknowledges, states in a region populated by other inward-looking states become more likely to acquire the bomb and vice versa.[9]

Likewise, Jacques Hymans's work on the role played by leader psychology in shaping the proliferation process could provide greater richness to our strategic framework of analysis.[10] Leaders' psychological makeup will, as Hymans points out, color their perceptions of threat. As a result, particular types of leaders, such as those who adhere to what Hymans labels a "national identity conception" of "oppositional nationalism," will be prone to inflate threats and, therefore, become more likely to, also according to our theory, possess the willingness to build the bomb.[11] At the same time, additional work on the psychology of nuclear proliferation should take into account the strategic setting in which leaders operate. It is implausible that the psychological makeup of a country's leadership is immune to strategic pressures.

---

[8] See: Solingen (2007).
[9] Ibid., 40–47.
[10] See: Hymans (2006).
[11] Ibid.

Our strategic framework can also accommodate Hymans's work on how technological and managerial incompetence may lead to nuclear forbearance.[12] According to our theory, a state's incompetence in the nuclear realm may affect proliferation in two ways. First, it may increase the cost of a nuclear program, making it less likely that the state is willing to acquire the bomb. Second, by delaying nuclear acquisition, it may facilitate nuclear forbearance if the security environment improves during this longer nuclear-development period. Only in the first case can we talk of incompetence causing nuclear forbearance, however. In the second case, forbearance occurs only if the strategic environment improves. Regardless of how much longer the nuclear-development phase becomes, our theory explains why proliferation might occur nonetheless as long as the security environment continues to provide the state with both the willingness and the opportunity to go nuclear. This logic also highlights the benefits of incorporating strategic dynamics into future work on the role that technological and managerial competence plays in the proliferation process.

A similar logic applies to work on how norms against nuclear proliferation and institutions such as the NPT affect the spread of nuclear weapons.[13] Our theory speaks to normative concerns and institutional effects by incorporating them into the strategic environment. At a minimum, institutions may reduce the likelihood that member states would be able to build the bomb undetected. According to our theory, the NPT may take away the ability of weak unprotected states – those that, if threatened, would enjoy a higher benefit of proliferation – to acquire the bomb by exposing their development efforts, making them vulnerable to preventive attack. In addition, institutions can help lower states' perception of the level of security threat in a coordinated manner, by generating lower expectations of future proliferation and conflict.

Finally, arguments about the effectiveness of restrictions to the supply of nuclear materials and technology as a means of deterring proliferation, which have recently enjoyed significant popularity, would have much to gain from accounting for the strategic dynamics at the core of our theory.[14] Without placing supply-side efforts in

---

[12] See: Hymans (2012).
[13] See: Tannenwald (1999); Rublee (2009).
[14] See: Fuhrmann (2009a, 2009b; 2012); Kroenig (2009a; 2009b; 2010).

their strategic context, it is not clear what effect they will have on the rate of proliferation. Existing supply-side theories, such as Matthew Fuhrmann's and Matthew Kroenig's, tell us which states are more or less likely to provide others with nuclear assistance: more powerful states, which have more to lose from proliferation among faraway states, are most likely to withhold assistance. But often alternative suppliers are available, and, in any case, the benefit of nuclear proliferation may be so great that a state is willing to pursue the bomb even if it must develop its program indigenously. As R. Scott Kemp has recently argued, "[a]longside a few highly visible programs that relied on technology transfers, the historical record contains many more lesser-known examples of states developing nuclear weapon capabilities without foreign assistance."[15]

To connect supply-side arguments to the odds of proliferation, we need to place supply constraints in the context of our broader strategic framework. When we do so, it becomes clear that supply-side efforts may deter proliferation in two ways. First, they may condition the cost of a nuclear program. If the cost of developing a nuclear weapon without international supply is sufficiently high to overcome the security benefit of proliferation, the state will no longer possess the willingness to nuclearize. Although this is a theoretical possibility, we know of no historical case in which this calculation occurred. Second, supply-side restrictions have often been employed by a powerful country such as the United States in an attempt to coerce one of its allies to remain nonnuclear. Such efforts – as with any other sticks-based approach to nonproliferation – are only likely to succeed if the protégé is relatively weak vis-à-vis its adversaries. A strong protégé would maintain the opportunity to nuclearize even if Washington abandoned it, and would thus likely attempt to circumvent such restrictions. What causes nonproliferation in the case of a weak protégé is therefore the strategic logic of proliferation, not the supply-side effort per se, the success of which is merely a symptom of the strategic environment inhabited by the potential proliferator. In other words, the effectiveness of restrictions to the supply of nuclear materials and technology is largely underpinned by the consequences of threats of abandonment. The efficacy of sticks-based nonproliferation policies must thus be evaluated in toto.

[15] Kemp (2014, 40).

Implications for U.S. Nonproliferation Policy

The history of proliferation is to a great extent the history of efforts to stymie the spread of nuclear weapons. Likewise, our strategic theory of nuclear proliferation is also a theory of nonproliferation and counterproliferation. Were it not for the fact that a potential proliferator's adversaries and allies have an incentive to deter its nuclear acquisition, it is likely that many more states would possess nuclear weapons. Because nuclearization is perhaps the largest step shift in the balance of power that a state can effect, preventive dynamics play a central role in regulating it.

Possessing interests, alliances, and forward-deployed forces throughout the globe, the United States is foremost among the states that have attempted to deter others from crossing the nuclear threshold. Washington possesses defense agreements with sixty-eight countries, accounting for one in four human beings and 75 percent of the world's economy.[16] Given this vast scope of U.S. security interests – and the unparalleled military capabilities that back them – nuclear acquisition by any other state limits Washington's ability to pursue its goals and increases the costs it pays, and the risks it incurs, to ensure the security of its many protégés. Washington is therefore likely to continue to place nuclear nonproliferation among its preeminent foreign-policy goals. Efforts to deter the spread of nuclear weapons will continue to be a central feature of U.S. security policy. Our theory has implications for these efforts.

Most obviously, the United States is likely to remain opposed to nuclear acquisition by any of its adversaries. As was the case with the recent effort to deter Iranian nuclearization, if the nuclear activities of another state outside the U.S.-led system of alliances raise suspicion, U.S. policymakers are likely to keep "all options on the table" – Washington's expression of choice to connote that it contemplates military action in pursuit of a goal. As our theory makes clear, the ability to deter an adversary from acquiring nuclear weapons depends on the credibility of such threats of preventive military action, even when implicit. Whether these threats are credible depends on a simple strategic calculus. On one plate of the scale, U.S. policymakers must weigh the cost of whatever preventive counterproliferation military

---

[16] See: Beckley (2015, 7).

operation is required to ensure the continuation of the target's nonnuclear status. On the other, they must weigh the expected detrimental consequences of the target's nuclearization for Washington's ability to fulfill its security goals. If the cost of immediate military action is lower than the expected consequences of the target's proliferation, threats of preventive action are credible. When this is the case, Washington is likely to be able to bring its adversary to the negotiating table and to persuade it to forego its nuclear ambitions. Should this adversary prove obdurate in its nuclear development, a U.S. preventive counterproliferation strike would be likely to ensue. Either way, the potential proliferator will likely see its nuclear designs foiled by U.S. coercive efforts.

When, on the contrary, U.S. threats of military action are not credible, then Washington is unlikely to be able to keep an adversary nonnuclear. In the absence of an underlying credible threat of preventive counterproliferation strike, a potential proliferator is unlikely to be thwarted by economic sanctions or other diplomatic efforts. Since the willingness to nuclearize requires the presence of a dire security threat, it is highly unlikely that a state would forfeit the great benefit to its security that would result from nuclear acquisition in order to accrue economic or diplomatic gains. Therefore, only powerful U.S adversaries – those capable of putting up a good fight in case of U.S. preventive counterproliferation military action – are likely to acquire nuclear weapons.

Given this logic, the preponderance of conventional power that the United States has enjoyed since the end of the Cold War presents great advantages for hampering nuclear proliferation. According to a belief common at the outset of the post–Cold War era, U.S. power preponderance would drive states that felt imperiled by U.S. designs to procure nuclear weapons. While that is correct, U.S. preponderance does not only boost their willingness to proliferate; it also hinders their opportunity to do so. Since U.S. adversaries are unlikely to find a security sponsor capable of projecting enough power over their territory to deter dominant U.S. conventional capabilities, it is likely that in the majority of future cases of attempted proliferation, U.S. threats of preventive action will remain credible – and proliferation will therefore be thwarted. In net terms, therefore, U.S. conventional preponderance places a powerful brake on the spread of nuclear weapons.

While Washington's ability to deter proliferation among its adversaries is an important asset, given the vastly superior number of U.S. allies in today's world, Washington's efforts to stymie the nuclearization of its protégés may be even more important in averting future proliferation.

The first thing to note in this respect is that, as our theory shows, U.S. protégés will only possess the willingness to build nuclear weapons if U.S. security guarantees do not reliably protect their territory and whatever broader security goals they may possess. A U.S. protégé that considers its security interests to be reliably protected by Washington will not possess the willingness to build the bomb. Therefore, the most effective way of deterring nuclear proliferation would be to extend reliable security guarantees to all U.S. protégés – not only guarantees that the United States will protect their territory, but also assurances of U.S. support for any other security goals that U.S. protégés may have.

Such an approach is no doubt unrealistic. The problem with it is that deterring nuclear proliferation is not the only goal of U.S. foreign and security policy; nor is it a goal worth pursuing at any cost. The role of U.S. policymakers, therefore, is to weigh proliferation concerns against other U.S. security goals, and to achieve their nonproliferation goals at the minimum possible cost. Therefore, in practice, our theory highlights a dynamic that is typical of the nuclear age and that is likely to continue into the future: the reliability of U.S. commitments to the security of an ally may be insufficient to undermine the protégé's willingness to nuclearize, prompting it to start a nuclear development program, and in turn leading the United States to engage in a nonproliferation effort toward that protégé. In some cases, Washington will be able to coerce its protégé to forfeit its nuclear ambitions out of fear that the United States would abandon it without making any additional commitments to its security. In other cases, however, U.S. nonproliferation efforts will require additional U.S. commitments to the security of its protégé. Our theory identifies these two key approaches in Washington's nonproliferation toolkit – carrots and sticks – and provides guidelines on their relative effectiveness depending on the strategic circumstances enveloping each case of nuclear development by a U.S. ally.

When a U.S. protégé is capable of deterring a preventive counterproliferation strike by its adversaries on its own, Washington will only succeed in ensuring this protégé retains its nonnuclear status if it employs a carrots-based approach to nonproliferation by extending additional security guarantees of protection. An attempt to keep a relatively strong protégé nonnuclear by threatening to abandon it – i.e., by employing a sticks-based approach to nonproliferation – is doomed to fail. In fact, it may well result in additional willingness to build a nuclear weapon on the part of the protégé, out of fear for the loss of U.S. security guarantees. Given that the protégé would have the opportunity to nuclearize even if Washington abandoned it, proliferation is likely to ensue.

Therefore, an effort to ensure the continuation of the nonnuclear status of protégés that are relatively strong vis-à-vis their adversaries will demand that Washington incur additional costs and risks in protecting them. Such is the prerogative of the strongest among U.S. allies. Since they would have the opportunity to nuclearize if abandoned by the United States, Washington will have to address their security concerns if it wants them to forfeit building the bomb. This dynamic is in part responsible for the vast network of U.S.-led alliances created during the nuclear age; it is also likely to lead to additional commitments of U.S. resources in the decades ahead.

Beyond the costs and risks entailed by reliable commitments to the security of a U.S. ally, the carrots-based approach needed to thwart a strong protégé's nuclear ambitions poses a second problem for U.S. policymakers. Often, Washington is unwilling to extend robust security guarantees to some of its protégés because of the ripple effect these might have in relations with other states. It may be the case that extending additional U.S. security guarantees to a loose ally will lead other loose allies to demand similar terms, triggering a cascade of requests for additional U.S. commitments. Or it may be that extending security commitments to one state will lead its adversaries to feel alienated, worsening U.S. relations with them. These reasons may lead Washington to withhold additional security guarantees from a state engaged in nuclear development. For example, as we saw, during the 1960s, U.S. policymakers resisted extending greater support to India and Israel in part out of fear that doing so would upset U.S. relations with other countries, respectively, Pakistan and the Arab states. Taking stock, vis-à-vis strong protégés, U.S. nonproliferation efforts are likely to succeed as long as Washington is willing to extend security guarantees sufficiently reliable to extinguish their willingness to nuclearize.

When, on the contrary, a U.S. protégé does not possess sufficient military capabilities to deter a preventive counterproliferation strike by its adversaries on its own, Washington has a second – and less costly – tool it can employ to thwart the protégé's nuclear designs. With such weaker allies, the United States can successfully employ a sticks-based approach to nonproliferation, issuing threats of abandonment if the protégé persists in its designs to develop nuclear weapons, withholding pledges of commitment, limiting deployments of U.S. forces, and restricting sales of U.S. weaponry; and also using its leverage to demand inspections of nuclear facilities and, more generally, the cessation of any nuclear activities that might be part of a military program. When employed toward weak U.S. protégés, this more forceful coercive approach is likely to result in nuclear forbearance out of fear for the loss of U.S. security guarantees. The weaker the protégé is in relation to its adversaries, the greater the effectiveness of a sticks-based nonproliferation approach, and the smaller the required minimum level of security commitment necessary to grant Washington sufficient nonproliferation leverage.

With weak protégés, therefore, Washington does not, in general, need to extend additional security commitments in order to ensure the maintenance of their nonnuclear status. The only exception to this rule stems from the fact that nonproliferation is only one among several goals Washington has in its relations with each of its allies. When one of these other goals trumps nonproliferation and features higher in Washington's priorities, an ally invested in nuclear development may use this tension to diminish or even neutralize Washington's leverage on the proliferation issue. If Washington needs the cooperation of a particular protégé to achieve another security goal, it will be difficult to coerce this protégé to remain nonnuclear when it has the willingness to build the bomb. Threats of abandonment would likely only ensure that the protégé would no longer cooperate in the pursuit of other vital U.S. goals. For as long as the protégé has the willingness to nuclearize, therefore, Washington must choose between two unpalatable options: either it forfeits its other strategic goals and coerces its protégé to maintain its nonnuclear status; or it enlists its protégé in pursuit of its other strategic goals but countenances its nuclearization. The only way out of this dilemma is to undermine the protégé's willingness to go nuclear. Thus, employing a carrots-based approach and extending additional security guarantees may prove to be the only effective nuclear nonproliferation approach vis-à-vis a weak ally when Washington needs this protégé's cooperation in pursuit of another important security goal.

We saw this dynamic in the past with Pakistan, when Washington turned a blind eye toward its nuclear development during the 1980s in order to secure Islamabad's cooperation in undermining the Soviet occupation of Afghanistan. We may see it again in the future. It is conceivable, for example, that in the aftermath of Iran's hypothetical nuclearization, Washington would be unable to coerce Saudi Arabia to remain nonnuclear while remaining an active U.S. partner in combating terrorism, ensuring the free flow of oil at a reasonable price, and pursuing other U.S. goals in the Middle East.

Overall, then, U.S. efforts to deter proliferation among its allies are hindered by two issues. First, Washington's unwillingness to extend reliable security guarantees to all of its allied and friendly states, either because of the costs or risks involved in doing so, or because of the consequences that doing so would have for U.S. relations with other countries. Second, Washington's determination to pursue other security interests beyond nonproliferation, which in some cases may limit its coercive nonproliferation leverage over protégés whose cooperation is essential to the pursuit of these other goals. The worst possible situation for U.S. nonproliferation efforts, therefore, emerges when these two dynamics are present: Washington is unwilling to extend reliable security guarantees to a protégé that is essential to achieving other U.S. goals. When this happens, it is likely that U.S. nonproliferation efforts will fail, as happened in the case of Pakistan.

When dealing with allies, this discussion highlights the importance of grouping the multiple nonproliferation policies in the U.S. toolkit – deployment of troops and nuclear weapons to the ally's territory; sale of military equipment and training of military forces; extension of formal and public security guarantees; and also diplomatic pressure, economic sanctions, withholding of military aid or sales, demands for inspections of nuclear facilities, and attempts to thwart foreign supplies of nuclear materials and technology – according to whether they undermine the potential proliferator's willingness or opportunity to build a nuclear weapon. These are the two most relevant categories of nonproliferation tools: differences between the two are highly consequential; differences within the two less so.

Therefore, U.S. policymakers must evaluate whether the strategic circumstances surrounding a protégé's nuclear development are more conducive to achieving success in nonproliferation efforts by undermining the protégé's willingness to nuclearize or by taking away its opportunity to do so. When the strategic environment calls for eroding the protégé's willingness to build the bomb, Washington will be well advised to employ a combination of carrots, such as deploying troops and nuclear weapons to the ally's territory, selling military equipment and training its military forces, and extending formal and public guarantees of its security. When, on the contrary, the strategic environment requires the removal of the U.S. protégé's opportunity to nuclearize, Washington should deploy an assortment of sticks, such as diplomatic pressure, economic sanctions, withholding of military aid or sales, demands for inspections of nuclear facilities, and attempts to thwart foreign supplies of nuclear materials and technology. Within each of these two sets of tools, different policies will work well in tandem and should be adjusted to the particular requirements of each individual case.

In sum, in a world in which U.S. military power is nonpareil, U.S. nonproliferation efforts will likely remain uniquely important in stopping the spread of nuclear weapons. In fact, U.S. counterproliferation and nonproliferation policies are likely to remain the strongest forces against additional nuclear proliferation.

The Future of Nuclear Proliferation

Nuclear acquisition is perhaps the most consequential step a state may take in ensuring its ability to deter threats to its security. Consequently, whenever a state acquires nuclear weapons, the states that more closely interact with it will face a transformed security landscape. The balance of power vis-à-vis adversaries will be greatly upset, with the new nuclear state enjoying a higher capacity to inflict costs on others. The ability of allied states to mold the behavior of the new nuclear state will be diminished. A regime that possesses nuclear weapons has the greatest possible insurance against external attempts to destabilize its government or conquer its territory. No technology of violence surpasses nuclear weapons in boosting the security of those that possess them.

Given these consequences of nuclearization, we can be sure that efforts to stymie the spread of nuclear weapons will remain a central

feature of the atomic age. States that consider nuclear-weapons development will continue to see their adversaries and allies go to great
lengths to prevent them from building a nuclear arsenal. Their adversaries will continue to issue implicit and explicit threats of preventive
military counterproliferation action. Their allies will remain firm in
their determination to keep their protégés nonnuclear, by extending them additional security guarantees or threatening them with
abandonment.

The United States, having the broadest set of security interests of
any contemporary state and possessing the most powerful military
forces on the planet, will remain primus inter pares in efforts to stop
proliferation. For global U.S. power, the spread of nuclear weapons
would impose serious constraints. Were its adversaries to build the
bomb, Washington would be more limited in its policy options – it
would be less able to deter aggression and less able to retaliate against
it. Were its allies to acquire a nuclear deterrent, Washington would be
less capable of controlling their behavior and ensuring the stability of
their regions. For a state as engaged in the world as the United States
has remained since the end of the Second World War, great power
comes with great responsibilities – and the costs and risks entailed by
these responsibilities are bound to increase with the further spread of
nuclear weapons.

Most recently, Iran has been at the center of proliferation concerns;
and the United States, at the center of efforts to deter Iranian nuclearization. It was only with the 2015 JCPOA that concerns about imminent
Iranian nuclear acquisition – and about the possibility of preventive
military counterproliferation action by U.S. or Israeli forces – could
be dispelled. As a relatively weak state involved in an adversarial relationship with the United States, Israel, and Sunni Arab states, and in
the absence of a powerful ally, Iran remains likely to possess the willingness to build nuclear weapons. A nuclear deterrent would make the
Iranian regime virtually immune to foreign threats to its survival and
might boost its bargaining position on other security issues. Yet, at the
same time, our theory makes clear why Iran is unlikely to have the
opportunity to nuclearize. For Tehran to acquire nuclear weapons, its
adversaries must estimate the security benefit of Iranian proliferation
to be lower than the cost of a preventive strike. Otherwise, a preventive strike is a rational option, and either Iran internalizes this threat
and abandons its nuclear investment or its program is likely to be

targeted. It should therefore come as no surprise that both U.S. and Israeli leaders have refused to take the military option off the table during negotiations with Iran over its nuclear program. Our theory predicts that, either through further comprehensive nuclear deals or as the result of a preventive strike, Iran will remain a nonnuclear-weapons state even beyond the fifteen-year horizon of the 2015 JCPOA. As long as Tehran is relatively weak vis-à-vis its adversaries and does not enjoy the protection of a powerful ally, nuclearization is beyond its reach.

Furthermore, our theory provides reason to doubt the widespread fear that eventual Iranian nuclearization would trigger a proliferation cascade in the Middle East involving Egypt, Saudi Arabia, or Turkey. None of these states is likely to pursue nuclear weapons as long as they continue to possess reliable U.S. security guarantees. At the same time, in order to persuade any of these allies to drop their eventual nuclear ambitions, Washington must continue to place nonproliferation at the top of its agenda. In the past, Washington has consistently succeeded in preventing clients from nuclearizing whenever it shared their security goals and privileged nonproliferation efforts over other strategic aims. This success is, to a great extent, responsible for the historical absence of "reactive proliferation."[17] We have no doubt that U.S. administrations will continue to place great importance on these states' security vis-à-vis a putative Iranian nuclear threat. Given the evolving nature of the Egyptian, Saudi, and Turkish regimes, however, it is less clear that Washington would be able to continue to place the goal of nonproliferation over all of its other policy aims vis-à-vis these states. In any case, our theory highlights an important cost Washington often pays to ensure the nonnuclear status of its allies: offering security guarantees to a burgeoning number of states. The ability and willingness of the United States to do so will have a great impact on the odds of future nuclear proliferation. Likewise it is with U.S. allies in East Asia. As China rises and North Korea's nuclear arsenal grows, it is crucial for nonproliferation efforts that Washington continue to extend reliable security guarantees to its allies in the region, lest it give Japan and South Korea the willingness to build the bomb.

U.S. willingness and ability to continue to deter nuclear proliferation in East Asia, the Middle East, and other regions of the globe will

---

[17] See: Bleek (2010b, 179).

depend greatly on the evolution of the systemic balance of power. As we saw, the preponderance of U.S. military power since the end of the Cold War has had an instrumental role in stopping the spread of nuclear weapons. But as other powers rise militarily vis-à-vis the United States, they will be better able to extend protection to third states engaged in nuclear development, hindering the effectiveness of threats of preventive U.S. action in countering proliferation. One might think this would lead to an increase in the odds of proliferation after a return to a bipolar or multipolar system. But this logic is incomplete. New great powers would likely have an interest in deterring proliferation among their allies too. So the transition to a world system in which U.S. military power is matched by that of others would be unlikely to cause a spike in nuclear proliferation. The only geopolitical scenario in which we can foresee an increase in proliferation is one in which the United States disengages from security commitments around the world without its role being taken over by one or more other powers willing and capable of deterring the spread of nuclear weapons. A lot hinges, therefore, on whether great military powers – be it the United States or others – will remain engaged in the world, willing to incur costs to stymie proliferation by adversaries and allies.

At the same time, the future patterns of proliferation will be shaped by two other crucial dynamics highlighted by our theory. The first is the tension between the measures taken by potential proliferators to increase the ambiguity surrounding their nuclear programs and the efforts of other states to detect activity that unquestionably aims at the construction of a nuclear weapon. Given the ineradicable dual nature of the technology, potential proliferators can always resort to some ambiguity in their nuclear endeavors, arguing that their nuclear efforts have entirely civilian purposes. Furthermore, potential proliferators can always attempt to hide their efforts by conducting their nuclear development covertly. In doing so, these countries attempt to lower their adversaries' and allies' estimates of the risks of nuclearization, thereby trying to avoid the preventive dynamics highlighted by our theory and escape other states' efforts to thwart proliferation. But the risk that some ambiguity will serve as cover for nuclear-weapons development will lead adversaries and allies to develop better approaches to detect other states' developments and intentions. Although this cat-and-mouse game is likely to continue to evolve in terms of the particular dissimulation and detection tactics employed, its central contours are likely to remain the same – as is the possibility of mistaken preventive military action against states that are suspected of having nuclear programs with military purposes but that in fact do not.[18]

A second inherent tension of the nuclear age that is likely to remain at the center of the proliferation process is that between actions taken by potential proliferators to increase the costs of eventual counter-proliferation military action and the efforts of other states to bring down the cost of disrupting their nuclear development. Preventive dynamics are, as we have shown, central to the proliferation process. Furthermore, whether they will successfully deter the spread of nuclear weapons (either by deterring nuclear development or by disrupting it through military action) depends crucially on the costs of preventive war. Therefore, efforts to manipulate this cost will remain the object of a great deal of attention by both the states considering nuclear acquisition and those likely to oppose it. We expect to see potential proliferators making key nuclear facilities costly to destroy by protecting them (say, by placing them underground) or positioning them in such a manner as to maximize collateral damage (say, by placing them in urban centers). At the same time, we expect to see those states interested in stymieing proliferation – first and foremost, the United States – developing technologies capable of disrupting another country's program at the lowest possible cost, for example, by developing cyber tools designed to disrupt nuclear facilities, targeting scientists rather than physical installations, and deploying weaponry (including, if necessary, low-yield nuclear weapons) capable of destroying targets while minimizing collateral damage. Like the cat-and-mouse game around dissimulation and detection, this interaction around lowering or raising the cost of preventive counterproliferation action is likely to remain a central feature of the proliferation process. As long as the technologies used to disrupt nuclear development keep up with those used to increase the costs of preventive action, the costs of preventive counterproliferation strikes will often remain lower than the costs that other states would pay as a consequence of the potential

---

[18] On these preventive dynamics, see: Debs and Monteiro (2014); Bas and Coe (2016a).

proliferator's nuclearization, making threats of preventive action credible, and thereby thwarting proliferation.

Through both these dynamics, the NPT plays a crucial role in ensuring the failure of proliferation attempts. To begin with, the intrusive regime to which NPT members are subjected makes it difficult for a state to inch its way toward the nuclear threshold while continuing to be seen as a bona fide member of the international community, unsuspected of having the willingness to build an atomic bomb. By decreasing the ability of potential proliferators to maintain their ambiguity, the NPT increases the odds that a state engaged in nuclear development be perceived as trying to develop a deterrent, in turn triggering the preventive dynamics at the core of our theory. Additionally, by revealing the location of a potential proliferator's nuclear facilities, the NPT contributes to lowering the costs of preventive war, making possible more limited, surgical military strikes. In doing so, the NPT regime boosts the effectiveness of preventive efforts to deter proliferation. Taken together, these two characteristics give the NPT a central role in the strategic logic of nuclear proliferation.

To some extent, these strategic benefits of the NPT account for its durability despite the intrinsic unfairness of the current nonproliferation regime, which separates states into nuclear haves and nuclear have-nots.[19] As the Canberra Commission on the Elimination of Nuclear Weapons stated two decades ago, "[n]uclear weapons are held by a handful of states which insist that these weapons provide unique security benefits, and yet reserve uniquely to themselves the right to own them." This is, in our view, an accurate characterization of the nuclear-nonproliferation regime. Further, we agree when the commission goes on to say that "possession of nuclear weapons by any state is a constant stimulus to other states to acquire them." Certainly, nuclear possession by one state is likely to increase the willingness to acquire nuclear weapons in its adversaries. Yet, we disagree when the commission concludes that "[t]he situation is highly discriminatory and thus unstable; it cannot be sustained."[20] Then like now, normative dynamics militate against the maintenance of a regime centered on such great

[19] See: Maddock (2010). For a powerful normative critique of the NPT, see: Tannenwald (2013).
[20] Canberra Commission on the Elimination of Nuclear Weapons (1996, 1).

iniquity. Yet, two decades later the NPT remains firmly in place, and the nonproliferation regime is as robust as ever despite the growing role of the so-called nonproliferation complex.[21] The NPT regime is robust not because it is fair but because it furthers the interests of the most powerful states in the world – the nuclear powers. In short, the NPT's resilience stems from the strategic pressures surrounding the spread of nuclear weapons, and from powerful states' determination to maintain other states nonnuclear.

Does this mean that we will no longer witness attempts at nuclear development? In fact, the number of states with active nuclear programs with military goals has decreased substantially over the last few decades and is now, to the best of our knowledge, at zero. (Iran and Syria were the last two states in this category; but at the time of writing, the former is implementing the 2015 JCPOA, and the latter is in the middle of a civil war that makes nuclear development exceedingly unlikely.) Still, it is possible that other states will (re)start a nuclear development effort. Strictly, our theory does not offer predictions about when states will start nuclear development, only about whether they will succeed in crossing the nuclear threshold. But why would a state start a nuclear development process and yet not conclude it and build a nuclear weapon? Here, we can offer four reasons. First, a state may – as many in history did – start a nuclear program with the aim of developing nuclear weapons and eventually drop it because it no longer has the willingness to nuclearize. Such was, as we have shown, the case with Sweden and South Korea. Second, a state may start in the pathway to nuclear acquisition but eventually realize it does not possess the opportunity to build a nuclear deterrent. Such was, as we have demonstrated, the case with Iraq, Iran, Taiwan, and West Germany. Third, a state may start a nuclear program for nonmilitary reasons, approaching the nuclear threshold and mastering the nuclear fuel cycle while having no intention to nuclearize. Such was the case, we argue, with Brazil and Japan. Finally, a state may start a nuclear program or manifest the willingness to develop nuclear weapons in order to acquire a bargaining chip it can use down the road with adversaries or allies. Specifically, a nuclear program might be traded in for additional security guarantees from a nuclear sponsor. South

---

[21] For an argument on how the burgeoning nonproliferation complex actually supports the iniquity at the core of the NPT, see: Craig and Ruzicka (2013).

Korea, which was earnest about its intention to develop a nuclear deterrent, ended up benefiting from additional U.S. guarantees aimed at undermining its willingness to nuclearize. A nuclear program might also be used as a bargaining chip with an adversary.[22] For example, during the Cold War, U.S. diplomats argued with their counterparts in West Germany that if they wanted to protect West Berlin, they would do well to remain nonnuclear, because the West could then threaten the Soviet Union that if the Soviet forces took over West Berlin, they would soon have to face a nuclear West Germany.[23] All in all, there are several reasons why we may witness renewed efforts of nuclear development. Whether those efforts will result in nuclear acquisition or forbearance, however, depends on the strategic dynamics on which our theory focuses.

Nuclear weapons give the states that acquire them remarkable deterrent capabilities. Their spread has therefore contributed to the lower incidence of war during the atomic age. At the same time, their deterring power makes them highly enticing for the nonnuclear states that are trying to mitigate serious security threats. For decades, we have understood how security threats drive up states' willingness to nuclearize. Now, we also understand how the features of the strategic environment in which the potential proliferator operates shape its odds of nuclearization. Rarely, it turns out, does the security environment fulfill the conditions necessary for a state to possess both the willingness and the opportunity to proliferate. The benefits of the nuclear revolution, therefore, are likely to remain limited to a few countries, while most states must continue to navigate the troubled waters of conventional deterrence and alliance politics in order to ensure their own security. Whereas nuclear weapons would be of greatest value for the weak and unprotected, these are precisely the states that cannot get them. So dictates the strategic causes of nuclear proliferation.

[22] See: Bas and Coe (2016b).
[23] We thank Marc Trachtenberg for this point.

Appendix I
Coding Rules

In this appendix we explain the procedures we applied to determine the position of each potential proliferator during the run-up to its nuclearization or abandonment in terms of two of our strategic variables – its relative power vis-à-vis its adversaries and the level of security commitment it received from a nuclear ally. Specifically, we lay out the method we used to determine which states are adversaries of the state engaged in nuclear development; and we lay out the rules we developed to determine whether each nuclear power was allied with a state developing nuclear weapons or its adversaries.

Rules for Coding Adversaries and Nuclear Allies

To determine where each potential proliferator was located during the run-up to its nuclear acquisition or abandonment in terms of our two key variables – relative power vis-à-vis its adversaries and the presence of a nuclear ally – we used the following coding rules:

We first code adversaries, which we define as countries perceived by the potential proliferator as independent direct security threats that could warrant the acquisition of nuclear weapons. Two states are independent direct security threats if they make independent decisions to engage in war, may care about different security problems, and may engage in war against the potential proliferator without the support of each other. To code them, we canvassed the secondary literature and, often, primary sources on each case in an effort to determine which states the potential proliferator considered to be independent direct security threats, against whom nuclear acquisition would provide additional security and bargaining power. These are the states that are most likely to consider a preventive attack against the potential proliferator.

We then investigate the role of nuclear powers as either allies of the potential proliferator or of its adversaries. In other words, we seek to determine which side, if any, nuclear powers would be likely to take in an eventual conflict between the potential proliferator – before or after its nuclearization – and its adversaries. We then code the type of alliance: whether it is formal or informal. We proceed as follows.

1. Side of the nuclear power: We look at the behavior of the nuclear power in past ICB crises, triggered after the beginning of the nuclear age in 1945 and terminated before the end of the calendar year in which the potential proliferator's nuclear program terminates. We look at the set of crises in which the potential proliferators and at least one of the adversaries were crisis actors on opposite sides.

    (a) If there is a crisis in which the potential proliferator and at least one of its adversaries were crisis actors on opposite sides, and the nuclear power was a crisis actor as well, we take the latest such crisis (i.e., the last such crisis to have taken place prior to the end of the potential proliferator's nuclear program). If the nuclear power was on the same side as the potential proliferator in the crisis, we code it as an ally of the potential proliferator. If the nuclear power was on the opposite side of the potential proliferator, we code it an ally of the potential proliferator's adversaries.[1]

    (b) If there is a crisis in which the potential proliferator and at least one of its adversaries were crisis actors on opposite sides, but none in which the nuclear power was a crisis actor as well, and the nuclear power is a superpower (i.e., the United States throughout the period or the USSR until the end of the Cold War in 1989), we take the latest crisis in which (i) the potential proliferator and at least one of its adversaries were crisis actors on opposite sides, (ii) the superpower was actively involved, and (iii) the involvement of the superpower was viewed favorably by one side and unfavorably by the other.[2] If at that time the superpower had no formal defensive alliance with the potential proliferator or any of the adversaries involved in the crisis, then

---

[1] We view Russia (1991–) as a different country from the USSR (1945–1991) so that the behavior of the USSR in ICB crises is not used to determine Russia's side between potential proliferators and their adversaries in the post–Cold War era.

[2] The ICB data set codes the level of involvement of the United States and the USSR in the variables "usinv" and "suinv," respectively. The superpower is

it is coded as an ally of the potential proliferator if its involvement is viewed favorably by the potential proliferator and unfavorably by one of the adversaries; and coded as an ally of the adversaries if its involvement is viewed unfavorably by the potential proliferator and favorably by one of the adversaries. If at that time the superpower had a formal defensive alliance with the potential proliferator and did not have a formal defensive alliance with at least one of the adversaries who were crisis actors, the superpower is coded as an ally of the potential proliferator. If at that time the superpower had no formal defensive alliance with the potential proliferator and had a formal defensive alliance with at least one of the adversaries who were crisis actors, the superpower is coded as an ally of the adversaries.[3]

(c) If there is no crisis where the potential proliferator and at least one of the adversaries were crisis actors on opposite sides, and the nuclear power is a superpower, we consider the configuration of formal defensive alliances of the superpower at the end of the potential proliferator's nuclear-weapons program. If the superpower had a formal defensive alliance with the potential proliferator and had no formal defensive alliance with any of the adversaries, we code it as an ally of the potential proliferator. If the superpower had no formal defensive alliance with the potential proliferator and had a formal defensive alliance with at least one of the adversaries, we code it as an ally of the adversaries. Otherwise the superpower is coded as an ally of neither the potential proliferator nor its adversaries.

"actively involved" in a crisis if its level of involvement is greater than "not involved" or "non-intervention or neutrality" (i.e., the variable "usinv" or "suinv" takes a value greater than 2). The perception of the involvement of the United States and USSR is codified in the variables "usfavr" and "sufavr," respectively.

[3] This means that we do not use the perception of the actors in cases in which the superpower has a formal defensive alliance with actor(s) on one side of the crisis. In such cases, the expectation is that the superpower would fight alongside its protégé in future crises. An expectation of support is compatible with the superpower having actively attempted to defuse past crises in order to avoid entrapment, causing its protégé to have viewed its involvement unfavorably. This need not mean that the superpower would not fight alongside its protégé were it to deem it necessary. Had it deemed it so in past crises, it would have been a crisis actor. At the same time, this

2. Format of the alliance: If the nuclear power is an ally of the potential proliferator, we code it a formal ally of the potential proliferator if, by the end of the potential proliferator's nuclear program, it has a formal defensive alliance with the potential proliferator, and an informal ally of the potential proliferator if it does not. If the nuclear power is an ally of the potential proliferator's adversaries, we code it a formal ally of the adversaries if, by the end of the potential proliferator's nuclear program, it has a formal defensive alliance with at least one of these adversaries, and an informal ally of the adversaries if it does not.[4]

rule means that except for the superpowers (the USSR from 1945 to 1989 and United States throughout the nuclear age), we do not consider a nuclear power to be an ally of either a potential proliferator or its adversary unless it has been an actor in a crisis opposing the potential proliferator and at least one of the adversaries during the period mentioned in 1a. Nuclear powers other than the superpowers are thus not coded as nuclear allies of either the potential proliferator or its adversaries even if they have a formal military alliance with one of these sides or have been involved in relevant crises and their involvement was viewed favorably by one side and unfavorably by the other. It is only for the superpowers that we use their formal defensive alliances and their involvement (short of being an actor) in relevant crisis – and the favorable/unfavorable perception of this involvement by the potential proliferator and its adversaries – to code them as allies of either side. This restriction on our criterion for coding nuclear states other than the superpowers as allies of either side has two justifications. First, in what concerns formal defensive alliances, nuclear allies that possess limited interests and power-projection capabilities (i.e., those that are not superpowers) often possess formal defensive alliances with superpowers. When the latter are involved as adversaries in a nuclear proliferation case, it would be incorrect to count their nuclear allies as co-adversaries. For example, it would not make empirical sense to count China as an adversary of Swedish or Swiss nuclearization alongside the USSR in the late 1960s despite China's nuclear status after 1964 and the Sino-Soviet Treaty of Friendship, Alliance, and Mutual Assistance. Likewise, given their limited power-projection capabilities, it would not make sense to count France or the United Kingdom as co-adversaries of China alongside the United States in the run-up to 1964 despite their nuclear status plus NATO and Manila Pact membership; or to count Pakistan as a co-adversary of Iraq alongside the United States in 1991 despite the U.S.-Pakistan Bilateral agreement. Second, in what concerns involvement in a crisis short of being a crisis actor, this information is unavailable in the ICB data set, and in any case would likely generate imprudent codings as allies of states that were unlikely or unwilling to intervene as a crisis actor in a future crisis between the potential proliferator and its adversaries.

[4] For information on formal alliances, we use the Alliance Treaty Obligations and Provisions Project (ATOP) data set. See: Leeds et al. (2002).

Appendix II
Other Cases of Nuclear Development

In this appendix, and following the coding rules laid out in Appendix I, we describe our coding decisions for each case.

Algeria

Dates of Nuclear Development: 1983–1993
Adversaries: Libya, Morocco
Allies: N/A
Adversaries' Allies: United States, informal

Coding of adversaries: Starting in 1963, Algeria had multiple clashes with Morocco over disputed areas of the Sahara desert, leading to an enduring rivalry from 1984 onward. In 1975–1976, 1979, and 1987, Algeria also clashed with Morocco over its support of the Polisario movement, which fought for the independence of Western Sahara, over which Morocco claimed sovereignty. Algeria's relations with Libya were close in some periods, leading the two countries to sign a mutual defense pact in 1975. Yet, relations soured when Algeria perceived that Libya was attempting to increase its regional influence. Algeria was concerned about Libya's announced merger with Chad in January 1981 and its growing influence over the Polisario movement. The border between Libya and Algeria, the subject of a conflicted, nonratified treaty from 1934, was also a major source of friction.[1]

Coding of nuclear powers: At the time Algeria abandoned its nuclear program in 1993, the United States, Russia, the United Kingdom, France, China, Israel, India, South Africa, and Pakistan were nuclear powers. The last crisis in which Algeria and any adversary (in this case, Morocco) were crisis actors on opposite sides, and in which the United

[1] See: Zartman (1987); Deeb (1989); Deutch (1991); Bennett (1998); Tertrais (2009).

States was actively involved and its involvement was viewed favorably by one side and unfavorably by the other, is ICB 261, Moroccan March (1975–1976). In this crisis, U.S. involvement was viewed favorably by Morocco, unfavorably by Algeria. Since the United States did not possess a formal defensive alliance with Morocco in 1993, we coded it as an informal ally of Morocco. There was no crisis between the end of the Second World War and the end of 1993 in which Algeria and either Libya or Morocco were crisis actors on opposite sides and any nuclear power was a crisis actor. Thus, Russia, the United Kingdom, France, China, Israel, India, South Africa, and Pakistan are coded as allies of neither side. In sum, we code the United States as Morocco's informal nuclear ally.

Australia I

> *Dates of Nuclear Development*: 1956–1961
> *Adversaries*: Indonesia, China
> *Allies*: United States, formal
> *Adversaries' Allies*: USSR, formal

Coding of adversaries: Since its inception in 1956, the Australian nuclear program was aimed at deterring a potential Chinese threat. Given Beijing's activist foreign policy, Canberra's government viewed China as Australia's main geopolitical threat. Australia's nuclear quest was a reaction to its worsening security situation vis-à-vis China as a consequence of the withdrawal of British forces from theaters east of Suez after the 1956 crisis. Given China's perceived intention to create its own sphere of influence in Southeast Asia and Australasia, Canberra decided to pursue nuclear weapons. At the beginning of the 1960s, Australia's military also feared a potential threat from Indonesia, given the activist, anti–status quo, and often belligerent policy of the Sukarno government (1945–1967).[2]

Coding of nuclear powers: At the time Australia abandoned its first nuclear program in 1961, the United States, Soviet Union, United Kingdom, and France were nuclear powers (plus China, which we

---

[2] See: Walsh (1997); Hymans (2006); Fitzpatrick and Huxley (2009); Leah (2012).

coded in the preceding text as Australia's adversary). There is no ICB crisis between the end of the Second World War and the end of 1961 in which Australia was a crisis actor. Thus, France and the United Kingdom are not coded as allies of either side. In 1961, the United States had a formal defensive alliance with Australia (ATOP treaty 3260 [Southeast Asia Collective Defense Treaty, a.k.a. Manila Pact]). We therefore code it as a formal ally of Australia. In 1961, the USSR had a formal defensive alliance with China (ATOP treaty 3200 [Sino-Soviet Treaty of Friendship, Alliance, and Mutual Assistance]). We therefore code it as a formal ally of China. In sum, we code the United States as Australia's formal nuclear ally and the USSR as China's formal nuclear ally.

Australia II

Dates of Nuclear Development: 1967–1972
Adversaries: China
Allies: United States, formal
Adversaries' Allies: USSR, formal

Coding of adversaries: China's nuclear acquisition in 1964 led Australia to reinitiate its nuclear efforts. Canberra's government was convinced that Beijing would be willing to resort to nuclear coercion and, if necessary, nuclear war in pursuit of its regional sphere of influence. Furthermore, the perception of a significant conventional threat emanating from China led the Australian military to recommend possession of tactical nuclear weapons. Given Sukarno's toppling and replacement with the more conservative Suharto's (1967–1998) regime in 1967, Indonesia was no longer a threat during this later period, leading us to code China as the sole adversary by the end of Australia's nuclear program.[3]

Coding of nuclear powers: At the time Australia abandoned its second nuclear program in 1972, the United States, Soviet Union, United Kingdom, France, and Israel were nuclear powers (plus China, which we coded above as Australia's adversary). There is no ICB crisis between the end of the Second World War and the end of 1972 in which Australia was

---

[3] See: Walsh (1997); Hymans (2006); Fitzpatrick and Huxley (2009); Leah (2012).

a crisis actor. Thus, the United Kingdom, France, and Israel are not coded as allies of either side. In 1972, the United States had a formal defensive alliance with Australia (ATOP treaty 3260 [Southeast Asia Collective Defense Treaty, a.k.a. Manila Pact]). We therefore code it as a formal ally of Australia. In 1972, the USSR had a formal defensive alliance with China (ATOP treaty 3200 [Sino-Soviet Treaty of Friendship, Alliance, and Mutual Assistance]). We therefore code it as a formal ally of China. In sum, we code the United States as Australia's formal nuclear ally and the USSR as China's formal nuclear ally.

Egypt

> *Dates of Nuclear Development*: 1955–1967
> *Adversaries*: Israel
> *Allies*: USSR, informal
> *Adversaries' Allies*: France, United Kingdom, and United States, informal

Coding of adversaries: Disputes between Egypt and Israel were recurrent since the latter's independence in 1948, leading to a prolonged rivalry between the two, which lasted until the Camp David Accords of 1979. In 1955, three years after coming to power, Gamal Abdel Nasser created the Atomic Energy Authority (AEA). The mission of the AEA was to focus on civilian applications but also to keep military options open. In 1959, upon learning that Israel was pursuing the bomb, Nasser declared that an Israeli bomb could trigger a war and insisted upon Egypt also obtaining the atomic bomb at any price. The Six-Day War of 1967 had a severe impact on the Egyptian economy and all AEA capital projects were canceled.[4]

Coding of nuclear powers: At the time Egypt abandoned its nuclear program in 1967, the United States, USSR, United Kingdom, France, and China (plus Israel, which we coded above as Egypt's adversary) were nuclear powers. The latest crisis to be initiated after the end of the Second World War and terminated by the end of 1967 in which Egypt and Israel are crisis actors on opposite sides, and the United States is a crisis actor, is ICB crisis 222, the Six-Day War (1967). In this crisis, the United States is on the same side as Israel. Furthermore, in 1967, the

---

[4] See: Bennett (1998); Walsh (2001); Einhorn (2004); Solingen (2007).

United States does not have a formal defensive alliance with Israel. We therefore code it as an informal ally of Israel. Also in this crisis, the USSR is on the same side as Egypt. In 1967, the USSR does not have a formal defensive alliance with Egypt. We therefore code it as an informal ally of Egypt. The latest crisis to be initiated after the end of the Second World War and terminated by the end of 1967 in which Egypt and Israel are crisis actors on opposite sides of the crisis, and the United Kingdom and France are crisis actors, is ICB crisis 152, the Suez Nationalization War (1956–1957). The United Kingdom and France are on the same side as Israel. In 1967, neither the United Kingdom nor France had formal defensive alliances with Israel. We therefore code the United Kingdom and France as informal allies of Israel. Finally, there is no ICB crisis between the end of the Second World War and the end of 1967 in which Egypt and Israel are crisis actors on opposite sides of the crisis and China is a crisis actor. Thus, we code China as an ally of neither Egypt nor Israel. To summarize, we code the Soviet Union as Egypt's informal nuclear ally and France, the United Kingdom, and the United States as Israel's informal nuclear allies.

Italy

Dates of Nuclear Development: 1957–1958
Adversaries: USSR
Allies: United States, formal
Adversaries' Allies: N/A

Coding of adversaries: Italy was a signatory of the North Atlantic Treaty in April 1949 and regarded the Soviet Union as its most serious external threat. Italy invested in close relations with its Western allies in order to gain access to the bomb and enjoy greater security. In 1955, it set up to host the U.S. Southern European Task Force (SETAF), which would soon be equipped with nuclear weapons. In 1957–1958, it secretly negotiated with France and West Germany for the joint production of nuclear weapons. A close alliance with the United States also offered great domestic political benefits for pro-Western Italian governments, given the strength of the Communist opposition in Italy.[5]

[5] See: Nuti (1993; 2011); Melissen (1994).

Coding of nuclear powers: At the time Italy abandoned its nuclear program in 1958, the United States and the United Kingdom were nuclear powers (plus the Soviet Union, which we coded in the preceding text as Italy's adversary). There is no crisis initiated after the end of the Second World War and terminated before the end of 1958 in which Italy and the Soviet Union are crisis actors on opposite sides of the crisis. Therefore we code the United Kingdom as an ally of neither Italy nor the Soviet Union. The United States is a formal ally of Italy because it is a superpower and has a formal defensive alliance with Italy in 1958 (ATOP treaty 3180 [Charter of the North Atlantic Treaty Organization]). To summarize, we code the United States as Italy's formal ally.

Libya

> *Dates of Nuclear Development*: 1970–2003
> *Adversaries*: United States
> *Allies*: N/A
> *Adversaries' Allies*: N/A

Coding of adversaries: Libya's nuclear program was initially aimed at boosting the country's role in its regional confrontation with Israel. During the 1980s, however, the Libyan regime gradually reconciled itself with a secondary role in that regard. At the same time, a different rationale emerged for the nuclear program: the need for a strategic deterrent capable of discouraging foreign intervention. This need became ever more important as Libya's relations with the United States worsened. Libyan anti-American actions included approving the 1979 attacks on the U.S. embassy in Tripoli; ordering Libyan jets to fire at U.S. aircraft in the Mediterranean in 1981; and, above all, the 1987 Lockerbie bombing, which killed 270 people, including several U.S. citizens. In fact, the previous year President Reagan had launched air strikes on Tripoli and Benghazi as punishment for Tripoli's ordering of a bombing in Berlin that killed two U.S. soldiers. Corroborating the view that the United States was becoming Libya's principal adversary, a 1990–1991 strategic reevaluation of the nuclear program conducted in Tripoli concluded that, without the Soviet counterweight, a U.S. preventive intervention was now more likely. This threat of U.S. action led Libya to make several attempts during the following decade to offer to end its nuclear program in exchange for the normalization of relations with the West. Seeing its openings rebuffed, and suspicious of U.S.

motives, Libya intensified its nuclear efforts in the mid-1990s in an attempt to develop the ultimate deterrent. This threat of U.S. intervention was perceived as having become graver after the 9/11 terrorist attacks, prompting a final push by the Qaddafi regime to trade its nuclear program. A more open U.S. administration accepted this offer, leading to the end of the Libyan nuclear program in 2003.[6]

Coding of nuclear powers: At the time Libya abandoned its nuclear program in 2003, Russia, the United Kingdom, France, China, India, and Pakistan were nuclear powers (plus the United States, which we coded above as Libya's adversary). There is no crisis in which Libya and the United States are crisis actors on opposite sides of the crisis and any other nuclear power is a crisis actor. Therefore, we code no other nuclear power as an ally of either Libya or the United States.

Romania

Dates of Nuclear Development: 1985–1993
Adversaries: N/A
Allies: N/A
Adversaries' Allies: N/A

Coding of adversaries: Romania purchased a nuclear reactor from Canada in 1977. The following year, Romanian dictator Nicolae Ceausescu (1965–1989) started a nuclear program, violating its commitment to the NPT, which it had ratified in 1970. Ceausescu appointed his wife Elena to supervise the effort, leading to widespread mismanagement. According to Mihai Balanescu, the former director of the Romanian nuclear research institute, the country's nuclear program had a military component aimed at the production of nuclear weapons. Starting in December 1985, Romania began to conduct illegal research for the production of weapons-grade plutonium. (This led the program to be coded as starting in 1985.) The regime failed to report this activity to the IAEA and refused international inspections. Despite access to Western technology, Romania's nuclear program "did not get very far down the road toward nuclear weapons. By the time Ceausescu was executed on

---

[6] See: Takeyh (2001); St. John (2004); Alterman (2006); Bowen (2006); Braut-Hegghammer (2006).

Christmas Day 1989, thanks to his incompetent administration, his decade-plus quest for the bomb had hardly left the starting gate."[7] The only program "achievement" had been the reprocessing of 100 mg of plutonium from its U.S.-supplied nuclear reactor. This lack of progress notwithstanding, during the regime's last year, Ceausescu announced to his government that the country possessed the technical capability to manufacture nuclear weapons. That same year, Hungarian foreign minister Gyula Horn (1989–1990) accused Romania of threatening the security of his country, when he shared that Romanian officials had announced that "their country was now capable of producing nuclear weapons and would soon make medium-range missiles."[8] A U.S. official at the time immediately denied that Romania possessed any of these capabilities. Had the regime continued, Balanescu estimates that around the year 2000 Romania would have acquired the eight kilograms of fissile material necessary for a crude bomb. The new Romanian authorities in the post-1989 era collaborated with the IAEA in shutting down the program, leading U.S. President Bill Clinton to praise their effort in September 1993. (This led the program to be coded as ending on this date.) Romania had loosened its ties with the Soviet Union during the 1950s and, particularly, 1960s, and had since experienced cool relations with Moscow. At the same time, Bucharest entertained warm relations with the West after distancing itself from the Warsaw Pact's policies. We therefore find no evidence that a potential nuclear deterrent would be aimed at a threat from the United States or its NATO allies. Gorbachev's accession to power in Moscow deepened Ceausescu's suspicions of Soviet aims, making him fearful that the opening policies of the new Soviet premier would lead Russia to attempt at replacing the Romanian leadership. It is possible that the Ceausescu regime saw a nuclear capability as a guarantee of regime survival during the quickly evolving Eastern European strategic setting of the late 1980s. Who exactly would be source of these threats remains unclear, leading us to code Romania as having no direct threats and, therefore, no adversaries.[9]

[7] See: Hymans (2008, 275–276).
[8] Henry Kamm, "Hungarian Accuses Rumania of Military Threats," *The New York Times,* July 11, 1989, p. A3.
[9] Ibid. See also: Garthoff (1995); Hymans (2008); Fuhrmann (2012); Williams (2012); Gheorghe (2013).

Coding of nuclear powers: N/A, since we are unable to identify Romania's potential adversaries.

Switzerland

Dates of Nuclear Development: 1946–1969
Adversaries: USSR
Allies: N/A
Adversaries' Allies: N/A

Coding of adversaries: A neutral country, Switzerland enjoyed friendly relations with neighboring (Western European) states and with the United States, from whom it purchased nuclear technology. Yet, Switzerland feared a possible conflict between the two Cold War blocs. The Bern government believed that, if such a conflict were to materialize, nuclear weapons – especially tactical nuclear weapons and atomic surface-to-air weapons – could improve Switzerland's ability to defend itself.[10]

Coding of nuclear powers: At the time Switzerland abandoned its nuclear program in 1969, the United States, United Kingdom, France, China, and Israel were nuclear powers (plus the Soviet Union, which we coded in the preceding text as Switzerland's adversary). There is no crisis between the end of the Second World War and 1969 in which Switzerland and the Soviet Union were crisis actors on opposite sides of the crisis. Therefore, the United Kingdom, France, and China are coded as allies of neither Switzerland nor the Soviet Union. The United States did not possess a formal defensive alliance with Switzerland in 1969. Therefore the United States is coded as an ally of neither Switzerland nor the Soviet Union.

Syria

Dates of Nuclear Development: 2001
Adversaries: Israel, United States
Allies: N/A
Adversaries' Allies: N/A

---

[10] See: Schwab (1969); Milivojevic (1990); Paul (2000).

Coding of adversaries: There is little information on the nuclear program attributed to Syria starting in 2001 – and of which one facility was reportedly bombed by Israel in 2007. The Syrian program is assumed to be aimed at deterring threats posed by Syria's neighboring rival, Israel. The two countries have fought four wars: the 1948 Arab-Israeli War, the 1967 Six-Day War, the 1973 Yom Kippur War, and the 1982 Israeli invasion of Lebanon, when Syria sent forces to support the PLO. Given the post-9/11 change in U.S. foreign policy toward a more proactive stance vis-à-vis unfriendly ("rogue") regimes such as Syria, along with Washington's effort to stymie the nuclear program developed by Syria's regional sponsor, Iran, we code the United States as a direct independent threat to Syria.[11]

Coding of nuclear powers: As of 2007, Russia, United Kingdom, France, China, India, Pakistan, and North Korea were nuclear powers (plus Israel and the United States, which we coded in the preceding text as Syria's adversaries). There is no crisis in which Syria and either Israel or the United States are crisis actors on opposite sides of the crisis and any other nuclear power is a crisis actor. (Note that, per our coding rules, Russia is considered a different country from the former USSR. Therefore, informal Soviet support for the Syrian regime, manifest during much of the Cold War, does not lead us to code Russia as a supporter of the Syrian regime.) We code all nuclear powers as allies of neither Syria nor Israel.

United Kingdom

Dates of Nuclear Development: 1945–1952
Adversaries: USSR
Allies: United States, formal
Adversaries' Allies: N/A

Coding of adversaries: Britain's foremost security threat from the end of the Second World War until British nuclear acquisition in 1952 was the

---

[11] See: Seymour Hersh, "A Strike in the Dark: What Did Israel Bomb in Syria?," *The New Yorker*, February 11, 2008; "U.S. Accuses Syria of Building Secret Reactor with North Korea's Help," April 25, 2008, Agence France Presse; "IAEA: Syria Tried to Build Nuclear Reactor," April 28, 2011, Associated Press; Makowsky (2012).

Soviet Union. The drive toward an independent British nuclear arsenal was based on London's perception that nuclear forces would be useful in countering Soviet coercion over secondary British security interests around the globe. Britain wished to be able to pursue its national security interests independently from the United States. London faced considerable financial pressure at the time, so that an independent nuclear arsenal appeared to be the most financially viable way of securing British interests and deterring Soviet power.[12]

Coding of nuclear powers: At the time the United Kingdom acquired nuclear weapons in 1952, the United States was a nuclear power (plus the Soviet Union, which we coded in the preceding text as the United Kingdom's adversary). The last crisis in which the United Kingdom and the Soviet Union are crisis actors on opposite sides of the crisis and the United States is a crisis actor is ICB crisis 123, Berlin Blockade (1948–1949). In this crisis, the United States is on the same side as the United Kingdom (according to the dyadic version of the data set). Furthermore, the United States had a formal defensive alliance with the United Kingdom in 1952 (ATOP treaty 3180 [Charter of the North Atlantic Treaty Organization]). We therefore code the United States as a formal ally of the United Kingdom.

United States

Dates of Nuclear Development: 1942–1945
Adversaries: Germany, Japan
Allies: N/A
Adversaries' Allies: N/A

Coding of adversaries: The United States developed its nuclear program between 1942 and 1945, the year it became the first nuclear power. Throughout this period, the United States was involved in an all-out war against Axis powers, most notably Germany and Japan. These two countries were therefore the main adversaries of U.S. nuclear acquisition. We code Germany and Japan as independent threats given their different war aims and fighting capabilities, demonstrated by

---

[12] See: Gowing and Arnold (1974); Malone (1984); Wheeler (1990); Goldstein (2000).

Japan's continued fighting for more than three months (until August 15, 1945) after Germany's surrender on May 7 that same year.[13]

Coding of nuclear powers: At the time the United States acquired nuclear weapons in 1945, there were no other nuclear powers.

Yugoslavia I

> *Dates of Nuclear Development*: 1954–1961
> *Adversaries*: USSR
> *Allies*: N/A
> *Adversaries' Allies*: N/A

Coding of adversaries: Yugoslavia started a nuclear program with military aims after having been expelled from the Soviet-led bloc. The Soviet Union's conventional superiority and, from 1949 on, its nuclear arsenal presented a serious threat to the survival and political independence of Yugoslavia's regime. This perception of Soviet threat was reinforced in Belgrade when Stalin encouraged an arms buildup by its allies neighboring Yugoslavia, especially Hungary. Furthermore, in 1949 the Soviet Union tried to eliminate Yugoslav leader Josip Broz Tito (1944–1980) through an attempted assassination followed by a coup. After both attempts failed, Soviet forces were assembled on Yugoslavia's borders. Finally, the Soviets imposed an economic blockade on Yugoslavia in an attempt to coerce it back into their bloc.[14] Therefore, we code the USSR as Yugoslavia's adversary, against which nuclear weapons would boost the security of the Belgrade government.

Coding of nuclear powers: At the time Yugoslavia interrupted its nuclear program in 1961, the United States, United Kingdom, and France were nuclear powers (plus the Soviet Union, which we coded in the preceding text as Yugoslavia's adversary). There is no crisis between the end of the Second World War and 1961 in which Yugoslavia and the Soviet Union are crisis actors on opposite sides of the crisis. Therefore, the United Kingdom and France are allies of neither Yugoslavia nor the

---

[13] See: Rhodes (1986); Weinberg (1994).
[14] See: Potter et al. (2000); Mukhatzhanova (2010).

Soviet Union. The United States did not possess a formal defensive alliance with either Yugoslavia or the Soviet Union in 1961. Therefore the United States is an ally of neither Yugoslavia nor the Soviet Union.

Yugoslavia II

Dates of Nuclear Development: 1974–1987
Adversaries: USSR
Allies: N/A
Adversaries' Allies: N/A

Coding of adversaries: After having interrupted its nuclear program in 1961, Yugoslavia restarted it in 1974. To the extent that this second Yugoslav program was prompted by security concerns, these were largely the same that were present during the earlier attempt at producing nuclear weapons, namely, the threat of a powerful nuclear Soviet Union, which controlled Eastern Europe around Yugoslavia and with which the Belgrade regime maintained tense relations.[15]

Coding of nuclear powers: By the time Yugoslavia abandoned its second nuclear program in 1987, the United States, United Kingdom, France, China, Israel, India, and South Africa were nuclear powers (plus the Soviet Union, which we coded in the preceding text as Yugoslavia's adversary). There is no crisis between the end of the Second World War and 1987 in which Yugoslavia and the Soviet Union are crisis actors on opposite sides of the crisis. Therefore, nuclear powers other than the United States are allies of neither Yugoslavia nor the Soviet Union. The United States did not possess a formal defensive alliance with either Yugoslavia or the Soviet Union in 1987. Therefore the United States is an ally of neither Yugoslavia nor the Soviet Union.

---

[15] See: Potter et al. (2000); Mukhatzhanova (2010).

Appendix III
Puzzling Cases of No Nuclear Development

In this appendix, we look at four cases of countries that, according to the quantitative literature on proliferation, were likely candidates for nuclearization and yet did not attempt to develop nuclear weapons. In each of these cases, we focus on the country's strategic environment – its relationship with both adversaries and allies – to show how their decision not to start a nuclear program with a military dimension is consistent with the causal mechanisms in our theory.

Greece

Greece has never pursued a nuclear-weapons capability. To confront powerful regional rivals, Athens instead chose to rely on a strong alliance with the United States.

At the outset of the Second World War, Athens was gripped by domestic turmoil. A Communist uprising escalated into the Greek Civil War (1946–1949), a bloody conflict that claimed more than 150,000 lives.[1] With neighboring Bulgaria and Yugoslavia supporting the Communists, Greece stood on the front line of the emerging Cold War. Romania, and the Soviet Union itself, also raised security concerns in Athens.[2] Together, these countries harnessed military capabilities much greater than Greece's. During the late 1940s, Yugoslavia spent four times as much on its military as Greece.[3] During the quarter-century following the Civil War, Romania and Bulgaria were nearly four times more powerful than Greece,[4] and the Soviet Union spent nearly 200 times as much as Greece did on its military.[5]

[1] See: Couloumbis (1983, 10).
[2] See: Rizas (2009, 369).
[3] See: Singer (1987).
[4] Ibid.
[5] Ibid.

Yet, tensions with these adversaries eventually abated. Relations with Yugoslavia improved in the early 1950s after the split between Josef Stalin and Marshal Tito. Then, relations with the Warsaw Pact improved after the death of Stalin in 1953.[6] By 1974, Greek prime minister Konstantinos Karamanlis (1955–1958, 1958–1961, 1961–1963, 1974–1980) stated that "[t]he old infamous Slavic threat does not exist today – at least in the way previous generations had perceived it – as a direct political and military threat against Greece.... Today relations with most of our northern neighbours are excellent."[7]

In contrast, relations with Greece's eastern neighbor, Turkey, worsened in the mid-1970s. The two countries quarreled over the control of islands and maritime areas in the Aegean Sea, as well as over the island of Cyprus, which Ankara invaded in 1974.[8] On July 15, 1974, members of the Cypriot National Guard, sponsored by the military junta in Athens, launched a coup d'état against the Cypriot government, and Ankara responded by invading the island five days later. After the collapse of the junta in Athens and unsuccessful peace talks in Geneva, Turkish forces again invaded Cyprus in mid-August. By then, Greek defense minister Angelos Averoff-Tossizza (1974–1981) conceded that while the largest threat traditionally "comes from the north, recent brutal developments force us to confront, chiefly ... the new danger from the east."[9] The following year, Prime Minister Karamanlis feared that "war between Greece and Turkey is a great possibility."[10]

After the end of the Cold War, however, relations between Greece and Turkey improved significantly. The two countries cooperated in the war in Kosovo and reciprocated in offering aid relief after earthquakes struck each other in the summer of 1999.[11] The "earthquake diplomacy" that resulted from these natural disasters set Greece and Turkey on the path to warmer relations.[12] By the turn of the century,

---

[6] See: Iatrides (1968, 115–116); Rizas (2009, 369, 371).

[7] Quoted in Kourkouvelas (2013, 1055).

[8] See: Couloumbis (1983, 88–97); Kourkouvelas (2013, 1063); Tsakonas and Tournikiotis (2003, 303); Rizas (2009, 368, 371).

[9] Quoted in Kourkouvelas (2013, 1054).

[10] Ibid., 1057.

[11] See: Tsakonas (2010, 73–75).

[12] Ibid., 111, 137–139, 156–167. See also: Larrabee (2012, 474).

the prospects of an all-out war between the two countries appeared slim[13] and concerns over Cyprus had receded.[14]

To confront its main foreign threats, Greece relied mainly on an alliance with the United States. Washington offered "instrumental" aid to Athens in confronting the Communist uprising[15] and lobbied for Greece's entry into NATO in early 1952.[16] Soon, NATO created Allied Forces Southern Europe and Allied Forces Mediterranean, covering Greece's strategic environment.[17] In 1953, Washington signed a basing agreement with Athens,[18] stationing an average of 3,300 U.S. troops throughout the Cold War.[19] The United States also deployed nuclear weapons on Greek territory between 1960 and 2001.[20]

With Greece and Turkey as NATO members, Washington could use its leverage to de-escalate possible conflicts between the two countries.[21] Over the years, Washington repeatedly intervened to defuse crises, starting with John Foster Dulles and Cyrus Vance's involvement over Cyprus in the 1950s and 1960s, and including Henry Kissinger's "triangular diplomacy" during conflicts over the Aegean.[22] As one analyst put it, "Washington was ... the determining factor for the containment of the Greek-Turkish conflict" during the Cold War.[23] This statement remains true.[24]

If Washington addressed Athens' security concerns, the relationship was not without frictions. At times, Greece feared abandonment from its American ally.[25] Often, Athens perceived that Washington favored Ankara when arbitrating conflicts between the two,[26] and therefore did not fully meet Athens' security needs. Such was the case in the Turkish

---

[13] See: Tsakonas and Tournikiotis (2003, 304).
[14] See: Larrabee (2012, 474).
[15] See: Rizas (2009, 369). See also: Couloumbis (1983, 13); Yilmaz (2012, 484).
[16] See: Couloumbis (1983, 15); Rizas (2009, 369).
[17] See: Kourkouvelas (2012, 199).
[18] See: Couloumbis (1983, 15).
[19] U.S. troop deployments decreased after the end of the Cold War, averaging 571 between 1991 and 2005. See: Kane (2006).
[20] See: Fuhrmann and Sechser (2014, 466); Kristensen (2005, 55–56).
[21] See: Tsakonas and Tournikiotis (2003, 306).
[22] On Dulles, see: Couloumbis (1983, 29); Krebs (1999, 361). On Vance, see: Couloumbis (1983, 54). On Kissinger, see: Rizas (2009, 368).
[23] Rizas (2009, 372). See also: Tsakonas (2010, 58).
[24] See: Tsakonas and Tournikiotis (2003, 307–308).
[25] See: Kourkouvelas (2012, 200).
[26] See: Krebs (1999, 367–368); Couloumbis (1983, 130).

invasions of Cyprus in the mid-1970s, and during a crisis over the Imia Islets in the Aegean in 1996.[27] Out of frustration with NATO's ineffectiveness during the Cyprus invasions, Greece pulled out of the military command structure in 1974, returning only six years later.[28] Nevertheless, as a result of U.S. commitments, Greece did not perceive a significant security benefit from acquiring an autonomous deterrent, and never developed a willingness to pursue a nuclear arsenal.

Greece's efforts in developing a nuclear industry have so far been minimal. The Greek Atomic Energy Commission (EEAE) was founded in 1954, and the following year Greece took advantage of the Atoms for Peace program to sign a bilateral research agreement with the United States.[29] By the end of the decade, the two countries had signed a defense-oriented agreement, and in the early 1960s Athens obtained an experimental research reactor from Washington.[30] Yet, despite this early start, Greece's nuclear industry never developed further.[31]

Looking ahead, it remains unlikely that Greece would perceive a move to an autonomous nuclear deterrent to be a productive investment. Greece's main security concerns are internal.[32] The Republic has seen hundreds of thousands of refugees and migrants come to its shores,[33] straining an already fragile economy, which has struggled with high unemployment and a crippling public debt.[34] In this financial situation, it would be very difficult to justify the cost of a nuclear-weapons program. Furthermore, the benefit of an autonomous deterrent appears vague. The Communist threat is gone, and the probability of conflict with Turkey is low. If relations with Turkey worsened, Greece might not have the opportunity to proliferate. At the turn of the century, Turkey's military spending was almost twice as high as Greece's, and its overall capabilities were about four times

---

[27] See: Tsakonas and Tournikiotis (2003, 306–307).

[28] See: Couloumbis (1983, 97, 142); Tsakonas (2010, 41). Throughout, Greece maintained its formal position in the alliance and its important relationship with the United States. See: Rizas (2009, 372).

[29] See: Krige (2006, 173).

[30] See: Andromidas and Baker (2014, 13).

[31] See: Dokos and Tsakonas (1998, 150).

[32] See: Larrabee (2012, 477).

[33] Greece received 857,363 migrants in 2015. See: IOM (2016).

[34] In 2014, Greece's debt was 177 percent of its GDP and its unemployment rate was 26.5 percent. See: IMF (2016).

those of Greece.[35] Recently, this disparity has grown even further: in 2015, Greece's military was almost a third of Turkey's.[36] Being considerably stronger, Turkey might consider a preventive counterproliferation operation. Yet, even before a conflict with Ankara escalated, Washington would probably intervene, as it has done in the past. Given Athens' conventional weakness, Washington should be able to use a sticks-based approach to ensure Greece's nuclear forbearance. In sum, Greece is likely to remain nonnuclear for the foreseeable future.

Saudi Arabia

Saudi Arabia is not known to possess a nuclear-weapons program. Enjoying high relative conventional military power vis-à-vis its two main regional rivals – Iran and, to a lesser extent, Israel – and benefiting from an informal security guarantee and abundant arms supplies from its loose ally, the United States, the Saudi kingdom has lacked the willingness to acquire nuclear weapons.

Saudi Arabia's principal security threat comes from Iran. Measured by military spending, Saudi Arabia is the stronger of the two countries. In 2014, the Saudis spent $73.7 billion on their military, compared with $11.5 billion spent by Iran.[37]

Prior to the 1979 Iranian Revolution, Saudi Arabia and Iran shared a common interest "in fighting socialist and radical-nationalist influences in the Gulf region, in ensuring a stable flow of oil and gas, and in increasing wealth through exports."[38] Since 1979, however, Saudi Arabia's pro-Western orientation and conservative Wahhabi interpretation of Sunni Islam contrasts with the anti-Western, revolutionary, and Shia-dominated Islamic Republic of Iran, resulting in political clashes between the two. For example, during the Iran-Iraq War (1980–1988), Saudi Arabia provided substantial financial support to Iraq. Riyadh and Tehran eventually resumed diplomatic

---

[35] Between 2000 and 2007, Turkey's military expenditure was, on average, 1.7 times that of Greece, and its CINC score was 3.7. See: Singer (1987).

[36] See: SIPRI (2016).

[37] See: SIPRI (2016). All figures in constant 2011 U.S. dollars; the last year for which data on Iran is available is 2011.

[38] Furtig (2007, 628).

relations after the end of the first Gulf War in 1991.[39] Relations between the two worsened again in the early 2010s, with each country supporting opposing proxies in several conflict theaters in the Middle East. In early 2016, Saudi Arabia severed diplomatic ties with Iran.[40] Competition with Tehran is central to Saudi strategic considerations.[41]

Despite growing tensions, the Saudi-Iranian relationship is best described as a "managed rivalry," in which the two "compete for influence in the region and throughout the Muslim world" while avoiding direct military conflict and regional destabilization.[42] Given Saudi military superiority, and Iran's lack of the industrial and technological base needed to produce the most advanced conventional weapons available, the most serious security concern for Riyadh emanating from Tehran in recent years has been the possibility of Iranian nuclearization. In the early 2010s, Iranian nuclear progress caused concern in Riyadh and fueled speculation that, if Iran were to acquire the bomb, Saudi Arabia would quickly follow suit.[43] But following the 2015 JCPOA nuclear deal between Iran, the P5 +1 countries (China, France, Russia, the United Kingdom, the United States, and Germany), and the European Union, Saudi Arabia declared itself "satisfied" that the agreement would prevent Iran from obtaining a nuclear weapon.[44] Therefore, the main potential driver of Saudi willingness to nuclearize is, for the time being, neutralized.

Saudi Arabia's next most significant regional rival is Israel. In 2014, Israel spent $15.3 billion in its defense, about one-fifth of Saudi military expenses.[45] Along with Saudi conventional strength, several other factors dampen the threat posed by Israel. The two countries do not

---

[39] See: Ibid., 629–630.
[40] See: Ben Hubbard, "Saudi Arabia Cuts Ties with Iran Amid Fallout from Cleric's Execution," *The New York Times*, January 4, 2016, p. A1.
[41] See: Al-Marashi (2010, 85).
[42] Lippman (2012, 241).
[43] See: Cordesman (2015). For the opposite view, see: Kahl et al. (2013, 5).
[44] See: Peter Baker, "Obama and Saudi King Sidestep Dispute over Iran Nuclear Deal," *The New York Times*, September 5, 2015, p. A7.
[45] See: SIPRI (2016). Iran and Israel are exceedingly unlikely to ally against the Saudis. Still, even if they were to compound their military power, the Saudi kingdom outspends them together by nearly three to one.

share a border. They also do not have directly competing economic interests in global petroleum markets. They share their key ally in the United States, and face a common enemy in Iran. In contrast with other Arab countries, Saudi Arabia has defended the peaceful resolution of the Arab-Israeli conflict, having supported multiple peace negotiations since the 1970s. Thus, the security rivalry between Saudi Arabia and Israel has not driven Riyadh to gain the willingness to acquire nuclear weapons.[46]

A final threat to Saudi security comes from domestic instability in Yemen. The upheaval facing this neighboring country is "likely to present Saudi Arabia with its most immediate security challenge for years to come."[47] Civil unrest in Yemen could reverberate in Saudi Arabia, weakening the rule of the House of Saud. While destabilizing, it is difficult to envision a scenario in which the Yemeni threat would prompt Riyadh to be willing to build nuclear weapons.

Saudi willingness to nuclearize is further undermined by its security relationship with the United States, which has for decades been a loose but consistent ally. Although Washington has extended no formal security guarantees to Riyadh, Saudi Arabia is the largest purchaser of U.S. arms.[48] Moreover, throughout the nuclear era, the United States has maintained a small troop presence in Saudi territory; usually fewer than 1,000 uniformed personnel, but averaging slightly over 2,000 troops during the 1990s.[49] For the United States "a self-confident Saudi Arabia, equipped with weapons powerful enough to help keep peace in the Gulf but not powerful enough to threaten Israel or, in the unlikely event of a change in regime, to threaten the United States, is much more of an asset than it is a potential liability."[50] In sum, Saudi Arabia's conventional strength vis-à-vis its adversaries, combined with

[46] See: Bahgat (2006, 429).
[47] Lippman (2012, 234).
[48] See: SIPRI (2016). Economic ties between the two countries are robust too, with Saudi Arabia in 2014 being the second largest supplier of oil to the United States. See: "U.S. Imports by Country of Origin," U.S. Energy Information Administration. Available at: www.eia.gov/dnav/pet/pet_move_impcus_a2_nus_ep00_im0_mbbl_m.htm. Last accessed: May 1, 2016.
[49] See: Reiter (2014).
[50] Lippman (2012, 263).

loose U.S. support, have led Riyadh not to possess the willingness to nuclearize, or even to start a nuclear program with a military dimension.

Saudi Arabia possesses an incipient civilian nuclear program, lacking a nuclear-power reactor.[51] In 2008, Riyadh signed a Memorandum of Understanding on Nuclear Energy Cooperation with the United States through which Washington pledged to "assist the Kingdom of Saudi Arabia to develop civilian nuclear energy for use in medicine, industry, and power generation," while the Saudis stated they will "not pursue sensitive nuclear technologies."[52] Despite a 2015 announcement of plans to build sixteen reactors over the next several decades, the lack of industrial infrastructure and a skilled workforce in the nuclear sector has led to widespread skepticism about this possible development.[53]

Certainly, a worsening security environment might lead Riyadh to become willing to build nuclear weapons. If that were to happen, there has been some speculation that the Saudis might be able to acquire a nuclear weapon from Pakistan, whose own nuclear program the Saudis are rumored to have bankrolled. By purchasing a nuclear weapon, Riyadh might be able to compress the prevention window in which the mechanisms described in our theory are at work. In any case, since the moment Riyadh is suspected of wanting to purchase a weapon, the preventive dynamics described in our theory would condition the Saudi kingdom's opportunity to acquire a nuclear deterrent.

Saudi Arabia's relative conventional strength makes it unlikely that its adversaries would be able to use preventive military action to deter its nuclearization. (Although Israeli military capabilities are in reality greater than defense spending numbers indicate.) Likewise, Washington would likely be unable to prevent Riyadh's nuclearization

---

[51] See: "Saudi Arabia," March 2016, Nuclear Threat Initiative (NTI). Available at: www.nti.org/country-profiles/saudi-arabia/nuclear/. Last accessed: May 1, 2016.

[52] "U.S.-Saudi Arabia Memorandum of Understanding on Nuclear Energy Cooperation," May 16, 2008, U.S. Department of State Archive. Available at: http://2001–2009.state.gov/r/pa/prs/ps/2008/may/104961.htm. Last accessed: May 1, 2016.

[53] See: Brooke Anderson, "Saudis Make Push for Nuclear Energy," *The Wall Street Journal*, September 15, 2015. Available at: www.wsj.com/articles/saudis-make-push-for-nuclear-energy-1442350064. Last accessed: December 29, 2015.

using a sticks-based approach to nonproliferation, more appropriate when dealing with relatively weak protégés. Yet, given the degree to which Saudi military power depends on U.S. sales and military aid, it remains unclear why Saudi Arabia would ditch its loose alliance with Washington, which supplies it with the advanced conventional weaponry Tehran cannot match, in favor of "a Pakistani deal rooted in cultural bonds, cash and secondary and tertiary strategic interests."[54] Furthermore, Washington could, if faced with Riyadh's resolute nuclear ambitions, implement a carrots-based nonproliferation approach, extending additional protection to the security of Saudi Arabia. In short, barring a major adverse transformation in the U.S.-Saudi relationship, Saudi Arabia's nonnuclear status is likely to remain unchanged for the foreseeable future.

Spain

Since the outset of the nuclear age, Spain has faced a low level of threat to its security and enjoyed U.S. security assurances – including substantial deployments of troops and nuclear weapons on its territory. The U.S.-Spanish security relationship was regulated through bilateral agreements starting in 1953. From 1982 onward, Spain has been a NATO member. The combination of these two factors has curbed Spain's willingness to pursue nuclear weapons. An incipient interest in a nuclear deterrent emerged during the dictatorship of Francisco Franco (1936–1975) but was dropped after the democratic transition of 1976. In 1987, Spain became a nonnuclear signatory of the NPT. Madrid's nuclear activity is limited to civilian power generation capability.

Having remained neutral but sympathetic to Axis powers during the Second World War, Spain entered the nuclear age internationally isolated. Its main foreign security threat was, as for other Western European powers, the possibility of Soviet aggression. Lesser threats emanated from Morocco and the United Kingdom. Morocco to this day contests Spanish sovereignty over the autonomous cities of Ceuta and Melilla, located on the Mediterranean coast of Northern Africa and surrounded by Moroccan territory. The United Kingdom, for its part,

[54] Kahl et al. (2013, 30).

controls Gibraltar, a rock of great strategic interest located on Spain's southernmost tip and controlling the gateway to the Mediterranean; Madrid has demanded its return to Spanish sovereignty consistently since the 1960s.

Moroccan and British threats would hardly justify Spanish willingness to nuclearize. Spain outspends Morocco in defense nearly five times. With such a conventional advantage – which is vastly greater when technology and training are factored in – Madrid has no need for a nuclear arsenal to deter a hypothetical Moroccan attack against its possessions in North Africa.[55] Furthermore, although the United Kingdom spends almost four times more than Spain on its military, the two countries share membership in NATO and it is difficult to imagine a scenario in which London would decide to coerce additional territorial concessions from Madrid.[56] Nuclear weapons would also be of little value to support Spanish interests on Gibraltar. In sum, of all the security threats faced by Spain, only the Soviet menace during the Cold War might have prompted the development of an autonomous nuclear arsenal.

Keen on alleviating its political isolation and in part to mitigate the Soviet threat, Spain started its rapprochement with the United States soon in the postwar era. When NATO was created in 1949, however, Spain did not join the alliance. A powerful faction of the Spanish military "opposed an alliance that could make Spain a target of reprisals;" some NATO members considered that "Spain was neither economically nor politically in tune with the major Western powers."[57] Still, Spain signed a bilateral pact with the United States on September 1953 – the Pact of Madrid – through which Washington pledged to supply military (and economic) aid to the Iberian country, contributing to overcome Franco's international isolation. In exchange, the treaty allowed the United States to build and use bases for air and naval forces on Spanish territory; of these, the Morón Air Base and the Rota Naval Station remain under joint U.S.-Spain operation. Specifically, the Pact allowed Washington to station nuclear-missile-armed submarines

---

[55] See: SIPRI (2016).
[56] Ibid.
[57] Seth S. King, "Spain Enters NATO as First Country to Join since 1955," *The New York Times*, May 31, 1982, p. A1.

in Spain (at Rota) and to fly nuclear-armed U.S. bombers over Spanish territory.[58] Between 1954 and the end of the Franco regime in 1976, there were on average over 9,000 U.S. troops stationed in Spain.[59] U.S. nuclear weapons were deployed in Spain between 1957 and 1979.[60]

The U.S.-Spanish nuclear relationship was the object of much scrutiny in the aftermath of the so-called Palomares incident of 1966. On January 17, a U.S. B52 bomber carrying thermonuclear weapons collided with a tanker airplane during a midair refueling just off the southeastern coast of Spain, dropping the four hydrogen bombs on board. The nonnuclear explosives in two of the bombs detonated and, while not causing a nuclear explosion, led to the radioactive contamination of the area around the fishing village of Palomares.[61] A week after the crash, and under growing public pressure, "the Spanish government formally prohibited the flight of US planes carrying nuclear weapons over its territory."[62] Franco also used the incident to push for additional economic and military aid. As a result, "throughout the 1960s Spain was always among the ten countries in the world that received the most North American military aid."[63] More importantly, U.S. nuclear weapons remained in Spain for more than a decade longer. The submarine-launched Poseidon missiles would only be removed from the Rota naval base by July 1979.[64]

When Spain's *transición* to democracy came about after Franco's death in 1975, the nature of the U.S.-Spain relationship was the object of renewed public scrutiny, reinforcing "the perception that the United States supported Franco's regime."[65] This negative perception compounded an aversion to nuclear weapons that had resulted from the Palomares incident.[66] By 1981, as Madrid was concluding

[58] See: Chislett (2005, 20).
[59] See: Reiter (2014).
[60] Ibid. See also: Office of the Assistant to the Secretary of Defense, "History of the Custody and Deployment of Nuclear Weapons: July 1945 through September 1977," Appendix B, "Deployments by Country, 1951–1977," 1978. Available at: www.dod.mil/pubs/foi/Reading_Room/NCB/306.pdf. Last accessed: April 25, 2016.
[61] See: Stiles (2006, 1).
[62] Ibid., 59.
[63] Powell (1995, 44), our translation.
[64] See: Chislett (2005, 30).
[65] Cantalapiedra (2009, 2).
[66] See: Portela (2014, 7).

its negotiations to join NATO, 43 percent of the Spanish population opposed membership in the alliance.[67] Many in Spain argued that NATO would be unable to protect Spain's principal security interests. NATO's "area of responsibility" under Article 6 is defined in a manner that excludes eventual Moroccan challenges to Spanish sovereignty over Ceuta and Melilla. In addition, Spanish attempts to gain sovereignty over Gibraltar from the United Kingdom would likely also go unheeded "because it could be assumed that other NATO members would support Britain on this issue."[68]

Nevertheless, Spain did join NATO in 1982, so that a mere three years after the last nuclear weapons stationed in Spain had been removed, the country was once again under the U.S. nuclear umbrella. In 1986, Madrid called for a referendum on Spanish continuation in the alliance. The socialist government supported a vote for NATO membership, which ultimately carried the day, but demanded three conditions in exchange: "Spain would not join NATO's integrated military structure; the ban on nuclear weapons in Spain would remain and, most importantly, there would be a gradual reduction of the US military presence in Spain."[69] Washington and Madrid then negotiated a new security agreement, leading to a reduction of around 40 percent of U.S. forces stationed in Spain to "4,500 military personnel and 500 civilians ... concentrated in Rota and Morón."[70] Moreover, the renewed agreement included a clause prohibiting "the 'deployment, storage and introduction of nuclear weapons' in Spanish territory." Still "the terms of the agreement failed to prohibit the transit of nuclear weapons."[71] Therefore, Spain's nonnuclear status does not necessarily imply the absence of (U.S.) nuclear weapons in Spanish territory at any given time.

In this environment of abundant security and robust U.S. security guarantees, the only period in which Spain entertained the possibility of developing a nuclear program with military aims was during the

---

[67] See: Rodrigo (1995, 96).
[68] Solsten and Meditz (1988, 263).
[69] Chislett (2005, 31).
[70] Ibid., 32.
[71] Portela (2014, 6). As Portela notes, "it is the policy of several NATO allies not to disclose the nature of the cargo of their vessels," and "the US and Spain renounced reciprocally to request information on the nature of the armaments transported in their respective vessels."

later years of the Franco regime. Facing relative political isolation as a dictator, Franco considered the nuclear option. According to him, a nuclear arsenal would be useful "to strengthen Spain's international position, due to the country's international isolation, threat perceptions and security problems."[72] Franco's rationale was that Spain could not count on the United States in case of a conflict with Morocco, "because Morocco was an important US ally in North Africa facing pro-Soviet Algeria."[73]

Such a rationale was weak, and the Spanish government never as much as granted "political authorization to explore the [nuclear] option," which would have put the country in our list of states that engaged in nuclear development.[74] A 1974 report from the CIA argued that some attention should be paid to the possibility of Spanish nuclearization, but that it would only become a risk if Spain's security environment were to suffer a profound transformation. According to the report:

Spain is the one European country that is deserving of some attention as a possible proliferator in the years ahead. It has indigenous uranium reserves of moderate size, an extensive long-range nuclear power program (three reactors in operation, seven under construction and up to 17 more planned), and a pilot [uranium] separation plant.[75]

At the same time, the report concluded:

Only an unlikely combination of circumstances, growing out of Spain's location with respect to Gibraltar, Portugal and North Africa – coupled with the loss of security ties to the US or NATO, and perhaps a post-Franco government unsure of itself – seems in any way plausible as a reason for Spain to develop a nuclear capability unless such weapons become commonplace.[76]

---

[72] Cantalapiedra (2009, 2).
[73] Ibid.
[74] Singh and Way (2004, 866–867).
[75] Special National Intelligence Estimate 4-1-74, "Prospects for Further Proliferation of Nuclear Weapons," August 23, 1974, in National Security Archive (NSA) Electronic Briefing Book (EBB) 240, "In 1974 Estimate, CIA Found That Israel Already Had a Nuclear Stockpile and That 'Many Countries' Would Soon Have Nuclear Capabilities," Doc. 1, p. 37.
[76] Ibid.

Such a confluence of events never came to pass. By the same logic, Spain is likely to remain nonnuclear for the foreseeable future.[77]

Turkey

Turkey has never attempted to develop a nuclear-weapons capability. While the country is located in a turbulent region, its military superiority over its regional adversaries, combined with its NATO membership and, especially, its tight alliance relationship with the United States, has led decisionmakers in Ankara to lack the willingness to pursue nuclear weapons.

Situated geographically at the intersection of Europe, Asia, and the Middle East, Turkey has faced a variety of security threats during the nuclear era. Its first major concern was the Soviet Union, which vastly outmatched Turkey in terms of military and economic power.[78] In the early years of the Cold War, Moscow's military spending exceeded that of Turkey roughly eighty fold.[79] This adverse balance of power was a grave source of insecurity for Ankara, driving it into NATO by 1952.

A second source of threat stemmed from Turkey's old rival, Greece. Greek-Turkish disagreements smoldered through the 1950s and 1960s but were reignited in the 1970s with territorial and maritime disputes in the Aegean Sea and with the crises over the island of Cyprus. These crises culminated in Turkey's twin invasions of the island in 1974, through which 37 percent of Cypriot territory came under Turkish control, in the process creating 180,000 Greek Cypriot refugees.[80] Despite this conflictual relationship, the threat from Greece was manageable, as Turkey had a significant power advantage over its local rival. Through most of the Cold War, Turkey spent 50 percent more than Greece on its military.[81] As Turkish defense minister İlhami Sancar's put it in 1975 (1961–1965, 1973–1974, 1974–1975), "in the Aegean Sea, the balance is obviously in Turkey's favor."[82]

---

[77] On how Spanish nuclear policy has exhibited a remarkable consistency since the early years of the democratic regime four decades ago, see: Portela (2014, 7).
[78] See: Couloumbis (1983).
[79] See: Singer (1987).
[80] See: Couloumbis (1983, 97).
[81] See: Singer (1987).
[82] Quoted in Krebs (1999, 367).

Relations with Greece began to improve in the post–Cold War, and took a marked turn for the better in 1999, when the two countries cooperated in the aftermath of an earthquake which struck both, as well as over the war in Kosovo. Since then, the two have signed numerous bilateral agreements and engaged in a variety of confidence-building measures. Today, Cyprus is no longer the flashpoint it was during the 1970s and 1980s and, as a result, Turkish perceives less of a Greek threat. Moreover, Turkey spends almost three times as much as Greece on its military, perpetuating a favorable balance of power.[83]

A third and more recent source of threat results from instability in the Balkans, Caucasus, and the Middle East. According to Turkey's 2000 Defense White Paper, this is "where the new threats and risks are concentrated."[84] The most serious of these threats come from neighboring Syria, Iraq, and Iran – all three of these countries have pursued their own nuclear programs; all three have been (or remain) involved in major wars, both civil and interstate. Yet, as with Greece, Turkey faces a favorable balance of power vis-à-vis these Middle Eastern neighbors. In the post–Cold War years, Turkey has spent roughly twice as much in its military as Iran, four times as much as Iraq, and over five times more than Syria.[85]

Finally, Turkey faces two nonstate threats, from groups that have carried out numerous terrorist attacks on Turkish territory and threaten to carve out segments of the Turkish state: the Kurdistan Worker's Party (a. k. a. PKK), a separatist Kurdish militant organization; and, more recently, the Islamic State of Iraq and the Levant (ISIL). Given their nature, however, it is difficult to see how nuclear weapons might prove useful in dealing with these nonstate threats.

Taking stock, Turkey faced three sets of threats against which a nuclear deterrent might bring a security benefit: the threat of Soviet expansionism and Greek rivalry during the Cold War; and the enduring threats from neighboring Iraq, Iran, and Syria. Whereas the Soviet Union was vastly more powerful, the remaining sources of threat to Ankara are significantly weaker than Turkey.

To meet its security needs, Turkey has relied on its own conventional forces and on an alliance with the United States. Turkey became a NATO

[83] See: SIPRI (2016).
[84] Quoted in Fuerth (2004, 152).
[85] See: Singer (1987).

member alongside Greece in 1952. Although the main goal of joining NATO was to mitigate the Soviet threat, membership in the alliance also helped manage Greek-Turkish relations by constraining their potential for military conflict. Furthermore, Turkey has pursued an especially deep security relationship with the United States – a veritable "*alliance within the Alliance*."[86] The two countries signed a basing agreement in 1954.[87] As a result, Turkey has hosted sizable U.S. military deployments, averaging over 6,500 personnel until the end of the Cold War and roughly 3,000 since.[88] The United States has also been Turkey's most important supplier of conventional arms throughout the nuclear period, averaging over $500 million in annual sales, far more than any other source.[89] Moreover, in early 1959, the two countries signed a secret bilateral defensive alliance agreement, paving the way for the placement of U.S. nuclear weapons in Turkish territory.[90] An initial deployment of mid-range Jupiter missiles was replaced in the early 1960s by B61 gravity bombs, peaking at 500 warheads in the 1980s.[91] Today, Washington continues to station an estimated 60 to 70 warheads on Turkish soil.[92] U.S. nuclear weapons have been an essential part of Turkey's security calculus throughout the nuclear era. As a Turkish ambassador to Canada remarked in the mid-1990s, "NATO without the U.S. nuclear weapons deployed in Turkey would mean nothing to the Turks."[93]

Bilateral security relations with the United States are particularly important for Turkey given the country's concerns about NATO, particularly in the post–Cold War period. With the collapse of the Soviet Union, Turkish leaders began to worry that their position in the Atlantic alliance would be diminished.[94] Furthermore, the lack of solidarity between members displayed during the Gulf War of 1990 and the Iraq War of 2003 fostered doubts in Ankara about the alliance's effectiveness.[95]

[86] Kibaroglu (2005, 445), Kibaroglu's emphasis.
[87] See: Couloumbis (1983, 15).
[88] See: Kane (2006).
[89] See: SIPRI (2016).
[90] See: Fuhrmann and Sechser (2014, 466); Stein (2013). Some argue that the initial deployment was made in 1961. See: Kibaroglu (2015, 162); Ergun (2015, 66).
[91] See: Ergun (2015, 68); Kasapoglu (2015, 97).
[92] See: Kasapoglu (2015, 97).
[93] Quoted in Kibaroglu (2005, 455).
[94] See: Güvenc and Özel (2012, 536–537).
[95] On the Gulf War, see: Lesser (2005, 93); Ülgen (2012, 12). On the U.S. invasion, see: Güvenc and Özel (2012, 534).

Turkey's relationship with the United States has not been without problems, however. Turkish abandonment fears first emerged over the Kennedy administration's shift to a strategy of "flexible response" and its removal of the Jupiter missiles from Turkey in the aftermath of the Cuban missile crisis.[96] Then, the 1974 Turkish invasions of Cyprus led Washington to place in storage its nuclear weapons deployed in Turkey, for fear of command-and-control problems; and to declare a three-year arms embargo on the country.[97] Turkey retaliated the following year by declaring all bilateral basing agreements to be invalid.[98] This measure, however, did not impact actual U.S. arms sales or deployments of U.S. forces.[99] In the post–Cold War period, U.S.-Turkish relations reached their nadir with Turkey's refusal to allow U.S. troops to use its territory in the 2003 invasion of Iraq; and when, months into the war, U.S. military personnel accidentally captured and detained Turkish Special Forces personnel operating in northern Iraq.[100] Still, despite this friction, Washington remains Ankara's most important external source of security – making the United States, in the Turkish government's eyes, "the key to its own survival in a region beset by instability."[101]

Although Turkey is not known ever to have pursued a nuclear program with military goals, the country possesses an active nuclear energy program. In 1955, Washington and Ankara signed a cooperation agreement under the U.S. Atoms for Peace program, followed a year later by the establishment of the Turkish Atomic Energy Authority (TAEK).[102] In 1959, Turkey began work on a 1 MW research reactor, which became operational three years later,[103] and in 1963 Turkey began a feasibility study for the construction of a fully operational nuclear power plant.[104] From the 1960s onward, Turkey planned to build at least a dozen reactors, but none have materialized. Turkey has signed nuclear cooperation agreements with a wide array of countries, including Argentina, Canada, China, France, Germany, Japan, Jordan, Pakistan, Russia, South Korea,

---

[96] See: Ergun (2015, 66–67).
[97] See: Güvenc and Özel (2012, 535).
[98] See: Couloumbis (1983, 151).
[99] See: Kane (2006); SIPRI (2016).
[100] See: Udum (2007, 61); Güvenc and Özel (2012, 542).
[101] Ülgen (2012, 4).
[102] See: Stein (2013).
[103] Ibid.
[104] See: Kumbaroglu (2015, 9).

and the United States, but, to date, it has yet to progress in its nuclear program beyond the research and development stage.[105]

Turkey has also been a solid member of the nuclear-nonproliferation regime. It signed the NPT in 1969 and, although it took until 1980 to ratify the treaty, it accepted IAEA safeguards in 1981, and signed the IAEA additional protocol in 2000. Beyond the NPT, Turkey has ratified the CTBT and nearly a dozen other international agreements related to the production and use of nuclear-weapons technology and other WMD.[106]

With the evolution of Iran's nuclear program over the past decade, some in Turkey have advocated a reexamination of the country's traditional nonnuclear stance.[107] A Turkish minister claimed in 2000 that "our possession of the nuclear bomb [would] strengthen our security and enhance our deterrence amid this nuclear environment."[108] Still, not even under this added pressure has Turkey's nuclear calculus changed toward development. The country continues to maintain a favorable balance of power vis-à-vis its neighboring adversaries: Iraq, Iran, and Syria.[109] Furthermore, Turkey maintains a tight alliance with the United States, Ankara's largest source of weapons procurement, maintaining roughly 2,000 troops and dozens of nuclear weapons stationed on Turkish territory.[110] Turkey's relative strength vis-à-vis its regional rivals, combined with robust U.S. security commitments, has so far been sufficient to undermine Ankara's willingness to develop an independent nuclear deterrent. As the Turkish foreign ministry stated in 2006, "[t]he common security umbrella provided by NATO to its allies gives Turkey the capacity for nuclear deterrence."[111]

---

[105] For an overview, see: Kumbaroglu (2015).

[106] See: Ergun (2015, 77).

[107] See: Kibaroglu (2004).

[108] Quoted in Fuerth (2004, 159). For scholarly debate on the possibility of Turkish nuclearization, see: Lesser (2005); Udum (2007); Varnum (2010); Perkovich and Ülgen, ed. (2015).

[109] In 2015, Turkey spent nearly twice on its military compared with Iran. Turkey defense expenditures exceeded those of Iraq as well. Data for Syria is unavailable. Since Iraq faces considerable domestic unrest and Syria is mired in a civil war, neither country poses a serious conventional threat to Turkey that might be mitigated by a nuclear deterrent. See: SIPRI (2016).

[110] See: Ülgen (2012, 1). For troop numbers, see: IISS (2016, 151). For weapons sales, see: SIPRI (2016).

[111] Quoted in Varnum (2010, 229).

Appendix IV
Formal Theory

This appendix presents our formal model of proliferation (for an informal presentation, see Chapter 2). Section 1 considers a baseline model with a potential proliferator and its adversary. Section 2 adds a third state, an ally of the potential proliferator, to the strategic interaction. Section 3 extends the game to an infinite-horizon setup. Section 4 concludes. Proofs are contained in section 5.

1 Adversaries and Proliferation

Consider a one-shot game between a potential proliferator P and its adversary Ad. P decides whether to invest in a nuclear-weapons program.[1] Such an investment costs $k > 0$ to P and produces an effect e at the end of the game. e is a benefit accruing to P at the expense of Ad. We will say that P *nuclearizes* if it obtains nuclear weapons. To prevent P's nuclearization, Ad may launch a preventive war. Assume for simplicity that any nuclearization attempt succeeds if there is no preventive war, and that any preventive war succeeds in preventing P's nuclearization.

P's investment decision is imperfectly observable. Let there be a signal s about P's investment decision I. If P does not invest $(I = 0)$, then $s = 0$. If P invests $(I = 1)$, then $s = 1$ with probability $p_s \in [0,1]$ and $s = 0$ with probability $1 - p_s$. Intuitively, $s = 1$ represents an unambiguous signal of P's nuclearization, while $s = 0$ is an ambiguous signal.

After receiving its signal, Ad decides whether to declare war. To explain why war can occur even if it is costly and destructive, we allow

---

[1] This model is a revised version of the two-period game of Debs and Monteiro (2014). One substantive difference with Debs and Monteiro (2014) is that we focus on nuclearization, not just on preventive war. One technical difference with Debs and Monteiro (2014) is that we black box the effect of nuclearization, instead of endogenizing it in a second period of interaction. We endogenize the effect of nuclearization in section 3.

for peaceful bargaining (Fearon, 1995). *Ad* can divide a pie of size 1 with *P*, offering z to *P* and keeping $1 - z$. *P* accepts or rejects the offer. If *P* accepts, the offer is implemented. If *P* rejects, war ensues.

A war is won by *P* with probability p, and by *Ad* with probability $1 - p$, with the winner obtaining the whole pie. However, war is costly, imposing a cost c_i on state *i*, $c_i > 0 \ \forall i$. We call $c_P + c_{Ad}$ the *cost of a preventive war* and assume that the cost of a preventive war is larger than the cost of the investment k. We define a preventive war to be *mistaken* if it is made against a state that is not investing in a nuclear-weapons capability.

Ultimately, we wish to understand the effect of the security environment on the odds of nuclearization and preventive war. We focus on two variables: *P*'s conventional capabilities κ (greater values of κ indicate that the balance of conventional capabilities is more favorable to *P*) and the probability p_c of future conflict between *P* and *Ad*. By "future conflict" we mean that the states will have conflictual preferences, so that the use of force would at least be considered, even if it may not lead to war.

First, we assume that the probability that *P* wins a war is increasing in its conventional capabilities. We write p as a function of $p(\kappa)$, which is increasing in κ.

Second, we assume that the effect of nuclearization is decreasing in *P*'s conventional capabilities and increasing in the probability of future conflict. Intuitively, nuclear weapons are often called the "weapons of the weak," in that states with weaker conventional capabilities benefit the most from nuclearization. Also, the greater is the probability that the two states have conflictual preferences, the greater is the benefit of having improved military capabilities, even if they are only used as a threat. We write e as a function $e(\kappa, p_c)$, which is decreasing in κ and increasing in p_c, and we assume that if there is no future conflict, then nuclear weapons produce no security benefit, that is, $e(\kappa, 0) = 0 \ \forall \kappa$.

Third, we assume that the cost of preventive war is increasing in *P*'s conventional capabilities. The greater are *P*'s conventional capabilities, the costlier it is to destroy its nuclear-weapons program. We write $c_P + c_{Ad}$ as a function $c_P(\kappa) + c_{Ad}(\kappa)$, which is increasing in κ.

Finally, we assume that κ is taken from an interval $[\kappa_L, \kappa_H]$, where κ_L is "small" and κ_H is "large" (so that $e(\kappa_L, p_c) > c_P(\kappa_L) + c_{Ad}(\kappa_L)$

and $e(\kappa_H, p_c) < k \quad \forall p_c > 0$, and every interesting interval of the parameter space is covered).

Summing up, the game proceeds as follows:

- P decides whether to invest in a nuclear-weapons capability;
- Nature sends the public signal s about P's decision;
- Ad decides whether to declare war or offer a share z of the pie;
- If Ad offered a share z of the pie, then P decides whether to accept or reject the offer;
- The outcome of P's nuclearization attempt, if any, becomes known and payoffs are accrued.

We solve for Perfect Bayesian Equilibria (PBE) of this dynamic game of imperfect information. This requires that at each information set, play is sequentially rational given beliefs, and beliefs are updated using Bayes's rule whenever possible.[2]

1.1 Solution

We note first that if the effect of nuclearization is smaller than the cost of the investment, then nuclearization is not rationalizable. P would not want to invest in a nuclear-weapons capability, even if it knew that the investment would come to fruition.

Proposition 1. For any quality of information p_s, if the effect of nuclearization is smaller than the cost of the investment $\left(e(\kappa, p_c) < k \right)$, then in equilibrium nuclearization does not occur and peace prevails.

Proof. See section 5.1.

Intuitively, the cost of the investment acts as a "willingness threshold," and nuclearization does not occur if the willingness threshold is not met. Therefore, we conclude that if the probability of conflict p_c between P and Ad is sufficiently low, then P will not see the investment as productive, and will choose to remain nonnuclear.

Result 1. There is a value $\underline{p_c}$ such that if $p_c < \underline{p_c}$, then nuclearization does not occur.

---

[2] Fudenberg and Tirole (1991, 325–326). If there is no investment in equilibrium, we assume that off-the-equilibrium-path beliefs after $s = 1$ are that P invested, the only decision that could generate this signal.

Proof. Follows from the preceding, the fact that $e(\kappa, p_c)$ increases in p_c and $e(\kappa, 0) = 0 < k$.

If the effect of nuclearization is greater than the cost of the investment, then P is willing to acquire nuclear weapons. Let us now determine whether it can successfully do so.

If the effect of nuclearization is smaller than the cost of preventive war, then preventive war is not rationalizable for Ad. Even if it knew that P were investing in nuclear capabilities, it would not want to strike preventively. In this situation, P nuclearizes unimpeded.

Proposition 2. If the effect of nuclearization is greater than the cost of the investment and smaller than the cost of preventive war $\left(k < e(\kappa, p_c) < c_P(\kappa) + c_{Ad}(\kappa)\right)$, then in equilibrium nuclearization occurs and peace prevails.

Proof. See section 5.1.

If the effect of nuclearization is greater than the cost of preventive war, then the threat of preventive war is credible. P wants to acquire nuclear weapons, but Ad wants to prevent it from doing so. Because nuclearization is a costly investment with delayed returns, Ad has the advantage and can successfully prevent proliferation if the signal is sufficiently informative. If it is not, then strategic uncertainty remains. P may try to proliferate, and Ad may decide to go to war, even if it receives an ambiguous signal of proliferation.[3]

Proposition 3. If the effect of nuclearization is greater than the cost of preventive war $\left(k < c_P(\kappa) + c_{Ad}(\kappa) < e(\kappa, p_c)\right)$, then the outcome depends on the quality of the signal.

(i) If the signal is sufficiently informative, i.e.,

$$\left(1 - p_s\right) e(\kappa, p_c) < k \tag{1}$$

then in equilibrium nuclearization does not occur and peace prevails;

---

[3] Technically, the equilibrium is in mixed strategies. Such an equilibrium captures the strategic uncertainty inherent in this interaction, where both nuclearization and preventive war are rationalizable, and information is sufficiently imperfect. Note that a mixed-strategy equilibrium can be understood as the pure strategy equilibrium of a close-by game of incomplete information, with private shocks on the players' payoffs. See: Harsanyi (1973).

(ii) If the signal is not sufficiently informative (condition (1) fails), then

nuclearization occurs with probability $\dfrac{\dfrac{k}{e(\kappa, p_c)}}{p_s + (1 - p_s)\dfrac{e(\kappa, p_c)}{c_P(\kappa) + c_{Ad}(\kappa)}}$

and war occurs with probability $1 - \dfrac{\dfrac{k}{c_P(\kappa) + c_{Ad}(\kappa)}}{p_s + (1 - p_s)\dfrac{e(\kappa, p_c)}{c_P(\kappa) + c_{Ad}(\kappa)}}$.

Proof. See section 5.1.

We have now completed our analysis of the strategic interaction between P and Ad, when P is interested in acquiring nuclear weapons (or the "willingness threshold" is met). Let us now evaluate the effect of our main independent variables on the odds of nuclearization and preventive war.

Consider first the benchmark case of perfect information $(p_s = 1)$, so that condition (1) holds. Nuclearization occurs if and only if the threat of preventive war is not credible. In turn, the threat of preventive war is not credible if and only if the effect of nuclearization is smaller than the cost of preventive war. As a result, the odds of nuclearization increase with P's conventional capabilities, since greater conventional capabilities reduce the effect of nuclearization and increase the cost of preventive war. Certainly, weaker states benefit more from acquiring nuclear weapons, but their adversary benefits more from preventing proliferation. Since nuclearization is a costly investment with delayed returns, the adversary has the advantage and deters proliferation more effectively:

Result 2. Consider the benchmark case of perfect information $(p_s = 1)$. Assume that the willingness threshold is met $(e(\kappa, p_c) > k)$. The probability of nuclearization increases with P's conventional capabilities (κ).

Proof. Follows from the preceding.

Now, consider the more realistic case where the signal is sufficiently uninformative (or condition (1) fails if the threat of preventive war is credible, i.e., $p_s < 1 - \dfrac{k}{c_P(\kappa_L) + c_{Ad}(\kappa_L)}$). The conclusion of the benchmark case continues to apply. The more credible is the threat of preventive war, the less likely is nuclearization. As a result of imperfect information, however, preventive war may occur, and it may be mistaken. *P* hopes to nuclearize undetected. When it is caught, a preventive war ensues. Even if the signal does not clearly reveal a nuclearization attempt, *Ad* may still launch a preventive war, worried that it missed such an attempt. The greater is the quality of the signal, then, the more *P* is deterred from investing, so that war is less likely, and it is less likely to be mistaken:

Result 3. Assume that the signal is sufficiently uninformative $\left(p_s < 1 - \dfrac{k}{c_P(\kappa_L) + c_{Ad}(\kappa_L)} \right)$ and the willingness threshold is met $\left(e(\kappa, p_c) > k \right)$. We conclude:

(i)   The probability of nuclearization increases with P's conventional capabilities (κ);
(ii) The probability of preventive war decreases with the quality of the signal (p_s);
(iii) The probability that a preventive war is mistaken decreases with the quality of the signal (p_s).

Proof. See section 5.1.

2 Adversaries, Allies, and Proliferation

Now let us add a third player to the strategic interaction, a nuclear ally *Al* for *P*. *Al* may share *P*'s preferences and may come to its defense in war.

If peace prevails and *P* receives a share z, let *Al*'s payoff be oz, where o measures the overlap of preferences between *Al* and *P* (Morrow, 1994). For simplicity, we assume that o takes one of two values, $o \in \{0,1\}$, where $o = 0$ is a low overlap of preferences and $o = 1$ is a high overlap of preferences. It is common knowledge that $o = 1$ with probability $p_o \in [0,1]$ and the value of o is private information of *Al*'s.

If *P* and *Ad* are in war, *Al* can join the war on the side of *P* ($j = 1$ if it does; $j = 0$ if it does not). We assume that *Al*'s support increases the probability of *P*'s victory and increases the cost of preventive war. For simplicity, though, such a decision does not affect the effectiveness of a preventive war, i.e., an investment in nuclear weapons comes to fruition if Ad does not launch a preventive war, and a preventive war ensures P's nonnuclearization. Formally, we write $p(\kappa, j)$ for the probability that P defeats Ad. We assume that $p(\kappa, j)$ is increasing in κ $\forall j$ and $p(\kappa, 1) > p(\kappa, 0)$ $\forall \kappa$. We write $c_i(\kappa, j)$ for the cost of war of state i, and call $c_P(\kappa, j) + c_{Ad}(\kappa, j)$ the cost of preventive war. We assume that $c_P(\kappa, j) + c_{Ad}(\kappa, j)$ is increasing in κ $\forall j$, $c_P(\kappa, 1) + c_{Ad}(\kappa, 1) > c_P(\kappa, 0) + c_{Ad}(\kappa, 0)$, and $c_P(\kappa, j) + c_{Ad}(\kappa, j) > k$ $\forall \kappa$, j. We also assume that $0 < c_{Al}(\kappa, 1) - c_{Al}(\kappa, 0) < p(\kappa, 1) - p(\kappa, 0)$ $\forall \kappa$, i.e., it is strictly costly for Al to join a war, but the increase in cost is lower than the effect on the war outcome.[4]

The presence of the ally also impacts the effect of nuclear weapons. The more likely the overlap of preferences between P and Al is to be high, the more likely Al is to support P in a future conflict, reducing the need for an autonomous nuclear deterrent. We write $e(\kappa, p_c, p_o)$ for the effect of nuclear weapons. $e(\kappa, p_c, p_o)$ is a benefit accruing to P at the expense of Ad, which is decreasing in κ, increasing in p_c, and decreasing in p_o. Consistent with the above, $e(\kappa, 0, p_o) = 0$ $\forall \kappa, p_o$. κ_L is "small" and κ_H is "large" (i.e., $e(\kappa_L, p_c, p_o) > c_P(\kappa_L, j) + c_{Ad}(\kappa_L, j)$ and $e(\kappa_H, p_c, p_o) < k$ $\forall p_c > 0$, p_o, j). The effect of P's nuclearization on Al's payoff can be written e_{Al}; we impose no restriction on e_{Al}.[5]

Summing up, the game proceeds as follows:

- P decides whether to invest in a nuclear-weapons capability;
- Nature sends the public signal s about P's decision;
- Ad decides whether to declare war or offer a share z of the pie;
- If Ad offered a share z of the pie, then P decides whether to accept or reject the offer;
- Nature determines whether Al has a high or a low overlap of preferences with P, and if war erupted between P and Ad, then Al decides whether to join the war on the side of P;
- The outcome of P's nuclearization attempt, if any, becomes known and payoffs are accrued.

---

[4] Thus, Al wants to join a war if the overlap of preferences is high ($o = 1$).
[5] Presumably, e_{Al} could be positive, and increase with the overlap of preferences, but our results do not depend on any assumption on e_{Al}.

Again, we solve for Perfect Bayesian Equilibria (PBE) of this dynamic game of imperfect information.

2.1 Solution

Consider *Al*'s decision to fight a war on behalf of *P*. *Al* joins a war if and only if the overlap of preferences is high, because it values the greater expected share of the pie, and is thus willing to pay the cost of war:

Lemma 1. *Al* joins a war on the side of *P* if and only if the overlap of preferences between *Al* and *P* is high.

Proof. Since *Al*'s decision has no effect on *P*'s nuclear status, holding fixed *P*'s investment decision and *Ad*'s decision to declare a preventive war, then *Al* chooses $j = 1$ if and only if $p(\kappa, 1)o - c(\kappa, 1) > p(\kappa, 0)o - c(\kappa, 0)$, which holds if and only if $o = 1$.

Thus, while *P* and *Ad* do not know whether *Al* would join *P* in war, they can form expectations about its response. Write $p(\kappa, p_o)$ for the expected probability that *P* defeats *Ad* and $c_P(\kappa, p_o) + c_{Ad}(\kappa, p_o)$ for the expected cost of preventive war, where

$$p(\kappa, p_o) = p_o p(\kappa, 1) + (1 - p_o) p(\kappa, 0) \tag{2}$$

$$c_i(\kappa, p_o) = p_o c_i(\kappa, 1) + (1 - p_o) c_i(\kappa, 0) \tag{3}$$

We conclude first that there is a willingness threshold for proliferation:

Proposition 4. If the effect of nuclearization is smaller than the cost of the investment $(e(\kappa, p_c, p_o) < k)$, then in equilibrium, nuclearization does not occur and peace prevails.

Proof. See section 5.2.

As a result, nuclearization does not occur if the probability of conflict is sufficiently low:

Result 4. There is a value $\underline{p_c}$ such that if $p_c < \underline{p_c}$, then nuclearization does not occur.

Proof. Follows from the above, the fact that $e(\kappa, p_c, p_o)$ increases in p_c and $e(\kappa, 0, p_o) = 0 < k$.

Also, consistent with the previous section, *P* nuclearizes unimpeded if the effect of nuclearization is greater than the cost of the investment, but smaller than the expected cost of preventive war:

Proposition 5. If the effect of nuclearization is greater than the cost of the investment and smaller than the expected cost of preventive war $\left(k < e(\kappa, p_c, p_o) < c_P(\kappa, p_o) + c_{Ad}(\kappa, p_o)\right)$, then in equilibrium nuclearization occurs and peace prevails.

Proof. See section 5.2.

Finally, if the effect of nuclearization is greater than the expected cost of preventive war, then nuclearization is deterred if the signal is sufficiently informative, and otherwise nuclearization, war, and mistaken preventive war are possible outcomes:

Proposition 6. If the effect of nuclearization is greater than the expected cost of preventive war $\left(k < c_P(\kappa, p_o) + c_{Ad}(\kappa, p_o) < e(\kappa, p_c, p_o)\right)$, then the outcome depends on the quality of the signal:

  (i) If the signal is sufficiently informative, i.e.,

$$\left(1 - p_s\right) e(\kappa, p_c, p_o) < k \tag{4}$$

then in equilibrium nuclearization does not occur and peace prevails;

  (ii) If the signal is not sufficiently informative (condition (4) fails), then

nuclearization occurs with probability $\dfrac{\dfrac{k}{e(\kappa, p_c, p_o)}}{p_s + (1 - p_s)\dfrac{e(\kappa, p_c, p_o)}{c_P(\kappa, p_o) + c_{Ad}(\kappa, p_o)}}$

and war occurs with probability $1 - \dfrac{\dfrac{k}{c_P(\kappa, p_o) + c_{Ad}(\kappa, p_o)}}{p_s + (1 - p_s)\dfrac{e(\kappa, p_c, p_o)}{c_P(\kappa, p_o) + c_{Ad}(\kappa, p_o)}}.$

Proof. See section 5.2.

Taking stock, we can now make predictions on the odds of nuclearization and war, assuming that the willingness threshold is met. Consider first the benchmark case where the signal is perfectly informative ($p_s = 1$, so that condition (4) holds). As in the previous section, the greater are *P*'s conventional capabilities, the less credible are *Ad*'s threats of preventive war, and the more likely is nuclearization:

Result 5. Consider the benchmark case of perfect information $\left(p_s = 1\right)$. Assume that the willingness threshold is met $\left(e(\kappa, p_c, p_o) > k\right)$. The probability of nuclearization increases with P's conventional capabilities (κ).

Proof. See section 5.2.

Now consider the effect of the ally. *Al*'s support in a future conflict reduces the effect of nuclearization, thus reducing *P*'s willingness to nuclearize. However, *Al*'s support in a current conflict increases the cost of preventive war, thus increasing *P*'s opportunity to nuclearize. The net effect of these countervailing forces depends on *P*'s conventional capabilities.

If *P* is strong, the effect of nuclearization is low. Preventive wars are not credible even without *Al*'s support. *Al*'s support, by reducing the effect of nuclearization, may turn nuclear weapons into an unproductive investment. If *P* is weak, in contrast, the effect of nuclearization is high. By increasing the cost of preventive war, *Al*'s support reduces the credibility of counter-proliferation threats, thus increasing the odds of nuclearization.

Result 6. Consider the benchmark case of perfect information $(p_s = 1)$. For any p_o and any $p_c > 0$, there is a value $\overline{\kappa}(p_c, p_o)$ with the following properties:

(i) If $\kappa > \overline{\kappa}(p_c, p_o)$, then nuclearization does not occur. $\overline{\kappa}(p_c, p_o)$ is decreasing in p_o;

(ii) If $\kappa < \overline{\kappa}(p_c, 1)$, then the probability of nuclearization increases in p_o.

Proof. See section 5.2.

Now consider the more realistic case where the quality of the signal is sufficiently uninformative (or condition (4) fails if the threat of preventive war is credible, i.e., $p_s < 1 - \dfrac{k}{c_P(\kappa_L, 0) + c_{Ad}(\kappa_L, 0)}$). Preventive wars, and mistaken preventive wars, can occur in equilibrium, and the conclusions of the baseline model still apply:

Result 7. Assume that the signal is sufficiently uninformative $\left(p_s < 1 - \dfrac{k}{c_P(\kappa_L, 0) + c_{Ad}(\kappa_L, 0)} \right)$ and the willingness threshold is met $\left(e(\kappa, p_c, p_o) > k \right)$. We conclude:

(i) The probability of nuclearization increases with *P*'s conventional capabilities (κ);

(ii) The probability of preventive war decreases with the quality of the signal (p_s);

(iii) The probability that a preventive war is mistaken decreases with the quality of the signal (p_s).

Proof. See section 5.2.

Now, turning our attention to the effect of the presence of the ally, we see as in the case of perfect information that it either decreases or increases the odds of nuclearization, depending on *P*'s conventional capabilities:

Result 8. Assume that the signal is sufficiently uninformative $\left(p_s < 1 - \dfrac{k}{c_P(\kappa_L,0) + c_{Ad}(\kappa_L,0)} \right)$. For any p_o and any $p_c > 0$, there is a value $\bar{\kappa}(p_c, p_o)$ with the following properties:

(i) If $\kappa > \bar{\kappa}(p_c, p_o)$, then nuclearization does not occur. $\bar{\kappa}(p_c, p_o)$ is decreasing in p_o;

(ii) If $\kappa < \bar{\kappa}(p_c, 1)$, then the probability of nuclearization increases in p_o.

Proof. See section 5.2.

3 Infinite-Horizon Game

Now consider an infinite-horizon version of the above game.[6] By modeling the states' interaction after nuclearization, we can enrich our analysis of the benefit of nuclearization, endogenizing $e(\kappa, p_c, p_o)$. By allowing for multiple attempts at proliferation, we can introduce the possibility of "nonproliferation deals," i.e., concessions made by enemies to ensure nonproliferation.[7] This enriches the strategic calculation of each player, who must think about the future terms and stability of nonproliferation deals, allowing us to test the robustness of the above conclusions.[8]

In each period, Nature first determines the intensity of conflict between *P* and *Ad*. With probability p_c, it is high. In that case, *P* can

---

[6] The model generalizes the two-player infinite-horizon game of Debs and Monteiro (2014) to a three-player setting. Note that the former is a special case of the latter, where $p_o = 0$.

[7] See: Debs and Monteiro (2014); Bas and Coe (2016b).

[8] We might worry that the efficient outcome – peace under some nonproliferation deal – is always enforceable, if players are sufficiently patient, questioning the robustness of our above conclusions. However, we show that such a concern is not warranted.

invest in nuclear weapons. If it does so at t, then it obtains nuclear weapons at the end of t if and only if Ad does not strike preventively. P's possession of nuclear weapons becomes common knowledge and P remains a nuclear-weapons state from then on. Use $N_t \in \{0,1\}$ for P's nuclear status in period t ($N_t = 1$ if and only if P possesses nuclear weapons at t), where subscript t refers to the value of a variable at t. With probability $1 - p_c$, the intensity of conflict is low. In that case, the game ends and player i receives a fixed per-period payoff of u_i. Intuitively, low conflict means that the dispute between P and Ad has been resolved, and neither considers the use of force.

If P does not possess nuclear weapons and Ad launches a preventive war at t, then P remains nonnuclear and loses the option of nuclearizing for E periods, where E represents the *effectiveness* of a preventive war. Write $O_t \in t\{0,1\}$ for whether P has the option to nuclearize ($O_t = 1$ if and only if it does). Write $n_t \in \{0,...,E-1\}$ for the number of periods of the effectiveness of a preventive war that have passed already.

We allow P's nuclear status to affect the outcome and the cost of war. Write $p(\kappa, j_t, N_t)$ and $c_i(\kappa, j_t, N_t)$ for, respectively, the probability that P defeats Ad and for the cost of war of state i. We assume that $p(\kappa, j_t, N_t)$ is increasing in κ $\forall j_t$, N_t and that $p(\kappa, 1, N_t) > p(\kappa, 0, N_t)$ $\forall \kappa$, N_t. Call $c_P(\kappa, j_t, 0) + c_{Ad}(\kappa, j_t, 0)$ the cost of preventive war. We assume that $c_P(\kappa, j_t, 0) + c_{Ad}(\kappa, j_t, 0)$ is increasing in κ $\forall j_t$, and that $c_P(\kappa, 1, 0) + c_{Ad}(\kappa, 1, 0) > c_P(\kappa, 0, 0) + c_{Ad}(\kappa, 0, 0)$ $\forall \kappa$. In addition, we assume that $c_P(\kappa, j_t, 0) + c_{Ad}(\kappa, j_t, 0) > k$ $\forall \kappa$, j_t, and that $0 < c_{Al}(\kappa, 1, N_t) - c_{Al}(\kappa, 0, N_t) < p(\kappa, 1, N_t) - p(\kappa, 0, N_t)$, $\forall \kappa$, N_t.

Now turning to the effect of nuclearization, write $m(\kappa, j_t)$ for the *military effect of nuclear weapons*, where $m(\kappa, j_t) = [p(\kappa, j_t, 1) - c_P(\kappa, j_t, 1)] - [p(\kappa, j_t, 0) - c_P(\kappa, j_t, 0)]$. We assume that the military effect of nuclear weapons decreases with P's capabilities κ $\forall j_t$ and that it is lower if Al joins in a war than if it does not ($m(\kappa, 1) < m(\kappa, 0)$ $\forall \kappa$).

Summing up, the timing of the game is as follows. In period 1:

- Nature determines whether the intensity of conflict between Ad and P is high or low; if it is low, the game ends and player i gets payoff u_i every period from then on; if it is high, the game continues as specified in the following text:
- P decides whether to invest in a nuclear-weapons capability;

- Nature sends the public signal s_t about P's decision;
- Ad decides whether to declare war or offer a share z_t of the pie;
- If Ad offered a share z_t of the pie, then P decides whether to accept or reject the offer;
- Nature determines whether Al has a high or a low overlap of preferences with P, and if war erupted between P and Ad, then Al decides whether to join the war on the side of P;
- The outcome of P's nuclearization attempt, if any, becomes known and payoffs are accrued.

The timing of the game in period $t \geq 2$ follows the above timing if, in period $t-1$, P did not nuclearize and peace prevailed.

If in period t, P invests in nuclear weapons and Ad does not launch a preventive war, then each period from $t+1$ onward proceeds as follows:

- Nature determines whether the intensity of conflict between Ad and P is high or low; if it is low, the game ends and player i gets payoff u_i every period from then on; if it is high, the game continues as specified in the following text:
- Ad decides whether to declare war or offer a share z_t of the pie;
- If Ad offered a share z_t of the pie, then P decides whether to accept or reject the offer;
- Nature chooses whether Al has high or low overlap of preferences with P, and if war erupted between P and Ad, then Al decides whether to join the war on the side of P;
- The outcome of P's nuclearization attempt, if any, becomes known and payoffs are accrued.

If in period t, P has the option to invest in nuclear weapons and Ad launches a preventive war, then in periods $t+1$ to $t+E$, the game follows the timing of the preceding paragraph and in period $t+E+1$, the timing of the game reverts to the timing of period 1 (with the same rules determining the timing of the game in subsequent periods).

We solve for equilibrium strategies when the intensity of conflict is high, assuming a common discount factor δ. We impose that, at any information set, play is sequentially rational given beliefs, and beliefs are obtained using Bayes's rule whenever possible.

There can be multiple equilibria in an infinite-horizon game. First, restrict attention to the set of *Markov Perfect Equilibria* (MPEs). An

MPE requires that strategies are *Markovian*, i.e., they depend on history only through payoff-relevant state variables, here P's nuclear status (N_t), whether P has the option to nuclearize (O_t) and, if it does not, the number of periods (n_t) of the effectiveness of the preventive war that have passed already (by default, set $n_t = 0$). An MPE is a vector of Markovian strategies that are mutual best-responses, beginning at any date t for any value of the payoff-relevant state variables.

We then consider the set of *Perfect Public Equilibria* (PPEs). A PPE requires that strategies are *public*, i.e., they depend not just on the payoff-relevant state variables listed above, but on the full public history of the game, here the signals about P's investment decision, the offers from Ad, the decisions by P to accept or reject Ad's offers, and the decisions by Al to join a war on the side of P. A PPE is a vector of public strategies that are mutual best-responses, beginning at any date t for any public history.

If the efficient outcome cannot be sustained as part of an MPE, we ask whether it can be sustained as part of a PPE, if any public history revealing a deviation triggers the MPE. For simplicity, we restrict attention to the set of efficient PPEs in stationary strategies, where, along the equilibrium path, P does not invest in nuclear weapons, Ad makes a fixed offer $z_t = z^*$ after $s_t = 0$, which P accepts. If there is no efficient PPE in stationary strategies, countries play the MPE.

3.1 Solution

First focusing on MPEs, we note that if Ad does not declare a preventive war, the outcome is straightforward, since strategies are not history dependent.[9] Ad makes an offer that leaves P indifferent between war and peace, anticipating that Al would join a war if and only if the overlap of preferences in the current period is high, i.e., Ad offers $z_t = p(\kappa, p_o, N_t) - c_P(\kappa, p_o, N_t)$, where

$$p(\kappa, p_o, N_t) = p_o p(\kappa, 1, N_t) + (1 - p_o) p(\kappa, 0, N_t) \tag{5}$$

$$c_i(\kappa, p_o, N_t) = p_o c_i(\kappa, 1, N_t) + (1 - p_o) c_i(\kappa, 0, N_t) \tag{6}$$

---

[9] Also note that P's nuclear status is solely determined by its investment decision and Ad's preventive war decision.

Thus, after P's nuclearization, there is a unique MPE, where peace prevails and the division of the pie reflects P's enhanced military capabilities:

Proposition 7. If P possesses nuclear weapons at the start of period t', then in $t \geq t'$, there is a unique MPE where Ad offers $z_t^* = p(\kappa, p_o, 1) - c_P(\kappa, p_o, 1)$, which P accepts.

Proof. See section 5.3.

In contrast, while a preventive war is effective, there is a unique MPE, where peace prevails and the division of the pie reflects P's nonnuclear status:

Proposition 8. If a preventive war occurred in period t', then in $t' + 1 \leq t \leq t' + E$, there is a unique MPE where Ad offers $z_t^* = p(\kappa, p_o, 0) - c_P(\kappa, p_o, 0)$, which P accepts.

Proof. See section 5.3.

This suggests a particular angle on the benefit of nuclearization, i.e., that nuclear weapons allow P to obtain greater concessions from Ad.[10] Write $m(\kappa, p_o)$ for the expected military effect of nuclear weapons, i.e., $m(\kappa, p_o) = p_o m(\kappa, 1) + (1 - p_o) m(\kappa, 0)$. We can write the expected effect of nuclear weapons $e(\kappa, p_c, p_o)$ as $e(\kappa, p_c, p_o) = p_c m(\kappa, p_o)$, or

$$e(\kappa, p_c, p_o) = p_c \left\{ [p(\kappa, p_o, 1) - c_P(\kappa, p_o, 1)] - [p(\kappa, p_o, 0) - c_P(\kappa, p_o, 0)] \right\} \qquad (7)$$

Note that $e(\kappa, p_c, p_o)$ as defined here satisfies the assumptions of the previous section, where it was taken as exogenous.

Now, considering periods where P has the option to nuclearize, we show that the MPEs follow the structure of the PBEs of the one-shot game. There is an efficient MPE, where peace prevails and nuclearization does not occur, if an investment in nuclear weapons is not rationalizable or if it can be deterred, i.e., if the threat of preventive war is credible and the signal is sufficiently informative:

Proposition 9. Assume that P is nonnuclear in t and has the option to nuclearize, and consider an efficient MPE, where nuclearization does not occur and peace prevails. This MPE exists if and only if either (i) the expected effect of nuclear weapons, discounted and averaged over all periods of high-intensity conflict, is smaller than the cost of the investment

---

[10] On the political effect of nuclear weapons, see: Anderson, Debs, and Monteiro (2015).

$$\frac{\delta}{1 - \delta p_c} e(\kappa, p_c, p_o) \le k \tag{8}$$

or (ii) the expected effect of nuclear weapons, discounted and averaged over all periods of high-intensity conflict, is greater than the cost of preventive war

$$\frac{\delta}{1 - \delta p_c} e(\kappa, p_c, p_o) \ge c_P(\kappa, p_o, 0) + c_{Ad}(\kappa, p_o, 0) \tag{9}$$

and the signal is sufficiently informative

$$(1 - p_s) \frac{\delta}{1 - \delta p_c} e(\kappa, p_c, p_o) \le k \tag{10}$$

Proof. See section 5.3.

Similarly, there is an MPE where nuclearization occurs and peace prevails, if the investment is rationalizable and the threat of preventive war is not credible:

Proposition 10. Assume that P is nonnuclear in t and has the option to nuclearize, and consider an MPE where nuclearization occurs and peace prevails.[11] This MPE exists if and only if the expected effect of nuclear weapons, discounted and averaged over all periods of high-intensity conflict, is greater than the cost of the investment, i.e., condition (8) fails, and the expected effect of nuclear weapons, discounted and averaged over the effectiveness of a preventive war, is smaller than the cost of preventive war:

$$\frac{(1 - (\delta p_c)^{E+1})}{1 - \delta p_c} \delta e(\kappa, p_c, p_o) \le c_P(\kappa, p_o, 0) + c_{Ad}(\kappa, p_o, 0) \tag{11}$$

Proof. See section 5.3.[12]

Finally, there is an MPE where nuclearization and war are possible outcomes, if the investment is rationalizable, the threat

---

[11] We ignore knife-edge conditions in the parameter space, where nuclearization could occur with probability strictly between 0 and 1.

[12] Conditions (9) and (11) differ due to the one-deviation principle. For the efficient MPE, *Ad* must respond to $s_t = 1$ with preventive war, when in equilibrium P is deterred from investing. Here, *Ad* must not respond to $s_t = 1$ with preventive war, when in equilibrium P nuclearizes unimpeded.

of preventive war is credible, and the signal is not sufficiently informative:

Proposition 11. Assume that P is nonnuclear in t and has the option to nuclearize, and consider an MPE where nuclearization and war happen with positive probability.[13] Nuclearization occurs with probability

$$\frac{k}{\frac{\delta e(\kappa, p_c, p_o)}{1 - \delta p_c}} \left[1 + \frac{1 - p_s}{1 - \delta p_c} \left[\frac{1 - (\delta p_c)^{E+1}}{1 - \delta p_c} \frac{\delta e(\kappa, p_c, p_o)}{c_P(\kappa, p_o, 0) + c_{Ad}(\kappa, p_o, 0)} - 1 \right] \right]^{-1}$$

and preventive war occurs with probability

$$1 - \frac{k}{\frac{\delta e(\kappa, p_c, p_o)}{1 - \delta p_c}} \left[1 - p_s \left[1 - \frac{1 - \delta p_c}{\frac{1 - (\delta p_c)^{E+1}}{1 - \delta p_c} \frac{\delta e(\kappa, p_c, p_o)}{c_P(\kappa, p_o, 0) + c_{Ad}(\kappa, p_o, 0)} - \delta p_c} \right] \right]^{-1} .$$

This MPE exists if and only if the signal is not sufficiently informative, i.e., condition (10) fails, and the expected effect of nuclear weapons, discounted and averaged over the effectiveness of a preventive war, is greater than the cost of war, i.e., condition (11) fails.

Proof. See section 5.3.

With the MPEs mirroring the equilibria of the one-shot game of the previous section, we obtain a first result that nuclearization is averted if it is sufficiently unlikely that P and Ad have conflictual preferences in the future:

Result 9. There is a value $\underline{p_c}$ such that if $p_c < \underline{p_c}$, then nuclearization does not occur.

Proof. Follows from Proposition 9 and the fact that $\lim_{p_c \to 0} \frac{\delta}{1 - \delta p_c} e(\kappa, p_c, p_o) = 0 < k$, so that condition (8) holds.

Second, we obtain that nuclearization can be deterred if information is perfect $(p_s = 1)$, as long as the probability of conflict is sufficiently high and players are sufficiently patient:

---

[13] We ignore the possibility that Ad would respond to an unambiguous signal of a proliferation attempt with a mixed strategy, which is not a compelling possibility. Knowing that P is proliferating, Ad should pick a pure strategy.

Result 10. The efficient MPE exists if the signal is perfectly informative, the probability of conflict is sufficiently high and players are sufficiently patient, i.e., if $p_s = 1$, then there exists values $\underline{p_c}$, $\underline{\delta}$, such that if $p_c > \underline{p_c}$, $\delta > \underline{\delta}$, then the efficient MPE exists.

Proof. Follows from Proposition 9, the fact that

$$\lim_{\delta p_c \to 1} \frac{\delta}{1 - \delta p_c} e(\kappa, p_c, p_o) = \infty > c_P(\kappa, p_o, 0) + c_{Ad}(\kappa, p_o, 0), \text{ so that condi-}$$

tion (9) holds, and the fact that condition (10) holds if $p_s = 1$.

This result suggests that repeated interaction can work in favor of nonnuclearization. If *Ad* is sufficiently patient and the probability of conflict is sufficiently high, then *Ad*'s threat of preventive war becomes credible (condition (9) holds). Declaring war entails a short-term cost, since war is inefficient, but a long-term benefit, given that *Ad* avoids making greater concessions to the potential proliferator. Certain that a proliferation attempt would be caught, *P* is deterred from investing in nuclear weapons (condition (10) holds).

Under imperfect information, however, *P* may be tempted to invest. Yet, because nuclearization is a costly attempt to change the balance of power, which could trigger a preventive war, there should be some space for a nonproliferation deal. Let us try to construct an efficient PPE in stationary strategies, assuming that after any public deviation, players revert to the MPE. Unfortunately, we show that the efficient PPE may not exist:

Result 11. For any imperfect signal, if the probability of conflict is sufficiently high, players are sufficiently patient, and the effectiveness of preventive war reaches a minimum threshold, then the efficient PPE exists if and only if

$$\frac{(1 - p_s)\delta e(\kappa, p_c, p_o) - (1 - \delta p_c)k}{p_s + (1 - p_s)\delta p_c} \leq \frac{1 - \delta p_c}{1 - (\delta p_c)^{E+1}}$$

$$\delta p_c \left(c_P(\kappa, p_o, 0) + c_{Ad}(\kappa, p_o, 0) \right) \tag{12}$$

This condition fails if the probability of conflict is sufficiently high, players are sufficiently patient, and the effectiveness of preventive war is sufficiently high. Also, the greater is the quality of the signal, the more stringent are the conditions for war. Technically, $\forall p_s < 1$, there are values $\underline{E}(p_s)$, $\underline{p}_c$, $\underline{\delta}$, such that if $p_c > \underline{p}_c$, $\delta > \underline{\delta}$, $E > \underline{E}(p_s)$, then the efficient PPE does not exist. Moreover, $\underline{E}(p_s)$ is increasing in p_s.

Proof. See section 5.3.

The logic of the result is as follows. For any imperfect signal, if the probability of conflict is sufficiently high and players are sufficiently patient, then an investment in nuclear weapons is rationalizable and cannot be deterred with the threat of preventive war (conditions (8) and (10) fail). Investing in nuclear weapons entails a one-time cost but long-term benefits. Greater patience only increases the incentives to nuclearize. Similarly, launching a preventive war entails a one-time cost but long-term benefits during the period of time when the preventive war effectively removes P's ability to invest in a nuclear-weapons capability. Therefore, if the effectiveness of preventive war reaches a minimum threshold, then the threat of preventive war becomes credible (condition (11) fails).

The fact that nuclearization and preventive war are costly creates a bargaining space, shown in condition (12), where the left-hand side is P's minimum demand and the right-hand side is Ad's maximum offer. However, since deviations entail long-term benefits, greater patience only increases the incentives to deviate, making war inevitable if the probability of conflict is sufficiently high and the effectiveness of a preventive war is sufficiently long.

Note that increasing the quality of the signal facilitates peace. If the signal is of higher quality, a proliferation attempt is more likely to be caught, lowering P's minimum demand (as p_s increases, the left-hand side of condition (12) decreases). In turn, if P requests smaller concessions, then Ad is less tempted to renege on a nonproliferation deal. Put differently, better information reduces the cost of peace and makes peace more likely.[14]

When the efficient PPE does not exist, we can confirm the effect of our key variables on the odds of nuclearization and war. In addition, we conclude that the more effective a preventive war, the more credible the threat of a preventive war. As a result, nuclearization becomes less likely, and preventive wars are more likely to be mistaken:

[14] See: Debs and Monteiro (2014). For another perspective on costly peace, see: Coe (2012).

Result 12. If the signal is imperfectly informative, the probability of conflict is sufficiently high, the effectiveness of a preventive war is sufficiently long, and players are sufficiently patient, then in equilibrium the following hold (technically, if $p_s < 1$, then there are values $\underline{p}_c$, $\underline{\delta}$, $\underline{E}(p_s)$, such that if $p_c > \underline{p}_c$, $\delta > \underline{\delta}$, $E > \underline{E}(p_s)$, the following hold):

(i)   The probability of nuclearization increases with *P*'s conventional capabilities (κ);
(ii) The probability of preventive war decreases with the quality of the signal (p_s);
(iii) The probability that a preventive war is mistaken decreases with the quality of the signal (p_s);
(iv) The probability of nuclearization decreases with the effectiveness of the preventive war (E);
(v)   The probability that a preventive war is mistaken increases with the effectiveness of the preventive war (E).

Proof. See section 5.3.

Finally, we can confirm the effect of *AI*'s support on the odds of nuclearization: reducing them if *P* is strong (by eliminating its willingness to proliferate) and increasing them if it is weak (by increasing its opportunity to proliferate):

Result 13. If the signal is sufficiently uninformative $\left(p_s < 1 - \dfrac{k}{c_P(\kappa_L, 0, 0) + c_{Ad}(\kappa_L, 0, 0)} \right)$, then there are values $\underline{E}$, $\overline{E}$ such that for any $E \in [\underline{E}, \overline{E}]$, there are values $\underline{\delta}(E)$, $\underline{p}_c(E)$, such that if $\delta > \underline{\delta}(E)$, $p_c > \underline{p}_c(E)$, then for any p_o, there is a value $\overline{\kappa}(p_o, E)$ with the following properties:

(i)   If $\kappa > \overline{\kappa}(p_o, E)$, then nuclearization does not occur. $\overline{\kappa}(p_o, E)$ is decreasing in p_o;
(ii) If $\kappa < \overline{\kappa}(1, E)$, then the probability of nuclearization increases in p_o.

Proof. See section 5.3.

4 Conclusion

In sum, a strategic and security-based approach to proliferation yields powerful predictions, by modeling nuclear proliferation as a costly investment with delayed returns. Nuclear weapons can improve the security of a potential proliferator, but also threaten its adversaries. Since nuclear weapons take time to be developed, the adversary could destroy a program before it comes to fruition.

Our first result is that nuclear weapons are acquired only when the potential proliferator attaches an important security benefit to nuclear weapons. If the "willingness threshold" is not met, then the potential proliferator cannot justify the costly investment in nuclear weapons. Yet, meeting this willingness threshold is not sufficient, a potential proliferator must also have the opportunity to proliferate. The greater are the conventional capabilities of the potential proliferator, the less credible are the adversary's threats of preventive war, and the more likely is the potential proliferator to acquire nuclear weapons.

The presence of an ally of the potential proliferator has two opposing effects on nuclear proliferation. First, it reduces the potential proliferator's willingness to acquire nuclear weapons. Second, it increases its opportunity to acquire nuclear weapons. The effect of these two countervailing dynamics depends on the capabilities of the potential proliferator. Strong potential proliferators would have the opportunity to acquire nuclear weapons on their own, and they have a relatively low willingness to acquire nuclear weapons since they can rely on conventional forces. The presence of an ally is likely to reduce proliferation by eliminating the potential proliferator's willingness to acquire nuclear weapons. Weak potential proliferators would not have the opportunity to proliferate on their own, and they see a large benefit in acquiring nuclear weapons since they can rely less on conventional forces. The presence of an ally is likely to increase proliferation by increasing the potential proliferator's willingness to proliferate.

By extrapolation, the framework suggests some policy prescriptions for effective nonproliferation efforts. Nuclear sponsors may want to use assurances with strong potential proliferators and coercive threats with weak potential proliferators.

5 Proofs

5.1 Adversaries and Proliferation

Proof. (Proof of Proposition 1). If $e(\kappa, p_c) \leq k$, then equilibrium strategies are as follows: P does not invest; for any signal, Ad offers $z = p(\kappa) - c_P(\kappa)$; P accepts $z \geq p(\kappa) - c_P(\kappa)$.

To see this, proceed by backward induction. P's decision to accept or reject an offer does not affect its nuclear status. Thus, P accepts the offer if and only if $z \geq p(\kappa) - c_P(\kappa)$.

Moving up, consider Ad's decision to strike preventively or make an offer z. Ad strictly prefers $z = p(\kappa) - c_P(\kappa)$ to any other offer. Offers $z > p(\kappa) - c_P(\kappa)$ are also accepted but provide a strictly lower pay-off. Offers $z < p(\kappa) - c_P(\kappa)$ are rejected and generate a strictly lower payoff, since $c_P(\kappa) + c_{Ad}(\kappa) > 0$ and P's rejection does not affect its nuclear status. Next, we show that Ad strictly prefers offering $z = p(\kappa) - c_P(\kappa)$ to declaring war. Offering $z = p(\kappa) - c_P(\kappa)$ gives Ad at least $1 - p(\kappa) + c_P(\kappa) - e(\kappa, p_c)$, which is better than the payoff of preventive war, $1 - p(\kappa) - c_{Ad}(\kappa)$, since $e(\kappa, p_c) \leq k < c_P(\kappa) + c_{Ad}(\kappa)$.

Moving up, consider P's investment decision. P chooses to invest if and only if $k \leq e(\kappa, p_c)$, which fails by assumption.

Proof. (Proof of Proposition 2). If $k < e(\kappa, p_c) < c_P(\kappa) + c_{Ad}(\kappa)$, then equilibrium strategies are as follows: P invests; for any signal, Ad offers $z = p(\kappa) - c_P(\kappa)$; P accepts any $z \geq p(\kappa) - c_P(\kappa)$.

This follows from the same steps as the proof of Proposition 1, the difference being that P chooses to invest, since $e(\kappa, p_c) > k$.

Proof. (Proof of Proposition 3). If $k < c_P(\kappa) + c_{Ad}(\kappa) < e(\kappa, p_c)$, then equilibrium strategies are as follows:

(i) If condition (1) holds: P does not invest; after signal $s = 0$, Ad offers $z = p(\kappa) - c_P(\kappa)$; after signal $s = 1$, Ad declares war; P accepts any $z \geq p(\kappa) - c_P(\kappa)$.

(ii) If condition (1) fails: P invests with probability

$$q^* = \frac{1}{p_s + (1 - p_s)\dfrac{e(\kappa, p_c)}{c_P(\kappa) + c_{Ad}(\kappa)}}; \text{ after signal } s = 0, \text{ then } Ad \text{ offers}$$

$z = p(\kappa) - c_P(\kappa)$ with probability $r^* = \dfrac{k}{(1 - p_s)e(\kappa, p_c)}$ and declares war with probability $1 - r^*$; after signal $s = 1$, Ad declares war; P accepts any $z \geq p(\kappa) - c_P(\kappa)$.

To see this, note that given the proofs above, P accepts any offer $z \geq p(\kappa) - c_P(\kappa)$ and Ad chooses between offering $z = p(\kappa) - c_P(\kappa)$ and declaring war. If $s = 1$, Ad believes that $I = 1$ and strictly prefers to declare war, since $e(\kappa, p_c) > c_P(\kappa) + c_{Ad}(\kappa)$.

If condition (1) holds, P prefers not to invest since doing so gives at most $-k + p(\kappa) - c_P(\kappa) + (1 - p_s)e(\kappa, p_c)$. Since P does not invest, Ad offers $z = p(\kappa) - c_P(\kappa)$ after signal $s = 0$. This completes case (i).

Assume that condition (1) fails.[15] Let P invest with probability q^*. After signal $s = 0$, let Ad offer $z = p(\kappa) - c_P(\kappa)$ with probability r^* and declare war with probability $1 - r^*$. First, note that $q^* \in (0,1)$. If $q^* = 1$, then Ad prefers $r = 0$, so that P prefers $q = 0$, a contradiction. If $q^* = 0$, then Ad prefers $r = 1$, so that P prefers $q = 1$, a contradiction. Second, note that $r^* \in (0,1)$. If $r^* = 1$, then P prefers $q = 1$, a contradiction. If $r^* = 0$, then P prefers $q = 0$, a contradiction. Thus, q^*, r^* are given by the indifference conditions:

$$p(\kappa) - c_P(\kappa) = -k + p(\kappa) - c_P(\kappa) + (1 - p_s)r^* e(\kappa, p_c)$$

$$1 - p(\kappa) - c_{Ad}(\kappa) = 1 - p(\kappa) + c_P(\kappa) - e(\kappa, p_c)\frac{q^*(1 - p_s)}{1 - q^* p_s}$$

completing the description of equilibrium strategies in case (ii). In this case, the probability of nuclearization is $q^*(1 - p_s)r^*$ and the probability of war is $1 - (1 - q^* p_s)r^*$.

Proof. (Proof of Result 3). Consider claim (i). The probability of

nuclearization is $q^*(1 - p_s)r^* = \dfrac{\dfrac{k}{e(\kappa, p_c)}}{p_s + (1 - p_s)\dfrac{e(\kappa, p_c)}{c_P(\kappa) + c_{Ad}(a)}} < 1$ when

$e(\kappa, p_c) > c_P(\kappa) + c_{Ad}(\kappa)$, which increases with κ, since $e(\kappa, p_c)$

---

[15] Ignore the knife-edge condition where $k = (1 - p_s)e(\kappa, p_c)$.

decreases with κ and $c_P(\kappa) + c_{Ad}(\kappa)$ increases with κ, and jumps to 1 when $e(\kappa, p_c) < c_P(\kappa) + c_{Ad}(\kappa)$.

Consider claim (ii). The probability of preventive war is 0 when $e(\kappa, p_c) < c_P(\kappa) + c_{Ad}(\kappa)$ and does not vary with p_s. If $e(\kappa, p_c) > c_P(\kappa) + c_{Ad}(\kappa)$, then the probability of preventive war is

$$1 - \left(1 - q^* p_s\right) r^* = 1 - \frac{\dfrac{k}{c_P(\kappa) + c_{Ad}(\kappa)}}{p_s + (1 - p_s)\dfrac{e(\kappa, p_c)}{c_P(\kappa) + c_{Ad}(\kappa)}}, \quad \text{which is decreas-}$$

ing in p_s.

Consider claim (iii). There are no preventive wars when $e(\kappa, p_c) < c_P(\kappa) + c_{Ad}(\kappa)$. When $e(\kappa, p_c) > c_P(\kappa) + c_{Ad}(\kappa)$, the probability that a preventive war is mistaken is

$$1 - \frac{\left(1 - r^*\left(1 - p_s\right)\right)q^*}{1 - \left(1 - q^* p_s\right) r^*} = 1 - \frac{1 - \dfrac{k}{e(\kappa, p_c)}}{p_s + (1 - p_s)\dfrac{e(\kappa, p_c)}{c_P(\kappa) + c_{Ad}(\kappa)} - \dfrac{k}{c_P(\kappa) + c_{Ad}(\kappa)}}$$

which is decreasing in p_s.

5.2 Adversaries, Allies, and Proliferation

Proof. (Proof of Proposition 4). If $e(\kappa, p_c, p_o) \le k$, then equilibrium strategies are as follows: P does not invest; for any signal, Ad offers $z = p(\kappa, p_o) - c_P(\kappa, p_o)$; P accepts any $z \ge p(\kappa, p_o) - c_P(\kappa, p_o)$; Al joins a war if and only if $o = 1$.

The proof follows the same logic as the proof of Proposition 1 and uses Lemma 1, given the simplifying assumption that Al's decision does not affect P's nuclear status, holding fixed P's investment decision and Ad's decision to declare a preventive war.

Proof. (Proof of Proposition 5). If $k < e(\kappa, p_c, p_o) < c_P(\kappa, p_o) + c_{Ad}(\kappa, p_o)$, then equilibrium strategies are as follows: P invests; for any signal, Ad offers $z = p(\kappa, p_o) - c_P(\kappa, p_o)$; P accepts any $z \ge p(\kappa, p_o) - c_P(\kappa, p_o)$; Al joins a war if and only if $o = 1$.

The proof follows the same logic as the proof of Proposition 2 and uses Lemma 1.

Proof. (Proof of Proposition 6). If $k < c_P(\kappa, p_o) + c_{Ad}(\kappa, p_o) < e(\kappa, p_c, p_o)$, then equilibrium strategies are as follows:

(i) If condition (4) holds: P does not invest; after signal $s = 0$, Ad offers $z = p(\kappa, p_o) - c_P(\kappa, p_o)$; after signal $s = 1$, Ad declares war; P accepts any $z \geq p(\kappa, p_o) - c_P(\kappa, p_o)$; Al joins a war if and only if $o = 1$.

(ii) If condition (4) fails: P invests with probability

$$q^* = \cfrac{1}{p_s + (1 - p_s)\cfrac{e(\kappa, p_c, p_o)}{c_P(\kappa, p_o) + c_{Ad}(\kappa, p_o)}}; \text{after signal } s = 0, Ad \text{offers}$$

$$z = p(\kappa, p_o) - c_P(\kappa, p_o) \text{ with probability } r^* = \frac{k}{(1 - p_s)e(\kappa, p_c, p_o)}$$

and declares war with probability $1 - r^*$; after signal $s = 1$, Ad declares war; P accepts any $z \geq p(\kappa, p_o) - c_P(\kappa, p_o)$; Al joins a war if and only if $o = 1$.

The proof follows the same logic as the proof of Proposition 3 and uses Lemma 1.

Proof. (Proof of Result 5). This follows from the assumption that $e(\kappa, p_c, p_o)$ decreases with κ and the assumption that $c_P(\kappa, j) + c_{Ad}(\kappa, j)$ increases with κ for any j, so that $c_P(\kappa, p_o) + c_{Ad}(\kappa, p_o)$ increases with κ.

Proof. (Proof of Result 6). Given that $e(\kappa, p_c, p_o)$ decreases with κ, we conclude that there is a value $\bar{\kappa}(p_c, p_o) \in [\kappa_L, \kappa_H]$ such that $e(\kappa, p_c, p_o) \leq k$ if and only if $\kappa \geq \bar{\kappa}(p_c, p_o)$.

Consider claim (i). If $e(\kappa, p_c, p_o) \leq k$, then nuclearization is not rationalizable and does not occur. Since $e(\kappa, p_c, p_o)$ decreases with p_o, then $\bar{\kappa}(p_c, p_o)$ decreases with p_o.

Consider claim (ii). If $\kappa < \bar{\kappa}(p_c, 1)$, then $e(\kappa, p_c, p_o) > k \; \forall p_o$. We use the fact that $e(\kappa, p_c, p_o)$ decreases with p_o and $c_P(\kappa, p_o) + c_{Ad}(\kappa, p_o)$ increases with p_o. If $e(\kappa, p_c, 1) > c_P(\kappa, 1) + c_{Ad}(\kappa, 1)$, then the probability of nuclearization is 0 for any p_o. If $e(\kappa, p_c, 0) > c_P(\kappa, 0) + c_{Ad}(\kappa, 0)$ and $e(\kappa, p_c, 1) < c_P(\kappa, 1) + c_{Ad}(\kappa, 1)$, then there is a value $\underline{p_o} \in (0, 1)$

such that the probability of nuclearization is 0 for $p_o < \underline{p_o}$ and 1 for $p_o > \underline{p_o}$. If $e(\kappa, p_c, 0) < c_P(\kappa, 0) + c_{Ad}(\kappa, 0)$, then the probability of nuclearization is 1 for any p_o.

Proof. (Proof of Result 7). The proof follows the same logic as the proof of Result 3.

Proof. (Proof of Result 8). As in the proof of Result 6, we conclude that for any p_o, there is a value $\overline{\kappa}(p_c, p_o) \in [\kappa_L, \kappa_H]$ such that $e(\kappa, p_c, p_o) \le k$ if and only if $\kappa \ge \overline{\kappa}(p_c, p_o)$.

The proof of claim (i) follows the same steps as the proof of claim (i) in Result 6.

The proof of claim (ii) also follows the same steps as the proof of claim (ii) in Result 6. The difference is that if $e(\kappa, p_c, p_o) > c_P(\kappa, p_o) + c_{Ad}(\kappa, p_o)$, then the probability of nucleariza-

tion is $q^*(1 - p_s)r^* = \dfrac{\dfrac{k}{e(\kappa, p_c, p_o)}}{p_s + (1 - p_s)\dfrac{e(\kappa, p_c, p_o)}{c_P(\kappa, p_o) + c_{Ad}(\kappa, p_o)}}$ which increases

with p_o, since $e(\kappa, p_c, p_o)$ decreases with p_o and $c_P(\kappa, p_o) + c_{Ad}(\kappa, p_o)$ increases with p_o.

If $\kappa < \overline{\kappa}(p_c, 1)$, then $e(\kappa, p_c, p_o) > k$ $\forall p_o$. If $e(\kappa, p_c, 1) > c_P(\kappa, 1) + c_{Ad}(\kappa, 1)$, then for any p_o, the probability of nuclearization is $q^*(1 - p_s)r^*$ as given above, which increases with p_o. If $e(\kappa, p_c, 0) > c_P(\kappa, 0) + c_{Ad}(\kappa, 0)$ and $e(\kappa, p_c, 1) < c_P(\kappa, 1) + c_{Ad}(\kappa, 1)$, then there is a value $\underline{p_o} \in (0, 1)$ such that the probability of nuclearization is given by $q^*(1 - p_s)r^* < 1$ above for $p_o < \underline{p_o}$ and 1 for $p_o > \underline{p_o}$. If $e(\kappa, p_c, 0) < c_P(\kappa, 0) + c_{Ad}(\kappa, 0)$, then the probability of nucleariza-tion is 1 for any p_o.

5.3 Infinite-Horizon Game

Proof. (Proof of Proposition 7). If $N_t = 1$, then in an MPE, equilibrium strategies if the intensity of conflict is high are as follows: *Ad* offers

$z_t^* = p(\kappa, p_o, 1) - c_P(\kappa, p_o, 1)$; P accepts any $z_t \geq p(\kappa, p_o, 1) - c_P(\kappa, p_o, 1)$; *Al* joins a war if and only if $o_t = 1$.

To see this, write $V_i^{MPE}(N_t, O_t, n_t)$ for the value of the game in an MPE for player i given the state variables. Consider *Al*'s strategy. *Al* joins a war if and if only if $p(\kappa, 1, 1)o_t - c(\kappa, 1, 1) + \delta V_{Al}^{MPE}(1, 0, 0) \geq p(\kappa, 0, 1)o_t - c(\kappa, 0, 1) + \delta V_{Al}^{MPE}(1, 0, 0)$ or $o_t = 1$. Using the same logic, P and *Ad*'s equilibrium strategies are as given in the Proposition.

Proof. (Proof of Proposition 8). If $N_t = 0$, $O_t = 0$, then in an MPE, equilibrium strategies if the intensity of conflict is high are as follows: *Ad* offers $z_t^* = p(\kappa, p_o, 0) - c_P(\kappa, p_o, 0)$; P accepts any $z_t \geq p(\kappa, p_o, 0) - c_P(\kappa, p_o, 0)$; *Al* joins a war if and only if $o_t = 1$.

The proof follows the same logic as the proof of Proposition 7, since none of the decisions has an effect on the future value of the state variables.

Proof. (Proof of Proposition 9). If $N_t = 0$, $O_t = 1$, then in the efficient MPE, equilibrium strategies if the intensity of conflict is high are as follows: P chooses not to invest in nuclear weapons; after $s_t = 0$, *Ad* offers $z_t^* = p(\kappa, p_o, 0) - c_P(\kappa, p_o, 0)$; after $s_t = 1$, *Ad* offers $z_t^* = p(\kappa, p_o, 0) - c_P(\kappa, p_o, 0)$ if condition (9) holds and declares war otherwise; P accepts any $z_t \geq p(\kappa, p_o, 0) - c_P(\kappa, p_o, 0)$; *Al* joins a war if and only if $o_t = 1$.

To see this, note that using the logic of the previous propositions, we determine *Al*'s strategy and P's decision to accept an offer if and only if $z_t \geq p(\kappa, p_o, 0) - c_P(\kappa, p_o, 0)$.

Consider *Ad*'s decision. By the usual logic, *Ad* chooses either to offer $z_t = p(\kappa, p_o, 0) - c_P(\kappa, p_o, 0)$ or to declare war. In an efficient MPE, *Ad* must offer $z_t = p(\kappa, p_o, 0) - c_P(\kappa, p_o, 0)$ after signal $s_t = 0$. After signal $s_t = 1$, *Ad* prefers to declare war if and only if

$$1 - p(\kappa, p_o, 0) - c_{Ad}(\kappa, p_o, 0) + \delta V_{Ad}^{MPE}(0, 0, 0)$$
$$\geq 1 - p(\kappa, p_o, 0) + c_P(\kappa, p_o, 0) + \delta V_{Ad}^{MPE}(1, 0, 0) \tag{13}$$

where, given Propositions 7 and 8, and the fact that the efficient MPE is played, $V_{Ad}^{MPE}(0, 0, 0) = \dfrac{p_c(1 - p(\kappa, p_0, 0) + c_P(\kappa, p_o, 0)) + (1 - p_c)\dfrac{u_{Ad}}{1 - \delta}}{1 - \delta p_c}$

and $\qquad V_{Ad}^{MPE}(1,0,0) = \dfrac{p_c(1 - p(\kappa, p_0, 1) + c_P(\kappa, p_o, 1)) + (1 - p_c)\dfrac{u_{Ad}}{1 - \delta}}{1 - \delta p_c}$.

Thus, condition (13) reduces to condition (9).

Now let us evaluate the conditions under which the efficient MPE exists. *Ad*'s decision is clearly optimal, given that war is inefficient and *P* does not invest in nuclear weapons.

As for *P*, investing provides at most

$-k + p(\kappa, p_o, 0) - c_P(\kappa, p_o, 0) + \delta V_P^{MPE}(1,0,0)$, where

$V_P^{MPE}(1,0,0) = \dfrac{p_c(p(\kappa, p_0, 1) - c_P(\kappa, p_o, 1)) + (1 - p_c)\dfrac{u_P}{1 - \delta}}{1 - \delta p_c}$. Not

investing provides $p(\kappa, p_o, 0) - c_P(\kappa, p_o, 0) + \delta V_P^{MPE}(0,1,0)$, where

$V_P^{MPE}(0,1,0) = \dfrac{p_c(p(\kappa, p_0, 0) - c_P(\kappa, p_o, 0)) + (1 - p_c)\dfrac{u_P}{1 - \delta}}{1 - \delta p_c}$. Thus, invest-

ing is not a profitable deviation if condition (8) holds.

Now assume that condition (8) fails. If condition (9) fails, by the above, *P* prefers to invest. If condition (9) holds, then *P*'s payoff from investing is $-k + p(\kappa, p_o, 0) - c_P(\kappa, p_o, 0) + \delta[p_s V_P^{MPE}(0,0,0) + (1 - p_s)V_P^{MPE}(1,0,0)]$,

where $V_P^{MPE}(0,0,0) = \dfrac{p_c(p(\kappa, p_0, 0) - c_P(\kappa, p_o, 0)) + (1 - p_c)\dfrac{u_P}{1 - \delta}}{1 - \delta p_c}$, given

Proposition 8 and the fact that the efficient MPE is played. Thus, investing is not a profitable deviation if and only if condition (10) holds.

Proof. (Proof of Proposition 10). If $N_t = 0$, $O_t = 1$, then in an MPE where *P* invests with some probability and peace prevails, equilibrium strategies if the intensity of conflict is high are as follows: *P* invests; *Ad* offers $z_t^* = p(\kappa, p_o, 0) - c_P(\kappa, p_o, 0)$ $\forall s_t$; *P* accepts any $z_t \geq p(\kappa, p_o, 0) - c_P(\kappa, p_o, 0)$; *Al* joins a war if and only if $o_t = 1$.

To see this, note that *Al*'s strategy and *P*'s decision to accept an offer are straightforward. Now, since *P* invests with positive probability and peace prevails, then *Ad* must offer $z_t = p(\kappa, p_o, 0) - c_P(\kappa, p_o, 0)$ $\forall s_t$. Finally, since *Ad* makes the same offer for all signals, *P* must invest with probability 1 (ignoring knife-edge conditions in the parameter space).

Now let us consider the conditions under which such an MPE exists. *Ad* prefers to offer $z_t = p(\kappa, p_o, 0) - c_P(\kappa, p_o, 0)$ if and only if condition (13) fails (or holds with equality). Given Proposition 8 and equilibrium strategies, we obtain

$$V_{Ad}^{MPE}(0,0,0) = \frac{1-(\delta p_c)^E}{1-\delta p_c}[p_c(1-p(\kappa, p_o, 0)+c_P(\kappa, p_o, 0))$$

$$+ (1-p_c)\frac{u_{Ad}}{1-\delta}] + (\delta p_c)^E V_{Ad}^{MPE}(0,1,0) \qquad (14)$$

$$V_{Ad}^{MPE}(0,1,0) = p_c[1-p(\kappa, p_0, 0)+c_P(\kappa, p_o, 0)$$

$$+ \delta V_{Ad}^{MPE}(1,0,0)] + (1-p_c)\frac{u_{Ad}}{1-\delta} \qquad (15)$$

Thus, condition (13) fails (or holds with equality) if and only if condition (11) holds.

Finally, *P*'s decision to invest is optimal if and only if condition (8) fails.

Proof. (Proof of Proposition 11). If $N_t = 0$, $O_t = 1$, then in an MPE where nuclearization and war occur with positive probability, equilibrium strategies if the intensity of conflict is high are as follows (assuming that *Ad* does not respond to signal $s_t = 1$ with a mixed strategy): *P* invests with probability

$$q^* = \frac{1}{p_s + \frac{1-p_s}{1-\delta p_c}\left[\frac{1-(\delta p_c)^{E+1}}{1-\delta p_c}\frac{\delta e(\kappa, p_c, p_o)}{c_P(\kappa, p_o, 0)+c_{Ad}(\kappa, p_o, 0)} - \delta p_c\right]} \qquad (16)$$

After signal $s_t = 0$, *Ad* offers $z_t^* = p(\kappa, p_o, 0) - c_P(\kappa, p_o, 0)$ with probability r^* and declares war with probability $1-r^*$, where

$$r^* = \frac{1}{1-p_s}\frac{k}{\frac{\delta e(\kappa, p_c, p_o)}{1-\delta p_c}} \qquad (17)$$

P accepts any $z_t \geq p(\kappa, p_o, 0) - c_P(\kappa, p_o, 0)$; *Al* joins a war if and only if $o_t = 1$.

To see this, note that *Al*'s strategy and *P*'s decision to accept an offer are straightforward. Now, since war occurs with positive probability and *Ad* responds to signal $s_t = 1$ with a pure strategy, then *Ad* must declare war after signal $s_t = 1$. Let q^* be the probability that *P* invests. Let *Ad* respond to signal $s_t = 0$ by offering $z_t = p(\kappa, p_o, 0) - c_P(\kappa, p_o, 0)$ with probability r^* and declaring war with probability $1 - r^*$. We can show that $q^* \in (0,1)$ and $r^* \in (0,1)$, in an equilibrium where both nuclearization and war happen with positive probability (ignoring knife-edge conditions on the parameter space). Next, q^* and r^* must satisfy the indifference conditions:

$$1 - p(\kappa, p_o, 0) - c_{Ad}(\kappa, p_o, 0) + \delta V_{Ad}^{MPE}(0,0,0) = 1 - p(\kappa, p_o, 0)$$

$$+ c_P(\kappa, p_o, 0) + \delta \frac{q^*(1-p_s)}{1 - q^* p_s} V_{Ad}^{MPE}(1,0,0) + \delta \frac{1-q^*}{1-q^* p_s} V_{Ad}^{MPE}(0,1,0)$$

$$-k + p(\kappa, p_o, 0) - c_P(\kappa, p_o, 0) + \delta\left(1 - (1-p_s)r^*\right)V_P^{MPE}(0,0,0)$$

$$+\delta(1-p_s)r^* V_P^{MPE}(1,0,0) = p(\kappa, p_o, 0) - c_P(\kappa, p_o, 0)$$

$$+\delta(1-r^*)V_P^{MPE}(0,0,0) + \delta r^* V_P^{MPE}(0,1,0)$$

To solve for q^*, use *Ad*'s indifference condition and the equilibrium of Proposition 8 (equation (14)) to conclude that

$$V_{Ad}^{MPE}(0,1,0) = \frac{1}{1 - \delta p_c}\left[p_c(1 - p(\kappa, p_o, 0) + c_P(\kappa, p_o, 0)) + (1 - p_c)\left(\frac{u_{Ad}}{1 - \delta}\right)\right]$$

$$- \frac{1}{1 - (\delta p_c)^{E+1}} p_c[c_P(\kappa, p_o, 0) + c_{Ad}(\kappa, p_o, 0)] \tag{18}$$

Also, use the fact that

$$V_{Ad}^{MPE}(1,0,0) = \frac{p_c(1 - p(\kappa, p_0, 1) + c_P(\kappa, p_o, 1)) + (1 - p_c)\dfrac{u_{Ad}}{1 - \delta}}{1 - \delta p_c}.$$

To solve for r^*, use *P*'s indifference condition and the equilibrium of Proposition 8 (which produces the equivalent of equation (14) for *P*) to conclude that

$$V_P^{MPE}(0,0,0) = V_P^{MPE}(0,1,0) = \frac{p_c\left(p(\kappa,p_o,0) - c_p(\kappa,p_o,0)\right) + (1-p_c)\dfrac{u_p}{1-\delta}}{1 - \delta p_c} \tag{19}$$

Also,   use   the   fact

that $V_P^{MPE}(1,0,0) = \dfrac{p_c\left(p(\kappa,p_0,1) - c_p(\kappa,p_o,1)\right) + (1-p_c)\dfrac{u_p}{1-\delta}}{1-\delta p_c}.$

The probability of nuclearization is $q^*(1-p_s)r^*$ and the probability of war is $1 - r^*(1 - q^* p_s)$, which simplify to the expressions in the statement of the proposition, once we

rewrite $q^* = \dfrac{1}{1 + \dfrac{1-p_s}{1-\delta p_c}\left[\dfrac{1-(\delta p_c)^{E+1}}{1-\delta p_c}\dfrac{\delta e(\kappa,p_c,p_o)}{c_p(\kappa,p_o,0) + c_{Ad}(\kappa,p_o,0)} - 1\right]}.$

Now let us consider the conditions under which such an MPE exists. Clearly, no player has a strictly profitable deviation. We just need to verify that q^*, $r^* \in (0,1)$. $q^* \in (0,1)$ if and only if condition (11) fails; $r^* \in (0,1)$ if and only if condition (10) fails.

Proof. (Proof of Result 11). Fix $p_s < 1$, then $\lim\limits_{\delta p_c \to 1}(1-p_s) \times \dfrac{\delta}{1-\delta p_c} e(\kappa,p_c,p_o) = \infty > k$, so that condition (10) fails. Also,

$\lim\limits_{\delta p_c \to 1, E \to \infty} \dfrac{(1-(\delta p_c)^{E+1})}{1-\delta p_c} \delta e(\kappa,p_c,p_o) = \infty > c_p(\kappa,p_o,0) + c_{Ad}(\kappa,p_o,0)$, so

that condition (11) fails.

If conditions (10) and (11) fail, then in any period t along the equilibrium path of an efficient PPE, strategies if the intensity of conflict is high are as follows: P does not invest; after signal $s_t = 0$, Ad offers z^* such that

$$z^* \le p(\kappa,p_o,0) - c_p(\kappa,p_o,0) + \frac{1-\delta p_c}{1-(\delta p_c)^{E+1}}\delta p_c\left(c_p(\kappa,p_o,0) + c_{Ad}(\kappa,p_o,0)\right) \tag{20}$$

$$z^* \ge p(\kappa,p_0,0) - c_p(\kappa,p_o,0) + \frac{(1-p_s)\delta e(\kappa,p_c,p_o) - (1-\delta p_c)k}{p_s + (1-p_s)\delta p_c} \tag{21}$$

after signal $s_t = 1$, *Ad* declares war; *P* accepts any $z_t \geq p(\kappa, p_o, 0) - c_P(\kappa, p_o, 0)$; *Al* joins a war if and only if $o_t = 1$. In any period t following a public history of a deviation from the efficient PPE, then players play the MPE of Proposition 11.

To see this, consider period t if for all $t' < t$ *P* did not invest, *Ad* offered z^*, which *P* accepted. *Al*'s decision is straightforward, since *Al* moves only if there was a public deviation from the PPE, so that players expect the MPE to be played from then on.

Consider *P*'s decision to accept or reject an offer. If there was a public deviation in period t, *P* accepts any $z_t \geq p(\kappa, p_o, 0) - c_P(\kappa, p_o, 0)$. Otherwise, *P* accepts if $z^* + \delta V_P^{PPE}(0,1,0) \geq p(\kappa, p_o, 0) - c_P(\kappa, p_o, 0) + \delta V_P^{MPE}(0,1,0)$, which reduces to $z^* \geq p(\kappa, p_o, 0) - c_P(\kappa, p_o, 0)$, using equation (19) and the fact that $V_P^{PPE}(0,1,0) = \dfrac{p_c z^* + (1 - p_c)\dfrac{u_P}{1 - \delta}}{1 - \delta p_c}$.

Ad's decision to launch a preventive war after signal $s_t = 1$ is straightforward, since $s_t = 1$ reveals that *P* deviated, and condition (11) fails.

Now let us verify the condition under which this PPE exists. After signal $s_t = 0$, *Ad* could deviate either by declaring war or by offering $z_t = p(\kappa, p_o, 0) - c_P(\kappa, p_o, 0)$. *Ad* strictly prefers the latter if and only if $1 - p(\kappa, p_o, 0) + c_P(\kappa, p_o, 0) + \delta V_{Ad}^{MPE}(0,1,0) \geq 1 - p(\kappa, p_o, 0) - c_{Ad}(\kappa, p_o, 0) + \delta V_{Ad}^{MPE}(0,0,0)$, which holds given equations (14) and (18). *Ad* does not deviate to offer $z_t = p(\kappa, p_o, 0) - c_P(\kappa, p_o, 0)$ if and only if

$1 - p(\kappa, p_o, 0) + c_P(\kappa, p_o, 0) + \delta V_{Ad}^{MPE}(0,1,0) \leq 1 - z^* + \delta V_{Ad}^{PPE}(0,1,0)$,

which reduces to condition (20), given equation (18) and the fact that $V_{Ad}^{PPE}(0,1,0) = \dfrac{p_c(1 - z^*) + (1 - p_c)ac\dfrac{u_{Ad}}{1 - \delta}}{1 - \delta p_c}$.

P does not invest in nuclear weapons if and only if $-k + p_s[p(\kappa, p_o, 0) - c_P(\kappa, p_o, 0) + \delta V_P^{MPE}(0,0,0)] + (1 - p_s)[z^* + \delta V_P^{MPE}(1,0,0)] \leq z^* + \delta V_P^{PPE}(0,1,0)$, which reduces to condition (21).

An efficient PPE exists if and only if conditions (20) and (21) are compatible. As p_c and δ approach 1, the two conditions are compatible if and only if $E \le \underline{E}(p_s) = \dfrac{c_P(\kappa,p_o,0)+c_{Ad}(\kappa,p_o,0)}{(1-p_s)m(\kappa,p_o)}-1$. Clearly, $\underline{E}(p_s)$ is increasing in p_s.

Proof. (Proof of Result 12). Using Result 11, the conditions in the statement ensure that conditions (10) and (11) fail, so that the efficient PPE does not exist and the MPE of Proposition 11 is played.

Consider claim (i). The probability of nuclearization is $q^*(1-p_s)r^*$ as given in the statement of Proposition 11, which is increasing in κ, since $e(\kappa,p_c,p_o)$ is decreasing in κ and $c_P(\kappa,p_o,0)+c_{Ad}(\kappa,p_o,0)$ is increasing in κ.

Consider claim (ii). The probability of preventive war is $1-(1-q^*p_s)r^*$ as given in the statement of Proposition 11, which is decreasing in p_s.

Consider claim (iii). The probability that a preventive war is mistaken can be written as

$$1-\dfrac{\left(1-r^*(1-p_s)\right)q^*}{1-(1-q^*p_s)r^*}=1-\dfrac{1-\dfrac{\dfrac{k}{\delta e(\kappa,p_c,p_o)}}{1-\delta p_c}}{\dfrac{1-(1-q^*p_s)r^*}{q^*}} \tag{22}$$

This is decreasing in p_s, since $1-(1-q^*p_s)r^*$ is decreasing in p_s given claim (ii) and $\dfrac{1}{q^*}$ is decreasing in p_s.

Consider claim (iv). The probability of nuclearization is $q^*(1-p_s)r^*$, which is decreasing in E, since q^* is decreasing in E and r^* is invariant in E.

Consider claim (v). Given equation (22), the probability that a preventive war is mistaken increases in E since $\dfrac{1-r^*}{q^*}+r^*p_s$ increases in E, given that q^* decreases in E and r^* is invariant in E.

Proof. (Proof of Result 13). We show that there are values $\underline{E}$, $\bar{E}$ such that for any $E \in [\underline{E},\bar{E}]$, there are values $\underline{\delta}(E)$, $\underline{p}_c(E)$, such that if

$\delta > \underline{\delta}(E)$, $p_c > \underline{p}_c(E)$, then conditions (10) and (11) fail $\forall \kappa \in [\kappa_L, \kappa_H]$ and condition (12) holds if and only if $\kappa \in [\overline{\kappa}(p_o, E), \kappa_H]$, where $\overline{\kappa}(p_o, E)$ satisfies

$$\frac{(1-p_s)\delta p_c m(\overline{\kappa}(p_o, E), p_o) - (1-\delta p_c)k}{p_s + (1-p_s)\delta p_c}$$

$$= \frac{1-\delta p_c}{1-(\delta p_c)^{L+1}} \delta p_c \left(c_P(\overline{\kappa}(p_o, E), p_o, 0) + c_{Ad}(\overline{\kappa}(p_o, E), p_o, 0)\right) \qquad (23)$$

To see this, fix $p_s < 1$, then $\lim_{\delta p_c \to 1}(1-p_s)\dfrac{\delta}{1-\delta p_c} e(\kappa, p_c, p_o) = \infty > k$, so that condition (10) fails. Now, let $\underline{E} = \dfrac{c_P(\kappa_H, p_o, 0) + c_{Ad}(\kappa_H, p_o, 0)}{m(\kappa_H, p_o)} - 1$

and $\overline{E} = \dfrac{c_P(\kappa_H, p_o, 0) + c_{Ad}(\kappa_H, p_o, 0)}{(1-p_s)m(\kappa_H, p_o)} - 1$. Clearly, $\underline{E} < \overline{E}$.

$\underline{E} > 0$ is ensured by the assumption that κ_H is "large," so that $m(\kappa_H, p_o) < c_P(\kappa_H, p_o, 0) + c_{Ad}(\kappa_H, p_o, 0)$.

Next, note that $\forall E > \underline{E}$, then there are values $\delta'(E)$, $p_c'(E)$, such that if $\delta > \delta'(E)$, $p_c > p_c'(E)$, then condition (11) fails $\forall \kappa \in [\kappa_L, \kappa_H]$.

Also, we conclude that $\forall E < \overline{E}$, then there are values $\delta''(E)$, $p_c''(E)$, such that if $\delta > \delta''(E)$, $p_c > p_c''(E)$, then condition (12) holds if and only if $\kappa \in [\overline{\kappa}(p_o, E), \kappa_H]$, where $\overline{\kappa}(p_o, E)$ is defined above.

Consider claim (i). When conditions (10) and (11) fail, the efficient PPE exists if and only if condition (12) holds, or $\kappa > \overline{\kappa}(p_o, E)$. Note that $\overline{\kappa}(p_o, E)$ decreases with p_o, since $m(\kappa, p_o)$ decreases with κ and p_o and $c_P(\kappa, p_o, 0) + c_{Ad}(\kappa, p_o, 0)$ increases with κ and p_o.

Consider claim (ii). If $\kappa < \overline{\kappa}(1, E)$, then condition (12) fails $\forall p_o$. The probability of nuclearization is $q^*(1-p_s)r^*$, which increases in p_o, since $m(\kappa, p_o)$ decreases in p_o and $c_P(\kappa, p_o, 0) + c_{Ad}(\kappa, p_o, 0)$ increases in p_o.

Bibliography

Abraham, Itty. 1998. *The Making of the Indian Atomic Bomb*. London: Zed Books.

Abreu, Hugo. 1979. *O Outro Lado do Poder*. Rio de Janeiro: Nova Fronteira.

Academic Peace Orchestra Middle East. 2013. "Nuclear Disarmament in South Africa: Historic Events and the Lessons for the Middle East," Policy Brief Nos. 28/29, pp. 1–16.

Accinelli, Robert. 1996. *Crisis and Commitment: United States Policy toward Taiwan, 1950–1955*. Chapel Hill: University of North Carolina Press.

2007. "In Pursuit of a Modus Vivendi: The Taiwan Issue and Sino-American Rapprochement, 1969–1972," in *Normalization of U.S.-China Relations: An International History*, pp. 9–55. William C. Kirby, Robert S. Ross, and Gong Li, eds. Cambridge, MA: Harvard University Press.

Achen, Christopher H., and Duncan Snidal. 1989. "Rational Deterrence Theory and Comparative Case Studies," *World Politics*, Vol. 41, No. 2, pp. 143–169.

Agrell, Wilhelm. 1990. "The Bomb That Never Was: The Rise and Fall of the Swedish Nuclear Weapons Programme," in *Arms Races: Technological and Political Dynamics*, pp. 154–174. Nils Peter Gleditsch and Olav Njølstad, eds. London: Sage Publications.

Ahmed, Samina. 1999. "Pakistan's Nuclear Weapons Program: Turning Points and Nuclear Choices," *International Security*, Vol. 23, No. 4, pp. 178–204.

Ahmed, Samina, and David Cortright. 1998a. "Going Nuclear: The Weaponization Option," in *Pakistan and the Bomb: Public Opinion and Nuclear Options*, pp. 89–110. Samina Ahmed and David Cortright, eds. Notre Dame, IN: University of Notre Dame Press.

1998b. "Pakistani Public Opinion and Nuclear Weapons Policy," in *Pakistan and the Bomb: Public Opinion and Nuclear Options*, pp. 3–27. Samina Ahmed and David Cortright, eds. Notre Dame, IN: University of Notre Dame Press.

Ahonen, Pertti. 1995. "Franz-Josef Strauss and the German Nuclear Question, 1956–1962," *Journal of Strategic Studies*, Vol. 18, No. 2, pp. 25–51.

Albright, David. 1989. "Bomb potential for South America," *Bulletin of the Atomic Scientists*, Vol. 45, No. 4, pp. 19–20.

　　1994. "South Africa and the Affordable Bomb," *Bulletin of the Atomic Scientists*, Vol. 50, No. 4, pp. 37–47.

　　2002. "Iraq's Programs to Make Highly Enriched Uranium and Plutonium for Nuclear Weapons Prior to the Gulf War." Institute for Science and International Security. Available at: www.exportcontrols.org/iraqs_fm_history.html. Last accessed: January 26, 2015.

　　2010. *Peddling Peril: How the Secret Nuclear Trade Arms America's Enemies.* New York: Free Press.

Albright, David, and Corey Gay. 1998. "Taiwan: Nuclear Nightmare Averted," *Bulletin of the Atomic Scientists*, Vol. 54, No. 1, pp. 54–60.

Albright, David, and Mark Hibbs. 1993. "South Africa: The ANC [African National Congress] and the Atom Bomb," *Bulletin of Atomic Scientists*, Vol. 49, No. 3, pp. 32–37.

Albright, David, and Robert Kelley. 1995. "Has Iraq Come Clean at Last?" *Bulletin of the Atomic Scientists*, Vol. 51, No. 6, pp. 53–64.

Alcañiz, Isabella. 2000. "Slipping into Something More Comfortable: Argentine-Brazilian Nuclear Integration and the Origins of the Mercosur," in *Questioning Geopolitics: Political Projects in a Changing World-System*, pp. 155–168. Georgi M. Derluguian and Scott Greer, eds. Westport, CT: Greenwood Press.

Alexander, Yonah, and Allan Nanes, eds. 1980. *The United States and Iran: A Documentary History.* Frederick, MD: University Publications of America, Inc.

Al-Marashi, Ibrahim. 2010. "Saudi Petro-Nukes? Riyadh's Nuclear Intentions and Regime Survival Strategies," in *Forecasting Nuclear Proliferation in the 21st Century. Volume 2: A Comparative Perspective*, pp. 76–99. William C. Potter with Gaukhar Mukhatzhanova, eds. Stanford, CA: Stanford University Press.

Alteras, Isaac. 1993. *Eisenhower and Israel: US-Israeli relations, 1953–1960.* Gainesville: University of Florida Press.

Alterman, Jon B. 2006. "Libya and the US: The Unique Libyan Case," *Middle East Quarterly*, Vol. 13, No. 1, pp. 21–29.

Alvandi, Roham. 2014. "The Shah's Détente with Khrushchev: Iran's 1962 Missile Base Pledge to the Soviet Union," *Cold War History*, Vol. 14, No. 3, pp. 423–444.

Anderson, Nicholas D. 2016. "Anarchic Threats and Hegemonic Assurances: Japan's Security Production in the Postwar Era," *International Relations of the Asia-Pacific*, forthcoming.

Anderson, Nicholas D., Alexandre Debs, and Nuno P. Monteiro. 2015. "The Political Effects of Nuclear Proliferation," Yale University mimeo.

Anderson, Robert S. 2010. *Nucleus and Nation: Scientists, International Networks, and Power in India*. Chicago: The University of Chicago Press.

Andrade, Ana Maria Ribeiro de. 2006. *A Opção Nuclear: 50 Anos Rumo à Autonomia*. Rio de Janeiro: MAST.

Andromidas, Dean, and Marcia Merry Baker. 2014. "Greece and a Marshall Plan for the Mediterranean," in *The New Silk Road Becomes the World Land-Bridge*, pp. 9–13. Nancy Spannaus, ed. Leesburg, VA: Executive Intelligence Review.

Argüello, Irma. 2011. "The Position of an Emerging Global Power: Brazilian Responses to the 2010 US Nuclear Posture Review," *The Nonproliferation Review*, Vol. 18, No. 1, pp. 183–200.

Armstrong, David, and Joseph Trento. 2007. *America and the Islamic Bomb: The Deadly Compromise*. Hanover, NH: Steerforth Press.

Aronson, Shlomo. 2000. "Israel's Nuclear Programme, the Six Day War and Its Ramifications." *Israel Affairs*, Vol. 6, Nos. 3/4, pp. 83–95.

2009. "David Ben-Gurion, Levi Eshkol and the Struggle over Dimona: A Prologue to the Six-Day War and Its (Un) Anticipated Results," *Israel Affairs*, Vol. 15, No. 2, pp. 114–134.

Bahgat, Gawdat. 2006. "Nuclear Proliferation: The Case of Saudi Arabia," *Middle East Journal*, Vol. 60, No. 3, pp. 421–443.

Bajpai, Kanti. 2003. "Strategic Threats and Nuclear Weapons: India, China and Pakistan," in *Prisoners of the Nuclear Dream*, pp. 27–52. M. V. Ramana and C. Rammanohar Reddy, eds. Hyderabad, India: Orient Longman.

Bajpai, Kanti P., P. R. Chari, Pervaiz Iqbal Cheema, Stephen P. Cohen, and Sumit Ganguly. 1995. *Brasstacks and Beyond: Perception and Management of Crisis in South Asia*. New Delhi: Manohar.

Baker, Pauline H. 1989. *The United States and South Africa: The Reagan Years*. New York: Ford Foundation.

Barber, James, and John Barratt. 1990. *South Africa's Foreign Policy: The Search for Status and Security 1945–1988*. New York: Cambridge University Press.

Barbier, Colette. 1990. "Les négociations franco-germano-italiennes en vue de l'établissement d'une coopération militaire nucléaire au cours des années 1956–1958," *Revue d'Histoire Diplomatique*, Vol. 104, No. 1–2, pp. 81–113.

2012. "La France et la force multilaterale (MLF)," in *La France et l'OTAN*, pp. 285–305. Maurice Vaisse, Pierre Melandri, and Frederic Bozo, eds. Bruxelles: Andre Versailles.

Barletta, Michael. 1997. "The Military Nuclear Program in Brazil," Center for International Security and Arms Control, Stanford University working paper.

Barnett, A. Doak. 1977. *China and the Major Powers in East Asia.* Washington, D.C.: Brookings Institution Press.

Barnhart, Michael A. 1987. *Japan Prepares for Total War: The Search for Economic Security, 1919–1941.* Ithaca, NY: Cornell University Press.

Bas, Muhammet A., and Andrew J. Coe. 2012. "Arms Diffusion and War," *Journal of Conflict Resolution,* Vol. 56, No. 4, pp. 651–674.

2016a. "A Dynamic Theory of Nuclear Proliferation and Preventive War," *International Organization,* forthcoming.

2016b. "Give Peace a (Second) Chance: The Viability of Deals to Avoid Proliferation and War," Harvard University mimeo.

Bass, Gary J. 2013. *The Blood Telegram: Nixon, Kissinger, and a Forgotten Genocide.* New York: Vintage Books.

Bass, Warren. 2003. *Support Any Friend: Kennedy's Middle East and the Making of the U.S. – Israel Alliance.* Oxford: Oxford University Press.

Bates, Robert H., Avner Greif, Margaret Levi, and Jean-Laurent Rosenthal. 1998. *Analytic Narratives.* Princeton, NJ: Princeton University Press.

Beckley, Michael. 2015. "The Myth of Entangling Alliances: Reassessing the Security Risks of U.S. Defense Pacts," *International Security,* Vol. 39, No. 4, pp. 7–48.

Bell, Mark S. 2015. "Beyond Emboldenment: How Acquiring Nuclear Weapons Can Change Foreign Policy," *International Security,* Vol. 40, No. 1, pp. 87–119.

Bell, Mark S., and Nicholas L. Miller. 2015. "Questioning the Effect of Nuclear Weapons on Conflict," *Journal of Conflict Resolution,* Vol. 59, No. 1, pp. 74–92.

Bendjebbar, André. 2000. *Histoire secrète de la bombe atomique française.* Paris: Le Cherche Midi.

Bennett, D. Scott. 1998. "Integrating and Testing Models of Rivalry Duration," *American Journal of Political Science,* Vol. 42, No. 4, pp. 1200–1232.

Ben-Zvi, Abraham. 1998. *Decade of transition: Eisenhower, Kennedy, and the Origins of the American-Israeli alliance.* New York: Columbia University Press.

Betts, Richard K. 1987. *Nuclear Blackmail and Nuclear Balance.* Washington, D.C.: Brookings Institution Press.

1993. "Paranoids, Pygmies, Pariahs, and Nonproliferation Revisited," *Security Studies,* Vol. 2, Nos. 3/4, pp. 157–183.

2006. "The Osirak Fallacy." *National Interest,* Vol. 83, pp. 22–25.

Bhutto, Zulfikar Ali. 1969. *The Myth of Independence.* London: Oxford University Press.

Biddle, Stephen, James Embrey, Edward Filiberti, Stephen Kidder, Steven Metz, Ivan C. Oerlich, and Richard Shelton. 2004. *Toppling Saddam:*

Iraq and American Military Transformation. Carlisle Barracks, PA: U.S. Army War College, Strategic Studies Institute.

Bissell, Richard E. 1982. *South Africa and the United States: The Erosion of an Influence Relationship*. New York: Praeger.

Bleek, Philipp C. 2010a. "Does Proliferation Beget Proliferation? Why Nuclear Dominoes Rarely Fall." PhD dissertation, Georgetown University.

2010b. "Why Do States Proliferate? Quantitative Analysis of the Exploration, Pursuit, and Acquisition of Nuclear Weapons," in *Forecasting Nuclear Proliferation in the 21st Century: The Role of Theory*, Vol. 1, pp. 159–192. William C. Potter with Gaukhar Mukhatzhanova, eds. Stanford, CA: Stanford University Press.

Bleek, Philipp C., and Eric B. Lorber. 2013. "Security Guarantees and Allied Nuclear Proliferation," *Journal of Conflict Resolution*, Vol. 58, No. 3, pp. 429–454.

Blix, Hans. 2004. *Disarming Iraq*. New York: Pantheon.

Borstelmann, Thomas. 1993. *Apartheid's Reluctant Uncle: The United States and Southern Africa in the Early Cold War*. New York: Oxford University Press.

Botha, R. F. Pik. 2008. "Interview with Dr. Sue Onslow," *LSE Ideas*. Pretoria, South Africa.

Boutwell, Jeffrey. 1990. *The German Nuclear Dilemma*. Ithaca, NY: Cornell University Press.

Bowen, Wyn Q. 2006. *Libya and Nuclear Proliferation: Stepping Back from the Brink*. London: Routledge for the International Institute for Strategic Studies.

Bozo, Frédéric. 2001. *Two Strategies for Europe: De Gaulle, the United States and the Atlantic Alliance*. Lanham, MD: Rowman and Littlefield.

2012. "Chronique d'une decision annoncee: le retrait de l'organisation militaire (1965–1967)," in *La France et l'OTAN*, pp. 331–357. Maurice Vaïsse, Pierre Melandri, and Frédéric Bozo eds. Bruxelles: André Versailles.

2013. *Histoire Secrète de la Crise Irakienne: La France, les États-Unis et l'Irak. 1991–2003*. Paris: Éditions Perrin.

Bracken, Paul. 2012. *The Second Nuclear Age: Strategy, Danger, and the New Power Politics*. New York: Times Books.

Brady, Henry E. 2008. "Causation and Explanation in Social Science," in *The Oxford Handbook of Political Methodology*, pp. 217–270. Janet M. Box-Steffensmeier, Henry E. Brady, and David Collier, eds. Oxford: Oxford University Press.

Brady, Henry E., and David Collier, eds. 2004. *Rethinking Social Inquiry: Diverse Tools Shared Standards*. Lanham, MD: Rowman and Littlefield.

Brands, Hal. 2006. "Rethinking Nonproliferation: LBJ, the Gilpatric Committee, and U.S. National Security Policy," *Journal of Cold War Studies*, Vol. 8, No. 2, pp. 83–113.

2007. "Non-Proliferation and the Dynamics of the Middle Cold War: The Superpowers, the MLF, and the NPT," *Cold War History*, Vol. 7, No. 3, pp. 389–423.

2011. "Saddam and Israel: What Do the New Iraqi Records Reveal?" *Diplomacy & Statecraft*, Vol. 22, No. 3, pp. 500–520.

Brands, Hal, and David Palkki. 2011a. "Saddam, Israel, and the Bomb. Nuclear Alarmism Justified?" *International Security*, Vol. 36, No. 1, pp. 133–166.

2011b. "Why Did Saddam Want the Bomb?" *Foreign Policy Research Institute*. Available at: www.fpri.org/enotes/2011/201108.brands_palkki.iraqnuclear.html. Last accessed: March 9, 2014.

2012. "'Conspiring Bastards': Saddam Hussein's Strategic View of the United States," *Diplomatic History*, Vol. 36, No. 3, pp. 625–660.

Braun, Chain, and Christopher F. Chyba. 2004. "Proliferation Rings: New Challenges to the Nuclear Nonproliferation Regime," *International Security*, Vol. 29, No. 2, pp. 5–49.

Braut-Hegghammer, Målfrid. 2006. "Libya's Nuclear Turnaround: What Lies Beneath?" *The RUSI Journal*, Vol. 151, No. 6, pp. 52–55.

2011. "Revisiting Osirak: Preventive Attacks and Nuclear Proliferation Risks," *International Security*, Vol. 36, No. 1, pp. 101–132.

Brazinsky, Gregg Andrew. 2011. "Between Ideology and Strategy: China's Security Policy toward the Korean Peninsula since Rapprochement," in *Trilateralism and Beyond: Great Power Politics and the Korean Security Dilemma during and after the Cold War,* pp. 163–88, Robert A. Wampler, ed. Kent, OH: Kent State University Press.

Brecher, Michael, and Jonathan Wilkenfeld. 2000. *A Study of Crisis*. Ann Arbor: University of Michigan Press.

Bruzelius, Nils. 2008. "'Unilaterally if Necessary' – One Motive Behind the American Security Guarantee to Sweden," *Särtryck ur Tidskrift i Sjöväsendet*, Vol. 1, pp. 50–67.

Buckley, Roger. 1992. *US-Japan Alliance Diplomacy, 1945–1990*. New York: Cambridge University Press.

Buhite, Russell, and Wm. Christopher Hamel. 1990. "War for Peace: The Question of an American Preventive War Against the Soviet Union, 1945–1955," *Diplomatic History*, Vol. 14, No. 3, pp. 367–384.

Bullard, Monte, and Jing-dong Yuan. 2010. "Taiwan and Nuclear Weaponization: Incentives versus Disincentives," in *Forecasting Nuclear Proliferation in the 21st Century. Volume II: A Comparative Perspective*, pp. 182–202. William C. Potter with Gaukhar Mukhatzhanova, eds. Stanford, CA: Stanford University Press.

Bundy, McGeorge. 1988. *Danger and Survival: Choices about the Bomb in the First Fifty Years*. New York: Random House

Bunn, George. 1992. *Arms Control by Committee: Managing Negotiations with the Russians*. Stanford, CA: Stanford University Press.

Burgess, Stephen F. 2006. "South Africa's Nuclear Weapons Policies," *The Nonproliferation Review*, Vol. 13, No. 3, pp. 519–526.

Burgess, Stephen F., and Helen E. Purkitt. 2005. *South Africa's Weapons of Mass Destruction*. Bloomington: University of Indiana Press.

Burgess, Stephen F., Helen E. Purkitt, and Peter Liberman. 2002. "Correspondence: South Africa's Nuclear Decisions," *International Security*, Vol. 27, No. 1, pp. 186–194.

Burr, William. 2009. "A Brief History of U.S.-Iranian Nuclear Negotiations," *Bulletin of the Atomic Scientists*, Vol. 65, No. 1, pp. 21–34.

Burr, William, and Jeffrey T. Richelson. 2000–2001. "Whether to 'Strangle the Baby in the Cradle': The United States and the Chinese Nuclear Program, 1960–64," *International Security*, Vol. 25, No. 3, pp. 54–99.

Bush, Richard C. 2004. *At Cross Purposes: U.S.-Taiwan Relations since 1942*. London: M. E. Sharpe.

Buszynski, Leszek. 2013. *Negotiating with North Korea: The Six Party Talks and the Nuclear Issue*. New York: Routledge.

Byman, Daniel, and Jennifer Lind. 2010. "Pyongyang's Survival Strategy: Tools of Authoritarian Control in North Korea," *International Security*, Vol. 35, No. 1, pp. 44–74.

Calingaert, Daniel. 1988. "Nuclear Weapons and the Korean War," *Journal of Strategic Studies*, Vol. 11, No. 2, pp. 177–202.

Camargo, Guilherme. 2006. *O fogo os deuses: Uma historia da Energia Nuclear – Pandora 600 A.C.-1970*. Rio de Janeiro: Contraponto.

Campbell, Kurt M., Robert J. Einhorn, and Mitchell B. Reiss, eds. 2004. *The Nuclear Tipping Point: Why States Reconsider Their Nuclear Choices*. Washington, DC: Brookings Institution Press.

Campbell, Kurt M., and Tsuyoshi Sunohara. 2004. "Japan: Thinking the Unthinkable," in *The Nuclear Tipping Point: Why States Reconsider Their Nuclear Choices*, pp. 218–53. Kurt M. Campbell, Robert J. Einhorn, and Mitchell Reiss, eds. Washington, DC: Brookings Institution Press.

Canberra Commission on the Elimination of Nuclear Weapons. 1996. *Report of the Canberra Commission on the Elimination of Nuclear Weapons*. Canberra: Commonwealth of Australia.

Cantalapiedra, David García. 2009. "Spain, Burden-Sharing, and NATO Deterrence Policy," *Strategic Insights*, Vol. 8, No. 4.

Carasales, Julio C. 1995. "The Argentine-Brazilian Nuclear Rapprochement," *The Nonproliferation Review*, Vol. 2, No. 3, pp. 39–48.

1999. "The So-Called Proliferator That Wasn't': The Story of Argentina's Nuclear Policy," *The Nonproliferation Review*, Vol. 6, No. 4, pp. 51–64.

Cha, Victor D. 2001. "The Second Nuclear Age: Proliferation Pessimism versus Sober Optimism in South Asia and East Asia," *Journal of Strategic Studies*, Vol. 24, No. 4, pp. 79–120.

2002. "Hawk Engagement and Preventive Defense on the Korean Peninsula," *International Security*, Vol. 27, No. 1, pp. 40–78

2009–2010. "Powerplay: The Origins of the U.S. Alliance System in Asia," *International Security*, Vol. 34, No. 3, pp. 158–196.

2012. *The Impossible State: North Korea, Past and Future.* New York: Ecco.

Cha, Victor D., and David C. Kang. 2003. *Nuclear North Korea: A Debate on Engagement Strategies.* New York: Columbia University Press.

Chafetz, Glenn, Hillel Abramson, and Suzette Grillot. 1996. "Role Rheory and Foreign Policy: Belarussian and Ukranian Compliance with the Nuclear Nonproliferation Regime," *Political Psychology*, Vol. 17, No. 4, pp. 727–757.

Chakma, Bhumitra. 2004. *Strategic Dynamics and Nuclear Weapons Proliferation in South Asia: A Historical Analysis.* Bern: Peter Lang.

Chang, Gordon H. 1990. *Friends and Enemies: The United States, China, and the Soviet Union, 1948–1972.* Stanford, CA: Stanford University Press.

Cheema, Pervaiz Iqbal. 1987. "American Policy in South Asia: Interests and Objectives," in *The Security of South Asia: American and Asian Perspectives*, pp. 119–133. Stephen P. Cohen, ed. Chicago: University of Illinois Press.

Chellaney, Brahma. 1994. "India," in *Nuclear Proliferation after the Cold War*, pp. 165–90. Mitchell Reiss and Robert S. Litwak, eds. Cambridge, MA: Ballinger.

Chen Jian. 2001. *Mao's China and the Cold War.* Chapel Hill: University of North Carolina Press.

2004. "In the Name of the Revolution: China's Road to the Korean War Revisited," in *The Korean War in World History*, pp. 93–125. William Stueck, ed. Lexington: The University Press of Kentucky.

Chen Jian, and Yang Kuisong. 1998. "Chinese Politics and the Collapse of the Sino-Soviet Alliance," in *Brothers in Arms: The Rise and Fall of the Sino-Soviet Alliance 1949–1963*, pp. 246–294. Odd Arne Westad, ed. Washington, DC: Woodrow Wilson Center Press.

Chengappa, Raj. 2000. *Weapons of Peace: The Secret Story to India's Quest to Be a Nuclear Power.* New Delhi: HarperCollins.

Chestnut, Sheena. 2007. "Illicit Activity and Proliferation: North Korean Smuggling Networks," *International Security*, Vol. 32, No. 1, pp. 80–111.

Chinoy, Mike. 2008. *Meltdown: The Inside Story of the North Korean Nuclear Crisis*. New York: St. Martin's Press.

Chislett, William. 2005. "Spain and the United States: The Quest for Mutual Rediscovery." Madrid: Real Instituto Elcano de Estudios Internacionales y Estratégicos.

Choi, Kang, and Joon-Sung Park. 2009. "South Korea: Fears of Abandonment and Entrapment," in *The Long Shadow: Nuclear Weapons and Security in 21st Century Asia*, pp. 373–403. Muthiah Alagappa, ed. Stanford, CA: Stanford University Press.

Choi, Lyong. 2014. "The First Nuclear Crisis in the Korea Peninsula, 1975–76," *Cold War History*, Vol. 14, No. 1, pp. 71–90.

Christensen, Thomas J. 1996. *Useful Adversaries: Grand Strategy, Domestic Mobilization, and Sino-American Conflict, 1947–1958*. Princeton, NJ: Princeton University Press.

Chubin, Shahram, and Sepehr Zabih. 1974. *The Foreign Relations of Iran: A Developing State in a Zone of Great-Power Conflict*. Berkeley: University of California Press.

Claire, Rodger W. 2004. *Raid On the Sun: Inside Israel's Secret Campaign That Denied Saddam the Bomb*. New York: Broadway Books.

Clinton, Hillary. 2011. "America's Pacific Century: The Future of Geopolitics Will Be Decided in Asia, Not in Afghanistan or Iraq, and the United States Should Be Right at the Center of the Action," *Foreign Policy*, No. 189, pp. 56–63.

Coe, Andrew J. 2012. "Costly Peace: A New Rationalist Explanation for War," Harvard University Mimeo.

Coe, Andrew J., and Jane Vaynman. 2015. "Superpower Collusion and the Nuclear Nonproliferation Treaty," *Journal of Politics*, Vol. 77, No. 4, pp. 983–997.

Cohen, Avner. 1996. "Cairo, Dimona, and the June 1967 War," *Middle East Journal*, Vol. 50, No. 2, pp. 90–210.

1998. *Israel and the Bomb*. New York: Columbia University Press.

2005. "The Last Taboo: Israel's Bomb Revisited," *Current History*, Vol. 104, No. 681, pp. 169–175.

2007. "Crossing the Threshold: The Untold Nuclear Dimension of the 1967 Arab-Israeli War and Its Contemporary Lessons," *Arms Control Today*, Vol. 37, No. 5, pp. 12–16.

2008. "Israel: A Sui Generis Proliferator," in *The Long Shadow: Nuclear Weapons and Security in 21st Century Asia*, pp. 241–268. Muthiah Alagappa, ed. Stanford, CA: Stanford University Press.

Cohen, Avner, and Marvin Miller. 2010. "Bringing Israel's Bomb Out of the Basement: Has Nuclear Ambiguity Outlived Its Shelf Life?" *Foreign Affairs*, Vol. 89. No. 5, pp. 30–44.

Cohen, Michael J. 2005. *Strategy and Politics in the Middle East 1954–1960: Defending the Northern Tier*. London: Frank Cass.

Cohen, Stephen P. 2013. *Shooting for a Century: The India-Pakistan Conundrum*. Washington, DC: Brookings Institution Press.

Cohrs, Patrick. 2008. *The Unfinished Peace after World War I: America, Britain and the Stabilisation of Europe, 1919–1932*. Cambridge: Cambridge University Press.

Cole, Paul M. 1997. "Atomic Bombast: Nuclear Weapon Decision-Making in Sweden, 1946–72," *The Washington Quarterly*, Vol. 20, No. 2, pp. 233–251.

Conley, Jerome M. 2001. *Indo-Russian Military and Nuclear Cooperation: Lessons and Options for U.S. Policy in South Asia*. Oxford: Lexington Books.

Cooper, John Franklin. 1979. "Taiwan's Options," *Asian Affairs*, Vol. 6, No. 5, pp. 282–294.

Copeland, Dale. C. 2000. *The Origins of Major War*. Ithaca, NY: Cornell University Press.

Cordesman, Anthony H. 2015. "Military Spending and Arms Sales in the Gulf: How the Arab Gulf States Now Dominate the Changes in the Military Balance," Center for Strategic and International Studies. Available at: http://csis.org/files/publication/150428_gulfarmssales.pdf. Last accessed: December 29, 2015.

Corera, Gordon. 2006. *Shopping for Bombs: Nuclear Proliferation, Global Insecurity, and the Rise and Fall of the A. Q. Khan Network*. Oxford: Oxford University Press.

Costigliola, Frank. 1994. "Lyndon B. Johnson, Germany, and 'the End of the Cold War,'" in *Lyndon Johnson Confronts the World: American Foreign Policy, 1963–1968*, pp. 173–210. Warren I. Cohen and Nancy Bernkopf Tucker, eds. New York: Cambridge University Press.

Couloumbis, Theodore A. 1983. *The United States, Greece, and Turkey: The Troubled Triangle*. New York: Praeger.

Coutto, Tatiana. 2014. "An International History of the Brazilian-Argentina Rapprochement," *International History Review*, Vol. 36, No. 2, pp. 302–323.

Craig, Campbell, and Sergey Radchenko. 2008. *The Atomic Bomb and the Origins of the Cold War*. New Haven, CT: Yale University Press.

Craig, Campbell, and Jan Ruzicka. 2013. "The Nonproliferation Complex," *Ethics and International Affairs*, Vol. 27, No. 3, pp. 329–348.

Crawford, Timothy W. 2012. *Pivotal Deterrence: Third-Party Statecraft and the Pursuit of Peace*. Ithaca, NY: Cornell University Press.

Crescenzi, Mark J. C. 2003. "Economic Exit, Interdependence, and Conflict," *Journal of Politics*, Vol. 65, No. 3, pp. 809–832.

Crosbie, Sylvia. 1974. *A Tacit Alliance*. Princeton, NJ: Princeton University Press.

Cumings, Bruce. 1997. *Korea's Place in the Sun: A Modern History*. New York: W. W. Norton and Company.

2001. "U.S.-North Korean Bilateral Relations and South Korean Security," in *Korean Security Dynamics in Transition*, pp. 105–116. Kyung-Ae Park and Dalchoong Kim, eds. New York: Palgrave.

Dalsjö, Robert. 2014. "The Hidden Rationality of Sweden's Policy of Neutrality during the Cold War," *Cold War History*, Vol, 14, pp. 175–194.

Daniel, John. 2009. "Racism, The Cold War, and South Africa's Regional Security Strategies 1948–1990," in *Cold War in Southern Africa: White Power, Black Liberation*, pp. 35–54. Sue Onslow, ed. London: Routledge.

Debs, Alexandre, and Nuno P. Monteiro. 2012. "The Flawed Logic of Striking Iran," January 17, 2012. Foreign Affairs online. Available at: www.foreignaffairs.com/articles/middle-east/2012-01-17/flawed-logic-striking-iran. Last accessed: May 2, 2016.

2014. "Known Unknowns: Power Shifts, Uncertainty, and War," *International Organization*, Vol. 68, No. 1, pp. 1–31.

Debs, Alexandre, Nuno P. Monteiro, and David A. Lake. 2013. "What Caused the Iraq War? A Debate." *Duck of Minerva online*. July 30 – August 6. Available at: http://duckofminerva.com/tag/iraq-war. Last accessed: May 2, 2016.

Deeb, Mary-Jane. 1989. "Inter-Maghribi Relations since 1969: A Study of the Modalities of Unions and Mergers," *Middle East Journal*, Vol. 43, No. 1, pp. 20–33.

Department of Defense, Defense Science Board. 2014. *Task Force Report: Assessment of Nuclear Monitoring and Verification Technologies*. Washington, DC.

Deutch, John M. 1991. "The New Nuclear Threat," *Foreign Affairs*, Vol. 71, No. 4, pp. 120–134.

De Villiers, J. W., Roger Jardine, and Mitchell Reiss. 1993. "Why South Africa Gave Up the Bomb," *Foreign Affairs*, Vol. 72, No. 5, pp. 98–109.

Diamond, Alexis, and Jasjeet S. Sekhon. 2013. "Genetic Matching for Estimating Causal Effects: A General Multivariate Matching Method for Achieving Balance in Observational Studies," *Review of Economics and Statistics*, Vol. 95, No. 3, pp. 932–945.

Dokos, Thanos, and Panayotis Tsakonas. 1998. "Greece," in *Europe and Nuclear Disarmament: Debates and Political Attitudes in 16 European Countries*, pp. 147–160. Harald Müller, ed. Brussels: Presses Interuniversitaires Européennes.

Donaghy, Greg. 2007. "Nehru's Reactor: The Origins of Indo-Canadian Nuclear Cooperation, 1955–1959," in *Canada's Global Engagements and Relations with India*, pp. 267–278. Christopher Sam Raj and Abdul Nafey, eds. New Dehli: Manak.

Doner, Richard F., Bryan K. Ritchie, and Dan Slater. 2005. "Systemic Vulnerability and the Origins of Developmental States: Northeast and Southeast Asia in Comparative Perspective," *International Organization*, Vol. 59, No. 2, pp. 327–361.

Dower, John W. 1979. *Empire and Aftermath: Yoshida Shigeru and the Japanese Experience, 1878–1954*. Cambridge, MA: Harvard University Press.

Drezner, Daniel. 1999. *The Sanctions Paradox: Economic Statecraft and International Relations*. New York: Cambridge University Press.

Duelfer, Charles. 2004. "Comprehensive Report of the Special Advisor to the DCI on Iraq's WMD." September 30. Available at: www.cia.gov/library/reports/general-reports-1/iraq_wmd_2004/. Last accessed: March 15, 2016.

2009. *Hide and Seek: The Search for Truth in Iraq*. New York: Public Affairs.

Duncan, Peter J. S. 1989. *The Soviet Union and India*. New York: Council on Foreign Relations Press.

Dunn, Lewis A. 1982. *Controlling the Bomb: Nuclear Proliferation in the 1980s*. New Haven, CT: Yale University Press.

Du Preez, Jean, and Thomas Matteig. 2010. "From Pariah to Nuclear Poster Boy: How Plausible Is a Reversal?" in *Forecasting Nuclear Proliferation in the 21st Century. Volume 2: A Comparative Perspective*, pp. 302–334. William C. Potter with Gaukhar Mukhatzhanova, eds. Stanford, CA: Stanford University Press.

Duval, Marcel, and Dominique Mongin. 1993. *Histoire des Forces Nucléaires Françaises depuis 1945*. Paris: Presses Universitaires de France.

Easley, Leif-Eric. 2007. "Defense Ownership or Nationalist Security: Autonomy and Reputation in South Korea and Japanese Security Policies," *SAIS Review*, Vol. 27, No. 2, pp. 153–166.

Einhorn, Robert J. 2004. "Egypt: Frustrated but Still on a Non-Nuclear Course," in *The Nuclear Tipping Point. Why States Reconsider Their Nuclear Choices*, pp. 43–82. Kurt M. Campbell, Robert J. Einhorn, and Mitchell B. Reiss, eds. Washington, DC: Brookings Institution Press.

Engelhardt, Michael J. 1996. "Rewarding Non-Proliferation: The South and North Korean Cases," *Nonproliferation Review*, Vol. 3, No. 3, pp. 31–37.

Epstein, William. 1977. "Why States Go – And Don't Go – Nuclear," *Annals of the American Academy of Political and Social Science*, Vol. 430, No. 1, pp. 16–28.

Ergun, Doruk. 2015. "The Origins of Turkey's Nuclear Policy," in *Turkey's Nuclear Future*, pp. 63–85. George Perkovich and Sinan Ülgen, eds. Washington, DC: Carnegie Endowment for International Peace.

Erlander, Tage. 1976. *Tage Erlander 1955–1960*. Stockholm: Tiden.

Evangelista, Matthew A. 1982–1983. "Stalin's Postwar Army Reappraised," *International Security*, Vol. 7, No. 3, pp. 110–138.

Evron, Yair. 1994. *Israel's Nuclear Dilemma*. London: Routledge.

Fajardo, José Marcos Castellani. 2004. "Acordo Tripartite Itaipu-Corpus: ponto de inflexão entre a disputa geopolítica e a política de cooperação." Masters Thesis. Universidade Federal do Rio Grande do Sul.

Fearon, James D. 1991. "Counterfactuals and Hypothesis Testing in Political Science," *World Politics*, Vol. 43, No. 2, pp. 169–195.

1995. "Rationalist Explanations for War," *International Organization*, Vol. 49, No. 3, pp. 379–414.

2013. "The Nuclear Revolution, International Politics, and U.S. Foreign Policy." Stanford University Mimeo.

Ferguson, Niall. 2015. *Kissinger, Volume I: 1923–1968, the Idealist*. New York: Penguin Press.

Fig, David. 1999. "Sanctions and the Nuclear Industry," in *How Sanctions Work: Lessons from South Africa*, pp. 3–25. Neta C. Crawford and Audie Klotz, eds. New York: St. Martin's Press.

Fischer, Hannah. 2007. "North Korean Provocative Actions, 1950–2007," *CRS Report for Congress*, RL30004-1.

Fitzpatrick, Mark. 2010. "The Fragile Promise of the Fuel-Swap Plan," *Survival*, Vol. 52, No. 3, pp. 67–94.

Fitzpatrick, Mark, and Tim Huxley. 2009. *Preventing Nuclear Dangers in Southeast Asia and Australasia*. London: International Institute for Strategic Studies.

Foot, Rosemary J. 1988–1989. "Nuclear Coercion and the Ending of the Korean Conflict," *International Security*, Vol. 13, No. 3, pp. 92–112.

Foot, Rosemary. 1995. *The Practice of Power, U.S. Relations with China since 1949*. Oxford: Oxford University Press.

Frankel, Benjamin. 1993. "The Brooding Shadow: Systemic Incentives and Nuclear Weapons Proliferation," *Security Studies*, Vol. 2, Nos. 3–4, pp. 37–78.

Freedman, Lawrence. 2004. "War in Iraq: Selling the Threat," *Survival*, Vol. 46, No. 2, pp. 7–49.

Fudenberg, Drew, and Jean Tirole. 1991. *Game Theory*. Cambridge, MA: MIT Press.

Fuerth, Leon. 2004. "Turkey: Nuclear Choices among Dangerous Neighbors," in *The Nuclear Tipping Point: Why States Reconsider Their Nuclear Choices*, pp. 145–174. Kurt M. Campbell, Robert J. Einhorn, and Mitchell B. Reiss, eds. Washington, DC: Brookings Institution Press.

Fuhrmann, Matthew. 2009a. "Spreading Temptation: Proliferation and Peaceful Nuclear Cooperation Agreements," *International Security*, Vol. 34, No. 1, pp. 7–41.

2009b. "Taking a Walk on the Supply Side: The Determinants of Civilian Nuclear Cooperation," *Journal of Conflict Resolution*, Vol. 53, No. 2, pp. 181–208.

2012. *Atomic Assistance: How "Atoms for Peace" Programs Cause Nuclear Insecurity*. Ithaca, NY: Cornell University Press.

Fuhrmann, Matthew, and Sarah E. Kreps. 2010. "Targeting Nuclear Programs in War and Peace: A Quantitative Empirical Analysis, 1941–2000," *Journal of Conflict Resolution*, Vol. 54, No. 6, pp. 831–859.

Fuhrmann, Matthew, and Todd S. Sechser. 2014. "Nuclear Strategy, Nonproliferation, and the Causes of Foreign Nuclear Deployments," *Journal of Conflict Resolution*, Vol. 58, No. 3, pp. 455–480.

Furtig, Henner. 2007. "Conflict and Cooperation in the Persian Gulf: The Interregional Order and US Policy," *Middle East Journal*, Vol. 61, No. 4, pp. 627–640.

Gaddis, John Lewis. 1987. *The Long Peace: Inquiries into the History of the Cold War*. New York: Oxford University Press.

Gall, Norman, 1976. "Atoms for Brazil, Dangers for All," *Bulletin of the Atomic Scientists*, Vol. 32, No. 6, pp. 4–9, 42–48.

Gallicio, Marc. 2001. "Occupation, Dominion, and Alliance: Japan in American Security Policy, 1945–69," in *Partnership: The United States and Japan*, pp. 115–134. Akira Iriye and Robert A. Wampler, eds. Tokyo: Kodansha International.

Gallois, Pierre. 1976. "French Defense Planning – The Future in the Past," *International Security*, Vol. 1, No. 2, pp. 15–31.

Gamba-Stonehouse, Virginia. 1991. "Argentina and Brazil," in *Security with Nuclear Weapons? Different Perspectives on National Security*, pp. 229–256. Regina Cowen Karp, ed. Oxford: Oxford University Press.

Ganguly, Sumit. 1999. "India's Pathway to Pokhran II: The Prospects and Sources of New Delhi's Nuclear Weapons Program," *International Security*, Vol. 23, No. 4, pp. 148–177.

2008. "War, Nuclear Weapons, and Crisis Stability in South Asia," *Security Studies*, Vol. 17, No. 1, pp. 164–184.

Ganguly, Sumit, and Devin Hagerty. 2005. *Fearful Symmetry: India-Pakistan Crises in the Shadow of Nuclear Weapons*. Seattle: University of Washington Press.

Ganguly, Sumit, and S. Paul Kapur. 2010. *India, Pakistan, and the Bomb: Debating Nuclear Stability in South Asia*. New York: Columbia University Press.

Garris, Jerome H. 1973. "Sweden's Debate on Proliferation of Nuclear Weapons," *Cooperation and Conflict*, Vol. 8, No. 3–4, pp. 189–207.

Garthoff, Raymond L. 1995. "When and Why Romania Distanced Itself from the Warsaw Pact," *Cold War International History Project Bulletin*, Issue 5, p. 111.

Gartzke, Erik, and Dong-Joon Jo. 2009. "Bargaining, Nuclear Proliferation, and Interstate Disputes," *Journal of Conflict Resolution*, Vol. 53, No. 2, pp. 209–233.

Gartzke, Erik, and Matthew Kroenig. 2009. "A Strategic Approach to Nuclear Proliferation," *Journal of Conflict Resolution*, Vol. 53, No. 2, pp. 151–160.

Garver, John W. 1993. *Foreign Relations of the People's Republic of China*. Englewoods Cliffs, NJ: Prentice Hall.

Gat, Moshe. 2005. "Nasser and the Six Day War, 5 June 1967: A Premeditated Strategy or an Inexorable Drift to War?" *Israel Affairs*, Vol. 11, No. 4, pp. 608–635.

Gavin, Francis J. 1999. "Politics, Power, and U.S. Policy in Iran, 1950–1953," *Journal of Cold War Studies*, Vol. 1, No. 1, pp. 56–89.

2012. *Nuclear Statecraft: History and Strategy in America's Atomic Age*. Ithaca, NH: Cornell University Press.

2015. "Strategies of Inhibition: U.S. Grand Strategy, the Nuclear Revolution, and Nonproliferation," *International Security*, Vol. 40, No. 1, pp. 9–46.

Gavin, Francis J., and Mira Rapp-Hooper. 2011. "The Copenhagen Temptation: Rethinking Prevention and Proliferation in the Age of Deterrence Dominance," presented at the annual meeting of the American Political Science Association, Seattle, September.

Gazit, Mordechai. 2000. "The Genesis of the US-Israeli Military-Strategic Relationship and the Dimona Issue," *Journal of Contemporary History*, Vol. 35, No. 2, pp. 413–422.

Geddes, Barbara. 1990. "How the Cases You Choose Affect the Answers You Get: Selection Bias in Comparative Politics," *Political Analysis*, Vol. 2, No. 1, pp. 131–150.

2003. *Paradigms and Sand Castles: Theory Building and Research Design in Comparative Politics*. Ann Arbor: University of Michigan Press.

George, Alexander L., and Andrew Bennett. 2005. *Case Studies and Theory Development in the Social Sciences*. Cambridge, MA: MIT Press.

George, Alexander L., and Timothy McKeown. 1985. "Case Studies and Theories of Organizational Decision Making," in *Advances in Information Processing in Organizations*, pp. 21–58. Robert Coulam and Richard Smith, eds. Greenwich, CT: JAI Press.

Gerzhoy, Gene. 2015. "Alliance Coercion and Nuclear Restraint: How the United States Thwarted West Germany's Nuclear Ambitions," *International Security*, Vol. 39, No. 4, pp. 91–129.

Gheorghe, Eliza. 2013. "Atomic Maverick: Romania's Negotiations for Nuclear Technology," *Cold War History*, Vol. 13. No. 3, pp. 373–392.

Ginor, Isabella, and Gideon Remez. 2007. *Foxbats over Dimona: The Soviets' Nuclear Gamble in the Six-Day War*. New Haven, CT: Yale University Press.

Glaser, Bonnie, Scott Snyder, and John S. Park. 2008. *Keeping an Eye on an Unruly Neighbor: Chinese Views of Economic Reform and Stability in North Korea*. Washington, DC: United States Institute of Peace.

Glaser, Charles L. 2010. *Rational Theory of International Politics*. Princeton NJ: Princeton University Press.

Gleijeses, Piero. 2013. *Visions of Freedom: Havana, Washington, Pretoria, and the Struggle for Southern Africa, 1976–1991*. Chapel Hill: University of North Carolina Press.

Golan, Galia. 2006. "The Soviet Union and the Outbreak of the June 1967 Six-Day War," *Journal of Cold War Studies*, Vol. 8, No. 1, pp. 3–19.

2008. "A (Dubious) Conspiracy Theory of the 1967 War," *Diplomatic History*, Vol. 32, No. 4, pp. 669–673.

Goldemberg, Jose, and Harold A. Feiveson. 1994. "Denuclearization in Argentina and Brazil." *Arms Control Today*, Vol. 24, No. 2, pp. 10–14.

Goldenberg, Ilan, Elizabeth Rosenberg, Avner Golov, Nicholas A. Heras, Ellie Maruyama, and Axel Hellman. 2015. *After the Joint Comprehensive Plan of Action: A Game Plan for the United States*. Washington, DC: Center for a New American Security.

Goldschmidt, Bertrand. 1990. *Atomic Rivals*. Translated by Georges M. Temmer. New Brunswick, NJ: Rutgers University Press.

Goldstein, Avery. 2000. *Deterrence and Security in the 21st Century: China, Britain, France, and the Enduring Legacy of the Nuclear Revolution*. Redwood City, CA: Stanford University Press.

Goldstein, Lyle J. 2003. "When China Was a 'Rogue State': The Impact of China's Nuclear Weapons Program on US–China Relations during the 1960s," *Journal of Contemporary China*, Vol. 12, No. 37, pp. 739–764.

Goldstein, Steven. 2001. "Dialogue of the Deaf? The Sino-American Ambassadorial-Level Talks, 1955–1970," in *Re-examining the Cold War: U.S.-China Diplomacy, 1954–1973*, pp. 200–237. Robert S. Ross and Jiang Changbin, eds. Cambrige, MA: Harvard University Press.

Goncharov, Sergei N., John W. Lewis, and Xue Litai. 1993. *Uncertain Partners: Stalin, Mao, and the Korean War*. Stanford, CA: Stanford University Press.

Goodman, Michael S. 2007. *Spying on the Nuclear Bear: Anglo-American Intelligence and the Soviet Bomb*. Stanford, CA: Stanford University Press.

Goodson, Donald L. R. 2012. "Catalytic Deterrence? Apartheid South Africa's Nuclear Weapons Strategy," *Politikon: South African Journal of Political Studies*, Vol. 32, No. 2, pp. 209–230.

Gordin, Michael D. 2009. *Red Cloud at Dawn: Truman, Stalin, and the End of the Atomic Monopoly*. New York: Farrar, Straus, and Giroux.

Gordon, Michael R., and Bernard E. Trainor. 1995. *The Generals' War: The Inside Story of the Conflict in the Gulf*. Boston: Little Brown.

Gordon, Philip. 1993. *A Certain Idea of France: French Security Policy and the Gaullist Legacy*. Princeton, NJ: Princeton University Press.

Gowing, Margaret, and Lora Arnold. 1974. *Independence and Deterrence: Britain and Atomic Energy, 1945–1952*. London: Macmillan.

Granieri, Ronald J. 2004. *The Ambivalent Alliance: Konrad Adenauer, the CDU/CSU, and the West, 1949–1966*. New York: Berghahn Books.

Grant, Rebecca. 2002. "Osirak and Beyond," *Air Force Magazine*, Vol. 85, pp. 74–78.

Gray, William Glenn. 2009. "Abstinence and Ostpolitik: Brandt's Government and the Nuclear Question," in *Ostpolitik, 1969–1974: European and Global Responses*, pp. 244–268. Carole Fink and Bernd Schaefer, eds. Cambridge: Cambridge University Press.

2012. "Commercial Liberties and Nuclear Anxieties: The US-German Feud over Brazil, 1975–7," *International History Review*, Vol. 34, No. 3, pp. 449–474.

Green, Michael J. 1995. *Arming Japan: Defense Production, Alliance Politics and the Postwar Search for Autonomy*. New York: Columbia University Press.

Green, Michael J., and Katsushisa Furukawa. 2008. "Japan: New Nuclear Realism," in *The Long Shadow: Nuclear Weapons and Security in 21st Century Asia*, pp. 347–372. Muthiah Alagappa, ed. Stanford, CA: Stanford University Press.

Grillot, Suzette R., and William J. Long. 2000. "Ideas, Beliefs, and Nuclear Policies: The Cases of South Africa and Ukraine," *Nonproliferation Review*, Vol. 7, No. 1, pp. 24–40.

Gromyko, Andrei. 1989. *Memories*. Translated by Harold Shukman. London: Hutchinson.

Grosser, Alfred. 1963. "France and Germany in the Atlantic Community," *International Organization*, Vol. 17, No. 3, pp. 550–573.

Gunnarsson, Gösta, Wilhelm Carlgren, Leif Leifland, Yngve Möller, Olof Ruin, and Göran Rystad. 1994. *Had There Been a War: Preparations for the Reception of Military Assistance 1949–1969*. Stockholm.

Güvenc, Serhat, and Soli Özel. 2012. "NATO and Turkey in the Post-Cold War World: Between Abandonment and Entrapment," *Journal of Southeast European & Black Sea Studies*, Vol. 12, No. 4, pp. 533–553.

Hagerty, Devin T. 1998. *The Consequences of Nuclear Proliferation: Lessons from South Asia*. Cambridge, MA: The MIT Press.

Haggard, Stephan, and Marcus Noland. 2012. "Engaging North Korea: The Efficacy of Sanctions and Inducements." in *Sanctions, Statecraft, and Nuclear Proliferation*, pp. 232–260. Etel Solingen, ed. Cambridge: Cambridge University Press.

2015. *Hard Target*. Unpublished Manuscript.

Hahn, Peter L. 2012. *Missions Accomplished? The United States and Iraq since World War I*. Oxford: Oxford University Press.

Hamann, Hilton. 2001. *Days of the Generals*. Cape Town: Zebra Press.

Hamblin, Jacob Darwin. 2014. "The Nuclearization of Iran in the Seventies," *Diplomatic History*, Vol. 38, No. 5, pp. 1114–1136.

Harmer, Tanya. 2012. "Brazil's Cold War in the Southern Cone, 1970–1975," *Cold War History*, Vol. 12, No. 4, pp. 659–681.

Harrer, Gudrun. 2014. *Dismantling the Iraqi Nuclear Programme: The Inspections of the International Atomic Energy Agency in Iraq 1991–8*. New York: Routledge.

Harris, Verne, Sello Hatang, and Peter Liberman. 2004. "Unveiling South Africa's Nuclear Past," *Journal of Southern African Studies*, Vol. 30, No. 3, pp. 457–475.

Harris, William R. 1965. "Chinese Nuclear Doctrine: The Decade prior to Weapons Development (1945–1955)," *The China Quarterly*, No. 21, pp. 87–95.

Harrison, Selig S. 1987. "U.S. Policy in South Asia," in *The Security of South Asia: American and Asian Perspectives*, pp. 134–140. Stephen P. Cohen, ed. Chicago: University of Illinois Press.

Harsanyi, John C. 1973. "Games with Randomly Disturbed Payoffs: A New Rationale for Mixed-Strategy Equilibrium Points," *International Journal of Game Theory*, Vol. 2, No. 1, pp. 1–23.

Harvey, Frank P. 2012. "President Al Gore and the 2003 Iraq War: A Counterfactual Test of Conventional 'W'isdom," *Canadian Journal of Political Science*, Vol. 45, No. 1, pp. 1–32.

Hayes, Peter. 1992. "The Republic of Korea and the Nuclear Issue," *Pacific Focus*, Vol. 7, No. 1, pp. 23–57.

Herring, George C., and Richard H. Immerman. 1984 "Eisenhower, Dulles, and Dienbienphu," *The Journal of American History*, Vol. 71, No. 2, pp. 343–363.

Hersh, Seymour. 1991. *The Samson Option: Israel's Nuclear Arsenal and American Foreign Policy*. New York: Random House.

Hershberg, James G. 2004a. "The United States, Brazil and the Cuban Missile Crisis, 1962 (Part 1)," *Journal of Cold War Studies*, Vol. 6, No. 2, pp. 3–20.

2004b. "The United States, Brazil and the Cuban Missile Crisis, 1962 (Part 2)," *Journal of Cold War Studies*, Vol. 6, No. 3, pp. 5–67.

Hersman, Rebecca K. C., and Robert Peters. 2006. "Nuclear U-Turns: Learning from South Korean and Taiwanese Rollback," *The Nonproliferation Review*, Vol. 13, No. 3, pp. 539–553.

Heuser, Beatrice. 1998. *Nuclear Mentalities? Strategies and Beliefs in Britain, France, and the FRG*. London: Macmillan.

Hibbs, Mark. 2014. "Looking Back at Brazil's Boreholes." Arms Control Wonk blog, April 22.

Higgins, Holly. 2000a. "The Foundation Is Shaken," in *Solving the North Korean Nuclear Puzzle*, pp. 167–81. David Albright and Kevin O'Neill, eds. Washington, DC: The Institute for Science and International Security Press.

2000b. "Chronology of Events Related to U.S.-North Korean Agreed Framework: June 1998–March 2000," in *Solving the North Korean Nuclear Puzzle*, pp. 277–297. David Albright and Kevin O'Neill, eds. Washington, DC: The Institute for Science and International Security Press.

Hilali, A. Z. 2005. *US-Pakistan Relationship: Soviet Invasion of Afghanistan*. Burlington, VT: Ashgate Publishing Company.

Hilton, Stanley E. 1985. "The Argentine Factor in Twentieth-Century Brazilian Foreign Policy Strategy," *Political Science Quarterly*, Vol. 100, No. 1, pp. 27–51.

Hiroshima, Sean. 2015. "Divided Intentions: Iraqi Nuclear Weapons Policy between the First and Second Gulf Wars." CISAC Honors Thesis. May 22. Available at: https://searchworks.stanford.edu/view/sc049qn8269. Last accessed: March 14, 2016.

Hoey, Fintan. 2012. "The Nixon Doctrine and Nakasone Yasuhiro's Unsuccessful Challenge to Japan's Defense Policy, 1969–1971," *The Journal of American-East Asian Relations*, Vol. 19, No. 1, pp. 52–74.

Holloway, David. 1994. *Stalin and the Bomb: The Soviet Union and Atomic Energy, 1939–1956*. New Haven, CT: Yale University Press.

2010. "Deciding Not to Go Nuclear: The Swedish and Swiss Cases." Stanford University Mimeo.

Hong, Sung Gul. 2011. "The Search for Deterrence: Park's Nuclear Option," in *The Park Chung Hee Era: The Transformation of South Korea*, pp. 483–512. Byung-Kook Kim and Ezra F. Vogel, eds. Cambridge, MA: Harvard University Press.

Hughes, Christopher. 2004. *Japan's Re-Emergence as a "Normal" Military Power*. Oxon, UK: Routledge.

2007. "North Korea's Nuclear Weapons: Implications for the Nuclear Ambitions of Japan, South Korea, and Taiwan," *Asia Policy*, Vol. 3, No. 1, pp. 75–104.

2009. *Japan's Remilitarisation*. Oxon, UK: Routledge. (102–112)

Hughes Christopher, and Ellis S. Krauss. 2007. "Japan's New Security Agenda," *Survival*, Vol. 49, No. 2, pp. 157–176.

Hughes, Llewelyn. 2007. "Why Japan Will Not Go Nuclear (Yet)," *International Security*, Vol. 31, no. 4, pp. 67–96.

Hurrell, Andrew. 1986. "The Quest for Autonomy: The Evolution of Brazil's Role in the International System, 1964–1985." D. Phil dissertation, Oxford University.

Hussain, Zahid. 1998. "Deliberate Nuclear Ambiguity," in *Pakistan and the Bomb: Public Opinion and Nuclear Options*, pp. 29–46. Samina Ahmed and David Cortright, eds. Notre Dame, IN: University of Notre Dame Press.

Huth, Paul K. 1988. "Extended Deterrence and the Outbreak of War," *American Political Science Review*, Vol. 82, No. 2, pp. 423–443.

Hymans, Jacques E. C. 2001. "Of Gauchos and Gringos: Why Argentina Never Wanted the Bomb, and Why the United States Thought It Did," *Security Studies*, Vol. 10, No. 3, pp. 153–185.

2002. "Why Do States Acquire Nuclear Weapons? Comparing the Cases of India and France," in *Nuclear India in the Twenty-First Century*, pp. 139–160. D. R. SarDesai and Raju G. C. Thomas, eds. New York: Palgrave.

2006. *The Psychology of Nuclear Proliferation: Identity, Emotions, and Foreign Policy* Cambridge: Cambridge University Press.

2008. "Assessing North Korean Nuclear Intentions and Capacities: A New Approach," *Journal of East Asian Studies*, Vol. 8, No. 2, pp. 259–292.

2011. "Veto Players, Nuclear Energy, and Nonproliferation: Domestic Institutional Barriers to a Japanese Bomb," *International Security*, Vol. 36, No. 2, pp. 154–89.

2012. *Achieving Nuclear Ambitions: Scientists, Politicians, and Proliferation*. Cambridge: Cambridge University Press.

Iatrides, John O. 1968. *Balkan Triangle: Birth and Decline of an Alliance across Ideological Boundaries*. The Hague: Mouton.

Iklé, Fred Charles. 1960. "Nth Countries and Disarmament," *Bulletin of the Atomic Scientists*, Vol. 16, No. 10, pp. 391–394.

International Institute for Strategic Studies. 2002. *Iraq's Weapons of Mass Destruction: A Net Assessment*. London: International Institute for Strategic Studies.

International Institute for Strategic Studies. 2016. *The Military Balance*, Vol. 116, No. 1. London: International Institute for Strategic Studies.

International Monetary Fund. 2016. Data. Available at: www.imf.org/en/ Data. Last accessed: May 3, 2016.

International Organization for Migration. 2016. Available at: www.iom.int/. Last accessed: May 3, 2016.

Iriye, Akira. 1987. *The Origins of the Second World War in Asia and the Pacific*. New York: Longman.

Jersild, Austin. 2013. Introduction to "Sharing the Bomb among Friends: The Dilemmas of Sino-Soviet Strategic Cooperation," Cold War International History Project e-Dossier No. 43. Woodrow Wilson International Center for Scholars, October 8. Available at: www.wilsoncenter.org/publication/ sharing-the-bomb-among-friends-the-dilemmas-sino-soviet-strategic-cooperation. Last accessed: February 15, 2016.

Jervis, Robert. 1976. *Perception and Misperception in International Politics*. Princeton, NJ: Princeton University Press.

1989. *The Meaning of the Nuclear Revolution: Statecraft and the Prospect of Armageddon*. Ithaca, NY: Cornell University Press.

2010. *Why Intelligence Fails: Lessons from the Iranian Revolution and the Iraq War*. Ithaca, NY: Cornell University Press.

2013. "Getting to Yes with Iran: The Challenges of Coercive Diplomacy," *Foreign Affairs*, Vol. 92, No. 1, pp. 105–115.

Jo, Dong-Joon, and Erik Gartzke. 2007. "Determinants of Nuclear Weapons Proliferation," *Journal of Conflict Resolution*, Vol. 51, No. 1, pp. 167–194.

Jones, Matthew. 2008. "Targeting China: U.S. Nuclear Planning and 'Massive Retaliation' in East Asia, 1953–1955," *Journal of Cold War Studies*, Vol. 10, No. 4, pp. 37–65.

Jonter, Thomas. 2001. "Sweden and the Bomb: The Swedish Plans to Acquire Nuclear Weapons, 1945–1972," SKI Report 01:33.

2002. "Nuclear Weapons Research in Sweden: The Co-operation between Civilian and Military Research, 1947–1972." SKI Report 02:18.

2010a. "The Swedish Plans to Acquire Nuclear Weapons, 1945–1968: An Analysis of the Technical Preparations," *Science and Global Security*, Vol. 18, No. 2, pp. 61–66.

2010b. "Why Sweden Did N build the Bomb, 1945–1968," Unpublished manuscript.

2012. "The United States and Swedish Plans to Build the Bomb, 1945–68," in *Security Assurances and Nuclear Nonproliferation*, pp. 219–245. Jeffrey Knopf, ed. Stanford, CA: Stanford University Press.

Kahl, Colin H. 2012. "Not Time to Attack Iran: Why War Should Be a Last Resort," *Foreign Affairs*, Vol. 91, No. 2, pp. 166–173.

Kahl, Colin H., Melissa G. Dalton, and Matthew Irvine. 2013. "Atomic Kingdom: If Iran Builds the Bomb, Will Saudi Arabia Be Next?" Center for a New American Security. Available at: www.cnas.org/files/documents/ publications/CNAS_AtomicKingdom_Kahl.pdf. Last accessed: December 30, 2015.

Kahn, Herman. 1970. *The Emerging Japanese Superstate: Challenges and Responses*. Englewood-Cliffs, NJ: Prentice-Hall.

Kampani, Gaurav. 2014a. "New Delhi's Long Nuclear Journey: How Secrecy and Institutional Roadblocks Delayed India's Weaponization," *International Security*, Vol. 38, No. 4, pp. 79–114.

2014b. "Teaching the Leviathan: Secrecy Ignorance and Nuclear Proliferation." PhD dissertation, Cornell University.

Kampani, Gaurav, Karthika Sasikumar, Jason Stone, and Andrew B. Kennedy. 2012. "Correspondence: Debating India's Pathway to Nuclearization," *International Security*, Vol. 37, No. 2, pp. 183–196.

Kane, Tim. 2006. "Global U.S. Troop Deployment, 1950–2005," Heritage Foundation, May 24. Available at: www.heritage.org/research/ reports/2006/05/global-us-troop-deployment-1950–2005. Last accessed: December 9, 2015.

Kang, David C. 2003. "International Relations Theory and the Second Korean War," *International Studies Quarterly*, Vol. 47, No. 3, pp. 301–324.

Kang, Gordon. 2006. *Nuclear Showdown: North Korea Takes on the World*. New York: Random House.

Kaplan, Lawrence S., Denise Artaud, and Mark R. Rubin, eds. 1990. *Dien Bien Phu and the Crisis of Franco-American Relations, 1954–1955*. Wilmington, DE: SR books.

Kapur, Ashok. 2001. *Pokhran and Beyond: India's Nuclear Behaviour*. New Delhi: Oxford University Press.

Kapur, S. Paul. 2007. *Dangerous Deterrent: Nuclear Weapons Proliferation and Conflict in South Asia*. Stanford, CA: Stanford University Press.

Kapur, S. Paul, and Sumit Ganguly, eds. 2008. *Nuclear Proliferation in South Asia: Crisis Behavior and the Bomb*. London: Routledge.

Karpin, Michael. 2006. *The Bomb in the Basement: How Israel Went Nuclear and What That Means for the World*. New York: Simon and Shuster.

Karsh, Efraim. 1987. *The Iran-Iraq War: A Military Analysis*. Adelphi Papers 220.

1990. "Geopolitical Determinism: The Origins of the Iran-Iraq War," *Middle East Journal*, Vol. 44, No. 2, pp. 256–288.

2002. *The Iran-Iraq War, 1980–1988*. Oxford: Osprey Publishers.

Kasapoglu, Can. 2015. "Turkey's National Security Strategy and NATO Nuclear Weapons," in *Turkey's Nuclear Future*, pp. 87–105. George Perkovich and Sinan Ülgen, eds. Washington, DC: Carnegie Endowment for International Peace.

Kase, Yuri. 2001. "The Costs and Benefits of Japan's Nuclearization: An Insight into the 1968/70 Internal Report," *The Nonproliferation Review*, Vol. 8, No. 2, pp. 55–68.

Kassenova, Togzhan. 2014. *Brazil's Nuclear Kaleidoscope: An Evolving Identity*. Washington, DC: Carnegie Endowment for International Peace.

Kay, David. 2004. *Iraq's Weapons of Mass Destruction*. Miller Center Report 20.

Kelleher, Catherine M. 1975. *Germany and the Politics of Nuclear Weapons*. New York: Columbia University Press.

Kelly, George A. 1960. "The Political Background of the French A-Bomb," *Orbis*, Vol. 4, No. 3, pp. 284–306.

Kemp, R. Scott. 2014. "The Nonproliferation Emperor Has No Clothes: The Gas Centrifuge, Supply-Side Controls, and the Future of Nuclear Proliferation," *International Security*, Vol. 38, No. 4, pp. 39–78.

Kennedy, John F. 1963. "News Conference 61," State Department Auditorium, Washington, DC, September 12, 1963, 4:00 P.M. Available at: http://www.jfklibrary.org/Research/Research-Aids/Ready-Reference/Press-Conferences/News-Conference-61.aspx. Last accessed: December 30, 2015.

Kennedy, Andrew B. 2011. "India's Nuclear Odyssey: Implicit Umbrellas, Diplomatic Disappointments, and the Bomb," *International Security*, Vol. 36, No. 2, pp. 120–153.

Keohane, Robert O. 1984. *After Hegemony: Cooperation and Discord in the World Political Economy*. Princeton, NJ: Princeton University Press.

Khan, Feroz Hassan. 2012. *Eating Grass: The Making of the Pakistani Bomb*. Stanford, CA: Stanford University Press.

Kharnad, Bharat. 2002. *Nuclear Weapons and Indian Security: The Realist Foundations of Strategy*. New Delhi: Macmillan.

Khomeini, Ruhollah. 1981. *Islam and Revolution, Writings and Declarations of Iman Khomeini*, Translated and Annotated by Hamid Algar. Berkeley, CA: Mizan Press.

Kibaroglu, Mustafa. 2004. "Iran's Nuclear Program May Trigger Young Turks to Think Nuclear," Carnegie Endowment for International Peace, December 20.

2005. "Isn't It Time to Say Farewell to Nukes in Turkey?" *European Security*, Vol. 14, no. 4, pp. 443–457.

2015. "Turkey and Nuclear Weapons: Can This Be Real?" in *Turkey's Nuclear Future*, pp. 155–182. George Perkovich and Sinan Ülgen, eds. Washington, DC: Carnegie Endowment for International Peace.

Kim, Ilsu. 2009. "Kim Jong Il and Denuclearization of the Korean Peninsula," in *North Korea's Foreign Policy under Kim Jong Il: New Perspectives,* pp. 81–95. Tae-Hwan Kwak and Seung-Ho Joo, eds. Burlington, VT: Ashgate Publishing Company.

Kim, Seung-young. 2001. "Security, Nationalism and the Pursuit of Nuclear Weapons and Missiles: The South Korean Case, 1970–1982," *Diplomacy and Statecraft*, Vol. 12, No. 4, pp. 53–80.

2011. "Balancing Security Interest and the 'Mission' to Promote Democracy: American Diplomacy toward South Korea Since 1969," in *Trilateralism and Beyond: Great Power Politics and the Korean Security Dilemma during and after the Cold War*, pp. 50–88. Robert A. Wampler, ed. Kent, OH: Kent State University Press.

Kim, Tongfi. 2011. "Why Alliances Entangle but Seldom Entrap States," *Security Studies*, Vol. 20, No. 3, pp. 350–377.

King, Gary, Robert O. Keohane, and Sidney Verba. 1994. *Designing Social Inquiry*. Princeton, NJ: Princeton University Press.

Kirshner, Jonathan. 1997. *Currency and Coercion: The Political Economy of International Monetary Power*. Princeton, NJ: Princeton University Press.

Kissinger, Henry A. 1979. *White House Years*. New York: Little, Brown and Company.

Klein, James P., Gary Goertz, and Paul F. Diehl. 2006. "The New Rivalry Dataset: Procedures and Patterns," *Journal of Peace Research*, Vol. 43, No. 3, pp. 331–348.

Kogan, Eugene B. 2013a. "Coercing Allies: Why Friends Abandon Nuclear Plans." PhD dissertation, Brandeis University.

2013b. "Proliferation among Friends: Taiwan's Lessons from 1970s–80s." Paper presented at the NSRI conference, Austin, TX, October 16–18.

Kohl, Wilfred L. 1971. *French Nuclear Diplomacy*. Princeton, NJ: Princeton University Press.

Kourkouvelas, Lykourgos. 2012. "Denuclearization on NATO's Southern Front: Allied Reactions to Soviet Proposals, 1957–1963," *Journal of Cold War Studies*, Vol. 14, No. 4, pp. 197–215.

2013. "Détente as a Strategy: Greece and the Communist World, 1974–9," *International History Review*, Vol. 35, No. 5, pp. 1052–1067.

Kramer, Mark. 1995–1996. "The USSR Foreign Ministry's Appraisal of Sino-Soviet Relations on the Eve of the Split, September 1959," in *The Cold War in Asia*, pp. 170–185. James G. Hershberg, ed., Cold War International History Project Bulletin No. 6/7. Available at: www.wilsoncenter.org/publication/bulletin-no-67-winter-1995. Last accessed: May 2, 2016.

Krebs, Ronald R. 1999. "Perverse Institutionalism: NATO and the Greco-Turkish Conflict," *International Organization*, Vol. 53, No. 2, pp. 343–377.

Kreps, Sarah, and Matthew Fuhrmann. 2011. "Attacking the Atom: Does Bombing Nuclear Facilities Affect Proliferation?" *Journal of Strategic Studies*, Vol. 34, No. 2, pp. 161–187.

Krige, John. 2006. "Atoms for Peace, Scientific Internationalism and Scientific Intelligence," *Osiris*, Vol. 21, No. 1, pp. 161–181.

Kristensen, Hans M. 2002. "Preemptive Posturing," *The Bulletin of the Atomic Scientists*, Vol. 58, No. 5, pp. 54–59.

2005. *U.S. Nuclear Weapons in Europe: A Review of Post-Cold War Policy, Force Levels, and War Planning*. Washington, DC: National Resources Defense Council.

Kroenig, Matthew. 2009a. "Exporting the Bomb: Why States Provide Sensitive Nuclear Assistance," *American Political Science Review*, Vol. 103, No. 1, pp. 113–133.

2009b. "Importing the Bomb: Sensitive Nuclear Assistance and Proliferation," *Journal of Conflict Resolution*, Vol. 53, No. 2, pp. 161–180.

2010. *Exporting the Bomb: Technology Transfer and the Spread of Nuclear Weapons*. Ithaca, NY: Cornell University Press.

2012. "Time to Attack Iran: Why a Strike Is the Least Bad Option," *Foreign Affairs*, Vol. 91, No. 1, pp. 76–86.

2013. "Nuclear Superiority and the Balance of Resolve: Explaining Nuclear Crisis Outcomes," *International Organization*, Vol. 67, No. 1, pp. 141–171.

2014. "Force or Friendship? Explaining Great Power Nonproliferation Policy," *Security Studies*, Vol. 23, No. 1, pp. 1–32.

Kumaraswamy, P. R. 2010. *India's Israel Policy*. New York: Columbia University Press.

Kumbaroglu, Gurkan. 2015. "Turkey and Nuclear Energy," in *Turkey's Nuclear Future*, pp. 9–37. George Perkovich and Sinan Ulgen, eds. Washington, DC: Carnegie Endowment for International Peace.

Küntzel, Mathias. 1995. *Bonn and the Bomb: German Politics and the Nuclear Option*. London: Pluto Press.

Kunz, Diane B. 1991. *The Economic Diplomacy of the Suez Crisis*. Chapel Hill: The University of North Carolina Press.

Kusunoki, Ayako. 2008. "The Sato Cabinet and the Making of Japan's Non-Nuclear Policy," *Journal of American-East Asian Relations*, Vol. 15, No. 1, pp. 25–50.

Kutchesfahani, Sara Z. 2014. *Politics and the Bomb: The Role of Experts in the Creation of Cooperative Nuclear Non-Proliferation Agreements*. New York: Routledge.

Kux, Dennis. 2001. *The United States and Pakistan, 1947–2000: Disenchanted Allies*. Washington, DC: Woodrow Wilson Center Press.

Kyle, Keith. 2011. *Suez. Britain's End of Empire in the Middle East.* London: IB Tauris.

LaFeber, Walter. 1997. *Clash: A History of U.S.-Japan Relations.* New York: W. W. Norton.

Lake, David A. 2010–2011. "Two Cheers for Bargaining Theory Assessing Rationalist Explanations of the Iraq War," *International Security*, Vol. 35, No. 3, pp. 7–52.

Lake, David A., and Michael K. McKoy. 2011–2012. "Correspondence: Bargaining Theory and Rationalist Explanations for the Iraq War," *International Security*, Vol. 36, No. 3, pp. 172–178.

Lake, David A., and Robert Powell, eds. 1999. *Strategic Choice and International Relations.* Princeton, NJ: Princeton University Press.

Lamazière, Georges, and Roberto Jaguaribe. 1992. "Beyond Confidence-Building: Brazilian-Argentine Nuclear Cooperation," *Disarmament*, Vol. 15, No. 3, pp. 102–117.

Lanoszka, Alexander. 2013. "Protection States Trust? Major Power Patronage, Nuclear Behavior, and Alliance Dynamics," Princeton University Mimeo.

Larrabee, F. Stephen. 2012. "Greek-Turkish Relations in an Era of Regional and Global Change," *Journal of Southeast European and Black Sea Studies*, Vol. 12, No. 4, pp. 471–479.

Lavoy, Peter R. 1997. "Learning to Live with the Bomb? India and Nuclear Weapons, 1947–1974." PhD dissertation, University of California at Berkeley.

Lawrence, Mark Atwood. 2005. *Assuming the Burden: Europe and the American Commitment to War in Vietnam.* Berkeley: University of California Press.

Leah, Christine M. 2012. "U.S. Extended Nuclear Deterrence and Nuclear Order: An Australian Perspective," *Asian Security*, Vol. 8, No. 2, pp. 93–114.

Lee, Chae-Jin. 1998. "China and North Korea: An Uncertain Relationship," in *North Korea after Kim Il Sung*, pp. 193–210. Dae-Sook Suh and Chae-Jin Lee, eds. Boulder, CO: Lynne Rienner Publishers.

2002. "U.S. Policy toward North Korea: Engagement and Deterrence," in *The Challenges of Reconciliation and Reform in Korea*, pp. 167–194. B.C. Koh, ed. Washington, DC: KEIA.

2006. *A Troubled Peace: U.S. Policy and the Two Koreas.* Baltimore, MD: Johns Hopkins University Press.

Lee, Jongseok. 2011. "South Korean and U.S. Policy toward North Korea: A Strategy for Two Crises," in *Beyond North Korea: Future Challenges to South Korea's Security*, pp. 109–134. Byung Kwan Kim,

Gi-Wook Shin, and David Straub, eds. The Walter H. Shorenstein Asia/Pacific Research Center.

Lee, Jung-Hoon, and Chung-in Moon. 2003. "The North Korean Nuclear Crisis," *Security Dialogue*, Vol. 34, Vol. 2, pp. 135–151.

Lee, Ming. 2009. "North Korea's China Policy," in *North Korea's Foreign Policy under Kim Jong Il: New Perspectives*, pp. 161–178. Tae-Hwan Kwak and Seung-Ho Joo, eds. Burlington, VT: Ashgate Publishing Company.

Leeds, Brett Ashley, Jeffrey M. Ritter, Sara McLaughlin Mitchell, and Andrew G. Long. 2002. "Alliance Treaty Obligations and Provisions, 1815–1944," *International Interactions*, Vol. 28, No. 3, pp. 237–260.

Lesser, Ian O. 2005. "Turkey, Iran, and Nuclear Risks," in *Getting Ready for a Nuclear-Ready Iran*, pp. 89–112. Henry Sokolski and Patrick Clawson, eds. Washington, DC: Strategic Studies Institute.

Leventhal, Paul, and Sharon Tanzer, eds. 1992. *Averting a Latin American Nuclear Arms Race: New Prospects and Challenges for Argentine-Brazilian Nuclear Cooperation*. New York: Macmillan.

Levey, Zach. 2004. "The United States' Skyhawk Sale to Israel, 1966: Strategic Exigencies of an Arms Deal," *Diplomatic History*, Vol. 28, No. 2, pp. 255–276.

Levite, Ariel E. 2002–2003. "Never Say Never Again: Nuclear Reversal Revisited," *International Security*, Vol. 27, No. 3, pp. 59–88.

Levy, Adrian, and Catherine Scott-Clark. 2007. *Deception: Pakistan, the United States, and the Secret Trade in Nuclear Weapons*. New York: Walker Publishing Company.

Levy, Jack S. 2008. "Preventive War and Democratic Politics," *International Studies Quarterly*, Vol. 52, No. 1, pp. 1–24.

Lewis, Jeffrey. 2006. "How Long for Japan to Build a Deterrent?" Arms Control Wonk blog post, December 28. Available at: www.armscontrolwonk.com/archive/201339/japans-nuclear-status/. Last accessed: February 15, 2016.

Lewis, John W. and Xue Litai. 1988. *China Builds the Bomb*. Stanford, CA: Stanford University Press.

1994. *China's Strategic Seapower: The Politics of Force Modernization in the Nuclear Age*. Stanford, CA: Stanford University Press.

Li, Danhui, and Yafeng Xia. 2014. "Jockeying for Leadership: Mao and the Sino-Soviet Split, October 1961–July 1964," *Journal of Cold War Studies*, Vol. 16, No. 1, pp. 24–60.

Li, Gong. 2001. "Tension across the Taiwan Strait in the 1950s: Chinese Strategy and Tactics," in *Re-examining the Cold War: U.S.-China*

Diplomacy, 1954–1973, pp. 141–172. Robert S. Ross and Jiang Changbin, eds. Cambridge, MA: Harvard University Press.

Liberman, Peter. 2001. "The Rise and Fall of the South African Bomb," *International Security*, Vol. 26, No. 2, pp. 45–86.

2004. "Israel and the South African Bomb," *The Nonproliferation Review*, Vol. 11, No. 2, pp. 46–80.

Lin, Yang Bonny. 2012. "Arms, Alliances, and the Bomb: Using Conventional Arms Transfers to Prevent Nuclear Proliferation." PhD dissertation, Yale University. Available at http://search.proquest.com/docview/1038970618?accountid=15172. Last accessed: September 2, 2015.

Lippman, Thomas W. 2008. "Nuclear Weapons and Saudi Strategy," The Middle East Institute Policy Brief. No. 5. Available at www.mei.edu/content/nuclear-weapons-and-saudi-strategy. Last accessed: December 30, 2015.

2012. *Saudi Arabia on the Edge: The Uncertain Future of an American Ally*. Washington, DC: Potomac Books.

Little, Douglas. 1993. "The Making of a Special Relationship," *International Journal of Middle East Studies*, Vol. 25, No. 4, pp. 563–585.

Liu, Yanqiong, and Liu Jifeng. 2009. "Analysis of Soviet Technology Transfer in the Development of China's Nuclear Weapons," *Comparative Technology Transfer and Society*, Vol. 7, No. 1, pp. 66–110.

Logevall, Fredrik. 2012. *Embers of War: The Fall of an Empire and the Making of America's Vietnam*. New York: Random House.

Lorentzen, Peter L., Taylor M. Fravel, and Jack Paine. 2014. "Using Process Tracing to Evaluate Formal Models." MIT Political Science Department Research Paper No. 2014-3. Available at SSRN: http://ssrn.com/abstract=2407629. Last accessed: December 3, 2015.

Lytle, Mark Hamilton. 1987. *The Origins of the Iranian-American Alliance, 1941–1953*. New York: Holmes and Meier.

Mabon, David W. 1988. "Elusive Agreements: The Pacific Pact Proposals of 1949–1951," *Pacific Historical Review*, Vol. 57, No. 2, pp. 147–178.

Mackby, Jenifer, and Walter B. Slocombe. 2004. "Germany: The Model Case, a Historical Imperative," in *The Nuclear Tipping Point: Why States Reconsider Their Nuclear Choices*, pp. 175–217. Kurt M. Campbell, Robert J. Einhorn, and Mitchell B. Reiss, eds. Washington, DC: Brookings Institution Press.

Mackie, John L. 1965. "Causes and Conditions," *American Philosophical Quarterly*, Vol. 2, No. 4, pp. 245–264.

Maddock, Shane J. 2010. *Nuclear Apartheid: The Quest for American Atomic Supremacy from World War II to the Present*. Raleigh: University of North Carolina Press.

Mahoney, James. 2008. "Toward a Unified Theory of Causation," *Comparative Political Studies*, Vol. 41, No. 4–5, pp. 412–436.

Mahoney, James, Erin Kimball, and Kendra L. Koivu. 2009. "The Logic of Historical Explanation in the Social Sciences," *Comparative Political Studies*, Vol. 42, No. 1, pp. 114–146.

Makowsky, David. 2012. "The Silent Strike: How Israel Bombed a Syrian Nuclear Installation and Kept It Secret," *The New Yorker*, September 17.

Malheiros, Tania. 1993. *Brasil: A Bomba Oculta*. Rio de Janeiro: Gryphus. 1996. *Histórias Secretas do Brasil Nuclear*. São Paulo: Gryphus.

Mallea, Rodrigo. 2013a. "The First Attempt at Argentine-Brazilian Nuclear Cooperation and the Argentine Response, 1967–1972." *Nuclear Proliferation International History Project research update*. Washington, DC: Woodrow Wilson Center for Scholars, July 12.

2013b. "From the Indian Bomb to the Establishment of the First Brazil-Argentina Nuclear Agreement (1974–1980)." *Nuclear Proliferation International History Project research update*. Washington, DC: Woodrow Wilson Center for Scholars, July 24.

Mallea, Rodrigo, Matias Spektor, and Nicholas J. Wheeler, eds. 2015. *The Origins of Nuclear Cooperation: A Critical Oral History between Argentina and Brazil*. Washington, DC, and Rio de Janeiro: Woodrow Wilson International Center for Scholars and FGV.

Malone, Peter. 1984. *The British Nuclear Deterrent*. New York: St. Martin's.

Mann, James. 1999. *About Face: A History of America's Curious Relationship with China, from Nixon to Clinton*. New York: Alfred Knopf.

Mao Zedong. 1961. *Selected Works of Mao Tse-Tung*. Volume IV. Peking: Foreign Language Press.

1963. *Selected Military Writings of Mao Tse-Tung*. Peking: Foreign Language Press.

1977. *Selected Works of Mao Tsetung*. Volume V. Peking: Foreign Language Press.

Mao Zedong sixiang wansui. 1967–1969. 3 vols. Released by the Institution of International Relations, Taipei.

Martin, Philippe, Thierry Mayer, and Mathias Thoenig. 2008. "Make Trade Not War?" *The Review of Economic Studies*, Vol. 75, No. 3, pp. 865–900.

Marwah, Onkar. 1981. "India and Pakistan: Nuclear Rivals in South Asia," *International Organization*, Vol. 35, No. 1, pp. 165–179.

Mazaheri, Nimah. 2010. "Iraq and the Domestic Political Effects of Economic Sanctions," *Middle East Journal*, Vol. 64, No. 2, pp. 253–268.

McGarr, Paul M. 2013. *The Cold War in South Asia: Britain, the United States and the Indian Subcontinent 1945–1965*. New York: Cambridge University Press.

McNamee, Terence. 2005. "The Afrikaner Bomb: Nuclear Proliferation and Rollback in South Africa," in *Why Do States Want Nuclear Weapons? The Cases of Israel and South Africa*, pp. 13–23. Avner Cohen and Terence McNamee, ed. Oslo: Norwegian Institute for Defence Studies.

Mearsheimer, John J. 1990. "Why We Will Soon Miss the Cold War," *The Atlantic Monthly*, Vol. 266, No. 2, pp. 35–50.

Melissen, Jan. 1994. "Nuclearizing NATO, 1957–1959: The 'Anglo-Saxons,' Nuclear Sharing and the Fourth Country Problem," *Review of International Studies*, Vol. 20, No. 3, pp. 253–275.

Mian, Zia. 1998. "Renouncing the Nuclear Option," in *Pakistan and the Bomb: Public Opinion and Nuclear Options*, pp. 47–68. Samina Ahmed and David Cortright, eds. Notre Dame, IN: University of Notre Dame Press.

Michishita, Narushige. 2003. "North Korea's 'First' Nuclear Diplomacy, 1993–94," *Journal of Strategic Studies*, Vol. 26, No. 4, pp. 47–82.

Milani, Abbas. 2010. *The Myth of the Great Satan: A New Look at America's Relations with Iran*. Stanford, CA: Hoover Institution Press.

2011. *The Shah*. New York: Palgrave MacMillan.

Milivojevic, Marko. 1990. "The Swiss Armed Forces," in *Swiss Neutrality and Security*, pp. 3–48. Marko Milivojevic and Pierre Maurer, eds. New York: Berg.

Miller, Jamie. 2012. "Things Fall Apart: South Africa and the Collapse of the Portuguese Empire, 1973–74," *Cold War History*, Vol. 12, No. 2, pp. 183–204.

2013a. "Yes, Minister: Reassessing South Africa's Intervention in the Angolan Civil War, 1975," *Journal of Cold War Studies*, Vol. 15, No. 3, pp. 4–33.

2013b. Response to Chris Saunders. Available at: http://h-diplo.org/reviews/PDF/AR440-Response.pdf. Last accessed: May 2, 2016.

Miller, Nicholas L. 2014a. "The Secret Success of Nonproliferation Sanctions," *International Organization*, Vol. 68, No. 4, pp. 913–944.

2014b. "Nuclear Dominos: A Self-Defeating Prophecy?" *Security Studies*, Vol. 23, No. 1, pp. 33–73.

Mirchandani, G. G. 1968. *India's Nuclear Dilemma*. New Delhi: Popular Book Services.

Mitchell, Derek J. 2004. "Taiwan's Hsin Chu Program: Deterrence, Abandonment, and Honor," in *The Nuclear Tipping Point: Why States Reconsider Their Nuclear Choices*, pp. 293–313. Kurt M. Campbell, Robert J. Einhorn, and Mitchell B. Reiss, eds. Washington, DC: Brookings Institution Press.

Mochizuki, Mike M. 2007. "Japan Tests the Nuclear Taboo," *The Nonproliferation Review*, Vol. 14, No. 2, pp. 303–328.

Mongin, Dominique. 1997. *La Bombe Atomique Française, 1945–1958*. Bruxelles: Bruylant.

Monteiro, Nuno P. 2014. *Theory of Unipolar Politics*. Cambridge: Cambridge University Press.

Monteiro, Nuno P., and Alexandre Debs. 2014. "The Strategic Logic of Nuclear Proliferation," *International Security*, Vol. 39, No. 2, pp. 7–51.

2015. "An Economic Theory of War." Yale University Mimeo.

Monten, Jonathan, and Mark Provost. 2005. "Theater Missile Defense and Japanese Nuclear Weapons," *Asian Security*, Vol. 1, No. 3, pp. 285–303.

Montgomery, Alexander H., and Adam Mount. 2014. "Misestimation: Explaining US Failures to Predict Nuclear Weapons Programs," *Intelligence and National Security*, Vol. 29, No. 3, pp. 357–386.

Montgomery, Alexander H., and Scott D. Sagan. 2009. "The Perils of Predicting Proliferation," *Journal of Conflict Resolution*, Vol. 53, No. 2, pp. 302–328.

Moravcsik, Andrew. 1997. "Taking Preferences Seriously: A Liberal Theory of International Politics," *International Organization*, Vol. 51, No. 4, pp. 513–553.

Morrow, James D. 1994. "Alliances, Credibility, and Peacetime Costs," *Journal of Conflict Resolution*, Vol. 38, No. 2, pp. 270–297.

Motta, Marly. 2010. "As Peças do Quebra-cabeça: Rex Nazaré e a Política Nuclear Brasileira," *História Oral*, Vol. 13, No. 2, pp. 115–135.

Mueller, John. 1988. "The Essential Irrelevance of Nuclear Weapons: Stability in the Postwar World," *International Security*, Vol. 13, No. 2, pp. 55–79.

1989. *Retreat from Doomsday: The Obsolescence of Major War*. New York: Basic Books.

Mukhatzhanova, Gaukhar. 2010. "Nuclear Weapons in the Balkans: Why Yugoslavia Tried and Serbia Will Not," in *Forecasting Nuclear Proliferation in the 21st Century: A Comparative Perspective*, Vol. 2, pp. 205–228. William C. Potter with Gaukhar Mukhatzhanova, eds. Stanford, CA: Stanford University Press.

Müller, Harald. 2003. "Germany and WMD Proliferation," *Nonproliferation Review*, Vol. 10, No. 2, pp. 1–20.

Müller, Harald, and Andreas Schmidt. 2010. "The Little-Known Story of Deproliferation: Why States Give Up Nuclear Weapons Activities," in *Forecasting Nuclear Proliferation in the 21st Century: The Role of Theory*, Vol. 1, pp. 124–158. William C. Potter with Gaukhar Mukhatzhanova, eds. Stanford, CA: Stanford University Press.

Musharraf, Pervez. 2006. *In the Line of Fire: A Memoir*. New York: Free Press.

Myers, David J. 1984. "Brazil: Reluctant Pursuit of the Nuclear Option," *Orbis*, Vol. 27, No. 4, pp. 881–911.

Myers, Ramon H., and Jialin Zhang. 2006. *The Struggle across the Taiwan Strait*. Stanford, CA: Hoover Institution Press.

Nakdimon, Shelomoh. 1987. *First Strike: The Exclusive Story of How Israel Foiled Iraq's Attempt to Get the Bomb*. New York: Summit Books.

Narang, Vipin. 2009–2010. "Posturing for Peace? Pakistan's Nuclear Postures and South Asian Stability," *International Security*, Vol. 34, No. 3, pp. 38–78.

   2013. "The Promise and Limits of Quantitative Methods in Nuclear Studies." Paper presented at the NSRI conference, Austin, TX, October 16–18.

   2014. *Nuclear Strategy in the Modern Era: Regional Powers and International Conflict*. Princeton, NJ: Princeton University Press.

Nedal, Dani K., and Tatiana Coutto. 2013. "Brazil's 1975 Nuclear Agreement with West Germany." Nuclear Proliferation International History Project research update. Washington, DC: Woodrow Wilson Center for Scholars, August 13.

Newnham, Rendall E. 2004. "Nukes for Sale Cheap? Purchasing Peace with North Korea," *International Studies Perspectives*, Vol. 5, No. 2, pp. 164–178.

Nincic, Miroslav. 2012. "Positive Incentives, Positive Results? Rethinking US Counterproliferation Policy," in *Sanctions, Statecraft, and Nuclear Proliferation*, pp. 125–153. Etel Solingen, ed. Cambridge: Cambridge University Press.

Nixon, Richard M. 1967. "Asia after Viet Nam," *Foreign Affairs*, Vol. 46, No. 1, pp. 111–125.

Noorani, A. G. 1967. "India's Quest for a Nuclear Guarantee," *Asian Survey*, Vol. 7, No. 7, pp. 490–502.

Norris, Robert S., and William M. Arkin. 1993. "Nuclear Notebook: U.S. Weapons Secrets Revealed," *The Bulletin of the Atomic Scientist*, Vol. 49, No. 2, p. 48.

   1994. "Nuclear Notebook: Estimated U.S. and Soviet/Russian Nuclear Stockpiles, 1945–94," *The Bulletin of the Atomic Scientist*, Vol. 50, No. 6, pp. 58–59.

Norris, Robert S., William M. Arkin, and William Burr. 1999. "Where They Were," *Bulletin of the Atomic Scientists*, Vol. 55, No. 6, pp. 26–35.

Norris, Robert S., and Hans M. Kristensen. 2005. "North Korea's Nuclear Program, 2005," *The Bulletin of the Atomic Scientists*, Vol. 61, No. 3, pp. 64–67.

Norris, Robert S., Hans M. Kristensen, and Joshua Handler. 2003. "North Korea's Nuclear Program, 2003," *The Bulletin of the Atomic Scientists*, Vol. 59, No. 2, pp. 74–77.

Nuti, Leopoldo. 1993. "'Me too, please': Italy and the Politics of Nuclear Weapons, 1945–1975," *Diplomacy and Statecraft*, Vol. 4, No. 1, pp. 114–148.

1998. "The F-I-G Story Revisited," *Storia delle Relazioni Internationali*, Vol. 13, No. 1, pp. 69–100.

2007. *La sfida nucleare: la politica estera italiana e le armi atomiche, 1945–1991*. Bologna: Il Mulino.

2011. "Italy's Nuclear Choices." UNISCI Discussion Paper No. 25. January, pp. 167–182.

Nye, Joseph S., Jr. 1987. "The Superpowers and the Non-Proliferation Treaty," in *Superpower Arms Control: Setting the Record Straight*, pp. 165–190. Albert Carnesale and Richard N. Haass, eds. Cambridge, MA: Ballinger Publishing Company.

Obeidi, Mahdi, and Kurt Pitzer. 2004. *The Bomb in My Garden – The Secrets of Saddam's Nuclear Mastermind*. Hoboken, NJ: John Wiley.

Oberdorfer, Don. 1997. *The Two Koreas: A Contemporary History*. Reading, MA: Addison-Wesley Publishing Company.

O'Hanlon, Michael. 1998. "Stopping a North Korean Invasion: Why Defending South Korea Is Easier Than the Pentagon Thinks," *International Security*, Vol. 22, No. 4, pp. 135–170.

Oliveira, Odete Maria. 1996. *A Integração Nuclear Brasil-Argentina: Uma Estratégia Compartilhada*. Florianópolis: Editora da Universidade Federal de Santa Catarina.

Olsen, Edward A. 2009. "North Korean Policy toward the United States: Pyongyang Copes with an Evolving U.S. Context," in *North Korea's Foreign Policy under Kim Jong Il: New Perspectives*, pp. 137–159. Tae-Hwan Kwak and Seung-Ho Joo, eds. Burlington, VT: Ashgate Publishing Company.

O'Neill, Robert. 2000. "Weapons of the Underdog," in *Alternative Nuclear Futures: The Role of Nuclear Weapons in the Post-Cold War World*, pp. 191–208. John Baylis and Robert O'Neill, eds. Oxford: Oxford University Press.

OPEC. 2016. "OPEC Annual Statistics Bulletin." Available online at: http://asb.opec.org/. Last accessed: February 1, 2016.

Oren, Michael. 2002. *Six Days of War: June 1967 and the Making of the Modern Middle East*. New York: Oxford University Press.

Pabian, Frank V. 1995. "South Africa's Nuclear Weapon Program: Lessons for U.S. Nonproliferation Policy," *The Nonproliferation Review*, Vol. 3, No. 1, pp. 1–19.

Pahlavi, Mohammed Reza. 1961. *Mission for My Country*. London: Hutchinson.

Palkki, David D., and Shane Smith. 2012. "Contrasting Causal Mechanisms: Iraq and Libya," in *Sanctions, Statecraft, and Nuclear Proliferation*, pp. 261–294. Etel Solingen, ed. Cambridge: Cambridge University Press.

Pan, Liang. 2007. "Whither Japan's Military Potential? The Nixon Administration's Stance on Japanese Defense Power," *Diplomatic History*, Vol. 31, No. 1, pp. 111–142.

Pantsov, Alexander V., and Steven I. Levine. 2007. *Mao: The Real Story*. New York: Simon and Schuster.

Pape, Robert A. 1996. *Bombing to Win: Air Power and Coercion in War*. Ithaca, NY: Cornell University Press.

Park, John S. 2012. "Assessing the Role of Security Assurances in Dealing with North Korea," in *Security Assurances and Nuclear Nonproliferation*, pp. 189–218. Jeffrey Knopf, ed. Stanford, CA: Stanford University Press.

Park, John S., and Dong Sun Lee. 2008. "North Korea: Existential Deterrence and Diplomatic Leverage," in *The Long Shadow: Nuclear Weapons and Security in 21st Century Asia*, pp. 269–295. Muthiah Alagappa, ed. Stanford, CA: Stanford University Press.

Park, Kyung-Ae 2001. "North Korea's Defensive Power and U.S.-North Korea Relations," in *Korean Security Dynamics in Transition*, pp. 83–104. Kyung-Ae Park and Dalchoong Kim, eds. New York: Palgrave.

Park, Tong Whan. 1998. "South Korea's Nuclear Option: The Interplay of Domestic and International Politics," in *The US and the Two Koreas: A New Triangle*, pp. 97–117. Tong Whan Park, ed. Boulder, CO: Lynne Rienner.

Parsi, Trita. 2007. *Treacherous Alliance – The Secret Dealings of Iran, Israel and the United States*. New Haven, CT: Yale University Press.

2012. *A Single Roll of the Dice: Obama's Diplomacy with Iran*. New Haven, CT: Yale University Press.

Patrikarakos, David. 2012. *Nuclear Iran: The Birth of an Atomic State*. London: I. B. Tauris.

Patti, Carlo. 2012a. "Brazil in Global Nuclear Order." PhD dissertation, University of Florence.

2012b. "Origins and Evolution of the Brazilian Nuclear Program (1947–2011)." *Nuclear Proliferation International History Project research update*. Washington, DC: Woodrow Wilson Center for Scholars, November 15.

2013a. "The German Connection: The Origins of the Brazilian Nuclear Program and the Secret West German-Brazilian Cooperation in the Early 1950s." Unpublished manuscript.

2013b. *O Programa Nuclear Brasileiro: Uma História Oral*. Unpublished manuscript.

2014. "The Origins of the Brazilian Nuclear Programme, 1951–1955," *Cold War History*, forthcoming, pp. 1–21.

Paul, T. V. 1995. "Nuclear Taboo and War Initiation in Regional Conflicts," *Journal of Conflict Resolution*, Vol. 39, No. 4, pp. 696–717.

1998. "The Systemic Bases of India's Challenge to the Global Nuclear Order," *Nonproliferation Review*, Vol. 6, no. 1, pp. 1–11.

1999. "Great Equalizers or Agents of Chaos? Weapons of Mass Destruction and the Emerging International Order," in *International Order and the Future of World Politics*, pp. 373–392. T. V. Paul and John A. Hall, eds. Cambridge: Cambridge University Press.

2000. *Power versus Prudence: Why Nations Forgo Nuclear Weapons.* Montreal: McGill-Queen's University Press.

2012. "Disarmament Revisited: Is Nuclear Abolition Possible?" *Journal of Strategic Studies*, Vol. 35, No. 1, pp. 149–169.

Pelopidas, Benoit. 2015. "The Nuclear Straitjacket: American Extended Deterrence and Nonproliferation." in *The Future of Extended Deterrence: The United States, NATO, and Beyond*, pp. 73–105. Stéfanie von Hlatky and Andreas Wenger, eds. Washington, DC: Georgetown University Press.

Peres, Shimon. 1970. *David's Sling.* London: Weidenfeld and Nicolson.

Perkovich, George. 1999. *India's Nuclear Bomb: The Impact of Global Proliferation.* Berkeley: University of California Press.

2008. "Could Anything Be Done to Stop Them? Lessons from Pakistan's Proliferating Past," in *Pakistan's Nuclear Future: Worries beyond War*, pp. 59–84. Henry Sokolski, ed. Carlisle Barracks, PA: Strategic Studies Institute, Army War College.

Perkovich, George, Mark Hibbs, James M. Acton, and Toby Dalton. 2015. *Parsing the Iran Deal: An Analysis of the Iran Deal from a Nonproliferation Perspective.* Washington, DC: Carnegie Endowment for International Peace.

Perkovich, George, and Sinan Ülgen, eds. 2015. *Turkey's Nuclear Future.* Washington, CT: Carnegie Endowment for International Peace.

Person, James F. 2012. "The Cuban Missile Crisis and the Origins of North Korea's Policy of Self-Reliance in National Defense," in *The Global Missile Crisis at 50: New Evidence from behind the Iron, Bamboo, and Sugarcane Curtains, and Beyond*, pp. 121–129. James G. Hershberg and Christian F. Ostermann, eds. Cold War International History Project Issue 17/18. Available at: www.wilsoncenter.org/sites/default/files/CWIHP_Cuban_Missile_Crisis_Bulletin_17-18.pdf. Last accessed: October 23, 2015.

Peyrefitte, Alain. 1994. *C'était de Gaulle. Volume I: La France redevient la France.* Paris: Editions de Fallois: Fayard.

Pinheiro da Silva, Othon Luiz. 2010. "Interview with Matias Spektor, Lucas Assis Nascimento, and Tatiana Coutto." Projeto Memória Histórica e Estratégica da Energia Nuclear no Brasil. CPDOC, FGV, Rio de Janeiro.

Pinkston, Daniel A. 2004. "South Korea's Nuclear Experiments," in *CNS Research Story*. Monterey, CA: James Martin Center for Nonproliferation Studies.

2009. "DPRK WMD Programs," in *North Korea's Foreign Policy under Kim Jong Il: New Perspectives*, pp. 97–118. Tae-Hwan Kwak and Seung-Ho Joo, eds. Burlington, VT: Ashgate Publishing Company.

Pleshakov, Constantine. 1998. "Nikita Khrushchev and Sino-Soviet Relations," in *Brothers in Arms: The Rise and Fall of the Sino-Soviet Alliance, 1945–1963*, pp. 226–245. Odd Arne Westad, ed. Washington, DC: Woodrow Wilson Center Press.

Polachek, Solomon W., 1980. "Conflict and Trade," *Journal of Conflict Resolution*, Vol. 24, No. 1, pp. 55–78.

Polachek, Solomon W. and Jun Xiang. 2010. "How Opportunity Costs Decrease the Probability of War in an Incomplete Information Game," *International Organization*, Vol. 64, No. 1, pp. 133–144.

Polakow-Suransky, Sasha. 2011. *The Unspoken Alliance: Israel's Secret Relationship with Apartheid South Africa*. New York: Vintage.

Pollack, Jonathan D. 2003. "The United States, North Korea, and the End of the Agreed Framework," *Naval War College Review*, Vol. 56, No. 3, pp.11–49.

2011. *No Exit: North Korea, Nuclear Weapons, and International Security*. London: Routledge.

Pollack, Jonathan D., and Mitchell B. Reiss. 2004. "South Korea: The Tyranny of Geography and the Vexations of History," in *The Nuclear Tipping Point: Why States Reconsider Their Nuclear Choices*, pp. 254–292. Kurt M. Campbell, Robert J. Einhorn, and Mitchell B. Reiss, eds. Washington, DC: Brookings Institution Press.

Pollack, Kenneth. 2004. *The Persian Puzzle*. New York: Random House.

Poneman, Daniel. 1981. "Nuclear Policies in Developing Countries," *International Affairs (Royal Institute of International Affairs 1944–)*, Vol. 57, No. 4, pp. 568–584.

Popp, Roland. 2006. "Stumbling Decidedly into the Six Day War," *The Middle East Journal*, Vol. 60, No. 2, pp. 281–309.

Portela, Clara. 2014. "The Rise and Fall of Spain's 'Nuclear Exceptionalism,'" *European Security*, Vol. 23, No. 1, pp. 90–105.

Potter, William C., Djuro Miljanic, and Ivo Slaus. 2000. "Tito's Nuclear Legacy: Should the West Be Worried about Yugoslavia's Nuclear Weapons Potential?," *Bulletin of Atomic Scientists*, Vol. 56, No. 2, pp. 63–70.

Potter, William C., and Gaukhar Mukhatzhanova. 2008. "Divining Nuclear Intentions: A Review Essay," *International Security*, Vol. 33, No. 1, pp. 139–169.

Powell, Charles T. 1995. "Las relaciones exteriores de España, 1898–1975," in *Las relaciones exteriores de la España democrática*, pp. 25–52. Richard Gillespie, Fernando Rodrigo, and Jonathan Story, eds. Madrid: Allianza.

Powell, Robert. 1999. *In the Shadow of Power: States and Strategies in International Politics*. Princeton, NJ: Princeton University Press.

Presbo, Andreas. 2009. "The Blue and Yellow Bomb (Part Two)" Armscontrolwonk.org, November 26. Available at: http://guests.armscontrolwonk.com/archive/2547/the-blue-and-yellow-bomb-part-2. Last accessed: November 29, 2014.

Press, Daryl G. 2005. *Calculating Credibility: How Leaders Assess Military Threat*. Ithaca, NY: Cornell University Press.

Priest, Andrew. 2007. "From Hardware to Software: The End of the MLF and the Rise of the Nuclear Planning Group," in *Transforming NATO in the Cold War Challenges beyond Deterrence in the 1960s*, pp. 148–161. Andreas Wenger, Christian Nuenlist, and Anna Locher, eds. London: Routledge.

Pruessen, Ronald W. 2001. "Over the Volcano: The United States and the Taiwan Strait Crisis, 1954–1955," in *Re-examining the Cold War: U.S.-China Diplomacy, 1954–1973*, pp. 77–105. Robert S. Ross and Jiang Changbin, eds. Cambridge, MA: Harvard University Press.

Purkitt, Helen E., and Stephen F. Burgess. 2012. "South Africa's Nuclear Strategy: Deterring 'Total Onslaught' and 'Nuclear Blackmail' in Three Stages," in *Strategy in the Second Nuclear Age: Power, Ambition, and the Ultimate Weapon*, pp. 37–51. Toshi Yoshihara and James R. Holmes, eds. Washington, DC: Georgetown University Press.

Pyle, Kenneth B. 1988. "Japan, the World, and the Twenty-first Century," in *The Political Economy of Japan. Volume 2: The Changing International Context*, pp. 446–486. Takashi Inoguchi and Daniel I. Okimoto, eds. Stanford, CA: Stanford University Press.

Quester, George H. 1973. *The Politics of Nuclear Proliferation*. Baltimore, MD: Johns Hopkins University Press.

1974. "Taiwan and Nuclear Proliferation," *ORBIS*, Vol. 17, No. 1, pp. 140–150.

2000. *Nuclear Monopoly*. New Brunswick, NJ: Transaction Publishers.

Raas, Whitney, and Austin Long. 2007. "Osirak Redux? Assessing Israeli Capabilities to Destroy Iranian Nuclear Facilities," *International Security*, Vol. 31, No. 4, pp. 7–33.

Rabinowitz, Or. 2014. *Bargaining on Nuclear Tests: Washington and Its Cold War Deals*. Oxford: Oxford University Press.

Radchenko, Sergey. 2009. *Two Suns in the Heavens: The Sino-Soviet Struggle for Supremacy, 1962–1967*. Washington, DC, and Stanford, CA: Woodrow Wilson Center Press and Stanford University Press.

2010. "The Sino-Soviet Split," in *The Cambridge History of the Cold War*. Volume II: Crises and Détente, pp. 349–372. Odd A. Westad and Melvyn Leffler, eds. Cambridge: Cambridge University Press.

2011. "North Korea and the End of the Cold War," in *Trilateralism and Beyond: Great Power Politics and the Korean Security Dilemma during and after the Cold War*, pp. 189–212. Robert A. Wampler, ed. Kent, OH: Kent State University Press.

Raghavan, Srinath. 2010. *War and Peace in Modern India*. London: Palgrave Macmillan.

2013. *1971: A Global History of the Creation of Bangladesh*. Cambridge, MA: Harvard University Press.

Rahnema, Ali. 2015. *Behind the 1953 Coup in Iran: Thugs, Turncoats, Soldiers, and Spooks*. Cambridge: Cambridge University Press.

Ramazani, Rouhollah K. 1975. *Iran's Foreign Policy, 1941–1973: A Study of Foreign Policy in Modernizing Nations*. Charlottesville: University Press of Virginia.

2013. *Independence without Freedom: Iran's Foreign Policy*. Charlottesville: University Press of Virginia.

Ray, Jayanta Kumar. 2011. *India's Foreign Relations, 1947–2007*. New Delhi and Oxon: Routledge.

Redick, John R. 1978. "Regional Restraint: U.S. Nuclear Policy and Latin America," *Orbis*, Vol. 22, No. 1, pp. 161–201.

Redick, John R., Julio C. Carasales, and Paulo S. Wrobel. 1994. "Nuclear Rapprochement: Argentina, Brazil, and the Non-Proliferation Regime," *Washington Quarterly*, Vol. 18, No. 1, pp. 107–122.

Reiss, Mitchell. 1988. *Without the Bomb: The Politics of Nuclear Nonproliferation*. New York: Columbia University Press.

1991. "The Illusion of Influence: The United States and Pakistan's Nuclear Programme," *The RUSI Journal*, Vol. 136, No. 2, pp. 47–50.

1993. "Safeguarding the Nuclear Peace in South Asia," *Asian Survey*, Vol. 33, No. 12, pp. 1107–1121.

1995. *Bridled Ambition: Why Countries Constrain Their Nuclear Capabilities*. Washington, DC: Woodrow Wilson Center Press.

Reiter, Dan. 2006. "Preventive Attacks against Nuclear Programs and the 'Success' at Osiraq," *Nonproliferation Review*, Vol. 12, No. 2, pp. 355–371.

2014. "Security Commitments and Nuclear Proliferation," *Foreign Policy Analysis*, Vol. 10, No. 1, pp. 61–80.

Reynolds, Celia L., and Wilfred T. Wan. 2012. "Empirical Trends in Sanctions and Positive Inducements in Nonproliferation," in *Sanctions, Statecraft, and Nuclear Proliferation*, pp. 56–122. Etel Solingen, ed. Cambridge: Cambridge University Press.

Rhodes, Richard. 1986. *The Making of the Atomic Bomb*. New York: Simon and Schuster.

1995. *Dark Sun: The Making of the Hydrogen Bomb*. New York: Simon and Schuster.

2010. *The Twilight of the Bombs: Recent Challenges, New Dangers, and the Prospects for a World without Nuclear Weapons*. New York: Knopf.

Rice, Condoleezza. 2011. *No Higher Honor: A Memoir of My Years in Washington*. New York: Random House.

Richelson, Jeffrey T. 2006. *Spying on the Bomb: American Nuclear Intelligence from Nazi Germany to Iran and North Korea*. New York: Norton.

Riedel, Bruce. 2013. *Avoiding Armageddon: America, India, and Pakistan to the Brink and Back*. Washington, DC: Brookings Institution Press.

Ritter, Scott. 1999. *Endgame: Solving the Iraq Crisis*. New York: Simon and Schuster.

Rizas, Sotiris. 2009. "Managing a Conflict between Allies: United States Policy towards Greece and Turkey in Relation to the Aegean Dispute, 1974–76," *Cold War History*, Vol. 9, No. 3, pp. 367–387.

Robinson, Thomas W. 1981. "The Sino-Soviet Border Conflict," in *Diplomacy of Power: Soviet Armed Forces as a Political Instrument*, pp. 265–313. Stephen S. Kaplan, ed. Washington, DC: Brookings Institution.

Rodrigo, Fernando. 1995. "La inserción de Espanña en la política de seguridad occidental," in *Las relaciones exteriores de la España democrática*, pp. 77–103. Richard Gillespie, Fernando Rodrigo, and Jonathan Story, eds. Madrid: Alianza.

Roehrig, Terence. 2012. "North Korea's Nuclear Weapons Program: Motivations, Strategy, and Doctrine," in *Strategy in the Second Nuclear Age: Power, Ambition, and the Ultimate Weapon*, pp. 81–98. Toshi Yoshihara and James R. Holmes, eds. Washington, DC: Georgetown University Press.

Ro'i, Yaacov, and Boris Morozov, eds. 2008. *The Soviet Union and the June 1967 Six Day War*. Stanford, CA: Stanford University Press.

Romberg, Alan D. 2003. *Rein in at the Brink of the Precipice: American Policy toward Taiwan and US-PRC Relations*. Armonk, NY: Henry L. Stimson Center.

Rosenberg, David Alan. 1979. "American Atomic Strategy and the Hydrogen Bomb Decision," *The Journal of American History*, Vol. 66, No. 1, pp. 62–87.

1982. "U.S. Nuclear Stockpile, 1945 to 1950," *The Bulletin of the Atomic Scientist*, Vol. 38, No. 5, pp. 25–30.

1983. "The Origins of Overkill: Nuclear Weapons and American Strategy," *International Security*, Vol. 7, No. 4, pp. 3–71.

Ross, Robert S. 1995. *Negotiating Cooperation: The United States and China, 1969–1989.* Stanford, CA: Stanford University Press.

Ross, Robert S., and Jiang Changbin, eds. 2001. *Re-examining the Cold War: U.S.-China Diplomacy, 1954–1973.* Cambridge, MA: Harvard University Press.

Rovner, Joshua. 2010. *Fixing the Facts: National Security and the Politics of Intelligence.* Ithaca, NY: Cornell University Press.

Rubin, Barry. 1980. *Paved with Good Intentions: The American Experience and Iran.* New York: Oxford University Press.

Rublee, Maria Rost. 2009. *Nonproliferation Norms: Why States Choose Nuclear Restraint.* Athens, GA: University of Georgia Press.

2010. "The Nuclear Threshold States: Challenges and Opportunities Posed by Brazil and Japan," *The Nonproliferation Review*, Vol. 17, No. 1, pp. 49–70.

Ryan, Mark A. 1989. *Chinese Attitudes toward Nuclear Weapons: China and the United States during the Korean War.* Armonk, NY: M. E. Sharpe.

Sagan, Scott D. 1996–1997. "Why Do States Build Nuclear Weapons? Three Models in Search of a Bomb," *International Security*, Vol. 21, No. 3, pp. 54–86.

2011. "The Causes of Nuclear Weapons Proliferation," *Annual Review of Political Science*, Vol. 14, pp. 225–244.

2014. "Two Renaissances in Nuclear Security Studies." Introduction to H-Diplo/ISSF Forum, No. 2, "What We Talk about When We Talk about Nuclear Weapons," Issforum.org, June 15. Available at: http://issforum.org/ISSF/PDF/ISSF-Forum-2.pdf. Last accessed: November 1, 2015.

Sagan, Scott D., and Kenneth N. Waltz. 2012. *The Spread of Nuclear Weapons: An Enduring Debate.* New York: W. W. Norton.

Samore, Gary. 2015. *The Iran Nuclear Deal: A Definitive Guide.* Cambridge, MA: Harvard Kennedy School's Belfer Center for Science and International Affairs.

Samuels, Richard J., and James L. Schoff. 2013. "Japan's Nuclear Hedge: Beyond 'Allergy' and Breakout," in *Strategic Asia 2013–14: Asia in the Second Nuclear Age*, pp. 233–264. Ashley J. Tellis, Abraham M. Denmark, and Travis Tanner, eds. Seattle: National Bureau of Asian Research.

Sarkar, Jayita. 2015a. "The Making of a Non-Aligned Nuclear Power: India's Proliferation Drift, 1964–8," *The International History Review*, Vol. 37, No. 5, pp. 933–950.

2015b. "'Wean Them Away from French Tutelage': Franco-Indian Nuclear Relations and Anglo-American Anxieties during the Early Cold War, 1948–1952," *Cold War History*, Vol. 15, No. 3, pp. 375–394.

Sattar, Abdul. 2007. *Pakistan's Foreign Policy 1947–2005: A Concise History.* New York: Oxford University Press.

Saunders, Chris. 2013. Review of Jamie Miller's "Yes, Minister. ..." H-Diplo article review No. 440. December 20. Available at http://h-diplo.org/reviews/PDF/AR440.pdf. Last accessed: May 2, 2016.

Saunders, Chris, and Sue Onslow. 2010. "The Cold War and Southern Africa, 1976–1990," in *The Cambridge History of the Cold War. Volume 3: Endings*, pp. 222–243. Melvyn P. Leffler and Odd Arne Westad, eds. New York: Cambridge University Press.

Schaller, Michael. 1985. *The American Occupation of Japan: The Origins of the Cold War in Asia.* New York: Oxford University Press.

1997. *Altered States: The United States and Japan since the Occupation.* New York: Oxford University Press.

2001. "Détente and the Strategic Triangle Or, 'Drinking Your Mao Tai and Having Your Vodka, Too'," in *Re-examining the Cold War: U.S.-China Diplomacy, 1954–1973*, pp. 361–389. Robert S. Ross and Jiang Changbin, eds. Cambridge, MA: Harvard University Press.

Schelling, Thomas. 1960. *The Strategy of Conflict.* Cambridge, MA: Harvard University Press.

1966. *Arms and Influence.* New Haven, CT: Yale University Press.

Schneider, Jonas. 2014. "Nuclear Nonproliferation within the Context of U.S. Alliances – Protection, Status, and the Psychology of West Germany's Nuclear Reversal." Paper presented at the International Studies Association annual convention.

Scholtz, Leopold. 2013. *The SADF in the Border War 1966–1989.* Cape Town: Tafelberg.

Schultz, Kenneth F., and David A Grimes. 2012. "Case-control Studies: Research in Reverse," *The Lancet*, Vol. 359, pp. 431–434.

Schulzinger, Robert D. 2001. "The Johnson Administration, China, and the Vietnam War," in *Re-examining the Cold War: U.S.-China Diplomacy, 1954–1973*, pp. 238–261. Robert S. Ross and Jiang Changbin, eds. Cambridge, MA: Harvard University Press.

Schwab, George. 1969. "Switzerland's Tactical Nuclear Weapons Policy," *Orbis*, Vol. 13, No. 3, pp. 900–914.

Schwartz, David N. 1983. *NATO's Nuclear Dilemmas.* Washington, DC: Brookings Institution.

Schwarz, Hans-Peter. 1992. "Adenauer, le nucléaire, et la France," *Revue d'Histoire Diplomatique*, Vol. 106, No. 4, pp. 297–311.

1997. *Konrad Adenauer: A German Politician and Statesman in a Period of War, Revolution and Reconstruction.* Providence, RI: Berghahn Books.

Seaborg, Glenn T. 1987. *Stemming the Tide: Arms Control in the Johnson Years.* Lexington, MA: Lexington Books.

Sechser, Todd, and Matthew Fuhrmann. 2013. "Crisis Bargaining and Nuclear Blackmail," *International Organization*, Vol. 67, No. 1, pp. 173–195.

Segev, Samuel. 1988. *The Iranian Triangle*. New York: Free Press.

Selcher, Wayne. 1985. "Brazilian-Argentine Relations in the 1980s: From Weary Rivalry to Friendly Competition," *Journal of Interamerican Studies and World Affairs*, Vol. 27, No. 2, pp. 25–53.

Shalom, Zaki. 2005. *Israel's Nuclear Option: Behind the Scenes Diplomacy between Dimona and Washington*. Portland: Sussex Academic Press.

Sheetz, Mark. 2002. "Continental Drift: Franco-German Relations and the Shifting Premises of European Security." PhD Dissertation, Columbia University.

Sheikh, Ali T. 1994. "Pakistan," in *Nuclear Proliferation after the Cold War*, pp. 191–206. Mitchell Reiss and Robert S. Litwak, eds. Cambridge, MA: Ballinger.

Shepley, James. 1956. "How Dulles Averted War," *Life*, Vol. 40, No. 3, January 16, pp. 70–80.

Shubin, Vladimir. 2009. "Unsung Heroes: The Soviet Military and the Liberation of Southern Africa," in *Cold War in Southern Africa: White Power, Black Liberation*, pp. 154–176. Sue Onslow, ed. London: Routledge.

Sigal, Leon V. 1998. *Disarming Strangers: Nuclear Diplomacy with North Korea*. Princeton, NJ: Princeton University Press.

Siler, Michael J. 1998. "U.S. Nuclear Nonproliferation Policy in the Northeast Asian Region during the Cold War: The South Korean Case," *East Asia: An International Quarterly*, Vol. 16, pp. 41–86.

Singer, J. David. 1987. "Reconstructing the Correlates of War Dataset on Material Capabilities of States, 1816–1985," *International Interactions*, Vol. 14, No. 2, pp. 115–132.

Singh, Sonali, and Christopher R. Way. 2004. "The Correlates of Nuclear Proliferation: A Quantitative Test," *Journal of Conflict Resolution*, Vol. 48, No. 6, pp. 859–885.

Snyder, Glenn. 1961. *Deterrence and Defense*. Princeton, NJ: Princeton University Press.

Snyder, Jed C. 1983. "The Road to Osirak: Baghdad's Quest for the Bomb," *Middle East Journal*, Vol. 37, No. 4, pp. 565–593.

Snyder, Scott. 2009. "Assessing North Korea's Strategic Intentions and Motivations," in *North Korea's Foreign Policy under Kim Jong Il: New Perspectives*, pp. 39–56. Tae-Hwan Kwak and Seung-Ho Joo, eds. Burlington, VT: Ashgate Publishing Company.

  2010. "South Korean Nuclear Decision Making," in *Forecasting Nuclear Proliferation in the 21st Century: A Comparative Perspective, Volume*

2: *A Comparative Perspective*, pp. 158–181. William C. Potter with Gaukhar Mukhatzhanova, eds. Stanford, CA: Stanford University Press.

Snyder, Scott and Joyce Lee. 2012. "Infusing Commitment with Credibility: the Role of Security Assurances in Cementing the U.S.-ROK Alliance," in *Security Assurances and Nuclear Nonproliferation*, pp. 162–188. Jeffrey Knopf, ed. Stanford, CA: Stanford University Press.

Sobek, David, Dennis M. Foster, and Samuel B. Robison. 2011. "Conventional Wisdom? The Effect of Nuclear Proliferation on Armed Conflict, 1945–2001," *International Studies Quarterly*, Vol. 56, No. 1, pp. 149–162.

Solingen, Etel. 1994. "The Political Economy of Nuclear Restraint," *International Security*, Vol. 19, No. 2, pp. 126–169.

——— 1996. *Industrial Policy, Technology, and International Bargaining: Designing Nuclear Industries in Argentina and Brazil*. Stanford, CA: Stanford University Press.

——— 2007. *Nuclear Logics: Contrasting Paths in East Asia and the Middle East*. Princeton, NJ: Princeton University Press.

——— 2010. "The Perils of Prediction: Japan's Once and Future Nuclear Status," in *Forecasting Nuclear Proliferation in the 21st Century*. *Volume 2: A Comparative Perspective*, pp. 131–157. William C. Potter with Gaukhar Mukhatzhanova, eds. Stanford, CA: Stanford University Press.

Solsten, Eric, and Sandra W. Meditz, eds. 1988. *Spain: A Country Study*. Washington, DC: GPO for the Library of Congress.

Soutou, Georges-Henri. 1989. "La Politique Nucléaire de Pierre Mendès France," *Relations Internationales*, Vol. 59, pp. 317–330.

——— 1993. "Les Accords de 1957 et 1958: Vers Une Communauté Stratégique et Nucléaire entre la France, l'Allemagne et l'Italie?," *Matériaux pour l'Histoire de Notre Temps,* Vol. 31, No. 1, pp. 1–12.

——— 1996. *L'alliance incertaine. Les rapports politico-strategiques franco-allemands, 1954–1996*. Paris: Fayard.

——— 2012. "La sécurité de la France dans l'après-guerre," in *La France et l'OTAN*, pp. 21–51. Maurice Vaïsse, Pierre Melandri, and Frédéric Bozo, eds. Bruxelles: André Versailles.

Spector, Leonard S. 1987. *Going Nuclear*. Cambridge, MA: Ballinger.

Spector, Leonard S., and Jacqueline R. Smith. 1990. *Nuclear Ambitions: The Spread of Nuclear Weapons, 1989–1990*. Boulder, CO: Westview.

Spektor, Matias. 2006. "Equivocal Engagement: Kissinger, Silveira and the Politics of US–Brazil Relations (1969–1983)." DPhil. dissertation, Oxford University.

Squassoni, Sharon, and David Fite. 2005. "Brazil's Nuclear History," *Arms Control Today*, Vol. 35, No. 8, pp. 16–17.

St. John, Ronald Bruce. 2004. "Libya Is Not Iraq: Preemptive Strikes, WMD and Diplomacy," *The Middle East Journal*, Vol. 158, No. 3, pp. 386–402.

Stein, Aaron. 2013. "Turkey's Nuclear History Holds Lessons for the Future," in *WMD Junction*. Washington, DC: James Martin Center for Nonproliferation Studies (CNS). Available at: http://wmdjunction.com/ 130513_turkey_nuclear_history.htm. Last accessed: May 2, 2016.

Steyn, Hannes, Richardt van der Walt, and Jan van Loggerenberg. 2003. *Armament and Disarmament: South Africa's Nuclear Weapons Experience*. Pretoria: Network Publishers.

Stiles, David. 2006. "A Fusion Bomb over Andalucía: U.S. Information Policy and the 1966 Palomares Incident," *Journal of Cold War Studies*, Vol. 8, No. 1, pp. 49–67.

Stockholm International Peace Research Institute (SPIRI). 2016. "Databases." Available at: www.sipri.org/databases. Last accessed: May 3, 2016.

Stueck, William. 1995. *The Korean War: An International History*. Princeton, NJ: Princeton University Press.

    2011. "Ambivalent Occupation: U.S. Armed Forces in Korea, 1953 to the Present," in *Trilateralism and beyond: Great Power Politics and the Korean Security Dilemma during and after the Cold War*, pp. 13–49. Robert A. Wampler, ed. Kent, OH: Kent State University Press.

Stumpf, Waldo. 1995–1996. "South Africa's Nuclear Weapons Program: From Deterrence to Dismantlement," *Arms Control Today*, Vol. 25, No. 10, pp. 3–8.

Subrahmanyam, K. 1987. "India's Security Challenges and Responses: Evolving a Security Doctrine," *Strategic Analysis*, Vol. 11, No. 1, pp. 1–12.

    1998. "India's Nuclear Policy – 1964–98: A Personal Recollection," in *Nuclear India*, pp. 26–53. Jasjit Singh, ed. New Delhi: Institute for Defence Studies and Analysis.

Subramaniam, R. R. 1987. "U.S. Policy and South Asia: The Decision-Making Dimension," in *The Security of South Asia: American and Asian Perspectives*, pp. 141–153. Stephen P. Cohen, ed. Chicago: University of Illinois Press.

Suskind, Ron. 2006. *The One Percent Doctrine: Deep Inside America's Pursuit of Its Enemies since 9/11*. New York: Simon and Schuster.

Swango, Dane Eugene. 2009. "The Nuclear Nonproliferation Treaty: Constrainer, Screener, or Enabler?" PhD Dissertation, University of California, Los Angeles.

Szalontai, Balazs. 2006. *Kim Il-Sung in the Khrushchev Era: Soviet-DPRK Relations and the Roots of North Korean Despotism, 1953–1964*. Stanford, CA: Stanford University Press

    2011. "The Elephant in the Room: The Soviet Union and India's Nuclear Program, 1967–1989." Nuclear Proliferation International History Project Working Paper #1, Woodrow Wilson International Center for Scholars.

Szalontai, Balazs, and Sergey Radchenko. 2006. *North Korea's Efforts to Acquire Nuclear Technology and Nuclear Weapons: Evidence from Russian and Hungarian Archives.* Cold War International History Project. Working Paper #53, Washington, DC: Woodrow Wilson International Center for Scholars.

Takeyh, Ray. 2001. "The Rogue Who Came in from the Cold," *Foreign Affairs,* Vol. 80, No. 3, pp. 62–72.

2009. *Guardians of the Revolution: Iran and the World in the Age of the Ayatollahs.* New York: Oxford University Press.

Takubo, Masufumi. 2008. "Wake Up, Stop Dreaming: Reassessing Japan's Reprocessing Program," *The Nonproliferation Review,* Vol. 15, No. 1, pp. 71–94.

Tamsett, Jeremy. 2004. "The Israeli Bombing of Osiraq Reconsidered: Successful Counterproliferation?," *Nonproliferation Review,* Vol. 11, No. 3, pp. 70–85.

Tannenwald, Nina. 1999. "The Nuclear Taboo: the United States and the Normative Basis of Nuclear Non-Use," *International Organization,* Vol. 53, No. 3, pp. 433–468.

2013. "Justice and Fairness in the Nuclear Nonproliferation Regime," *Ethics and International Affairs,* Vol. 27, No. 3, pp. 299–317.

Tatsumi, Yuki. 2012. "Maintaining Japan's Non-Nuclear Identity: The Role of U.S. Security Assurances," in *Security Assurances and Nuclear Nonproliferation,* pp. 137–161. Jeffrey Knopf, ed. Stanford, CA: Stanford University Press.

Taubman, William. 2003. *Khrushchev: The Man and His Era.* New York: W. W. Norton.

Tenet, George. 2007. *At the Center of the Storm: My Years at the CIA.* With Bill Harlow. New York: HarperCollins.

Tertrais, Bruno. 2004. "Destruction Assurée: The Origins and Development of French Nuclear Strategy, 1945–1982," in *Getting MAD: Nuclear Mutual Assured Destruction, Its Origins and Practice,* pp. 51–122. Henry D. Sokolski ed. Carlisle, PA: Strategic Studies Institute.

2009. "The Middle East's Next Nuclear State." *Strategic Insights,* Vol. 8, No. 1. Available at: http://hdl.handle.net/10945/11438. Last accessed: May 2, 2016.

Thakur, Ramesh, and Carlyle A. Thayer. 1992. *Soviet Relations with India and Vietnam.* London: Palgrave Macmillan.

Thayer, Bradley A. 1995. "The Causes of Nuclear Proliferation and the Utility of the Nuclear Non-Proliferation Regime," *Security Studies,* Vol. 4, No. 3, pp. 463–519.

Thompson, Alexander. 2010. *Channels of Power: The U.N. Security Council and U.S. Statecraft in Iraq.* Ithaca, NY: Cornell University Press.

Thompson, William R. 2001. "Identifying Rivals and Rivalries in World Politics," *International Studies Quarterly,* Vol. 45, No. 4, pp. 557–586.

Thornton, Thomas Perry. 1970. "South Asia and the Great Powers," *World Affairs,* Vol. 132, No. 4, pp. 345–358.

Touhey, Ryan. 2007. "Troubled from the Beginning: Canada's Nuclear Relations with India during the 1960s," in *Canadian Policy on Nuclear Cooperation with India: Confronting New Dilemmas,* pp. 11–33. Karthika Sasikumar and Wade Huntley, eds. Vancouver: Simons Centre for Disarmament and Non-Proliferation Research.

Trachtenberg, Marc. 1999. *A Constructed Peace: The Making of the European Settlement, 1945–1963.* Princeton, NJ: Princeton University Press.

2011. "The French Factor in U.S. Foreign Policy during the Nixon-Pompidou Period, 1969–1974," *Journal of Cold War Studies,* Vol. 13, No. 1, pp. 4–59.

Troyanovsky, Oleg. 2000. "The Making of Soviet Foreign Policy," in *Nikita Khrushchev,* pp. 209–241. William Taubman, Sergei Khrushchev, and Abbott Gleason, eds. New Haven, CT: Yale University Press.

Tsakonas, Panayotis. 2010. *The Incomplete Breakthrough in Greek–Turkish Relations: Grasping Greece's Socialization Strategy.* London: Palgrave Macmillan.

Tsakonas, Panayotis, and Antonis Tournikiotis. 2003. "Greece's Elusive Quest for Security Providers: The 'Expectations–Reality Gap,'" *Security Dialogue,* Vol. 34, No. 3, pp. 301–314.

Tucker, Nancy B. 2001. *China Confidential: American Diplomats and Sino-American Relations, 1945–1996.* New York: Columbia University Press.

2009. *Strait Talk: United States-Taiwan Relations and the Crisis with China.* Cambridge, MA: Harvard University Press.

2012. "The Evolution of U.S.-China Relations," in *Tangled Titans: The United States and China,* pp. 29–52. David Shambaugh, ed. Lanham, MD: Rowman and Littlefield.

Udum, Sebnem. 2007. "Turkey's Non-Nuclear Weapon Status: A Theoretical Assessment," *ISYP Journal on Science and World Affairs,* Vol. 3, No. 2, pp. 51–59.

Ülgen, Sinan. 2012. "Turkey and the Bomb." Washington, DC: Carnegie Endowment for International Peace.

Ullman, Richard. 1989. "The Covert French Connection," *Foreign Policy,* No. 75, pp. 3–33.

Vaïsse, Maurice. 1991. "Un Dialogue de Sourds. Les Relations Franco-Américaines de 1957 à 1960," *Relations Internationales,* Vol. 68, pp. 407–423.

1992. "Le Choix Atomique de la France (1945–1958)," *Vingtième Siècle. Revue d'Histoire*, Vol. 36, pp. 21–30.

van Sant, John, Peter Mauch, and Yoneyuki Sugita. 2007. *Historical Dictionary of United States-Japanese Relations*. Historical Dictionaries of U.S. Diplomacy Series. Lanham, MD: Scarecrow Press.

van Wyk, Martha S. (Anna-Mart). 2007a. "The US Government and South African Nuclear Capability, 1949–1995." SHAFR 2007 paper.

2007b. "Ally or Critic? The United States' Response to South African Nuclear Development, 1949–1980," *Cold War History*, Vol. 7, No. 2, pp. 195–225.

2009. "The USA and Apartheid South Africa's Nuclear Aspirations, 1949–1980," in *Cold War in Southern Africa: White Power, Black Liberation*, pp. 55–83. Sue Onslow, ed. London: Routledge.

2010a. "South Africa's Nuclear Programme and the Cold War," *History Compass*, Vol. 8, No. 7, pp. 562–572.

2010b. "Sunset over Atomic Apartheid: United States–South African Nuclear Relations, 1981–93," *Cold War History*, Vol. 10, No. 1, pp. 51–79.

2013. "Apartheid's Atomic Bomb: Birth and Demise." Paper Presented at the Summer Institute of the Society for Historians of American Foreign Relations, Washington, DC.

Vargas, Everton. 1997. "Átomos na Integracão: a Aproximacão Brasil-Argentina no Campo Nuclear e a Construcão do Mercosul," *Revista Brasileira de Política Internacional*, Vol. 40, No. 1, pp. 41–74.

Varnum, Jessica C. 2010. "Turkey in Transition: Toward or Away from Nuclear Weapons?," in *Forecasting Nuclear Proliferation in the 21st Century. Volume 2: A Comparative Perspective*, pp. 229–254. William C. Potter with Gaukhar Mukhatzhanova, eds. Stanford, CA: Stanford University Press.

Velazquez, Arturo. 2004. "Civil-Military Affairs and Security Institutions in the Southern Cone: The Sources of Argentine-Brazilian Nuclear Cooperation," *Latin American Politics and Society*, Vol. 46, No. 4, pp. 29–60.

Wallin, Lars. 1991. "Sweden," in *Security with Nuclear Weapons? Different Perspectives on National Security*, pp. 360–381. Regina Cowen Karp, ed. Oxford: Oxford University Press.

Walsh, James J. (Jim). 1997. "Surprise Down Under: The Secret History of Australia's Nuclear Ambitions," *Nonproliferation Review*, Vol. 5, No. 1, pp. 1–20.

2001. "Bombs Unbuilt: Power, Ideas and Institutions in International Politics." PhD dissertation, Massachusetts Institute of Technology.

2012. "Security Assurances and Iran: Assessments and Re-Conceptualization," in *Security Assurances and Nuclear Nonproliferation*, pp. 111–136. Jeffrey Knopf, ed. Stanford, CA: Stanford University Press.

Walters, Vernon. 1978. *Silent Missions*. Garden City, NY: Double Day.

Waltz, Kenneth N. 1979. *Theory of International Politics*. Reading, MA: Addison-Wesley.

  1981. "The Spread of Nuclear Weapons: More May Better." Adelphi Papers, No.171. London: International Institute for Strategic Studies.

  2003. "More May Be Better," in *The Spread of Nuclear Weapons: A Debate Renewed*, pp. 3–45. Scott D. Sagan and Kenneth N. Waltz. New York: W. W. Norton.

Wang, Vincent Wei-cheng. 2008. "Taiwan: Conventional Deterrence, Soft Power, and the Nuclear Option," in *The Long Shadow: Nuclear Weapons and Security in 21st Century Asia*, pp. 404–428. Muthiah Alagappa, ed. Stanford, CA: Stanford University Press.

Wang, Zongchun. 2007. "The Soviet Factor in Sino-American Normalization, 1969–1979," in *Normalization of U.S.-China Relations: An International History*, pp. 147–174. William C. Kirby, Robert S. Ross, and Gong Li, eds. Cambridge, MA: Harvard University Press.

Way, Christopher. 2012. "Nuclear Proliferation Dates." Unpublished document. Available at: http://falcon.arts.cornell.edu/crw12/documents/Nuclear%20 Proliferation%20Dates.pdf. Last accessed: December 2, 2015.

Way, Christopher, and Jessica L. P. Weeks. 2014. "Making It Personal: Regime Type and Nuclear Proliferation," *American Journal of Political Science*, Vol. 58, No. 3, pp. 705–719.

Weinberg, Gerhard L. 1994. *World at Arms: A Global History of World War II*. Cambridge: Cambridge University Press.

Wendt, Alexander. 1999. *Social Theory of International Politics*. Cambridge: Cambridge University Press.

Wenger, Andreas. 2004. "Crisis and Opportunity: NATO's Transformation and the Multilateralization of Détente, 1966–1968," *Journal of Cold War Studies*, Vol. 6, No. 1, pp. 22–74.

Westad, Odd A. 1998. *Brothers in Arms: The Rise and Fall of the Sino-Soviet Alliance, 1945–1963*. Washington, DC: Woodrow Wilson Center Press.

  2003. *Decisive Encounters: The Chinese Civil War, 1946–1950*. Stanford, CA: Stanford University Press.

Wheeler, Nicholas. 1990. "The Atlee Government's Nuclear Strategy, 1945–51," in *Britain and the First Cold War*, pp. 130–145. Ann Deighton, ed. New York: St. Martin's.

Whiting, Allen Suess. 1968. *China Crosses the Yalu: The Decision to Enter the Korean War*. Stanford, CA: Stanford University Press.

Whitlark, Rachel E. 2013. "All Options on the Table? Nuclear Proliferation, Preventive War, and a Leader's Decision to Intervene. Chapter 3: JFK and LBJ Confront China's Nuclear Program." Paper presented at the NSRI Conference, October 17–19, Austin, Texas.

Williams, Kristen P. 2012. "Romania's Resistance to the USSR," in *Beyond Great Powers and Hegemons: Why Secondary States Support, Follow, or Challenge*, pp. 33–48. Kristen P. Williams, Steven E. Lobell, and Neal G. Jesse, eds. Stanford, CA: Stanford University Press.

Williamson Jr., Samuel R., and Steven L. Rearden. 1993. *The Origins of U.S. Nuclear Strategy, 1945–1953*. New York: St. Martin's Press.

Wing, Christine, and Fiona Simpson. 2013. *Detect, Dismantle, and Disarm. IAEA Verification, 1992–2005*. Washington, DC: United States Institute of Peace.

Wirtz, James J. 2012. "Conclusions," in *Security Assurances and Nuclear Nonproliferation*, pp. 275–290. Jeffrey Knopf, ed. Stanford, CA: Stanford University Press.

Wit, Joel S., Daniel B. Poneman, and Robert L. Gallucci. 2004. *Going Critical: The First North Korean Nuclear Crisis*. Washington, DC: Brookings

Wohlstetter, Albert. 1961. "Nuclear Sharing: NATO and the N+1 Country," *Foreign Affairs*, Vol. 39, No. 3, pp. 355–387.

Wohlstetter, Roberta. 1978. "The Buddha Smiles: U.S. Peaceful Aid and the Indian Bomb," in *Nuclear Policies: Fuel without the Bomb*, pp. 57–72. Albert Wohlstetter, Victor Gilinsky, Robert Gillette, and Roberta Wohlstetter, eds. Cambridge, MA: Ballinger.

Woods, Kevin M. 2008. *The Mother of All Battles: Saddam Hussein's Strategic Plan for the Persian Gulf War*. Annapolis, MD: Naval Institute Press.

Woods, Kevin M., David D. Palkki, and Mark E. Stout. 2011. *The Saddam Tapes: The Inner Workings of a Tyrant's Regime, 1978–2001*. New York: Cambridge University Press.

Wrobel, Paulo S. 1996. "Brazil and the NPT: Resistance to Change?," *Security Dialogue*, Vol. 27, No. 3, pp. 337–347.

Xia, Yafeng, and Zhihua Shen. 2014. "China's Last Ally: Beijing's Policy toward North Korea during the U.S.–China Rapprochement, 1970–1975," *Diplomatic History*, Vol. 38, No. 5, pp. 1083–1113.

Yang, Zie-eun. 2011. "South Korea's Nuclear Decision: Explanations for South Korea's Nuclear Motivation and Renouncement." MA dissertation, Georgetown University.

Yeaw, Christopher T., Andrew S. Erickson, and Michael S. Chase. 2012. "The Future of Chinese Nuclear Policy and Strategy," in *Strategy in the Second Nuclear Age: Power, Ambition, and the Ultimate Weapon*, pp. 53–80. Toshi Yoshihara and James R. Holmes, eds. Washington, DC: Georgetown University Press.

Yilmaz, Şuhnaz. 2012. "Turkey's Quest for NATO Membership: The Institutionalization of the Turkish-American Alliance." *Journal of Southeast European and Black Sea Studies*, Vol. 12, No. 4, pp. 481–495.

Yusuf, Moeed. 2009. "Predicting Proliferation: The History of the Future of Nuclear Weapons," Policy Paper, Brookings Institution.

Zaloga, Steven J. 1993. *Target America: The Soviet Union and the Strategic Arms Race, 1945–1964*. New York: Presidio Press.

Zartman, I. Willian. 1987. "Foreign Relations of North Africa," *Annals of the American Academy of Political and Social Science*, Vol. 489 (International Affairs in Africa), pp. 13–27

Zhang, Shugang. 1992. *Deterrence and Strategic Culture: Chinese-American Confrontations, 1949–1958*. Ithaca, NY: Cornell University Press.

Zhao, Tong. 2010. "Sanction Experience and Sanction Behavior: An Analysis of Chinese Perception and Behavior on Economic Sanctions," *Contemporary Politics*, Vol. 16, No. 3, pp. 263–278.

Zhihua, Shen. 2000. "Sino-Soviet Relations and the Origins of the Korean War: Stalin's Strategic Goals in the Far East," *Journal of Cold War Studies*, Vol. 2, No. 2, pp. 44–68.

Zubok, Vladislav. 2000. "The Case of Divided Germany, 1953–1964," in *Nikita Khrushchev*, pp. 275–300. William Taubman, Sergei Khrushchev, and Abbott Gleason, eds. New Haven, CT: Yale University Press.

Primary Source Collections

Acheson, Dean. 1949. "Letter of Transmittal," July 30, 1949, in United States. Department of State. 1949. *United States Relations with China: With Special Reference to the Period 1944–1949*. Washington, DC: U.S. Government Printing Office, p. XV.

   1950. "Crisis in Asia – An Examination of U.S. Policy," remarks made before the National Press Club, Washington, DC, Jan. 12, 1950 in *Department of the State Bulletin*, Vol. XXII, No. 551, Jan. 23, 1950, pp. 111–118.

Central Intelligence Agency. 1978. "South Korea: Nuclear Developments and Strategic Decisionmaking." Langley, VA: Central Intelligence Agency, National Foreign Assessment Center.

   1994. CIA Intelligence Memorandum 225. In *CIA Cold War Records: The CIA under Harry Truman*. Michael Warner, ed. Langley, VA: Central Intelligence Agency.

Digital National Security Archive, "Japan and the United States: Diplomatic, Security, and Economic Relations, 1960–1976." Available at: http://proquest.libguides.com/dnsa/japan1960. Last accessed: March 11, 2016.

"Japan and the United States, Part II: Diplomatic, Security, and Economic Relations, 1977–1992." Available at: http://proquest.libguides.com/dnsa/japan1977. Last accessed: March 11, 2016.

"The Kissinger Transcripts: A Verbatim Record of U.S. Diplomacy, 1969–77." Available at: http://search.proquest.com/dnsa_kt. Last accessed: December 20, 2015.

"The United States and the Two Koreas, Part II, 1969–2010." Available at: http://search.proquest.com/dnsa_kr/productfulldescdetail. Last accessed: March 11, 2016.

Eisenhower, Dwight D. 1959a. *Public Papers of the Presidents: Dwight D. Eisenhower: 1955: Containing the Public Messages, Speeches, and Statements of the President, January 1 to December 31, 1955.* (Washington, D.C.: U.S. Government Printing Office.)

1959b. *Public Papers of the Presidents: Dwight D. Eisenhower: 1955: Containing the Public Messages, Speeches, and Statements of the President, January 1 to December 31, 1958* (Washington, D.C.: U.S. Government Printing Office, 1959).

Foreign Relations of the United States, 1944. Volume VI, *China*, ed. William M. Franklin (Washington, D.C.: U.S. Government Printing Office, 1967).

Foreign Relations of the United States, 1945, Volume VII, *The Far East, China*, ed. William M. Franklin (Washington, D.C.: U.S. Government Printing Office, 1969). Available at: https://history.state.gov/historical-documents/frus1945v07. Last accessed: December 20, 2015.

Foreign Relations of the United States, 1949a, Vol. VII, Part 2, *The Far East and Australasia*, eds. John G. Reid and John P. Glennon (Washington, D.C.: U.S. Government Printing Office, 1976). Available at: https://history.state.gov/historicaldocuments/frus1949v07p2. Last accessed: December 20, 2015.

Foreign Relations of the United States, 1949b, Volume IX, *The Far East: China*, eds. Francis C. Prescott, Herbert A. Fine, Velma Hastings Cassidy (Washington, D.C.: U.S. Government Printing Office, 1974). Available at: https://history.state.gov/historicaldocuments/frus1949v09. Last accessed: December 20, 2015.

Foreign Relations of the United States, 1950a, Volume VI, *East Asia and the Pacific*, eds. Neal H. Peterson, William Z. Slany, Charles S. Sampson, John P. Glennon, and David W. Mabon (Washington, D.C.: U.S. Government Printing Office, 1976). Available at: https://history.state.gov/historical-documents/frus1950v06. Last accessed: December 20, 2015.

Foreign Relations of the United States, 1950b, *Korea*, Volume VII, ed. John P. Glennon (Washington, D.C.: U.S. Government Printing Office, 1976). Available at: https://history.state.gov/historicaldocuments/frus1950v07. Last accessed: December 20, 2015.

Foreign Relations of the United States, 1952–1954, Volume II, Part 1, *National Security Affairs*, ed. Lisle A. Rose and Neal H. Peterson (Washington, D.C.: U.S. Government Printing Office, 1979). Available at: https://history.state.gov/historicaldocuments/frus1952-54v02p1. Last accessed: December 20, 2015.

Foreign Relations of the United States, 1952–1954, Volume VI, Part 2, *Western Europe and Canada*, ed. William Z. Slany (Washington, D.C.: Government Printing Office, 1986). Available at: https://history.state.gov/historicaldocuments/frus1952-54v06p2. Last accessed: December 20, 2015.

Foreign Relations of the United States, 1952–1954, Volume X, *Iran, 1951–1954*, eds. Carl N. Raether and Charles S. Sampson (Washington, D.C.: U.S. Government Printing Office, 1989). Available at: https://history.state.gov/historicaldocuments/frus1952-54v10. Last accessed: December 24, 2015.

Foreign Relations of the United States, 1952–1954, Volume XIV, Part 1, *China and Japan*, eds. David W. Mabon and Harriet D. Schwar (Washington, D.C.: U.S. Government Printing Office, 1985). Available at: https://history.state.gov/historicaldocuments/frus1952-54v14p1. Last accessed: December 20, 2015.

Foreign Relations of the United States, 1952–1954, Volume XV, Part 1, *Korea*, ed. Edward C. Keefer (Washington, D.C.: U.S. Government Printing Office, 1984). Available at: https://history.state.gov/historicaldocuments/frus1952-54v15p1. Last accessed: December 20, 2015.

Foreign Relations of the United States, 1955–1957, Volume II, *China*, ed. Harriet D. Schwar (Washington, D.C.: U.S. Government Printing Office, 1986). Available at: https://history.state.gov/historicaldocuments/frus1955-57v02. Last accessed: December 20, 2015.

Foreign Relations of the United States, 1955–1957, Volume III, *China*, eds. Harriet D. Schwar and Louis J. Smith (Washington, D.C.: U.S. Government Printing Office, 1986). Available at: https://history.state.gov/historicaldocuments/frus1955-57v03. Last accessed: December 20, 2015.

Foreign Relations of the United States, 1955–1957, Volume XII, *Near East Region; Iran; Iraq*, eds. Paul Claussen, Edward C. Keefer, Will Klingaman, and Nina J. Noring (Washington, D.C.: U.S. Government Printing Office, 1991). Available at: https://history.state.gov/historicaldocuments/frus1955-57v12. Last accessed: December 22, 2015.

Foreign Relations of the United States, 1955–1957, Volume XXVII, *Western Europe and Canada*, eds. Madeline Chi, Stephen Harper, Nancy Johnson, Margaret Kohutanycz, and Lorraine Lees (Washington, D.C.: U.S. Government Printing Office, 1992). Available at: https://history.state.gov/historicaldocuments/frus1955-57v27. Last accessed: December 20, 2015.

Foreign Relations of the United States, 1958–1960, Volume VII, Part 2, *Western Europe*, eds. Ronald D. Landa, James E. Miller, David S. Patterson, and Charles S. Sampson (Washington, D.C.: U.S. Government Printing Office, 1993). Available at: https://history.state. gov/historicaldocuments/frus1958-60v07p2. Last accessed: December 20, 2015.

Foreign Relations of the United States, 1958–1960, Volume XII, *Near East Region; Iraq; Iran; Arabian Peninsula*, ed. Edward C. Keefer (Washington, D.C.: U.S. Government Printing Office, 1992). Available at: https://history.state.gov/historicaldocuments/frus1958-60v12. Last accessed: December 20, 2015.

Foreign Relations of the United States, 1958–1960, Volume XIII, *Arab-Israeli Dispute; United Arab Republic; North Africa*, ed. Suzanne E. Coffman and Charles E. Sampson (Washington, D.C.: Government Printing Office, 1992). Available at: https:// history.state.gov/historicaldocuments/frus1958-60v13. Last accessed: December 20, 2015.

Foreign Relations of the United States, 1958–1960, Volume XVIII, *Japan; Korea*, eds. Madeline Chi and Louis J. Smith (Washington, D.C.: Government Printing Office, 1994). Available at: https://history.state.gov/historical-documents/frus1958-60v18. Last accessed: December 20, 2015.

Foreign Relations of the United States, 1958–1960, Volume XIX, *China*, ed. Harriet D. Schwar (Washington, D.C.: U.S. Government Printing Office, 1996). Available at: https://history.state.gov/historicaldocuments/frus1958-60v19. Last accessed: December 20, 2015.

Foreign Relations of the United States, 1961–1963, Volume VI, *Kennedy-Khrushchev Exchanges*, ed. Glenn W. LaFantasie (Washington, D.C.: Government Printing Office, 1996). Available at: https:// history.state.gov/historicaldocuments/frus1961-63v06. Last accessed: December 20, 2015.

Foreign Relations of the United States, 1961–1963, Volume VII, *Arms Control and Disarmament*, eds. David W. Mabon and David S. Patterson (Washington, D.C.: U.S. Government Printing Office, 1995). Available at: https://history.state.gov/historicaldocuments/frus1961-63v07. Last accessed: December 20, 2015.

Foreign Relations of the United States, 1961–1963, Volume VIII, *National Security Policy*, ed. David W. Mabon (Washington, D.C.: U.S. Government Printing Office, 1996). Available at: https://history.state. gov/historicaldocuments/frus1961-63v08. Last accessed: December 20, 2015.

Foreign Relations of the United States, 1961–1963, Vol. XII, *American Republics*, eds. Edward C. Keefer, Harriet Dashiell Schwar, and

W. Taylor Fain III (Washington, D.C.: U.S. Government Printing Office, 1996). Available at: https://history.state.gov/historicaldocuments/frus1961-63v12. Last accessed: March 11, 2016.

Foreign Relations of the United States, 1961–1963, Volume XIII, *Western Europe and Canada*, ed. William Z. Slany (Washington, D.C.: Government Printing Office, 1994). Available at: https://history.state.gov/historicaldocuments/frus1961-63v13. Last accessed: December 20, 2015.

Foreign Relations of the United States, 1961–1963, Volume XVII, *Near East, 1961–1962*, ed. Glenn W. LaFantasie (Washington, D.C.: Government Printing Office, 1994). Available at: https://history.state.gov/historicaldocuments/frus1961-63v17. Last accessed: December 20, 2015.

Foreign Relations of the United States, 1961–1963, Volume XVIII, *Near East, 1962–1963*, ed. Glenn W. LaFantasie (Washington, D.C.: Government Printing Office, 1995). Available at: https://history.state.gov/historicaldocuments/frus1961-63v18. Last accessed: December 20, 2015.

Foreign Relations of the United States, 1961–1963, Volume XIX, *South Asia*, ed. Louis J. Smith (Washington, DC: US Government Printing Office, 1996). Available at: https://history.state.gov/historicaldocuments/frus1961-63v19. Last accessed: December 20, 2015.

Foreign Relations of the United States, 1961–1963, Volume XXII, *Northeast Asia*, eds. Edward C. Keefer, David W. Mabon, and Harriet Dashiell Schwar (Washington, D.C.: U.S. Government Printing Office, 1996). Available at: https://history.state.gov/historicaldocuments/frus1961-63v22. Last accessed: December 20, 2015.

Foreign Relations of the United States, 1964–1968, Volume II, *Vietnam, January–June 1965*, eds. David C. Humphrey, Ronald D. Landa, and Louis J. Smith (Washington, D.C.: Government Printing Office, 1996). Available at: https://history.state.gov/historicaldocuments/frus1964-68v02. Last accessed: December 20, 2015.

Foreign Relations of the United States, 1964–1968, Volume XI, *Arms Control and Disarmament*, ed. David S. Patterson (Washington, DC: Government Printing Office, 1997). Available at: https://history.state.gov/historicaldocuments/frus1964-68v11. Last accessed: December 20, 2015.

Foreign Relations of the United States, 1964–1968, Volume XIII, *Western Europe Region*, ed. Glenn W. LaFantasie (Washington, DC.: Government Printing Office, 1995). Available at: https://history.state.gov/historicaldocuments/frus1964-68v13. Last accessed: December 20, 2015.

Foreign Relations of the United States, 1964–1968, Volume XV, *Germany and Berlin*, ed. David S. Patterson (Washington, DC: Government

Printing Office, 1999). Available at: https://history.state.gov/historical-documents/frus1964-68v15. Last accessed: December 20, 2015.

Foreign Relations of the United States, 1964–1968, Volume XVIII, *Arab-Israeli Dispute, 1964–1967*, ed. David S. Patterson (Washington, D.C.: Government Printing Office, 2000). Available at: https://history.state.gov/historicaldocuments/frus1964-68v18. Last accessed: December 20, 2015.

Foreign Relations of the United States, 1964–1968, Volume XX, *Arab-Israeli Dispute, 1967–1968*, ed. David S. Patterson (Washington, D.C.: Government Printing Office, 2001). Available at: https://history.state.gov/historicaldocuments/frus1964-68v20. Last accessed: December 20, 2015.

Foreign Relations of the United States, 1964–1968, Volume XXV, *South Asia*, eds. Gabrielle S. Mallon and Louis J. Smith (Washington, D.C.: U.S. Government Printing Office, 1999). Available at: https://history.state.gov/historicaldocuments/frus1964-68v25. Last accessed: December 20, 2015.

Foreign Relations of the United States, 1964–1968, Volume XXIX, Part 2, *Japan*, ed. Karen L. Gatz (Washington, D.C.: Government Printing Office, 2006). Available at: https://history.state.gov/historicaldocuments/frus1964-68v29p2. Last accessed: December 20, 2015.

Foreign Relations of the United States, 1964–1968, Volume XXX, *China*, ed. Harriet Dashiell Schwar (Washington, D.C.: U.S. Government Printing Office, 1998). Available at: https://history.state.gov/historicaldocuments/frus1964-68v30. Last accessed: December 20, 2015.

Foreign Relations of the United States, 1969–1976, Volume XI, *South Asia Crisis, 1971*, ed. Louis J. Smith (Washington, D.C.: U.S. Government Printing Office, 2005). Available at: https://history.state.gov/historicaldocuments/frus1969-76v11. Last accessed: December 20, 2015.

Foreign Relations of the United States, 1969–1976, Volume XVII, *China, 1969–1972*, ed. Steven E. Phillips (Washington, D.C.: U.S. Government Printing Office, 2006). Available at: https://history.state.gov/historicaldocuments/frus1969-76v17. Last accessed: December 20, 2015.

Foreign Relations of the United States, 1969–1976, Volume XVIII, *China, 1973–1976*, ed. David P. Nickles (Washington, D.C.: U.S. Government Printing Office, 2008). Available at: https://history.state.gov/historicaldocuments/frus1969-76v18. Last accessed: December 20, 2015.

Foreign Relations of the United States, 1969–1976, Volume XXVII, *Iran; Iraq, 1973–1976*, ed. Monica L. Belmonte (Washington, D.C.: United States Government Printing Office, 2012). Available at: https://history.state.gov/historicaldocuments/frus1969-76v27. Last accessed: January 5, 2016.

Foreign Relations of the United States, 1969–1976, Volume XXXVII, *Energy Crisis, 1974–1980*, ed. Steven G. Galpern (Washington, D.C.: U.S. Government Printing Office, 2012). Available at: https://history.state. gov/historicaldocuments/frus1969-76v37. Last accessed: December 18, 2015.

Foreign Relations of the United States, 1969–1976, Volume E-4, *Documents on Iran and Iraq, 1969–1972*, ed. Monica Belmonte (Washington, D.C.: U.S. Government Printing Office, 2006). Available at: https:// history.state.gov/historicaldocuments/frus1969-76ve04.   Last accessed: December 19, 2015.

Foreign Relations of the United States, 1969–1976, Volume E-7, *Documents on South Asia, 1969–1972*, ed. Louis J. Smith (Washington, D.C.: U.S. Government Printing Office, 2005). Available at: https://history.state. gov/historicaldocuments/frus1969-76ve07. Last accessed: December 20, 2015.

Foreign Relations of the United States, 1969–1976, Volume E-8, *Documents on South Asia, 1973–1976*, eds. Paul J. Hibbeln and Peter A. Kraemer (Washington, D.C.: United States Government Printing Office, 2007). Available at: https://history.state.gov/historicaldocuments/frus1969-76ve08. Last accessed: December 20, 2015.

Foreign Relations of the United States, 1969–1976, Volume E-10, *Documents on American Republics, 1969–1972*, eds. Douglas Kraft and James F. Siekmeier (Washington, D.C.: U.S. Government Printing Office, 2009). Available at: https://history.state.gov/historicaldocuments/frus1969-76ve10. Last accessed: December 20, 2015.

Foreign Relations of the United States, 1969–1976, Volume E-12, *Documents on East and Southeast Asia, 1973–1976*, eds. Bradley Lynn Coleman, David Goldman, and David Nickles (Washington, D.C.: Government Printing Office, 2011). Available at: https://history.state.gov/historical-documents/frus1969-76ve12. Last accessed: December 20, 2015.

Foreign Relations of the United States, 1977–1980, Volume XIII, *China*, ed. David P. Nickles (Washington, DC: US Government Printing Office, 2013). Available at: https://history.state.gov/historicaldocuments/ frus1977-80v13. Last accessed: December 20, 2015.

Försvarsdepartmentet. 1968. "Säkerhetspolitik och försvarsutgifter: Betänkande av 1965 prs försvarsutredning," Statent Offentliga Utredningnar. Stockholm.

IAEA (International Atomic Energy Agency). 2009. Country Nuclear Power Profiles: Sweden. Available at: www-pub.iaea.org/MTCD/publica-tions/PDF/cnpp2009/ countryprofiles/Sweden/Sweden2006.htm. Last accessed: November 28, 2014.

Imprimerie nationale. 1991. *Documents diplomatiques français*, 1957, tome 2. Paris.

National Security Archive, Electronic Briefing Book 6: "India and Pakistan – On the Nuclear Threshold," ed. Joyce Battle. Washington, D.C.: The George Washington University. Available at: http://nsarchive.gwu.edu/ NSAEBB/NSAEBB6/. Last accessed: December 20, 2015.

National Security Archive, Electronic Briefing Book 20: "New Archival Evidence on Taiwanese 'Nuclear Intentions', 1966–1976," ed. William Burr. Washington, D.C.: The George Washington University. Available at: http://nsarchive.gwu.edu/NSAEBB/NSAEBB20/. Last accessed: December 20, 2015.

National Security Archive, Electronic Briefing Book 38: "The United States and the Chinese Nuclear Program, 1960–1964," ed. William Burr and Jeffrey T. Richelson. Washington, D.C.: The George Washington University. Available at: http://nsarchive.gwu.edu/NSAEBB/NSAEBB38/. Last accessed: December 20, 2015.

National Security Archive, Electronic Briefing Book 66: "The Beijing-Washington Back-Channel and Henry Kissinger's Secret Trip to China," ed. William Burr. Washington, D.C.: The George Washington University. Available at: http://nsarchive.gwu.edu/NSAEBB/NSAEBB66/. Last accessed: December 20, 2015.

National Security Archive, Electronic Briefing Book 79: "The Tilt: The U.S. and the South Asian Crisis of 1971," ed. Sajit Gandhi. Washington, D.C.: The George Washington University. Available at: http://nsarchive. gwu.edu/NSAEBB/NSAEBB79/. Last accessed: December 20, 2015.

National Security Archive, Electronic Briefing Book 80: "Iraq and Weapons of Mass Destruction," ed. Jeffrey Richelson. Washington, D.C.: The George Washington University. Available at: http://nsarchive.gwu.edu/ NSAEBB/NSAEBB80/. Last accessed: May 2, 2016.

National Security Archive, Electronic Briefing Book 87: "North Korea and Nuclear Weapons: The Declassified U.S. Record," ed. Robert A. Wampler. Washington, D.C.: The George Washington University. Available at: http://nsarchive.gwu.edu/NSAEBB/NSAEBB87/. Last accessed: December 20, 2015.

National Security Archive, Electronic Briefing Book 106: "Nixon's Trip to China," ed. William Burr. Washington, D.C.: The George Washington University. Available at: http://nsarchive.gwu.edu/NSAEBB/ NSAEBB106/. Last accessed: December 20, 2015.

National Security Archive, Electronic Briefing Book 167: "Saddam's Iron Grip: Intelligence Reports on Saddam Hussein's Reign," ed. Jeffrey Richelson. Washington, D.C.: The George Washington University.

Available at: http://nsarchive.gwu.edu/NSAEBB/NSAEBB167/. Last accessed: May 2, 2016.

National Security Archive, Electronic Briefing Book 181: "U.S. Intelligence and the South African Bomb," ed. Jeffrey Richelson. Washington, D.C.: The George Washington University. Available at: http://nsarchive.gwu.edu/NSAEBB/NSAEBB181/. Last accessed: December 20, 2015.

National Security Archive, Electronic Briefing Book 184: "U.S. Intelligence and the French Nuclear Weapons Program," ed. Jeffrey Richelson. Washington, D.C.: The George Washington University. Available at: http://nsarchive.gwu.edu/NSAEBB/NSAEBB184/. Last accessed: March 11, 2016.

National Security Archive, Electronic Briefing Book 187: "U.S. Intelligence and the Indian Bomb," ed. Jeffrey Richelson. Washington, D.C.: The George Washington University. Available at: http://nsarchive.gwu.edu/NSAEBB/NSAEBB187/. Last accessed: December 20, 2015.

National Security Archive, Electronic Briefing Book 189: "Israel Crosses the Threshold," ed. Avner Cohen. Washington, D.C.: The George Washington University. Available at: http://nsarchive.gwu.edu/NSAEBB/NSAEBB189/. Last accessed: December 20, 2015

National Security Archive, Electronic Briefing Book 221: "U.S. Opposed Taiwanese Bomb during 1970s," ed. William Burr. Washington, D.C.: The George Washington University. Available at: http://nsarchive.gwu.edu/nukevault/ebb221/. Last accessed: December 20, 2015.

National Security Archive, Electronic Briefing Book 240: "In 1974 Estimate, CIA Found That Israel Already Had a Nuclear Stockpile and That 'Many Countries' Would Soon Have Nuclear Capabilities," ed. William Burr and Jeffrey Richelson. Washington, D.C.: The George Washington University. Available at: http://nsarchive.gwu.edu/NSAEBB/NSAEBB240/. Last accessed: May 1, 2016.

National Security Archive, Electronic Briefing Book 268: "U.S.-Iran Nuclear Negotiations in 1970s Featured Shah's Nationalism and U.S. Weapons Worries," ed. William Burr. Washington, D.C.: The George Washington University. Available at: http://nsarchive.gwu.edu/nukevault/ebb268/. Last accessed: December 20, 2015.

National Security Archive, Electronic Briefing Book 286: "U.S. Intelligence and the Detection of the First Soviet Nuclear Test, September 1949," ed. William Burr. Washington, D.C.: The George Washington University. Available at: www2.gwu.edu/~nsarchiv/nukevault/ebb286/. Last accessed: May 2, 2016.

National Security Archive, Electronic Briefing Book 333: "The United States and Pakistan's Quest for the Bomb," ed. William Burr. Washington, D.C.: The George Washington University. Available at: http://nsarchive.gwu.edu/nukevault/ebb333/. Last accessed: December 30, 2015.

National Security Archive, Electronic Briefing Book 367: "The Nixon Administration and the Indian Nuclear Program, 1972–1974," ed. William Burr. Washington, D.C.: The George Washington University. Available at: http://nsarchive.gwu.edu/nukevault/ebb367/. Last accessed: December 20, 2015.

National Security Archive, Electronic Briefing Book 377: "New Documents Spotlight Reagan-era Tensions over Pakistani Nuclear Program," ed. William Burr. Washington, D.C.: The George Washington University. Available at: http://nsarchive.gwu.edu/nukevault/ebb377/. Last accessed: December 20, 2015.

National Security Archive, Electronic Briefing Book 418: "The Iraq War Ten Years After," ed. Joyce Battle and Malcolm Byrne. Washington, D.C.: The George Washington University. Available at: http://nsarchive.gwu.edu/NSAEBB/NSAEBB418/. Last accessed: March 15, 2016.

National Security Archive, Electronic Briefing Book 423: "China May Have Helped Pakistan Nuclear Weapons Design, Newly Declassified Intelligence Indicates," ed. William Burr. Washington, D.C.: The George Washington University. Available at: http://nsarchive.gwu.edu/nukevault/ebb423/. Last accessed: December 20, 2015.

National Security Archive, Electronic Briefing Book 446: "Pakistan's Illegal Nuclear Procurement Exposed in 1987," ed. William Burr. Washington, D.C.: The George Washington University. Available at: http://nsarchive.gwu.edu/nukevault/ebb446/. Last accessed: December 30, 2015.

National Security Archive, Electronic Briefing Book 451: "Proliferation Watch: U.S. Intelligence Assessments of Potential Nuclear Powers, 1977–2001," eds. William Burr and Jeffrey T. Richelson. Washington, D.C.: The George Washington University. Available at: http://nsarchive.gwu.edu/nukevault/ebb451/. Last accessed: December 20, 2015.

National Security Archive, Electronic Briefing Book 474: "The United States and the Two Koreas, Part II: 1969–2010," ed. Robert A. Wampler. Washington, D.C.: The George Washington University. Available at: http://nsarchive.gwu.edu/NSAEBB/NSAEBB474/. Last accessed: December 20, 2015.

National Security Archive, Electronic Briefing Book 488: "China's First Nuclear Test – 50th Anniversary," ed. William Burr. Washington, D.C.: The George Washington University. Available at: http://nsarchive.gwu.edu/nukevault/ebb488/. Last accessed: December 20, 2015.

National Security Archive, Electronic Briefing Book 510: "The U.S. Discovery of Israel's Secret Nuclear Project," eds. Avner Cohen and William Burr. Washington, D.C.: The George Washington University. Available at: http://nsarchive.gwu.edu/nukevault/ebb510/. Last accessed: December 20, 2015.

National Security Archive, Electronic Briefing Book 518: "The Gas Centrifuge Secret: Origins of a U.S. Policy of Nuclear Denial, 1954–1960," ed. William Burr. Washington, D.C.: The George Washington University. Available at: http://nsarchive.gwu.edu/nukevault/ebb518-the-gas-centrifuge-secret-origins-of-US-policy-of-nuclear-denial-1954-1960/index.html. Last accessed: March 9, 2016.

National Security Archive, Electronic Briefing Book 531: "The United States and the Pakistani Bomb, 1984–1985: President Reagan, General Zia, Nazir Ahmed Vaid, and Seymour Hersh," ed. William Burr. Washington, D.C.: The George Washington University. Available at: http://nsarchive.gwu.edu/nukevault/ebb531-U.S.-Pakistan-Nuclear-Relations,-1984-1985/. Last accessed: December 30, 2015.

National Security Archive, Electronic Briefing Book 541: "Nuclear Weapons on Okinawa Declassified December 2015," eds. William Burr, Barbara Elias, and Robert Wampler. Washington, D.C.: The George Washington University. Available at: http://nsarchive.gwu.edu/nukevault/ebb541-Nukes-on-Okinawa-Declassified-2016/. Last accessed: March 11, 2016.

National Security Archive, Electronic Briefing Book 547: "Concerned About Nuclear Weapons Potential, John F. Kennedy Pushed for Inspections of Israel," eds. Avner Cohen and William Burr. Washington, D.C.: The George Washington University. Available at: http://nsarchive.gwu.edu/nukevault/ebb547-Kennedy-Dimona-and-the-Nuclear-Proliferation-Problem-1961-1962/. Last accessed: April 28, 2016.

National Security Archive, *Israel and the Bomb* by Avner Cohen, documents, ed. Avner Cohen. Washington, D.C.: The George Washington University. Available at: http://nsarchive.gwu.edu/israel/. Last accessed: December 20, 2015.

ÖB-utredningarna 1957, *Kontakt med Krigsmakten*, no. 10-12, 1957.

Sveriges Socialdemokratiska Arbetareparti. 1960. *Neutralitet, Försvar, Atomvapen*. Stockholm: Tiden.

United Nations Data. 2013. Available at: http://data.un.org/. Last accessed: September 2, 2013.

Wilson Center Digital Archive, "Brazilian Nuclear History," Washington, D.C.: Wilson Center. Available at: http://digitalarchive.wilsoncenter.org/collection/167/brazilian-nuclear-history. Last accessed: December 20, 2015.

"Chinese Nuclear History," Washington, DC: Wilson Center. Available at: http://digitalarchive.wilsoncenter.org/collection/105/chinese-nuclear-history. Last accessed: December 20, 2015.

"Foundations of Chinese Foreign Policy," Washington, D.C.: Wilson Center. Available at: http://digitalarchive.wilsoncenter.org/collection/227/foundations-of-chinese-foreign-policy. Last accessed: March 3, 2016.

"French Nuclear History," Washington, D.C.: Wilson Center. Available at: http://digitalarchive.wilsoncenter.org/collection/83/french-nuclear-history. Last accessed: December 20, 2015.

"Indian Nuclear History," Washington, D.C.: Wilson Center. Available at: http://digitalarchive.wilsoncenter.org/collection/44/indian-nuclear-history. Last accessed: December 20, 2015.

"Israeli Nuclear History," Washington, D.C.: Wilson Center. Available at: http://digitalarchive.wilsoncenter.org/collection/153/israeli-nuclear-history. Last accessed: December 20, 2015.

"North Korean Nuclear History," Washington, D.C.: Wilson Center. Available at: http://digitalarchive.wilsoncenter.org/collection/113/north-korean-nuclear-history. Last accessed: December 20, 2015.

"Saddam Hussein's Iraq," Washington, D.C.: Wilson Center. Available at: http://digitalarchive.wilsoncenter.org/collection/168/saddam-hussein-s-iraq. Last accessed: April 29, 2016.

"Sino-Soviet Split, 1960–1984," Washington, D.C.: Wilson Center. Available at: http://digitalarchive.wilsoncenter.org/collection/73/sino-soviet-split-1960–1984. Last accessed: December 20, 2015.

"South African Nuclear History," Washington, D.C.: Wilson Center. Available at: http://digitalarchive.wilsoncenter.org/collection/95/south-african-nuclear-history. Last accessed: December 20, 2015.

"South Korean Nuclear History," Washington, D.C.: Wilson Center. Available at: http://digitalarchive.wilsoncenter.org/collection/128/south-korean-nuclear-history. Last accessed: December 20, 2015.

"Warsaw Pact," Washington, D.C.: Wilson Center. Available at: http://digitalarchive.wilsoncenter.org/collection/88/warsaw-pact. Last accessed: December 20, 2015.

Index

CAMBRIDGE STUDIES IN
INTERNATIONAL RELATIONS